GENEVA 1954

GENEVA
1954

The Settlement of the

Indochinese War

BY ROBERT F. RANDLE

PRINCETON UNIVERSITY PRESS

PRINCETON, NEW JERSEY

1969

Standard Book Number: 691-07529-8

Permission to quote from the following books is gratefully acknowledged:

The White House Years: Mandate for Change, 1953–56. Copyright © 1963 by Dwight D. Eisenhower. Reprinted by permission of Doubleday & Company, Inc.

Full Circle: The Memoirs of Anthony Eden, by Anthony Eden. Copyright © 1960 by The Times Publishing Co., Ltd. Reprinted by permission of Houghton Mifflin Company.

Ho Chi Minh on Revolution: Selected Writings, 1920–1966, edited by Bernard B. Fall. Copyright © 1967 by Frederick A. Praeger, Inc. Reprinted by permission of the publisher.

Printed in the United States of America
by Princeton University Press
Princeton, New Jersey

This book has been composed
in Linotype Caledonia.

To my father and mother

Herbert and

Lillian Randle

Preface

I have tried in this book to tell as complete a story of the Geneva Conference of 1954 as the available documents permit. Part I, Prelude to Geneva: The Diplomacy of Nonintervention, and Part II, the Geneva Conference and World Politics, are largely narrative and historical analyses. Part III, the Geneva Agreements: Analysis and Implementation, includes a legal analysis of the Conference documents —what they purported to accomplish and the situations their implementation engendered—and my assessment of the significance of the Conference and the documents produced at Geneva.

It is never sufficient to confine oneself to the mere language of treaties, and this is particularly true, as in the case of the Geneva agreements, when the language is ambiguous and the settlement they embody, incomplete. To understand these agreements—and more, to understand the complex process by which the Indochinese War was ended—it is necessary to study the diplomacy of the Geneva Conference, both in its Korean and Indochina phases, against the background of extra-Conference diplomacy and the global events that very greatly influenced the conduct and decisions of the chief negotiators. Events in the pre-Conference period also affected the bargaining at the Palais de Nations and in the villas of Geneva in fundamental ways. For it was between January and May 1954 that the military situation in Indochina and the political situations in the capitals of the leading states determined the limits of the bargaining at Geneva. Thus, in order to tell this story as I believe it should be told, and in order adequately to analyze the relevant events and documents, I have been impelled to write this book of moderate length.

I have approached the subject matter less as an historian than as a specialist in international relations and international law. In the chapters of Parts I and II that are predominantly analytical (Chapters 3, 7, 8, 11, and 20) as well as in the chapters that are principally narrative, I have sought to achieve five objectives:

1. To show the effects of their domestic political conditions and domestic political trends upon the diplomacy of the principal states.

2. To show how, and with what effects, the foreign policy of each major state continuously interacted with the policies of other states throughout the period of the study.

3. To show the extent to which political and military events contemporaneous with negotiations for the settlement of the war bore upon the conduct of those negotiations.

4. To emphasize the point that when great powers are involved in a crisis, diplomacy becomes truly global. Thus the settlement of the

Indochinese War and the ratification by France of the European Defense Community Treaty became interrelated; the experience of the Korean War, its settlement, and the Korean phase of the Geneva Conference influenced the attitudes of the diplomats in the Indochina phase of the Conference; and the responses of statesmen to the problems of divided polities (Germany, Korea, Laos, and Vietnam) were similar.

5. To describe how a few particularly important events were viewed by the leading officials of each principal state. This approach necessitated repetition, but it has been valuable to me—as I hope it will be to the reader—in discovering the perspectives and motives of the leading diplomats and the presuppositions of their policies and in more fully appreciating how their attitudes and approaches were shaped by their particular national interests. It is an interesting experiment in examining how men of different nationalities perceived the same crisis.

The legal analysis of Part III will no doubt be controversial, partly because of my assumptions (which I have tried to make explicit) and partly because of my selection of facts. The reader who is not familiar with public international law must, however, appreciate that much of the controversy also will be due to the lack of substantive law or disagreement among legal authorities on principles that were crucially relevant to the settlement for Vietnam (for example, various aspects of state succession, sovereignty, recognition, and the obligatory force of the resolutions and general acts of multilateral conferences).

The approach I have used in assessing the obligations of the states that participated in the Conference was designed to be at once systematic, and at least partially fair to some of the variety of opinions on the legal questions involved in this complex subject. In Chapter 23, which examines the question whether, and to what extent, the State of Vietnam was bound by the Vietnam Cease-Fire Agreement and the Final Declaration of the Conference, I have not based my argument upon a preliminary conclusion that the Diem government of the State of Vietnam was—or was not—a duly constituted government of a sovereign state in July 1954. Rather, I have assumed, on one hand, that the government was duly constituted when the Conference ended, and on the other hand that it was not so constituted. Some fairly definite conclusions about the SVN's responsibility can be made with this approach.

Chapter 24 is a kind of legal history of the implementation of the various provisions of the Geneva settlements for Vietnam. I have tried to avoid questions relating to the legality of United States intervention in Vietnam in the sixties because too many issues beyond those that concern merely the Geneva Agreements are involved. This chapter (and the earlier chapters as well) may provide the supporters and critics of United States foreign policy with material that variously supports their arguments. I have felt, however, that this book could not be extended to deal with several current issues *in the terms in which the antagonists discuss them today*. In addition to the legality of U.S. action in Vietnam, I include in this category the questions whether, in 1954, U.S. policy toward the Malenkov regime was conducive to peace or to improved relations with the Soviet Union and whether, as a practical political matter, support for the regime of Ngo Dinh Diem was wise or unwise.

Chapters 25 and 26 are similar in approach to Chapter 24 and relate, respectively, to the settlements for Cambodia and Laos. In the case of Laos, I have dealt briefly with the 1962 settlement because United States officials have frequently coupled the 1954 and 1962 agreements, implying that both settlements created a "regime" for Indochina upon which all future settlements and decisions must, in part, be based. Chapters 27 and 28 summarize the legal and political problems to which the 1954 agreements gave rise. Also, an attempt is made to assess the accomplishments of the Geneva documents, the determination being based upon those matters about which there was a consensus among the negotiators.

I offer the following as some of the significant findings and conclusions of this book. In Parts I and II:

1. President Eisenhower and Secretary of State Dulles concluded, no later than the first or second of April 1954, that the United States should not become militarily involved in the Indochinese War unless the Chinese intervened. Both men adopted a policy of caution, to which they adhered throughout April and throughout the period of the Conference. Mr. Dulles's real policy was masked by an ostensible policy of threats and warnings of United States, and possibly Allied, intervention.

2. Dulles's responses to the Indochina crisis and his approach to allies and adversaries in the world arena and within the United States were, for the most part, characterized by astuteness and an acute sense of political realities and the limits they imposed and the possibilities they offered. My study of Mr. Dulles had led me to conclude that accounts that picture the late Secretary of State as an inflexible exponent of his own, puritanically inspired views of world politics are probably inaccurate and grossly oversimplified. Such assessments are certainly not correct in respect of his performance in 1954. I believe, therefore, that a fresh approach to Mr. Dulles as Secretary of State is required.

3. The diplomacy and politics of the European Defense Commu-

nity were intimately related to the diplomacy of the Geneva Conference. The EDC Treaty was rejected, on a procedural vote, by the French National Assembly in August 1954. Premier Mendès-France refused to make the question of EDC a matter of confidence. Rumor, particularly in the United States, had it that the Premier had made a "deal" with Soviet Foreign Minister Molotov: EDC in exchange for an honorable settlement in Indochina. I have concluded that the rumor was baseless, that there was no deal.

In Part III:

4. The Geneva Agreements (the cease-fire agreements, the Final Declaration, and the unilateral declarations) were vaguely worded at crucial points. Indeed, they were incomplete and legally defective in various essentials. Thus in most instances it is meaningless to speak glibly of this or that state violating the "Geneva Accords."

5. The Geneva Agreements purported to undertake both military and partial political settlements of the Indochinese War. However, it was only with respect to a cease-fire and related technical military matters that there was a consensus among the diplomats at Geneva. As the story of the Conference reveals, it was a formidable task to reconcile conflicting national interests and achieve even this modicum of agreement for formulating conditions for ending the war.

6. The form and procedures of the settlements for Laos and Vietnam were inadequate for preserving the peace of these countries, given the political conditions then existing as well as those that might reasonably be anticipated.

7. Irrespective of one's present estimate of the value of SEATO, in its origins and the form it assumed at its inception in September 1954, the collective defense scheme provided the United States and its allies with several positive legal and political advantages.

That these conclusions may elicit controversy, I have no doubt. However, I hope the reader who disagrees will carefully consider the development of the arguments in the text and the evidence adduced to support them.

A cursory review of the notes and bibliographical citations will show that I have relied heavily upon newspaper accounts, public documents, speeches, and the memoirs of the leading policymakers. To attain greater accuracy, I have sought the "best evidence" for a particular fact by comparing, whenever possible, several accounts of various events. Thus *New York Times* reports were compared with those in the *New York Herald Tribune*, and occasionally with other domestic and foreign newspapers; and these in turn were compared with the public statements and with descriptions in the memoirs of key statesmen. Where there were several interpretations of important questions and events, I have described them. Where the evidence was inconclusive, I have tried to be consistent and candid in admitting inconclusiveness. The private papers of John Foster Dulles provided some insights, and the interviews and statements of Mr. Dulles's friends and associates, filed with the Dulles Oral History Collection at the Princeton University Library, were very useful. In most cases, I have documented my assertions in such a way that scholars will be able to check the available authorities against my account.

Of the secondary sources upon which I have relied, mention must be made of *La Fin d'une Guerre: Indochine, 1954* by Jean Lacouture and Philippe Devillers, the first fairly complete account of the end of the Indochinese War and the Geneva Conference. The authors have relied, in part, upon interviews with leading French policymakers of the 1954 period. Although my analysis has led me to disagree with the Lacouture-Devillers book on several important questions, it is a well-written and informative work, and I have used it to help recreate the history of the period insofar as that history concerns French decisions and French approaches to problems related to the war. Among secondary accounts, I recommend this book to the reader—as well as the works of Bernard Fall, E. J. Hammer's *The Struggle for Indochina*, an excellent history of the politics of the Indochinese War up to 1954, and Donald Lancaster's *The Emancipation of French Indochina* and Coral Bell's *Survey of International Affairs, 1954*, both of which contain rather good though short accounts of the Geneva Conference.

I THANK Richard D. Challener, W. T. R. Fox, John Norton Moore, and Howard Wriggins for reading and commenting upon the manuscript; David S. Smith for his encouragement and support, and for providing me with secretarial assistance; and Benjamin Bock, formerly of the State Department Historical Office, for his suggestions and comments during the early research phase of my projects. Alexander P. Clark, Curator of Manuscripts at the Princeton University Library, and his able and charming assistants, Wanda M. Randall and Nancy Bressler, gave me their invaluable cooperation during my researches into the Dulles Papers and the Dulles Oral History Collection. I also express my gratitude to the Dulles Committee for its permission to use the Dulles Papers. To Daniel McCarthy for his suggestions and his thorough and detailed editing of the manuscript; and to John Downing, for his constructive criticisms, for his hostility to bad hypotheses and faulty reasoning, and for his willingness to hear me go on (and on) about the Geneva Conference, I owe my deepest thanks. William McClung, Social Science Editor of the Princeton University Press, and Sarah George, also of the Press, gave me particularly valuable advice during the period of the preparation of the manuscript for publication.

I also thank Thomas F. Reddy, Jr., James Laist, R. Morton Adams, and Frank Scheck, and the firm of Pennie, Edmonds, Morton, Taylor and Adams for their good will and forbearance while a lawyer made up his mind whether he wanted to practice law or to teach. Without their support, this book would not have been written. Finally, I thank Karl Klare for his help with the microfilms of back issues of the *New York Herald Tribune*, and my students at Columbia University who so patiently listened to my theories.

Robert F. Randle

Perth Amboy and New York City
January 1969

Contents

PART III: THE GENEVA AGREEMENTS: ANALYSIS AND
IMPLEMENTATION

List of Illustrations

Abbreviations Used in the Text and Notes

Cmd. 9186	*Documents relating to the Discussion of Korea and Indochina at the Geneva Conference*, Misc. No. 16 (1954), Cmd. 9186 (London: Her Majesty's Stationery Office, 1965)
Cmd. 9239	*Further Documents relating to the Discussion of Indochina at the Geneva Conference*, Misc. No. 20 (1954), Cmd. 9239 (London: Her Majesty's Stationery Office, 1954)
C.P.R.	Chinese People's Republic
DDE	D. D. Eisenhower, *Mandate for Change, 1953–1956* (Garden City, N.Y.: Doubleday, 1963)
Docs., 1954	P. V. Curl (ed.), *Documents on American Foreign Relations, 1954* (New York: Harper & Row, 1955)
DRVN	Democratic Republic of Vietnam
DSB	*Department of State Bulletin*
E	Anthony Eden, *Full Circle* (Boston: Houghton Mifflin, 1960)
Econ.	*The Economist* (London)
Ely	Paul Ely, *Mémoires—L'Indochine dans la Tourmente* (Paris: Plon, 1964)
Falk	R. A. Falk (ed.), *The Vietnam War and International Law* (Princeton: Princeton University Press, 1968)
FMM	*Foreign Ministers' Meeting, Berlin Discussions, January 25–February 18, 1954*, Department of State Publication No. 5399 (1954)
ISC	International Supervisory Commission; also known as International Commission for Supervision and Control or International Control Commission
JO	*Journal Officiel, Débats Parlementaires* (Paris: Imprimerie des Journaux officiels, 1954)
L&D	Jean Lacouture and Philippe Devillers, *La Fin d'une Guerre: Indochine, 1954* (Paris: Seuil, 1960)
NYHT	*New York Herald Tribune*
NYT	*New York Times*
OHP	The John Foster Dulles Oral History Collection at Princeton University Library, Princeton, New Jersey
PAVN	People's Army of Vietnam
RVN	Republic of Vietnam (the political entity south of the provisional demarcation line after 26 October 1955)

SVN   State of Vietnam (of which Bao Dai was chief of state
                —the political entity south of the provisional
                demarcation line after June 1948 but before 26
                October 1955)

TIAS   U.S. Department of State, *Treaties and Other
                International Acts Series*

T/L   *Times of London*

PART I

Prelude to Geneva: The Diplomacy
of Nonintervention

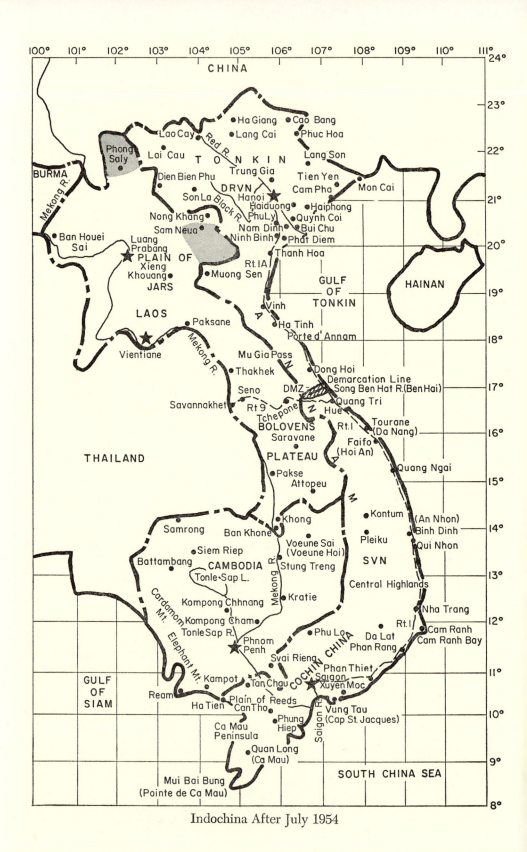

Indochina After July 1954

Chapter 1

THE SEVEN-YEAR WAR

[I]

When the Korean armistice was signed in July 1953, the Franco-Vietminh war[1] was in its seventh year.[2] France had had few military or political successes in Indochina during the course of its war; in fact, it was no nearer in 1953 than it had been in 1946 to achieving decisive military success or to resolving the issues of independence for the Associated States of Indochina.[3] The political debacle was in part a result of the instability of the successive French governments of the Fourth Republic and in part an inability, or perhaps even a refusal, to take specific steps toward granting independence to the Associated States, steps that would be satisfactory to the nationalists groups in Indochina, particularly the Vietnamese nationalists. Some Vietnamese nationalists demanded complete independence, others some modicum of autonomy in formal association with France.

The character of the Indochinese War had changed in late 1949 with the victory of the Chinese Communists over the Kuomintang. A regime sympathetic to Ho Chi Minh's Democratic Republic of Vietnam (the latter was established in 1946) now bordered on Laos and Tonkin, parts of which were more or less controlled by Vietminh forces. The civil or internal war fought by the Vietminh since 1946 had become "internationalized," the Communist Chinese supplying matériel to the Vietminh and—beginning in mid-1950—the United States supplying funds and arms to the French to support their military effort in Indochina. The decision of the Truman administration to provide this assistance was, of course, closely related to the revised East Asian security policies of the United States after the establish-

[1] "Vietminh" is derived from the name of a united-front organization assembled by the Indochinese Communist Party and known as the Viet Nam Doc Lap Dong Minh Hoi ("League for the Independence of Vietnam"); Ho Chi Minh was elected its general secretary. The league was disbanded but "Vietminh" has persisted in use and refers to the Vietnamese who had rebelled against French colonial authorities and conducted a war of independence against the French. Thus the Vietminh was a Vietnamese nationalist movement; it was also a movement guided by the principles of Marxism and Leninism.

[2] It is generally agreed that the war began on 19 December 1946. I shall refer to the war as the "Indochinese War" although it has been called the "Franco-Vietminh War," and more recently the "First Indochinese War."

[3] The constitution of the Fourth French Republic (articles 60-82) provided for the establishment of the French Union, an entity comprising an association of France with her colonies or former colonies. The union concept was roughly analogous to the concept upon which the British Commonwealth was based.

ment of the Chinese People's Republic (C.P.R.) and the outbreak of the Korean War.

In June 1948, France established a provisional central government for the State of Vietnam, with the former Emperor, Bao Dai, chief of state. France recognized the independence of Vietnam as an Associated State within the French Union; and in February 1950 the United States and Great Britain recognized the State of Vietnam, Laos, and Cambodia. In the course of time a number of states established formal diplomatic relations with the Bao Dai regime. The C.P.R. and the Soviet Union recognized the Democratic Republic of Vietnam (DRVN) in early 1950.[4]

The political incapacity of the French governments was matched by a corresponding military incapacity, a failure to achieve any really decisive victories over the Vietminh. The French Union forces fought with valor, as did their opponents, but by 1953 the French had made little progress militarily. With the Korean truce, political pressures in France for a negotiated settlement of the Indochinese War mounted during the summer and fall of 1953. This sentiment had existed well before mid-1953, but the end of the Korean War, after two years of bitter negotiations, persuaded the French advocates of negotiation that a similar solution of the Indochinese War was possible. Such sentiments were strengthened by hints, and eventually by explicit offers from Communist governments. The general policy of the Soviet Union under Malenkov was, at least ostensibly, one of détente with the United States and Western Europe; in other words, a policy of "peaceful coexistence." Moreover, with the end of its Korean involvement, the C.P.R.—though hardly less hostile toward the United States—began a policy of persuading Asian states of the Chinese Communist regime's peaceful intentions. In August and September 1953, radio broadcasts from Peking and Moscow hinted at the possibility of a truce in Indochina. A French economic mission returned to Paris from Peking that fall and reported that China would not oppose a solution to the Indochinese War that might entail Vietnam's remaining within the French Union.

Then, on 29 November 1953, the *Stockholm Expressen* published an exchange of telegrams between Ho Chi Minh and the managing editor of the *Expressen* in which the Vietminh leader declared the Vietnamese people would carry the war to a victorious end if the

[4] The reader should consult Dr. Ellen J. Hammer's *The Struggle for Indochina, 1940-1955* (Stanford: Stanford University Press, 1954), an excellent political history of France in Indochina for the years 1940-1953. The official statements of recognition of the Vietnam regimes by the United States, Great Britain, the Soviet Union, and the Chinese People's Republic are collected in A. B. Cole (ed.), *Conflict in Indo-China and International Repercussions* (Ithaca: Cornell University Press, 1956), pp. 117, 120-122.

French continued their war of conquest. If, however, the French government wished "to bring about an armistice and solve the Vietnam problem through negotiations, the people and Government of the Democratic Republic of Vietnam will be prepared to discuss the French proposal."[5] When asked about the prospects and the terms of an armistice, Ho replied: "The French Government must suspend hostilities. An armistice will then become a reality. The basis for such an armistice is that the French Government really respect the independence of the Vietnam" (sic).[6] Nothing was said about the role in peace negotiations of the government of the State of Vietnam (the Bao Dai regime).

Ho's statements in the *Expressen* suited the peace program of influential groups of Frenchmen, both among the attentive public and among deputies of the National Assembly—a program that envisaged direct negotiations with the Vietminh. The military forces of the French Union, directed by the French high command, and those of the Vietminh were the active belligerents, and only these parties—according to this view—ought to sit down together and arrive at an honorable and mutually satisfactory armistice.

One of the leaders of this program, Pierre Mendès-France, a former cabinet minister and now a deputy, as well as a longtime critic of official French policy in Indochina, was an advocate of negotiations to end the war and a proponent of a program for granting genuine independence to the Indochinese. Mendès-France had missed becoming Premier in June 1953 by thirteen votes, and Joseph Laniel, who had won enough votes for investiture, had formed a government and vowed to perfect the independence of the Associated States. Although negotiations to this end between the Laniel government and the State of Vietnam (Bao Dai) began in August, the usual difficulties were encountered. Georges Bidault, Laniel's Foreign Minister, resolutely opposed granting unrestricted independence to the Associated States. They must be joined in the French Union, Bidault believed, with impediments upon their sovereignty. Ardent Indochinese nationalists were sure to reject this kind of "independence," but, whatever the attitude of the Indochinese, Bidault's views were shared by many deputies of the right and the center.

When, in late November, the *Expressen* exchange appeared, Franco-Vietnamese talks had not made substantial progress, but the statements by the DRVN Premier strengthened the position of French advocates of direct negotiations with the Vietminh. In fact, they were probably designed to do precisely that. The Indochinese debate in France had never really ceased throughout 1953, but Premier Ho Chi

[5] Cole, *op. cit.*, pp. 148-149.   [6] *Ibid.*, p. 149.

Minh's statements seemed to spark renewed debate.[7] By fall of 1953 a large and growing number of non-Communist French were becoming tired of this war, which had consumed 25 percent of the officers and 40 percent of the noncommissioned officers of the French army— a war that had been singularly devoid of glory and appeared to offer no future gains for Frenchmen or for France. If France should emerge victorious, she must soon grant independence to a Vietnam that would be tied to the *métropole* by the most tenuous links: through a French Union whose form was shadowy and unsubstantial. Many Vietnamese nationalists had made it clear to Paris that they would be satisfied with nothing less than complete independence, withdrawal of the French army, and relations with France not substantially privileged above Vietnamese relations with any other state. What was the point or profit of continuing a war, some French critics asked, for Vietnamese who might demonstrate such ingratitude toward their defenders upon becoming independent? Why, then, should Frenchmen fight for the government of Bao Dai?

There was, moreover, little feeling in France for continuing this war on the margins of China simply because the Vietminh were Communists and because an American policy of containment required it. By the end of 1953 many Frenchmen were unwilling to view the Indochinese War as a struggle against communism; hence the concluding statement of Ho Chi Minh in the *Stockholm Expressen* was particularly pregnant with implications:

> Today it is not only the independence of Vietnam that is exposed to serious attacks. Even the independence of France is being seriously threatened. On the one hand, American Imperialism is making French Colonialists carry on and extend the war of conquest in Vietnam for the purpose of rendering France weaker and weaker and taking over her position in Vietnam. On the other hand, the American Imperialists are forcing France to sign the EDC pact, which implies that German militarism will be reborn.[8]

Were the *Expressen* statements of Ho Chi Minh offered for purely propagandistic reasons or was this a genuine offer to negotiate? I think it is possible that they were formulated and published primarily for propagandistic effects—although the DRVN Premier, in fact, outlined what he regarded as the Vietminh "first offer" in any future negotiations. In November 1953, Ho Chi Minh could not have ex-

---

[7] Debate among officials and deputies was largely informal but nonetheless vehement. In the National Assembly, two interpellations for Premier Ho's "peace offer" were shunted aside as the Assembly debated the 1954 budget. See *JO*, 1 December 1953, 2d sess., p. 5772, and 2 December 1953, 2d sess., p. 5839.

[8] Cole, *op. cit.*, p. 149.

pected the Laniel government to ignore Bao Dai's government; but this is what his "peace offer" implicitly required.

The SVN,[9] after all, had been recognized by France, the United States, and Great Britain. Acceptance of the *Expressen* "peace offer" and the concomitant official discarding of Bao Dai would have precipitated a crisis in Franco-American relations. Even apart from the exigencies of her foreign relations, France's domestic politics would not have permitted Laniel, nor perhaps even Mendès-France, to deal directly with the Vietminh in late 1953. So long as hope of a military victory against the Vietminh persisted, the parties of the center and right would have joined to overthrow any government that dared deal with these Vietnamese "rebels." Despite the anti-war sentiment most French officials continued to feel, throughout the winter of 1953/1954, that victory was possible.

While in retrospect it is possible to say that France could not abandon the SVN in order to respond to a putative peace offer from Ho Chi Minh, Vietnamese (SVN) officials in Saigon were not sure that France would not abandon them. They were aware of the sentiment in France for a negotiated settlement of the Indochinese War, even if this meant negotiations with the Vietminh. They probably could not assess the strength of that sentiment, nor determine its possible effects upon Fourth Republic politics. They were alarmed by the *Expressen* statements and by the prospect of the support such statements might give pacifist opinion in France. Bao Dai was somewhat reassured by Laniel's declaration that representatives of the Associated States must be brought into negotiations for settling the war; but the Vietnamese nationalists were not reassured. Uneasy over the possibility of a "sell out" and dissatisfied with the progress of negotiations for genuine independence, the nationalists pressed Bao Dai to dismiss Premier Nguyen Van Tam, who they thought was too subservient to French wishes. The chief of state bowed to this pressure and asked for Tam's resignation in December 1953. In January 1954 he requested his cousin and advisor, Prince Buu Loc, to form a government, which the prince did, pledging renewed efforts to achieve "total independence" for the State of Vietnam.

The *Expressen* "peace feelers" were repeated on two occasions, in similarly vague and general terms, in mid-December 1953. The first such feeler was a Vietminh information agency release, which in a roundabout way was broadcast to the world from Moscow;[10] the

[9] The acronym SVN means the State of Vietnam of which Bao Dai was chief of state.

[10] *NYT*, 14 December 1953. The announcement read in part: "If the French Government really respects the independence of Vietnam and is ready to start negotiations with the People's Government of Vietnam to end this war, the people and government of the DRVN will be ready to accept the French proposal."

second was a speech by the DRVN Premier on the seventh anniversary of the Indochinese War.[11] As in the *Expressen* statements, these feelers implicitly claimed that the DRVN represented the people of Vietnam and, explicitly, that France and the DRVN should negotiate with each other as the only two sovereign entities involved in the war.

[I I]

By early fall of 1953 the Vietminh controlled more than half of Vietnam; their holdings comprised most of northern and northwestern Tonkin, the central highlands area of Annam, and several important sectors in the Mekong delta in Cochin China. The Red River delta, with its two major cities of Hanoi and Haiphong was controlled by French Union forces, as were Hué and Tourane in central Vietnam and the major cities of Cochin China, including Saigon. Outside the cities, the rural areas were largely the preserve of the Vietminh.

In the spring of 1953, General Vo Nguyen Giap, commander in chief of the People's Army of Vietnam (PAVN), thrust into Laos, only to withdraw several months later. In October, apparently with more serious intent, General Giap moved his armies into the Annamite mountains of Laos and Tonkin. In December he opened an offensive westward and southward from the Annamite mountains, driving deep into Laos and capturing Thakhek on the Mekong River. By January 1954, Savannakhet was threatened. At this time units of the PAVN controlled more than half of Laos and small areas of northern Cambodia.

These moves caused consternation and alarm in Saigon and Paris. The December "peace offers" of the DRVN were viewed by an increasingly concerned segment of French opinion as a realistic basis for negotiation. When General Giap made his first moves into the Annamite mountains in October 1953, General Henri Navarre, commander in chief of the French Union forces, anticipated a broadened war effort in the west, including a second invasion of Laos and a repeat of the offensive in April. He agreed with Maurice Dejean, French High Commissioner for Indochina, that Laos would have to be defended: France, they felt, was obliged to defend Laos under the terms of the Franco-Laotian treaty of 22 October 1953, which had guaranteed Laos independence within the French Union. On 20 November 1953, six battalions of parachutists of the French Union army occupied the basin at Dien Bien Phu in northwestern Tonkin; and,

[11] *NYT*, 18 December 1953. Ho Chi Minh, *Selected Works* (Hanoi: Foreign Languages Publishing House, 1961), 3: 431.

in December, General Navarre declared that Dien Bien Phu must be held at all costs.

FRENCH MILITARY strategy in Indochina in 1953 and 1954 must be viewed in relation to a broadly conceived political-military plan of the French commander, General Navarre. The Navarre Plan, as it came to be called, envisaged the buildup of French Union forces to an estimated strength of 550,000 men. The bulk of this increase would consist of Vietnamese, whose contribution would be raised from 200,000 to about 300,000 men, but in addition, about 50,000 non-Vietnamese French Union troops would be sent to Indochina, increasing the strength of the non-Vietnamese contingent to 250,000 men. But to attract Vietnamese recruits, thus permitting proponents of the Navarre Plan to anticipate success in the crucial troop-buildup phase, some concessions on genuine independence for the State of Vietnam would have to be made. Certainly it would be unrealistic to expect the Vietnamese to rally to a French colonial cause, to fight the Vietnamese of the Vietminh with only unreliable promises of something described as "free association" within the French Union. Yet, substantial official opposition in France against perfecting SVN independence immediately called into question the efficacy of this or any other military plan that relied upon Vietnamese forces. Moreover, increases in the troop strength of the French Union forces would take time: offensive action against the Vietminh in the north would not be possible until Vietnamese recruits were trained; and the requisite training, it was estimated, would take more than a year. In the interim, what could be accomplished? General Navarre suggested that, south of the 18th parallel, French Union forces continue to stage limited operations against the Vietminh; north of the 18th parallel, however, French forces would go on a "strategic defensive," avoiding major engagements.

Professional military men, including the army chief of staff, General Paul Ely, warned the government that the Navarre Plan would not permit General Navarre to hold Laos, and might even result in the loss of the Red River delta if the Vietminh launched a determined offensive.[12] Despite these opinions the Navarre Plan became the official strategy of the French in Indochina after mid-1953.

The operational part of the plan produced neither success nor failure south of the 18th parallel, perhaps because Vietminh strategy called for no offensive action in the south of the type that was soon to develop in Tonkin. North of the 18th parallel, the Navarre operational

[12] *Le Monde*, 15 May 1953, and discussion in L&D, pp. 39-42. Cf. General Ely's more recent statement in *Memoires: L'Indochine dans la Tourmente* (Paris: Plon, 1964), pp. 23-26.

plan worked quite well from July through October 1953, until General Giap moved into the Annamite mountains and thence into Laos. French Union forces were unable to stop the Vietminh offensive, which eventuated in the capture of Thakhek in late December. General Giap did not reduce the pressure against French Laos until late February 1954. Before that, on 27 January, the PAVN struck at Luang Prabang, the royal capital of Laos.

[I I I]

In May 1950 the United States government formally announced its intention of providing the French with economic aid and military equipment to enable them to bring stability and order to Indochina.[13] This aid was increased annually, particularly after the Korean War began and the Truman administration became more conscious of overseas security considerations, in East Asia and elsewhere. Declarations of concern by American officials for the outcome of the Indochinese War became more frequent in 1953. With a truce in Korea the avowed goal of his administration, President Eisenhower (inaugurated in January) told the American Society of Newspaper Editors, on 16 April 1953, that "any armistice in Korea that merely released aggressive armies to attack elsewhere would be a fraud."[14] Two days later Secretary of State John Foster Dulles warned that Communists in the Far East could "no longer count on winning by shifting their strength and by focussing attack on one or another free world position that is isolated from the others."[15]

When the PAVN invaded Laos in April 1953, the United States responded by supplying C-119 troop transports to the Royal Laotian government. The military situation remained under constant review in Washington throughout the spring and summer of 1953. Administration spokesmen expressed their concern about the security of Thailand and announced that the Bangkok government would be provided military assistance. Communist Chinese assistance to the Vietminh had been extended to the DRVN in 1950 and had been continued irregularly through the years of Chinese involvement in the Korean War. During the summer of 1953, however, Chinese aid began to increase substantially, a fact that did not escape the attention of the intelligence agencies of the French and Vietnamese in Saigon nor those of the United States. With hard evidence of this Chinese

---

[13] *DSB*, 22 May 1950, p. 821, reporting the statement of Secretary of State Dean Acheson at a ministers' meeting in Paris, 8 May 1950.

[14] P. V. Curl (ed.), *Documents on American Foreign Relations, 1953* (New York: Harper & Row, 1954), p. 31.

[15] *NYT*, 19 April 1953. Mr. Dulles asserted that new priority had been given to Far Eastern affairs.

assistance in matériel and noncombatant manpower, Secretary Dulles on 2 September 1953 declared:

> Communist China has been and now is training, equipping and supplying the communist forces in Indochina. There is the risk that, as in Korea, Red China might send its own army into Indochina. The Communist Chinese regime should realize that such a second aggression could not occur without grave consequences which might not be confined to Indochina.[16]

In November, Vice President Richard Nixon echoed earlier administration statements of the strategic importance of Indochina and the necessity for a French victory.[17]

The 1953 statements of the President, his Secretary of State, and others were designed to clarify American intentions ahead of time, thereby, it was felt, deterring an adventurous adversary.[18] This policy of the new Republican administration—of apprising the aggressor of American intentions—was to run into difficulty in early 1954, as we shall see.

American concern also extended to Franco-Vietnamese relations and to the inability of the French to solve the problem of Vietnamese independence. Unless the charge of colonial repression could be avoided—unless the French could be persuaded to give the Vietnamese genuine independence—the government of the State of Vietnam could not win the allegiance of the Vietnamese nationalists and the Navarre Plan could not succeed. A report of the House Committee on Foreign Affairs stated in June 1953:

> The testimony before the Committee indicates that until the peoples of the Associated States are assured of receiving their ultimate

[16] *DSB*, 14 September 1953, p. 342. The Secretary of State made this remark in a speech to the American Legion at St. Louis, Missouri.

[17] *NYT*, 5 November 1953.

[18] Secretary of State Dean Acheson's exclusion of Korea from the United States' East Asian defense perimeter was believed to have invited the North Korean invasion. Mr. Acheson's perimeter included Japan, the Ryukyus, and the Philippines; but he omitted Formosa and Korea, which he (perhaps too simply) referred to as "other areas."

Mr. Acheson said: "So far as the military security of other areas in the Pacific is concerned, it must be clear that no person can guarantee these areas against military attack. . . . Should such an attack occur . . . the initial reliance must be on the people attacked to resist it and then upon the commitments of the entire civilized world under the Charter of the United Nations which so far has not proved a weak reed to lean on by people who are determined to protect their independence against outside aggression." See Raymond Dennett and R. K. Turner (eds.), *Documents on American Foreign Relations, January 1-December 31, 1950* (Princeton: Princeton University Press, 1951), pp. 431-432.

General Douglas MacArthur had similarly excluded Korea from the "defense perimeter," even urging prompt withdrawal of American troops from Korea. He believed the Republic of Korea army was strong enough to defend South Korea. See *NYT*, 2 March 1949.

independence, success in driving out the communist invaders will be difficult, if not impossible to achieve.[19]

The United States had long pressured the French to give the Vietnamese, Laotians, and Cambodians an independent status sufficient to compete with the nationalistic propaganda of the Vietminh—substantial enough, United States policymakers reasoned, to be worth the fight against the Communist-inspired Vietminh movement. Also, there were constant bipartisan reminders that the United States must not associate itself with a French effort to preserve France's colonial empire. But in spite of numerous American declarations opposing colonialism, in spite of American dissatisfaction with French conduct of the Indochinese War, the Eisenhower administration would not and could not bring itself to press the Laniel government for real concessions to the Bao Dai regime. Why this should be so can be seen in the factors that affected first French and then American diplomacy

FRENCH DIPLOMACY

1. The French regarded the Indochinese War as primarily a domestic matter, and France successfully resisted efforts to bring the question of the war to the United Nations, relying upon the provisions of article 2 (7) of the United Nations Charter, which removes matters of domestic jurisdiction from the competence of that organization.

2. Until early 1954, France was wary of increased American involvement in the war, particularly in the form of ground forces and training cadres. Influential segments of French opinion viewed the war as a conflict in a former French colonial preserve and wanted neither U.N. intervention, which might have the unintended effect of increasing C.P.R. aid to the Vietminh, nor U.S. intervention, which might result in France's being eased out of Indochina by the omnipresent Americans—first by U.S. armed forces, then by American officials, and finally by American businessmen.[20]

3. In spite of Laniel's promises to grant independence to Vietnam, Laos, and Cambodia, there was constant and effective opposition to this step by the French right, which included important figures in the government itself—Foreign Minister Bidault among others. By the fall of 1953 it became clear that *absolute* independence for the Associated States was out of the question. The reasons for this were

[19] U.S. Congress, House of Representatives, Committee on Foreign Affairs, *Report on H. R. 5710, a Bill to Amend Further the Mutual Security Act of 1951,* H. R. Report No. 569, 83d Congress, 1st sess., 16 June 1953, p. 37.

[20] General Navarre was supposed to have often complained of American commercial and military activities in Indochina. Ely, p. 32.

various: the states would be unable to resist aggression if they were completely independent; the French constitution required a particular status for the Associated States that placed restrictions upon their sovereignty, and to change this status would require a constitutional amendment; independence for the Associated States would cause the collapse of the prospective French Union and increasingly vehement demands for independence by other colonies, such as Tunisia, Morocco, and Algeria; and, finally, if the French withdrew voluntarily from Indochina—or what was worse, were asked to leave by a newly independent Indochina[21]—French prestige would sustain a shattering blow. No French government could survive such an eventuality, nor perhaps even the Fourth Republic itself.

4. The Communist character of the Vietminh did not disturb the French policymakers as much as it did their American allies.

American Diplomacy

1. Although critics of American policy in Southeast Asia in the 1960s have frequently asserted that the Eisenhower administration (and later administrations) did not appreciate the fact that the Indochinese War was a colonial war, based on the nationalist sentiments of the Indochinese, and not a war of the international Communist movement, there is no valid basis for such criticism. The Eisenhower administration, and many congressmen, were aware that this war was different from the Korean War, that the Vietminh was a popular movement, that the DRVN had substantial popular support in areas it controlled, and that the war had political aspects that made the outlook very bleak for French military efforts. The Communist nature of the Vietminh, however, was undeniable. Moreover, the DRVN had diplomatic relations with the Soviet Union and with the C.P.R., only lately the enemy of the United States in a very costly and frustrating war.

The Communist character of the Vietminh, for all practical purposes, overshadowed all other facts of the Indochinese War in 1953 and 1954. But these other facts were not ignored, they were relegated to secondary status.

2a. Although the United States government could press the French to widen the war, the war was becoming increasingly unpopular in

---

[21] It was not entirely unlikely that the French would be asked to leave after the cessation of hostilities. In October 1953 a national congress of the State of Vietnam recommended recognition of the SVN as a totally independent state, and also recommended abrogation of the treaties and conventions in force between France and the SVN. The congress declared that an "independent Vietnam cannot participate in the French Union in its present form." See Cole, op. cit., pp. 168-170.

France, and the Americans could easily be accused of being willing to fight to the last French soldier.

2*b*. The United States could press the French to allow an American training mission to expedite the Navarre Plan, but this would be—and was—resisted. The Indochinese War was a French affair and United States intervention was suspect.

2*c*. The United States could commit its own armed forces to Indochina. In 1953 the administration had not yet faced this issue, although Vice President Nixon had hinted that American troops might conceivably be committed. Congressional reaction to Mr. Nixon's remarks indicated that he had touched upon a sensitive issue.

2*d*. The United States could increase its diplomatic pressure to persuade the French to grant independence to the Associated States. This could result in the French pulling out of Indochina altogether, which, in view of the popularity of the Vietminh in many areas of Indochina (a fact appreciated in high government circles), would result in a Vietminh takeover of Vietnam, and possibly even Laos and Cambodia. If, on the other hand, this increased pressure did not eventuate in a withdrawal of French Union forces, it would antagonize the French, weaken the Western alliance, and most certainly jeopardize the European Defense Community treaty, which had not yet been ratified by the French National Assembly.

3. Premier Ho Chi Minh had asserted that American imperialists were forcing the French to sign the EDC treaty, which would permit the rebirth of German militarism. In broaching the subject of the EDC in the context of a peace offer in Indochina, Ho Chi Minh had made no merely fortuitous connection between two seemingly disparate problems of two widely separated geographical areas, Europe and Indochina. EDC and an Indochina armistice were to become subtly interrelated in the ensuing months, but even in November 1953 the Vietminh Premier knew that many French were opposed to German rearmament and to the supranational structure that would facilitate that rearmament.

IT WOULD be wise to break our narrative at this point to consider, however briefly, the EDC and its effects upon the policies of the Western allies.

After the outbreak of the Korean War the Truman administration determined that Europe (as opposed to East Asia) was still the primary area of United States strategic concern. To ensure against the possibility that the Korean action might be a feint for a Soviet military move against Western Europe, the United States decided to strengthen NATO and to rearm West Germany and invite her to join the Atlantic Alliance. As might be expected, there was much opposition to this policy, particularly in France. René Pleven, the French Premier, proposed a scheme for integrating German combat teams into the divisions of a supranational European army, a scheme roughly analogous to the previously established European Coal and Steel Community. The American reaction to the plan was negative at first, being viewed as an effort to obstruct German rearmament. Subsequently, however, this view changed and the United States became the staunchest advocate of the Pleven plan, with this understanding: German units were to be integrated into the European army on a basis of complete equality with the units of other participants. This European Defense Community, as it became known, was regarded not only as the framework for German rearmament, and thus for the buildup of NATO strength as well, but also as a further means for promoting the political and economic integration of Europe and ensuring West Germany's alliance with the West.

The EDC plan became embodied in the treaty of that name, signed 27 May 1952 by the continental European NATO allies (neither Britain nor the United States was a signatory). Concurrently, representatives of France, Britain, and the United States concluded a contractual agreement with West Germany, ending the military occupation. When all the NATO signatories had ratified the EDC treaty, it was agreed that West Germany would receive full sovereign powers.

By the end of 1953 ratification of EDC had been debated exhaustively in Europe's national parliaments. There were problems with Italian ratification and West German implementation, but a vote against ratification seemed a possibility only in France, where a mere 40 percent of the National Assembly could be counted as real supporters of the EDC. The Communists and the Gaullists were uniformly opposed; the Socialists, Radical Socialists, and Independents were divided in their sentiments; and the M.R.P. (Popular Republican Party) deputies were generally favorable. This parliamentary division was reflected in the cabinet itself, where even Laniel was less than enthusiastic about the project.

French ratification had been tied by successive governments to the Europeanization of the Saar and to obtaining firmer commitments from Britain and the United States to maintain sufficient forces in Europe to counterbalance the German contribution to the European army. Bidault had appealed (unsuccessfully) to Churchill and Eisenhower at the Bermuda Conference in December 1953 for a formal declaration embodying such guarantees. The French had also obtained concessions from her cosignatories in the form of a series of protocols that somewhat reduced French obligations under the treaty. All these preconditions, all the juridical, political, and military details that were the subject of lengthy debate in the National Assembly, reflected the widespread opposition in France to German re-armament and the EDC. Proponents of the treaty might point out that integration of combat units offered a means for controlling the German military; but opponents could argue that Germany might become dominant on the continent, particularly if the United States and Britain should decide that conditions warranted withdrawal of their forces. German dominance was no mere fantasy or speculative possibility inasmuch as the French army was fighting in Indochina and was committed to the defense of French North Africa.

The Eisenhower administration supported the EDC and its policy received the backing of the 83d Congress. Various means were employed to induce France to ratify the treaty, both behind-the-scenes diplomatic efforts and public action. For example, an amendment to the Mutual Security Program appropriation for 1953–1954, known as the Richards Amendment," made one-half of the appropriation for Europe contingent on the adoption of the EDC treaty. As might be expected, this congressional action was the cause of some resentment in Paris; but by far the most astringent French reaction came after Mr. Dulles's speech to the North Atlantic Council on 14 December 1953, in which the secretary said:

> If . . . the European Defense Community should not become effective; if France and Germany remain apart so that they would again be potential enemies, then indeed there would be grave doubt whether Continental Europe could be made a place of safety. That would compel an agonizing reappraisal of basic United States policy.[22]

President Eisenhower subsequently endorsed the warning implicit in his secretary's choice of the phrase "agonizing reappraisal," one of several such phrases that immediately gained notoriety.[23]

4. Indochina was regarded as strategically important by Washington, and with every policy pronouncement in 1954 it seemed to become ever more important. Indochina in the hands of a Communist regime would be a victory for international communism. In 1953 the possibilities of Ho Chi Minh's becoming a Southeast Asia Tito were not appreciated; and perhaps it is asking too much that they should have been. In any event, the fact of Vietminh success was appreciated: in Tonkin, in the Vietminh invasion of Laos, and in the guerrilla incursions in Cambodia. American policymakers, moreover, suspected that Premier Ho wanted to establish a federated state in the Indochina peninsula with the DRVN exercising some form of control over

[22] *NYT*, 15 December 1953.
[23] The President's endorsement of 23 December 1953 appears in *DSB*, 4 January 1954, p. 7.

Cambodia and Laos.[24] Declarations from administration officials in Washington on the strategic significance of a Vietminh victory described the situation in such metaphors as a "chain reaction," a "cork in a bottle," and a "row of dominoes"—implying that all Southeast Asia would become Communist if the Vietminh should emerge victorious. The policy of "containment," which had provided one rationale for United States involvement in Korea, would have failed were Communist military action to succeed elsewhere in Asia, and particularly in Indochina.

THUS CONCERN over the possible success of the Communist Vietminh, and what Washington (even in 1953) regarded as the strategic implications of that success, predominated over other concerns, the most important of which was satisfying the nationalist aspirations of Vietnamese elites. The Laniel government had, after all, begun negotiations with representatives of the State of Vietnam, and these talks continued throughout the winter of 1953/1954. The French government continued to assure the administration that these negotiations would eventuate in real independence for the Vietnamese; and for the time being American officials were encouraged.

Although expert military opinion in Washington expressed doubts about the efficacy of the Navarre Plan, there was no persuasive evidence that it would not work. Even the PAVN success in Laos in December and January did not, and as a matter of fact could not, prove that the plan was not going to succeed: operational results were not expected until late fall of 1954. The Navarre Plan, moreover, was the official strategy of the Laniel government, and there was no reason why the Eisenhower administration should ask the French to adopt an alternative.

The policy line adopted in Washington was one that would not offend French sensibilities; namely, the war in Indochina was primarily a French concern and a French responsibility. The United States would continue to provide funds and military hardware to the French for use by French Union–Vietnamese forces; and Washington would support the Laniel government's rejection of negotiating directly with the DRVN. It is likely that United States diplomats did much more, and urged such rejection, although even this was done cautiously.

The Indochinese War had not yet caught the attention of the American public, and radically anti-Communist elements in the Eisenhower administration had not yet made it a matter of principle to prevent France, at all costs, from dealing even at arm's length with

[24] See Ho Chi Minh (*op. cit.*, 2: 125-126, 147), but compare the DRVN Premier's statement about the equality of Cambodia, Laos, and Vietnam (*ibid.*, 3: 206, 246).

the DRVN. Thus American foreign affairs policymakers could still adopt a prudent "Indochina is a French affair" policy without antagonizing the right wing of the Republican Party. These halcyon days would end with the spring crisis. For the time being, however (i.e. at the end of 1953), the estimate in Washington was that Laniel could still outflank the proponents of negotiation to end the war because he was in fact prepared to negotiate for that end and could persuade the deputies that he was amenable to ending the war. Laniel, on the other hand, could reject the Ho Chi Minh "peace feelers" on grounds that appeared reasonable to the parliamentary right and center parties: the Vietminh were rebels and therefore could not demand to be treated as a legitimate entity, particularly since France and her allies had recognized another government of the Vietnamese people.

[I V]

Stalin had been dead about nine months when Ho Chi Minh made the statements that were published in the *Expressen*. In this interval the Soviets had tested a hydrogen bomb; they had ostensibly adopted a domestic policy that emphasized light industry, consumer goods, and agriculture; and they professed to have adopted a policy of peaceful coexistence with the West. In place of a solitary dictator, the Soviet Union was governed by the principle of "collective leadership" under Premier Georgy Malenkov. In the Panmunjom negotiations, it is possible that Soviet diplomatic pressure upon Peking was at least partially responsible for the Chinese relenting on their demands for prisoner repatriation, thus enabling a Korean armistice to be signed in July 1953; and in the fall of that year the Soviets, along with the Chinese, hinted at the possibility of a cease-fire in Indochina. The policy of détente had this merit: it would persuade the policymakers of Europe, and particularly the policymakers of the nonaligned states of Asia, that the Malenkov regime was indeed reasonable and determined to negotiate differences to reduce world tensions. Obstinacy by the United States, France, or any other state would result in a rather important propaganda victory for the Soviet Union. Even apart from the propaganda value of a détente policy, it is possible —and probable in the opinion of many Soviet experts—that Malenkov and his supporters wanted to explore ways of improving relations with the West.

In line with such policies, the Soviets favored and even pressed for a meeting of the Big Four foreign ministers. The ministers had last met in May and June 1949, and now there was much sentiment in both Britain and France for a ministers' meeting, in part as a means for testing Soviet intentions. Other European governments also favored such a meeting. The Adenauer government in West Germany and the Austrian government hoped the ministers could agree to end the occupation regimes and the *de facto* partition of their countries. American officials were not enthusiastic about a Big Four ministers' meeting but the administration eventually agreed to participate, more to please its allies than in the expectation of positive achievements. Besides, the United States had to show the world it was at all times ready to negotiate with the Soviet Union if improved relations between the two states were in prospect. Nevertheless, Washington was concerned that a Big Four conference would permit the Soviets to exploit matters that might produce disunity in the Western alliance: German rearmament, the EDC, and the Indochinese War.

Whether a great-power conference should be held at all, and on what terms, was the subject of a series of diplomatic exchanges throughout the fall of 1953. Eventually a modicum of agreement was achieved between the Western allies and the Soviet Union, in spite of the fact that the latter had pressed for a conference that would include the Chinese People's Republic. This, of course, was rejected by the United States, but the Soviet Union agreed to a Four Power conference and its decision was welcomed at the conference President Eisenhower, Prime Minister Churchill, and French Foreign Minister Bidault[25] held in Bermuda in early December 1953.

At Bermuda the two heads of state and Bidault discussed a variety of mutual problems, including the Indochinese War, and the three participants agreed that the French war effort was of "vital importance." Their communiqué emphasized the importance of Western unity within NATO as the foundation of a common policy of the alliance. It also emphasized the need for the EDC as an integral part of NATO defense efforts.[26] It was reported, unofficially, that Bidault promised he would refuse to consider the "peace feelers" of the DRVN government.[27]

Before the Four Power ministers' conference opened, the Western allies had made a number of procedural concessions to the Soviet Union. They accepted a delay in the start of the conference, postponing it from 4 January to 25 January. They offered an indefinite agenda to the Soviets, knowing the advantage this gave them to touch upon various problems, including China's participation. And they agreed to hold the conference in Berlin rather than in Lugano. Later,

[25] Premier Laniel was ill at the time and could not attend the conference.
[26] Curl (ed.), *op. cit.*, pp. 216-218.
[27] *NYT*, 9 December 1953.

after the ministers had convened in Berlin, they agreed that sessions of the conference would be held for approximately equal periods of time in the Western and the Eastern sectors of the city.[28]

The United States and its allies prepared intensively for the Berlin Conference; they hoped to anticipate every tactic the Soviet representative, Foreign Minister Vyacheslav Molotov, might employ. They had agreed that the Berlin Conference should be given full publicity and that no time limit would be imposed, although Dulles indicated that he would have to leave on 1 March to attend the Tenth Inter-American Conference at Caracas, Venezuela. Anticipating Soviet efforts to cause dissension but unsure whether their traditional adversary might not be willing to resolve vital questions of European security, the Western allies attempted to reach a common ground of understanding and agreement on the issues the Soviets or they themselves would raise at Berlin. If the conduct of Western diplomacy at the conference was any indication, the preparatory efforts had indeed solidified and harmonized the positions of the Big Three; the cooperation and coordination of effort achieved by Eden, Bidault, and Dulles was a tribute to the vitality of the Western alliance.

All this, however, would be sorely taxed as the Indochina situation rapidly deteriorated in the months after the Berlin Conference.

[28] *NYT*, 15 January 1954.

Chapter 2

THE BERLIN CONFERENCE AND
ITS POLITICAL CONTEXT

[I]

Talks on a Korean political settlement, which began in Panmunjon in late October 1953, had collapsed in December when Arthur Dean, the U.S. delegate, broke off discussions after Huang Hua, the C.P.R. delegate, accused the United States of conspiring with the Republic of Korea to subvert prisoner exchanges. It was conceivable that the Korean discussions would resume without the participation of the C.P.R. The same might be said of any possible talks on the Indochinese War. In September 1953, Dulles had declared that a prospective Korean conference agenda *might* be amended to include the Indochinese War *if* the Chinese were disposed to stop supporting aggression in Indochina.[1] Any suggestion at Berlin, particularly by the French, that the Big Four consider the situation in Southeast Asia was bound to occasion a Soviet proposal that China be brought into this and any future conference dealing with East Asian problems.

At Berlin, none of the Western allies had any illusions about the possibilities of finding mutually agreeable means for unifying Germany. Nevertheless, the British and French believed there was a basis for hoping the conference would reduce tensions in the mere fact that the Big Four foreign ministers were negotiating again. French officials were somewhat worried lest the Soviets drag out the conference, using it for propaganda purposes and appealing to those in France who might welcome a neutral Germany or peace in Indochina in exchange for nonratification of the EDC treaty. Bidault was in a fairly strong position to avoid this tactic, however. During the first week of January the French National Assembly had given the Laniel government a vote of confidence; and in the week preceding the opening of the conference the cabinet had given Bidault leave to refuse to bargain over EDC. The majority of ministers in the Laniel cabinet apparently agreed with their Foreign Minister that bargaining with the fate of EDC was not the way to obtain peace.[2] But Bidault could not refuse the offer of negotiations over Indochina in exchange for the participation of the C.P.R. in those negotiations;

[1] Press conference statement of 3 September 1953, in *DSB*, 14 September 1953, pp. 342-343.
[2] *JO*, 6 January 1954, p. 19. The vote was 319 for the government, 249 against. See also *NYT*, 10 January 1954.

and this, Bidault felt, the United States government must be made to realize.[3]

German rearmament, in or out of EDC, was unpopular in many circles in Britain and France, and the Soviet Union could use this issue as a lever for forcing the Western allies apart. The Soviet press, which had already accused the United States of wanting to foster a resurgence of German militarism, suggested that the conference would fail because of the American policy of rearming the mortal enemy of the war that had ended only a decade ago. In the House of Commons and in the British press, and from both the left and the right, the Churchill government was urged to repudiate the policy of German rearmament in exchange for German unification and to agree to meet with the Communist Chinese in exchange for an Austrian peace treaty.[4]

The Four Power Berlin Conference opened on 25 January in the Allied Control Authority Building in the American sector of Berlin. In attendance (with their staffs) were Britain's Foreign Secretary, Anthony Eden, France's Bidault, the Soviet Union's Molotov, and Secretary of State Dulles. In his opening statement Molotov introduced his proposal for a *five-power* conference, that is, a conference of the Big Four plus the C.P.R.[5] Also, Molotov hinted that Southeast Asia (as well as Korea) could be discussed at a five-power conference. Bidault said he was ready to discuss a settlement of the Indochinese War at any time, but how was this possible, he asked, when the C.P.R., by arming and training the Vietminh, had committed— and continued to commit—aggression against the French? The Chinese would have to make "pledges of good will" before restoration of peace in Asia was possible, the French minister asserted.[6] But this was not Bidault's final word. The ministers agreed to take up the question again the following week, ostensibly after giving it further study.

On two occasions in this early stage of the conference Dulles made

[3] See *NYT*, 9 January 1954, and Walter Lippmann's "The Nettle of Indo-China," *NYHT*, 11 February 1954.

[4] *NYT*, 22 January 1954. Neither the British nor the French government was overly optimistic about the prospects for German unification. *NYT*, 20 January 1954.

[5] *Foreign Ministers' Meeting, Berlin Discussions, January 25-February 18, 1954*, Department of State Publication 5399 (1954), p. 23 (hereafter referred to as *FMM*). See also Anthony Eden's account (E, pp. 65-85) and the accounts in R. P. Stebbins, *The United States in World Affairs, 1954* (New York: Harper & Row, 1956), pp. 102-132, and Coral Bell, *Survey of International Affairs, 1954* (London: Oxford University Press, 1957), pp. 131-137.

[6] *FMM*, p. 47. Eden favored a five-power conference, provided the United States could be induced to participate. E, p. 97.

his views clear on meeting with Communist China across the baize table. On 26 January he said:

I would like to state plainly and unequivocally what the Soviet Foreign Minister already knows—the United States will not agree to join in a five-power conference with the Chinese Communist aggressors for the purpose of *dealing generally with the peace of the world*. The United States refuses not because, as is suggested, it denies that the regime exists or that it has power. We in the United States know that it exists and has power, because its aggressive armies joined with the North Korean aggressors to kill and wound 150,000 Americans who went to Korea with British, French, and other United Nations forces to resist that aggression . . . we do not refuse to deal with it where occasion requires. We did deal with it in making the Korean Armistice.[7]

Two days later, however, Dulles said he would agree to discuss *particular* or *specific* questions with the Chinese if other interested parties also were present. The Korean armistice had been such a question, Dulles indicated, but the Eisenhower administration would not consent to negotiate with the C.P.R. over general questions of world security or the reduction of tensions in East Asia and elsewhere.[8]

By the end of the second week of the conference, after plans for German unification had been submitted by Eden for the Western delegations and by Molotov for the Soviet Union, the Western ministers concluded that the Soviets would not change their position on German unification. The Soviet plan was unacceptable to the Western ministers because, in their view, it would give undue weight and prestige to the East German government. It was, moreover, unacceptable to the Bonn government. On the other hand, the plan submitted by Eden the week before on behalf of the Western allies was unacceptable to the Soviet Union because it would probably result in the eventual liquidation of East Germany and its absorption in a state that was sure to be closely allied with the West. The Russians were under no illusions about the results of all-German elections held according to the procedure of the Western plan. West Germany had a substantially greater population than East Germany and the West Germans could be expected to support the Bonn government and West German candidates in any all-German elections, with the result that control of a constituent assembly would rest in West German hands. After the East Berlin riots in June 1953, the Soviets had every reason to believe that all-German elections would result in a defeat for the Pankow regime. Finally, the unification of Germany and its

[7] *FMM*, pp. 27-28. Emphasis added.
[8] *FMM*, pp. 50-51.

alliance with the West might fatally weaken the Soviet bloc in Eastern Europe. Thus the Soviets must hold firm. The Western ministers concluded that the Soviet Union had no intention of seeking a solution of the German problem.[9]

Although Molotov was blamed for preventing agreement on both the German and the Western security questions, and had in effect said no, he had refused in such a way that he could not be accused of being intransigent or unreasonable. Here was Molotov more flexible than the West had known in all the earlier postwar years. Moreover, his proposals were in some respects attractive to several sectors of public opinion in Britain and on the Continent. His collective-security treaty project would require the withdrawal of foreign troops from Europe, a not unwelcome event, particularly in left-of-center circles where the diminished fear of a Soviet attack led to the advocacy of a neutralized, demilitarized Europe. Reiterating a statement of I. G. Kabarov of the Ministry of Foreign Trade, Molotov had also suggested that, with improved security conditions in Europe, the Soviet Union would be amenable to purchasing more than a billion dollars' worth of industrial goods from Great Britain over a three-year period.[10] During the first week of the ministers' meeting, when the participation of Communist China in an enlarged conference was being discussed, Molotov had briefly described the commercial benefits of normalized trade with the C.P.R. and had argued that recognition of China's great-power status would have economic as well as political benefits.[11]

Thus the Western ministers' efforts to appear blameless for the failure to achieve results at Berlin were made difficult by the Soviet ministers' offers, which demonstrated neither the Soviet Union's peaceful intentions nor its warlike proclivities. Molotov adopted a more difficult intermediate approach—as Richard P. Stebbins wrote—

> too uncompromising to warrant a conclusion that Soviet hostility to the free world had generally abated, yet too conciliatory to hold the present policy of drift and galvanize the West into renewed solidarity and effort.[12]

(The ministers turned to the Austrian treaty on 12 February and discussed their proposals throughout the fourth and last week of the conference. Much to the disappointment of the Austrian delegation,

[9] According to the *New York Times*, experts had predicted that the Soviets would treat Berlin as a "holding" conference; that is, they would hold firm to their basic positions on Germany but try to divide the allies, wreck the EDC, and obstruct European integration. *NYT*, 22 January 1954.

[10] *Daily Telegraph* (London), 5 February 1954; *NYT*, 7 February 1954.

[11] *FMM*, p. 46.

[12] Stebbins, *op. cit.*, p. 114.

which had been invited to attend this phase of the conference, no agreement on Austria was reached by the Big Four ministers.)[13]

In a series of restricted sessions (for which no verbatim minutes are available) during the last two weeks of the conference, the ministers again took up the Korean political settlement, the Indochinese War, and the participation of the C.P.R. in any conference dealing with these questions. Because of domestic pressures for settling the Indochinese War, which were stimulated by a very timely Vietminh advance upon the Laotian royal capital of Luang Prabang in January and February, Bidault sought to obtain agreement of the foreign ministers to an international conference to deal with Indochina. He recognized that China must participate in such a conference; but in line with his earlier declaration that C.P.R. aid to the Vietminh be halted, he told Molotov that if such aid were stopped, France would negotiate.[14] Bidault argued with Dulles that it was as logical to negotiate with the Chinese on the Indochina problem as it was to negotiate with them on the Korean armistice.[15] Because Dulles had said the United States would not oppose a meeting with the Chinese on specific international issues provided other interested parties were present, Bidault's task was to convert Dulles from his position of non-opposition to a conference on Indochina to one in which the United States would consent to participate in such a conference. At the same time, Bidault had to maintain a firm position on Chinese aid to the Vietminh to make such a United States agreement a bit easier.

On 11 February Bidault is reported to have proposed a four-power conference on Korea and Indochina to be attended by delegates of the C.P.R. and other interested parties.[16] *Pravda*, responding obliquely to Bidault's earlier proposal, insisted that France take steps to end the war without a prior commitment of the Chinese to halt their aid to the Vietminh. The *New York Times* reported that Communist sources in Berlin had disclosed that Molotov offered to arrange a conference between Bidault and Premier Ho Chi Minh, which Bidault was reported to have declined.[17] On 12 February the Western allies proposed a conference to deal with both Korea and Indochina on 15 April. China would be invited to attend. Presumably, there was still a great deal of disagreement over the status of the C.P.R. (and other matters) because the ministers discussed the subject again on 15, 17, and 18 February and Molotov gave no definite reply. It was significant, however, that Dulles agreed to go along with the

[13] *FMM*, pp. 175-208.
[14] *Econ.*, 20 February 1954, p. 520; *FMM*, p. 47.
[15] *NYT*, 10 February 1954.   [16] *NYT*, 12 February 1954.
[17] *Ibid.*

proposal for an East Asia conference with Chinese participation. On his return to Washington at the end of February, he would be called upon to defend that decision. But in view of the pressures upon Bidault to negotiate, a refusal by Dulles to participate in a Korea-Indochina conference would have promoted Western disunity. London would have regarded his refusal as an unnecessarily obstinate or unreasonable response. In Paris such refusal would have confirmed the view (held by many) that the United States government was willing to see French soldiers sacrificed in a desperate war rather than negotiate with the Chinese.

The terms of a formal proposal for an East Asian conference occupied the delegates and their staffs during their last week at Berlin, and the ministers came up against what at first appeared to be an insurmountable procedural obstacle. Should the C.P.R. be regarded as an "inviting" or "convening" power of the forthcoming conference on Korea and Indochina, along with Britain, France, the Soviet Union, and the United States? Molotov insisted that the C.P.R. be treated, from the start, as a fully equal participant in a five-power conference. Dulles and Bidault insisted that only the Berlin powers should convene an Indochina conference, that invitations should be sent by these four powers to other interested states, including Communist China. The deadlock was broken by a text submitted by the British delegation that omitted the distinction between inviting and invited powers.[18]

Molotov was reported to have resisted a provision Dulles wanted to insert in the final communiqué, to the effect that Chinese participation in the five-power conference would not constitute recognition of the C.P.R. by the United States; but Molotov finally yielded.

The Berlin Conference ended on 18 February and a communiqué that reflected the rather meager accomplishments of the ministers was issued. It recorded that a conference of the representatives of the United States, France, Britain, the Soviet Union, the Chinese People's Republic, North and South Korea, "and other countries the armed forces of which participated in the hostilities in Korea" would meet in Geneva on 26 April "for the purpose of reaching a peaceful settlement of the Korean question."[19]

The communiqué continued:

[The Foreign Ministers] *agree* that the problem of restoring peace in Indochina will also be discussed at the Conference, to which

[18] E, p. 99. According to L&D (p. 58) and the *NYT* (12 February 1954), Bidault proposed the formula for the communiqué whereby the distinction between "inviting" and "invited" powers would be eliminated.

[19] Department of State Press Release, No. 84, 19 February 1954; *FMM*, pp. 217–218.

representatives of the United States, France, the United Kingdom, the Union of Soviet Socialist Republics, the Chinese People's Republic and other interested states will be invited.

It is understood that neither the invitation to, nor the holding of, the above-mentioned conference shall be deemed to imply diplomatic recognition in any case where it has not already been accorded.

On disarmament, the ministers stated there would be a future "exchange of views"; and on European problems, which had occupied so much conference time, the communiqué merely stated:

> The four Ministers have had a full exchange of views on the German question, on the problems of European security and on the Austrian question. They were unable to reach agreement upon these matters.[20]

[II]

General Vo Nguyen Giap had moved sizable PAVN forces into Laos in December 1953, had divided Laos in two by the capture of Thakhek on the Mekong River, and in the last days of January (during the first week of the Berlin Conference) had advanced westward toward Luang Prabang. He continued this advance throughout most of February.[21] Bidault's efforts to obtain agreement on an Indochinese conference must therefore be viewed with appreciation that Vietminh military successes were a constant and influential goad.[22] In Paris these successes provoked high-level discussions that sought to estimate the effects of the recent developments on the conduct of the war. In February the chiefs of staff and their president, General Paul Ely, concluded that a military decision could not now be obtained in Indochina and that the only possible policy was to seek favorable military conditions for a political resolution of the conflict.[23] In spite of indications that the Vietnamese recruitment and training aspect of the Navarre Plan was having very limited success, the chiefs of staff hoped to use an enlarged Vietnamese army to obtain the successes necessary for producing favorable negotiating conditions.

[20] The three Western foreign ministers issued a tripartite communiqué on 19 February (*FMM*, pp. 218–219) that defended the positions the ministers had taken at Berlin on the German and Austrian questions. The three Western governments, it said, "will continue their efforts to achieve German reunification in freedom and by peaceful means."

[21] The PAVN advanced to within 30 miles of Luang Prabang and then halted, possibly because of supply difficulties (DDE, p. 342). In February the French eliminated the PAVN salient across southern Laos.

[22] *Econ.*, 2 January 1954, p. 11.

[23] Ely, pp. 43-49.

France, they believed, could not afford to commit any more troops to Indochina.

The successes of the Vietminh also worried Washington. Dulles, in late December, had sought to allay the fears in some sectors of opinion by declaring there was no good military reason for alarm because of the Vietminh advances. They were merely a political move, he said, for Ho Chi Minh had renewed his offers to negotiate after his victory on the Mekong.[24] Dulles still was confident that the Navarre Plan would enable the French and Vietnamese to win in about a year's time.[25] His position may have been overly optimistic, but it is well to remember that in December there was as yet little concrete evidence that the Navarre Plan would not or could not be effective— nor was it possible to say that the French government must rush to the negotiating table because the military situation was rapidly deteriorating. The secretary's *public* optimism would serve to reassure both the French and American publics.[26]

Nevertheless, within the next five weeks the basis for optimism evaporated.[27] The military situation in Vietnam had not changed substantially but the success of the Vietminh in Laos increased the pressure on the Laniel government to negotiate. This pressure was accompanied by statements expressing fear that the Indochinese War could not be won, and it reflected a growing sentiment among the French that perhaps, after all, the war wasn't worth winning. The conclusion of the chiefs of staff, in February, that no military decision could be obtained was an official (unpublicized) military estimate

[24] Press conference statement on 29 December 1953 (Press Release 678), in *DSB*, 11 January 1954, p. 43.

[25] *Ibid.*

[26] President Eisenhower established an *ad hoc* committee to study the steps the United States government might take to support the Navarre Plan. The committee was comprised of the Joint Chiefs of Staff, Under Secretary of State Walter Bedell Smith, Deputy Secretary of Defense Roger Kyes, and CIA Director Allen Dulles. The President also designated Lt. General John W. O'Daniel as chief of the U.S. Military Assistance Advisory Group (MAAG) in Saigon. Whether or not General O'Daniel was an expert on Indochina, as the Alsops said (*NYHT*, 3 February 1954), he was intimately acquainted with problems of jungle warfare and had the confidence of President Eisenhower (DDE, p. 341).

[27] The *New York Times* reported that the Vietnamese training program had been a disappointment to the Pentagon, and Secretary of Defense Charles E. Wilson said things were going "as well as can be expected" (*NYT*, 4 February 1954). At his press conference on 3 February, President Eisenhower implied that the Vietnamese people lacked enthusiasm in their desire to fight with the French forces against the Vietminh (*ibid.*, p. 14). Eisenhower's press secretary, James C. Hagerty, issued a "clarification" of the President's remarks after the conference: The President, he said, in no way wished to reflect upon the fight being waged by the armies of Vietnam, Laos, or Cambodia, or on the leadership of their governments. He merely meant to say that a number of people in Indochina had not committed themselves to the struggle against communism. *Ibid.*, p. 6.

that was quite similar to a series of earlier pessimistic declarations of Frenchmen in high and in low places alike.[28]

In an address on 12 January, Mr. Dulles repeated his September warning to the Chinese that their open aggression in Indochina would have "grave consequences which might not be confined to Indochina."[29] At his news conference on 3 February, President Eisenhower announced that the U.S. Military Assistance Advisory Group in Indochina would be increased by about 200 men, mostly technicians and airplane mechanics. In addition, about forty medium bombers (B-26s) would be supplied to the French (the United States had earlier provided the French with C-119 troop transports). Mr. Eisenhower explained that the technicians would be sent to assist in servicing the aircraft presently in Indochina as well as the additional aircraft that were to be sent there.[30]

Congressional reaction over the implications of the MAAG increase was immediate. Was the United States going to send troops to Indochina? Why hadn't Congress been advised or consulted before the decision to send American servicemen to Indochina had been announced? The President, referring to the Indochinese War at his news conference on 10 February, said there could be "no greater tragedy for America than to get heavily involved in an all-out war in any of those regions."[31] About one week later, in Mr. Dulles's absence, Acting Secretary of State Walter Bedell Smith appeared before the Senate Foreign Relations Committee. In response to the criticism of Senator H. Alexander Smith (Rep., N.J.) against sending technicians to Indochina without informing Congress, Bedell Smith promised that, in the future, no major moves of this sort would be made without prior congressional consultation. He was of the opinion that reports of Vietminh successes had been exaggerated and he added that the administration had no intention of putting American troops in Indochina. William Knowland, the Senate majority leader and a Republican from California, assured his fellow senators that the administration had no plans to send combat troops to Indochina.[33] Senator Leverett Saltonstall (Rep., Mass.), chairman of the Senate Armed

[28] There were rumors that Bidault and Marc Jacquet, minister for the Associated States, had said that the National Assembly would insist on the recall of the French expeditionary force unless the allies provided "reinforcements" in the form of a massive increase in aid. *NYT*, 9 January 1954.

[29] *DSB*, 25 January 1954, p. 108.

[30] *NYT*, 4, 5, 6, 7 February 1954.

[31] DDE, p. 341; Dwight D. Eisenhower, *Public Papers of the Presidents of the United States* (Washington, D.C., 1960), p. 250; *NYT*, 11 February 1954. See also *Econ.*, 20 February 1954, p. 538.

[32] *NYT*, 17 February 1954. See also DDE, pp. 343-344.

[33] *Econ.*, 27 February 1954, p. 611.

Services Committee, said he had been assured that the air force technicians would be withdrawn from Indochina by mid-June.[34]

Some officials and analysts regarded these statements as neither felicitous, timely, nor desirable. The Eisenhower administration had announced on 3 January that two U.S. divisions were to be removed from Korea.[35] Coupled with the February statements on Indochina by the President and other officials, this step could be interpreted as a firm American policy of avoiding involvement in Indochina. Critics said it was a tacit invitation to the Communists to step up their military pressure on the French, and they compared it to the 1950 speech of Secretary of State Dean Acheson that had excluded Korea from the United States East Asia defense perimeter. Moreover, the statements could support the French politicians who had been arguing that the war was hopeless.

Although the technicians assigned to MAAG had a functional role to perform, their dispatch was certainly a gesture of support for the French and a warning that the United States considered Indochina vital: the contingent of technicians (which was soon to be sent to Saigon) might be only the first in a series of ever increasing increments of American military personnel. But the President's statement and the declarations of General Bedell Smith and Senators Knowland and Saltonstall destroyed the symbolic deterrent effect of the dispatch of the technicians. The French were not measurably reassured; and the Vietminh, the Chinese, and the Soviets might well conclude that the Indochinese War was indeed a wholly French affair: it would not be internationalized to the extent of enlisting United States combat divisions. A wider range of policy options and bargaining tactics was at the disposal of the Communist states if the probability of United States intervention was small.

[I I I]

In the fall of 1953 Indochina was described by high administration officials as an area of great strategic significance, vitally necessary to the security of the United States. If the Indochinese War had gone so badly for the French army that victory of the Vietminh was likely, the United States would be faced with a difficult choice: whether to permit all of Vietnam, or indeed all Indochina, to come under the control of Premier Ho's DRVN or to commit American combat troops to the area to support French Union troops, in hope of ensuring victory. Even if the C.P.R. sent troops to assist the Vietminh, the choice of an appropriate response would not be easy. If the Chinese re-

[34] *Congressional Record*, C., Pt. 2, p. 1506.
[35] *NYT*, 3 January 1954.

stricted their assistance to supplying merely matériel and "techni-cians" and the Vietminh won battle after battle, the choice would be even more difficult. And, of course, there was the problem of the very nature of the war: "a French colonial war." If the Chinese intervened actively, presumably France would invite American combat troops. In the absence of such Chinese intervention, it was likely that the French would not request active American assistance until the war had reached a critical stage, and then it might be too late. Through the end of February 1954, even as increasing amounts of Chinese ma-tériel were transported to the Annamite mountain regions of Tonkin and Laos, the French officially maintained that the situation was under control; not even an American training mission was deemed necessary. (It was, in fact, unwelcome.) But even if the French gov-ernment was willing to ask for the dispatch of combat troops, the United States was anxious to avoid the charge of supporting a colonial power in the Indochinese War because most of Vietnam's attentive public, whether or not it was affiliated with Communist political or-ganizations, was anxious to achieve complete political and economic autonomy. But successive French governments had failed to grant the Vietnamese autonomy, and hence the task of justifying Ameri-can intervention to the American public would be a bit more diffi-cult than in the Korean decision, which had not been tainted by charges of colonialism.

The government of the United States would have to make a deci-sion and would have to forge a viable policy for Southeast Asia. It had not done so in January 1954.[36] (There are critics who say the administration *never* did so, but they are incorrect, as we shall see.) Nevertheless, American policy for Southeast Asia in 1954 gave rise to bitter criticism in the press—at home, in Europe, and in Asia. It may not be possible fully to understand why administration officials be-haved as they did, but explanation (a hypothetical explanation be-cause of the nonavailability of official documents) can be facilitated by considering the factors that conditioned the decisions of the Presi-dent and his policymakers.

Nineteen fifty-four was an election year, and two years earlier, in the presidential campaign, the Republican Party had criticized the Truman administration on a number of grounds, but particularly for its handling of the Korean truce negotiations and its inability to bring the war to an end. Mr. Eisenhower had promised to make special, renewed efforts to achieve an armistice. With the American public profoundly disenchanted by the Korean War, frustrated by its prog-

---

[36] See Roscoe Drummond, "Have We a Policy in Indo-China?" *NYHT*, 17 Feb-ruary 1954; Walter Millis, "Our Major Military Problem," *NYHT*, 11 February 1954.

ress, disturbed by its casualties, and irritated by the inconveniences it caused, the Republicans had won a great victory in November 1952, after which the new administration sought to fulfill its campaign promises by diplomatic efforts in early 1953. The Chinese no doubt also were disturbed by the costs of their involvement in the war: direct costs in matériel and appallingly heavy casualties and indirect costs in the war's postponement of economic development and communization programs. The Kremlin's "collective leadership" after Stalin's death in March 1953, may have attempted to persuade the Chinese to liquidate their commitment, and it also is possible that the threats by spokesmen of the new administration to carry the war to the Chinese mainland may have exerted some influence. Whatever their reason, the Chinese slowly—grudgingly—agreed to the terms of the armistice. The Republican Party took (and no doubt received) credit for ending the war.

It is no wonder that the party that had accomplished this should be wary of the situation in Indochina. The anxiety of congressional opinion was due partly to the deepening crisis in Southeast Asia and partly to the realization that a Republican administration, however reluctantly, might have to re-involve the United States in a war in East Asia in an election year—and less than a year after the Korean War had ended. The Republicans would be unable to capitalize on the Korean peace and might suffer heavy election losses for involving American forces in a new war.

The perennial problem of congressional prerogatives in the executive's conduct of foreign relations had become peculiarly acute in the early years of the Eisenhower administration. A constitutional amendment that would have severely limited the President's and the Senate's treaty-making powers had been prepared and submitted to Congress in 1952 by Senator John Bricker, a Republican of Ohio.[37] From 1952 to 1954, the Bricker amendment in several forms, was a subject of acrimonious Senate debate. The amendment expressed, in legal form, a widely shared resentment (particularly among Republican congressmen) that President Roosevelt, by the Teheran, Yalta, and Potsdam agreements, and President Truman, by his decision to commit American troops to Korea, had abused their executive authority. Presidents Roosevelt and Truman, moreover, had failed to seek the advice of Congress on many foreign-policy matters. The Bricker amendment supposedly would restore the Constitution to its pristine form, in which the Congress would be almost the equal of the President in the execution of foreign policy.

[37] S. J. Resolution 1, Sen. Rept. 412, 83d Congress, 1st sess., 15 June 1953; P. V. Curl (ed.), *Documents on American Foreign Relations*, 1953 (New York: Harper & Row, 1954), p. 102.

In January, about the time the Senate began renewed debate, President Eisenhower sent a letter to Senator Knowland in which he opposed the Bricker amendment in the form it then assumed.[38] After five more weeks of debate, the last of a long series of votes revealed that the support of two-thirds of the Senate could not be won for the Amendment. The feeling that the Constitution ought not be tampered with, at least not in this way, had become too strong, but Congress was adamant that it be consulted on such things as sending troops abroad. The Eisenhower administration, because it opposed the Bricker amendment, had to be explicit—often excessively so—in its words and actions in assuring the Congress that congressional leaders would be consulted frequently in matters as serious as the commitment of United States combat troops to crisis areas around the world.

The year of the Geneva Conference was also the climactic year of the phenomenon known as McCarthyism. In fact, the well publicized Army-McCarthy hearings were contemporaneous with the crises in Indochina and the Geneva negotiations. Senator McCarthy's crusade against communism had the support of a large sector of public opinion in the United States, a fact that the Eisenhower administration could not ignore, no matter how offensive the senator's behavior might be. The exigencies of domestic politics required that the President keep peace in his Republican family. There was, moreover, more than a little political expediency in calculating the electoral benefits of branding the Democrats the party of treason. But Senator McCarthy became too importunate; he interfered excessively in the domains of the executive. Resistance, very cautious at first, increased among his fellow Republicans, not because they found his methods repugnant to individual civil liberties but simply because he was interfering in affairs they believed were none of his business. Ultimately, a quiet policy of nonopposition and noncooperation paid off, and Senator McCarthy's conduct eventually was curtailed by the censure of the Senate. Nevertheless, for the first eighteen months of its tenure the Eisenhower administration was burdened with a man who constantly intruded into the operation of several executive agencies.

European opinion was stirred by the McCarthy phenomenon. Press comment was generally critical, often condemnatory, and at the very least concerned for the effects and implications of this brand of anticommunism upon American foreign policy. Extreme statements were expected from Washington, and, when pronounced, seemed only to confirm the partially correct view that Senator McCarthy's influence on the GOP was strong, that policy was being shaped by him or at least was shaped to please him. The sentiment grew that American

[38] Letter dated 25 January 1954, in *DSB*, 8 February 1954, p. 195. See also *NYT*, 20 February 1954.

policy in Europe and in East Asia must be moderated, but the party of Joseph McCarthy, it was felt, would not be willing to conciliate, and conciliation was necessary in the new age of the hydrogen bomb. Indeed, conciliation was feasible because of internal changes in the C.P.R. and the Soviet Union.

The East Asian policy of the United States still operated in a state of trauma as a result of the so-called loss of China in 1949. The best explanation for this catastrophe, in the view of right-wing Republicans, was the bad, possibly treasonous China policy of the State Department in the immediate postwar years. This explanation accorded nicely with the general view that the foreign policies of Presidents Roosevelt and Truman were responsible for the gains that international communism had won—policies that had, in fact, been shaped by fundamentally disloyal persons.

The new regime in China had intervened directly in the Korean conflict, and on a large scale, just thirteen months after its formal establishment; and this intervention had snatched a brilliant victory from predominantly American combat forces. The Korean War had continued for another two and a half years without the kind of victory most Americans wanted and expected. Thus the Communist Chinese were responsible for the frustrating experience of a protracted war and protracted peace negotiations.

The most vigorous group of critics of the East Asia policy of President Truman's administration was known as the "China Lobby," which was headed by Senators Knowland and Styles Bridges (Rep., N.H.). This lobby, and many other critics, correctly assumed that in 1950 Secretary of State Dean Acheson was planning to adopt a policy of "living with" the C.P.R., an attempt at a *modus vivendi* in East Asia. An invasion of Formosa, where Chiang Kai-shek and his reduced Kuomintang following had retreated in 1949, was expected and would not be resisted by the United States. After the outbreak of the Korean War, and particularly after the intervention of Chinese volunteers, the State Department was accused by these critics of having plotted to sacrifice Chiang to a regime whose aggressiveness and Communist nature it had, with startling lack of foresight (if not deliberately), failed to recognize. For the China Lobby, the Communist character of the C.P.R. was the paramount fact and Formosa was the Chinese bastion of resistance to Chinese communism on the Asiatic mainland. Support for Chiang must be continued. He must eventually be allowed to redeem mainland China from the regime established by the Chinese Communist Party.

Senator Knowland was the Senate majority leader in 1954, at the time of the Indochinese crisis and the Geneva Conference; he was also one of the most outspoken supporters of the Chinese Nationalists and one of the most implacable enemies of the C.P.R. His opposition to United States recognition of the C.P.R. and to its admission to the United Nations, supported by many influential figures in the Eisenhower administration, was generally in accord with American public opinion at the time. Knowland's hard line on China had this support largely because of the Korean experience, but it often caused inconvenience for Mr. Dulles's policies, as we shall see.

Throughout the summer and fall of 1953 a new national security policy was evolving in Washington. This policy, known as the "New Look," had its roots in two or three basic aims of the Eisenhower administration: the reduction of taxes and expenditures and a balanced budget. The threat to national security came to be regarded as a long-term threat and the strategy of the Communist antagonists as that of forcing the United States to expend large sums of money on its national defense establishment over a long period of time, thereby causing inflation or depression. To avoid economic crises and thereby counter this more subtle threat, a policy of fiscal soundness was imperative. Budget stability over the "long haul" or "long pull" must be the aim. Secretary of the Treasury George M. Humphrey and Joseph M. Dodge, Director of the Bureau of the Budget, were the principal advocates of this theory.[39] The intimate relationship between budgetary stability and defense expenditures, which was realized from the outset by the proponents of the New Look, meant that reduction of the inherited Truman deficit and avoidance of future deficits depended upon the extent to which defense expenditures could be reduced. Such a step called for a reevaluation, at the highest levels, of national security policy and foreign policy.

Briefly stated, American strategy after 1950 contemplated the maintenance and expansion of America's nuclear war capability and the expansion of its ability to fight limited wars. The former element was necessary to the United States to pursue a deterrence strategy against the Soviets, who now possessed atomic weapons; the latter was necessary because the Soviets had a conventional war capability superior to that of the United States and its allies. The United States had to be able to deter and wage an all-out nuclear war and a conventional war (while prosecuting the Korean War in a theater that was regarded as secondary to Europe, where, it was believed, the primary threat lay).

As Samuel P. Huntington has written, the New Look strategy was based upon one central fact:

[39] See C. P. Huntington, *The Common Defense* (New York: Columbia University Press, 1961), pp. 64-88, and G. H. Snyder, "The 'New Look,' of 1953," in W. R. Schilling, P. Y. Hammond, and G. H. Snyder, *Strategy, Politics, and Defense Budgets* (New York: Columbia University Press, 1962, pp. 379-524.

overwhelming American superiority in nuclear weapons and the means of delivering them. In 1950, SAC could not have prevented the Soviets from occupying western Europe. By 1954, with its fleet of B-47's, its overseas bases, its large stockpile of improved fission bombs, and the increased readiness and competence of its crews, it could have effectively destroyed the Soviet Union with little likelihood of serious reprisal against the United States. The years of the New Look were the high-water mark of relative American military strength in the Cold War.[40]

In August 1953 the newly appointed Joint Chiefs of Staff submitted a report (known as the Sequoia Paper) to the President. It recommended:

1. Expanding and developing America's strategic deterrent forces;
2. Increasing the effectiveness of the continental defense network;
3. Reducing the size of America's conventional forces abroad and relying principally upon the military forces of our allies for their own local defense; and
4. Creating a highly mobile strategic reserve force.[41]

A National Security Council paper (NSC 162/2), which was approved by the President on 30 October, underscored the importance of a strategic retaliatory air force and tactical nuclear weapons for deterrence. It declared that the armed forces were *no longer* to place undue emphasis upon preparations for conventional or limited wars.[42] By 9 December the JCS had worked up military plans that were commensurate with the New Look guidelines of the Sequoia Paper. (Pursuant to recommendations of this JCS report, two divisions were ordered withdrawn from Korea in January 1954.)[43]

The American public became apprised of the fact that a new security policy was evolving by a series of announcements and speeches by administration officials in December 1953 and January and February 1954. By far the most noteworthy was a speech by Secretary of State Dulles before the Council on Foreign Relations on 12 January in which the secretary sought to explain the New Look and

---

[40] Huntington, *op. cit.*, p. 65.   [41] Snyder, *op. cit.*, p. 414.
[42] *Ibid.*, pp. 436-443, 451-456.
[43] At approximately the same time the announcement of troop withdrawals from Korea was made, the administration revealed that a mutual defense treaty had been signed with the Republic of Korea on 1 October 1953. On 26 January the Senate had advised and consented to the treaty by a vote of 84 to 6. The text of this treaty appears in *Documents on American Foreign Relations, 1953*, pp, 312-313.

analyze some of its assumptions, corollaries, and implications.[44] He stated that local defense alone could not contain communism: massive retaliatory power must back up local defenses. But a maximum deterrent at a bearable cost had to be achieved, and this could be done by a "community security system so well equipped to punish any who break in and steal" that aggressors would be deterred.[45] "The way to deter aggressors, is for the free community to be willing and able to respond vigorously at places and with means of its own choosing." The President had made a very basic policy decision, Mr. Dulles declared: "The basic decision was to depend primarily upon a great capacity to retaliate, instantly, by means and at places of our choosing."[46]

Secretary Dulles and other officials were soon called upon to explain this strategy of "massive retaliation" as Congress, allied governments, and the foreign and domestic press began to analyze the doctrine and its implications. Through March and April, in particular, a great "strategic debate" was waged. That debate will be considered in chronological context below, but at this point we should mention several problems that were associated with the application of the New Look to two relevant areas.

a. Events in Indochina were becoming increasingly serious. How —and where—would the United States strike massively in Indochina if the Vietminh were on the verge of defeating France and taking over all Vietnam or Indochina? How would the United States conduct combat operations in Indochina should the administration feel compelled to intervene? These questions were important because the New Look envisaged a cutback in army and Marine Corps troop strength.[47]

b. Getting the EDC treaty approved by European parliaments became more difficult if the New Look entailed primary reliance on strategic and tactical nuclear weapons. If these weapons were really as effective as they were touted to be, why shouldn't the European states simply rely upon the United States' strategic umbrella? Why must there be German rearmament? Why the EDC at all? For the French, in particular, there was yet another implication of the New Look: If the United States intended to reduce its troop commitment to NATO, what would be left to counterbalance a rearmed Germany within the EDC? Again, why the EDC at all?

---

[44] *Docs., 1954*, pp. 7-15. See also *NYT*, 17 January 1954.
[45] *Docs., 1954*, p. 9. [46] *Ibid.*, p. 10.
[47] Walter Millis, "Barren Ground for Politicking," *NYHT*, 16 February 1954, and Walter Lippmann, "The New Look and Its Critics," *NYHT*, 18 February 1954.

AN ADDITIONAL item of international concern ought to be mentioned in the context of our present discussion. The debate on the New Look in the first half of 1954 (and even during the time of the Geneva Conference) took place against a backdrop of revelations about the force of the relatively new hydrogen bomb. In mid-February, Representative Sterling Cole disclosed that the detonation of a 5-megaton thermonuclear device at Eniwetok in November 1952 had destroyed an entire atoll and devastated an area more than 6 miles in diameter.[48] At the beginning of March, the Atomic Energy Commission initiated a new series of tests, and three weeks later it was revealed that scientists had underestimated the blast effects of an approximately 20-megaton thermonuclear device that had destroyed their measuring instruments.[49]

The weapons had awesome capabilities, destroying structures by fire up to 25 miles from ground zero and dispersing radioactive fallout over many thousands of square miles. If it was the eleventh hour for the French in Indochina it was also, according to a widely shared view, the eleventh hour for mankind.

[48] *NYT*, 18 February 1954.   [49] *NYT*, 21 March 1954.

Chapter 3

THE DECISION TO NEGOTIATE

[I]

Secretary of State Dulles kept a busy schedule in his first full week in Washington after his return from the Berlin Conference. On Monday, 22 February, he met with sixteen Republican and Democratic congressional leaders; on Tuesday and Wednesday he testified before the Senate Foreign Relations Committee and the House Foreign Affairs Committee;[1] and on Wednesday evening he appeared on a nationwide telecast to deliver his "Report on Berlin" to the American public. Even before his return there had been criticism of the decision to commit the United States to attend a conference on Indochina with Communist China, and various congressional leaders expressed concern that this might be the first step toward formal recognition of the Peking regime.

The meeting with congressional leaders on Monday, 22 February, confirmed the expectations of those who predicted Mr. Dulles would be subjected to intensive questioning. Republican leaders were particularly critical, and although Senator Alexander Wiley, the chairman of the Senate Foreign Relations Committee, tended to support Secretary Dulles, Senator Knowland seemed to represent the consensus of the GOP leaders when he asserted that the administration would be held responsible for the outcome at Geneva. The administration, Knowland said, would be held accountable for any "slip." This was interpreted to mean any indication that the United States was moving toward diplomatic recognition of China, as well as any action that might result in involving the United States in a war in Indochina. Later, in a speech to the New York County Republican Committee, Knowland vehemently criticized Dulles for having agreed to a conference at all. He said there was no justification for the United States' consenting to the inclusion of the Indochina question on the Geneva agenda and he warned that the American people would not consent to a Far Eastern Munich.[2]

Dulles was thought to have argued, in his defense, that consideration of the Indochina problem at Geneva would improve Franco-American relations. His argument, however, is open to conjecture inasmuch as the meetings of Monday through Wednesday (22–24 February) were held in secret. But Mr. Dulles offered a public de-

---

[1] *NYT*, 21, 23 February 1954.   [2] *NYT*, 23 February 1954.

fense in his Wednesday evening telecast on 24 February. Referring to the paragraph in the Berlin Conference communiqué that dealt with Indochina (i.e. "the problem of restoring peace in Indochina will also be discussed at the conference"), Mr. Dulles said:

> This portion of the Resolution was primarily and properly the responsibility of France. The United States has a very vital interest in developments in this area and we are helping the French Union forces to defeat communist aggression by helping them out with grants of money and equipment.
>
> But the French and peoples of the Associated States of Indochina are doing the actual fighting in a war now in its eighth year. They have our confidence and our support. We can give counsel and that counsel is welcomed and taken into account. But just as the United States had a special position in relation to the Korean armistice so France has a special position in Indochina.[3]

This public statement confirms what Dulles is reported to have told congressmen in private: This is France's war; but if France wants to negotiate a settlement, the United States cannot obstruct such efforts unless it is prepared to sacrifice the EDC and, what is more important, continued good relations with France, and ultimately the unity and integrity of the Western alliance. What Dulles said about the possibility of a French collapse and an eventual communist takeover of Indochina, we do not know. We know, however, that the Republican leaders—on Monday—had told Dulles he would be held accountable for a "slip," which was said to include the dispatch of American ground troops to Indochina. The secretary might therefore have responded in this fashion: If we won't negotiate, and if we won't fight, what alternatives do we have and what alternatives can we offer the French?

In the speech of 24 February Secretary Dulles also argued that the Geneva Conference did not imply United States recognition of the C.R.P. He described what had happened at Berlin.

> I had told Mr. Molotov, flatly, that I would not agree to meet with the Chinese Communists unless it was expressly agreed and put in writing that no United States recognition would be involved.
>
> Mr. Molotov resisted that provision to the last. He sought by

[3] *Report on Berlin*, Press Release No. 93, Series S, No. 9 (Washington, D.C.: Department of State, Public Services Division), p. 10. See also Mr. Dulles's remarks of 19 February upon his return from Berlin (*DSB*, 8 March 1954, p. 347). Drew Pearson reported that Dulles told the Senate Foreign Relations Committee: "I secured an agreement in writing that the Geneva Conference would not constitute recognition of Communist China, but even so I can't seem to please you gentlemen. It looks as if there's just no way we can conduct foreign relations to your liking." *NYT*, 8 March 1954.

every artifice and device, directly and through our allies, to tempt us to meet with Communist China as one of the five great powers. We refused, and our British and French allies stood with us. When we went into the final session last Thursday afternoon, I did not know what Mr. Molotov's final position would be. So far, he had not accepted my position. We were to adjourn at seven o'clock. At six o'clock—just 60 minutes before the final adjournment—Mr. Molotov announced that he would accept our non-recognition proviso.

A Soviet concession of that order ought not to be ignored.[4]

Dulles then repeated his statement of 26 January in which he had said the United States would not meet with representatives of the C.P.R. for the purpose of dealing *generally* with the peace of the world. This implied that the agenda for the forthcoming Geneva Conference was in agreement with this policy, for the participants would discuss only two *specific* problems: Indochina and Korea.

The television speech did not end the debate. During the ensuing months Republican critics often raised the question, Why had Mr. Dulles agreed to a conference on Indochina? On 10 March, after Dulles had left Washington to attend the Tenth Inter-American Conference of the American States at Caracas, the President made a public gesture of support for his secretary when he said he knew of no one who could have better represented United States interests than Dulles had done at the several foreign ministers' meetings.[5]

It would be a useful exercise, even now, to attempt an answer to the question, Should Secretary of State Dulles have agreed to the inclusion of the Indochina problem on the agenda of a Far Eastern conference on Korea? First, however, we should canvass the important reactions of America's allies to the results of the Berlin Conference.

[II]

The French press generally was more concerned with the fact that Bidault had arranged for a conference on Indochina than with the failure of the foreign ministers to solve the problems of European security. Bidault himself underlined what had been accomplished when he said, on his return to Paris: *"The concrete result* of the conference is the decision to call the Geneva meeting to discuss peace in Indochina and Asiatic problems."[6] French public opinion and opinion in the National Assembly was reasonably satisfied that talks, which might lead to an end of the fighting in Indochina, would finally

[4] *Report on Berlin*, pp. 8-9.
[5] *NYT*, 11 March 1954; *DSB*, 10 May 1954, p. 702.
[6] *NYT*, 21 February 1954. Emphasis added.

begin. Mendès-France did *not* represent an important segment of opinion when he charged that the five-power conference was a pretext for avoiding direct dealings with Ho Chi Minh. He argued that the conference would postpone a settlement of the Indochinese War until such time as the United States and China had reached a *modus vivendi* in East Asia.[7]

At the end of February, Bidault recommended that the cabinet put the EDC treaty to a vote (Laniel had promised in November 1953 to push EDC ratification soon after the Berlin Conference),[8] which inspired rumors of a deal between Dulles and Bidault at Berlin: the French would actively support the EDC in exchange for American consent to an East Asia conference on Indochina. Further, it was reported that Dulles had told congressional leaders on 22 February that he now looked forward with confidence to French ratification of EDC.[9] Unofficial evidence seems to indicate there was an "understanding" between the French Foreign Minister and the American Secretary of State, but the substance of Bidault's "promises" is unknown. In any case, Bidault could not "deliver" ratification; he could merely encourage the cabinet to make the decision to bring the treaty to a vote in the French Assembly. The cabinet seemed to be in no hurry to do this, however: no attempt had been made to settle the Saar question, which France had made a precondition for action on the treaty. More significantly the National Assembly's Foreign Affairs Committee had called only witnesses who opposed the EDC; none of its supporters had yet been called.[10]

Moreover, a new and important realization was beginning to form in the minds of the French policymakers: the Soviets vigorously opposed the EDC, and settlement of the Indochinese War at a conference attended by Soviet representatives would require at least Russian good will and very likely Russian support. Antagonizing the Soviets by actively pushing, or perhaps (more remotely) even by ratifying the EDC treaty, would cost the French whatever cooperation the Russians were prepared to give.[11]

By the first week in March, two weeks after the end of the Berlin conference, Washington was showing impatience with these most recent French delays. A spokesman for the administration announced that the United States would make no declaration about keeping its troops in Europe until the French cabinet had fixed a voting date for the EDC treaty.[12] Thus the EDC continued to be the major source of irritation between Washington and Paris.

[7] *NYT*, 20 February 1954.   [8] *NYT*, 28 February 1954.
[9] *NYT*, 23 February 1954.   [10] L&D, p. 98.
[11] *NYT*, 20 February 1954.   [12] *NYT*, 3 March 1954.

IN GREAT BRITAIN, there was disappointment with the results of the Berlin Conference, and left-wing Labour and Conservative newspapers voiced criticism of Mr. Eden's conduct. First, there was impatience over the American policy of not recognizing the C.P.R., a regime with which the British had formal diplomatic relations, tenuous and generally bad relations but relations nonetheless. The American policy of nonrecognition, some Labourites felt, barred a reduction of tensions in the Far East. Second, the critics argued that Eden had followed the Dulles lead too closely and too often at Berlin. This was a facet of the growing sentiment that British foreign policy was much too dependent upon the United States. It was often said that British policy was no longer made in London but rather in Washington.[13]

Under the détente policy of the Malenkov regime, the demand for trade with Communist-bloc nations had increased in Britain, and with economic dependence upon the United States diminishing, there was a growing desire for a British "declaration of independence" from the United States. It was felt that the Eisenhower administration was not willing to explore, in a flexible and pragmatic fashion, the possibilities of improved relations with the Soviet Union, the government of which was now at least ostensibly different from its predecessor. In the case of Germany, in particular, with both Conservative and Labour opinion opposing German rearmament, critics accused Mr. Eden of slavishly adopting American policy; namely, favoring rearmament over unification. Labour's left wing advocated opening immediate negotiations on Germany and seeking a compromise that would entail the neutralization and unification of Germany.

There was also some opposition to the EDC, although the Churchill government and the Labour Party opposition, led by former Prime Minister Clement Attlee, supported the treaty. But the Labour left, led by Aneurin Bevan, opposed the EDC, primarily because it envisaged German rearmament and would increase rather than reduce tensions in Europe. In a Labour Party caucus, Bevan's opposition to the EDC proved unsuccessful, but the Labour moderates (who supported the government's position) won only narrowly, by a vote of 112 to 108.[14]

[13] *NYT*, 15, 21 February 1954.

[14] *NYT*, 28 February 1954. See also *NYT*, 7 February 1954, in which James Reston wrote that there was a diminished and diminishing fear of the Red army in Europe. He noted that American economic aid was petering out, that the Soviet Union was appealing to the growing sense of independence in Europe, bidding for trade with the West, and at the same time extolling the possibilities of new markets in China. But "the Western Powers have not yet begun to deal effectively with these new developments within the Grand Alliance and the Communist nations. More important, they are not talking to one another, or planning with one another in accordance with the realities of the day." Reston also criticized the administration for practicing "sudden diplomacy": for announcing the massive-retaliation strategy without advanced discussions with the

On 19 February in Saigon, Vietnamese leaders of the SVN indicated that they favored an international conference to deal with the Indochinese War, but they believed certain safeguards were necessary. There should be no settlement without the agreement of the governments of the State of Vietnam, Laos, and Cambodia. China must end its support of the Vietminh. The Vietminh must be destroyed. Vietnam must remain a united state. And the Western powers must guarantee the territorial integrity of Vietnam against Chinese interference.[15]

The announcement of this "program" coincided with the arrival in Saigon of Harold Stassen, director of the U.S. Foreign Operations Administration. He had gone to Saigon to examine the operations related to America's rapidly expanding aid program in Indochina.

BOTH THE government of the Republic of Korea and the Nationalist Chinese regime on Taiwan issued protests after the Berlin communiqué had been published. Taipei declared that its representatives would not sit with C.P.R. delegates and that the government would not recognize conference decisions. The ROK ambassador to the United States, You Chan Yang, termed the Berlin Conference "a diplomatic victory for the Soviets."[16] On 26 February the United States formally delivered invitations to the Korean Political Conference to the Republic of Korea and to the thirteen states that had provided military contingents for the U.N. force during the Korean War.[17]

---

allies (this was not entirely true); for suddenly warning Europe—and France, in particular—of a possible American retreat from Europe if the EDC treaty was not approved; for offering a "sudden solution" for the Trieste dispute between Italy and Yugoslavia; for providing military assistance for Pakistan, thereby antagonizing India and Israel; and for suggesting that Spain be admitted to the NATO alliance. Later, Reston would call the administration's handling of the Indochina crisis another example of "sudden diplomacy."

Mr. Dulles had been criticized, in the United States and abroad, for seeking to bring about an alliance between Turkey and Pakistan by promoting the negotiations that led to the conclusion of a mutual defense assistance agreement on 19 May (*Docs.*, 1954, pp. 379-383). The President, moreover, had approved Pakistan's request for military assistance at the end of February. The Indian government was very critical of these developments, which Nehru regarded as the first step in the "return" of foreign troops to Asia. In view of the poor relations between Pakistan and India, American military assistance to Pakistan could have been construed as increasing the probability of a military clash in South Asia in spite of the fact that Pakistan undertook to use the aid only for internal security and national defense.

[15] *NYT*, 20 February 1954.   [16] *NYT*, 21 February 1954.

[17] *DSB*, 8 March 1954, p. 347. The United States sent invitations to Australia, Belgium, Canada, Colombia, Ethiopia, Greece, Luxembourg, The Netherlands, New Zealand, the Philippines, the Republic of Korea, Thailand, Turkey, and the Union of South Africa. The Soviet Union invited the Chinese People's Republic and the Democratic People's Republic of Korea. Great Britain and France would also attend the Geneva Conference.

Two weeks later President Syngman Rhee declared that Korea had been "kept in the dark" during the four-power conference at Berlin. His final decision to accept the invitation to Geneva and to send delegates would await further information from Secretary Dulles. Korea must, however, "have iron-clad assurances there will be no sellout."[18] Even as late as 23 March, President Rhee declared that his government had not decided whether to accept or reject the invitation to the Geneva Conference. He did say, however, that if the United States would underwrite expansion of the ROK army, he would attend the conference.[19]

Rhee's opinion that Geneva would turn out to be "further useless talk," and the very similar position of the Taipei government tended to support those persons in the United States who had opposed any agreement to hold such a conference.

[I I I]

Should Secretary of State Dulles have agreed to United States participation in a conference that would deal with Indochina? The answer must be yes because the alternatives were very much less attractive, judged in terms of the events of early February 1954.

The simplest reason for Mr. Dulles's agreement was that Bidault wanted to discuss Indochina at a conference that included the C.P.R., and the conditions and qualifications for C.P.R. participation became less and less important to Bidault as the Berlin Conference progressed.[20] He wanted the conference because he felt, in view of public opinion in France at the time, that failure to schedule such a conference could result in a governmental crisis and possibly in the fall of the Laniel government.[21] It could be made to appear that the French cabinet was not interested in settling the war, nor even willing to explore the possibilities of negotiations with the Communist powers—all this despite Laniel's promises to end the Indochinese War and, in the right circumstances, negotiate a settlement. General Giap's offensive in Laos persuaded a few of the French hold-outs that victory, if obtainable at all, was a long way off—in a war already more than seven years long.[22] Bidault's return from Berlin without the

---

[18] NYT, 11 March 1954.   [19] NYT, 24 March 1954.

[20] Bidault felt increasingly pressed to obtain a conference on Indochina and was less inclined, by the last week of the Berlin Conference, to insist upon such conditions as proof of good faith or peaceful intent on the part of the C.P.R.

[21] As Eisenhower wrote later: "The life of the Laniel government was important to United States policies. We were convinced that no succeeding government would take a stronger position than his on the defense of Indochina, or in support of the European Defense Community." DDE, p. 343.

[22] Needless to say, General Ely's opinion that a military decision could no longer be obtained in Indochina was not public knowledge.

promise of negotiations would be viewed as evidence of the utmost insensitivity on the part of the Foreign Minister or France's Allies to the loss of French soldiers in Indochina. It would, moreover, reinforce the arguments of those, such as Mendès-France, who advocated direct negotiations with the Vietminh.

At Berlin, Bidault of course realized that discussions of the Indochinese War required the presence of Chinese diplomats, which would be opposed by Dulles—at the very least because of opposition in the administration's own party to dealings with the C.P.R. But Dulles could be convinced by a good argument and Bidault was a persuasive man. The Secretary of State could certainly see that withholding consent to United States participation would irritate French opinion and endanger Western unity, and the Western ministers had agreed that Molotov's primary objective at Berlin would probably be to weaken that unity. Refusal also would endanger the Laniel government and might bring into office someone who would be willing to negotiate directly with the Vietminh and make strategically dangerous concessions in order to obtain a peace settlement.

Refusal by Mr. Dulles would also antagonize British opinion, which did not share the aversion to Chinese Communists that was held by an important segment of American opinion. Eden almost at once recognized the French need for discussions on Indochina and realized that Chinese participation was imperative.[23] America's refusal could be viewed as unreasonable and as neglectful of the interests of its allies and would give support to the critics who had been questioning the wisdom of American foreign policy and British association with that policy.

There was also a logical reason for the United States to consent to negotiate a specific issue in the presence of the Chinese: it had been done before, at Kaesong and Panmunjom, in an effort to obtain a cease-fire in Korea, and it could be done again.

The Secretary of State—who had to take into account the fact that the policy of nonrecognition of the C.P.R., which at the time had the support of almost the entire Congress—was surely aware of international law on the recognition of states and governments. Both *de jure* recognition (recognition of a government as legally constituted) and *de facto* recognition (recognition that a government in fact controls a particular territory and population) require a formal and usually an explicit act or declaration of a government. Mutual consent to sit at a negotiating table is not necessarily such an act. There is, however, a rule that recognition may be presumed to have been extended to Y by government X by the actions of X; that is, by X's commer-

---

[23] E, pp. 98-99.

cial or political dealings with Y, for example, at multilateral conferences. But such a presumption usually can be rebutted by an express reservation to the effect that X does not mean to imply the recognition of Y by virtue of current dealings. Hence Mr. Dulles had demanded such a proviso at Berlin in the final communiqué.[24]

The influential anti-C.P.R. segment of the Republican Party (the China Lobby) feared that the agreement to negotiate with China at the Geneva Conference was the opening wedge of a policy of Chinese recognition and admission to the U.N. This group was well aware of the arguments that had been advanced, particularly in Britain and India, for achieving a compromise with China over the Taiwan question, and it was opposed to such arguments. Although Dulles's explanations for consenting to negotiate with China were plausible to some Republicans, other men, such as Senators Knowland, H. A. Smith, and Hubert Humphrey (who was running for reelection in 1954), nevertheless desired assurances that the nonrecognition policy was still firmly part of American Far East policy.[25] Such assurances were given several times, and from the highest sources, throughout the spring and summer of 1954.

There were, nevertheless, differences between negotiating with the Chinese at the forthcoming Geneva Conference and negotiating at the earlier conferences at Panmunjom. Geneva was to be a conference of the great powers, called to discuss East Asian problems, albeit two *specific* East Asian problems. It would meet in the famous Swiss city that had served as the meeting place of the League of Nations and had hosted other international conferences. Panmunjom had been a conference of Korean War belligerents, almost on the field of battle, and the conferees had discussed a single, narrow, functional issue: the terms of a Korean cease-fire. Geneva, which would bring a modicum of international prestige to the Chinese, might open abundant opportunities to a government intent upon demonstrating to the world that it was reasonable and fully capable of behaving like a great power. It was this "semblance of recognition" by participation—prestige by the mere fact of China's presence—to which Senator Knowland and others objected. No matter how plausible Dulles's arguments, no matter how good the reasons he advanced, his consent to the Geneva Conference was abhorred by these men; and the man who had given his consent was put on notice that he must not let this process of recognition by function or implication go any further.[26]

[24] Hersch Lauterpacht, *Oppenheim's International Law* (8th ed.; London: Longmans, Green, 1958), 1: 146-147.

[25] *NYT*, 21 February 1954.

[26] London, it was reported, felt that the Senate's reaction to the decision to

Various Communist broadcasts and news releases heralded Geneva as a five-power conference and exploited the fact of Chinese participation, but only in mid-March, after maintaining silence on this subject, did Peking radio announce that the C.P.R. would attend the Geneva Conference in the capacity of a great power with a recognized role in international affairs, in spite of the United States reservations and views on the matter.[27] Dulles in his television speech of 24 February had declared that "the Chinese Communist regime will not come to Geneva to be honored by us, but rather to account before the bar of world opinion."[28] There followed a series of statements in the same vein.

W. P. McConaughy, director of the Office of Chinese Affairs in the State Department, asserted that the Geneva Conference was not a five-power conference but rather a multipower conference. China would be present because of its aggressive role and "will be called upon to give an accounting for its aggression."[29] In response to critics in the United States and in Korea who had argued that Geneva would merely produce more "useless talk," McConaughy said the United States would not allow an unproductive conference to drag on indefinitely. On 23 March it was reported that Secretary Dulles had given President Rhee a promise to end the conference within three months if the Communists appeared to be using it as a propaganda device.[30]

Thus throughout the post–Berlin Conference period Dulles was very much on the defensive against critics of his agreement to negotiate with the Chinese at Geneva. By the end of March the criticism was beginning to have an effect, for it was hinted that General Bedell Smith, the Under Secretary of State, would do most of the negotiating at Geneva. A Washington newspaper correspondent, W. S. White, suggested that the administration was now attempting to play down Geneva.[31]

INDEED, other factors may have entered into Mr. Dulles's thinking: the entire New Look strategy and congressional opposition to send-

---

participate in the Geneva Conference would prevent the Secretary of State from patiently and thoroughly exploring the Soviet and the Communist Chinese positions. Since the United States would not recognize the C.P.R., the Communists, it was believed, could tie almost any issue to recognition and thereby exploit the "stubbornness" of the United States. *NYT*, 13 March 1954. See also T. J. Hamilton in the *NYT*, 21 February 1954, and Walter Lippmann, "A Booby Trap for Geneva," *NYHT*, 2 March 1954.

[27] *NYT*, 14 March 1954; *Econ.*, 27 March 1954.
[28] *Report on Berlin*, p. 9.
[29] *DSB*, 15 March 1954, p. 405.
[30] *NYT*, 24 March 1954.
[31] *NYT*, 26 March 1954.

ing American troops to Indochina. However, there were really only three alternatives to a multipower conference on Indochina.

1. Refusal to negotiate. This would entail continuation of the war and even greater losses of French Union troops. This alternative was not acceptable to the French.

2. Negotiating with the Vietminh. This would enhance the status of the Vietminh and the DRVN and might result in handing over at least part of Indochina to a Communist regime. In February this alternative was not acceptable to the United States nor (as yet) to the incumbent French policymakers.

3. Not negotiating *at the present time*. This was open to the same objections as the first alternative, unless the French could eliminate the Vietminh or force it to dissolve the DRVN and accept a relatively minor role in the SVN government. But the French had not succeeded in doing this after approximately seven years of war and, in view of recent military developments, it was something that could not be done *unless* the French invited U.S. combat troops to help them. In February 1954, as before, this request—as well as the alternative—was not acceptable to the French.

Let us assume, as Dulles may have conjectured in Berlin, that the Laniel government decided to change its policy and in March or April or May asked the United States to send troops. What then? The New Look security policy required a reduction in personnel strength of American armed forces; in fact, even with the Indochina crisis the Eisenhower administration pushed these reductions. In 1954 the effective strength of the army and the Marine Corps was cut by 10 percent. The New Look, when it was formulated, simply did not allow for a major *unilateral* American commitment of combat ground troops to supplement French Union forces in Indochina. Such a commitment would require a major revision of the New Look military strategy as well as a revision of the budget upon which that strategy was based. Of course, the Eisenhower administration policymakers cannot fairly be criticized for having failed to predict the crisis in Indochina, but whether they should have anticipated a crisis *like* the Indochina crisis is another matter. In any event, Mr. Dulles may well have concluded in February 1954 that the United States could not and would not dispatch ground troops to Indochina even if the French requested such action. New Look policy would be nullified even before it began; and the secretary's conclusion may well have been reinforced by congressional reaction, negative in some quarters, to the announcement of the dispatch of technicians.

Of the various alternatives listed, none was more generally acceptable to the Western foreign ministers, and particularly Secretary of State Dulles, than the course that was adopted: consent to a multipower conference on Indochina with C.P.R. representatives in attendance.

[IV]

As Secretary Dulles described it in his address of 24 February, Molotov held out until one hour before the end of the Berlin Conference before he consented to insertion in the communiqué of the proviso on nonrecognition of the C.P.R. Had the Soviet Foreign Minister made a real or merely an apparent concession? It may be argued that he got the five-power conference he had persistently demanded during the first week at Berlin. Even though it had been formally stipulated that the participation of the Chinese did not imply recognition of the Peking regime, wasn't the fact of China's participation enough? Wasn't this an admission by the Western allies that the C.P.R. had a right to be consulted on East Asian affairs? Indeed what kind of *concession* had Molotov made?

A proper response to such questions requires a great deal more evidence than is presently available. But if we contrast what was decided (as recorded at Berlin in the final communiqué) with what the Soviet Union and the C.P.R. had been demanding, we can make a good argument that Molotov had made a real concession and that he had held out for more than a week because Kremlin policymakers were trying to persuade Chinese diplomats that, for the present, they must be content with what Molotov had been able to obtain at Berlin.

1. Molotov had demanded a five-power conference to deal very broadly or generally with international tensions. He got his five-power conference, but it was limited to the problems of Korea and Indochina. Hence neither the status nor the future of Taiwan would be discussed, nor could the Chinese properly argue that America's policy of nonrecognition and opposition to C.P.R. admission to the U.N. was productive of conflict.

2. The Chinese had demanded that invitations to the Korean peace conference be sent to the neutral Asian states,[32] a demand that was not met. The communiqué prescribed the composition of the Korean Conference and it did not list the Asian states that had been neutral during the Korean war.

The Berlin agreement on Korea was, in fact, a concession to the Soviet Union, but not to the C.P.R. The Korean peace talks in the fall of 1953 had made little progress because of a procedural issue: the status of the U.S.S.R. at a Korean peace conference. The Communist position was that the Soviets should participate and should participate as a "neutral," along with the other neutral states they said must be

[32] *Econ.*, 27 February 1954, p. 588.

invited. The U.S. delegate was willing to have the Soviets attend, but only as a belligerent; the conference, in Arthur Dean's view, was to be a conference of belligerents only. The Berlin Conference had produced this result: the Soviet Union not only would attend a Korean conference, it would be a sponsoring power as well! Its neutrality or belligerent status during the Korean War was avoided, but no other "neutral" state was invited to attend this phase of the Geneva Conference.[33]

3. The Soviet press had long demanded the formal establishment of the international legal rights of the C.P.R. and its recognition as a great power, which China in fact was. By virtue of the proviso inserted in the communiqué at Mr. Dulles's insistence, this establishment of legal rights was *formally* avoided. There is every reason to believe the C.P.R. and the Soviets were as much interested as the United States in the *form* as well as the substance of international recognition of C.P.R. status. Consent to the proviso came grudgingly from Molotov, after much delay, and it must have been granted even more reluctantly by whatever C.P.R. diplomats were in behind-the-scenes contact with Molotov and the Soviet Foreign Ministry. Peking, surprisingly silent about the Berlin decision and the Geneva Conference for more than two weeks, then announced that China would attend the conference as a great power despite the declared United States position.

Apart from the important fact of participation, the C.P.R. did not benefit from Molotov's concession; indeed the concession was made at China's expense. The Soviets could make capital of the fact that they had agreed to a conference, which suited the détente policy of the Malenkov government, but Molotov made no concessions on the European matters discussed at Berlin. His inflexibility, however, could be at least partially concealed by a demonstrated willingness to negotiate on pressing East Asian problems, while Germany and Austria remained divided and a sympathetic East German regime would retain its authority. The Soviets might also have reasoned that the EDC could be stalled, perhaps even defeated, in the French parliament by playing upon the hopes of the French for a settlement of the Indochinese War. But all these factors were of little concern to Peking at the moment, which no doubt perceived the benefits Russia had obtained. The Chinese leaders were probably disappointed by the nonrecognition proviso, and may even have been irritated with their Russian allies, but they must have felt they had to acquiesce.

Thus Molotov's concession was primarily a concession at China's expense, but it was a real concession from the Soviets' standpoint

[33] See the summary in the *NYT*, 21 February 1954.

because it permitted an important question of "form" to be resolved against them. The Berlin communiqué, instead of omitting reference to the status of the C.P.R. which would have implicitly admitted China's claims to great-power status—together with her participation in the conference—explicitly precluded recognition of China by the United States. Molotov's concession could be regarded as merely an apparent concession only by those who started from the premise that the Soviets never make concessions in negotiations and by those who are willing, on the basis of evidence *after* the fact, to attribute to Molotov and the Kremlin leaders the ability to have foreseen the outcome of the Indochinese War.

[V]

Secretary Dulles had warned Bidault, just before they left Berlin, that the French could expect the Vietminh to stage major offensive operations in an effort to obtain a victory that would place them in a strong negotiating position at Geneva.[34] Under Secretary of State Bedell Smith likewise believed that the Vietminh offensive in Laos in January and February had been designed to create a crisis situation that would yield favorable decisions at Berlin. The offensives generated great anxiety in Paris and Washington, which no doubt influenced the ministers, and there is some circumstantial evidence that supports Bedell Smith's theory.

On 24 February the PAVN advance on Luang Prabang suddenly stopped. On the 26th, PAVN units began to pull back, and subsequently converged on Dien Bien Phu, where French airborne battalions had been ensconced since late November 1953. It was then— less than a week after the conclusion of the Berlin Conference— that General Giap halted his limited but successful Laotian campaign and moved back into the mountains of northwest Tonkin to besiege the village that was soon to achieve world reknown. On 13 March the Vietminh launched their first major attacks against the village, and heavy ordnance, particularly artillery and mortars, and other supplies flowed in increasing quantities to the area along the highways from southeastern China through Lang Son and Cao Bang. Dien Bien Phu was to be the victory the Vietminh needed to enable their Communist allies, and perhaps even themselves, to "negotiate from strength."

[34] DDE, p. 343. See also *NYT*, 22 March 1954.

Chapter 4

WASHINGTON ON THE
EVE OF THE CRISIS

[I]

Only in March would Washington be apprised of the seriousness of the French debacle in Indochina, which in early February President Eisenhower described as one long crisis.[1] Although disturbed by General Giap's Laotian offensive and his reaching the Mekong River, the administration still assumed that the French would continue to fight, and certainly would not withdraw precipitously, leaving all Indochina to the Vietminh or their protégés in Laos and Cambodia.

There were, of course, doubts in some quarters about the validity of these assumptions: although it had not led to any disasters in Vietnam, the Navarre Plan was not yielding results. Vietnamese troop training was not making headway. The French Union forces seemed to have lost their mobility. The Laniel government appeared unable to win over public opinion in Vietnam, or bring itself to grant genuine independence to the Vietnamese. Nor was the French government able to win over opinion in France so that the war would be prosecuted with the vigor required to put its diplomats in a strong negotiating position at Geneva. Nevertheless, Washington's assumption that France would continue to fight generally prevailed. Officials who had doubts were loath to express them publicly: public expressions of pessimism could only weaken the resolve of the French and at the same time stiffen the will of the Vietminh. The French government was sensitive about its conduct of the war because it was regarded as a French affair and because its political life depended upon associated events. In any case the United States would continue to supply money and hardware, at least until the policymakers could see what would happen at or after Geneva. Surely the French could hold until that time.

In Paris the Laniel government had become ever more alarmed. Chinese fighter aircraft (MIG-15s) appeared over Tonkin in early March; they did not engage in combat but their appearance forced the French to realize that Communist China might actively intervene in the war. Peking's intentions were not immediately clear, but the appearance of Chinese jets made intervention a very real possibility in the opinion of Premier Laniel's military advisors. This was fur-

[1] *NYT*, 4 February 1954.

ther support for those in France who wanted an end to the war rather than its intensification or internationalization. At the same time Vietminh raids continued throughout Vietnam. On 13 March, units of the PAVN carried out its first major assaults against Dien Bien Phu; and it was reported that the Vietminh had destroyed between ten and twenty American troop-transport aircraft on the ground. The Vietminh did not seem unwilling to test American intentions.[2]

Within two days after the first attacks on Dien Bien Phu, General Navarre and Maurice Dejean, the High Commissioner for Indochina, were alleged to have concluded that the village and its garrison would be lost unless there was some form of external military assistance, a relief force or perhaps aerial bombardment of Vietminh positions.[3] Even if Dejean did not inform the cabinet ministers of his appraisal, the intensity of the Vietminh attacks upon Dien Bien Phu might lead them to suspect that the "fortress" could not be held, and a loss of this sort would surely bring on a governmental crisis. Although the French troops dug in at Dien Bien Phu were only a small percentage of the entire French Union forces, their loss would be a tremendous psychological defeat (and a not inconsiderable military victory for the PAVN) in a war heretofore devoid of dramatic wins and losses.

On 5 March the President of the Conseil d'Etat transmitted to the National Assembly a list of conditions that must be satisfied for the government to accept a cease-fire:

1. Evacuation of Cambodia and Laos by the Vietminh;
2. Evacuation of the Tonkin delta by the Vietminh and establishment of a zone of security around the delta; and
3. The regrouping of Vietminh forces in central Vietnam in predetermined zones.

On 10 March the DRVN announced that it was "disposed to welcome" these propositions, but nothing further came of this exchange.[4]

[2] *NYT*, 18 March 1954.

[3] L&D, p. 68.

[4] L&D, p. 65. On 9 March the National Assembly passed a resolution that authorized the government to negotiate a settlement of the Indochinese War. It declared: "The National Assembly . . . Recalls solemnly that France sustained the armed conflict in Indo-China by virtue of the framework of the Constitution relative to the French Union to which the Associated States had already voluntarily adhered and that the complete repudiation of these arrangements by the said States will relieve France of its obligations in respect to them and permit France to consider the dictates of its interests inseparable from the free world." *JO*, 9 March 1954, p. 764.

The resolution reflected the growing impatience of French deputies and officials with the Vietnamese (SVN) diplomats who were then in Paris negotiating Vietnam's future status in association with the French Union. In the French view, Prince Buu Loc, the SVN Premier and head of the Vietnamese delegation, was being overly independent and stubborn (see *Econ.*, 13 March 1954). But the

René Pleven, the French Minister of Defense, having just returned from Indochina, had been invited to Washington in February to confer with American military advisors and officials of the Eisenhower administration.[5] On 11 March, Paris announced that, within ten days, General Paul Ely, president of the French Chiefs of Staff, would fly to Washington instead of Pleven.[6] Presumably, the French general would be able to give American policymakers an accurate picture of the situation in Indochina. Meanwhile, on or about 6 March, the National Security Council met in Washington to examine the situation in Indochina. The council's report to the President was said to have described Indochina as the strategic key to the Far East, both in terms of geopolitics and natural resources (minerals and rice) that were essential to Japan and the United States. The NSC recommended that all possible measures be taken to prevent a Communist government from controlling Indochina. This recommendation was hedged, however: the United States, the NSC report was alleged to have said, should take such measures only in concert with its allies.[7]

On 20 March, General Ely arrived in Washington, and his visit was to be an educational experience for the officials of the Eisenhower administration: during his stay in Washington the anxiety of the few became the profound concern of many. Crucial decisions had to be made soon; the crisis was no longer remote nor contingent upon unlikely possibilities of major French military defeats. General Ely had come to Washington to learn the American reaction to a Chinese intervention and to get an assurance of air support against a possible attack by Chinese aircraft on French Union defense positions. He also tried to have American military assistance accelerated.[8]

Publicly optimistic on his arrival, Ely stated that Vietminh losses at Dien Bien Phu were very heavy, which increased the French hope of victory. He said that the French could hold Dien Bien Phu if the delivery of matériel to the French Union forces could be speeded up. Whether the general was all this optimistic in his private conversations with American policymakers we cannot say with certainty. Nor

---

prince was under considerable pressure from the Vietnamese nationalists who were demanding full independence and—*if* Vietnam was to be in the French Union—completely equal associate status with France; that is, Vietnam must be fully sovereign and the equal of France within the union.

[5] *NYT*, 17 February 1954. For a discussion of the Pleven mission to Indochina, see Ely, Chapter II.

[6] General Ely had been invited to come to the United States by Admiral Arthur Radford, chairman of the American Joint Chiefs of Staff. Ely, p. 59.

[7] L&D, pp. 71-72. See also *U.S. News & World Report*, 18 June 1954, pp. 35-39, and 6 August 1954, pp. 21-23.

[8] *NYT*, 21 March 1954.

do we know whether he told his American allies that he and the French chiefs of staff had concluded earlier that the dispatch of available reinforcements would not change their estimate that French Union forces could not then win a decision in Indochina and, moreover, that the French government could not authorize such reinforcements because to do so might precipitate a governmental crisis. Did he know—and if he knew, did he tell the Joint Chiefs of Staff and others that General Navarre and Commissioner Dejean had determined that Dien Bien Phu could not be held? Did he have, and convey, an accurate impression of the morale of the French Union–Vietnamese army in Tonkin?

On 21 March, General Ely met with the JCS to discuss the nature of new American contributions to the war effort.[9] The United States could send additional troop-transport aircraft, which General Ely did not think was a priority matter. But in view of the French domestic political consequences of sending additional forces to Indochina, the general could not be expected to feel that the transports were particularly needed. More B-26 bombers might be supplied, which Ely regarded as a priority matter. Another twenty-five B-26s, he said, "would help clean out the communist artillery pockets that are giving the French defenders trouble . . ." at Dien Bien Phu.

The JCS suggested that the training of Indochinese pilots in the Philippines might be stepped up, implying that this was already an active program. General Ely's reaction to this proposal was not reported. The JCS also discussed the possibility of raising an international corps of pilots to fight in Indochina, financed by the United States. Here again, the general's reaction was not reported. Efforts could be made to persuade the French to permit the dispatch of an American training mission to Indochina to help train Vietnamese troops, but General Ely opposed this. The French were responsible for the war effort, he said, as American officials had stated on many earlier occasions. What General Ely probably did not say was that the French army could not concede that it had failed to train enough Vietnamese adequately, something the Americans might be able to do.[10]

But General Ely agreed that U.S. naval and air support would be essential if the Chinese intervened directly. Also, he told the JCS that the French were determined to kill as many Vietminh as possible "before the Vietminh vanish once more into the jungle."

[9] *NYT*, 22 March 1954. (The quotations of General Ely in the text are taken from this report.)

[10] The dispatch of American troop-training cadres to Indochina would undoubtedly be construed, in France and in the United States, as an admission that the Americans might succeed where the French had failed. Cf. Ely, p. 75.

On 22 March, Ely and Admiral Arthur Radford, chairman of the JCS, met with President Eisenhower. The President instructed Radford to do everything possible to satisfy French requests, with priority upon actions that would contribute to the success of the battle in progress.[11] The admiral took this instruction seriously, and literally.

On the afternoon of 24 March, General Ely again met with the JCS. It had been decided to supply France with an additional twenty-five B-26 bombers (bringing the total supplied up to that time to sixty or seventy).[12] The chiefs were of the opinion that a properly trained and equipped Vietnamese Army could defend Indochina against the Communists. To this end, the United States would step up material aid to the French command. The JCS apparently wanted the French to create an army with a combat capability similar to the army of the Republic of Korea, but the policy behind this idea would require the French to continue fighting for another year or two, until an anti-Communist government could win the allegiance of the Vietnamese people and the army of this government had gained military supremacy.[13] Because the French were not doing all they could to train the Vietnamese, General Ely was again pressed to allow the United States to assist in the training program.

The JCS attempt to involve the United States in the training program came one day after a press conference in which Secretary of Defense Charles E. Wilson announced that Lt. General John W. O'Daniel, U.S. Army Commander for the Pacific Area, had been ordered to Indochina.[14] O'Daniel was to become the chief of the Military Assistance Advisory Group in Saigon. Secretary Wilson underscored the purpose of this move (which was sure to irritate Paris and cause concern in Congress) when he implied that it was symbolic of an additional American commitment. General O'Daniel would not be going to Indochina, Wilson declared, if "we didn't think he had a good chance" of speeding up training. "Effective and aggressive training of Indochinese troops is essential if the war is to be brought to a successful conclusion." The use of American technicians to help train the Vietnamese was being studied, Wilson said, and in an effort to calm congressional (but apparently not French) sensibilities he added: "We are willing to assist in such training in any practical way, just as we have done in the case of a num-

[11] Ely, p. 64.

[12] *NYT*, 24, 25, 27 March 1954. See also Dulles's announcement at his press conference on 23 March. *DSB*, 5 April 1954, pp. 512-513, and Ely, pp. 62, 68, 77.

[13] *Econ.*, 2 January 1954, pp. 29-30.

[14] *NYT*, 24 March 1954. The decision had been made by the President well in advance of Wilson's press conference. DDE, p. 341.

ber of other countries. Such training in itself would not involve us in any war."

We do not know what General Ely said to the JCS on 24 March, after this announcement of the Secretary of Defense. In any case, O'Daniel's assignment to MAAG did not mean that the United States would in fact assist in the training program; prior agreement with the French was necessary and such an agreement never materialized. Only in the fall, several months after a cease-fire had been negotiated at Geneva, did the United States enter into a training agreement, but this was with the SVN government.

Secretary of State Dulles, who also held a news conference on 23 March, pledged whatever additional American equipment was needed for a French victory. As for the current major battle at Dien Bien Phu, Dulles paid his respects to the gallantry of the French Union defenders but he minimized the possible loss of the village and its garrison, declaring that the defenders were only a small portion of the French force in Indochina. He added: "I do not expect that there is going to be a communist victory in Indochina. By that I don't mean that there may not be local affairs where one side or another will win victories, but in terms of communist dominion of Indochina, I do not accept this as a probability."[15]

Mr. Dulles made another significant (perhaps extraordinary) assessment of the military situation in Indochina in commenting upon the Navarre Plan. "We have seen no reason to abandon the so-called Navarre plan. . . . There have been no serious reversals . . . and, as far as we can see, none are in prospect which could be of a character which would upset the broad time table and strategy of the Navarre plan."[16] In December, Dulles had expressed confidence in "the timetable of General Navarre's plan," which held in prospect (as Dulles had said on 23 March) "at least decisive military results" in about a year.

Was it possible for the American Secretary of State to be that confident of the Navarre Plan in December 1953? Was it conceivable that after the events of January, February, and March 1954 he would hold the same opinion? It is my opinion that neither in December nor in March was Dulles as confident of the Navarre Plan as he declared in his press conferences; his remarks, I believe, were calculated to reassure the French.[17] Taken with his other remarks at the 23 March press conference, his statements were meant to warn the French that

[15] *NYT*, 24 March 1954.   [16] *Ibid.*

[17] Melvin Gurtov, *The First Vietnam Crisis* (New York: Columbia University Press, 1967), does not agree with this assessment; see p. 50. Certainly Ely was more optimistic than his American counterparts (Ely, p. 62).

the Navarre Plan *must* be made to work. The United States would supply credits and hardware and, as Secretary of Defense Wilson had indicated on the same day, would assist in training the Indochinese. But who was to do the fighting while the Navarre Plan was so slowly implemented? A partial answer to this question was given in a major policy speech by the Secretary of State on 29 March before the Overseas Press Club of America.

IN THAT speech Mr. Dulles spoke first of Indochina and Communist China. He defended the American policy of nonrecognition of China and the reasons for United States opposition to its admission to the to the United Nations.[18] In the portion of his address devoted to Indochina, Dulles said that 30 million people were seeking the dignity of self-government in Vietnam, Laos, and Cambodia, and were "exercising a considerable measure of independent political authority within the French Union." The independence of these states was not yet complete, "but the French Government last July declared its intention to complete that independence, and negotiations to consummate that pledge are actively underway."[19] The Communists, however, were "attempting to prevent the orderly development of independence." He then described Ho Chi Minh's Communist affiliations and the extent of Communist Chinese support of the Vietminh.

> Military supplies for the Communist armies have been pouring into Vietnam at a steadily increasing rate.
> Military and technical guidance is supplied by an estimated 2,000 Communist Chinese. They function with the forces of Ho Chi Minh in key positions—in staff sections of the High Command, at the division level and in specialized units such as signal, engineer, artillery and transportation.[20]

It was after this discourse upon the importance of Indochina in terms of its desire for independence and Communist interference with the "development of independence" that the secretary emphasized the strategic importance of Indochina in Southeast Asia. It was an area rich in raw materials (tin, oil, iron ore, and rubber) and a rice-surplus area, he said.

> Southeast Asia is astride the most direct and best developed sea and air routes between the Pacific and South Asia. It has major naval and air bases. Communist control of Southeast Asia would carry a grave threat to the Philippines, Australia and New Zea-

[18] *The Threat of a Red Asia*, Press Release No. 165, Series S, No. 13 (Washington, D.C.: Department of State, Public Services Division, 1954), pp. 5-6.
[19] *Ibid.*, p. 1. [20] *Ibid.*, p. 2.

land, with whom we have treaties of mutual assistance. The entire Western Pacific area, including the so-called "offshore island chain," would be strategically endangered.[21]

The United States had supplied matériel to the French and American diplomatic efforts had sought to deter Communist China from open aggression. But China had "avoided the direct use of their own Red armies in open aggression against Indochina," using all means short of open invasion. Dulles then set forth United States policy in these often quoted terms:

> Under the conditions of today, the imposition on Southeast Asia of the political system of Communist Russia and its Chinese Communist ally, by whatever means, would be a grave threat to the whole free community. The United States feels that that possibility should not be passively accepted, but should be met by united action. This might involve serious risks. But these risks are far less than those that will face us a few years from now, if we dare not be resolute today.[22]

This speech was, of course, a major policy statement and was recognized as such by virtually all news analysts. Mr. Dulles meant to "educate the American public": the Eisenhower administration regarded Indochina as an area of "transcendent importance"[23] and the Dulles address intended to explain why this was so. It was also intended to warn Americans that the Chinese might force the administration to take action that could involve "serious risks," which the press interpreted as meaning another Korea-type action.[24]

The conditions that could persuade the administration to take these risks were carefully hedged. Imposition of a Communist system upon Southeast Asia, the secretary said, would be a grave threat that "should not be passively accepted." He did not say it *must* not be accepted nor did he say it *should* or *must* be actively resisted.[25]

---

[21] *Ibid.*, p. 3.   [22] *Ibid.*, p. 4.

[23] The President had used this expression in reference to Indochina at his press conference on 24 March. *NYT*, 25 March 1954.

[24] See the analysis of James Reston in the *NYT*, 30 March 1954. See also *Econ.*, 3, 10 April 1954; Walter Millis, "From Theory to Action," *NYHT*, 1 April 1954; and Hanson Baldwin, *NYT*, 1 April 1954. On the matter of risk-taking, Senator Alexander Wiley had told the sixth annual convention of the Military Government Association that there were indeed risks in sending technicians to Indochina, but this was a "world of risks." International communism, he said, thrived on the unwillingness of its enemies to take risks. *NYT*, 21 March 1954.

[25] A threat was obvious but implicit in Mr. Dulles's statement of American policy toward Indochina; it was cautiously conditioned to allow him an "out" if he later found that, under the circumstances, the United States should not or could not actively resist a Communist Vietminh success.

Mr. Dulles also declared that the threat was the imposition of a Communist system "by whatever means." When read with the earlier paragraphs, this appeared to widen the American commitment: the grave threat would follow not only from open Chinese intervention but also from the promotion of "aggression by all means short of open invasion."[26] But even this broadened warning was conditional; the possibility of the communization of Southeast Asia, Dulles said, "should be met by united action." The importance of this qualification appears to have escaped the attention of the French government, as we shall see. This principle of united action was to become extraordinarily significant in the diplomatic relations of the Western allies before and during the Geneva Conference.

At his press conference two days later, the President said he agreed completely with what Mr. Dulles had said in his Overseas Press Club speech. (He had, in fact, read and approved the speech on the morning of 29 March.)[27] He said it was not possible to lay down a general rule as to what the United States would do, but the government was committed, he said, to "united action" against a Communist effort to overrun Southeast Asia.[28]

Who, then, was to do the fighting in Indochina? Presumably the French would carry on the war, together with troops from the Associated States. To support this effort the United States was prepared to pledge equipment and credits and it would seek to improve the local troop-training phase of the Navarre Plan by providing training cadres. If, however, the military situation reached the point where Indochina was about to be communized, a coalition of states (of unspecified composition) might act to prevent this result. What this coalition might do, or how, or when it might intervene with combat troops—if this is what was implied—was left open. The Navarre Plan was still the basis for French operations; local defeats might be sustained, perhaps at Dien Bien Phu, but this would not radically alter the military situation in Indochina. The French, it was assumed, would eventually perfect the independence of the Associated

[26] *The Threat of a Red Asia*, p. 4.   [27] *NYT*, 29 March 1954.

[28] *NYT*, 1 April 1954. In February, Eisenhower had said he could think of no greater tragedy for America than to become involved in an all-out war in any of "those regions" (Indochina), which was later explained as a personal, not an official view. On 31 March, announcing that he agreed completely with Secretary Dulles, the President said there was a great disadvantage in deploying ground forces all around the world to meet every little situation as it arose. The United States and its allies must make their position strong enough to allow local situations to take care of themselves. *NYT*, 1 April 1954.

The President, it seems, was reluctant to admit the need for intervention by France's allies in the Indochinese War. But how might Congress, the Western allies, the Soviet Union, the C.P.R., and the Vietminh interpret the President's glosses upon his secretary's public declarations?

States; meanwhile, military operations would continue, along with expansion and training of an Indochinese army. Also, an effort would be made to win the allegiance of the Indochinese whom the Communists had subjected to "nationalistic anti-French slogans to win local support."[29] Within a period variously estimated at from one to two years, military and political action programs might eventuate in genuinely independent, anti-Communist governments in Laos, Cambodia, and Vietnam.

The Secretary of State expressed a lack of confidence in what might be achieved at Geneva when he said (at his news conference on 23 March) that peace would come through military supremacy rather than diplomatic negotiations at Geneva.[30] This was another reflection of the feeling that a military decision favorable to France would not be won for at least a year; and the Geneva Conference was only a month away. France and her allies would not be negotiating from strength, particularly if the Vietminh should succeed in taking Dien Bien Phu. Therefore, not much emphasis should be placed upon Geneva.[31]

[II]

We have as yet no reliable record of General Ely's reaction to the Dulles news conference and his address to the Overseas Press Club.[32] In his discussions with the JCS on 24 March, he was still very much concerned about the possibility of Chinese intervention. He felt that the United States should give China a firm and unequivocal warning. We do not know what the JCS told Ely, but Admiral Radford continued the discussion of the war with Ely after the other chiefs left. Radford and Ely met again on the 25th, and the admiral was concerned about the fate of the garrison at Dien Bien Phu. Because the President had instructed him to do everything possible to contribute to the success of the battle in progress, Radford suggested that a limited, tactical aerial bombardment of Vietminh positions around Dien Bien Phu would relieve the garrison. The bombardment would require several strikes from B-29s stationed at Clark Field in the Philippines and support by fighter aircraft of the Seventh Fleet.

General Ely returned to Paris on 26 March, informed Pleven of Radford's suggestion, and Pleven convened a committee of war on

---

[29] *The Threat of a Red Asia*, p. 2.   [30] *NYT*, 24 March 1954.

[31] See W. S. White, *NYT*, 26 March 1954, and Roscoe Drummond, "Washington," *NYHT*, 21 March 1954.

[32] In his memoirs, Ely mentions the Overseas Press Club speech only in passing, but shows misunderstanding of its purport. Ely, p. 87.

the 29th.[33] The committee weighed the risk of Chinese intervention but concluded that the risk was not great and that an air strike could succeed. Before it made a recommendation to the government, however, it sought General Navarre's advice, and a staff officer flew to Hanoi and returned to Paris with Navarre's approval on 4 April. The committee of war recommended that the government request the United States to implement this operation (Operation Vautour), and at 11:30 p.m., 4 April, Laniel and Bidault called on the American ambassador, Douglas Dillon, and requested aerial bombardment of the area around Dien Bien Phu. Dillon communicated this request to Washington; Secretary of State Dulles responded on the 5th; and Dillon immediately informed Bidault of Dulles's reply. As the secretary had explained to General Ely, the United States could not commit a belligerent act, such as the Radford plan envisaged, without the approval of Congress and consultations with France and other states.[34]

While the committee of war met in Paris, on and after 29 March, the JCS and administration officials debated the efficacy of the Radford plan and its possible consequences. On Saturday, 3 April, Dulles called a secret conference at the State Department,[35] attended by Admiral Radford, Under Secretary of Defense Roger Kyes, Secretary of the Navy Robert B. Anderson, Thruston B. Morton, Assistant Secretary of State for Congressional Relations, and eight congressmen. (It is significant, I think, that neither the President nor the Secretary of Defense attended the conference.) The congressmen were briefed on the military situation in Indochina and Admiral Radford told of his plan to save Dien Bien Phu. Upon questioning by the congressmen, the admiral admitted that his plan did not have the backing of the JCS and that it risked a war with China. Moreover, if the air strikes failed to relieve the garrison, U.S. ground troops would be used. The congressmen were reported to have been concerned about a plan that might lead to committing American ground troops in East Asia, especially without an understanding that the European and Asian allies of the United States would approve such intervention. Dulles, pursuing the policy announced in his Overseas Press Club speech, said that the administration would consult the allies shortly but that he had not yet done so. It appears that no decisions were taken at this meeting. The reticence of the congressmen

[33] Ely, pp. 76-78, 83-85.   [34] Ely, pp. 85-87.

[35] This account is based partly on a statement by Representative John McCormack (*NYT*, 23 January 1956) briefly describing the 3 April 1954 meeting and partly upon Chalmers H. Roberts's article "The Day We Didn't Go to War," *Reporter*, 14 September 1954, pp. 31-35. My analysis and conclusions differ substantially from those of Mr. Roberts.

vis-à-vis the Radford plan had been registered and the importance of having allies in a combat operation in Indochina was underlined.

This meeting, I submit, was a carefully considered move by Mr. Dulles for vetoing the Radford plan through the action of others. The Secretary of State and the President shared Radford's views that the situation in Indochina was bad and growing worse, but they did not believe the United States should commit belligerent acts without at least consulting its allies. Admiral Radford no doubt had the support of some highly placed officials, Vice President Nixon among them, but the intra-administration differences of opinion were to be resolved in favor of a policy of prudence and caution by having congressional opinion balance that of the administration "activists." What was more natural than to consult Congress on an issue such as this, just after the period when the Bricker amendment debate had so fully exposed the problem of executive-legislative powers and prerogatives in the formulation of American foreign policy?

Earlier Admiral Radford had urged the administration to push a resolution through Congress that would authorize the air strikes, but the Secretary of State, and the President, had been reluctant to do so. The meeting of 2 April would help convince Radford of congressional antipathy to such action; and the fact that President Eisenhower was not at the meeting indicated that he did not intend to ask for the resolution. There were several good reasons for *not* asking Congress for such a resolution at the time.[36]

1. If Congress approved such a resolution, the intra-administration pressures to act might become irresistible. Then—in spite of its effect upon our allies, in spite of the New Look strategy and its fiscal assumptions, in spite of the possibility of a war with China—the administration might have to order execution of the Radford plan. Its supporters had argued that the air strikes would not bring China into the war and would convince the Chinese that the United States was not merely talking. In other words, the Radford plan would deter the Chinese. This was conjecture, however, and Mr. Dulles was not disposed to take the risk.

2. If Congress disapproved the resolution (because it opposed a war in an election year or because it believed the air strikes would not succeed), this could be viewed by the Communist powers as an indication that the United States would not fight in Indochina. America's ability to deter by *threats* of intervention would be appreciably diminished.

Admiral Radford had spoken with Secretary Dulles on the 27th, just after General Ely had departed, and told him of his plan for

[36] DDE, p. 347.

air strikes at Dien Bien Phu. The secretary's reaction is not known,[37] but he probably told Radford that before any action was taken (including an air strike), public opinion would have to be prepared. The Overseas Press Club speech on 29 March was a major step in implementing the policy of educating the public, but, as far as the air strikes were concerned, Mr. Dulles—after reflection—had concluded that this "was a poor way for the U.S. to get involved" in the Indochinese War.[38] Thus at the meeting on 3 April, Dulles shared the view of several congressional leaders who doubted the efficacy of an air attack, who feared its consequences, and who regarded *unilateral* American intervention as undesirable.[39]

Between 27 March and 3 April the Secretary of State had conferred several times with the President about the effectiveness of air strikes and other means for supporting the French war effort, particularly a carefully considered defense program that would entail establishing a regional security alliance for Southeast Asia.[40] He met with the President again on Sunday evening, 4 April, to review the implementation of policies to help the French and to report the results of his meeting with the congressional leaders the day before. (Admiral Radford also was present.) Mr. Eisenhower, in *Mandate for Change*, wrote that Dulles had concluded it would be impossible to get congressional authorization for the United States to act alone. Congressional support would be contingent upon meeting three conditions:

(1) United States intervention must be part of a coalition to include the other free nations of Southeast Asia, the Philippines, and the British Commonwealth.

(2) The French must agree to accelerate their independence program for the Associated States so there could be no interpretation that United States assistance meant support of French colonialism.

(3) The French must agree not to pull their forces out of the war if we put our forces in.[41]

Mr. Eisenhower does not say whether he discussed Admiral Radford's air-strike plan with Dulles and Radford that evening, but he agreed that Dulles should go ahead with his plans to "talk to other

[37] L&D, p. 76.
[38] J. Shepley, "How Dulles Averted War," *Life*, 16 January 1956, pp. 70-80 (quotation on p. 72).
[39] J. R. Beal, *John Foster Dulles: A Biography* (New York: Harper & Row, 1957), pp. 207-208.
[40] *Ibid.*, p. 208.
[41] DDE, p. 347.

nations and tell them that if they would go along with our proposal we would be ready to participate in a regional grouping."[42]

Thus at the end of March the Dulles policy for Indochina was as follows.

1. American officials must reassure the French and stiffen their will to continue to fight; they must expedite the shipment of equipment the French had requested; and they must seek an agreement with France that would allow American cadres to train the Indochinese.

2. The administration must deemphasize Dien Bien Phu and the Geneva Conference. Building a position of strength for negotiations would take at least a year, possibly two, and would require granting genuine independence to the Indochinese and winning the allegiance of the people away from the Vietminh.

3. The military situation in Indochina was serious but not yet desperate. In France, however, popular revulsion to the war was growing. The Laniel government might collapse under a military setback and a new French government might be willing to pull out of Indochina and leave the Vietminh in control. Communization of Indochina should be resisted.

4. Resistance to communization would be effected by "united action." This, however, was primarily a policy of deterrence; no belligerent acts would be committed for the present.

5. If the deterrent function of a coalition policy should fail, the possibility of armed intervention could not be averted. The coalition would then act together, presumably with United States participation being supported by a congressional resolution.

Analysts such as Walter Lippmann and James Reston[43] asserted that the French would not be able to defeat the Vietminh and would not succeed in winning the allegiance of the Indochinese. Inability either to defeat the Vietminh or win the support of the non-Communist Vietnamese pointed up an important problem: if China did not actively intervene in Indochina and if the French could not obtain a military decision, the regime of Ho Chi Minh could become firmly established in Indochina. Was this eventuality covered by Dulles's "precondition" for united action, that is, "the imposition on Southeast Asia of the political system of Communist Russia and its Chinese Communist ally, by whatever means"? Presumably it was, since Premier Ho, an avowed Marxist, would impose the Communist political system of the Soviet Union upon Indochina if his armies or his diplomats were successful. This, at least, is what virtually every administration official believed. Certainly events in North Viet-

[42] *Ibid.* (emphasis added).
[43] Walter Lippmann, *NYHT*, 11 February, 29 March 1954; James Reston, *NYT*, 3 April 1954.

nam from the time of the Geneva settlements until mid-1956 seem to confirm the validity of this opinion, for in the two years immediately following the cease-fire the leaders of the DRVN emulated the Communist Chinese model of internal stabilization, rectification, and land reform and aligned North Vietnam firmly with the socialist bloc. But in the absence of Chinese intervention, could the Western allies agree to act according to the principles Dulles set down in his Overseas Press Club speech? Could the administration galvanize American public opinion sufficiently to permit it to take the necessary steps to prevent a Vietminh success in Indochina?

Dulles appeared before the House Foreign Affairs Committee on 5 April to testify on behalf of the administration's appropriations request for the fiscal 1955 Mutual Security Program, he declared that the United States must thwart the Communist effort to break the combat spirit of the French before the Geneva Conference began. "United action," he said, was required to discourage the Communists and to reassure the French and the Indochinese.[44] He also discussed the possibility of Chinese intervention in Southeast Asia. Observing that the Chinese were coming "awfully close" to direct aggression in Indochina, he again stated that United States reaction to overt Chinese incursions need not be restricted to Indochina. Dulles also declared that the communization of Southeast Asia "should not be passively accepted, but met by a unity of will and, if need be, unity of action."[45]

THE DULLES policy, as described above, was formulated in Washington without consulting America's allies, but consultations would follow, and, as we shall see, they revealed a reluctance by France and Britain that came somewhat as a surprise to administration officials.

Perhaps this should have been anticipated. The authors of the policy, principally the Secretary of State, were certainly aware of French opposition to the United States' sending training cadres to Indochina; they were aware, too, of the notorious instability of Fourth Republic governments. From March through early June 1954, the Laniel government was in a metastable condition, and so fearful were its officials of a governmental crisis that they did virtually nothing, merely hoping that American air power would save the military situation, and that American troops would not be dispatched to Indochina. Dulles was probably aware of the influential forces in France

[44] DSB, 19 April 1954, pp. 582-583.
[45] At his news conference of 7 April the President declared: "We must have a concert of opinion, and a concert of readiness to react in whatever way was necessary" (*NYT*, 7 April 1954). Mr. Eisenhower used the metaphor of the "falling dominoes" to describe the effect in Southeast Asia of the communization of Indochina.

that opposed continuation of the war, but whether he appreciated how intense this sentiment was we do not know. Probably he regarded it as only another factor to be taken into account, along with congressional opposition to the overseas use of U.S. infantry or marines and the incompatibility of the New Look strategy with a ground war in Indochina. His policy, intended to encourage and support the French war effort, might fail, but if it did, then—and only then—would crucial decisions be made.

Because Dulles policy was vague, it gave rise to rumors of impending United States intervention, both in Washington and in other capitals, but no doubt it was designed to do just this since its major function was to deter the Communist Chinese and, secondarily, the Soviet Union. It was only the first statement in a sustained program of statements, issued throughout the course of the Geneva negotiations and designed, at the very least, to make it appear that American intervention was always possible. It went beyond this, of course: in certain circumstances intervention was probable.[46]

Indeed, the unilateral pronouncement of a policy that would vitally affect America's allies should have been expected to cause irritation in London and Paris. Once more the United States had presumed to speak for Europe—when Europe, by 1954, had come to doubt the wisdom of some of its American partner's policies and a number of persons resented the assumptions that seemed implicit in America's dealings with her European allies: that, as the bloc leader, the United States could bind (or attempt to bind) its allies by unilateral public announcements of "allied" policy. Recent revelations of the power and effects of thermonuclear weapons heightened the fear that Indochina might lead to a war in which these weapons would be used.

Dulles has been criticized for not being aware of the interests of America's European allies. This simply was not true. His concern for the political situation in France was demonstrated during the Berlin Conference. He had no confidence in the Radford plan for air strikes at Dien Bien Phu, not only because he knew that Congress feared it would lead to the commitment of U.S. ground forces but because he knew that such an act of belligerency would horrify the British and their Commonwealth associates. In fact, it is difficult to criticize United States Southeast Asia policy as it stood in the first week of April 1954. It was deliberately tentative, requiring further events and consultations for defining America's responses to the actions of France and her adversaries.

Criticism of the New Look strategy is another matter, of course,

---

[46] Writing later, Mr. Eisenhower said that had the Chinese "adopted a policy of regular air support for the Vietminh, we would have assuredly moved in to eliminate this blatant aggression from without." DDE, p. 373.

and we shall see how the elements of that strategy figured in the events of April and May. The New Look was *so* new, however, that in the spring of 1954 its authors were still discovering many of its implications. During March and April, Secretary of State Dulles, the President, and other administration officials sought to explain the strategy to domestic critics and inquiring allies alike.

[III]

In his speech on 12 January before the Council on Foreign Relations, Dulles had announced that the President had made a basic strategic decision: the United States would "depend primarily upon a great capacity to retaliate, instantly, by means and at places of our choosing."[47] Critics seized upon the word "instantly" and asked whether the President would take such a momentous step without consulting Congress. At a press conference on 10 March, President Eisenhower stated emphatically: "There is going to be no involvement of America in war unless it is a result of the constitutional process that is placed upon Congress to declare it."[48] This assertion may have reassured those who were anxious to preserve Congress's rights in the constitutional process of declaring war, but others asked: Must Congress be consulted in all cases? What if an aggressor's move left little time to act? European critics asked why it would be necessary for the President to consult Congress if he were acting pursuant to the NATO treaty, which had been approved by the Senate.[49]

Dulles sought to answer these questions in a news conference on 16 March. In his view the President had the authority, without consulting Congress, to order instant retaliation against any attack upon the United States or its allies in Europe and the Western hemisphere. This authority was based, in part, upon the North Atlantic Treaty and the Rio Pact (1947), both of which the Senate had approved.[50] The next day the President held a news conference and, speaking on this same problem, declared that it was futile to speculate about hypothetical events. If the interests of the United States were threatened, the President would make a common-sense judgment at

[47] *Docs., 1954*, p. 10.

[48] *NYT*, 11 March 1954.

[49] Article 5 of the North Atlantic treaty reads: "The parties agree that an armed attack against one or more of them in Europe or North America shall be considered an attack against them all; and consequently they agree that, if such an armed attack occurs, each of them . . . will assist the Party or Parties so attacked *by taking forthwith*, individually and in concert with the other Parties, *such action as it deems necessary, including the use of armed force*, to restore and maintain the security of the North Atlantic area" (emphasis added).

[50] *NYT*, 17, 18, 21 March 1954. See also John Foster Dulles, "Policy for Security and Peace," *Foreign Affairs*, 32 (April, 1954): pp. 353-364 (released on 16 April). This article also appears in *DSB*, 29 March 1954, pp. 459-464.

such a time. If the situation were dire, he would commit American forces and then consult Congress; if time allowed, he would seek a declaration of war before he acted. Contrary to his position one week earlier, Mr. Eisenhower emphatically reaffirmed the President's power to fight or react instantly when confronted by an imminent attack, and to decide for himself, in an equivocal situation, when he must attack and when he must consult Congress.[51]

If European critics were concerned about the consequences of a delay while the President consulted Congress, others were at least equally apprehensive about the possibility of the United States' retaliating without consulting its allies.[52] On 16 March Secretary Dulles affirmed that there would be consultation "in most cases I can conceive of," in part because American air bases abroad could not be used without the consent of the host states. International cooperation was "implicit in our defense system."

> If you will read my address of January 12th, you will see that what I advocated there was a "capacity" to retaliate. In no place did I say that we would retaliate instantly. . . . The question whether or not you retaliate instantly and where you retaliate is a matter to be dealt with in accordance with the facts of each situation.[53]

In late March, Prime Minister Churchill announced that there would be instant consultation with the United States if either Britain or the United States were attacked, which President Eisenhower corroborated immediately. He added that this was particularly true since there were important U.S. air force bases in Great Britain.[54]

Former Secretary of State Dean Acheson, Adlai Stevenson, and Chester Bowles were perhaps the leading critics of the New Look, at least at this early stage.[55] Their basic criticism was that the New Look forced the United States to rely upon only one kind of military response: massive retaliation by aircraft carrying nuclear weapons. Small or limited wars and indirect aggression could not be effectively handled by this strategy. In a limited war, such as the Indochinese

[51] *NYT*, 18 March 1954.

[52] Canada's Secretary of State for External Affairs, Lester B. Pearson, asked for assurances that "instant retaliation" would not preclude prior consultation with America's allies. *NYT*, 21 March 1954.

[53] *NYT*, 17, 21 March 1954.   [54] *NYT*, 24, 25 March 1954.

[55] See Chester Bowles, "A Plea for Another Great Debate," *NYT*, 28 February 1954, and Dean Acheson, "Instant Retaliation: The Debate Continued," *NYT*, 28 March 1954. General Matthew B. Ridgway, Chief of Staff of the U.S. Army, also was a leading critic of the New Look. On 8 and 9 February, before the House Appropriations Sub-Committee, and again on 15 March, he criticized the proposed reductions in the strength of the army from nineteen or twenty divisions to seventeen divisions (*NYT*, 21 March, 16 April 1954). He argued that a lowering of U.S. capabilities was not possible without a corresponding decrease in U.S. responsibilities.

War, the United States would have the overly limited choice of turning it into a thermonuclear holocaust or, in the words of Stevenson, allowing Moscow and Peking "to nibble us to death." Since the Soviets had the hydrogen bomb and would soon have the capability of destroying American cities, the New Look invited an attack by the Soviets, according to Stevenson.

There was adequate evidence, moreover, that the strategy had aroused nervousness, suspicion, and repugnance among America's allies. Apart from their unwillingness to accept this apocalyptic defense policy, the allies' policymakers feared that the Eisenhower administration intended to reduce its overseas troop strength, which of course was envisaged in the original plans.

The administration responded to these criticisms in the Dulles press conference of 16 March (already mentioned), in a statement on the 19th, and in an article in the April 1954 issue of *Foreign Affairs*.[56] The purpose of the New Look, the secretary said, was to deter aggression, not to retaliate massively, and possession of the capacity to retaliate did not "impose the necessity of using it in every instance of attack." Strategic bombing was not the only means of deterring aggression: the United States would "retain a wide variety in the means and scope for responding to aggression." Secretary of Defense Wilson and Mr. Dulles repeatedly denied that the United States was planning to reduce its forces in Europe.

The "strategic debate" did not end with these reinterpretive and educative efforts of the administration. It was never explained, and perhaps could not be explained, how the budget could be balanced, the personnel strength of the armed forces reduced, and a strategy of massive retaliation pursued while the United States nevertheless retained "a wide variety in the means and scope for responding to aggression." On 19 March, ten days before his Overseas Press Club address, Secretary Dulles categorically declared that the policy of massive retaliation had "no application" to Indochina. Critics would certainly agree with that assertion inasmuch as there were no suitable targets in Indochina and the war was a complicated military-political struggle in which strategic air power was almost totally irrelevant. A policy of massive retaliation could only carry the war to China, where indeed there were suitable targets. Thus the question arose: If the policy of massive retaliation did not apply to Indochina, what was the government's policy in Indochina.

In March the administration began to grope its way toward such a policy. The Overseas Press Club speech was the first attempt (as I have argued, an *admittedly* tentative and provisional attempt) to announce publicly what that policy was, and indeed what it might be.

[56] See n. 50 above.

Chapter 5

UNITED ACTION

[I]

On Saturday, 3 April, the same day the Secretary of State had arranged for Admiral Radford to disclose his air-strike plan to congressional leaders, Dulles called in Henri Bonnet, the French ambassador, and explained to him what "united action" meant. A coalition would be formed, he is reported to have said, comprising France, Britain, the United States, Australia, New Zealand, Thailand, and the Philippines.[1] These nations would form a united front capable of resisting Communist aggression in Southeast Asia. Dulles wanted the prospective participants to take some positive, preparatory action immediately, that is, before the Geneva Conference opened, to demonstrate the resolve of the allies to the Communist powers. The latter would thereupon renounce their aggressive designs and their plan to exact major concessions from France at Geneva would be frustrated.

Having explained the concept of united action to the French ambassador, the administration had the task of consulting the British government, and the President wrote to Prime Minister Churchill on 4 April, broadly outlining his views on the crisis and urging cooperation in the formation of a regional security organization.

> Geneva is less than four weeks away. There the possibility of the Communists driving a wedge between us will, given the state of mind in France, be infinitely greater than at Berlin. I can understand the very natural desire of the French to seek an end to this war which has been bleeding them for eight years. But our painstaking search for a way out of the impasse has reluctantly forced us to the conclusion that there is no negotiated solution of the Indochina problem which in its essence would not be either a face-saving device to cover a French surrender or a face-saving device to cover a Communist retirement. The first alternative is too serious in its broad strategic implications for us and for you to be acceptable.[2]

Mr. Eisenhower went on to say that the Secretary of State, in a

---

[1] L&D, pp. 79-80. In view of later newspaper accounts, it is possible that Dulles included the Republic of Korea, the Associated States, and Taiwan as prospective coalition members in his proposal to Bonnet.

[2] DDE, pp. 346-347.

recent address, had sketched a preliminary plan for effecting the second alternative, a plan that called for united action by the allies.

I believe that the best way to put teeth in this concept and to bring greater moral and material resources to the support of the French effort is through the establishment of a new, ad hoc grouping or coalition composed of nations which have a vital concern in the checking of Communist expansion in the area. I have in mind in addition to our two countries, France, the Associated States, Australia, New Zealand, Thailand and the Philippines. The United States government would expect to play its full part in such a coalition. . . .

The important thing is that the coalition must be strong and it must be willing to join the fight if necessary. I do not envisage the need of any appreciable ground forces on your or our part.

During the week of 4 April, even before the British and French had replied to the proposed united-action demarche, administration officials contacted the ambassadors of New Zealand, Australia, the Philippines, Thailand, South Korea, and Taiwan in a concerted diplomatic effort to inform America's allies of what the United States would like to do by way of a united-action policy, to secure their advice, and hopefully their consent to the plan for such a coalition.[3] The joint issuance by the allies of a warning to China against intervening in Indochina also was discussed. The administration dispatched notes on these proposals to the ambassadors' governments on 6 April, at the same time publicly announcing the dispatch of these notes.[4]

The French refused to cooperate for the time being; a note of 6 April explained that French public opinion would not understand why the government had not done more to find a pacific solution. Also, the united-front tactic might harden the attitude of the Chinese and otherwise produce unfavorable conditions for negotiations at Geneva. It might even serve as a pretext for Chinese intervention. The French note suggested the matter be given further study,[5] at the same time postponing a reply to the United States' proposal for a joint warning to China.[6] The British, who were equally reticent, preferred not to take any steps that might compromise the chances of success at Geneva.[7]

[3] *NYT*, 10 April 1954. Dulles also discussed united action with Sir Roger Makins, the British ambassador, thus supplementing the President's direct approach to the Prime Minister.
[4] *NYT*, 6 April 1954.   [5] L&D, p. 81.
[6] *NYT*, 7 April 1954.
[7] DDE, p. 347; E, pp. 102, 104.

The cautiousness of the two major allies stemmed predominantly from fear of a larger war in Southeast Asia but also from a desire to explore with the Soviets and the Chinese the possibilities for a negotiated settlement on Indochina and the reduction of friction between Communist- and non-Communist-bloc states. There was, in addition, a great deal of uncertainty about the nature and function of the united action the United States was advocating. The French and, perhaps, the British concern for the attitude of the C.P.R. may have been caused by an almost immediate hostile reaction in Peking. The Peking *People's Daily* had asked: "What will this so-called 'united action' lead to? The answer has already been given in the Korean War."[8] The *Daily* went on to say that the United States was afraid of negotiating at Geneva.

The prospect of another Korea-type war could not be welcome in London. For one thing, the British army was already deeply committed in an anti-guerrilla war in Malaya; for another, the Mau Mau emergency in Kenya had become a major police operation. The French, of course, were continuously apprehensive of Chinese intentions. A statement that united action might lead to another Korea could only elicit—no doubt was designed to elicit—a cautious approach to United States undertakings in Asia.

Drew Middleton reported that the Churchill government was not opposed to a joint declaration warning China against a move into Indochina but questioned the administration's desire to issue the warning before the Geneva Conference began.[9] While skeptical of the prospects of success at Geneva, the British government believed they should not be diminished by a resounding declaration that might provoke and anger the Communists rather than make them more conciliatory. Middleton also reported British concern over the threat to Thailand and said that the British government would support a "regional grouping" in Southeast Asia. Some London papers seemed to support the idea of a coalition rather than "action," which seemed to indicate confusion in London over the meaning of "united action." If it meant a coalition, the British *might* go along; if it meant a warning declaration, or concerted belligerent action, the British were opposed, at least until after Geneva. The organization of a coalition would, in any case, require the same protracted and detailed diplomatic efforts as the NATO treaty. The question was *when* these organizing steps should begin.

Although responding negatively to the American proposal, the French government said that if the Geneva Conference failed to bring

[8] *NYT*, 3 April 1954.
[9] *NYT*, 8 April 1954. This was confirmed in Eden's *Full Circle* (p. 103). See E, 103.

about a cease-fire, it would be willing to permit other states to take an active part in the Indochinese War. The United States, in particular, would be *asked* to assume a greater role in the prosecution of the war.[10] Premier Laniel, who delivered a major policy address to the National Assembly on 9 April, just before the parliament recessed for the Easter holidays, said his policy was, first, to employ all means for a successful defense of Dien Bien Phu; second, to maintain the military effort in Indochina with American material assistance; and third, to negotiate for peace in Indochina at the forthcoming international conference.[11] The United States, Laniel declared, believed in the deterrent effect of repeated warnings to the Communists and that, by removing all doubts about America's intentions, Communist domination of Southeast Asia might be avoided. Just as some of the French ministers were opposed to any more warnings before Geneva, Laniel was reported to feel that Dulles's Overseas Press Club speech had already warned the Chinese sufficiently, that enough "deterrence" had been supplied for the time being.[12]

Dulles, not satisfied with the British and French reception of his plan for united action,[13] consulted the President, secured an "invitation" from the British, and decided to fly to London and to Paris for talks with allied officials. He wished to eliminate whatever mis-

[10] *NYT*, 9 April 1954.

[11] *JO*, 9 April 1954, pp. 1972-1973. See also the critical speech of the Socialist deputy, Gaston Defferre (*ibid.*, pp. 1973-1974).

[12] *NYT*, 12 April 1954.

[13] Arthur Krock of the *New York Times* reported that Dulles's coalition proposals were "leaked" in London and Paris (*NYT*, 10 April, 18 April 1954), which enabled the opposition parties in these capitals to criticize and attack the incumbent governments before the latter had adequate time to study the proposals. We know that the proposal for a joint warning to Peking was made public by the State Department. A collective defense for Southeast Asia was broached in a letter or cable from the President to the Prime Minister and through private conversations of Mr. Dulles with Henri Bonnet and Roger Makins. It is quite possible that the Secretary of State would have preferred secrecy: if the proposals were rejected, there would be no publicity for what could be regarded as an allied disagreement, or even disunity, upon an urgent problem. On the other hand, if and when the governments assented to begin negotiations for establishing a Southeast Asia alliance, Dulles could announce the fact and, theoretically, achieve optimal deterrent and propaganda effect. A "leak" would frustrate these calculations. But diplomatic activity in Washington throughout the first week of April was intense, and either there were leaks in the capital or news correspondents more or less guessed what had happened. If the foreign ministries of France or Britain leaked Dulles's proposals, part of the blame for early disclosure might be assigned to the administration.

At his press conference on 7 April the President again underscored the strategic importance of Indochina. He said the United States was making efforts for united action to cope with the crisis in Southeast Asia but that it was too early to assess the results. Secret negotiations with Britain, France, Australia, New Zealand, the Philippines, Thailand, and the Associated States were under way, he said. *NYT*, 8 April 1954.

understandings existed with respect to the united-action concept. The Secretary of State issued a statement on 10 April, the day of his departure for London:

> I am going in order to consult with the British and French governments about some of the very real problems that are involved in creating the obviously desirable united front to resist Communist aggression in Southeast Asia. . . .
>
> Unity of purpose calls for a full understanding. It seemed that this understanding would be promoted if I would personally go to London to talk to the British government and go to Paris to talk to the French government so that there could be a more satisfactory exchange of views than is possible by the exchange of cabled messages.[14]

When Secretary Dulles left Washington, he had one acceptance of his coalition plan to show his British and French allies. The day before, 9 April, the ambassador of Thailand had accepted the American "invitation to join in arranging a united front against aggression in Southeast Asia";[15] thus Thailand had shown immediate interest in the united-action concept.

Manila had been more cautious, but within a week Vice President Carlos P. Romulo announced that the Philippines would support a United States–sponsored Pacific alliance provided its prospective Western allies agreed to grant independence to the Asian territories under their rule.[16] President Ramon Magsaysay had also conditioned the Philippines' support upon an unequivocal guarantee of assistance from the United States in the event of an attack[17] (although its security was already guaranteed by a mutual security pact with the United States). The former condition, however—the grant of independence to Asian colonies—might cause some problems, depending upon how Manila interpreted the status of the Associated States within the French Union—whether membership in the union was compatible with the sovereignty and independence upon which the Philippine government conditioned its cooperation. But no real difficulties emerged, and the Philippine delegates at Geneva would support the concept of a Southeast Asia collective defense organization.

[14] *NYT*, 10 April 1954. Dulles was accompanied by (among others) Livingston T. Merchant, Under Secretary of State for Political Affairs, Winthrop W. Aldrich, the American ambassador to Britain, and Douglas MacArthur II, a State Department counselor.

[15] Private Papers of John Foster Dulles, Minute of 9 April, 1954, File I.G.; see also File IX for 1954.

[16] *NYT*, 18 April 1954; see also *NYT*, 9 April 1954.

[17] *NYT*, 19 April 1954.

During the first week of April, Dulles was reported to have spoken with the ministers from Australia, New Zealand, the Associated States, Taiwan, and South Korea. The results of these demarches are unknown at present, but Taiwan's Foreign Minister publicly urged the establishment of an anti-Communist alliance before the Geneva Conference convened.[18]

[II]

Washington was in an unsettled state during the first three weeks of April because of rumors of American intervention in Indochina. One rumor had the United States intervening unilaterally by a strategic air strike; another had it that intervention would be in the form of American ground forces; and still another rumor said that intervention would be collective, that the administration even now was preparing the basis for collective action. Certainly the diplomatic consultations during this period excited curiosity and anxiety and encouraged speculation. This also was true of the secret meeting on 3 April, attended by Dulles, Admiral Radford, administration officials, and congressional leaders, after which Senator Wiley said merely that Congress had been briefed on Indochina. Two aircraft carriers of the Seventh Fleet had taken up stations in the South China Sea, while Admiral Radford and others were worrying officials with the seriousness of the French military situation and the need for action to save Dien Bien Phu.

The vague language of the Dulles address of 29 March was conducive to the circulation of rumors; perhaps the secretary had even hoped for the propagation of rumors, for no immediate attempt was made to check them, to clarify the situation, nor to brief even the highest administration officials. Certainly Mr. Eisenhower's press conference on 7 April served none of these purposes. The President spoke of a chain reaction of disasters if Indochina were conquered by the Communists. He likened the strategic situation to a row of falling dominoes: first Vietnam would be communized, then Burma and Thailand, and America's island defense chain (Japan, Taiwan, the Philippines) would be flanked, Australia and New Zealand threatened.[19] At every turn the urgency of the situation was apparent.

Debate revealed that the French Indochina policy had no friends in the Senate.[20] Senators John F. Kennedy (Dem., Mass.) and Mike

[18] *NYT*, 16 April 1954.
[19] *NYT*, 8 April 1954.
[20] *Ibid.* and *NYT*, 15 April 1954. *Congressional Record*, 6 April 1954, pp. 4401-4410. Senator Stuart Symington (Dem., Mo.), while in Paris, was reported to have received a no from unidentified French persons in response to these questions: Did the French see a military or a political solution to the Indochinese War? Would

Mansfield (Dem., Montana) argued that the Indochinese could not be expected to continue fighting without complete, and guaranteed, independence. Senator Everett Dirksen (Rep., Ill.) expressed concern over France's monopoly of administrative talent in Indochina: if they should leave tomorrow, the political situation they left behind them would deteriorate catastrophically. Nevertheless, Dirksen believed that a target date for independence must be set soon. The Senate accepted Dulles's declaration that united action "must be undertaken" to prevent the communization of Southeast Asia. As the *New York Times* reported, the Senate was resigned to intervention in a "collective context."[21]

In the absence of detailed consultations with Britain and France in this period, it was only too easy for London and Paris to be confused about American intentions. Even if Dulles had been fully explicit in his discussions with Ambassador Bonnet and others, even if he had clearly explained to them what united action meant, British and French observers in Washington would report the substance of the rumors to London and Paris. They would describe Washington as it then *appeared* to be, with not one but several ostensibly authoritative voices speaking for the administration, but each voice telling a different story and describing a different version of United States policy in Southeast Asia. Dulles's trip to London and Paris was indeed necessary. Apart from his intention to persuade his hosts to support a united-action strategy, he would have to explain the official American policy.

[III]

Secretary Dulles and his staff arrived in London on Sunday, 11 April, and immediately began the first of a series of talks with Anthony Eden and others of the British Foreign Office; the talks continued through Tuesday, 13 April. Dulles assured the British that the United States was not attempting to prejudice the success of the Geneva Conference, but a united stand was necessary, he said, in order to put the West in a strong bargaining position. This would, in fact, enhance the prospects of the conference. Eden felt that the joint issuance of a warning to China would hinder progress at Geneva and play into the hands of the Communists. If the warning was meant to halt Chinese aid to the Vietminh, the Foreign Secretary argued, it would not succeed. The Chinese would "lose face" by withdraw-

---

the French use troops offered by the Republic of Korea or Taipei? If the French left Indochina and the United States took over the war, would France agree to give the Associated States freedom? *NYT*, 8 April 1954; see also Walter Lippmann, "The Indo-China Emergency," *NYHT*, 12 April 1954.

[21] W. S. White's report in the *NYT*, 5 April 1954.

ing their support of the Vietminh in the face of a public warning
of the kind Mr. Dulles contemplated.[22]

Any precipitate action before the Geneva Conference that might
eventuate in the use of British armed forces in Indochina was opposed by Mr. Eden. For one thing, it might alienate several members
of the Commonwealth, India in particular, who regarded the Indochinese War as a French colonial war. Eden's rather negative reaction to the prospect of open involvement in the war in Indochina
came about after Dulles described the decision made by the President the preceding Sunday evening (4 April). Dulles said he no
longer believed in the efficacy of a joint warning directed at Peking;
he wanted a regional security organization established in Southeast
Asia. This in itself would deter China and make military intervention
in Indochina unnecessary. Eden expressed his willingness to recommend that Britain join the defense organization Dulles had in
mind, but its establishment must be preceded by consultations among
the interested states.[23] Eden seems to have agreed that priority
should be given to coordinating allied policy at the conference, including preparations for a united front at Geneva. In short, he accepted the necessity for Western unity of intention and action but
felt this should come about through preparations for a united front
rather than through a joint warning to China or the other Communist
states. It is not clear, however, what the negotiators meant by "preparations" for a united front and it is difficult to say whether there was
a meeting of minds on when such preparations should begin. But it
is certainly clear that Eden believed that extended, careful conversations were prerequisite for establishing a collective defense organization for Southeast Asia similar to NATO.

Eden and Dulles issued a joint statement on 13 April, at the conclusion of their discussions. Recognizing that the Communist forces
in Indochina posed a threat, not only for the states directly involved
in the war but also for the entire area of Southeast Asia, the ministers
announced:

> [We] are ready to take part, with the other countries principally
> concerned, in an examination of the possibility of establishing a
> collective defense, within the framework of the Charter of the
> United Nations, to assure the peace, security and freedom of South-
> east Asia and the Western Pacific.
>
> It is our hope that the Geneva Conference will lead to the restora-
> tion of peace in Indochina. We believe that the prospect of

---

[22] E, pp. 104-105. Eden was joined by Selwyn Lloyd and by W. D. Allen,
Deputy Under Secretary for Far Eastern Affairs (among others).
[23] E, pp. 107, 105. *NYT*, 12, 13 April 1954.

establishing a unity of defensive purpose throughout Southeast Asia and the Western Pacific will contribute to an honorable peace in Indochina.[24]

Secretary Dulles went to Paris on Tuesday, the 13th. The Franco-American conversations lasted all day Wednesday, and the participants released a joint statement at the conclusion of their meeting similar to the Eden-Dulles statement the day before.[25] Bidault is reported to have told Dulles that every effort must be made at Geneva to achieve an honorable peace in Indochina: the French domestic political situation required it. Any step that would harden Chinese attitudes before the conference should be avoided since peace in Indochina depended upon China's amenability to compromise. Dulles argued that because the Soviets were as worried as the allies about the possibility of the Indochinese War becoming internationalized and leading to a nuclear war, a warning by the allies of their determination to prevent the communization of Indochina would compel the Soviets to press the Chinese and the Vietminh to compromise. Moreover, having conferred with congressional leaders, Dulles asserted that he could not very well ask Congress to approve United States intervention in Indochina (if that should be necessary) without evidence of the willingness of America's allies to join in a united action. Bidault, like his British counterpart, expressed reservations about the timing of Dulles's proposed moves. The Laniel government must at least appear to be sincere in its efforts to obtain a cease-fire in Indochina, he said, no matter how dim the prospects. If, however, the Geneva Conference failed, France would be confronted with the problem of internationalizing the war.[26]

[24] Department of State Press Release, No. 192, 13 April 1954; *Docs., 1954,* pp. 257.

[25] *Docs., 1954,* p. 259. The release read in part: "We recognize that the prolongation of the war in Indochina, which endangers the security of the countries immediately affected, also threatens the entire area of Southeast Asia and of the Western Pacific. In close association with other interested nations, we will examine the possibility of establishing, within the framework of the United Nations Charter, a collective defense to assure the peace, security and freedom of this area."

[26] L&D, pp. 83-84. According to Eisenhower, Laniel and Paul Reynaud promised total independence for the Associated States (DDE, p. 348). The Franco-American news release of 13 April, noting the Communist aggression in Indochina and its climax at Dien Bien Phu (and elsewhere), declared: "The independence of the three Associated States within the French Union, which new agreements are to complete, is at stake in these battles." *Docs., 1954,* p. 258.
At the beginning of April, Roger Makins told Secretary Dulles of the British Foreign Office opinion that, in the event of negotiations, partition of Vietnam would be the "least damaging solution" (E, pp. 102, 97). Neither Dulles nor Bedell Smith, apparently, regarded partition acceptable at this date. In Paris, on 14 April, Bidault was reported to have told Dulles that he would not discuss partition at Geneva. Joseph and Stewart Alsop, "Indo-China and Geneva," *NYHT,* 21 April 1954.

We do not know whether Dulles and Bidault discussed the substance of the American-British statement of the day before. Douglas Dillon stated that when Dulles arrived in Paris, he believed he had Eden's agreement to begin exploratory talks on a Southeast Asia collective security organization before the Geneva Conference opened.[27] Dulles must have informed Bidault of this, but we do not yet know what the official French view was.

Moscow watched the United States' diplomatic moves with acute interest. *Pravda* attacked the Overseas Press Club speech as a "transparent slanderous provocation intended exclusively to poison the atmosphere on the eve of the Geneva conference and to intensify tension in international relations."[28] On 11 April, the day the Eden-Dulles conversations began in London, Harrison Salisbury said a *Pravda* editorial had charged the United States with planning military action against China with weapons of mass destruction. Indochina, *Pravda* declared, was being prepared as a new Korea and would serve as the bridgehead for an attack against China. *Pravda* also accused the United States of preventing France from starting armistice negotiation on the Indochinese War, and hailed France, as a great nation, capable of making its own decisions.[29]

The Cominform *Journal* accused the United States of intimidating its allies, and *Izvestia* called the American plan for a Southeast Asia collective defense organization an attempt to suppress the "national liberation movement of Asian peoples" to preserve colonial domination by the imperialist powers.[30] On 12 April *Pravda* declared that the United States was having trouble lining up allies behind its united-action policy. American actions, it was said, had alienated almost all Asian opinion.[31] After the release of the Eden-Dulles statement, Tass said: "Mr. Dulles could not achieve support in Britain for his policy of 'united action' in Indochina—at least for the time being." *Pravda's* London correspondent praised the British resistance to proposals for united action as farsighted.[32]

[27] See the OHP statement (p. 13) of Douglas Dillon, confirmed in DDE (p. 348): Dulles expressed his belief to President Eisenhower that "he [Dulles] had accomplished much toward dispelling the British reluctance to say or do anything before Geneva." See also the OHP statement (pp. 25-26) of Robert Bowie, director of the Department of State policy planning staff: It was his impression that Eden went along with Dulles's idea. Finally, Dulles himself asserted that he thought he had the agreement of Churchill and Eden (and the reluctant agreement of Bidault, who preferred the U.S. to intervene alone, if at all). James Shepley, "How Dulles Averted War," *Life*, 16 January 1956.
[28] Reuters dispatch of 8 April 1954.
[29] *NYT*, 12 April 1954.
[30] *NYT*, 21 April 1954.
[31] *NYT*, 13 April 1954.
[32] Reuters dispatch, reprinted in *NYT*, 14 April 1954.

DULLES RETURNED to Washington on 15 April. Had his trip been as empty of accomplishment as the Soviet press (and Senator Knowland) said?[33] Probably not. He found no support in London or Paris for a joint warning against the Communists, at least before the Geneva Conference, but the British had indicated interest in a collective defense organization for Southeast Asia. Although the establishment of such an organization would take time, and although (as we shall see) there was no meeting of minds on the time negotiations for its establishment should begin, the mere agreement of the British to work toward this end was a positive accomplishment from the administration's point of view. It also was evidence of a firm British-American desire to preserve the unity of their efforts in East Asia as well as in Europe.

Dulles certainly seems to have believed he had Eden's agreement to the opening of discussions on a defense organization, and after his return to Washington he invited the French, the British, and other "interested powers" to attend preparatory discussions on 20 April.[34] This date was less than a week before the Geneva Conference was scheduled to open. On Easter Sunday, 18 April, Sir Roger Makins, the British ambassador, informed Dulles that he had been instructed not to attend the meeting on the 20th.[35] Dulles was shocked; public embarrassment was avoided, to some extent, by converting the meeting into a discussion of a Korean political settlement, which also would be a subject of discussion at Geneva. On this basis, Makins attended the 20 April meeting.[36] Bitter recriminations were exchanged, however, and the debacle became (and remains) a topic of debate. Eden, we know, was rather piqued; his instructions to Makins had concluded with these words:

> Americans may think the time past when they need consider the feelings or difficulties of their allies. It is the conviction that this tendency becomes more pronounced every week that is creating

[33] Senator Knowland criticized the Anglo-American communiqué of 13 April for failing to mention Taiwan or the Republic of Korea, which together had 1,100,000 men in arms. The senator insisted that a Southeast Asia collective defense organization must include South Korea and Taiwan. "I hope," he said, "the prejudices of Her Majesty's Government, no matter what they might be, may not be raised again to eliminate these republics from a Pacific collective security pact." *NYT*, 15 April 1954. See also Roscoe Drummond, "What Dulles Brought Home," *NYHT*, 18 April 1954, and Walter Lippmann, "The Dulles Trip and Indochina," *NYHT*, 19 April 1954.

[34] *NYT*, 19 April 1954.

[35] E, p. 111.

[36] *Ibid.* U.S. *News & World Report* (13 June 1954, p. 36) also reported that Dulles was "furious."

mounting difficulties for anyone in this country who wants to maintain close Anglo-American relations.[37]

What had happened? First, it is important to realize that this outcome was not merely a consequence of Dulles's scheduling the preparatory meeting before the opening of the Geneva Conference, although this was very much involved. The impasse resulted, in part, from a disagreement over the composition of the conference the Secretary of State had scheduled for the 20th, and from a disagreement about the future membership of the Southeast Asia defense organization. At the London meeting on 11 April Eden had declared that India and other Asian Commonwealth nations should not be excluded from any defense pact.

Dulles, according to Eden's memoirs,

> hoped that any indication that India might be invited to join would be avoided. He [Dulles] explained that if there was any question of extending the security arrangements westwards to include India, there would be a "strong demand" in the United States to extend it eastwards as well, to include Nationalist China and Japan. He therefore suggested that the controversial issues of India on the one hand and Formosa on the other should be avoided, and that the discussions should be limited to South-East Asia proper.[38]

The matter seems to have been left there. Eden merely recorded that no final decision was made, and about three days after the conclusion of the London talks Dulles scheduled the preparatory meeting for the 20th. This was Eden's reaction, as he described it some six years later:

> [It] appeared that Mr. Dulles had taken steps to settle the question of membership in advance, on his own terms. . . . This was an extremely serious matter. *Quite apart from the timing of such a matter*, it was clear to me that it would . . . be regarded as already constituting the proposed organization. I could not possibly accept this. Not only had India been given no opportunity to express her views, but Burma, too, was closely concerned and there had been no time for proper consultation with either the Indian or the Burmese Governments. To hold a *mass meeting* at this stage would be insulting to them both and consequently harmful in its effects on the Geneva Conference.[39]

If we accept this account at face value, it seems clear that Dulles

---

[37] E, p. 110. At the time, the American public knew little, if anything, about this misunderstanding.

[38] E, p. 109.   [39] E, p. 110 (emphasis added).

did not appreciate how sensitive Eden was about Indian participation in a Southeast Asia security organization;[40] and this insensitivity might be regarded as one instance of a broader kind of official behavior by the Eisenhower administration: the tendency, noted by many American news analysts, to formulate alliance policy unilaterally on the assumption the United States could speak for its allies with only minimal discussion beforehand. This tendency was deserving of criticism, of course, but the fact that Eden chose to bridle at this issue is significant, as is his reference to scheduling the meeting of ambassadors before the Geneva Conference began.

The British Foreign Secretary must have known that India would not agree to participate in the proposed Southeast Asia pact or any other form of united action. India's avowed policy up to this time had been strict neutrality, but a neutrality the United States viewed as favorable to the Communist bloc. A news release from Bombay on 15 April suggested that Prime Minister Jawaharlal Nehru might take countermeasures against the collective organization for Southeast Asia at the forthcoming conference of the Colombo powers, scheduled to meet on 28 April.[41] The Eden-Dulles statement was taken as a new challenge to Nehru's idea of an "independent peace area" in Asia. The *Times of India* had said that Britain's acquiescence in this matter was "dangerously near a spineless appeasement of an importunate ally." The proposed alliance, it was said, was a new attempt to reimpose foreign dominion in countries newly free or still struggling for independence.

Eden's suggestion for consultations with India could be viewed by Dulles only as a means for delaying the beginning of talks on the organizational form of united action. Dulles wanted some action taken before or during the Geneva Conference in order to warn the Communists, at least symbolically, that the West was preparing to resist the communization of Southeast Asia. He probably had raised the prospect of the participation of Taiwan because he knew influential persons in Washington would favor Nationalist Chinese participation, but he also knew that a security arrangement with Taiwan might not deter the C.P.R.; indeed, would antagonize that regime. Dulles might have felt he was making a small concession by omitting Tai-

---

[40] On the other hand, Eden did not seem to appreciate the difficulties under which Dulles labored, with Senators Knowland and McCarthy and others closely observing the secretary's conduct of foreign relations and critical of any policy that was less than openly hostile to the Communist-bloc states or their "neutralist sympathizers" (i.e. India, Burma, Indonesia).

[41] *NYT*, 16 April 1954. The Colombo powers—Burma, Ceylon, India, Indonesia, and Pakistan—were to meet in Colombo, Ceylon, during the first week of the Geneva Conference and consider various problems arising from the remnants of colonialism in Asia. The date for the Colombo Conference had been set before the Big Four ministers met in Berlin.

wan and that Eden was prepared to do the same vis-à-vis India. No final decision was taken, however, and apparently Dulles thought that Eden was not really prepared to delay consultations by conditioning them upon India's reply, which could only be negative. In any event, there was a misunderstanding on this point. In actual fact, Eden felt himself under heavy pressure to delay taking any steps until the possibilities for a cease-fire had been fully explored at Geneva.

First, if the news releases referred to above are any indication, India (and perhaps Burma) must have made the most vigorous diplomatic protestations against the Eden-Dulles statement of the 13th and the Asian policy it portended.[42] Britain, having so recently divested itself of its holdings in South Asia but still maintaining a substantial colonial empire in Africa, Southeast Asia, and elsewhere, would not welcome criticism by India as a participant in a colonial war in Indochina and as an unreformed "colonial-imperial" power. Britain's Commonwealth relations would be irreparably damaged if the metropolitan focus of that organization were to be accused by one of its leading members as unresponsive to the demands and sentiments of colonially governed peoples. The Indochinese War was unpopular in India, primarily because it was viewed as a colonial war, but also because the Indian government feared it might result in a thermonuclear exchange between the United States and the Soviet Union. In late April, New Delhi announced that no American planes carrying French troops would be allowed to fly over Indian soil.[43] Thus the Eden-Dulles statement could appear to New Delhi only as a British move toward an American policy of reliance upon threats against China rather than upon negotiations at Geneva. Nehru undoubtedly was well aware of the American effort to denigrate the forthcoming conference, and disagreed with that view most definitely. Whether the United States merely wished to threaten China to deter her further interference in Indochina or whether actual intervention was contemplated did not really matter to the Indian policymakers. Neither policy was conducive to peace in Asia, which, at this time, was in India's immediate interests.

Eden also felt pressed because of a domestic political event of great significance. On 14 April Aneurin Bevan resigned from the Labour Party's "shadow cabinet."[44] The move was interpreted (correctly) as Bevan's bid for leadership against the Labour moderates,

[42] *NYT*, 18 April 1954. Eisenhower later wrote: "On April 19 Foster [Dulles] gave me his guess that the British insistence on calling off this meeting was possibly due to pressure from Nehru, who had very little sympathy with any efforts to assist the French." DDE, p. 349.
[43] *NYT*, 25 April 1954.
[44] *NYT*, 15 April 1954.

who were led by Clement Attlee. Bevan had long been a bitter critic
of German rearmament, the EDC, and Britain's following America's
lead in Western alliance policy formulation. On the 14th, Bevan announced he could no longer support a party leadership that in turn
supported a government that was prepared to cooperate with the
United States in establishing a Southeast Asia collective defense
organization. There was the feeling in certain British circles that
Bevan would not have attempted to make his bid at this time unless
he had support in the House of Commons and unless he expected
public opinion to support his move.[45] Indeed, while most commentators criticized Bevan, they seemed sympathetic to his demand for
a truly independent British foreign policy.

Drew Middleton had reported, in early April, that the Prime Minister and the Foreign Secretary, under attack from the left and from
some Conservatives, had to admit to the House of Commons that the
United States had not consulted Britain about the March series of
thermonuclear tests in the Pacific.[46] At the end of March the Soviet
government had expressed its readiness to consider the admission
of the Soviet Union to NATO, a suggestion that was rejected out of
hand by Secretary Dulles without consulting Britain.[47] Some British
observers believed the offer was not as preposterous as the Americans
said it was. On the 10th, the day Mr. Dulles was to go to London, the
New York Times reported that the British were eager to discuss the
problems that had arisen from America's failure to consult Britain
with respect to the H-bomb tests and the Soviet proposal to join
NATO. Labour spokesmen, for two consecutive days, had argued that
there must be mutual coordination of policy or the United States must
be asked to remove its air bases from the British Isles.[48]

The Soviet proposal and the H-bomb tests were only two recent
irritants that strained Anglo-American relations. In February, James
Reston warned that the allies were not dealing with, nor even talking to each other about the consequences of "new developments
within the Grand Alliance and the Communist nations,"[49] namely,
the Malenkov policy of détente, a diminished European fear of the
Red army, Soviet appeals to the growing sense of independence
in Europe, and the Soviet bid for trade with the West. Yet the United
States was more demanding, Reston added, rather than less demanding. He listed instances of what he called Dulles's "sudden diplomacy," diplomacy undertaken unilaterally and without extensive

[45] *NYT*, 18 April 1954.
[46] *NYT*, 4 April 1954.
[47] *NYT*, 1 April 1954. The Soviet proposal was formally rejected on 7 May.
[48] *NYT*, 10 April 1954.
[49] *NYT*, 7 February 1954.

consultation with the allies: the proposals for ending the Italian-Yugoslavian dispute over Trieste, moves to establish a defense organization in the Middle East (including Iraq and Pakistan), preliminary efforts to bring Spain into the Atlantic Alliance, and the announcement of the strategy of "massive retaliation." Whether or not one accepts Reston's examples, it would not be difficult to find similar instances of a lack of discussion on a variety of specific matters of vital concern to the alliance partners.

Thus by April 1954 there was ample evidence, even for those in Britain who were staunch supporters of the Anglo-American tie, that the United States was persisting in unilateral pronouncements of policy. At a time when London was beginning to see world political developments from a perspective very different from that of Washington, American actions could only increase the demand for an independent British policy. Bevan's revolt highlighted this sentiment in London; and Clement Attlee was not the only person concerned with this challenge from the left. Eden now had to concern himself with the opposition, for if Bevan's bid was successful, Attlee's leadership would have been repudiated and Eden could no longer count on the usually equable support of the Labour Party in foreign-policy matters. Should Bevan succeed, the Labour Party would be transformed into a radical political party acting on a political platform that was anathema to the incumbent Foreign Secretary. If Makins had attended a Southeast Asia organization conference in Washington a week after the Eden-Dulles communiqué (which was, in part, responsible for Bevan's resignation from the shadow cabinet)—a conference that excluded Asian Commonwealth participation—Bevan could have used this as evidence of Britain's toadying to her American ally, without concern for the Commonwealth and the possibilities for peace the Geneva Conference offered.

Nor should one forget the prospect for Mr. Eden's political career. He was expected to succeed Churchill as Prime Minister when Sir Winston retired (as was expected) in 1954. It was not easy for critics to say that Prime Minister Churchill had slavishly followed the American policy line, but this would not hold true for Eden, if only because the Foreign Secretary did not have Churchill's prestige. Eden, therefore, would be very sensitive to the charge of subordinating Britain's interests to those of the United States.

Finally, there seems to have been something in Dulles's manner and official behavior that profoundly antagonized Eden, which was most unfortunate for both the United States and Great Britain, not only in 1954 but in 1956 as well, prior to and during the Suez debacle. Most scholars who have delved into the Dulles-Eden relationship have tended to sympathize with Eden, partly because they have accepted the canon of facts set forth by the former Foreign Secretary in his *Full Circle*, a typically self-serving memoir. From all accounts, moreover, Dulles was much less congenial than Eden; that is, until one "came to know" the Secretary of State. In overly simplistic terms, scholars have tended to criticize Dulles's policy as overly legalistic, naïve, deluded, or boorish—as Presbyterianism applied to world affairs.[50] It seems to me that praise of Secretary Dulles has too often been dismissed as partisan political attachment or qualified posthumous tribute to a man who was remarkably courageous in the face of mortal illness. Perhaps, to put it quite simply, Dulles was a great Secretary of State, but historians will need a longer perspective before a full or balanced evaluation can be made.

But Eden decided that Makins was not to attend the preparatory conference on the 20th despite his agreeing to the communiqué: "[We] are ready to take part . . . in an examination of the possibility of establishing a collective defense." Perhaps he felt this public language was subject to two conditions that were not publicized: (1) India and other Asian Commonwealth nations must not be excluded, or must at least be consulted, and (2) the "examination" must wait until the intentions and attitudes of the Communist states had been appraised at the Geneva Conference. Dulles did not regard the communiqué as conditioned in this way. His eagerness to begin discussion only one week after leaving London surprised, and seems to have affronted, the Foreign Secretary. However, the general language of the Eden-Dulles statement had brought condemnation from the left and, at the very least, unofficial criticism from the Indian press.[51]

It is my hypothesis that Eden had second thoughts; he wanted to retreat to the standard British policy position of March and April: no action and no commitment to act until the Geneva Conference had tested Soviet and Chinese intentions. This position, which had the support of the Labour Party, would save Attlee any embarrassment by Bevan and his supporters, who opposed "warning" the Communists, and any other steps which they believed would doom the Geneva Conference to failure before it began. Moreover, as a prospective prime minister, Eden wanted to prove that he was responsive to Commonwealth opinion and that British policy was an independent variable in America's foreign-policy equations.

[50] Herman Finer, *Dulles Over Suez* (Chicago: Quadrangle Books, 1964); Joseph Buttinger, *Vietnam: A Dragon Embattled* (New York: Praeger, 1967); Victor Bator, *Vietnam: A Diplomatic Tragedy* (Dobbs Ferry, N.Y.: Oceana, 1965); Sherman Adams, *First-Hand Report* (New York: Harper & Row, 1961).

[51] It very likely brought official Indian remonstrations as well; see n. 42 above.

[IV]

Ratification of the European Defense Community treaty was subordinated to united action in the crisis month of April. This is not to say the EDC was no longer a matter of concern; it was, in fact, a matter of constant concern. The United States had pressed the Laniel government to set a date for the ratification debate in the National Assembly,[52] but throughout March and most of April the French cabinet appeared to be pursuing dilatory tactics. The French government's position was precarious: ratification of the treaty would offend the Soviet Union, its defeat would offend the United States. The cooperation of both states with France was essential for an "honorable settlement" of the Indochinese War at Geneva, if such a settlement was at all attainable. Thus there was no hurry in Paris to schedule debate on the EDC.

On the 13th of April, when Britain's proposals for her formal association with the EDC were approved by plenipotentiaries of Belgium, The Netherlands, Luxembourg, Italy, West Germany, and France,[53] the British government agreed to place armed forces in Europe under a European army commander and committed itself to station air and ground forces on the continent for as long as "the threat exists to the security of Western Europe and of the European Defense Community." But the French signature to the association agreement brought on a cabinet crisis.[54] Gaullists and several Radical Socialists protested, and Laniel explained that the signature did not bind the National Assembly to similar action and was not an approval of the association agreement nor the EDC, an explanation that deeply disturbed supporters of the treaty. The dual crisis was settled, however, when the Premier promised to hold a cabinet meeting on Thursday, 15 April, to discuss the scheduling of Assembly debate on the treaty. At the Thursday meeting the cabinet set the 18th of May merely to discuss the *date* for debate.[55]

In mid-April, after consultation with congressional leaders of both parties, President Eisenhower prepared and sent a message to the

[52] Senators Knowland and Wiley suggested that Congress delay appropriations for NATO states that refused to take action on the EDC treaty (*NYT*, 9 April 1954). The U.S. High Commissioner for Germany, James B. Conant, warned that if the French failed to ratify EDC, West Germany would be given full sovereign powers. The British refused to associate themselves with Conant's views. *NYT*, 3 April 1954.

[53] *Memorandum regarding United Kingdom Association with the European Defense Community*, Misc. No. 10 (1954), Command Doc. 9126 (London: Her Majesty's Stationery Office, 1954). See p. 15.

[54] *NYT*, 14 April 1954.

[55] Thus the cabinet would not necessarily set a date for debate but merely discuss alternative dates, with no promise of a decision on the question. *NYT*, 16 April 1954.

governments of the six signatories of the EDC treaty.[56] The President urged these governments to expedite the creation of the EDC, making it an integral part of the Western community and an adequate instrument for Western defense. Mr. Eisenhower pledged that after the treaty had been ratified by the six countries, the United States would continue to maintain a "fair share" of a joint defense and would work for the integration of American forces under SACEUR. This pledge, together with Britain's association with the EDC signatories, it was assumed, would still French fears of a possible Anglo-American withdrawal from the continent and would help the Laniel government obtain EDC ratification. But there was to be no early ratification. In fact, debate on the treaty was never scheduled by the Laniel government. Thus, the Western allies would go to Geneva without agreement upon united action in either Southeast Asia or in Europe.

[56] *Docs., 1954*, pp. 85-87.

Chapter 6

AVOIDING INTERVENTION

[I]

By mid-April neither the American public, the press, nor even the best-informed Washington observers knew what the administration would do about Indochina. Mr. Dulles had gone to London and Paris and had returned, so it appeared, with the agreement of the allies to begin consultations leading to the establishment of a NATO-like defense organization for Southeast Asia. At Dien Bien Phu there had been a lull in the fighting for more than two weeks, and rumors of active intervention continued to circulate around Washington, but much diminished in intensity. There appeared to be no rationale for intervention, nor even for promoting a crisis atmosphere in which intervention would seem possible or probable, when the military news from Indochina was undramatic and was relegated to the back pages and when it seemed that the administration's diplomatic moves might soon produce a united front to deter the communization of Indochina. There was, of course, a great deal of uneasiness among the attentive public because of uncertainty about the administration's response in the increasingly probable event that the French suffered one or a series of military defeats. It was in this atmosphere, on 16 April, that an "unidentified source," high in the administration, made a statement that once more convinced many observers that American intervention in Indochina was indeed probable.[1]

The official declared that the situation in Indochina was serious, and he implied that the French might stop fighting and withdraw; in this event, Indochina would become Communist within a month. The United States would have to send troops if the situation required it, and perhaps without substantial contributions from her allies. "It is hoped that the United States will not have to send troops there, but if this government cannot avoid it, the Administration must face up to the situation and dispatch forces."[2] The United States was the only state in the Western alliance strong enough to pursue policies that would save Asia from communization; moreover, the official stated, the French had lost their will to win. The loss of Dien Bien Phu would be a catastrophe for them, and they would then seek a settlement at almost any cost. And the British government wanted neither to antagonize China nor the Labour Party. Troops, therefore, would have to come from the United States, inasmuch as Vietnamese

[1] *NYT*, 17 April 1954.　　　[2] *Ibid.* and 18 April 1954.

troops were not yet able to offer effective resistance. America must realize, the official said, that internal subversion rather than overt aggression was the real danger in Southeast Asia, and the United States must associate itself with the aspirations of the Asian peoples, which included independence from foreign domination, recognition of equality, and peace.

The administration official also took a pessimistic view of the prospects for success at Geneva. No progress would be made, he said, toward a free, independent, and unified Korea; the Korean Conference would end in an impasse. However, Communist intransigence on Korea might convince France and Britain of the futility of negotiations. In any event, negotiations with the Communists on the Indochinese War could result in a division of the country that, in turn, could result in Communist domination of a vital new area. If Indochina were communized, Communist pressures upon Thailand, Malaya, Indonesia, Burma, and even Japan would increase.

France-Soir identified Richard Nixon as the source of these statements. The *Times of London* had worded its report in terms that unmistakably pointed to the Vice President. American newspapers, on the 17th identified Nixon as the source (the occasion for his remarks was a convention of the American Society of Newspapers Editors)[3] and Nixon later confirmed that he had made the statements and had asked not to be identified. His remarks, he said, were only his personal views and had not been cleared with the administration. Whether or not these *were* the Vice President's personal views, the immediate question was the extent to which they reflected official thinking. Also on the 17th, the State Department declared that the dispatch of American troops to Indochina was highly unlikely and French withdrawal an improbable hypothesis.[4] The State Department also said that Nixon's remarks enunciated no new United States policy and were, in fact, in full agreement with previous statements of the President and the Secretary of State. But this did not clarify matters, for the Vice President had uttered too many new ideas and had placed new emphasis upon some old ideas.

Senator Knowland agreed with the Vice President, but did not believe that the United States would have to send troops. Senator Wiley agreed with Knowland. Knowland, in any case, was opposed to "another Korea," where the United States bore 90 percent of the burden of fighting, and before a new commitment was made the President should "come to Congress and lay the facts before it with his recommendations." "[The] reaction of the Congress," he added, "would to a considerable extent be influenced by what nations would con-

[3] *NYT*, 18 April 1954.   [4] *Ibid.*

tribute to collective action." Senators Saltonstall, Bourke Hickenlooper (Rep., Iowa), and Estes Kefauver (Dem., Tenn.) said they were opposed to the use of American troops; Senator Ralph Flanders (Rep., Vt.), and Senators Kennedy and Humphrey again underlined the necessity of completing the independence of the Associated States.[5]

The day before Vice President Nixon's remarks, Secretary of Defense Wilson—and Admiral Radford—had told the Senate Foreign Relations Committee there was no present need for American intervention in Indochina. On the 20th, Wilson assured Senator Saltonstall there had been "no change in the policies of the Department of Defense" on the dispatch of troops to Indochina.[6] Senator Wayne Morse (Rep., Ore.) declared, however, that this assurance was not enough; the administration, he said, ought to give the facts to the people. Thus uncertainty among the senators persisted: none was certain whether Mr. Nixon's remarks reflected a change in administration policy; but this was due, in part, to the fact that most of the senators had not been entirely certain of the administration's policy even before the Vice President made his statements on the 16th.

Nor was it clear why Nixon made the remarks at that time. Arthur Krock of the *New York Times* said Nixon had launched a "trial balloon" with the "official stamp" of the administration. James Reston, on the same day in the same newspaper, denied that the statement was a "trial balloon."[7] Reston's is the better view. On the 19th, after emerging from a meeting with the President, who was vacationing in Augusta, Georgia, Secretary Dulles said he thought it unlikely that American combat troops would be sent to Indochina and the possibility of French withdrawal too hypothetical even to discuss. Dulles remarked that these were his own opinions; he was not speaking for the President, nor had he spoken with the President about the use of troops. He also said that Nixon's remarks had been made off the record and were Nixon's personal views.[8]

Vice President Nixon, in a speech in Cincinnati on 20 April, said the Indochinese War was not just a civil war but a war of aggression.[9] The Chinese People's Republic controlled, supported, and directed the war, he said. Nevertheless, the United States would seek an "honorable and peaceful settlement" at Geneva but would oppose outright surrender to the Communists. The administration, he assured

[5] *Ibid.*   [6] *NYT*, 20 April 1954.
[7] *Ibid.* Roscoe Drummond concurred with Reston (*NYHT*, 22 April 1954).
[8] *NYHT*, 20 April 1954. Mr. Nixon has continued to insist that his remarks on 16 April expressed his own views, were not those of Mr. Dulles, and were not a "trial balloon"; see Nixon's OHP statement.
[9] *NYT*, 21 April 1954.

his audience, was striving to avoid sending troops to Indochina, but
the loss of that area to the Communists would jeopardize all Southeast
Asia and Japan. It might also lead the Kremlin to believe that it was
an advantageous time for a world war. The administration aimed
to hold Indochina if it could.

Nixon's statements of 16 April agreed with Dulles's Overseas Press
Club address in emphasizing the importance of Indochina and the
possible need to take small risks now rather than greater risks later.
The public was put on notice that the warnings administration officials had been issuing might yet require fulfillment. A significant
change of his personal attitude—of perhaps even the official attitude
—toward the Geneva Conference was expressed in Nixon's remark
at Cincinnati on the 20th that the United States would seek an "honorable and peaceful settlement" at Geneva. This contrasted with
his remarks of the 16th, and the chastening effect of Eden's refusal
to allow Roger Makins to attend the conference on the prospective
collective defense organization may have produced this change.

[I I]

Vietminh attacks on Dien Bien Phu were renewed during the
week of 11 April, and by 23 April the enemy had advanced to within
a quarter-mile of the central stronghold and had captured a portion
of the airfield, rendering supply by air almost impossible. A letter
from General Navarre in Saigon, dated 21 April and warning that
French forces in the beleaguered village could not hold out much
longer without immediate and massive aerial interdiction of Vietminh supply routes, produced great anxiety within the French cabinet.[10] It also gave rise to new efforts to obtain American consent to
bombarding the enemy's positions and supply lines in the areas around
Dien Bien Phu. Contact between French and American military
advisors had been maintained—particularly communication between
General Ely and Admiral Radford—since early April, when Dulles
had, in effect refused the first French request for aerial bombardment. Admiral Radford continued to feel that the United States must
use its air power to assist the French military effort in Indochina.

Dulles arrived in Paris on Wednesday, 21 April, and attended a
NATO council meeting on Friday.[11] After the NATO meeting, Bi-

[10] Ely, pp. 106-109; L&D, pp. 85-87.
[11] Before he left, Mr. Dulles issued a statement. Referring to his recent trip
(10 to 15 April) to Britain and France, he said: "I found in both capitals [London
and Paris] recognition that the armed Communist threat endangered vital free
world interest and made it appropriate that the free nations most immediately
concerned should explore the possibility of establishing a collective defense." He
praised the gallantry of the Dien Bien Phu defenders, and continued: "The violent

dault, Eden, and Dulles met to discuss their prospective positions and tactics at the Geneva Conference, which would begin on Monday, the 26th. An agitated Bidault informed Dulles, on the 23d, that Navarre had warned the cabinet that Dien Bien Phu could not hold out much longer and that its capture could permit the Vietminh to redeploy its forces toward the vital Red River delta, possibly before the monsoon season.[12] Bidault asked Dulles to reconsider his early April decision, which had had the effect of denying American aerial support to the French. Bidault no longer opposed internationalization of the war, and, urging immediate action, he discounted the value of a British contribution.[13]

Dulles, who informed the President of Bidault's request, recounted that the Foreign Minister had shown him a copy of a cable from Navarre to Laniel warning the Premier of the imminent fall of Dien Bien Phu.

> He [Bidault] will talk to me further on subject at dinner tonight but, in brief, situation at Dien Bien Phu is desperate. Attempt to regain Huguette has claimed last reserves. Only alternatives Navarre sees are (1) operation Voutour [*sic*] which would be massive B-29 bombing (which I understand would be U.S. operation from U.S. bases outside Indochina) or (2) request for cease fire (which I assume would be at Dien Bien Phu and not throughout all Indochina).
>
> I told Bidault B-29 intervention as proposed seemed to me out of question under existing circumstances but that I would report all this urgently to the President and that I would discuss it with Admiral Radford immediately upon latter's arrival in Paris tomorrow evening.[14]

---

battles now being waged in Vietnam and the armed aggressions against Laos and Cambodia are not creating any spirit of defeatism. On the contrary, they are rousing the free nations to measures which we hope will be sufficiently timely and vigorous to preserve these vital areas from Communist domination. . . .

"I leave for Geneva confident that the Western Allies are closer than ever before to a unity of purpose with respect to world problems, not only of the West, but of the East." *DSB*, 3 May 1954, pp. 668-669.

On the 21st and the 22d the NATO ministers and officials met privately. On Friday, 23 April, the report of the NATO "standing group" was the point of departure for discussions and exchanges of views on Soviet intentions. The report delineated recent important increases in Communist-bloc war capabilities, including the rearmament of East Germany and the Soviet delivery of jet aircraft to several East European Communist states. *NYT*, 22 April 1954.

[12] *U.S. News & World Report*, 6 August 1954, p. 21; L&D, p. 88.

[13] DDE, p. 349. According to Marquis Childs, Francis La Coste, a senior official in the French Foreign Office, appealed to Assistant Secretary of State Livingston Merchant for an air strike to save Dien Bien Phu. *The Ragged Edge: The Diary of a Crisis* (New York: Doubleday, 1955), p. 125.

[14] DDE, p. 350; *NYT*, 25 April 1954.

Dulles had given Bidault the same explanation he had given Bonnet on 5 April: The use of strategic aircraft to bombard the Vietminh at Dien Bien Phu was a belligerent act that required the authorization of Congress[15] and Congress was not likely to give such authorization unless the United States was assured that any intervention would be on a united-front basis, that is, in common with its allies. Apart from Dien Bien Phu, if a collective defense organization could be established in short order, Indochina could be held; and, with a united front, the request for air support at Dien Bien Phu might be regarded differently in Washington. In the opinion of the military advisors with whom Dulles had been in contact, it was too late to save the Dien Bien Phu garrison, but its fate, in any case, would not alter the strategic situation in Indochina. Dulles was aware of the significance of the fall of Dien Bien Phu, as was shown in this message to President Eisenhower:

> The situation here [Paris] is tragic. . . . There is, of course, no military or logical reason why loss of Dien Bien Phu should lead to collapse of French will, in relation both to Indochina and EDC. It seems to me that Dien Bien Phu has become a symbol out of all proportion to its military importance.[16]

But, of course, it *had* become a symbol, both for the French and for the Vietminh. President Eisenhower telephoned Bedell Smith, and both men agreed with Dulles: "There would be no intervention without allies."[17]

Late that same afternoon (Friday, 22 April), Dulles also told Eden about Navarre's letter and the French request, but Eden was opposed to aerial intervention because it could not be decisive and because a belligerent act of this kind could have "far-reaching consequences." Dulles, according to Eden's description of the conversation, again brought up the subject of Britain's and the United States' acting in concert to support the French. Eden rejected this proposal since he did not believe "that conditions in Indo-China could be remedied by outside intervention alone at this hour."[18] He added that Britain was ready to discuss a joint guarantee for Thailand in the event the French withdrew entirely from Indochina.

Admiral Radford arrived in Paris on Saturday morning and he and Dulles conferred with the British Foreign Secretary. The three

---

[15] L&D, p. 88; DDE, p. 351. See also the accounts in *U.S. News & World Report*, 18 June 1954, p. 37, and Chalmers Roberts, "The Day We Didn't Go to War," *Reporter*, 14 September 1954, pp. 31-35.

[16] DDE, p. 350.

[17] DDE, p. 351.

[18] E, p. 113.

men discussed the possible ways in which the French military effort might be sustained both at Dien Bien Phu and in the rest of Indo-china, but no firm conclusions were reached.[19] In the afternoon Dulles and Eden met again with Bidault. At this meeting, Eden reported, Secretary Dulles

> produced the draft of a letter, which the United Kingdom delegation was allowed to glance at briefly, and handed it to M. Bidault with the offer to send it to him formally if it would be helpful. So far as we could make out, the sense of the letter seemed to be that although it was unfortunately now too late for American support to be provided at Dien Bien Phu, the United States was nevertheless prepared, if France and the other allies so desired, to move armed forces into Indo-China and thus internationalize the struggle and protect South-East Asia as a whole. M. Bidault hesitated for several minutes. He then announced that he was prepared for Mr. Dulles to send him the letter officially.[20]

After the meeting ended, Dulles left Paris for Geneva; Eden, who decided he must return for consultations with the Prime Minister and the cabinet, flew to London Saturday night.

Eden records in his memoirs:

> Mr. Denis Allen sent me a message after my departure from Paris to say that Bidault was, on reflection, far from enthusiastic about the American proposals. If Dulles pressed the matter, it was prob-

---

[19] According to Eden, Dulles "wished to make it plain that there was no possibility of United States participation in the Dien Bien Phu battle, because the President had not the power to act with such speed, and because it was perfectly clear that no intervention could now save the fortress, where the situation was desperate" (E, p. 114). Admiral Radford was very concerned, however; he said that "there must be some military effort to assist the French without delay. . . . Admiral Radford went on to say that he thought it most likely that when Dien Bien Phu fell, the whole military situation in Indo-China would get out of control within a few days. . . . The only way he saw of preventing this was to demonstrate that France now had powerful allies in the fight." E, pp. 114-115.

Eden persistently misidentified the positions of Dulles and Radford; the views of the two men on the Indochina crisis were *not* the same, although Dulles did not openly or explicitly disassociate himself from the admiral's views. In Chalmers Roberts's account (*op. cit.*), Radford was alleged to have done most of the talking at this Saturday morning meeting, which comports fairly well with Eden's version (and Eisenhower's [DDE, p. 351]). But, Roberts wrote, "Dulles said that if the allies agreed, the President was prepared to go to Congress on the following Monday, April 26 . . . and ask for a joint resolution authorizing such action [i.e. an air strike]. Assuming quick passage by Congress, the strike could take place on April 28." I do not believe this is quite accurate. It agrees with neither Eden's nor Eisenhower's version, nor with the reports in *U.S. News & World Report* (13 June 1954, pp. 35-39, and 6 August 1954, pp. 21-23). See also Marquis Childs, *op. cit.*, pp. 130-131.

[20] E, p. 116.

able that Bidault would advise Laniel not to accept American intervention.[21]

Bidault, in fact, conferred with the French cabinet after the Saturday afternoon meeting with Dulles and Eden. Then the French decided to contact the American Secretary of State again,[22] and Bidault prepared a letter, on the afternoon of 24 April, that stated that French military experts believed Dien Bien Phu could be saved by the immediate bombardment of Vietminh positions by American aircraft. Moreover, the deployment of Vietminh troops in the area offered a unique opportunity for the destruction of the enemy by a properly placed air strike. This letter was dispatched to Dulles and reached him the *next day* in *Geneva*. Bonnet, the French ambassador to the United States, was informed of the contents of the Bidault letter and saw Under Secretary of State Bedell Smith immediately, on Saturday afternoon, the 24th. Bedell Smith, apprised of the contents of the letter, told Bonnet he must see the President before giving Bonnet an answer to this most recent demarche.[23] But the letter Bidault addressed to Dulles late on the 24th of April did not relate to the subject of the letter Dulles showed Eden and Bidault at their meeting earlier in the day, that is, the alleged offer of American troops.

Lacouture and Devillers, citing J. R. Tournoux's *Secrets d'Etat*[24] as their authority, state that the only letter that could be found in the official French dossiers for this period was the letter Bidault sent to Dulles, a copy of which was dispatched to Bonnet in Washington. These authors also relate that a government official contacted Eden on the evening of the 24th (after the afternoon meeting of the three ministers). This official, according to this account, requested that the British government at least symbolically associate itself in the concerted action France and the United States were preparing.[25] Presented with this request, Eden decided to return to London for talks with the cabinet. Eden stated that Maurice Schumann, French Secretary of State for Foreign Affairs, telephoned him late in the day to say that he hoped Eden would urge his colleagues in London to "agree to proceedings on the lines desired by Dulles."[26] There is no mention by Eden of Britain's symbolic association in the concerted action that allegedly was being prepared by France and the United States. Then, according to Eden's account, he received a message from Denis Allen that Bidault, on reflection, would probably advise Laniel not to accept American intervention. On Sunday afternoon, 25 April, according to Eden, René Massigli, the French ambassador in Lon-

---

[21] *Ibid.*   [22] L&D, p. 89.   [23] *Ibid.*
[24] (Paris: Plon, 1960), p. 54. Extracts of a letter from Dulles to Bidault appear on pp. 462-463; a letter from Bidault to Dulles on p. 463.
[25] L&D, p. 90.   [26] E, p. 116.

don, told Eden that Dulles's letter had been delivered to the French government, that is, the letter offering American ground troops![27]

Is IT POSSIBLE to determine what really happened in Paris that Saturday, the 24th of April? First, there is no reason to doubt Eden's story of the letter Dulles had apparently drafted and had shown to Eden at the meeting of the ministers that afternoon. Dulles asked Bidault if he wanted this letter sent to him formally and Bidault said he did. Second, it is doubtful that Eden would be mistaken about Massigli's informing him that a letter had been sent. This was on the afternoon of Sunday, 25 April. Did Dulles actually send, through official channels, the letter referred to in Eden's memoirs?

Lacouture and Devillers, who evidently had access to the French archives, report that they could find no such letter. Perhaps the letter was never sent; but why would Massigli have told Eden the letter *had* been sent? On the basis of the evidence now available, I am inclined to believe that *no* letter was sent, and that Dulles and Bidault agreed upon a scheme (a scenario!) to force the British to make a definitive decision on the 24th or 25th of April, before Dien Bien Phu was captured and before the Geneva Conference opened. Dulles would draft a letter offering combat troops; Bidault would agree that this letter should be sent to him; Massigli was instructed to tell Eden that *a* letter (not necessarily *the* letter) had been received. This, of course, is only a theory, but it is strengthened by a very important consideration namely, the substantive content of the letter: Dulles's statement that the United States was prepared to move armed forces into Indochina if France and the other allies desired. This offer was so different from anything Dulles had said up to that time that I think it improbable the Secretary of State would have sent such a letter. On 23 April, in his message to President Eisenhower, and on the 24th, when he informed Bidault of the difficulties entailed in acceding to the French request for an air strike at Dien Bien Phu, Dulles opposed the strike for the same reasons he had given Bonnet on the 5th of April. It was a belligerent act that would require congressional authorization, which would take time, and the consent of Congress depended upon the willingness of America's allies to join in united action, which Britain was reluctant to do because of the impending Geneva Conference.

Bidault, and many other French ministers, were in an extreme state of anxiety on 23 and 24 April. The French were now asking their American ally for help, and an outright refusal might create serious problems for the United States in its relations with France. But Dulles

[27] E, p. 119.

had conditioned his consent to action upon a political agreement with the British who did not seem to appreciate how serious the situation was.[28] Eden was in Paris on the 24th and was preparing to leave for Geneva that day or the next. Up to that time Eden had told the French that the British preferred to negotiate rather than commit themselves to united action. However, no definitive cabinet decision appears to have been taken in London at any time before the 25th of April; that is, no cabinet decision that would convince the French government, now desperately (and belatedly) seeking ways to save Dien Bien Phu, that Britain would *not* take action. Thus Bidault and Dulles could agree that Eden must return to London and must secure a decision from the cabinet before he went on to Geneva. The United States could not (or would not) make any commitment unless the British agreed to concerted action in some form or other (perhaps only symbolically). The question of action at this late hour could be settled only by a British decision.

Bidault may have held to the hope that the British would yet come around to an agreement of the kind Dulles ostensibly wanted, but Eden, of course, would have to be impressed with the gravity of the situation in Indochina. Secretary Dulles, however, very likely had little doubt about the British cabinet's decision when confronted with this problem that required an immediate decision; it would refuse to commit itself. Thus, Dulles reasoned, the onus of refusing the French requests could be shifted to Britain and the United States would escape the consequences of having refused to meet the French requests. Dulles hit upon the idea of the letter. He and Bidault agreed that if the former offered to send the letter formally and Bidault accepted this offer, Eden would be compelled to return to London and secure a cabinet decision, especially as the letter contained the offer to send armed forces to Indochina. Bidault probably hoped the British would also agree to at least a symbolic commitment. Even at this late hour he was, no doubt, unhappy about the prospect of American troops fighting in Indochina. But the terms of a united action could be decided among Eden, Dulles, and himself after the British cabinet gave its consent.

Dulles, on the other hand, believed that the letter would emphasize the seriousness with which he viewed the Indochina situation and the prospective certainty of French weakness at the negotiating table. If the British consented to join in united action, Dulles thought this would substantially improve the French position at Geneva, not because he intended to recommend to the President that troops be sent to Indochina but because he believed a united front would

[28] That is, it was Dulles's and Radford's opinion that the British did not appreciate the seriousness of the situation. DDE, p. 351.

do two things: (1) deter the Communists from further military action in Indochina and (2) provide the West an improved bargaining position by demonstrating its unity of will on Indochina. If the British refused, which was probable, they would bear much of the onus of the refusal—not the United States or the Secretary of State.

At the meeting between Bidault, Dulles, and Eden on Saturday afternoon (24 April), Bidault described the situation in Indochina. After a brief discussion, Dulles showed a draft of his letter to Eden, then to Bidault, and the latter agreed that it should be sent to him formally. The meeting ended and Eden "at once" sent this telegram to the British Foreign Office:

> It is now quite clear that we shall have to take a decision of first-class importance, namely whether to tell the Americans that we are prepared to go along with their plan or not. It seems essential that I should discuss this with my colleagues and I am, therefore, returning to London tonight.[29]

Thus Dulles and Bidault would get their definitive British decision.

Eden left for London that night; Dulles, however, left for Geneva, and for the next two days seems to have been strangely inaccessible. While "great decisions" were being made in London and Paris, while the French attempted to influence British decision-making, Dulles prepared for the Geneva Conference. Odd behavior indeed for a Secretary of State who had just offered to commit American armed forces to Indochina.

EDEN ARRIVED in London late in the evening of 24 April and met with Prime Minister Churchill at midnight. According to Eden, he and Churchill agreed that it was too late to save Dien Bien Phu and that the action the Americans contemplated would be ineffective, and might well lead to a major war.[30] The British cabinet met at 11 a.m. Sunday, 25 April—its first Sunday meeting in many years. After its discussion the cabinet unanimously approved a directive Churchill and Eden had composed during their conversation in the early hours of Sunday morning. This directive read, in part:

> 2. We are not prepared to give any undertaking now, in advance of the Geneva Conference, concerning United Kingdom military action in Indo-China. . . .
>
> 4. We can give an assurance now that if a settlement is reached at Geneva, we shall join in guaranteeing that settlement and in setting up a collective defence in South-East Asia . . . to make that joint guarantee effective. . . .

[29] E, p. 116.   [30] E, p. 117.

6. If no such settlement is reached, we shall be prepared at that time to consider with our Allies the action to be taken jointly in the situation then existing.

7. But we cannot give any assurance now about possible action on the part of the United Kingdom in the event of failure to reach agreement at Geneva for the cessation of hostilities in Indo-China.[31]

[III]

Let us shift our attention back to Paris and to the evening of 24 April.

The French cabinet met once again and instructed Bidault to make a new approach to the Americans on the proposal of an air strike at Dien Bien Phu. This was done by way of a letter to Mr. Dulles, as described earlier. Dulles received the letter in Geneva on the 25th, but his reactions are not recorded. A copy of the letter was sent to Henri Bonnet in Washington, who showed the letter to Bedell Smith, who consulted President Eisenhower late Saturday night.[32] Bedell Smith, after speaking with the President, informed Bonnet that a decision could soon be made if a declaration of intent to establish a collective security organization for Southeast Asia were published with the signatures of the interested states. Everything depended upon the British, Bedell Smith asserted: there was no question of the willingness of the other states; it was Britain's consent that was important. Bedell Smith also told Bonnet that, given British consent, an agreement among the ambassadors could be concluded by Monday, 26 April. The Under Secretary of State let it be known that a resolution authorizing the President to employ air and naval forces in Indochina had already been drafted and could be approved by Congress by Wednesday, the 28th.[33]

---

[31] E, p. 118. The British chiefs of staff and service ministers were present at the cabinet meeting. *NYT*, 26 April 1954.

[32] L&D, p. 89. The time of the receipt of the copies of the communication may be important. Dulles did not receive the letter until the 25th, presumably early in the morning; the message was cabled to Bonnet in Washington, which is some six or seven hours behind Paris or Geneva time. Thus Bedell Smith probably was apprised of the contents of the Bidault letter before Dulles had read it. The President and Bedell Smith consulted, and the latter again spoke with Bonnet late in the evening of the 24th. Apparently they held these meetings without seeking Dulles's advice.

[33] Tournoux, *Secrets d'Etat, op. cit.,* p. 55. The version in *U.S. News & World Report* (18 June 1954, pp.37-38) is somewhat different: "WASHINGTON, *April 25*—French Ambassador Henri Bonnet called on Under Secretary Walter Bedell Smith. Bedell Smith reviewed U.S. aid to France and said that the U.S. could not intervene in Indo-China save under 'united action' agreements and unless Congress gave approval. . . . A garbled version of this talk, published later in the French press, suggested that Bonnet had learned that President Eisenhower was prepared

Bonnet communicated this information to Paris and Paris, in turn, apprised the French ambassador in London, Massigli, of this most recent American proposal. Massigli went to the British Foreign Office on Sunday morning, met Mr. Eden after the Foreign Secretary returned from the cabinet meeting (described above), and told him of the conversation between Bonnet and Bedell Smith.[34] Eden was dismayed that the Americans had not contacted the British ambassador in Washington but had allowed the proposal to reach Eden through the French. At 4 p.m. on Sunday the British cabinet met again and rejected the proposal. Massigli was then informed of the British decisions. Eden flew to Geneva late that afternoon, stopping briefly at Orly Airport in Paris, where he met Bidault and informed him of the decisions of the cabinet.[35]

Laniel did not give up; on Monday, the day the Geneva Conference formally convened, the French Premier instructed Massigli to see the British Prime Minister and again ask for his consent to an air strike at Dien Bien Phu. On Tuesday, the 27th, Massigli saw Churchill, who told the French ambassador that the British government had made its decision: It would not agree to any such action, the effect of which would be to destroy any chance of success at Geneva.[36] After this meeting with Massigli, Churchill went to the House of Commons, where he declared "Her Majesty's Government are not prepared to give any undertaking about the United Kingdom military action in Indo-China in advance of the results of Geneva."[37] The Prime Minister was cheered by both benches. He further assured the House of Commons that Britain had not entered into "any new political or military commitments" with Mr. Dulles or M. Bidault. The Vietminh campaign was certainly not without significance, Churchill said, but it should not "prejudice the sense of world proportion which should inspire the conference and be a guide to those who are watching its progress."

Informed of the British decisions on the 25th, Bedell Smith independently—without discussing the matter with Secretary Dulles—conceived the idea of bypassing British participation or even its symbolic association in a coalition. His idea was simple: there would be

---

to go before Congress to ask for a joint resolution to permit American intervention in Indo-China. The President had no such plans." See also *U.S. News & World Report*, 6 August 1954, pp. 21-22.

[34] E, p. 119. Massigli also told Eden that the Dulles letter had been sent. (Was it that mysterious letter offering American troops for Indochina?)

[35] E, pp. 119, 120. Admiral Radford arrived in London on the 25th and delivered a message from the U.S. government (*T/L*, 27 April 1954). I have not been able to determine the content of the admiral's message.

[36] L&D, pp. 91-92; Tournoux, *op. cit.*, pp. 56-57.

[37] *H. C. Debates*, 5th Series, Vol. 526, coll. 1455-1456; *NYT*, 28 April 1954.

joint action by the ANZUS pact powers—Australia, New Zealand, and the United States. He sounded out Australian and New Zealand officials or diplomats on the evening of the 26th, suggesting concerted military intervention in Indochina by the ANZUS powers.[38] Their reaction seems to have been favorable, for on the 27th, someone (probably Bedell Smith) informed the President of what had happened: "I was informally told," the President wrote, "that both Australia and New Zealand were ready to listen to any proposals the United States government might make to them for collective action *for entering the Indochina war.*"[39]

Bedell Smith then contacted Dulles at Geneva and asked for his opinion. I have not been able to determine whether Dulles was receptive or whether he attempted to discourage his colleague. However, on 29 April, according to Eisenhower, Bedell Smith reported that "Australia and New Zealand had withdrawn from their original position favorable to united action."[40] Later, "Bedell Smith at my direction was to go to Geneva the next afternoon and invite the ANZUS deputies to meet with him that evening. Bedell was not at all sure that merely because the British had turned down our invitation to join a regional grouping we should abandon the whole effort."[41]

Mr. Eisenhower's memoirs do not clarify the distinction between two different forms of united action: (1) joint military intervention in Indochina (this, ostensibly, was Bedell Smith's conception on 26 April) and (2) cooperation in establishing a Southeast Asia regional security organization.

These were the options upon which the policymakers of Australia and New Zealand had a change of mind on or before 29 April—which Bedell Smith was directed to discuss with the ANZUS allies when he arrived in Geneva on the 30th. Rejection of the second option would almost certainly entail rejection of the first, but why had officials of Australia and New Zealand appeared willing, on Monday, to listen to proposals "which the United States might make for entering the war" but, on Thursday, indicated they were no longer willing to contemplate associating themselves in a regional defense organization? The answer seems to lie in the differences of time and place. On Monday, when Bedell Smith saw the Australian and

[38] L&D, p. 92. In view of his advocacy of this plan, Bedell Smith either favored intervention at this time to prevent a Vietminh victory (not necessarily to save Dien Bien Phu) or he understood Dulles's deterrent policies and sought to assist the Secretary of State in implementing them.

[39] DDE, p. 352 (emphasis added). Mr. Eisenhower did indicate, however, that he would have been unhappy about united action in Indochina without Britain's participation.

[40] DDE, p. 354.   [41] DDE, pp. 354-355.

New Zealand officials in Washington, their response was favorable enough for the Under Secretary of State to report to the President that their countries were at least willing to listen to proposals for military intervention. Thursday, after making a survey of diplomatic events at *Paris and Geneva* and speaking with Dulles at least once, Bedell Smith reported that the ANZUS allies did not favor associating themselves in a regional defense organization until after Geneva. By Thursday, Australian and New Zealand policymakers had probably determined that they must follow the lead of Britain, their Commonwealth partner.[42] Their response on the preceding Monday was simply an unofficial expression of interest by officials comparatively low in the policymaking hierarchy.

Since Bedell Smith obtained much of his intelligence of diplomatic events at Geneva from Dulles, it would be interesting to discover Dulles's reaction to his colleague's scheme and the effect his negative reaction would have upon discussions of that scheme at Geneva between the ANZUS partners. My own opinion is that Dulles had as many reservations about implementing the united-action concept without Britain as the President, and probably more and greater reservations, particularly about military intervention. A dispatch to the *New York Times* from Geneva dated Tuesday, 27 April,[43] mentioned that Dulles was still trying to stiffen the resolve of France and the non-Communist governments of Southeast Asia. He was reported to be trying to form a coalition with France, Thailand, the Philippines, and the Associated States—without Britain—but there was no mention of Australia or New Zealand.

Dulles, of course, was still interested in a collective security arrangement for Southeast Asia, and he pursued a policy of establishing such an organization for that area throughout the course of the Geneva Conference and afterward, until September, when the SEATO treaty was signed. But probably he did not approve of Bedell Smith's plan for this particular use of the ANZUS alliance (that is, for military intervention in Indochina) because the Associated States, Thailand, and the Philippines were not members of this "Anglo-Saxon" alliance; hence intervention could more easily be termed "imperialist" or "colonialist." What is more important, Dulles was in fact opposed to military intervention *at this time.*

On Monday, the day *before* Bedell Smith called Dulles for his opinion on his ANZUS plan, President Eisenhower had made a very significant speech to the U.S. Chamber of Commerce.[44] The Indochinese War, he said, would affect future relations between Japan,

---

[42] 1954 also was an election year in Australia.
[43] *NYT*, 28 April 1954. [44] *NYT*, 27 April 1954.

the states of Southeast Asia, and the rest of the world. Indochina was indeed important, but the United States could not be the "gladiator" of the world. Communist aggression was a problem for all free nations and each should contribute what it can. If the principle of joint responsibility was accepted, the United States *might* be willing to intervene in Indochina with naval and air power. The President said he was opposed to the use of American ground forces, however, and further explained that, under the principle of joint responsibility, mere "token forces" from America's allies would not be sufficient. The United States' "purpose" in Southeast Asia would be to arrive at some arrangement "that at least we could call a 'modus vivendi.'"

The President held a press conference on 29 April in which he elaborated on the theme of his Chamber of Commerce speech.[45] The United States, he said, was steering a middle course. We were opposed to a partition of Indochina but were willing to pursue a middle road of getting along with the Communists in Asia. A Communist conquest of Southeast Asia was of course unacceptable, but a satisfactory peace was unattainable. Because it might be possible to arrive at an agreement that would stop the bloodletting, the United States would wait to see what diplomacy could achieve at Geneva before it took any new steps to support France in Indochina.

To what extent the President's speech of the 26th and his press conference of the 29th reflected a policy change remained to be seen; the President had modified and reinterpreted his remarks on past occasions. He did not reject the possibility of intervention in Indochina *with allies*, but it seemed unlikely that anything would be done to save the garrison at Dien Bien Phu. On Thursday, the day of the President's press conference, the cabinet and the National Security Council met, and Eisenhower recorded that the question of an air strike at Dien Bien Phu again arose. By the 25th, however, despite Admiral Radford's earlier support and advocacy of the plan, the Joint Chiefs of Staff had concluded that an air strike, under the circumstances then existing, could not be efficacious:[46] the defenders

---

[45] *NYT*, 30 April 1954; DDE, p. 353.

[46] *NYT*, 26 April 1954. General Matthew Ridgway, Army Chief of Staff, opposed the Radford air-strike plan, insisting that the only effective form of intervention would be with ground troops. And the air strike, he argued, would eventually lead to the use of American troops. He estimated that ten divisions would be required, but these were not available; and the New Look policy required reduction rather than an increase in the strength of both the army and the Marine Corps. Ridgway also maintained that China's possible reaction must be considered; if American intervention brought about a Chinese intervention, the troop requirement would be much higher than the ten-division estimate. Ridgway's opposition to intervention was in line with his criticism of the New Look, which he regarded as dangerously impairing U.S. conventional war capabilities.

of the village would be killed along with the Vietminh. The JCS therefore recommended against an air strike. As Eisenhower wrote, "there was some merit in the argument that the psychological effect of an air strike would raise French and Vietnamese morale and improve, at least temporarily, the entire situation."[47] But apparently the President remained cautious: "I remarked that if the United States were, unilaterally, to permit its forces to be drawn into conflict in Indochina and in a succession of Asian wars, the end result could be to drain off our resources and to weaken our over-all defensive position."[48] He did not say it was decided *not* to carry out an air strike, but, presumably, with the JCS recommending against it and with the President's fear of being drawn "unilaterally" into the Indochinese War, the proposal was finally laid to rest. There was no air strike.

A French Union relief force of about 3,000 men was turned back by the Vietminh without difficulty. After 25 April, another attempt was made to relieve the garrison: a gallant but militarily insignificant force of 450 men was parachuted into Dien Bien Phu. On 7 May, the day the Indochina phase of the Geneva Conference began, Dien Bien Phu was captured by the Vietminh.

See *NYT*, 16 April, 13 June 1954; *Saturday Evening Post*, 28 January, 1956; Matthew B. Ridgway, *Soldier* (New York: Harper & Row, 1956), pp. 275-277; and Ridgway's OHP statement.

Eisenhower later characterized the idea of an air strike as "silly." Eisenhower OHP statement, p. 25.

[47] DDE, p. 354.   [48] *Ibid.*

Chapter 7

THE WESTERN ALLIANCE
IN THE INDOCHINA CRISIS

[I]

From the time, in late March, when the gravity of the French situation in Indochina was brought home to American policymakers until after the Geneva Conference had begun, the Secretary of State responded cautiously as the crisis problems presented themselves. Dulles, in short, was reluctant to become involved in the Indochinese War. The President was similarly reticent, and he and his Secretary of State, possibly with the tacit support of Secretary of Defense Wilson, guided the administration along a course that perhaps was less belligerent than they themselves realized, and certainly was less belligerent than the allies perceived.

Dulles, of course, was aware of the need to impress the Soviet Union and the C.P.R. with the firmness of the administration's resolve to prevent the total communization of Southeast Asia. This eventuality did not present itself in 1954; and the difficult decision of going to war never had to be made. Nevertheless, the administration had the unhappy task of supporting the French and at the same time limiting whatever gains the Communist Vietminh might make. These tasks could be accomplished, in part, by deterring the C.P.R. and the Soviet Union—by creating enough doubt about American intentions in the minds of the Communist policymakers to compel them to respond more prudently than otherwise they might. Admiral Radford, Vice President Nixon, and others (possibly Under Secretary of State Bedell Smith for one) were active supporters of intervention, in one form or another. They were convinced that it was as vitally necessary to deny gains to Communists in Indochina as it had been in June of 1950 to halt North Korean aggressions. If American air power, perhaps even ground troops, were required in Indochina, the administration and the public ought to face up to this need.

Although Secretary Dulles appeared to associate himself with the Radford position, he never pursued policies that could be termed "activistic." Dulles was troubled by a variety of factors.

1. The Indochina War was a French war. Until April, the French accepted only American credits and equipment and steadfastly refused American military advice and cadres for training the Indo-

chinese. They also refused to contemplate the active cooperation of United States armed forces. The war, again, was a French affair.[1]

2. Many persons in the United States may have denied that the Indochinese War was a colonial war, a war fought to preserve the French Empire; on the other hand, a great deal could be said for the proposition that the French military debacle was the result of a form of colonialism. Many Asian peoples, and a goodly share of Europeans, believed this; and Communist propaganda played effectively upon the theme of colonialism. The dilatory tactics of the French in granting independence to the Indochinese only confirmed the view that they were intent on maintaining their empire. But Dulles was fundamentally opposed to colonialism and believed that the Indochinese must have genuine independence. Moreover, as a policymaker fully aware of the propaganda potentialities for the Communists of a French colonial war, he believed the French were providing their adversaries with a powerful propaganda weapon by their reluctance to expedite negotiations with representatives of the SVN. Dulles, therefore, was wary about associating United States policy too closely with French policy in Indochina. He did not want the United States to be accused of supporting French colonialism.

3. Dulles was a lawyer who appreciated the role of law even in the quasi-anarchic relations between states.[2] The commission of a unilateral act of belligerency by means of an air strike without the support of a rule of law deeply troubled him. Indeed, involvement in the Indochinese War posed all sorts of difficult legal questions. Since it was a French affair, French consent would be required; but Dulles probably felt that more was needed. Overt aggression by the Chinese would of course provide a rationale for intervention,[3] but the Chinese had not overtly intervened. Collective self-defense, pursuant to a United Nations resolution or by means of a regional security arrangement (authorized by article 51 of the United Nations Charter), offered alternatives, and Dulles decided to pursue the latter alterna-

[1] In the view of the President, Dulles, and many administration officials, including the President's military advisors, the war had been—and continued to be—incompetently executed. DDE, pp. 350-353, 358, 362-364, 372-373, and Eisenhower's OHP statement. (Note: Many of the author's assertions in this chapter have been documented in the preceding three chapters and will not be redocumented here.)

[2] OHP statement of Loftus Becker.

[3] "Had the Chinese adopted a policy of regular air support for the Vietminh, we would have assuredly moved in to eliminate this blatant aggression from without. This would have necessitated striking Chinese air fields and would have created some risk of general war with China." DDE, p. 373. See also DDE, pp. 361-362, 354; James Shepley, "How Dulles Averted War," *Life*, 16 January 1956, and the account in Dulles's testimony before the House Foreign Affairs Committee on 5 April (*NYT*, 6 April 1954).

tive in his efforts to shape a Southeast Asia regional defense organization.[4]

4. The secretary, it seems, always was ready to threaten the use of military force but reluctant to use it. A close associate recollected that Dulles was very unhappy about sending American troops to Lebanon in 1958.[5] Perhaps in 1954 Dulles calculated that the American people were not ready to undertake prosecution of a war in Indochina so soon after the war in Korea had ended. Perhaps, on the other hand, the secretary was simply hesitant to employ force.

5. Finally, the New Look strategy imposed constraints upon the policymakers of the Eisenhower administration. In its formulation, which took many months of labor—from July 1953 to December 1953 —it had the support both of those in the cabinet who believed in budgetary stability over the long haul and the air-power strategists. It would have been very difficult to revise the New Look in March or April 1954. The political pressures against such a move would have been too great.[6]

As was pointed out earlier, the New Look ruled out another Korea-type action; the defense budget would be cut; and the personnel strength of the army and the Marine Corps would be reduced. Thus General Ridgway could ask how intervention in Indochina could be contemplated when adherence to the New Look strategy made such intervention almost impossible, and at best ineffective.

Admiral Radford, no doubt aware of the implications of the new strategy, probably felt that his plan for an air strike at Dien Bien Phu, because it relied only upon United States air and naval power, was fully compatible with the New Look. He seems to have felt that the strike would have accomplished its objectives—the relief of Dien Bien Phu, the deterrence of China, the increase in French morale— without the dispatch of combat troops. He may have been correct, but this is conjecture. The President, the Secretary of State, the Joint Chiefs of Staff, and several congressional leaders seemed to feel that an air strike would provoke rather than deter the Chinese and, rather than limit an American commitment, would be the prelude to increased involvement.

The President himself had many misgivings about involvement in

[4] An effort was made by Thailand, with United States support, to involve the United Nations in the Southeast Asia crisis in May and June; see Chapter 13 below.

[5] OHP statement of General Nathan Twining.

[6] Secretary of Defense Wilson announced, on 26 April, that the administration would take a second "new look" at military plans and expenditures. This reevaluation, he said, had been forced upon the United States by events in Asia and Europe (in the latter case he meant the delays in the ratification of the EDC treaty) (*NYT*, 27 April 1954). Nothing ever came of this reevaluation.

the Indochinese War. The same questions that troubled Dulles also troubled him: the colonialist character of the war,[7] an unflattering image of French political and military ineptitude, and a fundamental aversion (in spite of his military background) to the use of force.[8] His reluctance to intervene in Indochina was revealed in his frequently spontaneous press conference utterances. Eisenhower and Dulles were of one mind in their desire to permit the use of American military force only if the communization of all Indochina were threatened or if the Communist Chinese intervened overtly. The fall of Dien Bien Phu was not a precondition for intervention, even though Dulles may have had some moments of doubts in Paris on 23 and 24 April.

Let us briefly review the events of late March and April and see the extent to which they bear out the hypothesis that both Dulles and Eisenhower responded very cautiously to the crisis in Indochina, to the demands of the more militant members of the National Security Council, and to the pleas of America's French ally.

As WE HAVE seen, the Washington mission of General Paul Ely emphasized the gravity of the French military position in Indochina. The NSC had discussed the Indochinese War before Ely's visit and, so far as we can tell without access to the still secret records, had determined that Southeast Asia was of vital strategic importance to the United States and its allies. Conversely, its loss to the Communists must be prevented by the United States *in cooperation with those allies*. If the NSC discussions of early and mid-March were somewhat academic or hypothetical (apparently it was believed that the French war effort would not precipitously collapse), any NSC meeting after General Ely's visit would have had to consider the very real possibility of a French political or military collapse should Dien Bien Phu fall.

Admiral Radford, among others, appreciated the psychological significance of a victory of the Vietminh at Dien Bien Phu. He proposed to Ely, on 24 and 25 March, that the United States carry out an air strike against the Vietminh attackers of the fortress; but this operation posed two questions. (1) Would an air strike succeed, and would it destroy a substantial proportion of the Vietminh forces and their ordnance, thereby relieving the pressure on the French garrison at Dien Bien Phu? Saving Dien Bien Phu would prevent the dangerous consequences of its capture, that is, the fall of the Laniel government and either French withdrawal from Indochina or negotiating a peace

---

[7] DDE, pp. 373-374, and Eisenhower's OHP statement.

[8] Sherman Adams, *First-Hand Report* (New York: Harper & Row, 1961), pp. 462-463; E. J. Hughes, *The Ordeal of Power* (New York: Atheneum, 1963), pp. 103-154.

at any price. (2) If the air strike failed, what then? Even if the air strike succeeded, should the United States become involved in the Indochinese War by this means?

At an early date—that is, by 28 or 29 March, and certainly no later than 4 April—Dulles concluded that:

1. An air strike might not succeed;
2. It was a belligerent act, in any case;
3. This was not the best way to become involved in the war; and
4. American troops might have to be used in Indochina after the strike.[9]

By mid-April, many of the administration's military advisors had concluded that an air strike *could not* succeed, and by 25 April, at the latest, the JCS recommended against such an operation.

The policy that was to be followed was outlined by Dulles in his Overseas Press Club speech on 29 March. With American assistance, he implied, the French must continue the war until they achieved the victory envisaged by the Navarre Plan; they must grant independence to the Indochinese; and sufficient time must be gained to allow the new governments in Vietnam, Laos, and Cambodia to win the allegiance of their people. The loss of Dien Bien Phu was indirectly

---

[9] "After careful reflection and several National Security Council meetings on the subject, Dulles concluded that a carrier strike, against Dienbienphu's attackers was a poor way for the U.S. to get involved" (Shepley, *op. cit.*, p. 72). Herman Phleger, a legal advisor in the Department of State during the Eisenhower administration, stated that Secretary Dulles concluded that a carrier-based strike against Dien Bien Phu was not desirable. He had only committed himself to *explore* the idea (OHP statement). J. R. Beal, *John Foster Dulles: 1888-1959* (New York: Harper & Row, 1959), pp. 208-209; Adams, *op. cit.*, p. 122.

Georges Bidault, in *Resistance* (New York: Praeger, 1967 [p. 196]), declared that Dulles offered the French government two atomic bombs! "What he did do, however, was to ask me if we would like the U.S. to give us two atomic bombs. I think that he spoke to others about this project, for he always liked to ask different people's advice, however unseemly or embarrassing. But it was I who answered without having to do much thinking of the subject, 'If those bombs are dropped near Dien Bien Phu, our side will suffer as much as the enemy.'" Lacouture and Devillers do not mention this offer, but Tournoux does (*Secrets d' Etat* [Paris: Plon, 1960], p. 48). The Secretary of State is alleged to have asked Bidault *"Et si on vous donnait deux bombes atomiques pour sauvez Dien-Bien-Phu?"* Dulles is said to have asked this question at the Quai d' Orsay, but when? Neither Bidault nor Tournoux answer this question. Dulles was at the Quai d' Orsay on 14 April, when he was in Paris to explain the united-action concept, and again on 23 and 24 April, but it is my opinion that Dulles asked Bidault a hypothetical question only, perhaps sarcastically. The administration would not have given France two atomic bombs, nor *could* it have; federal law forbade it. Bidault might be willing to impugn Dulles's ability to discern the limitations upon the use of atomic weapons at Dien Bien Phu but I find this hard to do. Finally, if the secretary meant that the U.S., not France, would make an air strike and drop two atomic bombs upon Dien Bien Phu, he could not have been serious; by the end of the first week in April Dulles had concluded that an air strike was neither feasible nor desirable.

depreciated when the Secretary of State admitted that the loss of local engagements must be expected. Two messages were implicit in this latter statement: first, the French, who had sufficient manpower and matériel, must continue to fight even after the fall of Dien Bien Phu; second, the fall of the fortress would not be a cause for American intervention because it was not regarded as having sufficient strategic importance. All this did not reflect naïve faith in the Navarre Plan nor ignorance of political conditions in France. Dulles was aware of the unpopularity of the war in France, the all too likely consequences of the loss of Dien Bien Phu, and the limitations of the Navarre Plan, but he could not voice these misgivings without producing psychological gains for the Communists either in Indochina or Geneva.

The formal expressions of optimism, masking real pessimism, were supplemented by the announcement of a policy of united action to prevent the communization of Southeast Asia.[10] This ambiguous concept, formally announced in the "present American policy" paragraphs of the Overseas Press Club speech, was the subject of discussion (and a cause of confusion) during most of April. Dulles wanted a regional defense arrangement for Southeast Asia similar to the North Atlantic Treaty Organization, an idea that had occurred to him at least by late February 1954, after the Berlin Conference.[11] He was to press the idea until it eventuated in the Southeast Asia Treaty Organization, the treaty and protocol of which were signed on 8 September 1954. The concept of united action gave rise to much speculation and many official and unofficial interpretations, which no doubt confused the policymakers in London and Paris, despite the fact that President Eisenhower, in his communication to Churchill on 4 April, was fairly explicit in his description of the coalition he hoped to see formed. But the rumors of intervention and the manifold interpretations given the term "united action" had the not undesirable consequence of raising doubts in the minds of Soviet and Chinese policymakers.

When, on 4 April, the President, Secretary Dulles, and Admiral Radford met in the White House, the President decided that any American military action in Indochina had to be based upon the satisfaction of three conditions: cooperation of the allies; a French grant of independence to Vietnam, Laos, and Cambodia; and the promise of the French to continue the fight should American forces intervene. These conditions were explicitly formulated the day after

[10] The President had called for "united action" to meet the threat of communism in Southeast Asia in a speech of 16 April 1953; this remark was resurrected by the Secretary of State after the Berlin Conference.
[11] Beal, *op. cit.*, pp. 205-206.

Dulles, Radford, and others had met with eight congressional leaders and the congressmen had expressed deep concern over the Radford plan for an air strike—as Dulles no doubt had predicted they would react in their desire for American action only in concert with the British, the French, and other allies. Thus, when on 5 April Bonnet informally requested an air strike at Dien Bien Phu, Secretary Dulles informed him that the only action the United States could take would be united action in a coalition. For the next two weeks Dulles tried to explain the concept of united action to the allies and unsuccessfully sought to initiate discussions pertaining to the security organization proposal before the Geneva Conference began on 26 April.[12]

The conditions for America's consent to intervention were not satisfied until after the Geneva Conference had ended in July—when, for the time being, a cease-fire removed the reasons for American involvement. These conditions, in effect, allowed the administration to avoid deciding whether it must commit American armed forces in Indochina. Other important conditions, which were implicit in the Overseas Press Club speech and other Dulles pronouncements were never satisfied: the Chinese did not overtly intervene in the war and Communists (of one kind or another) did not succeed in taking over all of Indochina.

Inasmuch as these explicit conditions[13] had the effect of keeping the United States away from "the brink," we might inquire whether they were imposed for this reason; in other words, did the administration deliberately impose preconditions for intervention in order to *avoid* intervention? Dulles consistently responded to French pleas

---

[12] On 5 April, the day after President Eisenhower, Dulles, and Radford agreed upon the conditions for American intervention in the Indochinese War, the Secretary of State briefed the House Foreign Affairs Committee. He related, in some detail, the extent of Communist Chinese involvement in the war. He called the committee's attention to his Overseas Press Club speech and underlined the phrase "aggression by whatever means," suggesting that perhaps the results of aggression (rather than the act of aggression) ought to be the basis for retaliation. *NYT*, 6 April 1954.

In view of Dulles's charges of Chinese interference in the war, one might conclude that the administration was contemplating intervention; however, the secretary emphasized the point that appropriate retaliatory measures ought to be carried out with "unity of will and . . . unity of action." Dulles's remarks were unduly publicized and lent force to rumors that the administration would intervene. In my view, the primary purpose of these remarks was to deter the C.P.R. Intervention was not entirely out of the question in early April, however, since Chinese intentions were unknown. Hence Congress and the American people had to be made aware of various contingencies.

[13] That is, the conditions agreed upon by the President, Dulles, and Radford on 4 April: concerted action in a coalition; the grant of independence to the Indochinese, particularly the SVN; and a guarantee from the French government that it would sustain its war effort in Indochina prior to and during a coalition's intervention.

for assistance by saying that congressional approval was required before the United States could commit a belligerent act, and congressional approval, he usually added, was dependent upon America's securing allies. We should inquire, however, if Congress, even in effect, required the administration to impose conditions upon intervention in Indochina. The following analysis will attempt to answer this inquiry.

1. Conditions for the intervention of American armed forces in Indochina were imposed. This is certain, and is in itself significant in the context of events through late March and April. Thus, despite the gravity of the situation from the French point of view, the administration was not going to "rush into" the war. Attaching conditions also was a way of holding tight rein on the activists in the NSC, at least for a time.

2. Secretary Dulles and the President no doubt believed that the formation of a "NATO" for Southeast Asia would take months of consultations, but they certainly seem to have expected that the prospective participants would consent to beginning these consultations immediately, that is, before the Geneva Conference. Dulles was disappointed and angry when Eden instructed Roger Makins not to participate in early discussions that would lead to the formation of the coalition. President Eisenhower's description of the Indochina crisis leads us to believe that he and his Secretary of State sought to obtain the agreement of the allies, at least in principle, to a security pact for Southeast Asia. Dulles wanted this agreement before Geneva, since it could at least symbolize the resolve of the allies to resist further Communist encroachments in Southeast Asia and thus strengthen the bargaining position of the non-Communist states at the Geneva Conference. A fully formed regional defense organization was not a prerequisite for intervention, if in fact the administration felt compelled to intervene, but the allies' agreement in principle, particularly Great Britain's, was essential if the administration (a) intended to intervene *only with its allies* or (b) wanted the agreement merely as a bargaining counter at Geneva.

Since we know that Dulles intensively sought such agreement of the allies before Geneva, he must have believed that their agreement was *possible*. Therefore, we cannot conclude that the condition of allied cooperation was imposed to avoid intervention before the Geneva Conference since his diplomatic activity was compatible with both of the conclusions listed above.

3. With respect to the independence of the Associated States, negotiations over Vietnamese independence were still in progress in Paris. On 14 April, Foreign Minister Bidault and Paul Reynaud told Dulles that a formula for independence had finally been reached

that both the Vietnamese and the Laniel government could agree upon. Thus the secretary might have expected that the French would implement this agreement shortly. The fact that several Gaullist ministers were unhappy about this formula, which delayed agreement for two more months, did not really matter if independence remained a possibility. On the other hand, Dulles may well have asked whether the French would continue to pursue delaying tactics, as they had done since 1946. But if American intervention was contingent upon independence, as indeed it was, this in itself might speed up Franco-Vietnamese negotiations. If the Laniel government wanted active American assistance badly enough, it might feel compelled to concede to the Vietnamese nationalists the kind of independence the latter demanded. The condition of independence could have been satisfied in time to permit intervention, and satisfaction of this condition was not immediately necessary for beginning consultations toward the establishment of a regional defense organization. Thus we cannot conclude that this condition was imposed in order to avoid intervention.

4. Could the President and Secretary Dulles have believed that France would promise to remain in the war if the United States committed its armed forces? If, instead, France agreed to join a regional defense organization, this *might* have been sufficient.

Did it occur to Dulles to ask what the United States would do if the French pulled out of Indochina entirely? This was a very pertinent concern, for the Vietminh would then have overrun all of Vietnam and, at the very least, established sympathetic Communist regimes in Laos and Cambodia, which Dulles would have regarded as a very basic reason for intervention. Thus imposition of the condition that France agree to remain in the war until its successful conclusion could imply that

a. The administration was not prepared to intervene even if Indochina were communized. (In my opinion, this must be dismissed.)

b. The implications of this condition were not realized by Dulles at this time.

c. If the French withdrew, they would relinquish whatever residual advantages might have accrued to them after the Associated States became independent. The French Union would receive a damaging blow. It may have been Dulles's opinion that the Laniel government would not be prepared to take this drastic step, but, given the political instability of the governments of the Fourth Republic, the possibility that a successor government might take this step ought not to have been overlooked.

In my opinion the consequences of this condition were not thought through. Such a policy betrays excessive caution, for a policymaker who is bent upon action is necessarily economical in the formulation of conditions that will permit him to take action.[14] An undue multiplication of conditions suggests reluctance to act.

On the evidence available (which is not terribly conclusive), it appears that Secretary of State Dulles mentioned only the first two conditions (concerted action and independence for the Associated States) on the two separate occasions he informed the French that United States consent to intervene was conditioned: on 5 April he mentioned the conditions to Ambassador Bonnet and on 24 April to Foreign Minister Bidault.

Thus the conditions laid down by President Eisenhower on 4 April did not exclude the possibility of intervention but they do, indeed, manifest a prudent program. The conditions reflect the anti-colonialist sentiments of both the President and the Secretary of State and a resolve not to act alone—possibly for reasons related to the problematic legitimacy of such unilateral action, possibly because of fear that the United States alone might have to bear the human cost of intervention. I doubt whether the President or Dulles purposely conditioned the consent to intervene with the object of preventing it. The fact that none of the conditions was satisfied before the beginning of the Geneva Conference does not mean that they *could not* have been satisfied. By 18 April, however, when Dulles knew the British would not even consent to participating in critical discussions on the establishment of a regional defense organization, the likelihood that the conditions of 4 April would be satisfied before the conference began was remote.

Did the President and the Secretary of State impose the conditions we have analyzed because congressional leaders required them to do so? Dulles seems continually to have told the French that congressional approval would be required if the United States were to commit a belligerent act. But three observations are in order before we answer this question.

1. The meeting on 3 April between Radford, Dulles, and the eight congressional leaders was arranged, I have hypothesized, to persuade Radford (and, through the admiral, other activists in the administration) that Congress would have reservations about either an air strike or the use of combat troops. The questions the congressional leaders raised were the same questions the moderates on the NSC had raised: Shall we become involved in a war in an election year, and so soon after the Korean War had ended? Shall we involve ourselves in a war that seems to be tainted by colonialism? Shall we go in alone? This meeting did not veto involvement in the war, nor did it

[14] This might be termed an extension of Occam's razor. The preconditions for intervention were multiplied even further in late May and in June.

frustrate any hope Dulles had for getting approval of a resolution that would authorize an air strike (which he was said to be carrying in his pocket).[15] Neither the President nor Dulles wanted to ask Congress for such a resolution at the time. The President did not even attend the meeting. The meeting of 3 April gave Dulles greater freedom to pursue a more cautious policy within the administration than the activists were prepared to allow.

2. The President and his Secretary of State were unquestionably aware of congressional sensitivity over the conduct of the executive in foreign affairs. In January the President had finally taken a firm stand in opposition to the Bricker amendment, and the Senate's action in February *seemed* to have dealt the amendment at least temporary quietus. Now, only one month later, a question of the war-making powers of the executive presented itself. The President and his advisors could be expected to seek congressional approval for an act of belligerency and congressional opinion in formulating their policy relative to Indochina.

3. Although content to condition intervention upon congressional approval, neither the President nor Dulles sought congressional support for intervention during the crisis. If the President wanted an air strike, or perhaps blanket authorization to intervene, he could have attended the 3 April meeting and lent his request the prestige of his person and his office. During the crisis period and until the fall of Dien Bien Phu, W. S. White, the *New York Times* Washington correspondent, said that if the President wanted the authority to intervene, he could have mustered sufficient support in Congress.[16] It is noteworthy that major addresses on public policy for Indochina were made by Dulles, Nixon, and others during this period, *not* by President Eisenhower. The policy seemed to stress the importance of Indochina; it hinted that intervention was under consideration and hence always possible, and it allowed such rumors to circulate, but it never officially signaled that a decision was imminent (to be announced in a presidential broadcast or telecast to the people). Some were disturbed by this policy "drift." After explaining that his remarks on America's "facing up" to the use of troops in Indochina were his personal views, Vice President Nixon declared that the response to these remarks persuaded him that the American people had not been made aware of the significance of Communist gains in Indochina.[17]

[15] Chalmers Roberts, "The Day We Didn't Go to War," *Reporter*, 14 September 1954.
[16] *NYT*, 25 April 1954; *Econ.*, 24 April 1954, p. 285; *Congressional Record*, Vol. 100, Pt. 4, 83d Congress, 2d sess., pp. 5281, 5289-5294, 5613-5614.
[17] James Reston in the *NYT*, 20 April 1954.

Administration policy (by which I mean principally the policy of the President and Mr. Dulles) was not formulated in the attempt to lead Congress toward a decision for war; rather, the policy relied upon a symbiosis of sentiment between reticent congressional leaders and cautious elements in the administration.

Thus (in answer to the second question) Congress did not require the President to impose conditions upon the decision to intervene in the war. The President probably believed it was necessary to consult Congress, but he did not permit congressional opinion to determine national policy in this case. Rather, he took advantage of congressional sentiment to reinforce or support the policy that he, Dulles, and other moderates on the NSC had already formulated. This congressional card was played against France, which sought an air strike at Dien Bien Phu. It was also played against the activists on the NSC who favored the air strike and, perhaps, the dispatch of American combat troops to Indochina.

United States policy in Indochina after early April entailed creating a regional defense organization for Southeast Asia that would be *capable* of preventing further Communist gains. The agreement of the prospective participants, it was hoped, would be obtained before the Geneva Conference opened, primarily to strengthen the negotiating position of France and thus permit the French to resist Communist demands. Secondly, it entailed creating the appearance or possibility of American intervention. This would deter Chinese and Soviet intervention in the war and would persuade the Soviets, who were anxious to avoid a confrontation with the United States, that they must press the Chinese and the Vietminh to make concessions to the French. Thirdly, in the event the Geneva Conference failed to achieve peace in Indochina and the war continued (both events were expected in early April), the United States would continue to supply credits and equipment to the French. If it appeared that the Communists were undeterred by American threats and the new defense organization, collective intervention could be undertaken to prevent the communization of Southeast Asia.

The British attitude hindered the execution of this policy as the Churchill government wanted to give the Geneva Conference a better chance of succeeding. This was in accord with its policy of exploring possible ways of reducing international tensions by negotiating with a Soviet Union that apparently had become more amenable to this approach. Intervention, or even the threat of intervention, could change what was hoped would be a conciliatory Russian line at Geneva to the all too familiar intransigence. The American policy also would harden the attitude of the Chinese. Eden did not believe that British policy would result in the communization of Indochina, a consequence he hoped to avoid, but Indochina was not expected to fall in the two or three weeks it would take to allow the Geneva Conference to get under way.

Dulles, however, did not share the belief that the Soviets had become more tractable; if anything, their foreign policy had become more flexible, more subtle, and therefore more dangerous. Neither did he, nor most policymakers in the administration, hold much hope for negotiating a settlement at Geneva. What really disturbed Dulles, given his assumption about the Soviets and the Chinese, was the unwillingness of the British to create for the French and for the West— and therefore for themselves—an adequate bargaining position. After 18 April it was clear that the British were not even sympathetic to the deterrent aspect of American policy; that is, they opposed creating fear in the minds of the Soviets that the United States might intervene. They opposed what Eden would later call Dulles's "noising off."[18]

Critics have said that the administration formulated an Indochina policy in March and early April 1954 without consulting its British ally and, after its formulation, did not keep the British properly informed. Nor did Dulles, it was said, attempt to still the rumors of intervention or explain what he meant by united action. It is true there had been little or no consultation with Britain in the making of the policy Dulles so vaguely announced in his address of 29 March, but its deterrent aspect would have been destroyed if the secretary had explained in great detail what the United States would and would not do in Indochina. The British might very well have informed India, or even the Soviet Union, that the United States did not really mean to intervene. In the context of the events of April, Dulles did not and could not know what the United States would do in the various hypothetical futures that seemed possible, and, given the estrangement between Eden and Dulles after 18 April, the Secretary of State probably would not want to be completely candid with the Foreign Secretary.

When Dulles went to Paris in late April to attend the NATO council ministers' meeting, he knew that Dien Bien Phu would soon fall but undoubtedly was shocked by the despondency, irresoluteness, and pessimism of many of the ministers in the Laniel government. Not only would Dien Bien Phu fall, which at the beginning of April was regarded in Washington as likely, but now it was likely that the capture of the garrison would signal the deterioration of the French mili-

---

[18] Eden either did not understand a policy of deterrence or, understanding it, gave it no credence (E, pp. 101-102, 104). "I found it hard to see how pretending that we might be going to do so [i.e., help the French] would really help anybody." E, p. 124.

tary position throughout Tonkin, the collapse of the Laniel government, and the installation in Paris of a government that would be willing to make peace at any price. What had earlier been discussed in Washington as merely possible had, in the atmosphere of Paris in late April, become almost real for the Secretary of State.

Did Dulles's attitude undergo a change? Did he become less cautious? I think not. On 23 April, Bidault asked for an air strike at Dien Bien Phu; on 24 April, Dulles told Bidault that an air strike would not be efficacious and, in any case, would come too late to save the garrison. He again remarked that an air strike was a belligerent act, requiring congressional authorization,[19] which in turn depended upon the United States' securing the participation of its allies and the French giving independence to the Associated States.

Bidault, Dulles, and Eden met again on the afternoon of the 24th; and we have noted the incident of the mysterious letter in which Dulles offered to send ground troops to Indochina. While Eden returned to London late on the 24th to secure a definite cabinet decision on British cooperation in a joint allied intervention, Secretary Dulles left for Geneva. No records are available, as yet, to show what Dulles did or what he wrote on these two crucial days, 25 and 26 April, while the British cabinet met twice, while Massigli pleaded for British cooperation, and while Bedell Smith tried to expedite his scheme for intervention by the ANZUS powers. Dulles seems to have spent these two days preparing for the opening of the conference on 26 April and attempting to line up the allies behind his coalition scheme. He was, no doubt, in touch with Washington, and he spoke with Bedell Smith on the 26th.

Dulles may have had moments of doubt in these crucial days. He may have felt that, after all, intervention would be necessary sometime in the future. But the practical effect of his actions—and of whatever decisions were made in Washington or by Dulles in Paris and Geneva—was to refuse intervention and to wait upon the results of negotiations at the Geneva Conference and the results of French and Vietminh military operations in Indochina.

[II]

Eden's decision on or about 18 April ordering Ambassador Makins not to attend the preliminary conference on the Southeast Asia collective defense organization dramatically highlighted the divergence between British and American cold war policy. Let us put aside questions of who misunderstood whom or whether Eden changed his mind after his 13 April meeting with Dulles. Let us, instead, attempt

[19] Confirmed in E, p. 114.

to understand British foreign policy in the crucial months preceding the Geneva Conference.

In February the British press generally welcomed the scheduling, by the ministers at Berlin, of a conference on Korea and Indochina, but it expressed concern over the criticism Dulles received on his return to Washington. The British believed that the critics, in the Senate or elsewhere, could prevent Dulles from effectively negotiating with the Communists at Geneva;[20] and negotiation was of primary importance. If one idea dominated the Churchill government in late 1953 and in 1954, it was the idea that negotiations with the Communist-bloc states were necessary. By this means the intentions of the Malenkov regime could be explored and tested and the Sino-Soviet alliance could be reconnoitered and its strengths and weaknesses assessed. Also, the conflict in Southeast Asia might be liquidated before it enlarged into a major war. Thus the British were eager to see what results the Berlin and Geneva Conferences might produce.[21]

Throughout March and April, while Washington's utterances tended to deprecate the Geneva Conference, the British government cautiously but firmly insisted on the value of such a conference and optimistically forecast some positive results. The British press questioned the soundness of the United States attitude toward the conference, one commentator going so far as to say that American reluctance to negotiate was undermining the Western allies' position in Asia.[22] In early April, soon after Dulles's Overseas Press Club address, the British government declared that it was not willing to take steps that would antagonize the Soviets and the Chinese before the Geneva Conference had begun. Dulles was eager to go to Britain to explain United States intervention, but the British, it appears, were not terribly interested in this. Go he did, nevertheless, on 11 April. The Eden-Dulles communiqué of 13 April provided the basis, so Dulles believed, for scheduling talks on the new defense organization. These, however, had to be canceled because of Eden's reassertion of a policy of negotiating at Geneva and doing nothing that might prejudice the success of the talks. Much to Dulles's dismay,

[20] *NYT*, 13, March 1954.

[21] Throughout 1954 the British and Soviet governments exchanged a series of notes on European collective security. For a time the British hoped for some concrete results, but nothing was achieved in 1954. See *Text of a Note from the Soviet Government regarding Collective Security*, Misc. No. 9 (1954), Command Doc. 9122; *Text of a Note from the Government of the United Kingdom*, Misc. No. 13 (1954), Cmd. 9146; *Further Correspondence*, Misc. No. 26 (1954), Cmd. 9281; *Further Correspondence*, Misc. No. 34 (1954), Cmd. 9327 (London: Her Majesty's Stationery Office, 1954).

[22] *NYT*, 25 April 1954.

this was construed by the British to include not only intervention (which, I have argued, Dulles did not want) but discussions that could lead to a declaration of intent to form a regional defense pact. This would disappoint the French, but, more importantly, it appreciably diminished the effectiveness of a policy of keeping the Communists guessing while deterring them.

Eden explained that he adhered to the policy of waiting upon the results of Geneva because he did not wish to widen the Indochina War just as a conference that might end the fighting was about to begin. There is no question that there was much apprehension in Britain that the United States intended to intervene and "escalate" the war. There was, moreover, fear that the Eisenhower administration might use atomic weapons and the new thermonuclear devices whose tests were nearing completion in the Pacific. After all, spokesmen for the administration had been expatiating upon the massive retaliatory aspects of the New Look since the preceding winter, and a widened war in Indochina would very likely mean Chinese intervention, which would mean the strategic bombing of China. This, in turn, could actuate the Sino-Soviet alliance and bring the Soviet Union into the war. The world war that all agreed must be avoided would have begun, simply because the United States had not been willing to wait several weeks until the Geneva Conference opened. It might be as unproductive as the Berlin Conference had been, but all chance for its success should not be destroyed even before the diplomats gathered in Geneva. Besides, the intelligence benefits to the West might be substantial, so the policymakers of the British cabinet reasoned, and so reasoned many influential individuals among the British public.

Eden also opposed allied intervention to save Dien Bien Phu: it was too late to do this and the air strike would not be effective. The American JCS (before 25 April) had reached the same conclusions; and Dulles himself had decided an air strike was not the best way to intervene in the war, if the United States must intervene. He reached this conclusion very early in April, soon after Admiral Radford told him of the plan. Thus there was no essential disagreement between the British and the Americans on this point. It seemed, moreover, that Dulles had not really pressed for a joint allied warning aimed at Peking. This scheme was shelved, at the latest, by 11 April, when Eden and Dulles and their staffs conferred in London.

In his account of the Indochina crisis in *Full Circle*, Eden did not discuss the efficacy of a deterrence policy; that is, a policy of creating doubts in the Communist states concerning the possible reactions of the West to the successes of the Vietminh in Indochina. Such a policy, in Dulles's view, would strengthen the negotiating positions of the French (and other United States allies) at Geneva. Possibly Dulles told Eden that he must *threaten* intervention; probably he did not tell the Foreign Minister that he did *not favor* intervention, for the reasons mentioned earlier. But even if Dulles attempted to persuade Eden of the necessity for a deterrent-type diplomacy (and Eden's memoirs do not suggest that he did this), Eden would not have been receptive for he was loathe to create, before Geneva, a diplomatic atmosphere other than one that would help persuade the Soviets of Britain's good will and its attitude of conciliation and compromise: in other words, its readiness to negotiate in good faith without threats, explicit or implicit.

Although this wholly admirable commitment to negotiations and the pursuit of world peace no doubt had its basis in a sincere desire to prevent a thermonuclear holocaust and a continued loss of life in Indochina, British foreign policy, of course, was firmly rooted in the British government's perception of British national interests.

1. In the first place, the British were not militarily prepared for intervention in Indochina. Their guerrilla action in Malaya was proving costly in terms of troop commitment and its effect upon the economy. An additional commitment in Indochina would severely tax an overextended defense budget. Britain, moreover, was moving toward a "new look" of its own: reliance upon a modest strategic nuclear capacity accompanied by cutbacks in its conventional forces. Such a defense policy could not permit a large military presence in Indochina.

2. There was hope for increased trade with the Soviet Union and even with the C.P.R. On several occasions at the Berlin Conference, Molotov held out prospects of improved commercial relations with the British, at one point declaring that the Soviets were willing to purchase, over a three-year period, a billion dollars' worth of industrial goods. A policy that led to intervention in Indochina, or even threatened such action, could hardly encourage such developments.

3. The Attlee Labour moderates supported the foreign policy of the Churchill government but Aneurin Bevan was a constant critic. His dramatic resignation from the shadow cabinet on 14 April came ostensibly over the issues of British dependence upon American policy and a "proper" approach to the Indochinese War. If Bevan could persuade the Labour Party that British policy was not sufficiently conciliatory, that it supported an American policy that was likely to result in the use of atomic weapons in East Asia, he might be able to wrest control of the Labour Party from Attlee and even become Prime Minister. This could only be viewed with extreme apprehension by the government whose leader was soon to retire. Eden, of course, would be even more concerned; as Churchill's successor, he was anxious to demonstrate his leadership ability in two important respects.

(a) British policy would be formulated in the British Foreign Office, not in Washington, and would continue to follow an independent line. (b) Eden, as Prime Minister, would be peace-maker: he would use every opportunity to improve relations between the Communist and non-Communist powers. He would negotiate at Geneva and would attempt to act as "honest broker" between the French and the Communists. Success at Geneva would materially improve his image as a statesman who was worthy to be Prime Minister in his own right. Also, it would deflate Bevan's charges against the Tories and the Labour moderates.

4. The British wanted a settlement in Indochina that would provide a non-Communist buffer zone north of Malaya, where British troops were already involved in fighting a Communist-led insurrection. They also wanted guarantees for Laos, Cambodia, and Thailand, which, together with a buffer state in southern Vietnam, would form a Southeast Asian *cordon sanitaire* for the Commonwealth nations of Burma, India, and Malaya. Thus the British appreciation of the situation in Southeast Asia had as firm a geopolitical base as the Americans'. Eden has said he began to think of partition as a possible solution to the Indochinese War in early 1954,[23] and certainly by April this type of solution was under active study in London.

Eden therefore was willing to offer guarantees to Thailand if the French withdrew from Indochina,[24] and was agreeable to associating Britain in a regional defense pact *after* he had decided whether Geneva offered prospects of satisfying British interests. Before the end of April, when it became evident that the French position in Indochina was critical, the British government seemed to think the Geneva negotiations might lead to the Chinese halting aid to the Vietminh, thus allowing the French to pacify the country. By late April it was certain that the French had neither the capability nor the will to pacify all of Indochina; hence a solution such as partition seemed to offer the best political advantages to the West.

BUT LET US speculate a moment upon British thinking before the grave crisis in late April. The Foreign Office might have asked itself how the Communist Chinese could be induced to halt their aid to the Vietminh. The British rejected threats,[25] but concessions might have this effect. It could not be forecast with certainty, but the Soviets were expected to be willing to compromise at Geneva, at least on matters that would permit the settlement of the Indochinese War. According to the British view, the war was peripheral to Soviet interests as they were understood by Malenkov and his supporters in 1954, who therefore were willing to press the Vietminh to settle

[23] E, p. 97.   [24] E, p. 114.   [25] E, pp. 104-105.

the war in exchange for concessions benefitting the Soviets. The Chinese, the British believed, did not want to intervene in Indochina. Wanting primarily to get on with their economic programs within China, they also were willing to press the Vietminh to settle the war, and would even halt their assistance to them if certain guarantees or concessions were made, for example, no American troops or U.S. military bases in Indochina, China's admission to the United Nations, and its recognition by the United States. The French, of course, had little to offer the Chinese, but could offer the defeat of EDC to the Russians.

Only the United States, however, was in a position to make the concessions that could permit a settlement at Geneva. Only the United States could offer, to the satisfaction of the Chinese, the "neutralization" of Indochina. Inasmuch as the United States had prevented admission of the C.P.R. to the U.N. and had steadfastly refused recognition, there may have been hope in Britain (and France as well) that the China policy of the United States would change in 1954. The American domestic political situation could not permit such a change, but this was not clear to many Englishmen before and during the Geneva Conference. Efforts were made to persuade American policymakers of the reasonableness of extending recognition to the C.P.R. and admitting it to the U.N.,[26] but these efforts stimulated the fears of the China Lobby (and others) that a change of China policy was indeed in the offing. The administration had continually to assure its critics that this was not the case. For example, the American delegate to the U.N., Henry Cabot Lodge, asserted in late March and again in late April that the United States would not hesitate to use its veto to prevent the C.P.R.'s admission.[27]

The British were unhappy with what appeared to them an unrealistic and unwise policy. They reasoned that if Geneva produced no positive achievements, the conference could indeed be turned against the West: Soviet and Chinese concessions could be conditioned upon American recognition of China. Knowing that Washington's policymakers were adamant and would not change their stand on the international status of China, the Communists could contrast their attitude of reasonableness with that of the intransigent Americans. This would offer significant propaganda victories.[28]

5. Relations with colonies and former colonies were a matter of very great importance for a state like Great Britain, which was making the painful transition from an imperial power to an undetermined role as the focus of a new and loosely organized aggregation of states

---

[26] *NYT*, 21, 28 March 1954.
[27] *NYT*, 21 March, 20 April 1954.
[28] *NYT*, 22, 25 April 1954.

known as the Commonwealth. British intervention in the Indochinese War, therefore could be represented as a return to "imperialist" practices (collaborating with the French in a colonial war) and could destroy the ideological basis of the Commonwealth. Moreover, good Commonwealth relations required consultation with the member nations and evidence of a willingness to accommodate British foreign policy to the policies of these members. Thus India's opposition to the Indochinese war and her desire to reduce tensions in East Asia were a factor the Churchill government had continually to take into account in the spring of 1954.

Prime Minister Nehru and his special envoy, V. K. Krishna Menon, were convinced that the death of Stalin and the truce in Korea offered the world an opportunity to liquidate the tensions of the cold war. Nehru sincerely believed that peaceful coexistence with the Soviet Union and China was possible, and the Geneva Conference would offer the practical means for giving real significance to that term;[29] he therefore would oppose any policy that would tend to prejudice the success of the conference. Dulles's "united action" concept, whatever it meant, portended a program that would destroy the hypothesized peaceful attitudes of the Chinese and the Soviets, and when Dulles traveled to London and secured Eden's consent to "an examination of the possibility" of establishing a Southeast Asia defense pact, the Indian press condemned the British step as appeasement. Nehru, moreover, publicly criticized the idea of a Southeast Asia alliance as provocative and antagonistic to the Chinese.[30] On 28 April the South Asian states of India, Pakistan, Ceylon, Burma, and Indonesia met in Colombo, Ceylon, and throughout the conference Nehru deprecated the idea of a Southeast Asia alliance. We do not yet know the extent to which India pressured the British to refuse to cooperate in a regional pact, but Dulles believed the pressures were substantial.[31]

Nehru played an independent peace-making role. In late April, in an address before the Indian Parliament, the Prime Minister asked

[29] *Jawaharlal Nehru's Speeches* (New Delhi: Ministry of Information and Broadcast, 1958), 3: 245-246.

[30] *NYT*, 16 April 1954; *T/L*, 29 June 1954.

[31] For the relationship between the Geneva Conference and the Colombo Conference, see Chapter 10 below. Before the convening of the Colombo Conference, it was believed that the delegates of the Colombo powers would direct their attention principally to colonialism in Asia and the Indochinese War. In addition, economic questions (stabilized commodity prices and the expansion of technical and economic assistance) would be discussed. *NYT*, 28 April 1954.

New Delhi impliedly denied having officially contacted the British government or pressed it to refuse participation in preliminary talks relating to the coalition for Southeast Asia before the Geneva Conference opened. "There had been no exchange of views between the Government of India and any of the governments who are concerned [with the proposed coalition]." *NYT*, 18 April 1954.

Britain, the United States, China, and the Soviet Union to make a formal agreement not to intervene in Indochina.[32] This proposal was in line with independent India's frequent espousal of the principles of sovereignty and noninterference in the domestic affairs of Asian states. Nehru had also called upon the Communist and the non-Communist powers to refrain from acts that would destroy the hopes or chances for negotiating a settlement of the Indochinese War at Geneva. In his speech to the Parliament, Nehru also proposed a peace plan for Indochina, which was later aired at the Colombo Conference. His plan called for (*a*) an immediate cease-fire in Indochina, (*b*) a guarantee by France of independence for the Associated States, (*c*) direct negotiations between the belligerents in the conflict (i.e. between France and the Vietminh), (*d*) nonintervention by third states and cessation of military aid to the belligerents, and (*e*) keeping the United Nations informed of the progress of the Geneva negotiations. Nehru stressed that the good offices of the U.N. must be used for conciliation and not for sanctions.

Nehru's speech was criticized in the United States[33]—although some senators tended to agree with Nehru that, from the point of view of the Vietminh, the Indochinese War was basically anti-colonialist in character and nationalist sentiment was its driving force. The British Labour Party, but particularly the Bevanites, tended to support Nehru's views. On 1 May the Labour Party's national executive committee passed a resolution endorsing an amended form of Nehru's peace proposal.[34] Labour's support, as well as concern for Commonwealth relations generally, made it all the more necessary for the Churchill government to be guided by India's Indochina policy.

Thus, although we may attribute the *manner* in which Eden dramatized his disagreement with American policy to his dislike or mistrust of the Secretary of State, the *substance* of their policy differences rested upon distinctly divergent interpretations of the national interests of the sovereign states of which these men were ministers. It would be utopian to suggest there should not have been such divergences. However, it would only be realistic to have expected the policymakers of Britain and the United States to have sought to recognize the bases for their differences and to have attempted to bridge the gap between them. By the time the Geneva Conference opened, no such efforts had been made.

[32] *Nehru's Speeches, op. cit.*, pp. 251-252; *NYT*, 25 April 1954.
[33] *NYT*, 25 April 1954.
[34] *Econ.*, 1 May 1954, p. 360.

[III]

Premier Joseph Laniel's speech to the National Assembly in early April outlined his government's policy in Indochina: Dien Bien Phu would be defended; the war effort in Indochina would be continued with United States material assistance; and negotiations at Geneva would be aimed at securing a cease-fire with appropriate regard for the rights of "interested parties." The Laniel government had already indicated, however, that if the Geneva Conference failed to achieve an honorable settlement of the Indochinese War, the United States and other interested states would be asked to assume greater responsibility.[35] While the war had taken on a new aspect with increased deliveries of Chinese ordnance to the Vietminh, there was no proof of Chinese combat troops in Indochina, and the Laniel government would not request American troops. The French ministers, in fact, were quite cautious in commenting upon the remarks Dulles had made in his Overseas Press Club speech about the extent of Chinese involvement in the war. In addition, Dulles's speech and his other remarks were kept out of the Indochinese press by order of the French High Commissioner.[36]

When Secretary Dulles traveled to Paris on 14 April, seeking to obtain French support for his united-action proposal, spokesmen for the Laniel government had expressed fear that the war might expand into a general war with China and possibly the Soviet Union. Although they believed the United States had given the Communists sufficient warnings, they apparently approved of the plan for creating a collective defense arrangement for Southeast Asia (but this is not entirely clear from the available evidence). By the end of April the French were pressing Dulles to proceed with his plan for the coalition, even without the British if need be.[37]

By the time of the NATO council ministers' meeting on 23 April, the Laniel government seems to have reached a point of desperation. Perhaps the cable from Navarre on 21 April, warning that Dien Bien Phu could not be held without a massive air strike, precipitated the alarm; in any case, realization that the French garrison at Dien Bien Phu had just about reached the limit of its ability to resist again turned the attention of the ministers to the Radford plan (the outcome of the French demarches has been described above). The French, particularly distressed by Prime Minister Churchill's statement in the House of Commons that the British would not make

[35] *NYT*, 7, 13 April 1954.
[36] *NYT*, 8 April 1954.
[37] *NYT*, 30 April 1954.

any commitments in advance of the Geneva Conference, felt the statement was brutal and untimely in view of the imminent collapse of the Dien Bien Phu garrison. Robert Schuman then informed the cabinet that Britain had refused to join the United States in efforts to save the garrison. The government felt let down by its allies, and by Great Britain in particular,[38] but even though it had failed to obtain the agreement of the United States and Britain to intervene, the Laniel government seems to have adhered to the policy announced in the National Assembly earlier in the month. France would press for a cease-fire at Geneva, but it must be an effective cease-fire: the Vietminh must not be able to resume hostilities nor subvert, by infiltration tactics, the civil order of areas controlled by the French or by the governments of the Associated States. The war effort would be continued until a satisfactory truce was concluded. If Geneva failed to produce such a settlement, the United States would be asked to intervene.

Bidault was greatly concerned about his weak bargaining position. Britain had publicly declared she was not prepared to take military action in Indochina, and, with this pronouncement, American intervention also had been ruled out for the time being. The Communists, therefore, would act with more assurance at the conference; with the decreased probability of military intervention by France's allies, Communist terms for a cease-fire could be onerous, and perhaps unacceptable. Bidault, moreover, wanted the Chinese to agree to halt their assistance to the Vietminh, which China might agree to do in exchange for concessions: U.S. recognition of the C.P.R., admission to the U.N., or the neutralization of Taiwan. But only the United States could make these concessions, and the Eisenhower administration had made it clear that under no circumstances would it pay this price for an Indochinese settlement. The administration seemed equally unreceptive to French suggestions that various commercial concessions be made.[39] The Soviet Union might be able to persuade China to withhold aid to the Vietminh and press the Vietminh to accept a cease-fire, but why would the Soviets be willing to take these significant steps?

1. Soviet concern for European security and Soviet efforts to bring about the defeat of the EDC treaty suggested that, if the French agreed not to ratify the treaty, the Soviets might be willing to try to arrange an end to the Indochinese War on terms satisfactory to the French. The United States, West Germany, and France's other

---

[38] Eisenhower later recorded that a Frenchman (unidentified) complained that the allies were letting France down. Eisenhower replied: "You've let yourself down." OHP statement, p. 25.

[39] *NYT*, 7, 11 April 1954.

European allies were apprehensive about the French striking a bargain such as this; indeed, the Laniel government's policymakers had rejected this bargaining tactic in March and Bidault had refused to countenance what he called *"marchandage planétaire."*[40] Nevertheless, for the reasons we suggested earlier, Laniel did not bring the EDC treaty to a vote in the Assembly: defeat of the treaty would antagonize the United States and its passage would anger the Soviet Union. The support of the former and willingness of the latter to conciliate and press their respective allies was necessary for the French at Geneva.

2. Bidault had rejected the tactic of bargaining over EDC, but what tactic would he use? One was at least tacitly offered by the American Secretary of State: the threat of military intervention by the United States, the internationalization of the war, and increased likelihood of Chinese and Soviet involvement. Should Geneva fail to bring about a settlement of the war, France would ask for the dispatch of American troops to Indochina. If the professions of the Malenkov regime were sincere, the Soviets would try to avoid an extension of the war, and to this end might use their influence upon the Chinese and the Vietminh. However, there were several difficulties in employing this tactic.

a. Britain had refused to make a commitment on and after 25 April and the United States did not intend to intervene unilaterally. Bidault could reason, however, that if the Communists were intransigent at Geneva and employed delaying tactics, the British would almost certainly, albeit reluctantly, agree to join a coalition, and this strategy would be more effective.

b. The tactic of relying upon threats would undoubtedly cause great concern in France. Many deputies opposed continuation of the war and many more feared its extension.[41] Later, Mèndes-France accused Bidault of playing *"poker infernale"* with Dulles.[42]

c. There were many imponderables. Was Dulles bluffing? Would the Soviets think that France and the United States were bluffing? What if the Soviets could not persuade the Chinese to suspend aid to the Vietminh? What if neither Russia nor China could persuade Ho Chi Minh to agree to a cease-fire that was agreeable to the French?

[40] Tournoux, *op. cit.*, p. 34. Bidault is quoted there as having said he did not want to put the EDC in the hole (*"le trou"*) in order to obtain a smile from Molotov. Also: *"On n'échange pas Adenauer contre Ho Chi Minh."*

[41] Raymond Aron wrote in *Le Figaro* on 26 April: "How could the American threat be effective if we proclaim that, in no circumstances, would we let it be executed? It is necessary, as far as this is possible, to avoid extension of the conflict; but it is necessary to assume the risk of this extension in order to obtain an honorable peace." Quoted in L&D, p. 99.

[42] *JO*, 10 June 1954, p. 2851.

If the conference failed to bring a truce, would French opinion countenance a continuation of the war? In spite of these problems, Bidault felt there was little else he could do, and he would employ the tactic of American threats to the extent that circumstances allowed. On 24 April the French cabinet gave Bidault a free hand for negotiating at Geneva. He must, however, report daily to Laniel. More importantly, his constant task would be to negotiate toward a truce in Indochina with the kind of guarantee the Laniel government required.[43]

IN FACT, there was an alternative approach to peace in Indochina: direct negotiations with the Vietminh, espoused by Mèndes-France, a leading advocate of this policy. In early March René Pleven had outlined the terms of a possible cease-fire and the Vietminh had cautiously welcomed the terms. No efforts were made to pursue the matter further, however, and the Laniel government seems to have adhered to the policy of refusing to deal with the Vietminh, maintaining the policy it had adopted in response to Ho Chi Minh's proposals in November and December 1953. It was believed, and correctly so, that direct dealings with the Vietminh would antagonize the United States and the State of Vietnam.

Having recognized the SVN in 1950, the United States would not approve any policy that gave other than rebel status to the Vietminh. Officials of the Eisenhower administration had urged the Laniel government to reject proposals for direct dealings with the Vietminh in the winter of 1953/54.

[IV]

Negotiations between French and Vietnamese representatives for defining an independent status for the State of Vietnam in the French Union had begun on 8 March in Paris. Similar negotiations had taken place several times before, and each time the French had refused to grant the Vietnamese meaningful independence. Each time the sovereign status of the State of Vietnam remained problematical. In March and April 1954, Vietnamese negotiators, led by Prince Buu Loc, demanded an unequivocal grant of independence. Adherence to the French Union was made contingent on this grant, much to the irritation of the French negotiators.

The parties had early agreed upon a procedural matter, however: two treaties were to be concluded. One treaty would grant independence to the Vietnamese; the other would define the status of the SVN in the French Union. But there was disagreement over the

---

[43] L&D, pp. 107-108.

words to be used in granting independence and over the exact definition of the status of the SVN. The difficulty lay in article 62 of the
constitution of the Fourth French Republic, which stated: "The
members of the French Union pool all the means at their disposal,
to guarantee the protection of the whole of the Union. The government of the Republic assumes the co-ordination of these means and
the control of the policy apt to prepare and ensure this protection."
The French read this article as meaning the French government
would assume direction of the foreign and defense policies of the
newly "independent" Vietnam. The Vietnamese, who argued that
sovereignty meant control over foreign policy, demanded full autonomy and everything this implied. They refused to be bound by
articles of the constitution of another member of the French Union.[44]

By the first or second week in April the French government had
come around to the view that the status of the SVN would be defined
entirely by the two treaties mentioned above, treaties negotiated by
sovereign equals. The French constitution would not be construed as
limiting the sovereignty of the SVN. Ministers on the right, particularly Gaullists, opposed this decision. They also opposed granting independence to the SVN, arguing that this step should not be taken
until after the Geneva Conference: the "threat" to grant independence to the State of Vietnam could be used as a bargaining device
against the Chinese or the Vietminh and to force Vietminh concessions favorable to the French. It is probable that the decision to
push ahead with the negotiations, in spite of opposition and Bidault's reluctance, was a consequence of United States pressure. The
political commission, which had been established by the parties to
the negotiations, produced drafts of the treaties on 21 April. The
first treaty granted independence to the State of Vietnam; the second treaty associated France and the SVN in the French Union.[45]

Bao Dai, who arrived in Paris in early April to take part in the
negotiations for independence, let it be known that he preferred
American rather than French protection. He hoped to speak with
Dulles on 13 April but had arrived too late to meet him.[46] On Dulles's
next visit to Paris, on 23 April, Bao Dai met Secretary Dulles and
pledged the adherence of the SVN to the proposed collective defense organization.[47]

Bao Dai and the other Vietnamese in Paris were profoundly dis-

[44] L&D, pp. 105-106.
[45] *Docs., 1954*, pp. 270-272. See Chapter 13 below for a discussion of the
initialing of these treaties by representatives of France and the State of Vietnam.
[46] *NYT*, 14 April 1954. In early April the Foreign Operations Administration
declared that it would reorient its aid in order to give more direct support to the
Vietnamese government and the Vietnamese fighting forces. *NYT*, 4 April 1954.
[47] *NYT*, 25 April 1954.

turbed by rumors that partition, as a solution to the Indochinese War, was being studied at the highest levels. We know, of course, that Eden favored this approach and has claimed to have had it in mind since the beginning of 1954. In April, Ambassador Makins communicated Eden's views to Dulles and Bedell Smith: a compromise with the Communists, Makins said, may be the only alternative in Indochina, and partition the "least damaging solution."[48] The plan was rejected by the United States, but these maneuvers came to the attention of the Bao Dai government and caused profound consternation among the Vietnamese ministers.

About 24 April a dispute in Paris caused further delays in the signing of the two Franco-Vietnamese treaties of independence and association. The *London Times* reported that the French government, acceding to Gaullist demands, had decided to defer signing the treaties until the details of association (i.e. economic and cultural relations, military affairs, technical assistance, etc.) had been worked out. Whether this was the reason is difficult to determine.[49] On 27 April *Le Monde* carried a statement that had been issued by the Bao Dai government on the 24th. The government of the SVN, the statement said, had for the time being decided not to sign the two treaties of independence and association. The SVN had not received specific assurances from the French that adequately guaranteed the unity and independence of the new republic. Proposals envisaging partition were denounced, as was the possibility that France would negotiate directly with the Vietminh rebels at Geneva. With respect to the Geneva Conference, the statement declared that "neither the Chief of State nor the government of Viet-Nam will consider themselves bound by the decisions" of a conference that ran counter to the independence or unity of the SVN.

We do not know who was responsible for the delay in signing the treaties. The statement of the Bao Dai government seems to indicate that it was the decision of that government, but it would not be beyond belief that the French government had again delayed an unequivocal grant of independence to the SVN and that the Vietnamese negotiators were so irate over the delay, the lack of a sense of urgency by the French, and the rumors of partition that they decided, unilaterally, to delay the signing. This result would certainly have been welcomed by the Gaullists, and perhaps by many more ministers in the Laniel government.

Several days later, on 28 April, the French and the Vietnamese diplomats published a statement of intention.[50] France and Vietnam, it said,

[48] E, pp. 102, 97.   [49] *L/T*, 29 April 1954.
[50] *Ibid.*; see also the references in n. 45.

affirm their agreement to settle their mutual relations on the basis of two fundamental treaties. The first of these treaties recognizes the total independence of Viet Nam and her full and entire sovereignty. The second establishes a Franco–Viet Nam association in the French Union founded on equality and intended to develop the cooperation between the two countries. Solemnly confirming their will to apply these two treaties on a parallel basis, the French and Viet Nam Governments agree to submit them simultaneously for ratification, as foreseen by their respective national laws.

The independent spirit of the Vietnamese also was demonstrated earlier that day when Bidault, meeting with the SVN Minister of Foreign Affairs, Nguyen Quoc Dinh, asked Dinh to sign a communiqué stating that the French and the Vietnamese would continue consultations at Geneva. Dinh refused to sign until the communiqué was amended to read that the parties would continue consultations "at Geneva or elsewhere."[51] The original form of the communiqué, Dinh argued, assumed that a delegate of the SVN would go to Geneva, which was by no means certain. A delegate could attend the conference only if the State of Vietnam was truly independent, and the treaties of independence had not yet been signed. If we couple these remarks with Bao Dai's announcement that the signing of the treaties would be postponed, it appeared for a time, that there would be no SVN minister at Geneva.

The reservation of Bao Dai that the State of Vietnam would not be bound by decisions made at Geneva in conflict with the unity of the state remained essentially unchanged throughout the conference. At the conclusion of negotiations in July, the SVN representative, Tran Van Do, announced that his government formally protested the substance of the cease-fire agreement concluded by France and the Vietminh and the final declaration issued in the name of the conference. He also issued a declaration that, in effect, disassociated his government from the settlement that was embodied in the conference documents, a step of momentous historical importance.

[51] L&D, p. 106.

Chapter 8

THE SINO-SOVIET ALLIANCE AND
THE INDOCHINA PERIPHERY

[I]

In an election campaign speech on 12 March 1954, Georgy Malen-kov, chairman of the Council of Ministers, declared that the Soviet Union was opposed to a continuation of the cold war. It was, he said, a "policy of preparation for a new world war that, with modern weapons of war, means the destruction of world civilization."[1] Krem-linologists considered this passage significant in that the Soviet Premier chose to say *world civilization* and not *capitalism* would be destroyed in any future world war. This was regarded as a marked change from the Stalinist attitude toward war and its "inevitable" outcome.

On 26 April Malenkov made another address of importance, and this time was joined by Nikita Khrushchev, first secretary of the Communist Party of the Soviet Union on the dais of the Supreme Soviet. Malenkov warned that senseless, atomic aggression against the Soviet Union would lead to the defeat of the aggressor by atomic arms. In a passage that contrasted sharply with his 12 March speech, Malenkov stated that any future war would "inevitably lead to the collapse of the capitalist system."[2] Both Malenkov and Khrushchev were critical of the United States. The Premier declared that American policies created an atmosphere of anxiety. Khrushchev attacked the U.S. Secretary of State:

> Mr. Dulles acts as if he had become sick with some sort of rage. We know that a person in a rage is mad. But is it fitting for a states-man to announce the foreign policy of his country when he is drunk with fury and malice toward other people?[3]

What had taken place to change the tenor at Malenkov's speeches and to cause him to reassert the traditional Communist view that a world war would result in the downfall of capitalism? We know that the Soviet press had attacked American policy in Southeast Asia on the grounds that Indochina was being prepared as a new Korea. Remarks of administration officials, particularly those of Secretary of

---

[1] *Soviet News*, 15 March 1954; *NYT*, 14 March 1954.
[2] *Soviet News*, 28 April 1954; *NYT*, 27 April 1954.
[3] "Speech of Deputy N. S. Khrushchev," *Izvestia*, 27 April 1954, quoted in H. S. Dinerstein, *War and the Soviet Union* (New York: Praeger, 1959), p. 113.

State Dulles, were said to have the object of poisoning "the atmosphere on the eve of the Geneva Conference" and intensifying tensions in international relations.[4] The United States was accused of planning aggression against China with weapons of mass destruction.[5]

We also know that the Soviets attached great importance to Geneva. Speeches by Malenkov and repeated references to the conference in the Soviet press held out the promise of reduced international tensions and collaboration among the states of the socialist bloc in foiling the plans of aggressors by peaceful methods. China was of obvious importance in this socialist collaboration, and *Pravda* continually emphasized the impossibility of deciding "a single disputed international question" without the Chinese People's Republic.[6] The Geneva Conference offered the means to demonstrate to the world the unity of the socialist camp and to demonstrate to China the genuine efforts the Soviet Union was making to have the C.P.R. recognized as a great power.

At the end of March a low-echelon Russian diplomat in London suggested to various Foreign Office contacts that partition of Indochina would be a possible solution to the Indochinese War. It was reported that Sergei Vinogradov, the Russian ambassador to France, told Bidault he was certain an acceptable formula for peace could be found, based upon a cease-fire and the creation of a buffer state in Indochina.[7]

Apart from these démarches, the Soviets must have been intently watching the pre-Geneva maneuvers of officials of the Eisenhower administration, particularly the statements and the movements of the American Secretary of State. The Soviet press made propaganda capital of the apparent failure of Dulles to interest the allies in his "united action" scheme. Although the policymakers of the Kremlin could look with satisfaction upon the British rebuff to Dulles's efforts, they could not be sure of what the United States would do. The announcement of the New Look strategy and its subsequent public elaboration was intensively studied in Moscow, as was the concept of united action, which was probably as confusing to the Soviets as it was to the British and the French (and to many observers in Washington). No responsible Soviet official could discount the *possibility* of American military intervention in Indochina, nor could anyone determine whether the United States might use atomic weapons against targets in China if the C.P.R. decided to intervene in Indochina as it had in Korea.[8] Finally the Kremlin could not exclude Soviet

[4] Reuters dispatch, 8 April 1954.   [5] *NYT*, 12 April 1954.
[6] *NYT*, 24 April 1954.   [7] *NYHT*, 9 April 1954; *NYT*, 13 April 1954.
[8] Soviet diplomats were alleged to have told French officials that Dulles was bluffing and would not support a policy of intervention that required sending U.S. troops to Indochina (Joseph and Stewart Alsop, "The Dulles Gamble,"

involvement in a war that extended from Indochina throughout East Asia. The New Look implied that the cities and military centers of the Soviet Union would be the targets of the American air force should war between the superpowers occur. As the position of the French garrison at Dien Bien Phu weakened, the sense of crisis in Paris grew and Western diplomatic activity became more intense. Even after the British refused to join in collective action in Indochina—even after the fall of Dien Bien Phu—the possibility of American intervention remained. Dulles, and to some extent Bidault (as long as he held the post of Foreign Minister), would make certain that it remained a possibility.

These realizations must have been the subject of serious discussion and debate among Kremlin policymakers. The Indochina crisis, against the backdrop of the American strategy of massive retaliation, however modified or re-interpreted in early 1954, must have significantly affected Soviet policymakers. One manifestation of the effect was the change in the tenor of Malenkov's speeches we noted earlier.

The period between the spring of 1953, soon after the death of Stalin, and February 1955, when Malenkov was deposed, was often marked by intense competition between two principal factions in the Kremlin: on one hand Malenkov and his supporters, who substantially controlled the apparatus of the state, and on the other hand Khrushchev and his supporters, controlling the party apparatus. In early August 1953, Malenkov launched the "New Course," a domestic program that scheduled tax reductions and price cuts and, most importantly, provided for a shift in emphasis from heavy industry to light industry, food processing, and increased production of consumer goods. The New Course was opposed by Marshals Bulganin and Zhukov and many army leaders who favored continued emphasis on the development of heavy industry. Khrushchev, elected first secretary of the CPSU in September 1953, also opposed the New Course; whether because he felt it was bad policy or because he op-

---

NYHT, 9 April 1954). Even if this were true, it seems to me that the Soviet policymakers had to regard the probability of U.S. intervention as positive and finite—low, perhaps, but finite. As for the factor of American reactions, the Malenkov regime might have been wary of even a low probability. The Alsops also reported that Dulles had warned Molotov at Berlin that the U.S. would fight, albeit reluctantly, to prevent the communization of Indochina. While the Soviets might have regarded the probability of U.S. intervention to save Dien Bien Phu as low, in my view they would have assigned higher probability to U.S. intervention as a response to the threatened loss of Hanoi, and still higher probability to the U.S. response to the destruction of the French expeditionary force or the loss of Vietnam to the Vietminh. It also seems to me that the Soviets would have calculated that, should the Geneva Conference fail to bring peace to Indochina, the mere fact of the war's continuing would sharply increase the probability of direct U.S. (and C.P.R.) involvement.

posed all of Malenkov's programs is a matter of dispute.[9] In any case, by fall of 1953 another domestic sector required attention: agriculture. After discussions in January and February 1954, Khrushchev, in early March, announced his "virgin-soil program" for increasing production in the agricultural sector, and implementation of this program would require increased production of agricultural machinery, products of heavy industry. Thus the virgin-soil program interfered to a considerable degree with Malenkov's New Course.

Khrushchev gradually consolidated his position in the CPSU by appointing his supporters to a number of key party secretaryships. The CPSU Central Committee secretariat and other party secretariats were enlarged and the new appointees invariably were supporters of the first secretary. Apparently Khrushchev's influence also extended into the conduct of Soviet foreign affairs. Paloczi-Horvath wrote that by July 1954 many career diplomats and associates of Molotov had been replaced by Khrushchevites.[10] By the fall of 1954 Malenkov's New Course was going rather badly, and Khrushchev on several occasions openly declared that heavy industry would continue to have top priority. On 8 February 1955 the Supreme Soviet accepted Malenkov's resignation as chairman of the Council of Ministers and elected Khrushchev and Marshal Bulganin to replace him.

The major policy dispute between the factions, as I have stated, was over the future course of Soviet economic development: whether heavy industry would continue to receive first priority in the allocation of resources or whether the New Course, and with it light industry, should claim a greater proportion of resources than before. The positions of protagonists and antagonists were largely determined by their attitudes toward a fundamental question: What was the probability of the Soviet Union's becoming involved in a war with the capitalist states? This question was the subject of intensive high-level debate throughout the period covered by this study. Malenkov's policy of détente generally, and his speech of 12 March in particular, represented the view that the probability of war with the United States was slight because of the satisfactory current (and future) level of Soviet nuclear capability. Hence Malenkov could declare that a world war would mean the destruction of civilization. Implicit in this assessment was the belief that the two superpowers mutually deterred each other.[11] In a speech at Erevan, Armenia

[9] For more detailed accounts, see Wolfgang Leonhard, *The Kremlin since Stalin* (New York: Praeger, 1962); George Paloczi-Horvath, *Khrushchev: The Road to Power* (London: Secker & Warburg, 1960); Myron Rush, *The Rise of Khrushchev* (Washington, D.C.: Public Affairs Press, 1958); Edward Crankshaw, *Khrushchev's Russia* (London: Penguin, 1962).

[10] *Khrushchev: The Road to Power*, op. cit., p. 162.

[11] Dinerstein, op. cit., Chapters 3 and 4.

(also on 12 March), Deputy Premier Anastas Mikoyan declared that the "danger of war has receded to a large extent in connection with the fact that we now have not only the atomic but also the hydrogen bomb. . . . Atomic and hydrogen weapons in the hands of the Soviet Union are a means for checking the aggressors and for waging peace."[12]

Khrushchev and many officers of the Soviet armed forces were not as sanguine as Malenkov about the unlikelihood of a major war or the deterrent effectiveness of the Soviet Union's nuclear capability. Marshal Bulganin argued:

> We would commit an irreparable error if we did not strengthen our armed forces. Very many facts indicate that the imperialist forces headed by the U.S. are openly conducting a policy of the preparation of a new war against us. . . .
> The most important thing in military affairs is the uninterrupted perfection of the armed forces. . . .
> We cannot assume that the imperialists expend enormous material and financial resources on armaments only to frighten us.[13]

Khrushchev made a speech on 6 March in which he said "the Communist Party and the Soviet government cannot but realize that there are reactionary forces in the capitalist countries which seek to find a solution to their economic difficulties and the exacerbated contradictions of the imperialist camp by the preparation of a new war."[14]

These views manifested a very different appreciation of the likelihood of war than Malenkov's speech of 12 March. With the announcement of the United States doctrine of massive retaliation and the trend of American policy in Southeast Asia, the pressure upon Malenkov to modify his strategic outlook must have intensified. Indeed, in his address of 26 April the Premier was less optimistic about the chances of peace, and he implied that an American war against the Soviet Union might not be prevented by the Soviet deterrent capability. Although significant, this forced reappraisal did not end the debate. After April, however, the Soviet press contained many editorials, speeches, and commentaries that stressed the aggressive intentions of the United States and the need for increased Soviet military strength and vigilance against a surprise attack.[15]

---

[12] "Speech of A. I. Mikoian," *Kommunist* (Erevan), 12 March 1954, and *Pravda*, 12 March 1954; quoted in Dinerstein, *op. cit.*, p. 71.

[13] "Speech of Comrade N. A. Bulganin at the Meeting of the Electors of the Moscow City Electoral District, March 10, 1954," *Izvestia*, 11 March 1954; quoted in Dinerstein, *op. cit.*, p. 104.

[14] Dinerstein, *op. cit.*, p. 103.

[15] *Ibid.*, pp. 119-128; see also A. L. Horelick and Myron Rush, *Strategic*

Thus it is very likely that the American response to the French debacle in Indochina—particularly the Dulles-Bidault strategy of threatening intervention and creating a Southeast Asia defense organization—had the effect of weakening Malenkov's position. Uncertain of America's intentions, a reaction that Dulles sedulously cultivated, the Kremlin policymakers revised their estimates of the probability of war and moved closer to the Khrushchev-Bulganin policies for the Soviet response to an increase, rather than decrease, in international tensions. The Indochina policy of the Eisenhower administration, coupled with the ostensible adoption of the New Look, was a strong argument against Malenkov's New Course.

[I I]

There appears to have been no disagreement between the Malenkov and Khrushchev factions on the desirability of coming to Geneva. Both factions could agree that the conference gave them an opportunity to sponsor their Chinese ally, who would be appearing at a high-level multilateral conference for the first time since the establishment of the C.P.R. in 1949. The mere presence of a C.P.R. delegation, the Soviets asserted, was an admission of its role as a "great power."[16] And perhaps more formal concessions could be extracted from the West, particularly the United States, at the conference. The cooperation of the Soviet Union with China at Geneva and the Soviets' championing the rights of the C.P.R. would enhance Sino-Soviet solidarity. Also, Geneva offered more direct benefits and opportunities that both factions in the Kremlin sought. The Soviets wished to prevent the rearming of West Germany and the ratification of the EDC treaty; and it was widely believed that they wished to promote disunity among the Western allies. Therefore the Soviets might offer to use their influence with the Chinese and the Vietminh to obtain a cease-fire in Indochina in exchange for a French promise of nonratification of EDC. They might try to demonstrate how America's China policy tended to prolong the war in Southeast Asia, and thereby further divide the allies. They might persuade the French to deal directly with DRVN representatives, thereby securing the Vietminh a measure of recognition, increased prestige, and a means for demoralizing the SVN regime. Malenkov might hope that if peace could be brought to Indochina, this accomplishment would so improve East-West relations that America's allies would conclude there was no need for EDC or German rearmament.

Power and Soviet Foreign Policy (Chicago: University of Chicago Press, 1966), Chapter 2.
[16] *NYT*, 1 April 1954.

Did the Kremlin policymakers want to end the Indochinese War? Did they wish to prevent an extension of that war? An attempt to answer these questions will be made after we have examined Molotov's conduct at Geneva. With respect to the second question, however, we can anticipate Geneva and say that the Malenkov faction probably wished to avoid a widening of the war. The Premier had asserted there was a diminished and diminishing probability of a world war and on this premise had formulated a radically different domestic program, which placed greater emphasis upon light industry. Malenkov, for a variety of reasons, no doubt came to regard the New Course as an end in itself. For one thing, he had committed himself to the program and he had become associated with it in the minds of his supporters and his opponents. For another, the New Course might have been viewed as inherently desirable in terms of what it would do for the Soviet people. In any case, because it had become a defined policy, its formulators and executors would want to avoid a war that could only mean abandonment of the New Course. This was an interesting situation, not uncommon in politics: Malenkov *assumed* there would not be a war and created a domestic program that was based on this assumption. But the program's execution required that Malenkov guarantee the continued validity of his assumption.

Thus, as far as the war in Indochina was concerned, Malenkov probably wished to avoid what we would today call escalation. The marshals of the Red army also may have wished to prevent Russian involvement in a war with the United States, but they objected to the timid stance that seemed to infuse Malenkov's policies. The constant emphasis upon the Soviet desire for peace and the proposed cutbacks in heavy industry were not correct, to their way of thinking, at a time when officials of the Eisenhower administration had just announced the decision to adopt a strategy of massive retaliation.

[III]

Toward the end of 1953 the Indian government decided it could not resist China's "integration" of Tibet into the C.P.R. and it began talks with the now amenable Chinese that were aimed at normalizing relations between the two states. On 29 April an agreement on trade and intercourse between India and the "Tibet region of China" was signed in Peking.[17] The preamble of this agreement recited the principles that were to govern its execution, namely, mutual respect

[17] *Notes, Memoranda and Letters Exchanged and Agreements Signed Between the Governments of India and China, 1954-1959*, White Paper No. 1, pp. 98-101 (New Delhi: Ministry of External Affairs, 1959).

for the other's sovereignty and territorial integrity, nonaggression, noninterference in internal affairs, equality and mutual benefit, and peaceful coexistence. These general principles, usually referred to as the Five Principles of Peaceful Coexistence or *Panch Shila*, later became the hallmark of Sino-Indian relations, and in June, during a recess in the Geneva Conference, Prime Minister Nehru and Premier Chou En-lai agreed that they were applicable to all outstanding problems between the two countries.[18] The improvement in relations between India and China, and its ideological embodiment in the Five Principles, reflected a definite turn in the C.P.R.'s conduct of her foreign relations. During this new phase of Chinese diplomacy, which has been termed the "Bandung phase," after the conference of Afro-Asian states of that name in April 1955, the C.P.R. cultivated its relations with the uncommitted states of Africa and Asia and seemed to have persuaded them that the Peking regime was dedicated to peace in Asia, to cooperation for mutual development, and to the elimination of the remnants of colonialism and imperialism.

The Soviet Union had continually proclaimed the C.P.R. a great power. The publication in mid-1954 of the results of the census of 1952–1953, showing China had a population of more than 650 million, underlined the reality of China's great-power status. Her participation in the Geneva Conference was evidence, in the opinion of many uncommitted states, that, by negotiating with France, Britain, the United States, and the Soviet Union, China had been admitted to "the club," however encumbered this admission was by legalistic reservations of American officials. China, as an Asian power, was the focus of attention of the Afro-Asian states after the Bandung Conference, and for several years Peking's Afro-Asian policy was moderate, equable, and ameliorative. When the Sino-Indian agreement on trade and intercourse was signed in April 1954, the "Bandung spirit" had not yet fully blossomed, but the enunciation of the Five Principles, in any case, was a signal event. Along with Chou En-lai's circumspect and amiable conduct of China's case at Geneva, the proclamation of *Panch Shila* and the improvement in Sino-Indian and Sino-Burmese relations heralded a new phase in C.P.R. diplomacy.

Peking seems to have attached great importance to the Geneva Conference, which was first and foremost the debut of the C.P.R. at a multilateral ministers' meeting. By participating, China achieved prestige and tacit recognition of her great-power status. Secondly, it was a means of demonstrating the style of diplomacy of this "newest" power to Asia and the world. We know now, of course, that Chou's

18 *Docs., 1954*, pp. 278-280.

moderation fitted well with the image of China he wished to cultivate among the Afro-Asian nations, but it was not known how he
would behave at the conference; certainly he and his delegation
aroused great interest and curiosity on their arrival in Geneva. Finally,
there was the rather important subject matter of the conference:
Korea and Indochina. At the very least, Peking was determined to
ensure that no settlement unfavorable to China's interests would be
made, and it is possible Peking believed it could extract concessions
from the Western powers—in exchange for a conciliatory attitude
on Indochina—that might take the form of recognition, admission to
the United Nations, modification of trade embargoes, or neutralization of Taiwan. (Our understanding of the American political scene
in 1954 should convince us how vain were Peking's hopes for such
concessions, if in fact she *had* such hopes.)[19] The course of events
at Geneva and in Indochina might, in China's view, permit Britain
and France to be persuaded of the need to press the United States
for concessions. The sensitivity of the Eisenhower administration to
an official change in America's China policy was no doubt due to the
influence of the right wing of the GOP, but it may also have been
due to some still confidential intelligence that indicated that the
Soviets and the Chinese were determined to obtain concessions as the
price for an Indochina settlement.

An address by Premier Chou En-lai on 28 April was significant:

> The international status and rights of the People's Republic of
> China has been subjected to impermissible discrimination. The
> peaceful development and security of China are being constantly
> threatened. The extreme unreasonableness and extreme unfairness
> of this situation are very obvious. The continued existence of this
> situation obstructs the peaceful settlement of the pressing issues
> of the world, especially those of Asia, and aggravates the tension
> and uneasiness in international relations. It is clear that this situa-
> tion should not prevail any longer. Our conference should mark
> the beginning of change in this situation.[20]

[19] We cannot dismiss the possibility that influential C.P.R. policymakers believed they could win concessions at Geneva. Moreover, it is generally agreed that,
in its Bandung phase, the C.P.R. desired U.N. representation. If a truce were
arranged in Indochina, particularly with China's cooperation, prospects of the
C.P.R.'s admission to the U.N. would be greatly enhanced since Peking would
have shown itself to be "peace loving."

[20] This was the Chinese Premier's first address to the conference. *Documents
relating to the Discussion of Korea and Indo-China at the Geneva Conference*,
Misc. No. 16 (1954), Cmd. 9186 (London: Her Majesty's Stationery Office.
1954), p. 16. It also appears in a special supplement to *People's China*, 16 May
1954.

Chou did not elaborate upon the ways in which the conference might change the situation but he certainly seems to have hoped that changes would be brought about. And he seems to have had more in mind than the tacit recognition that came with attending a great-power conference.

Spokesmen for the C.P.R. were indeed sensitive about its "international status and rights." Having monitored broadcasts from China throughout the spring of 1954, a Hong Kong source noted the continued emphasis they placed upon participation by the C.P.R. in all discussions pertaining to the solution of Asian (and world) problems.[21] No matter what the United States said, the Geneva Conference was a *five*-power conference, Peking declared: and the Soviet Union repeated the same line.[22] The Soviets, no doubt aware of the feelings of their Chinese ally on status, made repeated efforts before the Geneva Conference opened to secure various signs of recognition for the C.P.R. At the end of March, *Pravda* asserted that Dulles had agreed at Berlin to permit the C.P.R. to attend the Geneva Conference on equal footing with the other powers.[23] The next day, State Department officials denied that the United States had accepted China as the fifth great power; the Berlin communiqué, they argued, implied that the Big Four would be the hosts and would invite the other states.[24] The British Foreign Office also rejected the *Pravda* assertion that the Big Four had agreed to accept the C.P.R. as an equal.[25] When Eden, Dulles, and Bidault met in Paris on 23 April, they reaffirmed their policy of treating China as an "invited" power and not as an "inviting" power.[26] This may very well have been done at Dulles's insistence: it was reported that he had warned the British and French the United States would walk out of the conference if the C.P.R. was regarded as an inviting power.[27]

One wonders what the Chinese told the Soviets during the preparations for the conference. In Washington it was rumored that the Soviets were having difficulties with their ally since it had taken so long

[21] *NYT*, 11 April 1954.   [22] *NYT*, 15 March 1954.   [23] *NYT*, 1 April 1954.

[24] *NYT*, 2 April 1954. The State Department issued this statement, which read in part: "Characterization of the Geneva Conference as a conference of the representatives of the United States, France, the United Kingdom, the Chinese People's Republic and the Soviet Union did not correspond either to the letter or the sense of the agreement reached by the four ministers at Berlin on February 18" (*NYT*, 15 April 1954). Reference was made to Dulles's opening statement at the Berlin Conference: "I would like to state here plainly and unequivocally what the Soviet Foreign Minister already knows—the United States will not agree to join in a five power conference with the Chinese Communist aggressors for the purpose of dealing generally with the peace of the world." *FMM*, pp. 27-28.

[25] *NYT*, 2 April 1954.   [26] *NYT*, 24 April 1954.   [27] *NYT*, 23 April 1954.

to arrive at an agreement on preparatory and procedural matters.[28] For example, the Soviets objected to seating arrangements they believed implied inferior status for the Chinese delegation. (It was subsequently agreed to seat the delegates alphabetically around the table.)[29]

Soviet concern for Chinese sensibilities also was manifested by constant consultation between the two participants before and during the Geneva Conference. But we can say no more than that conversations were held; we do not know to what extent the Chinese expressed discontent with the Berlin communiqué or the Soviets' way of representing the C.P.R. in Big Four talks. We do not know to what extent the distinction between invited and inviting powers and the nonrecognition paragraph in the Berlin communiqué injured Chinese pride. We may guess that it did: the comparative dearth of comment in the Chinese press for several weeks after the Berlin Conference confirms this hypothesis to some extent.[30]

Later (in October 1954) the Soviets, on the occasion of the anniversary of the establishment of the C.P.R., agreed to a series of measures that had the effect of making China the sovereign coequal of the Soviet Union.[31] Russian troops were to be withdrawn from the naval base at Port Arthur and the base transferred to the C.P.R. without compensation. The regimes of four Sino-Soviet joint stock companies (nonferrous metals, petroleum, shipbuilding, aircraft construction) were ended and it was agreed that the Soviet shares would be transferred to the C.P.R. A joint declaration on general policy called for the continued cooperation of the two states in strengthening general peace. To this end, the Five Principles of Coexistence were to be strictly observed. The United Nations Charter, the declaration continued, recognized the responsibility the great powers bore for keeping the peace, and the Geneva Conference had emphasized the necessity for the participation of all the great powers in resolving problems that threatened the peace. This Sino-Soviet declaration, after the Geneva Conference, indicated the importance the two Communist allies attached to it.

[28] On 16 March Dulles declared it was his impression that the Soviets were stalling and he surmised that this was due to China's displeasure over the arrangements made at Berlin (*NYT*, 17 March 1954). On the same day the Soviets agreed to a number of pre-conference procedural items, giving the impression (so the *New York Times* said) that whatever delays there had been were a result of normal consultations between the C.P.R. and Soviet governments. *NYT*, 18 March 1954.

[29] *NYT*, 27 April 1954.   [30] It is, however, only a hypothesis.

[31] *NYT*, 12 October 1954.

[IV]

Apart from the C.P.R.'s international status, which Peking hoped the Geneva Conference would enhance, the security of China continued to be a pressing problem. The C.P.R. was not yet five years old and a rival Chinese regime, under Chiang Kai-shek on Taiwan, challenged the legitimacy of the Peking government—and the United States supported Chiang's claims and aspirations. Moreover, after late March 1954, the possibility of American intervention in the Indochinese War could not be discounted. The Vietminh were doing quite well without the help of Chinese volunteers, but Secretary Dulles's Overseas Press Club address had implied that the United States might have to intervene in Indochina to prevent its communization, even in the absence of overt Chinese intervention. Peking must then make the difficult decision of how it should respond to this new American presence in Asia. Finally, there was the multiple problem of America's New Look, the significance of massive retaliation, and the implications of this strategic theory for China in the context of the Vietminh successes in Indochina.

There was no significant change in one of these problems—that is, the existence and verbal belligerency of the Nationalist Chinese on Taiwan—in the two-month period before the Geneva Conference opened. However, the possibility of American intervention in Indochina and the difficult task of understanding the meaning of the massive retaliation strategy were undoubtedly uppermost in the minds of Peking's policymakers. In 1954 the mainland China press, while proclaiming the good will of the C.P.R. for the peoples of the world and Peking's desire for peaceful coexistence, maintained an attitude of hostility toward the United States.[32] This is not wholly incomprehensible, of course; the American policy of nonrecognition of the C.P.R., coupled with its recognition of the Taipei regime, was a constant challenge to the right of the C.P.R. to exist. Then, after late March, the possibility of American intervention in Indochina provoked the Chinese press to more militant attacks. The United States was accused of trying to sabotage the Geneva Conference, of creating a tense atmosphere unfavorable to negotiation. "United action," said the *People's Daily*, was meant "to create a tense situation . . . in preparation for extending the Indochina war."[33]

Dulles, another account said, had fabricated the charge of Chinese participation in the Indochina War in order to create a pretext for further American intervention.[34] The *New China News Agency* issued

[32] *NYT*, 11 April 1954.
[34] *NYT*, 9 April 1954.

[33] *People's Daily*, 3 April 1954, p. 1.

a vague warning in early April when it declared that "united action" could mean a "new Korea."[35] Later in the month Peking rather solemnly vowed: "We advocate peace and oppose war. But we certainly will not take it lying down if anyone else's armed aggression is directed against us." The statement also accused the United States of speeding plans to take a direct part in the war.[36] Other than the hint that the Indochinese War might become another Korea-type war, no firm warning was uttered and there was no commitment to action; it was still too early for that. The United States had not intervened or committed a belligerent act. The Chinese—as well as the British—could afford to wait for the Geneva Conference to produce some results. At the same time the Chinese, no less than the British, were uncertain of the intentions of the Eisenhower administration. They must have realized that a Vietminh victory, which would lead to the establishment of a DRVN that comprised all Vietnam (a noteworthy Communist success that Chinese ordnance and Chinese training and technical cadres would have helped achieve), might lead to the dispatch of American troops to Indochina, with or without British assistance. How would Peking have responded to this eventuality? The Chinese never had to make such a decision but surely they discussed it. And in their thinking and in their debates about the likelihood of a new war with the United States, the Chinese had to weigh another factor: massive retaliation and the New Look.

We know that in London, Moscow, and Washington in late 1953 and most of 1954 policymakers and their military advisors were groping toward an understanding of the role of nuclear weapons in the defense postures of their respective nations. In Peking, the leaders of the C.P.R. were wrestling with similar problems, in their case somewhat magnified because they did not possess atomic weapons and would have to rely upon the Soviet nuclear "umbrella." Alice Langley Hsieh, in her study of China's strategy, suggested that 1954 saw an important development: it was in 1954 that the C.P.R.'s policymakers began to realize the implications of nuclear warfare.[37] This process was undoubtedly affected by whatever information the leaders obtained of the strategic debate that was raging in the Kremlin in the spring of 1954.[38] There was remarkably little commentary about this in the Chinese press, however, and almost nothing that

[35] *NYT*, 3 April 1954.   [36] *NYT*, 22 April 1954.
[37] A. L. Hsieh, *Communist China's Strategy in the Nuclear Era* (Englewood Cliffs, N.J.: Prentice-Hall, 1962), p. 15.
[38] We may guess that whatever decisions the Chinese made during 1954 were, to some extent, affected as well by the Malenkov-Khruschchev rivalry, which had political, strategic, and ideological implications of the greatest import.

offers the analyst an insight into Chinese thinking on the subject. The hydrogen bomb tests were mentioned briefly. The radioactive contamination of the Japanese fishing vessel *Fortunate Dragon*,[39] an unusual propaganda opportunity, was passed over. And, until late March there was virtually no comment on Dulles's massive-retaliation speech, delivered in January. (The Soviets themselves did not offer detailed remarks on that speech until about the same time.)[40] A *People's Daily* editorial on 3 April accused American leaders of increasing world tensions:

> Among the recent activities of the political leaders of the United States are the publicizing of their so-called "new look" military policy, the boosting of the atomic threat, the mad spreading of war hysteria, the hydrogen bomb experiments on the Marshall Islands in the Pacific, the naval manoeuvres in Indochina, and the air manoeuvres in South Korea.[41]

The movement of two American aircraft carriers into the South China Sea in early April provoked a vigorous response as the *People's Daily* of 21 April accused the United States of speeding its plans for extending the Indochina War.[42] But there was no mention of an atomic strike against China.

Dr. Hsieh concluded, having surveyed the Chinese press at the time, that complete silence had been maintained on the possibility of a nuclear retaliatory strike against China should the C.P.R. become involved in the Indochinese War.[43] We do not know whether this omission in the Chinese news releases reflected a policy of caution purposely adopted after an analysis of the possibility of a nuclear strike by the United States against China or whether the news silence was based upon a lack of information or understanding. The Chinese press observed and commented upon the deployment of American air forces in the Pacific and suggested that this was a deliberate effort to "encircle" the C.P.R. and the Soviet Union with a "global air force 'ring.'" After her analysis of the Chinese press releases, Dr. Hsieh stated:

[39] The crew of this vessel was fishing in Marshall Islands waters, about 80 miles from Bikini (and 20 miles outside the restricted zone proclaimed by the U.S. government), when a thermonuclear device was detonated on the morning of 1 March. Three hours later the crew, the vessel, and the catch were contaminated by radioactive fallout from the blast. The incident provoked a storm of indignation in Japan and widespread apprehension.

[40] Dinerstein, *op. cit.*, pp. 106-107.

[41] "Survey of China Mainland Press," No. 781, 3-5 April 1954 (p. 3), quoted in Hsieh, *op. cit.*, p. 6.

[42] *NYT*, 22 April 1954.   [43] Hsieh, *op. cit.*, p. 5.

In view of the inadequacy of China's air defense and early warning systems vis-à-vis the enhanced United States striking power . . .
the significance of a Chinese re-evaluation of the United States base
structure and air power in the Far East should not be underestimated. It is difficult to determine whether this new concern with
United States air power grew directly out of China's awareness of
a growing United States striking power, or whether it reflected
China's reaction to the Soviet debate on strategy of 1953–54.[44]

Dr. Hsieh also suggested that the Soviets and the Chinese may have
concluded that the United States, at least temporarily, possessed
superior nuclear capability, both in terms of weapons stockpiles and
delivery means.[45] Hence a policy of caution may have been enjoined
upon them.

Except for warnings that an act of aggression against the C.P.R.
would not be taken "lying down," there was no indication of the
manner in which the Chinese would respond to an American dispatch of combat troops to Indochina. The Chinese press and radio,
which condemned United States maneuvers as productive of tension and as widening the war, also condemned "united action" and
the concept of a collective defense organization for Southeast Asia.
These verbal attacks were never incompatible with the C.P.R.'s
propaganda efforts in Asia, however. Their attack on the proposal for
a Southeast Asia "NATO" was in complete accord with official Indian
sentiment—and in fact with the current predispositions of Asian governments that felt military alliances tended to produce rather than
prevent wars.

After the Dulles Overseas Press Club speech, and even after the
arrival of the two American aircraft carriers in the South China Sea,
Peking seems to have made no effort to persuade the Vietminh to ease
its pressure on Dien Bien Phu. In fact, deliveries of Chinese ordnance and other supplies to north and northwestern Tonkin continued at a fairly high level. We may attempt a tentative analysis of
the Chinese leaders' thinking in the week or two preceding the Geneva
conference.

1. The Chinese believed the Eisenhower administration was bluffing. This may have been true, but, like the Russians, Chinese policymakers could not exclude the possibility of American intervention.

2. Peking was alarmed neither by American threats nor the likelihood of American intervention. This may well be true; important
Chinese decision-makers may have believed their own propaganda
disparaging atomic weapons and their effect upon the outcome of

---

[44] *Ibid.*, p. 16.   [45] *Ibid.*, pp. 16-17.

war in Asia. They may have felt that, at any level less than the nuclear level, they were fully capable of meeting United States military action.

3. The probability of American involvement was slight (although some policymakers were apprehensive about massive retaliation), and the fall of Dien Bien Phu would not be the occasion for American intervention. Therefore a Vietminh victory at Dien Bien Phu would be welcome, particularly since it would weaken the French negotiating position at Geneva. Such a victory, however, certainly did not mean the Vietminh would succeed in winning Indochina or force the French to capitulate. Peking, according to this hypothesis, took heed of Dulles's statements that the loss of Dien Bien Phu would be a local defeat and not a strategic defeat and, as such, would not bring about American intervention.

4. Interruption in deliveries of matériel to the Vietminh after the first of April could not have persuaded General Giap to relieve his pressure against Dien Bien Phu. It is possible that by April the Vietminh was equipped to take the fortress without additional deliveries (unless the French substantially reinforced the garrison). If this were so, cessation of shipments to Tonkin would have had little effect upon the tactical military situation around Dien Bien Phu. More importantly, this step would have embarrassed the Chinese. It would very likely have produced an undesirable deterioration in Sino-Vietminh relations; moreover, it might be construed by the United States or France as a sign of timidity and might eventuate in the increased hostility of the Western powers.

In my view, Peking was aware of the risks and might well have imagined what massive retaliation could do to its program of socialist reconstruction. But the American threat had not "matured" by the first of May, let alone by the first of April. The preconditions for involvement had not been fulfilled; the President had not attempted to galvanize public opinion; the Secretary of State's remarks were vague and carefully hedged. The situation did not yet warrant bringing pressure upon the Vietminh. Certainly it did not warrant withholding shipments of supplies to the Dien Bien Phu area. The Chinese, in short, had decided to wait upon the results of the Geneva Conference.

[V]

Of all the relations between allies and adversaries we have touched upon to this point we know least about Sino-Vietminh and Soviet-Vietminh relations. Both the Soviet Union and the C.P.R. provided material assistance for Ho Chi Minh's troops; the C.P.R., additionally, provided military ordnance, political workers, training cadres, and technicians. The deliveries of equipment and the dispatch of Chinese noncombatant "advisors" undoubtedly contributed greatly to the capabilities of the PAVN, enabling it to launch its successful offensives against the French in Tonkin and Laos in late 1953 and in 1954.

Proposals for a settlement of the Indochinese War, made by Ho Chi Minh in his *Expressen* statement of November 1953, were repeated in December. The terms of the proposals were vague, but their acceptance by the French would have been a concession of supreme importance to Ho Chi Minh in his efforts to improve the international legal status of the DRVN. As the Vietminh saw it, direct negotiations between French and DRVN representatives would be a blow to the pretensions of the "puppet" Bao Dai regime and would aid materially in the very important process of legitimating the Vietminh. Recall that on 10 March[46] the Vietminh announced it was disposed to welcome the French conditions for a cease-fire that had been enunciated five days before by Premier Laniel.[47] (By the time the Vietminh indicated it could accept these conditions, Giap had deployed his forces around Dien Bien Phu and would begin his attack three days later.) Determining the location of the no-man's-land perimeter and the size and location of the Vietminh regroupment zone in central Vietnam would require Franco-Vietminh negotiations, and certainly Premier Ho attached importance to such negotiations.

Was Ho willing to settle for less than the whole of Vietnam in exchange for direct negotiations with the French? He would certainly favor accomplishing his objectives by diplomatic rather than military means, if he could; and if the French were willing to treat with him, and even perhaps legitimate his regime, this would constitute a signal victory over the rival Bao Dai regime. But these negotiations would not necessarily lead to the unification of Vietnam under the banner of the DRVN. The DRVN might be willing to remain in the French Union provided it was recognized as a sovereign state in full control of its domestic and foreign relations. It might also be willing to maintain French commercial and cultural arrangements. But most assuredly the Vietminh goal in any negotiations would be the elimination of the Bao Dai regime and consolidation of the DRVN. Thus direct negotiations with the French offered Ho a

---

[46] L&D, p. 65.

[47] These conditions were (1) evacuation of Vietminh forces from Cambodia and Laos, (2) establishment of a no-man's-land perimeter around the Red River delta, and (3) evacuation of Vietminh regulars from the Red River delta region. *JO*, 6 March 1954, pp. 713-715.

measure of legitimacy that correspondingly made the Bao Dai regime less legitimate. In addition, direct negotiations offered the possibility of French elimination of Bao Dai and even French suppression of other nationalist movements. This is not to say the French (at least the Laniel government) would agree to Vietminh demands, but they *might*. Finally, even if direct negotiations with the French did not produce the optimum results, they must place the Vietminh in such a position that it could achieve its aims in the months—at most one or two years—that followed any settlement.

The alternative to negotiations was, of course, continuation of the offensive against the French Union forces. This required the will, which the Vietminh had, and the means to do so. But Generals Ely and Navarre, among others, spoke of the heavy casualties the PAVN suffered in its assaults upon Dien Bien Phu and the probability that offensives during the current fighting season would be curtailed because of these casualties;[48] and the monsoon season would soon begin. Hence it was estimated that there would be little significant military action after Dien Bien Phu. This estimate was soon shown to be erroneous: the Vietminh was willing to commit its forces, however depleted, in a major offensive against the Red River delta. The Chinese, and to a lesser extent the Soviets, continued to provide supplies and equipment to the DRVN throughout May and June. Thus the PAVN would have the capability of sustaining the impetus of its offensive action. If the French would neither negotiate with the Vietminh nor make the concessions it demanded, the French must risk the loss of most of Tonkin.

Ho Chi Minh could reasonably calculate that a French defeat at Dien Bien Phu and a series of French defeats in the Red River delta would destroy their will to fight. Vietnam would then be his, perhaps with Laos and Cambodia associated with the DRVN. Could he obtain a decision in the delta? Not, it was obvious, before talks had begun and a settlement had been explored at Geneva. In the meantime, military pressure must be continued, and this would weaken the French bargaining position at Geneva.

What Ho Chi Minh could do, however, and what he could obtain, either by force or by diplomacy, was very much dependent upon what the great powers, including his Soviet and Chinese allies, would allow. This is not to deny that he could determine to go on fighting even though threatened with American intervention or the suspension of Soviet and Chinese aid. But he must have had to concern himself with the possibility of American intervention—and with an additional unknown, the sending of Chinese troops into Indochina

[48] L&D, pp. 156-157.

if the Americans intervened. Peking had warned that "united action" meant another Korea, and the intrusion of, say, half a million Chinese troops would have been a very unwelcome eventuality for Ho Chi Minh. Moreover, however unlikely the suspension of aid by its social-ist allies, there was no reason to believe that the DRVN, as a small state, would not be subject to the same pressures and promises to which small states have always been subjected in their relations with their great-power allies.[49] In the context of a great-power con-ference, the pressures upon the DRVN representatives could be-come irresistible if the alternative was isolation.[50]

[49] A. B. Fox, *The Power of Small States* (Chicago: University of Chicago Press, 1959).

[50] The Soviets had been willing to try various forms of persuasion on their East European allies; why should they not also persuade, or attempt to persuade, the Vietminh to accept their counsels? As I think I have indicated, the DRVN could not be persuaded to accept an obviously unreasonable settlement, but, were the Soviets and the Chinese able to secure a reasonable settlement—that is, one that the Soviets and Chinese themselves regarded as reasonable—Vietminh unwilling-ness to accept that settlement would be viewed as sheer intransigence. The DRVN would face the unhappy situation of appearing to reject a solution the Western powers felt was favorable to the Communists and the C.P.R. and U.S.S.R. deemed acceptable. Thus their isolation was a possibility, not only from their Communist allies but from the sympathetic regimes of Asia that, in principle, supported the Vietminh's aspirations but wanted the Indochinese War brought to an end.

PART II

The Geneva Conference and World Politics

Chapter 9

THE KOREAN CONFERENCE

[I]

The State Department delivered invitations for the Korean phase of the Geneva Conference to its United Nations allies on 26 February.[1] The Soviet Union was to invite the Chinese People's Republic and North Korea, and presumably had done this by mid-March at the latest. But agreement upon a number of other arrangements was delayed. By mid-March, the American ambassador in Moscow, Charles E. Bohlen, had had little success in obtaining Soviet agreement upon the composition of the conference secretariat, financial arrangements for the conference, and the choice of the building at Geneva. On 16 March the State Department hypothesized that the Russians were delaying the settlement of these matters because their Chinese ally was not entirely happy with the form of the Berlin communiqué.[2] Deputy Foreign Minister V. V. Kuznetzov, as if seeking to disprove the State Department's hypothesis, the very next day informed Bohlen that the Soviet Union agreed to hold the conference in the Palais des Nations. This agreement, it was suggested in a Tass news release, had been made after normal consultations with China.[3]

By 24 April a committee on arrangements had settled most of the procedural problems. Plenary sessions of the conference were to be scheduled daily, except Sunday, from 3 p.m. to 7 p.m. The sessions would be closed to the press and the public, but each delegation was to decide for itself what matters it wanted to release to the press. The official languages of the conference were to be English, French, Russian, Chinese, and Korean.[4] The Soviet Union representative had at first opposed making Korean an official language, presumably because, without it, the roster of languages would imply that the conference was a meeting of the "Big Five." The Soviets eventually came around on this point, but they were more adamant about the selection of a chairman for the Korean phase of the conference.

It is customary to rotate the chairmanship among the foreign-

[1] *DSB*, 8 March 1954, p. 347.

[2] *NYT*, 17 March 1954. The U.N. General Assembly had offered to provide a meeting place for an East Asian conference in August 1953 but Dag Hammarskjöld said he would do nothing until he received a formal request for such a conference from the governments of the Big Four.

[3] *NYT*, 18 March 1954.

[4] *NYT*, 25 April 1954.

minister participants of an international conference, but the United States refused to allow Chou En-lai or North Korea's Marshal Nam Il to chair the Geneva meetings. It had been suggested that a Swiss citizen, perhaps the President of the Swiss Federal Council, be asked to preside, but the Swiss government informed the committee that this would constitute intervention in a procedural dispute and refused to allow its President to participate.[5] This difficulty, and a dispute over seating arrangements, were resolved by an agreement between Eden and Molotov in a meeting between the two ministers on Monday morning, 26 April. The seating of delegations would be alphabetical, according to the English spelling of the names of the countries.[6] The chairmanship was to be handled in this fashion: for the Korean phase of the conference, Prince Wan Waithayakon of Thailand would preside at the first session, Molotov at the second session, and Eden at the third session, after which the chair would be rotated among these three men; for the Indochinese phase, Eden and Molotov would assume the duties of chairman on alternate days. The American delegation accepted this arrangement, which denied the prestige of the chairman's role to the C.P.R. and afforded the United States government a not unwelcome measure of detachment from proceedings in which, in March and April, it had continually voiced its lack of confidence.[7]

When the Korean phase of the conference officially convened, on Monday, 26 April, there was as yet no agreement upon which countries would be represented when the Indochina question was taken up; it was not even clear how or when this question would be placed on the agenda. It will be recalled that a disagreement arose in late March and early April over the conference status of the C.P.R., that the Berlin communiqué had been silent on the procedure for inviting the C.P.R. "and other interested states,"[8] and that Dulles had informed

[5] *Ibid.*

[6] *NYT*, 27 April 1954.

[7] The editors of the *Economist* wrote: "[The] episode of the chairmanship, which must have involved Mr. Molotov in some delicate explanations to the Chinese of his failure to press their claims to formal recognition as one of the 'Big 5,' may be taken as an indication that the communists do not want to wreck the Conference. The question remains, however, whether they really want to reach settlements in Korea and Indochina, or only to maintain the Conference as a forum for further ventilation of their demands in other directions." *Econ.*, 1 May 1954, p. 359.

[8] *FMM*, pp. 217-218; State Department Press Release, No. 84, 19 February 1954. The "communiqué formula" for the Korean Conference participants was as follows: The ministers proposed that a conference of representatives of the U.S., France, the United Kingdom, the U.S.S.R., the C.P.R., the Republic of Korea, the People's Democratic Republic of Korea, and other countries whose armed forces participated in the hostilities in Korea and who desired to attend "shall meet in Geneva on April 26 for the purpose of reaching a peaceful settlement of the Korean question."

Eden and Bidault that the United States delegation would walk out if China were accorded the status of an "inviting" power.[9] Yet even the status question was overshadowed during the first week of the conference by another procedural question: what "interested states" were to be invited to participate in the Indochinese phase?

There seems to have been early agreement among the Big Four that the Vietminh ought to be invited to participate in some way. (The *New York Times* correspondent in Geneva reported on 27 April that the United States wanted a "small Indochina Conference" with the Big Four, China, the three Associated States, *and* the Vietminh.)[10] Molotov had suggested that the conference include France, Britain, the United States, the Soviet Union, the C.P.R., Laos, Cambodia, Burma, Thailand, India, Pakistan, Indonesia, Australia, and both the SVN and the DRVN. Bidault wanted to exclude India and Indonesia but seems to have made no express reference to the Vietminh's participation. It was clear that the SVN would oppose sending an invitation to the Vietminh, but even the SVN's participation was in doubt. In late April the Vietnamese Foreign Minister, Nguyen Quoc Dinh, had told Bidault it was not certain that the SVN would send a delegation to Geneva. It is significant that very early in the conference both the United States and France apparently were willing to have a DRVN presence at Geneva, in some vague status on the fringes of the main diplomatic arena. The American position seems to have been that if France wished to invite the Vietminh, the United States would acquiesce.

In any case, resolution of the question was not easy. Dulles, Eden, and Bidault had met late in the afternoon of the 26th but had not reached specific conclusions on the composition of the Indochina Conference. On Tuesday Molotov and Bidault discussed this question (together with the evacuation of French and Vietnamese wounded from Dien Bien Phu, the battle for which was still in progress),[11] and it was at this meeting that Molotov suggested that the Colombo powers be invited to attend. On Wednesday morning Molotov urged Vietminh participation; and on the same day, subsequent to a warning from Bao Dai that the SVN would not participate in the confer-

[9] *NYT*, 23 April 1954.
[10] *NYT*, 28 April 1954.
[11] *Ibid.* The Big Four ministers were to meet Monday evening (26 April) but Molotov did not appear; instead, he conferred privately with Premier Chou En-lai and Marshal Nam Il. Could a procedural meeting of the Big Four foreign ministers, however informal, have been resented by the Chinese because they had been accorded a status different from that of the other great powers? Molotov may have understood this and hence refused to attend the Monday night meeting, or perhaps Chou reminded him of his obligation to support the great power aspirations of his Chinese ally.

ence if the Vietminh were invited, Marc Jacquet, French Secretary of State for the Associated States, flew to Cannes to meet with the Emperor. Jacquet was joined by Bidault's cabinet secretary, Pierre Falaize, and Donald Heath, United States ambassador to the SVN.[12] That same Wednesday, Molotov and Bidault met once again and this time reached an agreement: Russia and France would recommend participation by the Big Four, the C.P.R., and the three Associated States to their allies. Earlier, Molotov had asked simply for equal representation of the Vietminh, and Bidault then told him he must give the request some thought. Actually, Bidault's hesitancy seems to have been due not so much to his own opposition to the presence of a Vietminh delegation at the conference as to Bao Dai's opposition.[13] As we shall see, the French Foreign Minister would refuse to deal directly with any DRVN delegates, but apparently he had no reservations about the "mere presence" of those delegates in the Palais des Nations.

In his conversation with Jacquet on the 28th, Bao Dai averred that he still did not know whether he would agree to send a delegation to the conference. After Heath and Falaize pressed the Emperor, Bao Dai insisted upon receiving a letter of invitation from Britain, France, and the United States. He also insisted upon preliminary consultations with representatives of the Big Three and a guarantee that the participation of the Vietminh would not constitute recognition of the DRVN. In the meantime he would order his Minister of Foreign Affairs, Nguyen Quoc Dinh, and two other delegates (including Tran Van Do) to Saint-Julien-en-Genevois on the French-Swiss frontier. The ministers of the Big Three acquiesced, dispatched a formal tripartite letter of invitation to Bao Dai, and on the evening of 30 April the three-man SVN delegation crossed the Swiss frontier and arrived in Geneva, on Saturday, 1 May. On Sunday, Jean Chauvel, French ambassador to Switzerland and a member of the French delegation, informed Andrei Gromyko, the Soviet Deputy Foreign Minister, that the United States, Britain, France, and the SVN agreed to the participation of the Vietminh, but such participation implied no recognition of the DRVN.[14] Official invitations were then dispatched, on Monday, 3 May, to the SVN, the DRVN, Laos, and Cambodia;[15] and on 4 May the Vietminh delegation, up to that time biding its time in the Russian sector of Berlin, arrived in Geneva.

[12] NYT, 29 April 1954.
[13] L&D, p. 122, which is based upon interviews with Nguyen Quoc Dinh and Prince Buu Loc.
[14] L&D, pp. 122-123; NYT, 30 April, 1 May 1954.
[15] On 6 May the Chinese indicated that they would press for the participation of the Pathet Lao and Khmer Issarak, the insurgent "resistance governments" in Laos and Cambodia. This matter will be taken up in Chapters 11 and 12.

[II]

During the week of 25 April, while the Big Four ministers and their staffs sought to resolve the problem of the composition of the Indochina Conference, plenary sessions of the Korea Conference met daily. Participants in the Korean phase of negotiations included the delegations of the Big Four, the C.P.R., North and South Korea, and twelve other states[16] that had fought in Korea under the United Nations command. By the end of the first week of the conference the major proposals for the unification of Korea had been tabled. On 1 May a committee of representatives from North and South Korea, Britain, France, China, the Soviet Union, and the United States was set up with the task of attempting a reconciliation of the unification proposals in private sessions.[17]

The difficulties were indeed formidable. The Communists could be expected to oppose all-Korean elections, proposed by the Australian Minister of External Affairs, which would have the effect of winning for the incumbent North Korean regime—at the very most—a minority role (the north had only about a third of the total Korean population). Even if the people of North Korea returned Communist deputies in the prospective U.N.-supervised elections (which was by no means certain), these deputies probably could exert little effect upon the policies of an all-Korean government. On the other hand, the proposals of the North Korean delegate, Marshal Nam Il, were unacceptable to the states that had fought in Korea under the aegis of the United Nations. Nam Il's proposed all-Korean electoral commission would guarantee the Communists of North Korea weight equal to that of South Korea in the important task of drafting an election law and implementing elections. As Canada's Lester B. Pearson, Secretary of State for External Affairs, said on 4 May, the composition of the commission Nam Il wanted would give the North Korean Communists "a veto over the activities and decisions of that Commission. . . . It means that the all-Korean Commission would operate as the Communist members wished, or not at all."[18] The Western and the South Korean delegates were determined to see that the elections were observed and controlled by the United Nations, although the improbability of Communist acceptance of supervision, by whatever means *acceptable to the West*, was appreciated by most par-

[16] Australia, Belgium, Canada, Colombia, Ethiopia, Greece, Luxembourg, The Netherlands, New Zealand, the Philippines, Thailand, and Turkey.

[17] *NYT*, 2 May 1954.

[18] *Documents relating to the Discussion of Korea and Indo-China at the Geneva Conference*, Misc. No. 16 (1954), Command Doc. 9186 (London: Her Majesty's Stationery Office, 1954), p. 34.

ticipants at Geneva.[19] This, no doubt, was *one* reason Secretary of State Dulles left the conference on Monday, 3 May, assigning to Under Secretary of State Walter Bedell Smith the task of heading the American delegation.

The various East-West proposals for the unification of Korea were remarkably similar to the proposals for the reunification of Germany that had been tabled by the Big Four at Berlin. And, as had happened at Berlin, the Korean Conference would fail to bring about the merger of the Communist and non-Communist parts of divided Korea.

The positions of the Korean negotiators did not change appreciably throughout May. Eden, Bidault, and Belgium's Minister of Foreign Affairs, Paul Henri Spaak, emphasized the need for U.N. supervision of all-Korean elections, which must, moreover, take into account the distribution of population in North and South Korea. Molotov argued that the U.N. had deprived itself of standing to supervise elections by its "illegal" intervention in Korean affairs in 1950; Nam Il's proposal for an all-Korean commission, Molotov stated, would permit the Koreans to settle Korean affairs without external interference. Chou En-lai agreed, and likewise dismissed the proposal for supervision of general elections by the U.N.[20] Matters remained deadlocked when the formal Korean Conference was recessed on 14 May.

The delegations were by this time deeply involved in considering issues relating to the settlement of the Indochinese War. The first plenary session on Indochina had, in fact, convened on Saturday, 8 May, after which the two conferences ran concurrently but separately. The Korean Conference definitely took second place after the Indochina Conference began, both in terms of international press coverage and in terms of the significance of developments in and beyond Geneva. Plenary sessions on Korea were resumed on 22 May, and continued for about another month, but the Korean Conference had reached the same kind of impasse the Big Four had reached in Berlin in February. At the fourteenth plenary session, on 11 June, Eden, increasingly impatient with the attitude of the Soviet and Chinese delegations at both the Korean and Indochina Conferences, summed up the sentiment of the allied delegations:

It has also been said here that the United Nations have lost their moral authority and their competence to deal with the Korean problem impartially. The Delegation of the United Kingdom re-

[19] The Communist delegations were not opposed to supervision *per se.* Nam Il had, in effect, proposed elections that would be supervised by Koreans on an all-Korean commission in which North and South Korea would be equally represented.
[20] Cmd. 9186, p. 52.

jects this contention. We can never agree that, by taking up arms to fulfill their obligation and resist aggression, the United Nations have thereby forfeited their rights and duties as the supreme international organization. On the contrary, we believe that they have strengthened their authority.[21]

A. D. McIntosh, acting head of the New Zealand delegation, asserted that it would be wrong to disguise the fact that the conference was divided on the central issues of a settlement. Eden, also, seemed to imply that the conference was irrevocably deadlocked when he declared "there must be some sign that an agreement is possible." Britain, he said, would stand firmly upon the principles of free elections and the authority of the U.N.; if the differences over these two main issues could not be resolved,

> we shall have to admit that this Conference has not been able to complete its task. It is our view . . . that it would then be right to report back to that organization [the U.N.] upon the position we have reached. This would ensure that, while the existing military armistice agreement in any event remained in force, the search for political settlement in Korea could be resumed whenever the right moment came.[22]

The fifteenth plenary session, on 15 June, was the last meeting on the Korean question at Geneva. The speeches of Molotov, Chou, and Nam Il (and the speeches of Eden and others at the preceding session) showed that no immediate reconciliation of views was possible. Molotov had submitted a proposal for adoption by the conference: Pending final settlement of the Korean problem, no action would be taken by the conference participants that might constitute a threat to the maintenance of peace in Korea.[23] Premier Chou En-lai, in addition, proposed that the participants agree to continue their efforts toward achieving a peaceful settlement in Korea. Bedell Smith stated that the Korean armistice agreement (paragraph 62), which had been approved by the General Assembly on 28 August 1953, contained more formal and exact terms for the maintenance of peace in Korea than did Molotov's proposal.[24]

Prince Wan of Thailand then read the text of a "declaration of the sixteen" that was, in effect, a *final* and official statement of the non-Communist delegations at the conference. The declaration asserted that the signatories to the Armistice had made a number of proposals for bringing about the unification of Korea and that these proposals were to be understood as having been offered within the framework

[21] *Ibid.*, p. 87.
[23] *Ibid.*, pp. 90-91.
[22] *Ibid.*, p. 89.
[24] *Ibid.*, p. 96.

of two fundamental principles (referred to by Eden at the preceding session). (1) The U.N. was empowered to take collective action to repel aggression, to restore peace, and to extend its good offices in seeking a peaceful settlement in Korea; (2) genuinely free all-Korean elections should be held, under U.N. supervision, for certifying representatives to a national assembly in which representation would be in direct proportion to the population in Korea. But the Communists, the declaration continued, repudiated the authority and competence of the United Nations and insisted upon election procedures "which would make genuinely free elections impossible. . . . Plainly, they have shown their intention to maintain communist control over North Korea." The declaration concluded that further consideration of the Korean question therefore would serve no useful purpose for the present.[25]

Nam Il accused the sixteen nations of rejecting his government's proposals without justification and of breaking off negotiations. Prince Wan retorted that the sixteen would continue to work for the peaceful unification of Korea on the basis of the two fundamental principles of the declaration. Premier Chou En-lai said that he regretted the rejection of his proposal relating to future efforts by the participants of the conference toward unifying Korea. There was, he argued, no express provision that recorded the desire of the conferees to achieve a peaceful settlement. Eden, who chaired this last session, suggested that all the proposals made on that day, together with the interpretive and critical statements, be made a part of the conference record. There appears to have been no objection to this suggestion,[26] and the chairman brought the meeting to a close at 8:40 p.m. Thus the Korean Conference, for all practical purposes, ended in failure.

[III]

The deadlock ending of the Korean Conference seemed to confirm the opinion of many American policymakers of the futility of negotiating with the Communists. Well before the Geneva Conference opened, the official "line" in Washington, as we have said, depreciated the significance of the conference and expressed a lack of faith in the ability of its prospective participants to achieve any positive results. Even by the middle of May, many of the United States' allies had come to conclusions similar to the earlier pessimistic statements that had emanated from Washington, at least as far as Korea was concerned. Dulles, who was in Washington after 3 May, reported

[25] *Ibid.*, pp. 100-102.
[26] *Ibid.*, pp. 98-100.

that unification of Korea had not been accomplished; also, he expressed doubt whether the unification of Indochina, under conditions of peace and freedom, was possible. But, he added, "we never thought there was a good chance of accomplishing these results."[27]

By mid-June, the Indochina Conference had reached an impasse. Plenary and restricted high-level political sessions had been suspended while the French National Assembly dismissed one government and found another. The British by this time were pessimistic that Geneva would accomplish anything at all, and the day after the Korean meetings ended Eden announced that he and Prime Minister Churchill would travel to Washington within two weeks for talks with President Eisenhower and other American officials. Nevertheless, the state of affairs at Geneva had not fully confirmed the opinions of the anti-Geneva circles in Washington. The conference was not yet over, and the British, whatever they may have expected from the negotiations over Korea and Indochina, had at least *negotiated*. They had made their contribution to good Commonwealth relations; they had, in effect, "tested" the Russians and the Chinese; and probably they felt they had gathered some useful diplomatic intelligence. Nevertheless, the fact of deadlock could not be ignored.

Even before the first Korean plenary session convened, minor differences among the delegations of the U.N. allies over the proper approach to elections in Korea had been apparent, which tended to emphasize the impression of allied disunity at the time the Geneva Conference began. Within two weeks, however, the United States had come around to the Australian-Canadian-British view that elections should be held throughout Korea, not merely in the north. President Rhee himself acquiesced in this approach after receiving various assurances. Thus the appearance of disunity among the non-Communist delegations was transformed into real unity by the end of May. If the Communists sought to divide the allies or attempted to make capital of differences among them, they did not succeed in doing so at the Korean Conference.

Was there any alternative to the termination of the Korean Conference on 15 June? Premier Chou En-lai seems to have believed that discussion must continue; the C.P.R. delegation, he said, "had brought with it the spirit of negotiation and conciliation to participate for the first time in this [the Geneva] international Conference."[28] Both Chou and Nam Il accused the United States of obstructing Korean unification. Yet it is difficult to see what any additional meetings could or would have accomplished as Chou and Molotov persisted in impugning the authority of the United Nations to involve

[27] *DSB*, 24 May 1954, p. 781 (press release dated 11 May 1954).
[28] Cmd. 9186, p. 100.

itself in any settlement. Chou had said: "The illegal resolutions of the United Nations on the Korean question and the inability of the United Nations to deal with the Korean question impartially *are inseparable from the fact that the People's Republic of China has been deprived of its right to join the United Nations.*"[29] Chinese bitterness toward the U.N. was due in part to the ends to which the organization had lent itself in Korea and in part to the C.P.R.'s exclusion from U.N. membership. It is therefore unlikely that Chou would have changed his position against U.N. supervision of elections. Indeed, on 22 May he had said the participants ought not let the conference remain deadlocked for any length of time over a U.N. role in the settlement: "Our Conference has been convened for the purpose of finding *other ways* to achieve a reasonable solution of the Korean problem."[30]

Although appearing to concede the necessity for election supervision, and even offering a proposal for a neutral-nations supervisory commission, the Chinese Premier (and his Korean and Soviet allies) refused to retract his demand for an all-Korean electoral commission that would give North Korea a veto over provisions of the elections law and over administration of the election. The non-Communist delegations could not accept this, and the Communist representatives had to insist upon it if they wished to prevent the People's Republic of Korea, only one-third as populuous as South Korea, from being absorbed in the Republic of Korea—and this apparently was their design.

It is difficult for the historian to determine what alternatives were open to the conferees—what compromises were attempted or avoided (private discussions took place throughout the period of the conference but records of these discussions are not yet available). There was, however, one alternative that worried some delegates, namely, the resumption of hostilities. This course was favored by President Rhee, who had opposed the Geneva Conference because he feared concessions counter to South Korean interests would be made. After the Geneva Conference ended in July, Rhee came to Washington hoping to win support for his plans for the forcible unification of his nation, but his proposals received a cool reception, both from Congress and the administration. Yet, with the prospect of a conference deadlock in June, the resumption of hostilities was not entirely impossible.[31]

[29] *Ibid.*, p. 56 (emphasis added).
[30] *Ibid.*, p. 100.
[31] Peace and war in Asia may well have been indivisible. If the United States actively intervened in the Indochinese War, President Rhee's proposals may have had a different reception in Washington.

Molotov, as we have seen, proposed that the conference agree that no action be taken that would constitute a threat to the maintenance of peace in Korea, and Chou had supported this proposal. Did this betray a real concern for a reopening of Korean hostilities? The reader will also recall that Bedell Smith declared that the Korean armistice agreement contained sufficiently specific and formal terms for the maintenance of peace in Korea that these terms rendered Molotov's proposal superfluous. In rebuttal, Chou had argued that only the two belligerent states were bound by the armistice agreement, that the Geneva Conference had been convened on a broader basis and must have its own agreement, and Molotov had defended Chou's proposal. It was not surprising that the Soviet delegation should favor consolidation of peace in Korea, he said, in view of President Rhee's talk of an offensive against North Korea. While it would be difficult to draw any conclusions from the available documents, it seems that the Soviet proposal was at the very least a prudent propaganda move. The Chinese, and even more likely the Russians, preferred to see peace maintained in Korea probably as much as President Eisenhower and Secretary Dulles. Chinese policy aims in Asia, then in the process of revision, could be better accomplished by "peaceful coexistence," and would only have been hampered by a resumption of hostilities in Korea. The Soviets, for reasons discussed earlier, probably calculated that the risks of a new war in the peninsula far outweighed whatever benefits might accrue to them from such a war. The utility of peace in Korea was greater than the utility of having either or both of their allies engaged in a new war in Korea, and was certainly greater than the utility of Soviet involvement.

Thus the deadlock of the Korean Conference, perhaps, was only to be expected. There was no fighting in Korea; no ally was either on the verge of collapse or the verge of victory; and there was no likelihood of further outside intervention in the affairs of another state. Apart from the desires of the Korean people for unification, there were no pressing reasons for bringing unification about; none of the great powers was prepared to pay the price of unification. The Soviet Union was unwilling to see Syngman Rhee's regime take over all of Korea and because there was no prospect of Rhee's defeat in all-Korean elections in the near future, elections would have to be controlled by a commission that would give North Korea veto power over any procedures that might result in the disappearance of the Pyongyang regime. The non-Communist delegates, on the other hand, were not prepared to allow elections on any basis other than that upon which the more populous South Korean districts would return supporters of Rhee, or at least supporters of a government sympathetic to the West.

Unification, for the present, could be accomplished only by force. President Rhee saw this, and very probably the other delegates at Geneva saw this as well. But, because virtually everyone was opposed to the resumption of hostilities, Korea would remain divided.

Chapter 10

DIPLOMACY UNDER A PALL

[I]

Secretary of State Dulles had left Paris for Geneva on Friday evening, the 24th of April, after a day of conferences. He attended the early plenary sessions of the Korean Conference which opened on the 26th, and he promoted his proposed Southeast Asia regional defense organization, to which end he appears to have sounded out almost every ally. By the middle of the week Dulles knew that Canada, Australia, and New Zealand would coordinate their positions on the defense organization with that of Great Britain; that is, they would bide their time, waiting to see what might be achieved at Geneva. It was reported that Dulles was also trying for a coalition of a more limited kind, including the United States, France, the Associated States, Thailand, and the Philippines.[1]

By the end of the first week Dulles's progress was slight. Certainly the regional defense organization could not come into being in time to have an appreciable effect upon negotiations at Geneva; its preparatory discussions had not even been scheduled. Dulles met with the ANZUS pact states on 2 May, the day before he returned to Washington, to discuss military plans for the defense of Southeast Asia, but the ANZUS delegates again adopted a "wait and see" attitude. Dulles could not have been happy over his lack of success in lining up the allies for the regional defense organization; he believed that even preparations for such discussions would measurably strengthen the allies' bargaining position at Geneva and encourage the non-Communist governments of Southeast Asia. The British position, as we know, remained firm: the possibilities of the conference must not be prejudiced, neither by intervention in Indochina nor by an agreement on concerted intervention under such conditions as the American Secretary of State had in mind. Prime Minister Churchill's unequivocal statement in the House of Commons on 27 April seemed to have settled the question.

Both Britain and the United States were loath to commit a belligerent act in Indochina, but neither Britain nor France was certain that the administration was truly reluctant. Indeed, America's European allies were convinced that administration activists might bring the United States into the war, and they regarded Dulles as one of these adventurers. On the 30th, when Dulles and Eden met

[1] *NYT*, 28 April 1954.

for private talks, Dulles assured the Foreign Secretary that the United States was seeking neither a war with China nor large-scale intervention in Indochina, but the best way to avoid these contingencies Dulles argued, was a policy of firmness and a demonstration of allied unity. The Secretary of State, with some acerbity, complained that the British delegation had remained silent during the Korean plenary sessions in the face of Communist charges of American imperialist action.[2] He apparently charged Eden in a rather blunt fashion with having repudiated their mutual "understanding" of 13 April concerning preparations for a collective defense arrangement without offering an alternative. However Eden responded, we know that on his arrival in Geneva he had told Dulles that Britain would join the United States in guaranteeing a settlement produced by negotiation and, if the conference failed, that he would be willing to "examine the situation afresh."[3] Beyond this he was not willing to go. Then, at their meeting on the 30th, Eden reaffirmed the British position on both armed intervention and the proposed defense organization.

Bidault, as we have seen, regarded American threats and the possibility of American intervention as his only bargaining weapon; the French political and military position was weak and the loss of Dien Bien Phu would make their position even weaker. The Communists would make concessions to the French if the United States paid the price in recognition of the C.P.R., neutralization of Taiwan, or admission of China to the U.N., but the United States would not agree to such an exchange. They would also make concessions if they feared a widening of the war, but since only the United States would generate such a fear, Bidault had placed himself in the position where he must rely upon the verbal belligerency of his American ally to worry the Communists sufficiently to induce them to agree to an "honorable" cease-fire in Indochina. Bidault, Dulles, and Eden discussed France's negotiating position on the afternoon of 30 April, when Bidault somewhat gloomily asserted "he had hardly a card in his hand, perhaps just a two of clubs and a three of diamonds."[4] After Bidault left, Dulles again asked Eden if the opening of talks on the Southeast Asia defense organization would not hearten the French and demonstrate that the Western allies were preparing for any eventuality. Eden's reply highlighted the divergent approaches of the two governments: "If we were not preparing to go to the help of the French in Indo-China, [he] found it hard to see how pretending that we might be going to do so would really help anybody."[5] Dulles believed that "pretending" would help the French but Eden did not.

[2] DDE, p. 355.   [3] E, p. 121.   [4] E, p. 124.   [5] *Ibid.*

Although the secretary understood Bidault's need for a strategy of deterrence (he might even have persuaded Bidault to accept this strategy), President Eisenhower did not always demonstrate a similar understanding, and after Dulles left Geneva, Bidault had cause to doubt even the Secretary of State's position. The French Foreign Minister was much dismayed over a number of statements that emanated from Washington during the first few weeks of the Geneva Conference. For example, in the last week of April, President Eisenhower declared that the United States could not be the "gladiator of the world," that the United States must seek a middle road between the unacceptable loss of Indochina to the Communists and an unattainable victory over the Vietminh.[6] To this end, he said the United States would await the outcome of the Geneva Conference, hoping that the bloodshed could be stopped and a *modus vivendi* with the Communists achieved. But such a policy could only undermine Bidault's bargaining position by removing his sole support: the American deterrent. Dulles, who certainly understood this, was reported to have been greatly disturbed by the President's pronouncement.[7]

Eisenhower again found that he had to clarify his position. To Bedell Smith, who was to fly to Geneva on 30 April, the President explained that his *modus vivendi* statement was not intended to mean that United States policy on Indochina had weakened nor that the United States was putting pressure on the French to reach a settlement.[8] Moreover, since the President's remarks seemed to differ from Dulles's earlier declaration, it might appear to the secretary's GOP critics that he was no longer in favor, and the President did not mean to suggest that he was about to look for another Secretary of State. He sent a warm letter of support to Dulles in Geneva, assuring him that he valued his services highly.

In circumstances such as these there was every reason for Dulles to want to return to Washington. First, he must answer his critics; second, he must reach an understanding with the chief executive, and with his advisors in the cabinet and the NSC, on American policy in Indochina in view of the impending collapse of Dien Bien Phu; third, he wanted symbolically to disassociate himself from the bargaining at Geneva. Actually, Dulles had decided in February or March that he would not remain long at Geneva and that Under Secretary of State Bedell Smith would take charge of the American delegation after a week or so. The secretary's detachment from

[6] *NYT*, 27, 30 April 1954; *DSB*, 10 May 1954, pp. 702-704.
[7] Donald Lancaster, *The Emancipation of French Indochina* (London: Oxford University Press, 1961), p. 316.
[8] *NYT*, 5 May 1954.

the Premier of the Chinese People's Republic was perhaps symbolic during the Korean plenary sessions, when Dulles and Chou ignored each other. It was reported that Dulles even refused to shake the Premier's hand.[9]

In any case, Dulles prepared to leave Geneva[10] and Bedell Smith prepared for his duties as head of the United States delegation. Smith met with the President and Admiral Radford on 28 April and with the cabinet and the NSC on the 29th. On the 30th he left for Geneva, and closeted himself with the Secretary of State on his arrival.[11] To the best of our ability to determine what had been agreed upon in Washington and in Bedell Smith's conference with Dulles, the American appraisal of the situation seemed to be as follows. (1) The war in Indochina was still very much a French affair. (2) The United States were prepared to support French efforts to end the war provided American interests were not appreciably affected by such efforts.[12] (3) Partition of Indochina or the formation of a coalition government with Vietminh participation, which would probably result in the communization of Indochina, must be opposed. (4) Any cease-fire that placed the Vietminh in an advantageous position for resuming hostilities must be opposed. (5) Although Bidault assured Dulles that he would not agree to partition or a coalition government, the French might have no alternative but to accept such a solution, and the United States must disassociate itself from any settlement it did not like. There was an additional consideration: Dien Bien Phu could not hold out much longer, its capture might result in the fall of the Laniel government, and a succeeding government might ask for peace in Indochina at any price. Therefore, efforts toward the formation of a united front should go forward in the event the Geneva Conference did not bring an end to the war. As one aspect of coalition activity, Washington would continue to press for a regional defense organization whether or not peace came to Indochina.

On the evening of 1 May, Eden and Lord Reading dined with Bedell Smith and the members of the American delegation, and Eden termed the after-dinner discussions "exceptionally difficult." Nevertheless, Bedell Smith's relations with Eden were cordial, in contrast

[9] *NYT*, 2, 6 May 1954. One can well imagine how a photograph of Dulles shaking the Chinese Premier's hand would have been received in Washington, particularly by several GOP congressmen.

[10] *NYT*, 1 May 1954. The *Times* also reported that Dulles was returning to Washington to work on his Southeast Asia alliance, hopefully with the British, but without them if necessary.

[11] *NYT*, 30 April, 6 May 1954.

[12] *NYT*, 26 April 1954.

with the antipathy between Dulles and Eden, which is clearly evident in the latter's memoirs. Of the 1 May discussions, Eden wrote:

[The] conversation turned to the situation in Indo-China and we were subjected to a prolonged, and at moments somewhat heated, onslaught upon our attitude. Only Mr. Bedell Smith seemed to have any real comprehension of the reasons which had led us to take up our present position.[13]

The diplomats touched upon the possibility of Chinese intervention and the training of Vietnamese forces to defend Vietnam, and Reading asked Dulles what he thought of the fact that it would take two years to train an adequate indigenous force. In Eden's words, Dulles "replied that they would have to hold some sort of bridgehead as had been done in Korea until the Inchon landings could be carried out. Lord Reading commented that this meant things would remain on the boil for several years to come, and Mr. Dulles replied that this would be a very good thing."[14]

It was Eden's conclusion that the Americans were aggrieved by the British refusal to support them even though the Americans had no plans of their own. Eden, moreover, "was determined that we should not endorse a bad policy for the sake of unity."[15] He reported his impressions and decisions to London, and recorded having discussed a defense organization with Lester Pearson, Richard Casey of Australia, and Clifton Webb of New Zealand. The three men were in agreement with Eden's views on building such an organization, "with the widest possible Asian support, to guarantee and support whatever settlement can be achieved in Indo-China and to assure the security of the rest of the area."[16]

Dulles returned to Washington on 3 May and shortly thereafter testified before the Senate Foreign Relations Committee. The Secretary of State was the object of some rather stiff criticism on his return, and in addition to the outright critics there were also many congressmen who were confused by the policy the administration was pursuing. Many even asked whether there *was* a policy. The adverse reaction of the press and Congress upon Dulles's return was due to frustration, born of the realization that, in terms of bargaining at Geneva, the United States was in a bad position because the French were in a bad position. The exigencies of alliance policy were particularly burdensome, or seemed to be, at this stage of the conference. The Korean Conference, moreover, would very likely produce a deadlock—according to general opinion in Washington—after a week of discussions. Dulles said he had discovered no discernible difference

[13] E, p. 125.   [14] E, p. 127.   [15] *Ibid.*   [16] E, p. 128.

in Soviet and Chinese policies at Geneva. Their familiar, intransigent tactics, from the American point of view, would be extended to the Indochina negotiations. The prospects were poor: either a Communist victory at Geneva and on the battlefield or United States military involvement in Indochina.

Senator Knowland, one of the most vocal critics, argued that the United States should not wait for the results of the Geneva Conference nor British consent before acting—in a way he did not specify. Knowland, who implied that someone had suggested he do less vocalizing over the policy of his party's administration,[17] declared that he would not be quiet when United States interests were threatened. Worried that Geneva would become an Asian Munich, Knowland asserted that Britain was paralyzing American policy.[18] Others asked why the administration had not explored policy alternatives with congressional leaders when the situation in Indochina had begun to deteriorate. Why had Dulles proposed united action before consulting Congress or the allies? Why did he give the British an opportunity to refuse American requests for a concerted policy when the result was a public demonstration of Western disunity?[19]

To allay public confusion and assuage congressional irritation, Dulles appeared before the Senate Foreign Relations Committee and met with congressional leaders.[20] He attended an NSC meeting on the 6th and again on the 8th of May.[21] Press conferences of the next two weeks were devoted to the Indochina crisis, and the Secretary of State scheduled a national television address for 7 May. This program of consultation and orientation, it was hoped, would inform Congress and the public of the current Indochina policy of the United States.

The President, in a news conference statement of 5 May, briefly reviewed the diplomacy of the Indochina crisis. He said that Secretary Dulles's Overseas Press Club address of 29 April set forth no

[17] *NYT*, 4 May 1954.
[18] Drew Middleton wrote that the British felt they were being unjustly criticized for preventing "united action" when it was far from certain that such action would have been supported by the "accusers" (*NYT*, 4 May 1954). Insofar as "united action" meant U.S. intervention with ground troops under the current conditions in Indochina, it is this book's thesis that neither the President nor the Secretary of State was prepared to take such action. Although some French and American activists and independent observers may have suspected that this was the case, they had little evidence to support their suspicions. But Britain's reluctance was well known, and the British government could easily be blamed for frustrating coalition action in Indochina by those who wanted such action. Dulles himself assisted this attribution of blame by forcing the burden of saying no upon the British on 25 April (see Chapter 5).
[19] See James Reston's column, *NYT*, 3 May 1954.
[20] *NYT*, 5 May 1954.
[21] *NYT*, 8 May 1954.

really new policy; rather, it reaffirmed principles that had guided earlier American postwar foreign policy. More than that, it was a reminder to interested Asian allies that the United States was prepared to join with others in the application of those principles to the threatened area. Meanwhile, the President added, conversations leading to the realization of a Southeast Asia security arrangement were proceeding, but

> Obviously, it was never expected that this collective security arrangement would spring into existence overnight. There are too many important problems to be resolved. But there is a general sense of urgency. The fact that such an organization is in process of formation could have an important bearing upon what happens at Geneva during the Indochina phase of the Conference.[22]

When Dien Bien Phu fell, on 7 May, President Eisenhower immediately dispatched messages to President René Coty of France and to Bao Dai extolling the gallantry of the garrison and assuring the chiefs of state that the "free world [would] remain faithful to the causes for which they have so nobly fought."[23] Washington continued to insist that the loss of Dien Bien Phu was not a strategic defeat; it had been only one battle in a very large and very long war, and its garrison, however gallant and well trained, comprised less than 5 percent of the French Union forces in Indochina.[24] Nonetheless, the press in France and in the United States had almost continuously emphasized the battle of Dien Bien Phu since its beginning in early March, and, though the fall of the fortress did not receive as much publicity in the United States as it did in France, it produced pessimistic forecasts in both countries, to the effect that Indochina was lost, and with it all of Southeast Asia.

THE SECRETARY of State addressed the nation over the radio and television networks on the evening of 7 May in a speech that was in essence a briefing for the American public. First, Dulles explained that he could not have remained in Geneva for any great length of time because of the need for him to administer America's foreign affairs from Washington. He then examined the background of the Geneva Conference, emphasizing the Soviet concession at Berlin that the conference would not be a "five-power affair" and would confer no new international status upon Red China.[25] The Korean Conference, he

[22] *DSB*, 17 May 1954, p. 740.
[23] *Ibid.*, p. 745. Earlier, on 28 March, the President had sent President Coty a letter of tribute to the defenders of Dien Bien Phu.
[24] L&D, p. 136.
[25] *The Issues at Geneva*, Press Release No. 238, Series S, No. 15, 7 May 1954 (Washington, D.C.: Department of State, Public Services Division, 1954), p. 2.

said, was under way when he left Geneva, but whether the Communists would accept supervised elections in Korea remained to be seen. The plan they offered for Korean unification was quite similar to the Soviets' proposal at the Berlin Conference for the reunification of Germany, and was similarly objectionable. Dulles concluded his discussion of the Korean problem with a promise not to "surrender at the Council table at Geneva the freedom for which so many fought and died." And—in a passage that President Rhee ought to have considered seriously—he assured his audience that "the United States Delegation will do all that lies within its power to promote, *by peaceful means*, the independence and freedom and unity of Korea."[26]

Turning to Indochina, Dulles declared that American policy followed two complementary lines: strengthening resistance to communism in Indochina and building a broader community of defense in Southeast Asia. This policy required three things:

(1) The French should give greater reality to their intention to grant full independence [to the Associated States];

(2) There should be greater reliance upon the national armies who would be fighting in their own homeland . . . ;

(3) There should be greater free-world assistance.[27]

Discussing the implementation of these steps, Dulles took note of the growing feeling among the French that France was overextended. He spoke again of Chinese assistance to the Vietminh, the existing defense arrangements in East Asia, and the administration's efforts to begin discussions with interested allies in a Southeast Asia collective defense arrangement. Such conversations were now taking place and progress was being made. "We must agree," he said, "as to who will take part in the united defense effort and what their commitments will be." The key for a successful defense and for deterring attacks was an association for mutual defense. The United States was working for that objective, but in this process the administration had never sought "any sudden spectacular act such as an ultimatum to Red China."[28]

Referring to the hostilities in Indochina, Dulles praised the heroism of the garrison at Dien Bien Phu, which had that very day capitulated after a resistance of fifty-seven days. Briefly, he compared the Indochinese War to the Korean War and described the situation in Indochina as "far more complex."

[26] *Ibid.*, p. 3. (Emphasis added.)   [27] *Ibid.*, p. 5.
[28] *Ibid.*, p. 8.

The present conditions there do not provide a suitable basis for the United States to participate with its armed forces.

The situation may perhaps be clarified as a result of the Geneva Conference. . . . If they [the French] can conclude a settlement on terms which do not endanger the freedom of the peoples of Viet-Nam, this would be a real contribution to the cause of peace in Southeast Asia. But we would be gravely concerned if an armistice or cease-fire were reached in Geneva which would provide a road to a Communist takeover and further aggression. If this occurs, or if hostilities continue, then the need will be even more urgent to create the conditions for united action in defense of the area.[29]

The Secretary of State concluded his address with three remarks that were tantamount to a policy guideline to which the administration would adhere: First, congressional support for military action was essential; second, there must be mutuality of purpose in an adequate collective effort in Indochina; third, American participation in any collective effort should be "on a basis which recognizes fully the aspirations and cultures of the Asian peoples."[30]

With perhaps one exception, this address denoted no real change in policy but rather a continuation of the policy enunciated by the secretary before the Overseas Press Club. It distinguished between the long-range menace to Southeast Asian security and current hostilities. With respect to the former, it indicated that the United States was firm in its resolve to press for the eventual establishment of a regional defense organization. To that end, it emphasized that independence for the Associated States, the strengthening of national armies, and additional economic and military assistance from the United States were necessary. The possible change in policy was the declaration that the Indochina situation did not, at present, provide a basis for the participation of American armed forces. This declaration, however, should have surprised no one in view of the President's remarks the week before.

But the policy change was not so much the decision not to intervene (both the President and Dulles had reservations about this from the very beginning of the crisis) as its public declaration, proclaiming to the world what the United States would *not* do. This might damage the deterrent effect of American threats; perhaps it even meant the end of such threats. Dulles said that "present conditions" did not permit American participation; but Geneva might clarify the situation or, again, it might not. In effect, the United States must

<hr>

[29] *Ibid.*, pp. 9-10.   [30] *Ibid.*, p. 10.

reserve its decision until administration policymakers could determine what the conference would produce. If hostilities continued or if a negotiated armistice provided a "road for a Communist takeover," the time for a decision would be at hand. This was certainly a warning to the Communist negotiators at Geneva not to demand or expect too much, but its effectiveness was another matter. Dulles's caution was indicated by his statement concerning the consequences of a resumption of hostilities: The United States would not intervene unilaterally but would "create the conditions for united action in defense of the area."[31]

Had the Secretary of State meant to imply that he was resigned to the loss to the Communists of at least part of Vietnam? His address, together with other quasi-official statements from Washington, certainly created this impression in Paris. Dulles had expressed hope for a settlement at Geneva that did not "endanger the freedom of the peoples of Viet-Nam." The *New York Times* reported on 6 May that the National Security Council had decided the United States must support French efforts to conclude an armistice but, the report said, American efforts at Geneva should be directed to arranging a "protracted armistice," one in which the Communists would withdraw from Laos, Cambodia, and South Vietnam and in which a neutral zone would be set up in the Red River delta. In Paris and in the Communist capitals this language could be taken to imply that, apart from the Red River delta, the United States could not hope to see a Vietnam unified under the SVN flag. Bidault, moreover, could not have been happy about this reported NSC "decision." There would be no direct American intervention in Indochina in the foreseeable future.

Adding to French disquiet, or at least to the disquiet of Bidault and others in the government who agreed with his approach to negotiations, were such reports as that of 1 May in the *New York Herald Tribune*. Reliable sources, it was said, had stated that the United States would accept a partition of Indochina under satisfactory circumstances. On 3 May, editorials in several Saigon dailies also announced that the United States was willing to accept partition if (as in Korea) a defensible frontier could be established that would block the spread of communism.[32]

DULLES MET with the President and military and foreign policy advisors on the 10th. Afterward he indicated that the President was weighing possible defense budget increases and was again consider-

[31] *Ibid.*   [32] *NYT*, 6 May 1954.

ing universal military training.[33] On 11 May, Dulles testified in closed session before the House Committee on Foreign Affairs. He later held a press conference, his first after returning from Geneva, that was to cause further alarm in Paris. Dulles said he regarded the armistice proposals the French had offered at Geneva as acceptable (the first plenary session of the Indochina Conference had been held three days earlier on 8 May); but the Vietminh proposal for a cease-fire and withdrawal of French forces, he said, set the stage for a Communist takeover of all Vietnam and was completely unacceptable. He also touched upon the regional defense pact and the many difficulties in creating such an arrangement, but these difficulties were not insuperable, he said. Asked whether the pact would include the Associated States, Dulles said he could not forecast its membership; this depended upon France, Laos, Cambodia, and Vietnam. Asked what causes would activate the defense pact, Dulles replied: "If the states of Vietnam, Laos, and Cambodia are comprehended in this collective security pact, I would feel then it would be appropriate to use force to put down attacks such as are now going on there."[34] Then, in discussing the defense of Southeast Asia in general terms, Dulles remarked that if Indochina were lost, Southeast Asia could still be defended.

Later—how much later is uncertain, but definitely on the same day—he clarified his remarks; he had understood, he said, that they might be open to misinterpretation. Perhaps he had received the first expressions of alarm from Paris. In any case, he amended his last remark as follows.

> I see it has been said that I felt that Southeast Asia could be secured even without perhaps Viet-Nam, Laos, and Cambodia. I do not want for a minute to give the impression that we believe that they are going to be lost or that we have given up trying to prevent their being lost. On the contrary, we recognize that they are extremely important and that the problem of saving Southeast Asia is far more difficult if they are lost. But I do not want to give the impression either that if events that we could not control and which we do not anticipate should lead to their being lost, that we would consider the whole situation hopeless, and we would give up in despair. We do not give up in despair. Also, we do not give up Viet-Nam, Laos, or Cambodia.[35]

The clarification came a bit too late to prevent excitement in Paris and in Geneva. But before we describe the reaction to Mr. Dulles's

[33] *NYT*, 10 May 1954. [34] *DSB*, 24, May 1954, p. 782.
[35] *Ibid.*, p. 782.

remark and its aftermath, let us touch upon some other important events affecting the French role in the diplomatic drama.

[II]

After a three-week Easter recess the French National Assembly, agitated over the news of Bidault's efforts to get the Americans to intervene in Indochina, reconvened on 4 May.[36] The Communists and the Socialists attacked the government, arguing that Bidault did not believe in negotiating and did not want peace. The Gaullists, generally unhappy with Laniel's European policies, were only luke-warm in their support of the Premier, and distinctly irritated by the opportunities Bidault had given the Americans for interfering in French affairs. The left and the center parties demanded a full-scale Indochina debate within a week's time; and the left demanded an immediate cease-fire. Laniel argued that the cease-fire the opposition wanted was a "capitulation, pure and simple,"[37] and his government intended to negotiate for an armistice with guarantees. The Premier also insisted that a debate on Indochina would weaken the French bargaining position at Geneva and would hinder negotiations. But the pressures upon Laniel were so great that finally he agreed to schedule the Indochina debate for 14 May.

Bidault immediately protested. This move by Laniel amounted to a public withdrawal of support for his Foreign Minister and would so weaken the latter's hand as to render his efforts at Geneva completely ineffectual.[38] The Premier must not schedule a debate; if he did, Bidault would have no alternative but to resign. Laniel then changed his mind and revoked his promise of a parliamentary debate—which might also cause the fall of the government. This, in turn, might produce a result almost all the government's critics did not want: the adjourning of the Geneva Conference. Once adjourned, there could be no assurance that it would reconvene. On 6 May Laniel was successful; he received 311 votes against 262 on a motion temporarily postponing debate on the Indochina question.[39]

Bidault was still in a most difficult position. When he told Eden and Dulles on 30 April that he had little to bargain with, he had reason to be pessimistic. The United States and Britain had not given him the support he thought he needed, for, on 29 April, President Eisenhower had told the U.S. Chamber of Commerce that the United States would seek a *modus vivendi* with the Communists in Indo-

[36] *NYT*, 4 May 1954.
[37] *JO*, 5 May 1954, p. 2098 (sess. of 4 May).
[38] L&D, p. 133.
[39] *JO*, 7 May 1954, pp. 2188-2189 (sess. of 6 May).

china. The French had seized upon this remark, and Bidault, in particular, pointed out to Dulles that the Soviets would conclude the United States was willing to allow a part of Indochina to be surrendered to the Communists. Bedell Smith, in his briefing before his departure for Geneva, was instructed to tell the French (and Dulles?) that Eisenhower's speech—and his earlier press conference remarks —did not signify a weakening of the United States' Indochina policy. The day before he left Geneva, Dulles had told Bidault he would do all within his power to help France during the conference, and afterward as well, if the conference came to nothing.[40] On the day of his departure Dulles confirmed his support to Bidault in writing and told him he would press his efforts for a regional security organization. Nevertheless, Bidault could not be entirely certain that the Americans had *not* decided that part of Indochina would fall—or be assigned—to the Vietminh nor that the collective defense arrangement would secure territories in Laos and Vietnam that were not currently controlled by the Vietminh. It might even mean "drawing the line" at the Mekong.

In addition to Bidault's doubts about his allies, his government was under constant attack from critics of every political complexion in the National Assembly and in the press. The victory of 6 May, postponing an Indochina debate, was temporary at best. The fall of Dien Bien Phu, though long expected, stunned Paris and muted criticism for a time, but the attacks upon the government's Indochina policy would surely be renewed—and renewed with vigor if Bidault did not succeed, or did not appear to succeed, in bringing a ceasefire closer to realization.

THE FRENCH Foreign Minister was also having difficulties with his Communist counterparts at Geneva over evacuation of the wounded from Dien Bien Phu, and the consequence of this affair even further embittered Bidault's critics. On 26 April he had issued an appeal for the evacuation of French Union wounded from beleaguered Dien Bien Phu, which had been barred by the Vietminh, although the French commander, on 15 March, had agreed to a six-hour truce for the evacuation of Vietminh wounded.[41] The Geneva Conference, Bidault said, should open with this humane gesture. When, on 28 April, Bidault and Molotov met to discuss the question of participants in the Indochina Conference, Bidault again raised the matter of evacuating the Dien Bien Phu wounded.

What Molotov said and what the two ministers understood respecting the position of the other is a matter of dispute, but the net effect

[40] L&D, p. 170.
[41] *Econ.*, 1 May 1954, p. 386; *NYT*, 27 April 1954.

of the meeting was Soviet insistence that Bidault deal directly with the Vietminh on the evacuation. (Vietminh delegates were, in fact, waiting in Berlin for an invitation to the conference.) The Soviet delegation's account of the meeting, which was released to the press, reported that Bidault had told Molotov the question of the wounded should be taken up and settled before the question of the conference participants was resolved. Bidault, the Soviet report alleged, had promised to give Molotov a reply on the question of Vietminh participation after he consulted his allies.[42]

The French regarded the news release as an act of bad faith, designed to force Bidault to agree to Vietminh participation. The French delegation then issued a news release giving its account of the 28 April meeting. The foreign ministers had first discussed a Vietminh invitation to Geneva, and Bidault said he must consult his allies. After that, Bidault raised the matter of the French Union wounded, but Molotov refused to intervene. The French, he said (according to the French version), must make arrangements directly with the Vietminh delegation when it arrived in Geneva. Molotov subsequently denied that the release of his conversations with Bidault had any object other than correcting inaccuracies that had appeared in the French press. (The French had reported that their appeals to the Vietminh had gone unanswered and that aircraft sent to evacuate the wounded had been fired upon.)

Bidault made another effort, this time to enlist the Chinese as intermediaries in an attempt to get an agreement on evacuation without dealing directly with the Vietminh, but the Chinese also refused and insisted that the French must deal directly with the Vietminh. The matter remained unresolved for a week and a half, while more than 1,000 wounded waited upon an agreement. On 4 May the Vietminh delegation arrived in Geneva, having been invited pursuant to an agreement reached by the foreign ministers (described in Chapter 9). On 10 May, Pham Van Dong, Deputy Premier of the DRVN and head of the Vietminh delegation, offered to permit the evacuation of the seriously wounded,[43] and Bidault accepted the offer. But the matter did not end there; it produced further disagreement and recriminations, the effects of which would further strain French relations with the Communists and provide an additional basis upon which Bidault's Paris critics could challenge the sincerity of his efforts for a cease-fire.

The day after the fall of Dien Bien Phu (and Dulles's television address), Henri Bonnet conferred with the Secretary of State.[44] Bon-

[42] *NYT*, 29 April 1954.
[43] *Econ.*, 15 May 1954, p. 548.
[44] This account is based upon L&D, pp. 171-173.

net's impressions, which the ambassador conveyed to Paris, were disturbing, particularly because many French officials were close to despair. Bonnet felt that Dulles no longer believed the French could obtain the settlement they wanted, and he (Dulles) was now deeply concerned about the Communist expansion southward. It would be necessary to establish a security arrangement quickly, without Britain if need be, and discussions should begin immediately for studying ways of checking Communist expansion. Conveying these impressions to Paris, Bonnet asked whether it would not now be wise to ask the Americans what they would do if the Geneva Conference did not bring about a cessation of hostilities or the military situation in Tonkin deteriorated to such an extent that the French must request American intervention.

The French cabinet was studying Bonnet's dispatch and his suggestion for sounding out the Eisenhower administration when Dulles made the remark, on 11 May, that Southeast Asia could be held without Indochina. The fact that this remark was hypothetical and delivered in the informal context of a news conference was overlooked. Laniel's ministers were shocked. Bidault was notified and immediately asked Bedell Smith for confirmation or clarification. At 11 p.m., 12 May, Bedell Smith showed Bidault an exact text of Dulles's remarks. The French minister was reassured for the time being; his bargaining position was weak but it was not entirely untenable.

In the aftermath of Dulles's press conference remark, the French cabinet decided to pursue the suggestion of Henri Bonnet; that is, to inquire what the American government would do if Geneva did not produce an end to hostilities or the military situation in Tonkin deteriorated. The pursuit of answers to these hypotheticals is another story, the threads of which we will pick up later, but one thing should be made clear at this point, and that is the "gap" in American policy as viewed from Paris.[45]

The Eisenhower administration would support the French as long as they continued to fight in Indochina against the Vietminh, but the situation, as it then stood, did not provide the basis for the participation of American armed forces. In the long term, a security or defense pact would (or might) "guarantee" the frontiers of a non-Communist Southeast Asia. But what would the United States do if the grave consequences of which Dulles spoke on 7 May came to pass; that is, if hostilities continued or the Vietminh won an armistice that placed it in an advantageous position for the renewal of hostilities? Would not the collapse of French Union forces in the delta constitute a grave consequence for France's ally as well as for France

[45] L&D, p. 173.

herself? Would not the loss of part of Vietnam or Laos to the Vietminh establish a position from which the Vietminh could more easily
renew hostilities? And had not the American interventionists said
that the loss of Indochina would mean the loss of Southeast Asia?
Dulles, on 12 May, had in effect challenged this strategic appraisal
when he asserted that the loss of Indochina, if it should come about,
would not render the situation in Southeast Asia desperate or hopeless. The proposed defense pact would, in part, forestall the communization of Southeast Asia.

But, the French might ask, how determined was the administration
in its resolve to prevent the loss of part of Vietnam or Laos, particularly if

1. The situation, according to Mr. Dulles, did not now warrant the
participation of U.S. armed forces?

2. The war in Indochina was a French affair, which implied that
the outcome was beyond American control?

3. The decision to take action would wait upon the results of the
Geneva Conference?

4. American action was conditioned upon the cooperation of the
allies, the grant of real independence to the Associated States, and
the continued presence of French Union forces in Indochina?

Some members of the French cabinet might reasonably conclude
that, despite protestations that they were speaking hypothetically,
American policymakers were *not* determined to resist the loss of parts
of Indochina to the Vietminh. Indeed, they might determine not to
intervene unless Thailand and Malaya were threatened, which would
mean, of course, that they were resigned to the loss of Indochina.
This disturbing thought impelled the French cabinet to decide to
explore the sentiments, attitudes, and policies of the United States
government.

[III]

Anthony Eden and Vyacheslav Molotov dined together at the
British villa in Geneva on Wednesday evening, 5 May, and Eden
recalled that Molotov was very amiable, a very different person than
he had been at Berlin three months before. "This was a transformation," Eden theorized, "prompted . . . by worry over the situation in
Indochina."[46]

Molotov seems to have suggested, according to Eden's account, that
the success of the Indochina Conference depended upon the two of
them, "the implication being that we both had allies whose views on
the situation . . . might be more extreme than our own." Eden said

[46] E, p. 131.

that this was the most difficult conference in which he had ever taken part. Molotov agreed. Eden suggested that the Indochina situation was more dangerous than the Korean; hence the latter could be allowed to remain in suspense while the conference turned to Indochina. Molotov agreed. Eden expressed the view that the fighting should be halted by an acceptable cease-fire and the political positions sorted out later. Molotov agreed. Eden told the Soviet Minister that if the Geneva Conference produced no results, the "supporters of each side" would continue to increase their involvement until there was a clash between them. Molotov agreed. The two ministers then proposed that each share the task of chairing the Indochina plenary sessions, first one and then the other, on alternate days, and the proposal was subsequently accepted by the Chinese, French, and American delegations.

As was described earlier, the series of discussions between Dulles and Eden, before Dulles's departure from Geneva, touched upon the familiar subjects of a Southeast Asia collective security arrangement and measures (or gestures) that could be taken to support the French. Eden held to the view that, while Britain was interested in regional security, no steps should be taken, nor indeed would be taken by the British government, until after the Geneva Conference had been given an opportunity to produce results. In a memorandum he submitted to Dulles on 30 April, Eden set forth his views on Southeast Asia's defense. The Communist threat in the area was as much political as military, Eden wrote, and any defense effort must have the widest Asian support.[47] If the British and Americans could not secure the active support of the nations in the area, they must at least secure their benevolent neutrality. Pakistan and Ceylon had indicated to the Foreign Office that they would not oppose the defense arrangement, and Nehru had been persuaded not to condemn it "root and branch."

There is no indication in Eden's memoirs that Dulles commented upon the memorandum, nor any evidence that he acted upon any of its recommendations. This is not to say that he did not make any of the efforts Eden suggested. At the beginning of May, Assistant Secretary of State Robert Murphy spoke with the ambassadors of the Colombo powers in Washington and explained American intentions relative to a defense pact for Southeast Asia.[48] He may even have requested the "moral" support of Pakistan, Burma, and Ceylon. But whatever the results of these conversations, they could not have been terribly impressive from the administration's point of view.

Mr. Eisenhower has related that on 5 May he received a message from Bedell Smith outlining a proposal by Eden that "the United

---

[47] E, pp. 122-123.   [48] L&D, p. 171.

Kingdom take part at once with the United States, France, Australia and New Zealand, in an examination of the Indochina–Southeast Asia situation by a 'Five Power Staff Agency,' located in Singapore."[49] This proposal is especially significant because it might give us a clue to the evolution of British policy in this crucial period, and it was recognized as significant at the time by the President. As Mr. Eisenhower later wrote, the proposal "for the first time showed their [the British] willingness to try to do something before the end of the Geneva Conference."[50] Britain may have felt that talks for underwriting whatever settlement was reached at Geneva could begin before the Conference ended,[51] but Eden's suggestion was nevertheless a change in the Foreign Secretary's policy.

The memorandum Eden submitted to Dulles on 30 April contained the following paragraphs.

7. While we do not believe that a French collapse in Indo-China could come about as rapidly as the Americans appear to envisage, this danger reinforces the need to lay the foundations of a wider and viable defense organization for South-East Asia.

8. We propose therefore that the United States and the United Kingdon should begin an immediate and secret joint examination of the *political and military problems* in creating a collective defense for South-East Asia, namely: (*a*) nature and purpose; (*b*) membership; (*c*) commitments.[52]

It is conceivable that this was the proposal, in a more developed form, that five days later was transmitted to the President. But Eden's proposal of the 30th contained no mention of the "Five Power Staff Agency located in Singapore."

Another point of difference was the suggested participants—France, Britain, and the ANZUS powers—which contrasted with Eden's emphasis in his memorandum upon wide Asian support for any collective action. He may have believed that India, Indonesia, and Burma would oppose such talks, and therefore it might be better to exclude all Asian states. But a better theory seems to be that the British, at this time, distinguished between military and political talks. If military matters were to be the subject of conversations, only states that were willing and able to make a real and immediate military con-

[49] DDE, p. 364. The *NYT*, 5 May 1954, reported that Britain and the United States had completed plans for holding military staff talks at Singapore.

[50] DDE, p. 364.

[51] Coral Bell, *Survey of International Affairs, 1954.* (London: Oxford University Press, 1957), pp. 56-57.

[52] E, p. 123 (emphasis added).

tribution ought to take part; if, on the other hand, political talks were projected, such talks should be delayed until Britain and the United States could win the cooperation of the Colombo powers.[53] Nehru, however, could not have been pleased with this change in the British attitude, no matter what distinctions were drawn.

But if military talks were to be held, the President wanted the participation of all the states that would take part in a united action, particularly Thailand and the Philippines. Eisenhower, who thought that Eden's proposal had the drawback of being confined to "white" nations, declared that

> any reply to Eden (along with my acceptance of his proposal) should make clear that a Five Power Staff Agency along with other nations was not to the United States a fully satisfactory substitute for a broad political coalition of Southeast Asian countries in a cooperative defense effort.[54]

It seems that the President had learned British policy so well he was now using it against the British.

We do not yet know what diplomatic exchanges took place after the President accepted Eden's proposal, although there seems to have been enough disagreement to delay the start of the talks. On the 10th of May, Selwyn Lloyd, Minister of State for Foreign Affairs, emphasized the point that Britain was not committed to any course of action through the agency of any prospective staff talks. Their function, he said, was merely to examine all military contingencies in Southeast Asia.[55] The talks between Australia, France, Great Britain, New Zealand and the United States began on 2 June in Washington, not in Singapore, and Thailand, the Philippines, and the Associated States did *not* take part; they lasted until 11 June. The results were not made public, except for the announcement that the conferees had studied all the hypothetical military situations that might arise in Indochina. And it was emphasized (by Dulles, on 25 May) that the discussions were not designed to lay the basis for a Southeast Asia alliance.[56]

[53] *NYT*, 23 May 1954. But there is a difficulty in this theory too. Eden's memorandum of 30 April called for Anglo-American joint examination of political *and* military problems. E, p. 123.

[54] DDE, p. 364.

[55] *H. C. Debates*, 5th Series, Vol. 527, coll. 834-835. On 17 May the Prime Minister assured the House of Commons that the government had not embarked upon any negotiations involving commitments. He also distinguished between political and military matters, and declared that the staff talks were scheduled merely to examine military problems. *H. C. Debates*, 5th Series, Vol. 527, coll. 1692-1693; *NYT*, 18 May 1954.

[56] *DSB*, 7 June 1954, p. 864.

[IV]

Eden, who seems to have been rather optimistic about the outcome of the Colombo Conference, which began on 28 April, believed that the Colombo powers could contribute materially to the maintenance of peace in Indochina. He had in mind Asian support—in particular, a *guarantee*—of the Geneva settlement by the Colombo powers. On 5 May he received a message from Nehru, the Indian Prime Minister, saying that although he could make no commitments (presumably on guarantees of the Geneva settlement), India would "assist in promoting and maintaining a settlement in Indo-China."[57] At Colombo, the *Economist* reported, Nehru began to doubt whether the Colombo powers could offer to assume responsibility for peace in Indochina after a negotiated armistice.[58] There might have been practical difficulties in establishing a police force made up of contingents from the five Colombo states. In view of continuing poor relations, Indian and Pakistani soldiers might be unable to cooperate in police operations.

In any event, the Indochina War was the major topic of the Colombo conferees. Nehru's peace proposal, which he had offered in a speech on 24 April to the Indian House of the People, was not accepted by the conference, but a compromise proposal was adopted in its stead (after some debate). The amended peace proposal called for (1) an immediate cease-fire, (2) a declaration by France that genuine independence would be given to the Associated States, (3) negotiations for a cease-fire by the belligerent parties, and (4) an agreement among China, the United States, the Soviet Union, and Britain to take the steps necessary to prevent the resumption of hostilities.[59] The amended plan differed from Nehru's original plan in that the former did not call for a solemn declaration of nonintervention by the major powers.

Imperialism and aggression also were debated at Colombo. Referring to the Indochinese War, Ceylon's Prime minister asserted: "There can be no question of Ceylon's assisting in a colonial war, but Ceylon is definitely against Communist aggression and infiltration."[60] Nehru pointed out that the conferees could not single out communism for condemnation inasmuch as this would imply the end of a policy of neutrality. The ministers worked out a formula, which was included in the conference communiqué, declaring that the conferees were

[57] E, p. 128.

[58] *Econ.*, 1 May 1954, p. 360.

[59] The full text of the communiqué of the Conference of Prime Ministers of South and Southeast Asia appears in *Docs., 1954*, pp. 272-276; the "peace proposal" is on p. 273.

[60] *T/L*, 3 May 1954.

determined "to resist interference in their countries by external communist, anti-communist or other agencies."[61] The communiqué condemned colonialism and thermonuclear weapons testing; it urged giving the C.P.R. a seat in the United Nations; and it called for self-determination for Morocco and Tunisia.

[61] *Docs., 1954*, p. 275.

Chapter 11

SOLUTIONS

[I]

Before we describe the details of the negotiations at the Indochina Conference we would do well to review the alternative policies that were open to the delegates. We do not know, and perhaps can never know, all the calculations the participating diplomats made on what they could ask for and what they would accept in the way of a settlement or nonsettlement of the Indochina question. We can be sure, however, that studies of this kind were made and that solutions were discussed at the highest governmental levels.

Let us consider what kind of settlement the delegations of each principal state hoped for; that is, what each participant envisaged as the preferable outcome of the Geneva Conference. In this way we can compare the "ideal solutions" with the outcome of the conference, appreciate the extent to which positions varied during the negotiations and the extent to which concessions were made or forced, and perhaps determine whether the results could be termed a gain or a loss from the point of view of each state.

The SVN and the DRVN

Both the State of Vietnam and the Democratic Republic of Vietnam wanted peace in Indochina, based upon a unified, fully sovereign, and independent Vietnam. At the very most, the French could be given some commercial privileges, and some cultural ties with France might remain, but France would retain no control over domestic or foreign affairs. Each government apparently was willing, in principle, to associate with France—on the basis of complete equality—in the French Union, but Vietnam must be free to join other alliances and otherwise act as a sovereign state in world politics.

There were, of course, nationalists in both the SVN and the DRVN who wanted a complete break with France and the elimination of all economic and political ties; there were others who understood that trained personnel and technical, material, and financial assistance were needed for development. For the DRVN, this assistance could come from the Soviet Union, the C.P.R., and perhaps France; for the SVN, such assistance would come primarily from the United States, and perhaps from France and other Western European states or Commonwealth states such as Canada, Australia, and New Zealand.

Thus the SVN and the DRVN delegations wanted the Geneva Conference to end the war. They wanted the conference participants to recognize and to guarantee the independence, territorial unity, and territorial integrity of Vietnam.

LAOS AND CAMBODIA

Both the Laotian and the Cambodian delegations wanted an end to the war in Vietnam and an end to both conventional war and insurgent operations within the territorial limits of their respective states, from which they wanted the Vietminh to withdraw. The Laotians seemed content with the independence France had given Laos in the treaty of 22 October 1953; the Cambodians wanted independence. Both states were prepared to join and to remain in the French Union.

After Chou En-lai arrived in Geneva, he remarked that perhaps representatives of the "patriotic governments" of the Pathet Lao and Khmer Issarak ("rebels" to the non-Communist delegations) ought to be invited to Geneva. The Laotian and Cambodian governments, which regarded these "liberation governments" as illegal movements controlled and directed by the Vietminh, wanted these "rebels" disarmed, along with the withdrawal of the Vietminh.

FRANCE

The French government wanted a cease-fire and a continuation of French commercial, cultural, and economic privileges in Vietnam, Laos, and Cambodia. It also wanted the Associated States within the French Union and substantial influence over the internal political and economic decision-making processes of each state. Most French leaders of the center and right were not particularly interested in a unified Vietnam, only in a compliant Vietnam. They preferred to see a non-Communist government, rather than the Vietminh, directing the state because they felt their own political and economic interests would be better served thereby.

Their American ally, moreover, was anti-Communist, and, in the interests of viable Franco-American relations, the Laniel government was prepared neither to negotiate directly with the Vietminh nor to acquiesce officially in partition, either of which would imply partial or total recognition of DRVN authority in Vietnam. Further, French preference for a non-Communist regime was probably a consequence of their conclusion that Ho Chi Minh would press for closer relations with the Soviet Union or China, at France's expense. In other words, the French correctly concluded that, for the Vietminh, the ideology of international communism would be more attractive than the ideology of the French Union.

At Geneva, the French wanted to end the fighting because it was a drain on their manpower and other resources, which might better be committed either to North Africa, where terrorist activities were beginning to cause concern, or to Europe, to counterbalance an economically resurgent Germany that would soon be rearmed. The cease-fire had to be of a particular kind, however; it would have to provide for the security both of the French Union expeditionary force and the areas controlled by the French and their Indochinese allies. There would have to be insurance, in other words, against infiltration by Vietminh guerrillas so that real civil order would be restored.

THE UNITED STATES

The Eisenhower administration wanted a non-Communist Vietnam, Laos, and Cambodia. To achieve this result, it might be necessary for the French to continue the war, with substantial American assistance in the form of credits and ordnance, but not troops. There was little support in Washington for a negotiated settlement. Indeed, there was outright opposition from a few influential senators and analysts, who argued that

a. An agreement to negotiate was, in itself, a confession of weakness and an admission of the strength of the Vietminh.

b. A negotiated settlement might enable the Communists to take over all of Indochina.

We know that by late April the official American policy had been *publicly* reconciled to negotiations. The United States would be guided by French wishes and would support French efforts to achieve an honorable cease-fire, provided American interests were not adversely affected. If affected adversely, American policy was not clear, but certainly the administration would disassociate the United States from any agreement it did not like.

Faced with having to negotiate at Geneva, administration officials supported, and sought support for, a non-Communist Vietnam under the aegis of Bao Dai, whose government must try to win the allegiance of the Vietnamese people. The aims of American policy in Indochina would require:

a. An unequivocal grant of genuine and effective independence by France.

b. Time and money. The United States would supply money and other forms of assistance.

c. An SVN government sufficiently competent to bring stability to

Vietnam with American assistance. Non-Communist Vietnamese must provide that government.

d. Weakening the Vietminh so that it could not challenge the authority of the SVN government and bring about the communization of the state. The Geneva Conference must arrive at a settlement that would provide the requisite "situation of strength" for the SVN. In addition, the Bao Dai government would be encouraged to join an anti-Communist regional defense organization. However, rather than have the conference place the Vietminh in a position enabling them to resume hostilities, the United States preferred to see the Franco-Vietnamese forces continue the fight until the Vietminh was reduced to military and political impotency.

GREAT BRITAIN

The British, who wanted to end the fighting in Indochina, recognized the military and consequently the bargaining strength of the Vietminh, and were prepared to be "realistic" about the means for ending the war. They were willing, in short, to pay a price for peace, provided it was not exorbitant. They assumed that partition of Vietnam was a viable though not felicitous solution. But partition must allow the creation of a non-Communist buffer state between Thailand and Laos and Cambodia. The Geneva settlement, the British felt, should be guaranteed so as to stabilize the area and prevent the resumption of hostilities. In the non-Communist territories, the French would be permitted to remain in order to pacify the areas. The conference could assist in this process by obtaining China's consent to stop its military aid to the Vietminh and by persuading both the Soviets and the Chinese to use their influence with the Vietminh in bringing a halt to all hostile actions, including infiltration and subversion.

In addition to a willingness to accept partition—that is, to pay for peace in terms of territory—Eden was prepared to be conciliatory and amenable in dealing with the Communists and to grant concessions.

All this was correct policy only to the extent that one agrees with the British estimate of Soviet and Chinese (and to some extent Vietminh) intentions, intentions relative not only to Indochina but their global intentions as well. The price of peace in Indochina would be paid largely in French, not English, coin. This fact, and the British commitment to détente and to the Commonwealth, incurred unintended and unexpected costs—strains upon the Western alliance, serious differences of opinion, and (in the case of Dulles and Eden) personal animosity—that had important implications for future relations between the United States, Great Britain, and France. Even in 1954, many Frenchmen were bitter about Eden's willingness to make concessions at France's expense. Eden's desire for peace may have been sincere, but the kind of peace he wanted and his means for achieving it were grounded upon a British estimate of what British interests required, which was no less disinterested than American or French estimates.

THE SOVIET UNION

The Soviets, whose prime objective was that the writ of the DRVN run throughout Vietnam, also wanted three socialist states established in Indochina. But whether they were prepared to see Ho Chi Minh dominate Indochina (through an Indochinese federation under the DRVN) is difficult to determine. They were probably more concerned about the implications of Chinese involvement in Indochinese affairs. In spite of rather warm Sino-Soviet relations in 1954, the Kremlin competed with the Chinese for influence over new socialist states and their Communist parties.[1]

Most Soviet experts agree that the Malenkov regime probably wanted a cease-fire in Indochina, on the best possible terms of course. For the reasons discussed earlier, Malenkov's New Course (like the American New Look) assumed there would be no Soviet-American military confrontation in the near future; hence greater Soviet resources could be allocated to light industry. Again, because a continuation of the war involved the risk of American intervention, a Sino-American confrontation, and possibly a Soviet involvement, the Kremlin probably favored a cease-fire. While the Geneva Conference was in session, however, there was no reason why they should not encourage the Vietminh to press its offensive, thus bringing their ideal goal of Vietminh domination of Vietnam that much closer.

CHINA

China's ideal solution is difficult to estimate. On the one hand, Peking almost certainly favored the creation of a socialist state on her southeastern frontier; the C.P.R. would have better relations with a state governed by the Vietminh than one governed by non-Communist Vietnamese nationalists. A Vietnam controlled by the DRVN would "guarantee" China that it would not become a member of a Western-oriented regional security organization or, what was worse,

[1] In this connection, see F. C. Jones, "The Far East," Part IV of Peter Calvocoressi and Coral Bell, *Survey of International Affairs, 1953* (London: Oxford University Press, 1956), pp. 240-242; A. D. Barnett (ed.), *Communist Strategies in Asia* (New York: Praeger, 1963); and Adam Bromke (ed.), *The Communist States at the Crossroads: Between Moscow and Peking* (New York: Praeger, 1965).

provide bases for American military forces. On the other hand, aware of past Sino-Vietnamese rivalries and conflicts, the Chinese probably would not want the DRVN to dominate Laos and Cambodia. It is even possible that China preferred a small Vietnamese state, comprising Tonkin and northern or central Annam, rather than a unified Vietnam. Thus China might have been inclined to accept partition as a means of limiting the ambitions of a traditional rival.

INDIA

Although India was not a participant at the conference, the attitude of the Indian government, particularly that of Prime Minister Nehru, was very influential; indeed, Nehru managed to affect British policy in a significant way. In addition, the Indian special envoy, Krishna Menon, arrived in Geneva in late May and made persistent efforts to achieve a settlement that would be satisfactory to India. For all practical purposes, Menon was a participant in the Geneva Conference.

In the mid-1950s, Nehru had ambitions for India as the leading country of an uncommitted and nonaligned bloc of nations, globally and in the United Nations. Indian policy was embodied in the Five Principles of Peaceful Coexistence, or *Panch Shila* (described earlier), and regarded the Indochinese War as essentially anticolonial and nationalistic in character. The fact that the Vietminh was a Communist movement was not regarded as significant. A cease-fire must be obtained—according to the Indian view—France must grant real independence to Vietnam, Laos, and Cambodia, and there must be *no* interference in the internal affairs of the Associated States. It will be recalled that these items were the basis of Nehru's peace plan, which he announced to the Indian House of the People on 24 April.

It is significant that India's relations with France were not especially warm in 1954. New Delhi was pressing France to relinquish Pondicherry and other French colonial enclaves in India, and French resistance to such pressures was deemed of a piece with her dilatory practices in granting independence to the Associated States.

[II]

I should now like to examine, in rather schematic form, the options or alternatives for a resolution of the Indochinese War that were open to the policymakers of some of the states that participated in the Geneva Conference. For the present, I have omitted consideration of the situations in Laos and Cambodia and the policy options available to their conference delegations, but these will be taken up briefly at the end of the chapter.

The first alternative had to be faced by the French well before early May.

1. To continue the war or to negotiate.

If the decision were made to continue the war, there were three foreseeable consequences.

a. The Vietminh would defeat the Franco-Vietnamese forces and Vietnam would be united under the regime of Ho Chi Minh.

b. The Franco-Vietnamese army would defeat the Vietminh and Vietnam would be united under the aegis of Bao Dai.

c. The war would drag on, with neither belligerent decisively defeating the other. If this happened, the choice of continuing the war or negotiating its settlement would have to be redetermined in the future.[2]

The political situation within France and the military situation in Tonkin precluded 1*c*; the Laniel government felt it must negotiate. The United States would have preferred that the French continue the war, principally because the Vietminh was in a strong military position in the north and would compel the French to make political and territorial concessions at the bargaining table, concessions the United States could not approve in view of the strongly anti-Communist attitudes of its officials. Therefore, with American economic assistance, military equipment, and training cadres for Vietnamese forces, the United States policymakers hoped for 1*b*.

If, however, the Vietminh conquered Vietnam, or appeared to be well on the way to doing this, the Eisenhower administration would face a difficult decision. Statements by Dulles made it appear that, in this eventuality, there was a good chance of American intervention. This possibility could not be discounted by the Communists, nor can it be discounted by the historian until documentary evidence becomes available that clearly shows the administration decided it would *not* intervene if Vietnam fell to the Communists. In my opinion, such a decision was never made, and intervention remained a viable option throughout the period of the Geneva Conference.

2. If it was decided to negotiate, how, with whom, and under what auspices would the belligerents negotiate?

a. Directly with each other. This choice was rejected by the Laniel government and by the United States because of the prestige and status it would give the Vietminh.

b. Under the auspices of the United Nations. France had long been

---

[2] The scope of the war could of course become wider with the intervention of third-party states, such as the United States, China, the Soviet Union, etc.

opposed to U.N. involvement in the Indochinese War, presumably because the nonaligned states might characterize the war as colonialist. China, very much involved in the war though in an indirect way, also could be expected to oppose this choice because it had no seat in the U.N. and because the Korean War had been waged under U.N. authority. The U.N. General Assembly, moreover, had condemned the C.P.R. as an aggressor.

c. Under the auspices of one or several states. Because the Indochinese War had Communist-non-Communist and colonialistic-nationalistic aspects, no "honest broker" states seemed to be available. This alternative may not have been adequately investigated, but, since the Laniel government refused to deal directly with the Vietminh, it is difficult to see how this alternative could have been implemented.

d. At a great-power conference. This was the accepted alternative, as we know, and the decision was made at Berlin in February.

3. *Should a cease-fire be agreed to and put into effect before or after there was an agreement to negotiate?*[3]

In view of the military successes of the Vietminh in 1954, this was an important decision. If there had been a cease-fire before the French had agreed to negotiate, there would have been no military setbacks in Tonkin that could adversely affect the French bargaining position. We cannot say whether this question was given adequate consideration in Paris or Washington or whether the French could have obtained a cease-fire before agreeing to negotiate. The latter is doubtful, for the French refused to deal with the Vietminh in an official, formal way. Further, the Vietminh probably understood the implications of its military strength and would refuse to surrender this advantage by agreeing to a cease-fire before the French agreed to negotiate.[4]

4. *Negotiations having been agreed upon, what matters should be negotiated?*[5]

a. A military settlement only.

b. A military and a political settlement. Also, a cease-fire would

[3] See Walter Lippmann, "The Big Black Cloud," *NYHT*, 4 May 1954.

[4] In 1961 the United States insisted upon and obtained a cease-fire in Laos before agreeing to attend a reconvened "Geneva conference" on the Laotian question.

[5] The order of discussion of questions, that is, the agenda, also was of great importance; the postwar era had seen many disputes over the sequence of items on an agenda. The negotiations at Kaesong, Korea, in 1951 were only one of the most recent examples of such a dispute (see David Rees, *Korea: The Limited War* [New York: St. Martin's Press, 1964]). As the reader will note in the subsequent discussion, the agenda problem at Geneva took the form: Shall the conference discuss military or political questions first?

quickly be arranged and the conference participants would work toward a political solution in a more leisurely fashion.

c. Agreement upon the terms of a military and political settlement, after which a cease-fire would be put into effect.

Obviously, this is an oversimplified description of the choices that faced the diplomats at Geneva. Any purely military solution—a cease-fire and nothing more—would have been impossible. There would have to be troop movements and some control of the armed forces, if only control by the military commands of the respective belligerents, and these matters would entail political decisions. The alternatives are offered to emphasize the need for important procedural decisions by the conferees.

Item 4a poses this problem: Shall the conference attempt merely to arrange a cease-fire and establish concomitant military procedures for the maintenance of the cease-fire, resolve any immediately pressing political questions, and then adjourn? Shall the powers meet again, at a later date, to effect a political settlement? This was the procedure for the cease-fire in Korea: first a truce was arranged, in July 1953 (after two years of negotiations *between the belligerents*); then a political conference was held, first at Panmunjom, in the fall of 1953, and then at Geneva, from April until June 1954.

Obviously, this procedure would favor the French because it would end the war and take Vietminh pressure off the French Union forces. Thus the Vietminh would lose an important advantage and materially weaken its bargaining position at any future political conference. And thus the Communist delegations could be expected to oppose this procedure.

Although alternative 4b envisages a resolution of political questions at Geneva, the Communists might still oppose an early cease-fire. French military weakness in Tonkin could be exploited by the Communists during negotiations in order to obtain a more favorable political settlement. Hence the Communists would favor 4c. Because additional military reverses after the fall of Dien Bien Phu might endanger the security of the French Union army and bring down the Laniel government, the French would favor 4a or 4b.

5. *All the states at Geneva professed their desire for peace and agreed that a cease-fire should be arranged, but what kind of cease-fire —what terms, conditions, and procedures—should the delegates propose? There was no defined battle line between the belligerent principals in Indochina, as there had been in Korea.*

a. Guerrilla operations were important in the Indochinese War, and since the Vietminh, not the French, employed guerrilla tactics, the security of French-controlled areas would be of vital concern for the French high command, which would demand guarantees and control procedures to prevent the easy resumption of hostilities by the Vietminh.

b. If the Vietminh agreed to an armistice, it too would be concerned for the security of its forces. A reinforced French Union army could still defeat the Vietminh, particularly in conventional set-piece engagements. Hence the Vietminh terms for a cease-fire would place it in easily defensible areas if hostilities were resumed and would demand an agreement not to reinforce the French expeditionary force.

Other procedures for implementation, supervision, and control would have to be given careful scrutiny by the political and military advisors of the governments represented at Geneva. They will be considered in detail in later chapters.

It was almost certain the Geneva Conference would have to make an interim political settlement, but what kind of settlement would this be?

6. *A coalition government.*

This solution entailed the creation of a Vietnamese government made up of representatives of the DRVN and the SVN. Presumably, a provisional government would be set up, a constitution would be drafted, elections for a national legislature would be held, and a representative government established. The intricacies of such procedures would necessitate long discussions and be attended by disagreements and perhaps, stalemate. The United States did not favor this solution, nor, it seems, did Britain and France. Coalition governments had been tried in Eastern Europe after the Second World War, only to be subverted and replaced by Communist "popular democracies." The Western powers did not want another Czechoslovakian coup in Vietnam. Moreover, elections for a national legislature in the atmosphere of a Vietminh victory might lead to electoral success for nationalist-Communist deputies, and this could not be countenanced by the Eisenhower administration nor by many ministers in the Laniel government.

Nor was it clear that Ho Chi Minh would have accepted the solution of a coalition government; he might have rejected representation for non-Communist Vietnamese nationalists. If this solution enabled French Union troops to control areas that had been controlled by the PAVN, Ho would certainly have refused to participate in a coalition, no matter how good his chances for subverting the coalition or how bright his election prospects. Vietnamese Communist and non-Communist ministers and deputies would undoubtedly demand guarantees, as well as veto powers, to ensure preservation of their status and privileges in a coalition government. Such arrangements might so hinder government operations that hostilities would be renewed out of exasperation.

7. *Partition*

This solution envisaged a division of the "national territory" of Vietnam (i.e. Tonkin, Annam, and Cochin China) and the allocation of one or more areas to the DRVN and to the SVN. The British were known to favor this solution.[6] The Churchill government preferred pacification of Indochina and consolidation of the non-Communist SVN government, but had concluded that this was not possible. Partition, it believed, was the best *obtainable* solution. The SVN opposed partition, refusing (albeit ineffectually) to countenance any division of the national territory. The United States publicly supported the SVN on this issue, and no doubt pressed the Laniel government to clarify its position. The French government assured the United States that it would not be part of a settlement that delivered territory to the Communists,[7] but the SVN diplomats in Paris, and Bao Dai himself, were well aware that partition was being discussed.

In late April, Paris newspapers reported the suggestions of various correspondents and unnamed French officials to the effect that partition was the best solution. The *New York Herald Tribune* carried a story on the 1st of May that stated "reliable sources" in the Eisenhower administration had indicated the United States would accept partition under satisfactory circumstances. SVN recalcitrance in the dispatch of its delegation to Geneva was related to the anxiety and anger the Vietnamese felt as a result of such rumors. Bao Dai himself demanded clarification, and Dejean, the French High Commissioner in Saigon, issued this official statement to the press on 3 May: "The French government has no intention of seeking a settlement of the Indochinese problem based upon a partition of Vietnamese territory."[8] On 6 May, Bidault wrote to Bao Dai and stated that French efforts at Geneva would be directed to bringing about a cessation of hostilities in Indochina, not a definitive political settlement. Nothing would be more contrary to the intentions of the French government, he wrote, than "establishment, at the expense of the unity of Vietnam, of two states each having an international status (*une vocation internationale*)."[9] An SVN delegation was sent to

[6] *NYT*, 22 April 1954.
[7] *NYT*, 28 April 1954. Joseph and Stewart Alsop, in an article titled "Indo-China and Geneva" (*NYHT*, 21 April 1954), reported that Bidault had told Secretary Dulles he would not discuss partition at Geneva.
[8] *Le Monde*, 7 May 1954, L&D, p. 123.
[9] L&D, pp. 123-124.

Geneva, but the Vietnamese in Geneva, in Paris, and in Saigon (and Bao Dai in Cannes) continued to be apprehensive, even after Bedell Smith met with Bao Dai on 15 May and assured him that, contrary to the rumors, the United States continued to oppose partition.[10]

One indication of the state of French thinking relative to a settlement in Indochina is the response of General Navarre (dated 21 April) to a series of questions posed by Jean Chauvel, French Ambassador to Switzerland and a member of the French delegation. In the event that negotiations tended toward granting, however provisionally, one or several zones of influence to the Vietminh, Chauvel asked, what maximum limits should the French accept? (The questionnaire used the phrase *"d'une zone d'influence ou de plusieurs"* without elaborating upon its implications.) As to Vietnam, Navarre answered, France could accept a line of partition only at the 18th parallel. This would enable the French to retain the cities of Hué and Tourane and an area (Mu-Gia and Troc) that was militarily valuable. It would be necessary, he added, to continue, at least provisionally, the occupation of Hanoi and Haiphong and a corridor between them ("maintenir . . . la libre disposition de l'axe Hanoi-Haiphong"). The enemy might not be willing to accept a line north of the 16th parallel, Navarre warned, but French acquiescence in Vietminh demands on the location of the demarcation line would give the Vietminh the entire zone of French authority in central Vietnam.[11]

Chauvel's questions were hypothetical, and he used the phrase "zones of influence," but General Navarre responded in a definite fashion; he spoke of lines of partition. The general had evidently given partition a great deal of thought: he had a specific line in mind and envisioned (perhaps only provisionally) France's retention of Hanoi and Haiphong. The Chauvel-Navarre exchange, of course, does not prove that the Laniel government had decided upon partition by mid-April, but it demonstrates that the French were aware that they might have to accept such a solution. We may wonder, however, about the sincerity of the "unequivocal" assurances of opposition to partition given by Bidault and Dejean to the Vietnamese and to the Americans.

If, then, the conference agreed upon partition, important questions of space and time had to be resolved.

a. Should partition be temporary or permanent? If temporary, what procedures should be followed for "de-partitioning" the country? The SVN and the DRVN delegations were equally committed

[10] *NYT*, 16 May 1954.
[11] Ely, pp. 112-113; L&D, pp. 126-127, citing Note 1809, Géné. CC of 21 April 1954.

to a unified Vietnam. If either faction could be persuaded to accept partition, it would consent only upon the understanding that such a solution would be temporary. The great powers, on the other hand, would certainly be less dedicated than the Vietnamese to the idea of unity if their interests, as they perceived them, required the disunity of Vietnam. Thus, since the principal geopolitical basis for British support of partition was the creation of a buffer state in Indochina, there would be little enthusiasm among some British policymakers for the unification of Vietnam under the DRVN if this appeared to be the outcome of an amalgamation of the partitioned state.

In addition, the Soviets, the British, and the Americans (and perhaps the Chinese) might tend to favor permanent rather than temporary partition—unification of the state under the banner of their ideological protagonist, either the DRVN or the SVN—or a resumption of hostilities with its attendant risk of confrontation. What may or may not have been as clear to the diplomats in 1954 as it is for us today was the permanent character of the "temporary" partition solutions. Germany, Korea, and Palestine are only three examples of this phenomenon.

b. How much territory should be assigned to the SVN and how much to the DRVN?

i. Most of Vietnam would be assigned to the SVN. Obviously, the Vietminh would not accept such a division and would, no doubt, prefer to continue fighting.

ii. Most of Vietnam would be assigned to the DRVN. The United States would reject a partition that gave the bulk of Vietnam to the DRVN, but it is not entirely clear what the administration was prepared to do to prevent such a division. It might, of course, merely disassociate itself from such an arrangement—in effect, a more modern application of the Stimson doctrine. Or the United States might intervene. Britain and France also would probably reject the assignment of all or most of the territory to the DRVN, but we should not dismiss the possibility of an agreement between the Communists and the French whereby, in exchange for acquiescence in the extension of the DRVN territories to all of Vietnam, France would be given special economic and cultural privileges in Vietnam. Such a deal was never consummated, but the Eisenhower administration was concerned about such an eventuality, which could have caused irreparable damage to Franco-American relations.

iii. Vietnam would be divided in an approximately equal fashion. France and the United States, as we know, refused to accept partition, but if they had to accept such a solution, it would certainly take this form. Britain favored this alternative, with guarantees for the security and territorial integrity of Laos, Cambodia, Malaya, Burma, and Thailand.

    c. What form should the division of territory take?

    i. A division of Vietnam into a northern and a southern zone with a single line of partition between the two zones. Presumably the DRVN would be assigned the northern zone since the Vietminh controlled a greater proportion of territory in Tonkin than in Annam and Cochin China. But would the Red River delta, with the cities of Hanoi and Haiphong, also be assigned to the DRVN? The French would be most reluctant to agree to this, unless, of course, the Vietminh succeeded in capturing or seriously threatened to capture the delta.

Another important question was the location of the partition line. The French would want a line far to the north; the Vietminh one far to the south. But area was not the only factor involved in determining the location of the line; geopolitical factors would also have to be considered: natural obstacles; highways or geographical features providing access to Laos, Cambodia, and the zone of the opposite party; cities and ports; and the resources of various areas.

    ii. A "leopard's spots" solution, that is, partition of Vietnam into a plurality of zones. This form of solution, more complex than a north-south partition, might appeal to the belligerents because they could cease hostilities and retain control of the territories in their possession. The major cities would remain under French-SVN jurisdiction, but a great deal of rural territory would remain in Vietminh hands. Such a solution, however, would be difficult to police, and because of the multiplicity of lines of contact between formerly belligerent forces, there would be increased risk of incidents which might bring about a resumption of hostilities.

8. *Other solutions*

The Geneva Conference might consider the neutralization of Vietnam: A *unified* and *pacified* Vietnam would be enjoined from entering alliances; other states would agree to refrain from interfering in the affairs of the Vietnamese; foreign troops would be withdrawn and no additional troops or armaments would be introduced into the country. But this solution required an all-Vietnamese government, and the only satisfactory form for this government would have been a coalition government, subject to the same objections raised earlier in paragraph 6.

Although a kind of federal or confederal solution might have been worthy of consideration, this would have involved a partition of Vietnam into provinces or substates (the leopard's spots solution) and formation of a federal government based upon a constitution that

would at least temporarily protect the political influence and po-
litical-control bases of the Communist and the non-Communist Vietnamese in each area-province. The Geneva Conference might arrange
for a "basic law of federation" and then agree upon provisions for
the neutralization of Vietnam, but implementation procedures would
very probably cause as much disagreement as the analogous procedures for the unification of Germany or Korea.

[III]

In both Laos and Cambodia the Vietminh had been active, both
in combat operations and in support of local irregulars; in Laos it
was the Pathet Lao, in Cambodia the Khmer Issarak. How should
the Geneva Conference resolve the problems created by civil or internal war in these countries?

1. By withdrawing the Vietminh forces and disarming the irregulars (and perhaps by their subsequent assimilation into the national
armies of the two states). The non-Communist delegations favored
this solution, as did the representatives of the Royal Governments of
Laos and Cambodia.

Chou En-lai, on his arrival in Geneva, hinted that the C.P.R. and
the other Communist delegations might press for some form of recognition—however informal—of the status of the Pathet Lao and the
Khmer Issarak. Having achieved this, the Communists would be able
to demand, on behalf of these "liberation governments," political
concessions of the kind the Vietminh had won by force of arms in
Vietnam. The Communists could then support other solutions, such
as 2 and 3 below.

2. A coalition government, with, for example, the Pathet Lao participating in the Royal Government of Laos.

3. Partition. Some areas of either Cambodia or Laos would be
assigned to the insurgents and some to the incumbent government.

The non-Communist conferees believed that the PAVN had invaded Laos and Cambodia and had committed "aggression" against
them. They believed, moreover, that the Pathet Lao and Khmer
Issarak were puppets of the Vietminh and hence must oppose both
coalition or partition solutions. It remained to be seen how far the
Communist states would support the "liberation governments" of the
Pathet Lao and Khmers, particularly since these movements did not
have the prestige, status, or success of Ho Chi Minh's Vietminh.

Chapter 12

THE INDOCHINA PHASE

[I]

Convening the day after the fall of Dien Bien Phu, the Indochina phase of the Geneva Conference did not, from the point of view of France and her allies, begin under the most propitious circumstances. Eden chaired the first plenary session and Bidault was the first speaker. The French Foreign Minister paid tribute to the heroism of the French Union troops at Dien Bien Phu; he described the historical background of the conflict then in progress;[1] and then he set forth his proposals for a settlement.

1. There should be a general cessation of hostilities, based upon guarantees to protect the security of the troops of both parties and the civilian population. Measures for implementing a cease-fire should be established and the cease-fire should be supervised by an international commission.

2. Regular army units should assemble in areas defined by the conference.

3. All combat troops that did not belong either to the regular armies or to the police forces should be disarmed. Troop regroupment and the disarmament of irregulars should begin not later than the date the conference would fix for this.

4. All prisoners of war and civilian internees should be released.

5. Because Laos and Cambodia were not fighting a civil war but defending against invasion, this called for withdrawal of the invading Vietminh forces (regulars and irregulars) and restoration of the territorial integrity of these two states. All other military elements (i.e., Pathet Lao and Khmer Issarak), should be disarmed. The evacuation of Laos and Cambodia, and other provisions of the settlement, should be supervised by an international commission, as in the case of Vietnam.

6. "These agreements shall be guaranteed by the States participating in the Geneva Conference." In the event of a violation, the guarantor states would consult with the view of taking appropriate measures.[2]

Bidault emphasized that an immediate, guaranteed cease-fire was essential. Afterward, during a transitional phase, political problems could be progressively resolved, and this, in the last analysis, would

---

[1] Cmd. 9186, p. 109.   [2] *Ibid.*, p. 111.

depend upon the opinion of the government of Vietnam. In any case, such a solution could be assured only when the Vietnamese peoples were completely free to express their political choice in free elections.

Pham Van Dong, head of the DRVN delegation, who spoke after Bidault, noted that the people of France and most political circles in France wanted peace in Indochina. In fact, the peoples of the whole world wanted peace, and the conference must not miss this opportunity for achieving a just settlement. Before he presented his proposals for such a settlement, Pham Van Dong asked for discussion on a proposal that recognized the necessity of inviting representatives of the resistance "governments" of the Pathet Lao and the Khmer Issarak to the conference. These governments, he said, represented the great majority of Laotians and Cambodians, and their presence at Geneva would guarantee the success of negotiations since their representatives would bring the true aspirations and the proposals of the peoples of Laos and Cambodia to the attention of the conference.[3]

Bedell Smith rejected Pham Van Dong's proposal. "The United States," he said, "cannot agree . . . that non-existent, so-called governments or states, such as the so-called Pathet Lao or Free Cambodians, can in any way be considered as qualified for invitations to this Conference under the Berlin Agreement."[4] The Under Secretary of State also responded to newspaper reports that the invitation to the DRVN had been dispatched in the name of the Soviet Union *and* the C.P.R. He asserted that if these reports were true, the form of the invitation was at variance with the understanding of the foreign ministers at Berlin. Molotov did not challenge Bedell Smith's remark about the invitation; he simply recorded his support of Pham Van Dong's proposal for Pathet Lao and Khmer representation. A war of national liberation was being fought in Laos and Cambodia, he said, and the governments (as he called them) of the Khmer and Pathet Lao controlled considerable areas in those states. There was, therefore, no reason for denying these governments representation at the conference.

Sam Sary, head of the Cambodian delegation denied that the Khmer Issarak constituted a government. They were bandits, he said, not regular troops, and were controlled, in part, by the Vietminh. "[These] Khmers [Khmer Issarak] are foreigners who are being manipulated by a foreign bloc."[5] Speaking next, Phoui Sananikone,

---

[3] *Ibid.*, pp. 112-113.
[4] *Ibid.*, p. 114.
[5] *Ibid.*, p. 115.

head of the Laotian delegation, briefly recounted the history of the Pathet Lao in Laos and noted that it had dissolved itself in 1949. In 1953, with the invasion of Laotian territory by the Vietminh, a so-called government of the Pathet Lao had been set up in Vietminh-held territories under the leadership of Prince Souphanouvong. The prince, said Phoui, had no mandate from the Laotian people; he was a dupe of foreign elements and powers. "This so-called Pathet Lao represents absolutely nothing."[6]

Chou En-lai supported Dong's proposal; Eden and Bidault in turn rejected the proposal; and Eden agreed with Bedell Smith's earlier suggestion that the four "inviting" powers settle the question in a restricted session. Molotov asserted that if there was to be a restricted session, five powers, not four, must be represented: China's presence was indispensable. He then admitted that the C.P.R. had been made an "inviting" power: the invitations to the DRVN, prepared in and dispatched from Moscow, had listed the C.P.R. as such a power. Bedell Smith denounced this unilateral act of the Soviet Union as a violation of the Berlin "accords."[7]

With neither a decision on the question submitted by Pham (i.e. Pathet Lao and Khmer Issarak representation) nor resolution of the composition of the restricted meeting to consider this question, Eden adjourned the session.

The second plenary session, chaired by Molotov, convened on Monday, 10 May. Pham Van Dong, the first speaker, announced that the DRVN would permit the evacuation of seriously wounded French Union force prisoners from Dien Bien Phu, and Bidault accepted this "offer" at once.[8] Pham Van Dong then gave the Vietminh version of the background of the Indochinese War—to give the conferees a "more objective and just appreciation" of the facts than Bidault had imparted.[9] He accused the United States of having intervened in Indochina as early as 1946 and having sought to prolong and extend the war. The American objective, he said, was to convert Indochina into an American colony after the French had been ousted. Dong rejected the French proposals for a settlement, which proceeded from an "outworn imperialist colonial conception." A proper settlement, he said, must include military *and political* matters. He submitted his own proposals for a solution,[10] which are set out below, along with the corresponding French proposals or the French position on particular questions.

[6] *Ibid.*, p. 116.   [7] L&D, p. 141.
[8] *Econ.*, 15 May 1954, p. 548.   [9] Cmd. 9186, p. 120.
[10] *Ibid.*, pp. 116-118.

Vietminh Proposals	*French Proposals or Position*
1. Recognition by France of the independence of Vietnam and the Pathet Lao and Khmer Issarak.[11]	1a. France had already granted independence to the Republic of Vietnam and to Laos. b. Bidault rejected the proposition that the Pathet Lao or Khmer Issarak had status as governments.
2a. Withdrawal of all foreign troops from Vietnam, Cambodia, and Laos within the number of days to be fixed *by the belligerents.*	2a. Regroupment of regular belligerent forces (French Union *and* Vietminh) into *zones fixed by the conference.* Assembly into these areas to begin in a specified number of days *determined by the conference.*
b. Before withdrawal, assembly areas *for French troops* in Vietnam would be established, but the number of these areas should be held to a minimum.	b. All regular and nonregular Vietminh forces that had entered Laos and Cambodia should be evacuated.
c. French troops should refrain from interfering in the affairs of authorities in localities where they were stationed.	c. All forces in the Associated States that were not members of the army or police forces should be disarmed.
3a. Free, general elections in Vietnam, Cambodia, and Laos, supervised by advisory conferences composed of representatives of the belligerent parties. Pending the establishment of a single government in each of the three states, the governments of the "two parties . . . will administer the districts under their control."	3a. The immediate end of hostilities, with procedures for implementation determined by the conference.
b. Before this measure was implemented, there should be a cessation of hostilities (see paragraph 8 below).	b. No political solution until after a cease-fire and until the SVN government had been consulted. The French also envisaged a "transitional period" after the cease-fire; elections probably would not be held until the end of this period. c. No decision on a political solution until after a cease-fire.
4. The DRVN would examine the question of its association in the French Union. The Pathet Lao and Khmer Issarak would do the same.	4a and 5a. The French had concluded a treaty with Laos, granting it independence and defining its position within the French Union.
5. The DRVN, Pathet Lao, and Khmer would recognize French cultural and economic interests in their respective states.	b. France and the SVN had drafted treaties of independence and association in the French Union. They would be signed soon.
6. The belligerents would refrain from taking action against "collaborators."	
7. An exchange of prisoners of war would be arranged.	7. Release both of prisoners of war and interned civilians would be arranged.

[11] *Ibid.*, pp. 120-121.

8. A cease-fire would be concluded before the measures listed in paragraphs 1–7 were carried out; but agreements between France, the DRVN, Pathet Lao, and Khmer must provide for:

  a. Free passage to their assembly areas of the troops of one party across territories of the other party;

  b. An end to the entry of troops and arms into Indochina;

  c. Establishment of supervisory machinery to implement cease-fire agreements. Joint committees of representatives of the belligerent parties would be created in each of the three countries for this purpose.

8a. An immediate cease-fire would be concluded; political questions should be discussed at a later time.

  b. There must be international supervision of the evacuation of Vietminh forces from Laos and Cambodia and similar supervision of the provisions of a cease-fire (e.g. disarming nonregulars, regroupment of regulars, etc.).

  c. The cease-fire agreements should be guaranteed by the states participating in the Geneva Conference.

Eden subsequently made a statement indicating his support for Bidault's proposals for a settlement. He believed it was essential to bring about a cease-fire immediately, but a simple cease-fire would not be practicable. The opposing forces must be separated into distinct, clearly defined zones, and measures for preventing a resumption of hostilities must be agreed upon.[12] Bedell Smith, the last speaker of the day, approved Bidault's outline of a settlement as the basis for discussion but reserved the position of the United States on guarantees for the settlement. The United States, he said, would first want to know the obligations of the guarantors.[13]

AFTER THE close of the second plenary session, Jacques Baeyens, a spokesman for Bidault, held a press conference in which he declared that, while the Vietminh proposals appeared attractive, they would result in Communist governments in each Associated State. Dong, he said, had denounced American intervention but had said nothing about Chinese intervention. As for the DRVN's respecting the economic and cultural interests of France, how much value could France put upon this? The offer of the DRVN to associate in the French Union was comparable to the Soviet offer to join NATO.[14]

Some of the French journalists at the press conference inaccurately interpreted Baeyens' remarks as an official rejection of the Vietminh proposals, wired their newspapers accordingly, and late editions in Paris announced the "rejection." This caused an uproar among the Assembly deputies and within the government itself. The shock of the loss of Dien Bien Phu no longer constrained the anti-government forces in the Assembly, and debate on the government's Indochina policy had been informally renewed. These reports from

[12] *Ibid.*, p. 123.   [13] *NYT*, 10 May 1954.   [14] L&D, p. 144.

Geneva seemed to support the critics who had been saying that Bidault wanted to continue the war. On 11 May a French spokesman denied that the French delegation had rejected the Vietminh proposals; they were, instead, being given serious study. Nonetheless, the spokesman insisted that they openly sought to win the Vietminh an immediate political success and to establish three "popular democracies" within the French Union. The French, moreover, could not agree that a cease-fire depended upon a political settlement.[15]

In Paris, however, the opposition pressed ever more vehemently for an early debate on the government's Indochina policy.[16] On 11 May Laniel proposed that, instead of a debate, the Assembly appoint a permanent parliamentary commission on Indochinese questions whose first task would be to investigate the fall of Dien Bien Phu.[17] But this obvious delaying tactic pleased virtually no one in the Assembly. François Mitterand, long a critic of France's Indochina policy, argued that the National Assembly alone must decide whether or not the war should be widened and troop replacements sent to Southeast Asia.[18] The applause Mitterand received was an ill omen for Laniel. On 13 May, on a vote of confidence on the question of postponing debate, Laniel won by a mere two votes, 289 to 287, with 50 abstentions.[19] This gained the Premier, and his Foreign Minister, a little time; but no one—in Paris or Geneva—was under any illusion about the likelihood of the Laniel government's lasting much longer. Only a signal success at Geneva, or perhaps even a minor achievement that Bidault could dramatize as a step toward a cease-fire, might enable the Premier to prevail through the crisis.

But success at Geneva depended upon too many other parties, notably the Communists and the United States. It also depended upon military developments in Indochina, which began to take an alarming turn toward the end of May; General Giap had redeployed his PAVN forces and was ready to strike against the French Union defenses in the Red River delta. At the end of May the opposition again began to demand a debate on the Indochina situation. Parliamentary interpellations forced Laniel to ask for another vote of confidence, the third within six weeks, and this was to prove fatal.

---

[15] L&D, p. 145. At his press conference on 11 May, when Secretary Dulles was asked what he thought of the Vietminh proposal, he answered: "I think very little of it because it is the same pattern that has been applied in the past in Germany, Austria, and Korea; namely, to compel a withdrawal of the forces which sustain a free society and to set up a system under which the Communists can grab the whole area. It is certainly unacceptable in its totality, whether there is any particular word or phrase in it that is unacceptable I would not want to say without further study. But it is not acceptable in its totality." DSB, 24 May 1954, pp. 781-782.

[16] NYT, 12 May 1954.   [17] JO, 12 May 1954, p. 2336.
[18] Ibid., pp. 2343-2344.   [19] JO, 14 May, p. 2383.

[I I]

On Tuesday, 11 May, the Indochina Conference was in recess while the delegations of the great powers (and others) met in plenary session to consider a Korean settlement. On 12 May the third plenary session on Indochina was held. Nguyen Quoc Dinh, head of the delegation of the State of Vietnam, delivered the first speech and declared that his delegation was ready to consider any serious and positive effort made in good faith and leading to a military settlement.[20] But all proposals (1) must include adequate guarantees for the establishment of a real and lasting peace and the prevention of further aggression; (2) "must not involve any division, whether direct or indirect, definitive or temporary, *de facto* or *de jure*, of the national territory"; and (3) must provide for international supervision of a cease-fire.

Dinh then turned to the matter of a political settlement. Relations between France and Vietnam, he said, would be governed by the terms of two treaties (after they were signed): a treaty of independence and a treaty associating Vietnam with France in the French Union on the basis of sovereign equality. As for the political settlement the conference would negotiate, Dinh's proposal comprised the following elements.

1. Recognition that the government of Bao Dai was the sole representative of the Vietnamese nation.
2. Recognition of only one army, under the control of the State of Vietnam.
3. Free elections throughout Vietnam after the Security Council of the United Nations had determined that the authority of the State of Vietnam had been established. These elections should be controlled and supervised by the U.N.
4. A representative government would be established after the elections, under the aegis of Bao Dai.
5. Vietnam would undertake to refrain from prosecuting "collaborators."
6. The political and territorial integrity of Vietnam would be guaranteed by other states (including, presumably, all the Geneva powers).
7. Economic assistance would be furnished by the United Nations.

These extraordinary proposals in effect presumed the virtual surrender of the political and military gains the Vietminh had won to that date. Further, they envisaged the dissolution of the DRVN and the PAVN. Dinh's speech might be termed unreal or even fantastic

[20] Cmd. 9186, p. 123.

were it not for one fact: Bedell Smith, without elaboration or explanation, approved the proposals. The United States government, it appeared, would support the ambitions (pretensions, if you will) of the Bao Dai government. But how far the administration would be willing to go with such support was not yet known, not even among the highest policymakers in the government. Nor was the character of the prospective support, other than the espousal of the SVN delegation's proposals at the conference, quite clear to outside observers, although there had been indications that American economic assistance would, in the not too distant future, be channeled to the Vietnamese directly rather than through French intermediaries.

It is interesting to contrast the proposals of the two Vietnamese delegations. Each asked for recognition of the independence of Vietnam but each, naturally, had a very different idea of what government must rule this independent Vietnam. If Nguyen Quoc Dinh had been explicit in his claims for recognition of the Bao Dai regime, recognition of the DRVN was implicit in Pham Van Dong's proposals. Both ministers proposed all-Vietnamese elections after a cease-fire and both favored supervision of the elections, Dinh by a United Nations body and Pham Van Dong, by an advisory conference composed of representatives of "the two parties" (i.e. the French and the Vietminh).

The positions of the two delegations on election supervision were analogous to the positions of their Communist and non-Communist Korean counterparts in the Korean Conference, except that the Vietminh wanted the non-Communist Bao Dai regime excluded from the supervisory commission. It is, of course, obvious that Dong's proposal for an advisory conference had the defect (or advantage, depending upon one's point of view) of enabling the Vietminh to veto decisions that might operate contrary to its interests. Pham Van Dong's proposal for supervision of the cease-fire was similar to his proposal for the elections: he wanted joint committees of representatives of the belligerents (France and the Vietminh), and the Bao Dai regime excluded by implication. Dinh, on the other hand, proposed international supervision.

The DRVN Foreign Minister also put himself on record as resolutely opposed to partition. The Vietminh had not at this date accepted partition—they had not yet (at least publicly) resigned themselves to the necessity for it. Dong proposed the withdrawal of troops into regroupment areas, but these areas were not to become permanent enclaves. The French were to withdraw from their regroupment areas by a date set by the belligerents—*out* of Indochina

—and no new troops (neither French nor other foreign troops) were to be introduced.

The apparent unreality of Dinh's proposals resulted from two factors.

1. The Vietminh was a military force to reckon with; it had fought as a disciplined and independent army for several years and, moreover, had won several victories. The SVN army was not an independent entity and had virtually no independence of action; its operations and logistics were controlled by the French high command. Its troops had little esprit and, probably, little or no dedication to the government of Bao Dai or Bao Dai himself.

2. The DRVN had no capital city and occupied no important coastal cities, but the Vietminh occupied a substantial portion of rural Vietnam. It was a government independent of France and, like its army, tightly disciplined and not given to schism. The government of the SVN was neither unified, disciplined, nor truly independent. The French constantly interfered in its operations, even as late as spring of 1954. SVN premiers who did not meet with the approval of the French High Commissioner, the minister for the Associated States, or the French cabinet (usually because they were ardent nationalists) were forced to resign.

Thus the Vietnamese leaders of the DRVN had exercised real independence in the hills of Tonkin while the Vietnamese leaders of the SVN enjoyed neither independence in fact nor even unequivocal independence. Indeed, the *de jure* independence of the DRVN was no more questionable than that of the SVN. The *de facto* independence of the former coupled with military victory, would seem to render overly emphatic or ambitious claims of the SVN delegate almost unrealistic were it not for the possibility that the United States might eventually make such claims more plausible than they appeared to be on 12 May 1954.

PREMIER CHOU addressed the third plenary session after Nguyen Quoc Dinh and supported Pham Van Dong's proposals for a settlement of the Indochina question and for inviting representatives of the Pathet Lao and Khmer Issarak to Geneva. Foreign Secretary Eden delivered a short but characteristically pertinent speech. "I shall not follow some of the previous speakers in the re-writing of history or the passing of historical judgments," he said, "because I know we here are most unlikely to reach any agreement on such things. . . . If we differ on history, I hope that does not mean we must disagree on what should be done now."[21] Eden assumed that

[21] *Ibid.*, p. 126.

the conferees were agreed upon putting a stop to the fighting and he posed five questions.

1. Were the delegates agreed that the troops of both belligerent parties ought to be concentrated in predetermined areas?

2. Was it accepted that Laos and Cambodia were in a special category and that Vietminh forces ought to be withdrawn from these states? (The day before, Prince Wan Waithayakon of Thailand had suggested that Laos and Cambodia be separated from the more complex question of Vietnam to expedite the discussions.[22] His suggestion did not affect the issue of Vietminh withdrawal, but there was no question that the prince wanted the Vietminh to leave Laos and Cambodia, both of which border Thailand, and the French troops to remain in Indochina until a date determined by the conference.)

3. "Who is to work out the areas of concentration for Viet-Nam? Is it to be the Commanders-in-Chief with, I suppose, reference back to the Conference here?"[23]

4. Did the conference agree that irregulars ought to be disarmed after troops had been concentrated in the regroupment areas?

5. Were the conferees in favor of international supervision of the military and political procedures of a settlement? If so, what form?

Eden remarked that Britain favored U.N. supervision, which did not necessarily mean supervision by the combatants nor by any of the states represented at the conference table. He noted that the ministers of the Colombo powers had recently expressed favor of the use of the offices and machinery of the U.N. for furthering the purposes of the Geneva Conference and the implementation of conference decisions on Indochina. Bedell Smith and Bidault approved Eden's questions and said they hoped for early answers. The session then adjourned.

Unhappy with the public attitudes various speakers had struck, Eden suggested to Bedell Smith and Bidault that "we should continue our talks in restricted sessions, consisting of the heads of all nine delegations with only two or three advisors apiece."[24] The sessions would be secret and no detailed account of the proceedings would be given to the press. Bedell Smith and Bidault agreed. The next day Molotov and Chou En-lai were contacted by the Foreign Secretary and they too approved his idea. The first restricted session was scheduled for Monday, 17 May. There would, however, be one more public plenary session, on 14 May.

Molotov and Bidault were the principal speakers at the fourth plenary session, at which the Soviet Foreign Minister accused the United States of seeking to extend the Indochinese War and of inter-

[22] L&D, p. 145.   [23] Cmd. 9186, p. 127.   [24] E, p. 133.

vening in increasing strength in the affairs of Indochina. He also criticized Britain, France, and the United States for attempting to establish a military bloc in Southeast Asia, not for the defense of states in the area but for combating national liberation movements of the indigenous peoples. The end result of these efforts, he said, was the support of colonial regimes in Asia. Molotov urged support for the proposals of the DRVN delegation, which, he said, provided a basis for settlement, and he criticized the French proposals for not dealing with political problems. "The task of the Geneva Conference should be understood as meaning that it must bring about a cessation of the fighting in Indo-China as soon as possible, and at the same time reach such an agreement as would enable the legitimate claims of the Indo-Chinese peoples to be satisfied in regard to securing their national independence and democratic rights."[25]

Molotov promised to answer the five questions Eden had posed in the preceding plenary session but said it would be inappropriate to narrow the matter "down to these questions and to by-pass those problems of a military and political character that have already been raised by events in Indo-China." He made two more noteworthy observations.

1. He recognized, in principle, the acceptability of the French proposal that the conference guarantee its eventual settlements. In the event of violation of the agreements, there should be consultations among the guarantor states for adopting *collective* measures for implementing the agreements. He seems to have been unwilling to accept the French idea of consultations for the adoption of individual as well as collective measures. In any event, he said he felt it would be desirable for other conference participants to make known their views.

2. Because of the importance of reaching an agreement, Molotov said he would suggest an "addition" to the DRVN proposals: The agreement "must include provisions for the setting up of a supervisory commission composed of neutral countries."[26] Pham Van Dong had initially asked for joint committees of the belligerents to oversee the implementation of a cease-fire agreement; thus the "addition" suggested by Molotov was, in fact, a concession.

This was significant because it was Molotov who made it and because Bedell Smith (and probably Bidault and Eden as well) would not otherwise have accepted the truce supervision of Dong's joint commissions and Molotov probably realized this. The non-Communist delegations might be willing to accept the kind of supervision Molotov now proposed, provided the technical details could be agreed upon.

[25] Cmd. 9186, p. 129.   [26] *Ibid.*, p. 131.

The composition of a neutral nation supervisory commission would be crucially important, as experience had shown in the case of the Korean Armistice Commission (when representation was divided equally between non-Communist and Communist states—Sweden and Switzerland, Poland and Czechoslovakia—and the commission had been almost constantly deadlocked). Molotov did not, at this point, propose the membership of the Indochina commissions; he merely noted that the conference would encounter no insuperable difficulties in determining the composition of the commissions he proposed for supervising the implementation of an Indochina truce. It remained to be seen how substantial a concession the Soviet minister had made when the conference actually turned to the question of the commission membership. Nor did Molotov's proposal touch upon the international supervision of elections, which he might very well have opposed at this time. After all, in the Korean Conference Molotov refused to compromise on his plan for a joint North and South Korea commission to control and oversee elections.

As for the major points of disagreement between the Communist and non-Communist participants, Molotov adhered to the Communist position.

1. There must be recognition of the sovereignty and independence of the Pathet Lao and Khmer Issarak. (He said nothing about inviting representatives of these "governments" to Geneva, but he was on record as favoring such invitations.)

2. The conference must resolve some of the political problems arising from the war as well as reach an agreement on a cessation of hostilities. Bidault wanted only a cease-fire with guarantees, that is, only a military settlement. He did not want the conference to discuss political problems, which, he said, must be settled after a transitional period of peace and stability.

The French Foreign Minister spoke formally for the second time after Molotov concluded his address.[27] After treating the Vietminh proposals in detail, Bidault took up Eden's five questions. France wanted the troops of the belligerents concentrated in areas to be determined by the Geneva participants in consultation with the respective commanders in chief. Irregular troops must be disarmed and the cease-fire must be subject to international supervision. France, moreover, would consider any proposals for the composition of a supervisory commission. "If the principle of international supervision is accepted, then in Viet-Nam joint bodies might be employed, the terms to be settled by mutual agreement, to work under the Inter-

[27] Ibid., p. 134.

national Commissions and assist them in their task."[28] (It should be noted that Bidault did not mention the United Nations as the organization that might provide supervisory personnel. This was of a piece, however, with the long-standing French policy of keeping the U.N. out of the Indochinese War.) Finally, the Laotian and Cambodian questions ought to be considered separately, Bidault said, but Vietminh troops must be withdrawn from these countries immediately.

Before adjourning this fourth session, Molotov announced that the conference would next convene on Monday, 17 May, and the meeting would be "secret." A plenary session would not meet again until 8 June.

[III]

After the fall of Dien Bien Phu and the television address of the Secretary of State on 7 May, Washington continued to voice diverse views on the Indochina crisis. We have already noted Dulles's remark, at his news conference on 11 May, of the possible strategic consequences of the loss of Indochina to the Vietminh when he had said that Southeast Asia *could* be defended without Indochina. His earlier statement had produced a quick (and pained) reaction in Paris and in Geneva, and Dulles subsequently explained that he had been speaking hypothetically. The United States, he said, had not given up trying to prevent the loss of the Associated States. On the 12th, President Eisenhower emphasized the importance of Indochina; moreover, he felt that the free world ought not write off Indochina and that "we ought to look at this thing with some optimism and determination."[29] There was no disagreement on this matter between himself and the Secretary of State, he added.

On 14 May, Deputy Secretary of Defense Robert B. Anderson warned against piecemeal conquests by the Communists and asserted that collective defense was the best way to meet a threat of this kind.[30] On a CBS television program on Sunday, 16 May, Senator Knowland declared that it would be a mistake for the United States to become involved with ground troops on the continent of Asia unless Red China intervened in Indochina in force. Senator Mike Mansfield (Dem., Mont.), appearing with Knowland, said he opposed sending troops to Indochina because Red China and the Soviet Union could deploy forces superior to any the United States could at present furnish. Both men expressed the hope that Asian nations would join in a collective defense effort to protect their own interests. Secretary of Defense Charles Wilson, before setting off on an official trip to East Asia, associated himself with Dulles's views of the 7th;

[28] *Ibid.*, p. 136.   [29] *NYT*, 16 May 1954.   [30] *NYT*, 14 May 1954.

namely, that present conditions in Indochina did not provide a suitable basis for the participation of American troops, but collective defense plans could go ahead.[31]

During this period, when it was made plain that American combat forces would not be dispatched to Indochina *for the present*, administration policymakers continued their behind-the-scenes efforts to line up support for a regional defense alliance. To the Washington ambassadors of the Colombo powers, American officials explained that the United States did not intend to support colonialism in Southeast Asia; rather, it sought to establish an alliance of genuinely independent states that would be able to resist Communist imperialism.[32] These demarches may not have been entirely fruitless (they may have been efforts to prevent official condemnation by the Colombo powers of the defense-system scheme), but they did not seem to have won the support of the governments contacted. Although Britain remained the principal obstacle to preparatory talks, Eden was willing to permit military staff talks between the ANZUS states and his government, but he continued to oppose political talks of any kind. The French government was deeply concerned about this divergence in approach, and Schumann expressed his anxiety over the unity of the Communists at Geneva, which contrasted with the apparent disunity of the West.[33] The problem was almost certainly a topic of discussion between Bidault and Bedell Smith, who reported to Washington the strong feeling in Geneva that the United States must demonstrate Western unity and call a Southeast Asia–pact parley, even without Britain. This, he said, would show the United States' determination to prevent a settlement that would result in Communist control of Indochina.[34]

In Washington, there was a great deal of sentiment for getting on with an Asian alliance, and some bitter criticism of the British. For example, the *New York Times* reported that the American delegation in Geneva believed Britain was strengthening its ties with India and the Commonwealth at the expense of Anglo-American relations. The alleged influence of the Labour Party's left wing on British policy also was condemned.[35] Then, on 19 May, at his weekly news conference, the President asserted that Britain was not indispensable to a Southeast Asia alliance if it was made up of the appropriate Asian nations.[36] This created dismay in London and in the Commonwealth delegations at Geneva. Although Eden did not reply in a public statement, Clifton Webb, the New Zealand Minister of External Affairs, declared that an anti-Communist alliance in Southeast

[31] *NYT*, 17 May 1954.   [32] *NYT*, 14 May 1954.   [33] *NYT*, 15 May 1954.
[34] *NYT*, 12 May 1954.   [35] *NYT*, 16 May 1954.   [36] *NYT*, 19 May 1954.

Asia was inconceivable without Great Britain.[37] This, and another incident (which we will describe next), very probably caused Eden to return to London on 22-23 May for consultations with Prime Minister Churchill and the cabinet.

The reader will recall that, on 13 May, the Laniel government received a vote of confidence from the National Assembly on the question of putting off debate on its Indochina policy, by a margin of two votes. At a meeting the day before, the French cabinet had decided to ask what the United States would do if France could not secure an honorable cease-fire at Geneva or the military situation in the Red River delta seriously deteriorated,[38] and Bonnet, the French ambassador in Washington, was instructed to pose these questions to the State Department. (Douglas Dillon, the American ambassador in Paris, was informed of these questions on the evening of the 12th.) The purpose of this new démarche seems to have been to secure assurances of support from the administration, thus strengthening Bidault's position at Geneva. Also, the responses these questions elicited would enable the French to make a more realistic appraisal of their chances of securing a cease-fire with the security guarantees Bidault asked for at the first plenary session. On 13 May Bonnet and Dulles discussed these questions at length.

The decision of the French cabinet (to pose the hypothetical questions) and the approaches to the Eisenhower administration were made in secret, and we do not know the exact substance of Dulles's comments on 13 May, but Lacouture and Devillers—basing their account upon interviews with French officials—have pieced this story together.[39] Dulles understood that the French needed an alternative if they failed to get an honorable settlement at Geneva; He also understood that France could not continue the struggle alone. If the conference brought no acceptable results, Dulles said, it would be necessary to discuss the conditions of an eventual American intervention. (Such remarks are fully in accord with the substance of Dulles's speech of 7 May.) Congress must first approve military action, however, and it would not do this unless certain conditions were met: genuine independence for the Associated States and creation of a collective defense pact to ensure military action by or in the name of a coalition. (This accords with his Overseas Press Club speech of 29 March.) Dulles, however, seems to have added another condition according to Lacouture and Devillers: United Nations approval for intervention—an additional complication for United States intervention, which might even preclude it.

[37] *NYT*, 20 May 1954.
[38] *NYT*, 13 May 1954; L&D, p. 174.
[39] L&D, pp. 174-175.

Whatever the content of the Dulles-Bonnet conversations, by the 13th, the French démarche was no longer secret; the press reported the episode on the basis of "leaks" that might or might not have been correct. Reuters, for example, reported that France had asked for immediate American military assistance in Indochina. The *New York Times* of 13 May correctly reported that France wanted to know what the United States would do if an honorable cease-fire could not be arranged. This, it was said, would force the administration to make a decision among various positions and factions (activists and various types of prudent policymakers). Later editions of the *Times* and the *New York Herald Tribune*, however, spoke of Franco-American *military discussions*. If such there were they were of the most informal kind, and probably considered what *might* be done in various contingencies. In any case, officials of the Eisenhower administration discussed the new French approach and prepared a reply; it was ready for delivery by 15 May.

In Geneva, Eden learned of what he called "Franco-American discussions on the possibility of military intervention by the United States in Indo-China." He learned of these discussions, he said, from Swiss newspapers on the morning of 15 May and was startled that this issue had been "resurrected at such a moment." He asked Bedell Smith about the press reports, but the American ambassador knew nothing about them. He then approached Bidault, who, according to Eden, gave him a "vague denial." Somewhat later a French advisor to Bidault, acting on instructions from the French Foreign Minister, showed Eden a document that listed the conditions for American intervention.[40]

Now it was also on 15 May that Ambassador Dillon gave Maurice Schumann an official reply to the questions of the 13th. An examination of the possibility of American intervention, he said, depended upon the satisfaction of certain conditions. The President could ask Congress for the necessary authorization only if seven conditions were fulfilled.[41]

1. France and the three Associated States must request the United States for military assistance.

2. The same request must be addressed to the governments of Thailand, the Philippines, Australia, New Zealand, and Great Britain. If Thailand and the Philippines agreed to this request, if Australia and New Zealand indicated they would agree after the 1954 Australian elections were held, and if Britain at least acquiesced, the

[40] E, p. 133.
[41] DDE, p. 359; J. Laniel, *Le drame indochinois: De Dien Bien Phu au pari de Geneve* (Paris: Plon, 1957), p. 110.

United States would accept such responses as adequate bases for proceeding.

3. The United Nations must approve the request of Thailand, Laos, and Cambodia for the dispatch of a U.N. observation commission to Southeast Asia.

4. The French government must reaffirm the complete independence of the Associated States and give them unqualified freedom to withdraw from the French Union.

5. During the period of united action the French government must keep its forces in Indochina. American assistance (principally sea and air power) would supplement, not substitute for, French Union troops.

6. Military arrangements for the division of authority, the division of tasks, and training the SVN army must be concluded between France and the United States.

7. The French request for assistance must be approved by the French parliament as well as by the French cabinet.

Here indeed was a multiplication of conditions. Because it is difficult to see how any French government could have accepted them, they may have been formulated to put off a decision until the distant future, when a defense pact would have been negotiated, or perhaps to prevent the administration from having to make a decision.

This note of 15 May, with its seven conditions, was undoubtedly the same note the French advisor showed Eden on Bidault's instructions. The note Eden said "contained the conditions for United States intervention in Indo-China."[42] Eden was concerned and irritated. Late on the 15th the *New York Herald Tribune* arrived, reporting the "full details of the Franco-American negotiations." Eden, who could now discuss the situation with Bedell Smith without compromising his French source related that Bedell Smith was indignant over the inability of the administration to keep the discussions secret. He recorded his conversation with Smith as follows.

> I pointed out that for us the seriousness of the situation lay not only in the matter of the announcement, but in the fact that we had received no prior intimation whatever of these conversations. Bedell Smith said at once that it was intolerable that we should get information of this kind from a newspaper and that of course we should have been told. The United Kingdom Government were to have been informed, once French acceptance of the conditions was known. He emphasized that the matter was not nearly so serious as the newspapers had made it look. All that was contemplated,

[42] E, p. 134.

he said, was American assistance with the training of troops. Whatever the nature of the intended action, it was clear that the publicity given to these talks could do grave damage, and Bedell Smith and I agreed to limit it as best we could.

I told the Australian, New Zealand and Canadian delegates what had happened, and sent a reassuring letter to Mr. Nehru. I was relieved when Bidault informed me, two days later, that France would make no request for intervention while the Conference was still in session.[43]

Eden conveyed to Prime Minister Churchill his fears that renewed talk of intervention would weaken whatever chance remained of agreement at the conference. The Foreign Secretary believed the Franco-American discussions would convince the Chinese and Russians that the United States really intended to intervene. He did not believe that this would incline the Communists to compromise.[44]

Eden's fear of the consequences of renewed discussions of military intervention and their effect upon the course of negotiations at Geneva reflected, in part, the degree to which he was committed to the success of the conference. His behind-the-scenes efforts were aimed at bringing about a cease-fire on the basis of a partition of Vietnam and the withdrawal of Vietminh troops from Laos and Cambodia. The settlement negotiated at Geneva would be guaranteed, he hoped, by Asian states. Eden believed his success depended upon creating an atmosphere of mutual confidence and trust, conciliating disagreements, and winning explicit Soviet support for his goals— and he believed the Soviets wanted to end the Indochinese War as much as he did.

If Eden's premises were correct, it was possible that threats of intervention and discussions whose aim was the establishment of a collective defense system or the formulation of conditions for intervention might very well aggravate the Communists. Rather than expedite the negotiations, this would certainly slow them up; rather than elicit concessions from the Soviets, Chinese, and Vietminh, this could make them obdurate. But many American and French officials accepted neither Eden's premises nor his conclusions; they felt that British policy was a policy of weakness. Concessions from the Communists could be won only by a policy of deterrence (what Eden called "noising off"); a satisfactory cease-fire could be achieved only by being "tough"; and subsequent events seem to bear out this view rather than Eden's. The significant concessions were made at Geneva when one or another Western delegation made threats: threats either

[43] *Ibid.*   [44] E, p. 135.

to proceed with plans for some form of united action or threats to break off negotiations.

We cannot accurately measure the effects on the Communists of the French démarche of the 13th, the American response, and the British reaction. We know that the conference did not make any real progress for another two weeks, but it would be difficult to establish a causal relationship between the renewed talk of intervention and the lack of progress in the negotiations. If the British could conclude from everyday news reports that the French and Americans were planning formal military discussions without them, the Russians and the Chinese could have drawn the same conclusion. None of the news releases after 15 May, describing the conditions for American intervention, was ever complete. Independence for the Associated States, a request for intervention, and coalition action were listed in the newspaper reports, along with such additional conditions as United Nations approval of peace-observation teams and Franco-American military agreements, but an accurate list of the conditions that might elicit French disagreement did not appear in any of the French, British, or American papers of the period.[45] Today we may be able to argue that the French could not have accepted the conditions of the American note of 15 May, but the Communists could not have drawn that conclusion in May 1954. They would have had to conclude there was a risk, however small, of eventual United States intervention.

Eden, in his account of the incident, remarked that two days afterward, on 17 May, Bidault assured him France would not request help by intervention. In Paris, it seems, Laniel's immediate reaction to the seven conditions was a polite comment to the effect that they were not unacceptable.[46] But, according to Eisenhower, Laniel and Maurice Schumann (French Secretary of State for Foreign Affairs) told Dillon that they could not grant the Associated States the right of withdrawal from the French Union, which they did not regard as an important right in any case.[47] Several days later Schumann informed Dillon that his government contemplated a reduction of French troops in Indochina over the next few years; approval of the EDC, he said, could not be secured if the French would have to keep troops in Indochina for an indefinite period. Because the French were most reluctant to fulfill the seven conditions, Bidault could

---

[45] That is, a report that put explicit, public emphasis upon those conditions the French would probably not accept; namely, the right of the Associated States to withdraw from the French Union, French guarantees to keep troops in Indochina, and preliminary approval by the French Assembly of a formal governmental request for assistance.

[46] Laniel, *op. cit.*, p. 110.   [47] DDE, pp. 359-360.

assure Eden that his government would make no request for intervention during the conference.

IT APPEARS the administration had again parried a "request" for commitment from an importunate France; the American formulators of the seven conditions could not have believed France would be willing or able to fulfill them. Even had France been willing to, its agreement would have been illusory, since it could not have "delivered." The National Assembly would have balked, the debate on France's Indochina policy would have begun earlier, and Laniel would have lost a vote of confidence sooner than he did. But did the Eisenhower administration policymakers appreciate the consequences of an effort by Laniel to satisfy the conditions, an effort that would surely entail the collapse of his government? We know that American officials were pessimistic about the future of the Laniel government; they expected it to fall after the Assembly vote on 13 May. But, if this occurred, a governmental crisis in Paris would very likely coincide with the military crisis that was shaping up in Tonkin. Moreover, the succeeding government might be willing to make peace "at any price." Given this appraisal of the weakness of the Laniel government, it is difficult to understand how Dulles could have expected the French to accept conditions likely to bring on a governmental crisis.

On the other hand, the conditions were quite reasonable from an American point of view. France should make an explicit request for assistance to show that the United States and its allies were not officious meddlers in a French affair. The United Nations should approve the prospective course of action, if only by the dispatch of observation commissions, to dispel charges of colonialism. If the Associated States were truly independent and sovereign, they would of course have the right to withdraw from the French Union; such a right is an attribute of sovereignty. If the United States undertook to intervene in Indochina, France should provide assurances that her troops would not be withdrawn, leaving American troops to bear the burdens of combat. And if French and American troops were to conduct joint military operations, it was obvious that organization and command arrangements would have to be made. Finally, because the Laniel and any successor government might fall as a result of the Assembly's disagreements with Franco-American Indochina policies, the United States would want insurance against a political decision to repudiate a French government's request for assistance or its commitment to continue the war. This insurance would be in the form of parliamentary approval of a governmental request for assistance.

The rationale for the conditions is understandable; nevertheless, it is interesting to note that each condition embodied a form of protection against results the "party of caution" in Washington feared. The conditions, so imposed, would to a great extent allay the doubts and suspicions of "hesitant" administration officials and congressmen. The activists must either have agreed with some of the conditions or realized that they could not fairly object to them. They had, in effect, been finessed.

As EDEN indicated in his memoirs, he was irritated by the report of the Franco-American military discussions for two reasons: because the idea of intervention had been "resurrected," and because the British had not been informed of the discussions. Nevertheless, there had been reports in American and British newspapers on 13, 14, and 15 May about the new French démarche and the fact that Bonnet and Dulles had discussed the possibility of intervention in the event the Geneva Conference failed to produce an acceptable settlement.[48] It would be rather surprising if Eden was unaware of these reports. On 14 May the *New York Herald Tribune* carried a page 2 story by Ned Russell that was probably the story Eden referred to when he said the *Tribune* carried "full details of the Franco-American negotiations."[49] Yet neither this story nor any other *Tribune* account of that week carried "full details" of any such talks. The Russell article was merely one of many fragmentary accounts of discussions in Washington and Paris that had touched upon the question of American intervention. Russell's article, however, said that *formal* discussions were to be held in Paris, and it was probably this prospect that disturbed Mr. Eden.[50]

We might concede that the British ought to have been informed of all this, but the discussions were quite informal and the questions so hypothetical that the French and the Americans probably did not feel the British had to be informed at this stage. Paris sources expressed surprise at the British reaction and British suspicions, which

[48] *T/L*, 17 May 1954; *NYT*, 18, 20 May 1954.
[49] In the *NYHT* of 14 May 1954, there were no other accounts of prospective talks or talks then in progress of the kind Eden mentioned in his memoirs.
[50] The relevant portion of the Russell article read: "The U.S. and France will shortly begin discussion of the exact conditions on which the United States would consider military intervention in the French Indo-Chinese war, it was disclosed today.
"The Franco-American conference, according to informed diplomatic sources here, is intended to bolster the sagging position of French Foreign Minister Georges Bidault in his negotiations at Geneva for a cease-fire in Indo-China.
"Agreement on the conference, which is expected to be held at Paris, was understood to have been reached at a meeting here between Secretary of State John Foster Dulles and French Ambassador Henri Bonnet."

they said were unfounded.[51] There had been several well-documented "leaks," they added, that fairly well indicated the nature and scope of the discussions. Nevertheless, the British reaction was understandable. They had been accused of refusing to come to the assistance of France in late April and in early May, thereby preventing American action. Many British officials regarded this accusation as unjust and pointed out that there was strong opposition in the United States to involvement in Indochina. They believed they had been made the scapegoat for an *American* decision not to intervene. (They had.) In Washington there had been open talk of bypassing the British in organizing a collective defense in Southeast Asia, and press reports after 13 May gave conflicting interpretations of the nature of the Franco-American conversations. Thus it is not difficult to understand why British officials might conclude that they were being bypassed.

Prime Minister Churchill addressed himself to the Indochina crisis, intervention, and the state of Western alliance relations in remarks to the House of Commons on 17 and 20 May. He affirmed that the British government was still committed to the policy of attempting to negotiate an Indochina settlement at Geneva before taking actions that might prejudice the success of the conference.[52] This included embarking upon talks that could lead to the foundation of a defense arrangement for Southeast Asia. At the House of Commons session on the 20th (the day after Eisenhower's remark to the effect that Britain was not an indispensable party to a defense pact), Churchill stressed the seriousness of the differences that separated the Americans and the British. He associated himself with the sentiments of a Labour MP that the actions and words of American and French officials were contrary to the spirit of the Western alliance and the Entente Cordiale, but he refused to comment upon President Eisenhower's remarks. As for the Franco-American military discussions, he said merely that they were informal and exploratory and had not eventuated in commitments by either party.

Eden returned to London on 22 May for discussions with the British cabinet; strained Anglo-American relations, resulting from the events of the preceding week, required such a meeting. Britain faced a dilemma, according to Drew Middleton; it sought to preserve and improve its Commonwealth ties and its ties with the United States, but now the interests of these states had diverged and this divergency was keenly felt in London.[53] The British emphasis upon the primacy of negotiations, including negotiations with the Communists, had

[51] *T/L*, 19 May 1954.
[52] *H. C. Debates*, 5th Series, Vol. 527, coll. 1692-1693; *NYT*, 18 May 1954.
[53] *NYT*, 23 May 1954.

generated frictions between the United States and Britain. There were other differences as well: policies toward China and the efficacy of "threats" in forcing the Communists to be more amenable to French demands for a settlement of the war.

Whatever conclusions the cabinet reached in its meeting of 23 May, the policy of negotiation remained paramount. No immediate steps would be taken by Britain to help organize a Southeast Asia collective defense system.

Chapter 13

DEADLOCK

[I]

When the restricted sessions of the Indochina Conference convened for the first time on Monday, 17 May, a host of substantive problems would have to be solved, problems that would inevitably arise with the efforts to reconcile the various proposals submitted by the delegates at the earlier plenary sessions. The conferees took up two important procedural questions almost immediately.

1. Should the cessation of hostilities in Laos and Cambodia be treated separately from the Vietnam issue? The non-Communist delegations asserted that separate consideration was warranted because the Vietminh had invaded these two countries and, without Vietminh support, the Pathet Lao and Khmer Issarak would be ineffectual movements. The latter were Communist rebel groups, in any case; certainly not governments. The Communist delegates, on the other hand, argued that the "patriotic movements" in Laos and Cambodia were governments whose rights the conference must respect. The hostilities in all three Indochinese states must be similarly resolved, with due regard for the status and rights of the liberation governments.

2. How should the disagreement over the primacy of a military or a political solution in Vietnam be resolved? The Vietminh proposals of 10 May, supported by the Soviets and the Chinese, appeared to require that the conferees agree upon the terms of a political solution and cease-fire procedures, after which the cease-fire would be effected. The French, on the other hand, demanded a guaranteed cease-fire with discussion of political problems put off until later.

The conference discussed Indochina at the first restricted session, but only in general terms. Because the press was given little information about events at these sessions, we know only a few of the details, but we know that the general discussion on Indochina on the 17th produced no concrete achievement.[1]

Molotov seems to have yielded somewhat on the second procedural point, the priority of a military over a political solution; he suggested that the proposals of Bidault and Pham Van Dong be considered simultaneously, with priority given to a military solution.[2] By 24 May it was evident that the Vietminh would accept this sug-

[1] Econ., 22 May 1954, p. 624.
[2] Le Monde, 19 May 1954, pp. 1-2.

gestion, when Hoang Van Hoan, the DRVN ambassador to China, told a correspondent of *Le Monde* that it was necessary to achieve a cease-fire first of all.[3] He denied that the DRVN delegation had exacted prerequisite political conditions. If, in the Dong plan, political propositions preceded propositions for a cease-fire, it was only a formal matter of presentation, Hoang said. The DRVN's change of position was an important development, but it may be doubted that this DRVN concession indicated its desire for a cease-fire. The question remained: What kind of cease-fire and with what conditions?

The Communists must have realized (if the Korean truce and subsequent conferences were any example) that negotiations toward a political settlement would be protracted—and perhaps unproductive from their standpoint. Even the Communists would agree that, chronologically, there would have to be a cease-fire before a political solution could be effected. (The procedural question during the first weeks of the Indochina Conference was whether a political solution should be discussed and designed before a cease-fire was discussed and at least partially implemented.) Molotov's concession of 17 May, confirmed by Hoang on the 24th, showed that the Communists were willing to postpone discussion of a political solution; but it is well to remember that military arrangements would inevitably entail political consequences. The Communists would naturally try for the most advantageous cease-fire arrangement, which would necessarily be accompanied by informal political advantages. This decision of the Communists was essentially one of getting on with negotiations, of reaching—or rather evincing a desire to reach—more significant and substantive issues, where they could make more effective use of the leverage given them by the strong military position of the Vietminh.

The evacuation of wounded from Dien Bien Phu also was discussed on 17 May. The reader will recall that, on 10 May, Pham Van Dong offered to permit evacuation of the wounded French Union forces. Bidault had accepted this offer, and, on the 11th, General Navarre received orders to communicate with General Giap to make arrangements for the transfer of more than 1,000 wounded from Dien Bien Phu to Hanoi. Giap agreed to permit evacuation if Navarre would "neutralize" provincial route 41 between Dien Bien Phu and Son La; Navarre then issued an order prohibiting the bombardment of route 41, and the evacuation of wounded began. Two problems immediately arose, however: the Vietminh would not permit the evacuation of Vietnamese (i.e. those who had fought with the French),

[3] *Ibid.*, 25 May 1954, p. 2 (told to M. J. Schwoebel).

and Giap used route 41 to move his troops toward the delta. Bidault, for the second time, appealed to Molotov and asked him to notify Pham of these facts and have the DRVN minister rectify the situation. But Molotov again told Bidault to consult with Pham Van Dong directly, rather than work through an intermediary, and Bidault, it appears, refused to yield to this "blackmail."[4] On 16 May, Navarre announced suspension of the evacuation of wounded and resumption of the bombardment of route 41. This was the situation on the 17th, when the ministers discussed the problem in restricted session. The French relented in avoiding direct, formal dealings with the Vietminh delegation and Colonel Michel de Brébisson was authorized to meet with Colonel Ha Van Lau on 19 May to discuss the evacuation of the wounded and, in addition, a prisoner exchange.

On the 18th and 19th two more restricted sessions were held, at which the procedural treatment of Laotian and Cambodian hostilities was the principal subject of debate. Pham Van Dong and Chou En-lai insisted the Pathet Lao and Khmer Issarak be recognized and invited to Geneva, and would have to be consulted in any negotiations affecting the destiny of their respective countries.[5] The non-Communist participants uniformly agreed that such pretensions must be resisted. Eden, however, believed the Communists might reasonably expect concessions in Vietnam because of the military situation there, and, by insisting upon a blanket settlement for all of Indochina, the non-Communist bloc was in effect demanding that any concessions made to the Vietminh also be made to the "liberation governments" of Laos and Cambodia.[6] Thus no real progress had been made by late Wednesday.

The American delegation was impatient with the lack of progress after three days of private discussions. One of the Americans (whether Bedell Smith or someone else is not clear) showed Bidault and Eden a proposal for resuming public plenary sessions. Eden rejected the proposal;[7] he felt the procedure of restricted sessions ought to be given a "full and fair trial." Bidault commented that a return to public sessions would bring down his government. The American delegation did not thereafter formally demand a change in procedure.

There were no formal meetings on Thursday; the day was spent in informal talks among the various heads of delegations. Eden met with Premier Chou En-lai for an hour in the morning, and then spoke with Bidault and Bedell Smith. In the evening, Molotov and the Foreign Secretary dined together. Eden still held to his opinion that Molotov was anxious to reach a settlement and that the two

[4] L&D, p. 154.   [5] Econ., 22 May 1954, p. 634.
[6] E, p. 133.   [7] E, p. 135.

ministers had a special task to try to facilitate agreement. Eden later related this interesting exchange:

> He [Molotov] remarked that he read in papers that we and the U.S. were having differences, and he did not believe that. I said he was right not to, because allies often have to argue their respective points of view. Molotov said: "That is right, we have to do that amongst ourselves, too," and he emphasized to me once again that China was very much her own master in these matters.[8]

Molotov, at a restricted session on Friday, 21 May, proposed five points as the basis for a military solution: (1) a cease-fire, (2) regroupment of the troops of each belligerent into zones, (3) adoption of measures to prevent reinforcement of the belligerents after a cease-fire, (4) methods for controlling such arrangements, and (5) an international guarantee of any settlement.[9] Molotov's five points differed from Bidault's proposals of 8 May in that the former made no mention of disarming irregulars nor specified the methods for controlling the cease-fire arrangements. (The Vietminh had demanded Franco-Vietminh commissions, the French international commissions.) Aside from these differences, Bidault was pleased with the Soviet minister's Vietnam proposals and accepted them as a basis for negotiations.[10]

The conferees continued to discuss the French and the Vietminh proposals without making significant progress. The DRVN delegation refused to admit the need for withdrawing Vietminh troops from Laos and Cambodia. On 22 May (a Saturday) a Korean plenary session was held, and no Indochina talks were scheduled. Later in the day, Eden and Bidault left Geneva for consultations with their governments. In the evening, Molotov and Bedell Smith dined together, but the substance of their conversation was not disclosed. On Sunday there were a few limited and informal discussions, and on Monday, 24 May, the nine heads of the delegations again met in restricted session. Bidault, accepting Molotov's five points as comprising the essential elements of a cease-fire, suggested two more points: the disarming of Vietminh irregulars and the immediate liberation of prisoners.[11] After a week of private discussions the ministers had at least five points, and perhaps seven, to guide them in their negotiations, but it was not at all clear when they would put flesh upon the skeleton they had formed.

[8] E, p. 136.
[9] *Econ.*, 29 May 1954, p. 724.
[10] L&D, p. 186.
[11] *Econ.*, 29 May 1954, p. 724. Both Bidault and Eden had, by the 24th, returned to Geneva after consulting with their respective governments.

The following day, 25 May, Eden suggested that the conference get down to the business of discussing the terms and conditions of a cease-fire, including the regroupment of forces, troop transfers between the regroupment areas, and the disarmament of irregulars.[12] If the ministers could agree upon a cease-fire for even one of the Associated States, he said, it should be implemented immediately, whether or not agreement had been reached on a cease-fire for the other two states. The French and American delegations had accepted this idea the week before; now, with support from Molotov, the DRVN and the Chinese also accepted it. Since there was as yet no agreement upon the status of the Pathet Lao and the Khmer Issarak, the effect of accepting Eden's suggestion was to postpone or temporarily bypass the procedural issue of the representation of the "liberation governments" of Laos and Cambodia. The conference could now concentrate upon a separate cease-fire agreement for Vietnam. Later, it was hoped, similar and separate agreements would be negotiated for Laos and Cambodia.

Hoang Van Hoan had indicated, on the 24th, that the DRVN accepted the need for cease-fire discussions without a preliminary agreement on a political solution. At a restricted session on Tuesday, 25 May, Pham Van Dong made an even more significant statement: There should be a complete and simultaneous cease-fire throughout Indochina, he said, followed by a regroupment of regular military forces into zones established by the conference.[13] In defining the limits of these zones or areas of regroupment, the conference (and commissions in each of the three states) should consider the location of suitable areas, their size, their population, and their economic and strategic value. Each zone should be economically and politically viable, and controlled by only one authority in their "relatively extended" areas. Also, they should have facilities for independent or self-sustaining economic activity and administrative control. Wherever possible, a line of demarcation between them should follow easily recognizable terrain features and should not create communication and transportation problems for the authorities within each zone. This proposal represented the DRVN's acceptance of temporary *de facto* partition.

Nguyen Quoc Dinh, head of the SVN delegation, objected, as did Bidault, who had returned from Paris in time for the restricted session on the 27th.[14] Bidault insisted that the regroupment procedures of a cease-fire arrangement should not be regarded as a partition of

---

[12] E, p. 140.
[13] T/L, 27 May 1954; Econ., 29 May 1954, p. 724.
[14] NYT, 26 May 1954.

Vietnam.[15] This was certainly support for the SVN position, but whether it represented Bidault's real feelings was open to doubt. By this time the majority of the French delegation had come around to favoring some form of partition, but, in view of the official assurances France had given the SVN in early May (that the French government would not countenance partition), Bidault could not formally or publicly support Pham Van Dong's proposals.

The French Foreign Minister, however, proposed that representatives of the high commands of the belligerent parties meet in Geneva to make recommendations for a cease-fire. They should study and recommend the principles that might govern the regroupment of troops and determine the size and location of the regroupment zones. Meanwhile, the conference should turn its attention to other questions, Bidault said. After statements by Nguyen Quoc Dinh and Chou En-lai, the session ended with agreement upon a relatively insignificant procedural point: establishing a committee of experts that was to examine and, if possible, reconcile the various proposals that had been submitted to the conference during the preceding two weeks of restricted sessions. This committee met on the 28th but made no progress.[16]

On Saturday, 29 May, the British Foreign Secretary, having informally obtained the approval of Bidault, Bedell Smith, Molotov, and Premier Chou, formally submitted a proposal that embodied Bidault's suggestions for military staff talks to study conditions for a cease-fire. The text of the proposal, which the conference adopted, was as follows.

In order to facilitate the early and simultaneous cessation of hostilities it is proposed that:

(a) Representatives of the two commands should meet immediately in Geneva and contacts should also be established on the spot.

(b) They should study the dispositions of forces to be made upon the cessation of hostilities, beginning with the question of regrouping areas in Vietnam.

(c) They should report their findings and recommendations to the Conference as soon as possible.[17]

The session at which this proposal was adopted was acrimonious, and occasioned a tough speech by Pham Van Dong that was almost entirely unrelated to the preceding proposal. Molotov had to remind the Vietminh minister that the conference was discussing Eden's proposal for belligerents' staff talks. Subsequently, Bedell Smith indi-

[15] Econ., 5 June 1954, p. 814.   [16] Ibid.   [17] Cmd. 9186, pp. 136-137.

cated displeasure with the word "simultaneous" in the preamble, which he said might imply that the United States had accepted the Communist arguments for a blanket Indochina settlement. He wished to express an American reservation: the British proposal was not a departure from the principle that hostilities in Laos and Cambodia were very different and entirely separate from the Vietnamese problem.[18] Smith's reservation gave rise to debate, but the session ended with an agreement that representatives of the high commands of the belligerents would meet on 2 June, the following Wednesday. The conference then adjourned. At the end of the day Molotov left Geneva for Moscow for consultation with Kremlin leaders; he indicated that he would return by 1 June.

Thus, after two weeks in restricted session, the delegates had made only minimal progress.

1. They had tacitly agreed, for the time being, to bypass the problem of hostilities in Laos and Cambodia and the status of the Pathet Lao and Khmer Issarak. The conference was nowhere near a solution of these problems.

2. The delegates had agreed upon the priority to be accorded a military, as opposed to a political, settlement of the Vietnam question.

3. Finally, the delegates had agreed to establish a joint commission (later known as the "military commission"), made up of representatives of the belligerents. The primary duty of this body was to study methods for regrouping troops in Vietnam and determining the size and location of regroupment zones.

The conference had moved somewhat nearer partition as a solution to the Vietnam debacle. Eden, as we know, favored this solution, and by the end of May the Commonwealth representatives at Geneva also supported this approach. The bulk of the French delegation also inclined toward partition. Most important of all, Pham Van Dong, at the 25 May session—with Soviet and Chinese support—had tabled a proposal for the temporary *de facto* partition of Vietnam.

The significance of Pham's proposals should not be underestimated nor overestimated. He had, in effect, given notice to the non-Communist delegates that the Vietminh wanted a cease-fire and would accept, for the time being, less than the whole of Vietnam. It would not seek to unify Vietnam by military means once the conference had reached a satisfactory agreement upon the cessation of hostilities. Given the Vietminh's earlier demand for the unity of Vietnam, this was a substantial change in policy. Why, then, did the Vietminh agree to accept what amounted to partition, and what did the change in policy signify?

[18] *Sunday Times* (London), 30 May 1954; E, p. 142.

If we assume, as Eden assumed, that Molotov wanted a settlement, it is entirely possible that the Soviet Foreign Minister pressed
the DRVN delegation to accept what in his opinion was the optimum
solution at the time, namely, partition, with a line of demarcation as
far south as possible but with the DRVN-controlled zone to include
both Hanoi and Haiphong. He may have believed that French Union
forces could be defeated in the delta, and that after this defeat the
French would pull out of Indochina entirely, leaving Annam and
Cochin China (and Laos and Cambodia!) to the Vietminh. Many
Vietminh undoubtedly believed victory was within their grasp; but
what would the Americans do? Surely there was at least the possibility
of United States intervention, even though one discounted all the
bluster and bluffing of the preceding months. If American troops
were dispatched to Vietnam, the strategic picture would be completely altered. An American presence in Tonkin, moreover, might
force the Chinese to intervene, a consequence the Vietminh could
not welcome. Thus Molotov could have appealed to prudence in the
Vietminh; he could have used the possibility of American and
Chinese intervention to persuade them of the necessity for accepting
a *temporary* partition.

We cannot totally discount the hypothesis that the Vietminh themselves, perhaps even independently of external pressures, had decided to accept partition. They might have been able to sustain their
offensive pressure in the Red River delta, but they may have concluded that military operations in the south would take time to organize. This would require a buildup of the PAVN, both in personnel
and equipment. Thus they may have decided that, for the present,
it would be better to consolidate the DRVN in northern Vietman,
not only militarily but politically and economically as well. For this
purpose they would need a zone in which they had full and unchal-
lenged administrative control, and a zone that was economically viable.

To what extent these various factors (Molotov's hypothetical pressures, the possibility of American and Chinese intervention, the need
to rebuild and consolidate) entered into the decision to offer proposals for *de facto* partition we do not know, but it seems fairly
clear, from statements made by DRVN spokesmen at a later time and
from what we know of the pan-Vietnamese sentiments of the Vietminh leadership, that the kind of partition Pham proposed on 25 May
was strictly provisional and temporary. I submit that he would not
have indicated Vietminh willingness to accept temporary partition
unless he (and his colleagues) were convinced that the unification
of Vietnam could be achieved by peaceful means. Thus Pham did
not announce that the DRVN would accept temporary partition,
period; he was saying a good bit more. The Vietminh would accept

de facto partition if the conference agreed upon conditions for a settlement that, in the opinion of the Vietminh, would enable it to unify Vietnam under the aegis of the DRVN after the cessation of hostilities. Therefore, the task of the Communist delegations at Geneva after 25 May was to secure conditions for a settlement that would later work to the political benefit of the Vietminh in gaining a peaceful victory throughout Vietnam.

Whatever achievements had been made by the end of May were in no small way attributable to the efforts of Anthony Eden. He pursued his goal (and his government's goal) of negotiating for an end to the Indochinese hostilities with a singlemindedness that, as we have seen, often irritated the Americans and the French. But his patience was not unlimited; he received a mandate from the British cabinet (probably on 23 May during his return to London) to set a time limit on the negotiations at Geneva.[19] Sometime early in the week of the 23d, the British delegation let it be known that it expected results within two weeks. Eden was supposed to have told his diplomatic counterparts at Geneva that he would act as an intermediary and peace-maker for one or two weeks more, but not for three weeks. It is entirely possible that these warnings from the British delegation, together with Eden's peace-making efforts, were largely responsible for even the slight progress made at the restricted sessions during the week.

Krishna Menon arrived in Geneva on the evening of 22 May. In his role as a personal emissary of Prime Minister Nehru and an observer for a nonaligned but interested Asian state, he could have played an influential role in the negotiations. He continually made the rounds among most of the delegations. Although he at first refused to speak with newsmen, it was learned that he had offered the services and good offices of the Indian government in the supervision of an armistice.[20] He seems to have arrived too late to affect the progress of the restricted sessions during the week of 23 May, but afterward he entered into the complex interdelegation diplomacy with great enthusiasm. We may guess that some of his efforts were fruitful, but we cannot be sure of this.

ON MONDAY, 31 May, the conference began its third week of restricted sessions and turned to a new agenda topic, the composition and competence of an armistice supervisory commission, on which discussions would continue for two and a half weeks without progress. On Monday, Andrei Gromyko, seconding Molotov (who was returning from Moscow), suggested that the supervisory commission be com-

19 *NYT*, 30 May 1954; *Econ.*, 5 June 1954.
20 *NYT*, 27 May 1954; *T/L*, 31 May 1954.

posed of officials from Poland, Czechoslovakia, India, and Pakistan.[21] Bedell Smith retorted that the commission should be made up of representatives from "really neutral" independent states; Poland and Czechoslovakia, he said, were not in that category. At the restricted session on Wednesday, 2 June, the non-Communist delegates rejected Gromyko's proposal but did not submit proposals of their own.

Meanwhile, Colonel de Brébisson and Ha Van Lau met on 1 June and arranged a meeting of the military commission for the next day. They also reached an agreement on the evacuation of the Dien Bien Phu wounded. On Wednesday, while the conference discussed the armistice supervision commission in restricted session, the military commission met for the first time. General Henri Delteil, representing the French Union military high command, and Ta Quang Buu, representing the DRVN, jointly presided over the commission.[22] Included also were de Brébisson, Ha Van Lau, Colonel Fleurant, and Colonel Le Van Kim who represented the Vietnamese (SVN) army.[23] Two additional military commissions were established, one for Laos and another for Cambodia. The three commissions continued to meet on a fairly regular, uninterrupted basis until the end of the Geneva Conference in July. While political discussions proceeded in either plenary or restricted sessions, parallel (but secret) sessions of the military commissions gradually elaborated the technical terms and conditions of a cease-fire.

On Thursday, 3 June, Nguyen Quoc Dinh, rejecting Gromyko's proposal of 31 May, proposed that the United Nations be asked to form an armistice supervisory commission.[24] But Premier Chou En-lai rejected this suggestion. Such a commission, he said, must be made responsible to the nine delegations comprising the Geneva Conference and not to the United Nations. This was an understandable reaction because the C.P.R., though represented at Geneva, was not represented in the United Nations. Chou also distinguished between an "international commission," which would function throughout Indochina, and mixed supervisory commissions, which would be responsible for supervising the armistice in each of the three states. The mixed commissions, he insisted, should neither control nor be controlled by the international commission.

On the next day, 4 June, Eden indicated his approval of Chou's suggestion for making an international commission responsible to the

[21] *Econ.*, 5 June 1954, p. 814.
[22] L&D, p. 210. Ta Quang Buu at this time was the DRVN assistant defense minister.
[23] There was no SVN high command. Vietnamese troops were under the high command of the French expeditionary force, and units of Vietnamese soldiers, no larger than battalion size, were integrated into that force.
[24] *Econ.*, 12 June 1954, p. 906.

conference, and suggested that the conference establish a permanent organization for this purpose.[25] Aside from this proposal, the debate continued, with the non-Communist delegations supporting the view that an international commission should have authority over the mixed commissions. After this session adjourned, the conference did not meet again until Tuesday, 8 June, when it met in plenary, not restricted, session. At this point, however, we must break off our account of the conference proceedings and again turn to important extra-conference developments that influenced the negotiations at Geneva.

[I I]

The reader will recall that approval of the United Nations of any scheme for concerted action in Southeast Asia was one of the conditions for American intervention listed in the secret United States note to France of 15 May. More particularly, it specified U.N. approval of a plan for sending an observation commission to Indochina and its neighboring states. In the week following the dispatch of this note there were hints that the United States and Thailand were planning to ask the Security Council, and perhaps eventually the General Assembly, to take action on the Indochina problem.[26] Statements by Dulles and Prince Wan Waithayakon, confirming these rumors, were made on or about the 25th of May. At his news conference of the 25th, Dulles announced that the Thai government, in consultation with American officials, was preparing a complaint for submission to the United Nations, alleging that Communist aggression in Indochina threatened the security of Thailand.[27] The same day Prince Wan, then in Geneva, announced that his government would ask the U.N. to send observers to Indochina to investigate the Communist threat in that area. Thanat Khoman, Thailand's deputy representative to the U.N., would leave for New York after a stopover in Paris, Prince Wan said. At the U.N. headquarters, Khoman would canvass the attitudes of Security Council members and then formally submit a proposal. Should the Soviet Union veto the Thai request, the prince said, his government was prepared to submit the proposal to the General Assembly. The Vietminh invasion of Laos and Cambodia required a U.N. response, and the General Assembly was fully authorized to act under the terms of the Uniting for Peace Resolution, Prince Wan asserted.[28]

[25] *Ibid.*

[26] On 10 May the Thai government had offered bases on Thai territory for the use of the "free world" (*NYT*, 11 May 1954). Rumors of concerted Thai-American action in the U.N. began to circulate at that time.

[27] *NYT*, 25 May 1954.   [28] *Ibid.*

This Thai-American enterprise was widely discussed in the press for the next two weeks. Dulles and Henry Cabot Lodge, the American delegate to the U.N., discussed the plan on the 26th, and they were reported to favor a fourteen-member observation commission, with Soviet and American participation.[29] Thailand, it appears, favored a five-member committee, with representatives from India, Pakistan, Sweden, Uruguay, and New Zealand. In any event, there were indications that the United States and Thailand would take the matter to the General Assembly after the expected Soviet veto in the Security Council. Britain, India, and France, however, objected to the scheme. France, it was learned, had opposed a similar plan a year before. British officials argued that the plan might divert the attention of the delegates at Geneva and unduly complicate negotiations. India feared that it might even cause the collapse of the Geneva negotiations. The British also seem to have argued that U.N. involvement would complicate efforts to arrange for "united action" in Southeast Asia.

On 29 May the Thailand U.N. delegate formally requested the Security Council to place his government's complaint on the agenda. On 3 June the council voted 10 to 1 to put the matter on its agenda, the Soviet Union voting against and Britain and France reluctantly voting in support of the move. Then, having scheduled the Thai complaint, the Security Council adjourned for an indefinite period, in effect leaving the matter suspended while the interested states watched developments at the Geneva Conference.[30]

The Security Council reconvened in mid-June, while proceedings were deadlocked in Geneva, and the Thai proposal for a peace-observation commission was again considered. On 18 June, when the Soviet Union vetoed the resolution embodying the plan,[31] Thailand and the United States were in a position to take their proposal to the General Assembly (under the Uniting for Peace Resolution) but they seemed hesitant to do so. It was not at all clear when the two governments would take the necessary steps to apprise the General Assembly of the proposal or whether, in fact, they would do this.[32] The Laniel government had fallen on 12 June and had been succeeded by a government headed by Pierre Mendès-France. The new Premier had promised a cease-fire within a month or, failing that, his resignation.

It is possible that United States and Thai officials conferred with

[29] *NYT*, 28 May 1954.
[30] *NYT*, 23 June 1954.
[31] *NYT*, 19 June 1954. The text of the resolution also appears in *DSB* (28 June 1954, p. 975), along with statements by Dulles and Lodge on the Soviet veto.
[32] *NYT*, 19 June 1954.

their allies and agreed to wait until mid-July to see whether the conference would produce a cease-fire within the period Mendès-France had set for himself and for his government. It is also possible that sufficient votes for calling a special session of the General Assembly could not have been mustered until the new French Premier had been given an opportunity to achieve a truce and had failed. The Geneva Conference resulted in a cease-fire, and later that year the Southeast Asia Treaty Organization (SEATO) was established. These events rendered action along the lines projected by the Thai proposal unnecessary. Thus the Soviet veto on 18 June, coupled with the impact of events in Geneva and Paris, permanently disposed of the plan for a U.N. peace-observation commission.

[III]

Secretary Dulles, at his news conference on 25 May, remarked that the prospects for moral sanction of armed intervention in Indochina looked somewhat better, but he did not elaborate on this. In response to questions from the correspondents, he made these four points:

1. "We are not prepared to go in for a defense of colonialism. We are only going to go in for defense of liberty and independence and freedom. . . . We go in where the United Nations gives moral sanction to our action."[33] These statements apparently had a good effect in New Delhi, which approved the secretary's remarks, noted the delicate problem of Dulles's relations with Congress, and implied that the United States was acquiescing in moves at Geneva to draft India for an armistice supervisory role. This, New Delhi believed, was one of several indications of greater "elasticity" in American policy.[34]

2. The French, Dulles said, had as yet made no request for United States intervention, and the administration did not have such a request from the French government under consideration.

3. From the juridical point of view, the French had met the American conditions of independence for the Associated States, but, Dulles added, it takes time to turn "paper" independence into reality. "[It] is one thing to have the letter and another to have the spirit and I would say at the moment the principal deficiency is a translation of the spirit of liberty into the area and in the conduct of the French people in relation to the native peoples. There is quite a bit to be done, I think, in that practical respect."[35]

4. Asked about united action and the prospects for a Southeast Asia pact, Dulles said: "We don't go in alone; we go in where other

[33] DSB, 7 June 1954, p. 863.
[34] NYT, 27 May 1954.
[35] DSB, 7 June 1954, p. 863; NYT, 25 May 1954.

nations which have an important stake in the area recognize the peril as we do." Conversations with friendly governments were continuing, he said: Secretary of Defense Wilson and American military advisors were in Manila conferring with officials of the Philippines government. He also noted that preliminary discussions were being conducted between the ANZUS powers, Britain, and France for more formal talks on the military situation in Southeast Asia. (These conversations were preliminary to the Five Power military staff talks that began in early June; at this date there was no agreement on the details. Dulles made note of that fact.) He emphasized the point that the military talks were in no sense a substitute for continuing political discussions; but similar military talks were "neither going on or in contemplation with Thailand and the Philippines."

The same day as Secretary Dulles's conference, Prime Minister Churchill again declared that British policy would not change until the Geneva Conference had been given a chance to succeed. The British, however, had that week obtained the administration's consent to staff talks in Washington, limited to Australia, Britain, France, New Zealand, and the United States. Contrary to the administration's original desires, Thailand and the Philippines were not invited. Dulles, as we have seen, had stated that the five-power military talks were not a substitute for political discussions, but the British were more emphatic and more explicit: the staff talks were of a technical military nature, designed to inventory the military alternatives open to these powers should the Geneva Conference fail and hostilities continue. They were not, the British emphasized, preparatory conversations for a Southeast Asia pact. The talks began on 3 June in the Pentagon and a communiqué, issued on the first day of the talks, read in part: "The conversations, while not committing any of the nations represented, will be of value not only to countries represented, but to other countries in the region in further conversations which may take place later on a wider basis."[36]

The Eisenhower administration continued to examine intervention and the conditions of intervention in Indochina. On 28 May, Dulles, Admirals Radford and Cutler, and Deputy Secretary of Defense Anderson met with the President at the White House. One of the questions they discussed was the American response to an overt Chinese attack in Indochina. Various alternatives were discussed, but Mr. Eisenhower, writing some years later about this meeting, said that, although he approved contingency planning, he "did not believe overt Chinese Communist aggression was likely."[37]

[36] *NYT*, 3 June 1954.
[37] DDE, p. 361. Eisenhower wrote of the conversations of 28 May: "One of the renewed questions was that of United States response to overt military aggression

Exchanges between French and American diplomats continued after mid-May on the conditions for American intervention if hostilities continued in Indochina or the French Union forces were endangered by Vietminh attacks in the Red River delta. We have noted that the French were dissatisfied with several conditions in the American note of 15 May, and they continued to press the United States for a revision of its conditions for intervention. As for the National Assembly's approval of a request for intervention by France's allies, Laniel told Dillon that an attempt to secure parliamentary ratification would topple his government. In Geneva, Bidault made the same point with Bedell Smith,[38] who remarked that such an engagement must be durable and, in view of the instability of French governments, this was best assured by the National Assembly's committing itself to a request for intervention. This matter was carried no further by French officials.

The French also sought to change the terms of the condition which required a commitment to maintain their forces in Indochina for the duration of a coalition action. They also sought clarification of the nature of American participation. On 28 May Dillon received instructions from Washington, whose substance he conveyed to Maurice Schumann: France must understand that American and other allied forces that might intervene in the Indochina War would be additions to the currently engaged French Union forces and not substitutes for them. France must explicitly engage to maintain its forces in Indochina for the duration of collective action, including those presently engaged and those whose dispatch had already been decided upon. Troop rotation would continue in a normal fashion and French and allied troops would be withdrawn to the extent the military situation and the development of the SVN army permitted. Withdrawal of troops, in any case, would not be undertaken by one contributory state without preliminary consultations with the other allies.[39] The French cabinet regarded neither this condition nor Dillon's elaboration of it acceptable. Bidault proposed an alternative to Bedell Smith but seems to have been unsuccessful in changing the terms of the condition.

Dulles indicated in an informal fashion, at his 25 May press conference, that the French had given the Associated States juridical in-

by Communist China *or forces directed by them.* The Joint Chiefs of Staff agreed that we should not in such a circumstance rely upon a static type of defense as in Korea, but rather upon an offensive against Communist China—not, however, necessarily going to the industrial sources of Chinese power or destroying cities, but striking areas and facilities supporting a Chinese offensive, airfields, communications lines, and bases." (Emphasis added.) *Ibid.*

[38] L&D, p. 194.
[39] L&D, p. 195; confirmed in DDE, p. 359.

dependence. Whether he was correct in this assessment is open to dispute, but he was unquestionably correct in his estimate of the difficulty of translating juridical independence into actual independence; and he implied that the French had not accomplished this transformation. One of the original and continuously reasserted conditions demanded of France for American intervention, the grant of genuine independence to the Associated States, was the key factor in the administration's efforts to win Asian as well as non-Asian support for a collective defense arrangement for Southeast Asia. The United States would not be associated, in even the most tenuous way, with actions that could be characterized as colonialist, and until the SVN became a genuinely sovereign state, there was always this danger. The condition of independence, reasserted in the note of 15 May, was also the subject of further discussion between American and French diplomats. On 27 May Dillon apprised Alexander Parodi, secretary general of the Quai d'Orsay, of new instructions he had received from Washington for Vietnamese independence. Dillon's instructions set forth four principal points.

1. France, as soon as possible, would sign the two treaties of independence and association with the SVN. At the time of signature the President of France would affirm that the French Union was composed of free and sovereign states. The President of the United States would then publicly declare that, in his view, the Associated States had achieved the status of fully sovereign states.[40]

2. A truly national Vietnamese government would be formed.

3. The Associated States would receive American military assistance.

4. France would declare its intention of withdrawing its expeditionary corps when hostilities ended, with the understanding that reduced forces, consistent with French obligations to the French Union, might be based in Indochina.

In early May, the signing of the treaties of independence and association had been delayed by the French, who apparently preferred to wait until conventions on Franco-Vietnamese economic and cultural relations had been drafted. Bao Dai, learning of this new delay, indignantly announced that his government had decided to postpone signing the treaties for an indefinite period. But the Vietnamese, nonetheless, were greatly disturbed by mounting evidence that the participants at Geneva were moving toward partition; the proposals of Pham Van Dong of 25 May, which in effect called for a temporary *de facto* partition of Vietnam, persuaded the Vietnamese they must secure French agreement to sign the treaties immediately. From 25 through 27 May, Prince Buu Loc, the SVN Premier, met with

[40] L&D, p. 192.

Bedell Smith and Bidault and stressed the need for quick action on the treaties. The French, it seems, were still hesitant, and the Americans continued to press the French. On 27 May Dillon told Parodi of his new instructions (above), which "requested" the French to sign the treaties *as soon as possible*. There are two versions of subsequent events.

1. Paul Reynaud, vice president of the Council of Ministers, proposed to Prince Buu Loc that the treaties be signed before the prince left for Saigon.[41] The prince insisted the treaties be initialed since signature could be effected only by the respective chiefs of state. Reynaud acquiesced. On 4 June, at ceremonies in the Hotel Matignon in Paris, the treaties were *initialed* by Laniel and Prince Buu Loc. This version is puzzling, however, because Bao Dai and Rene Coty were both in France; thus the chiefs of state *could* have signed the agreements in Paris on 4 June. It would have been strange if Buu Loc's anxiety for independence had not been shared by Bao Dai, and stranger still if Buu Loc had initialed the treaties *without* the authority of his chief of state. Therefore, it would seem, the Vietnamese were not at all chary even about *signing* the treaties (as opposed to initialing them); the French—even at this late date—were reluctant to do more than *initial* them. This tactic would give the French the options, should future events require it, of disclaiming the juridical force of the treaties. Signature was unequivocal, and many ministers opposed the unequivocal grant of independence at this time. Others believed the treaties would create a host of legal problems. Some, in fact, thought the treaties' concomitant conditions of independence contravened the French constitution in the status they assigned the SVN within the French Union.

2. According to a second version of the events subsequent to 27 May, Prince Buu Loc and American officials continued to press the French for action on Vietnamese independence and Laniel thought it prudent to bow to this pressure. He would agree to *initial* the treaties with Buu Loc, but their formal *signature* was not possible because supplementary accords on Franco-Vietnamese military, economic, juridical, and cultural relations had not yet been drafted.[42] French legal experts, moreover, had advised President Coty of serious legal and constitutional problems if the President signed the treaties in their present form. On 4 June, therefore, Prince Buu Loc and Laniel *initialed* the treaties in Paris. In this version it was the French, not Prince Buu Loc, who insisted upon initialing the treaties.

The reader will no doubt perceive that the author prefers the second version, but it is well to remember there is still an element of doubt.

---

[41] L&D, p. 193.   [42] *NYT*, 5 June 1954.

When the relevant documents become available the historian may be able to confirm one or the other version briefly described above. The treaty of association, at any rate, did not specify the unconditional right of the Vietnamese to withdraw from the French Union, although it spoke of France and Vietnam as "sovereign States, equal in rights and duties."[43] Presumably, a fully sovereign state would have the right of withdrawal. But the two treaties were never formally signed nor ratified by either the French or the SVN government. Other events were to overtake these legal procedures.

Although the governments of France and the United States continued to discuss the terms and conditions of American intervention, agreement was no nearer at the end of May than it had been in the middle of the month—but, according to Eden, the "bogey of intervention was once again with us."[44] He recorded that on 29 May he received "late news from Paris that French and Americans had agreed some plan [*sic*] apparently for intervention in Indo-China." And later:

> Sir Gladwyn Jebb reported from Paris on May 31 that the United States had practically reached agreement with France on the conditions for intervention, should the Conference fail. Bidault confirmed to me on the same day that, if no agreement were to be reached at Geneva, American help was contemplated to the extent of three divisions.[45]

We know now that the United States had not "practically reached agreement with France on the conditions for intervention," not even on the contingency that the conference might fail. This was so principally because the Laniel government could not agree to maintain French troops in Indochina for the duration of a prospective coalition action, but also because it could not even attempt to secure the approval of the National Assembly for a request for intervention. Sir Gladwyn Jebb's intelligence may or may not have been faulty, for it had been reported that Bedell Smith told Bidault, on the 24th, that *six* (not three) divisions of marines could be committed to Indochina without congressional authorization.[46] This was nothing short of extraordinary, particularly in view of Bedell Smith's explicit promise to the Senate Foreign Relations Committee, on behalf of the administration, that there would be no major moves in East Asia without prior congressional consultations.[47] It also was extraordinary because it seems to suggest that Bedell Smith was ignorant of the American note to the French government of 15 May that listed the

[43] *Docs., 1954*, p. 271 (article 2).   [44] E, p. 142.
[45] E, p. 143.   [46] L&D, p. 194.
[47] *NYT*, 17 February 1954.

several preconditions for United States intervention. Such a possibility, in my view, was unlikely.

After the incident of mid-May, when Eden claimed he learned of Franco-American "military talks" from Bidault and from the *New York Herald Tribune*, Bedell Smith had attempted to allay the Foreign Secretary's fears.[48] Bedell Smith probably had been briefed by Washington on the nature of the French inquiry and the highly conditioned American response. Neither Bedell Smith, nor anyone else representing the administration, for that matter, attempted an elaborate interpretation for the British of the nature of the American response to the French inquiries of 13 May. The British would therefore remain confused, even confounded, by American intentions. Thus, to recur to the end of May, when the "intervention bogey" again confronted Eden, it is my opinion that Jebb and Eden were once again the object of an engineered "leak," designed to persuade the rumor mills of Geneva that intervention had not been laid to rest.

[48] E, p. 134.

Chapter 14

GIAP MOVES ON THE DELTA

[I]

After the fall of Dien Bien Phu the Vietminh did not give the French Union forces respite, contrary to the expectations of Generals Navarre and Cogny.[1] Limited but successful PAVN offensives were undertaken in southern Laos against French strong points and in the Annamite mountains of northern Laos and northwestern and western Tonkin. Preparatory Vietminh offensive activity had occurred in the south and southwestern sectors of the Red River delta as well, and hit-and-run acts of sabotage within the French-held delta region increased in mid- and late May. An even greater danger appeared in the movement toward the delta of the Vietminh forces that had formerly been deployed around Dien Bien Phu. This movement had begun on or about 13 May, and by mid-June four PAVN divisions were in position to attack the delta's defenses.[2]

On 14 and 15 May the French Committee of National Defense met to consider the military situation in Indochina, particularly the ability of the French Union forces to hold the delta's defense perimeter and, within it, the cities of Hanoi and Haiphong. After the Laniel government had barely won a vote of confidence on the 13th, Laniel's cabinet decided to ask the United States what form of military assistance it would provide the French if the Geneva Conference failed to produce peace or the situation in the Red River delta deteriorated. This latter contingency was the basis of painful discussions in the Committee of National Defense at the time officials of the Eisenhower administration were preparing an answer to the French inquiry.

Since the French Union forces had, for all practical purposes, lost their mobile reserves and their offensive spirit and, at least in Tonkin, those forces were highly dispersed, it was decided to consolidate the delta defenses by reducing the size of the defense perimeter. It would be necessary, in other words, to evacuate and abandon outlying posts. This was not an easy decision: any "retrograde" movements in the northeast could easily be characterized as a retreat. Not only would this tend to weaken Bidault's bargaining position at Geneva, it might even encourage early offensive action by the Vietminh, and would certainly tend to persuade the Vietnamese that a Vietminh

---

[1] Henri Navarre, *L'Agonie de L'Indochine* (Paris: Plon, 1956), pp. 262-263.
[2] *Ibid.*, p. 263.

victory was inevitable. Several ministers opposed extensive withdrawals in the delta area and argued, instead, for reinforcement of the French forces. René Pleven, Minister of National Defense, did not oppose withdrawals, but he believed that a reduction of the defense perimeter should appear to be a consolidation and not a retreat.[3] To ensure this, he (and General Ely) favored sending three divisions from the French metropolitan army to Indochina; and, in order partially to replace depleted French forces in Europe and North Africa, Pleven asked the cabinet to call up a second contingent of reserves. Laniel reserved his decision: a call-up of reserves might very well produce a governmental crisis.

The Premier and the cabinet were well aware that there must not be another Dien Bien Phu; the French expeditionary force must be protected and its security guaranteed. Therefore, withdrawals from advanced positions must be undertaken. The cabinet decided to send a special military mission to Indochina, composed of Generals Ely, Salan, and Pélissier, which arrived in Saigon on 18 May with a directive from the cabinet to the commander in chief of the French Union forces. In the present period, it said, the primary consideration was the security of the expeditionary corps.[4] General Navarre's principal duty, which he must regard above all other considerations (*"primant toutes autres considerations"*), would be to safeguard the corps. As for operational aspects of the French military plan, the directive instructed Navarre to "clean up" the situation south of the 18th parallel in order to prepare for a possible withdrawal and a defensive position south of that line should military or political developments require this. North of the 18th parallel, political considerations were not to be given primacy over military considerations.

Navarre, the directive continued, would begin withdrawals in the Red River delta to maintain "equilibrium" between French forces and the Vietminh. Initially, the withdrawals should enable the French to hold defensible portions of the delta.[5] Afterwards, further withdrawals should emplace the corps in the Haiphong redoubt, where marine transport would be provided (for evacuation?). But this second phase would be undertaken only upon the order of the government, or by General Navarre, if Vietminh pressure became irresistible. The commander in chief "must avoid the dispersion of our forces and, to this end, assure necessary regroupment in order that the battle of Tonkin would not risk the attrition of the Expedi-

[3] Ely, pp. 127-131, 120; L&D, p. 160.

[4] Joseph Laniel, *Le drame indochinois: De Dien Bien Phu au pari de Genève* (Paris: Plon, 1957), pp. 106-107; Ely, pp. 129-130.

[5] To accomplish this, General Ely suggested withdrawals in the south and in the west of the delta. Navarre, *op. cit.*, p. 268; Ely, pp. 121-123.

tionary Corps so that the general situation in Indochina would be compromised."[6]

The directive concluded with an injunction to safeguard the expeditionary corps and "elements of the Vietnamese population . . . notably . . . the families of the Vietnamese who were engaged in combat in the ranks of the Franco-Vietnamese forces."[7]

Navarre objected to his orders, but, as he could not alter their general sense, he proposed to execute them in this fashion. He would regroup the expeditionary corps around Hanoi and along the Hanoi–Haiphong road, and would allocate responsibility for the defense of the southern and western sectors of the delta to Vietnamese units. Ely approved Navarre's proposal, believing it was compatible with the spirit of the cabinet's directive.[8]

After a tour of the delta defenses, the French military mission returned to Paris, where it arrived on 25 May. General Ely and his colleagues, refusing to speak with reporters, reported directly to the Committee of National Defense on the 26th. Although this meeting was secret, the substance of Ely's report was leaked to the press. The "leak," perhaps unjustifiably, was attributed to Marc Jacquet, Secretary of State for the Associated States, who resigned his post on 29 May because of the incident. General Ely apparently gave a profoundly pessimistic and disturbing report to the committee: French losses had been heavy, the corps had lost its offensive spirit, the strategic reserve was almost gone, Vietnamese troops were neither reliable nor properly trained and equipped. Their morale was low, and Vietminh propaganda had persuaded the Vietnamese in Tonkin that a Vietminh victory was near. The delta had been heavily infiltrated by Vietminh guerrillas—toward which General Giap was moving his forces and against which, by late June, he could begin offensive operations. General Ely and his colleagues thought that, with reinforcements, urban centers could be held, but with tenuous communication between them. The generals, therefore, supported Pleven's earlier request for calling up a contingent of reserves.[9]

On 28 May the Council of Ministers decided to call up a portion of the 1954 reserves for assignment to units in Europe and North Africa; regular army troops from these areas would, in turn, be sent to Indochina. The council also decided to relieve General Navarre and Commissioner Dejean of their duties. On 2 June General Ely was named High Commissioner for Indochina and commander in chief of French Union forces. He left for Saigon on 6 June.[10]

[6] Laniel, *op. cit.*, p. 107.   [7] *Ibid.*
[8] Navarre, *op. cit.*, p. 269; Ely, pp. 143-144.
[9] Ely, pp. 148-150; L&D, p. 165; *NYT*, 30 May 1954; *Econ.*, 29 May 1954.
[10] *NYT*, 6 June 1954; DDE, p. 361.

[I I]

An article by Hanson Baldwin in the *New York Times* of 30 May revealed some of the facts of the military situation in Southeast Asia that so greatly disturbed the administration activists. Baldwin said that about two Vietminh divisions had partly infiltrated the delta region of Tonkin in the south and southwest and within two or three weeks the PAVN would be in a position to launch attacks against the French Union defenses. These attacks would be timed to coincide with uprisings in Hanoi, Phuly, and Namdinh and an impending political crisis in France. Outposts in Cambodia and Laos had already been abandoned. The strategy of the Communists, Baldwin said, was to bring down the Laniel government in the hope that its successor would be willing to make peace at any price.[11]

It was this worsening situation in Tonkin to which Admiral Robert Carney, Chief of U.S. Naval Operations, implicitly referred when he declared the United States was approaching a fork in the road. The danger, he said, was "imminent and increasing."[12] On 1 June it was revealed that Admiral Radford had appeared before a secret meeting of the House Foreign Affairs Committee and stated that if the decision were made to intervene in Indochina, the war should be on an "all-out basis"; atomic weapons should be used. The admiral emphasized that the *decision* to intervene was political; he was speaking only of what he would advocate *if* that decision were made. He assured the congressmen no decision had been made vis-à-vis Indochina about which they had not already been apprised.[13]

On 3 June General James A. Van Fleet, former commander of the Eighth Army in Korea, appeared before a secret joint session of the Senate Armed Forces Committee and the Senate Foreign Relations Committee. Van Fleet had been sent on a fact-finding tour of East Asia by the President in May but had been ordered to return to Washington for reasons that were not known. Although Senator Wiley, Chairman of the Foreign Relations Committee, was noncommittal at the end of the session, it was reported that Van Fleet's remarks had been "gloomy" and "depressing."[14] But these developments did not alter or signify a possible alteration in administration policy. On 2 June President Eisenhower said he had not yet decided to ask Congress for authority for armed intervention in Indochina. He emphasized that no decisions had been reached on intervention

[11] Baldwin estimated there were from 5,000 to 32,000 Chinese "advisors" in Tonkin and 300,000 to 380,000 Chinese troops were deployed across the frontier in Yunnan, Kwantung, and Kwangsi provinces in the C.P.R.
[12] *NYT*, 28, 30 May 1954.
[13] *NYT*, 2 June 1954.
[14] *NYT*, 4 June 1954.

but he assured the news correspondents the administration was daily exploring means for serving United States interests.[15]

Secretary of Defense Wilson, on his return from the Far East, asserted that intervention was "scarcely imminent." Halting communism, in Wilson's opinion, was more a political than a military matter.[16] Secretary Dulles appeared before the Senate Foreign Relations Committee on 4 June and asserted that the "situation in Indochina is fraught with danger, not only to the immediate area but to the security of the United States and its allies in the Pacific area."[17] The situation was grave, Dulles said, but not hopeless.

The Secretary of State, however, made these remarks as part of a larger statement in support of the administration's Mutual Security Program. He expressed hope that the Geneva Conference would find a formula for ending hostilities and for assuring the Indochinese true independence. But the Communists' attitude was not encouraging. "It is impossible to predict what the future holds."[18] Uncertainties in the Far East (and elsewhere), the secretary said, urged Congress to preserve and continue the provisions of the Mutual Security Program, which was designed to allow flexibility in its application and execution. Thus Dulles's statement was not a major policy pronouncement but rather a brief in support of the administration's Mutual Security Program.[19]

Some voices urged the United States to commit troops to Indochina while Franco-Vietnamese forces were still fighting, but the administration did not change its policy.[20] Dulles and the President were "protected" against the criticisms of Republican and various military activists because they appeared willing to take decisive action *pro-*

---

[15] *NYT*, 3 June 1954. The Defense Department announced that it would soon withdraw some 200 U.S. Air Force technicians from Indochina, thus honoring a pledge to the Senate Armed Services Committee made in early March. Volunteers might be permitted to remain, the announcement said.

[16] *Ibid.*

[17] John Foster Dulles, *Free World Unity*, Press Release No. 297, 4 June 1954, Series S, No. 18 (Washington, D.C.: Department of State, Public Services Division, 1954), p. 8. See also *DSB*, 14 June 1954, pp. 921-925.

[18] *Ibid.*, p. 9.

[19] Referring to the fact that France and Italy had not yet ratified the EDC treaty, Dulles declared that "these delays contribute a negative factor from the standpoint of the free world. Not only have they delayed a German military contribution to Western defense, but they have also prevented West Germany from joining the family of sovereign nations. . . . It is obvious that the present situation cannot continue much longer. . . . We have made it clear to our European allies that failure to approve and implement EDC would necessitate a thorough reexamination of American policies. It cannot now be said what the results of that reexamination would be. It can, however, safely be predicted that it would necessitate some basic changes and that certain attitudes and policies on our part, which seem to be taken for granted by certain of our allies, would have to be reviewed." *Ibid.*, pp. 3-4.

[20] *NYT*, 8 June 1954.

vided "entirely reasonable" preconditions were fulfilled. The very reasonableness of the conditions ensured a cautious policy. Asked at his press conference of 10 June whether he planned to ask for authority to act in Indochina before Congress adjourned, the President stated that he had no plan "as of this moment to ask for anything that was outside the normal traditional processes in the operation [of the government]." If the crisis became acute, he would lay the problem before Congress. "As of this moment," he said, "he had no such plan."[21]

On 3 June the NSC met again, and Eisenhower recalled that he used this meeting to clarify his attitude and opinions. Although there were misunderstandings between the United States and the French, he said, he was determined that none should exist among members of the administration.

> If the United States should, by itself, and without the clear invitation of the Vietnamese people and satisfactory arrangements with the French, undertake to counter Chinese Communist aggression, I said, this would, of course, mark the collapse of the American policy of united action. Moreover, if the nations of the Southeast Asian area showed a complete indifference to the fate of Indochina, it would be the signal for us to undertake a reappraisal of basic United States security policy. I was convinced that it was in our interest to commit United States armed forces in the event of overt Chinese aggression, but I was determined that Southeast Asian nations could not disclaim responsibility for their own safety, expecting the United States alone to carry all the burdens of Free World security. If I should find it necessary to go to the Congress for authority to intervene in Indochina, I wanted to say that we had allies such as Thailand, Australia, New Zealand, the Philippines, and above all, the bulk of the Vietnamese people, ready to join with us in resisting such aggression.[22]

Misunderstandings of the Indochina problem were evident on all sides, Eisenhower wrote. "People seemed to assume that the United States was carrying primary responsibility for the defense of Indochina, as we had in Korea,"[23] but the burden of the fighting rested

21 *NYT*, 11 June 1954. At his news conference the week before, the President declared that he had not decided whether to ask for congressional authority to take some form of action in Indochina (*NYT*, 3 June 1954). The NSC met on 3 June, and possibly it was at this session that the cautious policymakers voiced their real sentiments to the activists and obtained decisions to refrain from asking Congress for an intervention resolution and to acquiesce in the partition of Vietnam.

22 DDE, p. 362.
23 *Ibid.*

with the French and the Associated States, which implied that they would continue to bear it. And, since the burden of the fighting remained with these states, they must decide how long they would remain at Geneva. Dulles, at his press conference on 8 June, said substantially the same thing.

During their inquiries of mid-May and later, the French expressed fear that the Chinese air force might launch an attack against the Red River delta defenses and military installations that might destroy French air capability and damage the port of Haiphong, making it virtually impossible for the French to evacuate the delta if this should become necessary. Eisenhower noted that the French had expressed "once again the old threat," that if the French expeditionary force was defeated because the United States had not come to its rescue, France might have to make peace at any price. This "old threat" seems to have irritated the President, who later wrote:

> I could not see why we would be compelled to tell the French or any other ally, in advance, in what manner we would respond to Chinese Communist intervention, unless these same allies were prepared to join and cooperate with us effectively on a partnership basis, should this contingency arise.[24]

We do not yet know the extent to which the Laniel government pressed the United States for assistance, or merely for variations in the conditions for intervention, nor do we know the character of French remonstrations. There was, however, evidence of irritation with the French among the highest policymakers in the administration during early June—for example, in Dulles's public remarks during the first two weeks of June. The Secretary of State was scheduled to speak in Seattle on 10 June and in Los Angeles on the 11th, and on both occasions he delivered major policy statements, which we will examine below. While Dulles's speeches were in preparation, Robert Murphy appended to one of them a comment that bitterly decried French policy. The French, he said, had dragged their feet in Indochina, to the extent that they had even discredited the United States. The primary responsibility for the prosecution of the war, he emphasized, lay with France, not the United States.[25]

Similarly, Eisenhower's *Mandate for Change* contains an exchange of letters that were highly significant in revealing the President's attitude toward the French government. On 8 June he received a letter from General Alfred M. Gruenther that read in part:

[24] *Ibid.*
[25] Private Papers of John Foster Dulles, memorandum dated 26 March 1954, File I.B.

> Yesterday, Pleven asked me to come and see him to discuss cer-
> tain matters in connection with the 3 new divisions the French
> are about to activate to send to Indo-China—(Maybe!)....
>
> At one stage he said: "If we should lose the delta area it would
> be a catastrophe for France and a great set back for the whole
> Free World. It would start a wave of anti-allied outbursts in France
> with great bitterness because the Allies let us down."[26]

Gruenther, a close friend of the President, was one to whom the latter
could express his feelings straightforwardly, in nonofficial and non-
diplomatic language, and his reply gives us an unusual glimpse of an
angry President.

> Pleven knows as well as you and I do that, beginning in early
> 1951, every kind of presentation has been made to the French Gov-
> ernment to induce that government to put the Indo-China war on
> an international footing. . . . We urged further that France not only
> declare her intention of making Indo-China independent and that
> she was fighting for the right of Indo-China to be independent—
> but that she should take steps to place the issue before the U.N.
> At the very least, this latter action would have had the effect of
> legitimizing any kind of coalition that might then have been formed
> to fight the war.
>
> As the conflict has dragged on, the United States has more than
> once offered help of a kind that would tend to keep our participa-
> tion in the background, but could nevertheless be very effective.
> *I refer to our efforts to get a good guerrilla organization started in
> the region, our offer to take over a great part of the burden of train-
> ing native troops, and numerous offers of help in the logistic
> [sic] field.*
>
> Most of these have been rebuffed. . . .
>
> In recent months, the French government has begun to speak
> out of the other side of its mouth, and has been demanding help of
> various kinds. But it is noteworthy that all these requests for help
> have been for help on France's own terms—her government has
> consistently insisted upon promises from us of certain kinds of
> technical help which we would presumably turn over to them with-
> out question to be used by them as they saw fit.
>
> Yet at the same time, they have made no single effort to meet
> the conditions that we have insisted upon for three years as con-
> stituting the only sound basis on which any European govern-
> ment could be fighting in South East Asia. . . .
>
> . . . Take, for example, the fact that while the United States was
> sending conscripted soldiers to Korea to fight a war in which we

[26] DDE, p. 363.

as a nation never had any of our political or economic interests involved, the French refused to send conscripts to Indo-China, which
had been for years merely one of their colonies.[27]

After this letter appeared in his book, Mr. Eisenhower said: "During
this period I often expressed a thought in conversation with Secretary
Dulles. 'France ought to recall General de Gaulle,' "[28]

On Tuesday, 8 June—the same day President Eisenhower received
the above letter from General Gruenther—the Secretary of State held
a news conference at which he made five important comments in
response to questions from the correspondents.

1. The primary responsibility for negotiations at Geneva lay with
France, in association with the delegations from Vietnam, Laos, and
Cambodia.

2. "It seems that the Communist forces in Indochina are intensifying their activities. They have done so ever since the proposal for
peace in Indochina, which was taken at the Berlin Conference. There
has been, I think, a deliberate dragging out of the negotiations at
Geneva while the Communist military effort has been stepped up in
Indo-China itself."

3. *"The United States has no intention of dealing with the Indochina
situation unilaterally, certainly not unless the whole nature of the
aggression should change."*[29] Dulles also commented that such a change
might be "a resumption by Communist China of open armed aggression in that area or in any other area of the Far East."

4. There was no present plan for asking Congress for authorization
for American action in Indochina, and there had not been sufficient
acceptance by the allies of a program of action for the President to go
to Congress. (The President confirmed this at his press conference
on 10 June.)[30]

5. Asked to describe the objectives of united action, Dulles answered: "to retain in friendly hands as much as possible of the Southeast Asian peninsular and island area. Now the practicality varies
from time to time. What was practical a year ago is less practical today.
The situation, has, I am afraid, been deteriorating."

Bonnet met with the Secretary of State a short time after the press
conference, and, according to one account, Dulles was brutally
frank.[31] France, he told Bonnet, wished to have the option of determin-

[27] DDE, pp. 363-364 (emphasis added).
[28] DDE, p. 364.
[29] Department of State Press Release, No. 309, 8 June 1954; *DSB*, 21 June 1954,
pp. 947-949 (emphasis added).
[30] *NYT*, 11 June 1954.
[31] L&D, p. 201. No authority is cited, but one might speculate that the authors
based their account upon an interview with Bonnet.

ing American actions in Indochina and calling the forces of its allies to the rescue if things went badly at Geneva or in Indochina. France wanted to do this at its own convenience and at the hour of its choice, but the United States, he said, could not play this game (*"les États-Unis ne peuvent se prêter à ce jeu"*).[32] The question whether the United States was prepared to send marines to Indochina was, at this hour, "vain and without object."

The battle for the Red River delta, it would appear, must be fought by the French with whatever Vietnamese assistance they could muster. The United States was not going to intervene unilaterally. It might intervene in a coalition with other states, but the formation of such a coalition would take many weeks, and the first battles for the delta had already occurred. A major Vietminh offensive was expected by 15 June. Further, the French were pressing for a commitment from the Eisenhower administration without having fulfilled the conditions that were within their power to fulfill. There were, of course, conditions over which they had no power (e.g. British consent or acquiescence in coalition action), but the Laniel government was not prepared formally to ask France's allies for intervention or to secure parliamentary approval for such a request. Nor was Laniel prepared to assure the United States that French forces would be kept in Indochina during the period of collective action. Finally, although Dulles had publicly declared that the SVN was juridically independent, he could not have been pleased with the 4 June ceremony at the Matignon at which Prince Buu Loc and the French Premier had merely initialed the treaties of independence and association. He was too good a lawyer not to have been aware of the problems that might, at some future time, arise in connection with the juridical status of the SVN. Thus, not having met the preconditions, the French were again asking for American intervention to save the delta, and using what Mr. Eisenhower called the "old threat" of peace at any price. Administration officials, it seems clear, were irritated by these French importunities.

On the 3d of June, General Valluy, the French military representative to the Five Power staff talks in Washington, had informed American officers that the French expected an all-out Vietminh attack within ten days, but morale was low and the men of the French expeditionary force were tired. Valluy was not optimistic, Mr. Eisenhower later wrote, about their withstanding an attack. This was difficult for the President to understand as "French Union forces included seventy-nine battalions and eleven *groupes mobiles* available for defense of the delta, which should be highly useful in this open ter-

[32] *Ibid.*

rain."[33] Irrespective of the President's assessment, the French had distinct reservations about their ability to hold the delta, and it was doubtful whether they could even begin to transfer troops from the metropolitan army to Indochina before the decisive battles for the delta began.

[III]

Secretary Dulles delivered two important addresses on the West Coast on 10 and 11 June. The first, at the forty-fifth annual convention of Rotary International in Seattle, dealt with the theme of international unity built upon diversity. The second address, before the Los Angeles World Affairs Council on 11 June, was related to security in East Asia. In the Seattle address, Dulles discussed the origins of America's alliances, the concept of collective action, and the problems confronting America's alliance policy. With respect to Indochina, he noted that Thailand had asked the Security Council to send an observation commission to Southeast Asia, and the council had placed the request on its agenda.

It has been suggested that an affirmative response to Thailand's appeal might in some way impede the negotiations at Geneva with reference to possible peace in Indochina. That argument has little validity. A peace observation commission has no authority to make decisions. It is a reporting body. . . . It is difficult to see why negotiations at Geneva would be impeded by the fact that representatives of the United Nations were in the area reporting what was going on. Knowledge has never been an impediment to honest negotiations.[34]

(We have seen that the Soviet Union would veto the Thai proposal for an observation commission on 18 June, but despite the sentiments Dulles expressed in Seattle, the United States would not take the question to the General Assembly.)

Discussing colonialism, Dulles said that Ho Chi Minh, "a Moscow-indoctrinated Communist," had "utilized a revolutionary movement that attracted much genuine native support."[35] Ho had committed himself to efforts in Indochina, Dulles said, that could succeed only with external Communist assistance. "This created a dependence upon external Communist support such that if any of the peoples of Vietnam, Laos, or Cambodia should now end in the control of Ho Chi-

---

[33] DDE, p. 365.

[34] John Foster Dulles, *International Unity*, Press Release No. 316, Series S, No. 19 (Washington, D.C.: Department of State, Public Services Division, 1954), pp. 4-5. See also *DSB*, 21 June 1954, pp. 935-939.

[35] *Ibid.*, p. 6.

Minh, they would not, in fact, be independent." Noting that the
world conditions created by Communist strategy made the realization of genuine independence a task of "infinite difficulty and deli-
cacy," Dulles said the United States was "pushing for self-government"—and more forcefully than was publicly known because "open
pressures are rarely conducive to the best results." If the United States
had acted with restraint in pressing for the independence of colonies,
it was because its policymakers believed quick action would not
produce true independence and might "spell confusion and division
which would be the transition to a captivity far worse than present
dependence."[36]

Dulles then noted that the government had outlined conditions
that would justify the creation of a collective defense alliance in Southeast Asia. "At the head of the list of those conditions was the stipulation that there must be assurance that the French will, in fact, make
good on their July 3, 1953, declaration of intention to grant complete
independence [to the Associated States]. *The United States will never
fight for colonialism.*"[37]

Did this remark imply that Secretary Dulles was not satisfied with
the steps the French government had taken to fulfill the condition
of Vietnamese independence? Did it notify the French that they must
wage the battle for the delta alone? After all, these were questions the
ministers of the Laniel government probably discussed among themselves. (The President that very same day had said he did not intend
to ask Congress for authority to take direct action in Indochina.)
These questions cannot be answered with certainty, and the secretary let his listeners draw their own inferences, a familiar practice in
his policy pronouncements.

The second address, on 11 June in Los Angeles, did not answer the
questions posed above, and therefore the ministers of the Laniel government must have remained uncertain. Dulles reviewed the situation in Indochina in a fashion similar to some of his earlier historical
analyses. Disturbances, he said, had been fomented from Communist
China, but there had been no open invasion by China. The task of
pacification, under these circumstances, "cannot be successfully met
merely by unilateral armed intervention";[38] but if various conditions
were met or fulfilled—conditions the administration had consistently
delineated—the circumstances "*might* justify intervention." He listed
the five conditions of the secret note of 15 May to Ambassador Dillon
in such a way that the Laniel government would not be compromised.

[36] *Ibid.*, p. 7 (emphasis added).   [37] *Ibid.*
[38] John Foster Dulles, *Security in the Pacific*, Press Release No. 318, Series S,
No. 20 (Washington, D.C.: Department of State, Public Services Division, 1954),
p. 4. See also *DSB*, 28 June 1954, pp. 971-973.

(1) An invitation from the present lawful authorities; (2) clear assurance of complete independence to Laos, Cambodia, and Viet-Nam; (3) evidence of concern by the United Nations; (4) a joining in the collective effort of some of the other nations of the area; and (5) assurance that France will not itself withdraw from the battle until it is won.

Only if these conditions were realized could the President and the Congress be justified in asking the American people to make the sacrifices incident to committing our nation, *with others*, to using force to help to restore peace in the area.[39]

Dulles, of course, did not express the need for French parliamentary approval, although the mere mention of point 5 could give critical French deputies more ammunition for their attack against the Laniel government. In Paris, another major Assembly debate was even then in progress, a debate that ended two days later in Laniel's failure to win a vote of confidence. Dulles, moreover, appeared to have purposely omitted an explicit mention of British cooperation when, in point 4, he said that other nations "of the area" must join in a collective effort.

It is the writer's opinion that the Secretary of State could not have been more explicit on 10 and 11 June without materially harming Franco-American relations. But these two speeches, together with Dulles's remarks at his press conference of the 8th and the remarks in early June of President Eisenhower and Secretary Wilson, enable us to make four observations on American policy as of the second week of June 1954

1. The French government, with a battle for the delta rapidly shaping up, was panicking—just as it had panicked in late April before the fall of Dien Bien Phu. French spokesmen were pressing the United States for a commitment to save the French expeditionary corps and the cities of Hanoi and Haiphong if such help should become necessary, but administration officials were irritated by these most recent importunities. First, because the French appeared to lack the will to sustain their position in Tonkin. Second, because the Laniel government had not met any of the preconditions for American intervention. (We have noted, however, that probably no French government could have met the conditions in the note of 15 May. It can be argued, moreover, with some justification, that the conditions had been formulated with the intention of *preventing* American intervention, unless Chinese intervention or Vietminh victories in southern Vietnam created a "new war.") Third, the French seemed to be using the "old threats" of the defeat of EDC, the communization of Southeast

[39] *Ibid.*, pp. 4-5 (emphasis added).

Asia, and a possible anti-American reaction in France against a refusal of American support for France at this crucial time. And the
administration resented the implication that it was responsible for the
French debacle. Finally, the French conduct of their political and
military affairs impressed some officials as singularly dilatory and
even incompetent. The French had repeatedly reneged on granting
real independence to the Associated States and transforming paper
independence into fact. The Laniel government had held off a decision on reinforcing the French Union forces (by calling up reserves and by other means) until it was too late for such measures
to affect the campaign in Tonkin. Also, it had long retained officials
in Indochina (General Navarre and Maurice Dejean) who, committed
to a policy of *grandeur*, refused to implement a policy of independence for the Vietnamese. It had, in addition, rather consistently
painted an overly optimistic picture of the situation in Indochina
and, at least in the American view, had expressed its resentment toward Americans and fear of their involvement in Indochina by refusing to cooperate with MAAG officers and accept American advice,
whether proffered directly or through Paris.[40]

2. The administration had not decided *not* to intervene in Indochina; under the circumstances,[41] it could not have made such a decision. As noted earlier, however, intervention had been so hedged by
conditions that it was quite impossible for them to be fulfilled in time
for the United States to make a contribution that would (*a*) affect
the Geneva negotiations and (*b*) prevent a French defeat in the Red
River delta.

3. If the French had not been given a flat no by the administration,
it had been given something very close to it. The French government, therefore, could reasonably conclude that Washington believed the Indochinese War and the Geneva negotiations were primarily a French responsibility, and it must take the initiative in
securing the expeditionary corps in Tonkin and obtaining a satisfactory cease-fire at Geneva. As for Geneva, France could rely upon the
United States for diplomatic support, but she could not expect military support unless she met the conditions the administration had
formulated.

[40] DDE, pp. 364, 372-373. On 10 June the U.S. government refused to provide
an airlift to Indochina for 3,000 French troops in North Africa (it would, however,
fly about 1,000 Dien Bien Phu wounded out of Hanoi). The reasons for the refusal of the airlift were said to be political, related to India's decision not to allow
such flights over her territories. *NYT*, 11 June 1954.

[41] These circumstances included ignorance of Vietminh and Communist Chinese
intentions and the desire of various influential persons to have the United States
take a more active role in the military defense of Indochina (Nixon, Robertson,
and Radford).

4. It is this writer's opinion that, by 11 June at the latest, the administration had reluctantly concluded that some form of partition of Vietnam was inevitable, but its conclusion, obviously, was not made public.[42] After mentioning the Vietminh attacks against the Hanoi–Haiphong rail line *in early June* and the Communist stalling at Geneva, Eisenhower wrote: "By this time it was generally accepted that partition would occur in Vietnam and possibly even in the other Associated States."[43] He did not say it was "generally accepted" among the members of his administration, but such an inference is possible. Washington officials knew that the French planned to withdraw to a defense perimeter in the delta, which meant that almost all of Tonkin would come under Vietminh control. There even appeared to be some doubt that the delta could be held.

If the President was not prepared to ask Congress for the authority to intervene, if the preconditions for intervention had not been fulfilled, if the Geneva negotiations were primarily a French responsibility, and if the French wanted a cease-fire in Indochina, the French must do one of two things within the next month or two: (*a*) accept a cease-fire with the Vietminh, who were in control of Tonkin (i.e. accept partition), or (*b*) continue fighting until sufficient reinforcements arrived to alter the military situation. In my view, the administration was under no illusion that the French would continue the war: the French simply would not do this. In late March, or even in April, some American officials may have *hoped* that the French would persevere. After Dien Bien Phu, Laniel had solemnly declared that the French would continue the fight unless a satisfactory and honorable cease-fire could be won at Geneva, but with the threat to the delta, which developed so rapidly in May and June, the official attitude had changed. The primary objective became the security of the French expeditionary corps in its withdrawal from exposed positions, perhaps even its withdrawal from Tonkin. There seemed to be no thought of military action to improve the French position or maintain a military presence in the north. Bidault's bargaining position at Geneva had become untenable.

THUS IT SEEMS reasonable to conclude that the administration was aware of the implication of its refusal to intervene actively and of France's inability to improve its military and political position. The consequence was partition. No American government in the fifties could have been happy with this outcome. It was, after all, a breach of the doctrine of containment. A "vital new" area would come under

[42] This assessment might have been made at the NSC meeting on 3 June.
[43] DDE, p. 365.

Communist domination, Vice President Nixon declared.[44] But the alternative appeared equally undesirable. President Eisenhower and Mr. Dulles simply were not willing to commit American troops to Indochina in the spring of 1954 to prevent partition—the only way this could have been prevented, barring a highly improbable resurgence of the French martial spirit.

The American realization that partition was inevitable strengthened the official resolve not to associate the United States formally with a settlement that was based upon such a solution. The administration would adopt a kind of nonrecognition policy on the theory that the Vietminh had won territory by the illegal use of force. Dulles had warned, as early as March, that the United States would not associate itself with an agreement that resulted in Communist domination of the territory and peoples of Indochina. There was some evidence that Dulles was considering even American withdrawal from the Geneva Conference,[45] which would emphatically demonstrate American disapproval.

It is likely that American irritation with the French was in great part due to dissatisfaction with a situation America, *in effect*, had no capacity to resolve to its liking. Partition represented a victory for the Communists, and the French had made such a victory possible. The administration had wanted a victory over the Vietminh Communists without committing troops to Indochina and without using its strategic air and naval power, but, without the use of its military capabilities, it could not hope for a Vietminh defeat. Prudence, cautiousness, and a refusal to act unilaterally, all this translated into formal preconditions for intervention, precluded the use of force in Indochina or the commission of a belligerent act. In a word, Eisenhower's policymakers had denied themselves the alternative of force and therefore had to rely upon their French ally for its application. But France, by early June, could not prevent partition, and, having denied themselves the option of force, United States policymakers also were unable to prevent partition.

Vietnam partition, however, depended upon another important factor: acceptance by the Vietminh and, more basically, by the Soviet Union and the C.P.R. It was not known whether the Communists would accept partition, but Pham Van Dong's proposals of 25 May, supported by Molotov and Chou, appeared to envisage temporary

---

[44] *NYT*, 17 April 1954.

[45] In a memorandum to Dulles dated 5 June and commenting upon a draft of the speech the secretary was to deliver in Seattle, Carl W. McCardle, Assistant Secretary of State for Public Affairs, urged Mr. Dulles to educate the public on the reasons why "we will probably be phasing out of [the Geneva Conference]." Private Papers of John Foster Dulles, File I.B.1; Rotary International File, 10 June 1954.

de facto partition. Nevertheless, a division of territory, a cease-fire (and its implementation, control, and supervision), and resolution of the Laotian and Cambodian questions contained the possibility that hostilities might continue, and the possibility that China might overtly intervene. Against this latter eventuality, the administration was determined to make its intentions plain. On 11 June at Los Angeles, referring to the possibility of overt Chinese aggression in Indochina (or elsewhere), Dulles declared:

> If such overt military aggression occurred, that would be a deliberate threat to the United States itself. The United States would of course invoke the processes of the United Nations and consult with its allies. But we could not escape ultimate responsibility for decisions closely touching the United States and its allies. . . .
>
> Your Government wants peace, and the American people want peace. But should there ever be openly launched an attack that the American people would clearly recognize as a threat to our own security, then the right of self-preservation would demand that we—regardless of any other country—meet the issue squarely.[46]

The last sentence had been added to a draft of Dulles's address by President Eisenhower himself. After reading the speech and this important sentence, Carl W. McCardle, Assistant Secretary of State for Public Affairs, penned a note to Dulles asking whether "we want to give the impression that we will go it alone, regardless," even if an open attack were launched.[47] Secretary Dulles's reply does not appear in his private papers, but the sentence, of course, appeared in the final draft of his address. Did he agree with this candid declaration or had he retained it in deference to the chief executive? It is difficult to say; but certainly it offers a significant insight into the President's thinking at the time. Read in the context of the speech, the sentence warned that if the Chinese overtly intervened in Indochina, the United States might be compelled to act without allies in meeting the "issue squarely." How the United States would do this was left to inference, but agreement upon united action would no longer be a prerequisite for action.

[I V]

The administration's appraisal of Communist tactics at Geneva held to the view that the Communists were stalling.[48] This view con-

[46] *Security in the Pacific, op. cit.*, pp. 5-6.

[47] Private Papers of John Foster Dulles, memorandum of 8 June 1954; World Affairs Council, Los Angeles, 11 June 1954, File I.B.1. See also the President's notes to Dulles's speech and the cover letter of 8 June (*ibid.*).

[48] DDE, p. 365.

firmed the predispositions of Washington policymakers that the Soviets and the Chinese would use the conference to divide the allies
and capitalize upon the weaknesses of the French. President Eisenhower's reaction to the accomplishments of the Geneva Conference
after one month of negotiations was typical of opinion at the time.

> [The] Communists now began to prolong and stall the confer-
> ence, obviously taking advantage of the overwhelming military
> initiative they enjoyed in the Red River Delta. The longer they
> could stall, the more nervous the French would become—and In-
> dochina, particularly the delta, would go farther down the
> drain. . . .
>
> Now we were feeling the full impact of the earlier refusal to
> undertake any united action until after the Geneva Conference.
> The Communists realized that if they could draw out the confer-
> ence, they need fear little by way of any intervention by out-
> side powers.[49]

Writing in the *New York Times* of 5 June, T. J. Hamilton voiced
the sentiment of many Republican senators when he said it would
have been better if the Geneva Conference had not been held.[50] In
January and February the situation in Indochina had been stable,
Hamilton said, implying that the agreement to hold the conference
gave the Communists a special reason to push for victory. This is a
curious (and inaccurate) observation inasmuch as the Vietminh offensive had begun before the Berlin Conference, and one could
hardly call the situation "stable" in view of the Vietminh victories
in Laos. However, there was undoubtedly an element of truth in the
proposition that the Communists had decided to try for a stunning
military victory before the conference convened. On the other hand,
there is equal truth in the assertion that bad strategy made the French
decide to take a stand at Dien Bien Phu. Finally, and most important, the argument that the Geneva Conference should not have
been held—advanced by Hamilton (and several senators)—ignored
the very weighty factors that had impelled Secretary Dulles to agree
to a conference. (These factors have been discussed in detail in
Chapter 3.)

From an American point of view, the Communist delegations at
Geneva were in no hurry to reach a settlement. In this connection,
as President Eisenhower noted, there was the Vietminh buildup
in the delta and its desire to exploit the military weaknesses of the
French. There was also the feeling that the Communists knew the

---

[49] DDE, p. 358.
[50] Senator Knowland demanded that the Geneva Conference be ended. *NYT*,
13 June 1954.

Laniel government was near its end and also wanted to exploit the unstable political situation in Paris. In addition, the Communists might have wanted to cultivate the divergent stands and policies in the American and the British positions on the Indochinese War, the Geneva Conference itself, and the efficacy of negotiations. In assessing the Communists' bargaining strategy, we should remember that Molotov had made several minor concessions (the primacy of a military over a political solution and agreement upon "neutral" nations' supervision of a cease-fire) and Pham Van Dong had offered proposals that accommodated the kind of solution the British desired.

If the Communists were stalling, they were doing it cleverly— allowing just enough progress to confirm the British hope, and perhaps the hope of French public opinion as well, that the Communists desired a settlement. We do not know what tactics the Communists used, but we should remember that, until the military commission on Vietnam had met on 3 June, Bidault had refused to deal directly with the Vietminh. While direct dealings between the French and the Vietminh would have the symbolic significance of legitimizing a "rebel" force, they were regarded as intrinsically desirable by an important segment of opinion in Paris. And there is no reason for believing the Communists did not also feel such dealings were desirable and natural under the circumstances.

Whatever the Communists' tactics, their actions in mid-June and afterward tend to confirm the hypothesis that, though they might have wanted to delay the conference, they did not want it adjourned *sine die.* Nor, it seems, did the Soviets and the Chinese want to appear overly belligerent. Nevertheless, the buildup and prospective offensive in the delta produced that reaction in England. Was it possible, British opinion asked, that the Vietminh did not want a cease-fire? Did they feel they could win on the battlefield and therefore need not seek a negotiated settlement? The *Economist's* editors declared that if the Vietminh leaders were to seek a

> second spectacular victory . . . [at Hanoi, etc.], while the Geneva conference is still wrestling with the problem of bringing the Indochina war to an end, they will make nonsense of the Communists' argument that only their antagonists wish to extend the war. They will strengthen the hand of the extreme interventionist faction in Washington; and they will place Mr. Eden in an impossible position at Geneva.[51]

Eden, aware of this consequence of increased Vietminh activity in the delta, in the first week of June let it be known that he would

[51] *Econ.*, 12 June 1954, p. 877.

act as an intermediary for only one or two weeks more. His role as "intermediary" had been criticized in the American and the French press, and on a few occasions in British news articles. This role, Eden wrote, was open to "every kind of misrepresentation."[52] The Foreign Secretary therefore wanted the Communists to know that he could not persist indefinitely in his efforts at conciliation; he might have to consider breaking off negotiations, in which case hostilities would continue. Did the Communists want this? Did the Vietminh want to attempt to secure a victory in the delta before a cease-fire? Might they even have wanted to push their forces farther into Annam, Cochin China, Laos, and Cambodia? If the answers to these questions were affirmative, Eden's theories were wrong, and British opinion would be sorely disappointed—so disappointed, in fact, that Britain might immediately associate itself with the American plan for coalition action.[53]

[52] E, p. 144.
[53] *NYT*, 9 June 1954 (report by Drew Middleton).

Chapter 15

THE GENEVA NEGOTIATIONS AND THE GOVERNMENT CRISIS IN FRANCE

[I]

The worsening military situation in the Red River delta and the ostensible lack of progress at Geneva in achieving a cease-fire produced the expected reaction in Paris: the Communists and Socialists were joined by substantial numbers of deputies from the center and right, and all demanded a debate on the Laniel government's Indochina policy. In late May the Premier was compelled to agree to a debate and he scheduled it for early June. Bidault made plans to leave Geneva for Paris on the 7th in order to defend his government's policies and his own tactics at the conference. Soviet Foreign Minister Molotov, back from his trip to Moscow, had indicated that he wanted a plenary session on Tuesday, 8 June. Since a public statement by the Soviet minister after three weeks of restricted sessions was likely to be of unusual significance, Laniel succeeded in postponing the Assembly debate until the 8th.[1] The Premier proposed that Bidault be given an opportunity to reply to Molotov's speech.

The reader will remember that the conference, in restricted session, had turned to neutral nations' supervision of an armistice. Molotov had in principle agreed that such supervision was necessary, but the composition and competence of the supervisory commission he and the other Communist delegates envisaged was such as to assure, in the opinion of the non-Communist delegates, its inoperability. Over the weekend of 5 and 6 June, many individuals at Geneva and in the Western capitals expected Molotov to make a public gesture of compromise on at least armistice supervision. There was a great deal of anticipation within the French delegation and in Paris itself. Whatever Molotov and the other ministers might say at the forthcoming plenary sessions would have a very great influence upon the course of the National Assembly debate.

At the Tuesday session, on the 8th, Bidault spoke first, largely for his Paris audience, describing in some detail the French proposals that had been submitted to the conference since early May and

[1] *JO*, 9 June 1954, p. 2829 (2d sess., 8 June). Interpellations on the government's Indochina policy were discussed on 1 June (*JO*, 2 June, pp. 2736-2752 [2d sess.]) and 2 June (*JO*, 3 June, pp. 2777-2791). Discussions then ceased for about a week and were resumed on 8 June (*JO*, 9 June, pp. 2824-2829 [2d sess.]).

underlining the willingness of the French to compromise. When he turned to the subject of a supervisory commission, he made a number of suggestions. It should be installed throughout Vietnam, on a partly fixed, partly mobile basis, and equipped with modern transportation, communication, and observation facilities. The international supervisory commission (ISC) described by the French minister would be a fairly large organization, with a staff large enough to meet changing needs. The ISC would have at its disposal a number of joint commissions, composed of representatives of the two commands (the French and the Vietminh) and acting under the authority and pursuant to the instruction of the ISC in investigating incidents. "In the event of any violation, directly it is clear that the parties cannot reach agreement and that consequently the joint commissions are powerless, the International Commission will deal with the dispute and enforce its decisions. Decisions of the Commission will in all cases be taken by majority vote."[2] Bidault also proposed the creation of a body to which the ISC might appeal in the event of violations or similar circumstances. The appellate organ could, in turn, appeal to the members of the conference, who would act as guarantors of a cease-fire agreement.

After a short statement by the Cambodian delegate that called for a cease-fire in Cambodia and evacuation by Vietminh regulars and irregulars, Molotov addressed the conference. The general purport of his speech was made known to his audience quite early. "The time has come," Molotov said, "to postpone no longer the consideration of questions of a political settlement, the more so since the discussion has confirmed the fact that these two categories of questions [military and political questions] are closely inter-related."[3] He proposed that the conference examine, without delay, political problems created by the "situation" in Indochina, and suggested that the delegates might consider, on alternate days, military and political questions. The independence France had allegedly granted the Associated States was not real, Molotov said, and no Asian state attached importance to declarations of independence made by France or the colonialist regimes in Indochina.[4] The conference must, first of all, examine questions connected with the sovereignty of the Associated States, the holding of free, general elections, and the withdrawal of foreign troops. Finally, the conferees ought to ensure "the establishment of direct contact between representatives of *both sides* to discuss *political questions*."[5]

Molotov criticized the Bao Dai government, saying it did not rep-

[2] Cmd. 9186, p. 140.
[4] *Ibid.*, p. 147.

[3] *Ibid.*, p. 143.
[5] *Ibid.*, p. 151 (emphasis added).

resent the sentiments of the Vietnamese people. He denigrated the recent (4 June) agreement purporting to establish the sovereignty of Vietnam: "[It] still remains unsigned and therefore unpublished."[6] The DRVN, on the other hand, had genuine popular support, Molotov asserted. Witness Dien Bien Phu: It was defended "not by the forces of the French or the forces of the Vietnamese, but by the forces of all kinds of foreigners brought together there."[7] The PAVN, however, consisted of Vietnamese troops only. Why, therefore, must this colonial war be continued? Molotov asked.

It cannot mean anything else than a further deepening of the differences between France and the peoples of Indo-China. . . . If the Government of France is really anxious to establish the independence of the States of Indo-China, then in the present circumstances there are no grounds for continuing the war in Indo-China, since important pre-requisites for an amicable settlement of these mutual relations have been brought about. This settlement has now become possible on honourable terms for both sides. In any case, nobody is going to prove that the continuation of the war in Indo-China is required by the national interests of France. On the contrary, to refuse or evade negotiations on this question with the real representatives of the Vietnamese people, is, in our opinion, contrary to the national interests of France.[8]

The Soviet minister also reasserted his support for Pham Van Dong's proposals, particularly as they implied future amicable relations with France, perhaps even within the French Union.[9]

Molotov's remarks on the necessity for a discussion and resolution of political questions was a procedural step backward. His unequivocal assertion (quoted above) that France's national interest required direct dealings between the belligerents on the relevant political questions was, in the context of the political situation in Paris, a blow to Bidault. It could not help but strengthen the hand of the deputies who had urged direct negotiations with the Vietminh, especially Pierre Mendès-France.

Anthony Eden spoke to the conference after the Soviet Foreign Minister. He again emphasized the need for truce supervision and remarked that the delegates would likely agree that joint committees of the belligerents were a necessary supplement to international supervision. "These joint committees could probably render some

[6] *Ibid.*, p. 147.   [7] *Ibid.*, p. 148.

[8] *Ibid.*, p. 149. Molotov also criticized American efforts to establish a collective defense arrangement for Southeast Asia (p. 143) and Bidault's conceptions of the way peace should be brought to Indochina (p. 151).

[9] Cmd. 9186, p. 145.

useful service provided that it was clearly understood that their functions were mainly technical and clearly subordinate [to the authority of an ISC]."[10] Eden believed the best way to avoid the inevitable ISC deadlock that would result if the conference adopted Molotov's proposal—that is, a commission half Communist, half non-Communist —would be to have the five Colombo powers supervise the arrangements concluded at Geneva. These countries—Burma, Ceylon, India, Indonesia, and Pakistan—would be truly impartial, Eden said; they had recognized neither the Vietminh nor the Associated States.

> We are bound to agree that as Asian countries they have a particular concern in the restoration of peace in Indo-China and possess first-hand knowledge of the kind of problems confronting us there. Moreover, they are probably close enough to be able to provide and organize without undue difficulty the large staff of qualified observers that will be needed.[11]

Eden reminded the conference participants that they had two urgent tasks: reaching agreement on the composition and powers of the ISC and dealing with the special problems of Laos and Cambodia. He forcefully declared the Vietminh had committed "aggressive acts" in those states, and called for the withdrawal of foreign troops. The Cambodian representative, he remarked, had told the delegates that his government had no intention of allowing military bases on its territories, bases that might threaten the peace of Indochina. Hence the peoples of Cambodia and Laos, he said, should be allowed to work out their destinies in peace and under a form of international supervision designed to prevent interference from beyond their borders.

The plenary session adjourned after Eden's speech. Bidault boarded a train for Paris, where he must confront the formidable number of deputies who opposed his policies, not only his policies, on Indochina but, in the case of the Gaullists, his European policies as well.

[II]

The sixth plenary session, on 9 June, did nothing to improve the survival potential of the Laniel government. Premier Chou En-lai, who delivered an uncompromising address, agreed with Molotov that military issues and political questions were interrelated and could not be separated; both should be discussed simultaneously, he argued.[12] In discussing neutral nations' supervision of an armistice, Chou asserted that Communist states must be made members of such a supervisory commission if the conference expected to reach

---

[10] *Ibid.*, p. 152.   [11] *Ibid.*   [12] *Ibid.*, p. 164.

agreement upon its composition.[13] Also, the joint committees and the supervisory commission were distinct organizations; neither should be given authority over the other. The neutral nations' commission should conduct its business with the approval of the representatives of all its member nations. In other words, its basis of operation should be the principle of unanimity. Chou again dismissed the notion of U.N. supervision: "[The] United Nations is not suitable to perform the function of supervising the implementation of the armistice in Indo-China."[14] Finally, he insisted that, since the conference had agreed upon the principle of a simultaneous cease-fire throughout Indochina, the question of troop dispositions and regroupment should be studied for Indochina as a whole. On the withdrawal of foreign troops from Laos and Cambodia, Chou asked how it was possible for troops that had been organized by the Pathet Lao and Khmer Issarak to withdraw from territories in which the latter were the legitimate government. Thus by 9 June the delegates of the two leading Communist powers had taken public positions that threatened to deadlock the conference.

1. The Chinese Premier insisted that the hostilities in Laos and Cambodia had to be considered with the Vietnamese question. Moreover, Chou had insisted that the conference recognize the role of the Pathet Lao and the Khmer Issarak in determining the destiny of Laos and Cambodia.

2. Political questions must be discussed simultaneously with military questions. Both Molotov and Chou En-lai now demanded this procedure, which constituted a reversal of Molotov's compromise of 14 May. (Point 1, above, constituted merely *reactivation* of an issue that had been put aside by the conference. Molotov had once agreed to this, thereby impressing many as being willing to compromise.)

3. According to the Soviet proposal, a neutral nations' supervisory commission should be composed of representatives of Czechoslovakia, Poland, India, and Pakistan. The Chinese Premier added the stipulation that the commission operate on the principle of unanimity. If the Korean armistice had any didactic value, a commission of this kind would not accomplish very much. The equal representation of Communist and non-Communist nations would almost ensure a stalemate on most substantive issues.

4. The Franco-Vietminh joint commissions must not be subordinate to the neutral nations' commission but have parallel authority.

It is difficult to determine the reasons for the Communist insistence upon these four propositions, but Molotov had just returned from Moscow, where, we may imagine, it was decided to pursue a "tougher

[13] *Ibid.*, p. 161.   [14] *Ibid.*, p. 163.

line," at least temporarily. The generally accepted hypothesis was that the Soviets wanted to influence the Assembly debate in Paris, and bring about the fall of the Laniel government, in the hope that it would be succeeded by one more amenable to compromise. And perhaps the Soviets were dissatisfied with Bidault, who had consistently refused to negotiate with delegates of the DRVN and had not explored the implications of Pham Van Dong's proposals of 25 May for a temporary *de facto* partition. Thus they may have hoped for a more compromising French foreign minister, but not necessarily have expected Bidault's replacement to make significant concessions other than talk to the Vietminh at Geneva or agree to a temporary partition—and not be burdened, like Bidault, by a personal promise to the SVN Vietnamese not to accept partition. On the other hand, the Communists may have expected that a new French government would desire to end the war quickly and would be willing to pay a high price to the DRVN in terms of territory, influence on supervisory commissions, and a guarantee of future political control of the whole of Vietnam. The French might even be persuaded to make similar concessions to the Pathet Lao and Khmer Issarak.

Whatever the Soviets' (and Chinese) motives, they could not count upon a decisive victory at Geneva; that is, a victory that would turn the Associated States into people's republics or render such conversion inevitable. The United States, and even Great Britain, would resist negotiations that tended in that direction, and the parties of the center and right in the French National Assembly would resist concessions of the magnitude necessary to permit such a victory. In any case, the Soviets must have calculated that it was worthwhile to attempt to undermine Bidault and his government. After all, political instability in Paris would be advantageous to the Vietminh's military campaign in Indochina and the diplomatic competition in Geneva. Finally, we may surmise that the Kremlin leaders hoped that any new French government might be even less amenable to American pressures than was Laniel's because French unwillingness to coordinate European or Asian policies with the United States could increase the already noticeable strains in the Western alliance.

The only cost incurred by the Soviets and the Chinese in their newly adopted stance would be the confidence or good will of the *temporarily* worried nonaligned states of Asia, such as India, Burma, Pakistan, and Indonesia. Their governments would feel—and the Indian government believed—that the Communists had become more intransigent and were no longer interested in the Geneva negotiations. This "loss," however, could be remedied within a week or two by appropriate propaganda efforts.

In Paris there was a heated Assembly debate on Wednesday, 9 June. Mendès-France accused Bidault of playing "infernal poker" in asking for American intervention and risking general war.[15] He explained that the Communist states were now primarily interested in internal economic and social problems, and the time had come for a basic revision of Western strategy. He believed the Communists were desirous of achieving a cease-fire in Indochina; and France should seek peace, Mendès-France argued, on honorable terms, on terms that did not amount to a capitulation.[16] After other prominent deputies pursued the attack against the government, Laniel submitted a resolution requiring the Assembly to pass on to other business, but this was defeated by a vote of 322 to 263 early in the morning of 10 June.[17] Since the vote was on a procedural question and not a vote of confidence, it did not create a situation in which Laniel must resign, but it was quite clear that, barring extraordinary developments at Geneva, the Premier would be forced into a very difficult, if not untenable, position when the Assembly voted on the question of confidence on Saturday, 12 June.[18]

[I I I]

Having presented his case to the National Assembly, Bidault left Paris late on the 10th and arrived in Geneva at dawn on 11 June, after the Indochina Conference had met in another plenary session on the 10th (the third since public sessions had been resumed). Eden, Molotov, and Bedell Smith had each made statements, the latter having earlier informed President Eisenhower that he believed the British were running out of patience. On the 10th, Eisenhower had cabled Smith and told him that if the French should insist on continuing negotiations "in spite of their obvious futility, our best move would be to reduce our delegation in stature rather than completely withdraw it." Bedell Smith would return to Washington, and the message suggested that the diplomat advise Britain to follow suit.[19] Eden did not see this message until the 15th, and he and Bedell Smith did not leave Geneva until 20 June.[20]

The Molotov and Bedell Smith speeches at the plenary session had been little more than short declaratory statements of minor importance. Eden's address, though likewise short, went right to the issues that divided the delegates. Expressing regret that the statements of the preceding two days had deepened the differences, he

---

[15] *JO*, 10 June 1954, p. 2851 (sess. of 9 June).
[16] *Ibid.*, pp. 2854-2855.   [17] *Ibid.*, pp. 2876, 2888-2889.
[18] *Ibid.*, p. 2876.   [19] DDE, p. 365.
[20] E, p. 144.

noted there was agreement about a simultaneous cessation of hostilities and international supervision of an armistice. He urged support of his earlier proposal for an ISC made up of representatives of the Colombo powers, although the proposal had "been ignored by certain delegations." Eden was "convinced that a group of four powers, two supporting the views of either side, can only lead to deadlock. My reason for refusing to accept such a proposal is not ideological. It is simply that it wouldn't work."[21] He opposed the rule of unanimity as an obstructive veto device and supported the role of an ISC as a body that could reconcile differences between the belligerent representatives on the joint commissions; where differences existed, such an ISC would have authority to make binding decisions. Finally, Eden touched upon the Vietminh invasions of Laos and Cambodia and likened them to Hitler's invasion of Czechoslovakia; all were equally unjustified. The divergencies among the conference delegates on the Laotian and Cambodian questions were wide and deep, and, "unless we can narrow them now without further delay, we shall have failed in our task." The United Kingdom, he said, "is still willing to attempt to resolve . . . [the differences], here or in restricted session, or by any other method which our colleagues may prefer. But if the positions remain as they are today, then it is our clear duty to say so to the world, and to admit that we have failed."[22]

The session adjourned after it agreed to Eden's suggestion that he and Molotov, as the conference co-chairmen, meet to discuss the future course of negotiations.[23]

[IV]

Although the conference appeared to be settling into stalemate during the second week of June, modest progress was made by the members of the military commission.[24] On 9 June, Colonel de Brébisson, acting upon a suggestion of Jean Chauvel, approached Colonel Ha Van Lau of the DRVN and proposed that they discuss the implications of Pham Van Dong's proposals of 25 May. De Brébisson wanted particularly to know what Dong had meant by an "exchange of territories." On the 10th, Ha Van Lau told de Brébisson that Pham Van Dong was very interested in the latter's proposal and in his thoughts on the size and nature of zones of regroupment. He then suggested that he, de Brébisson, General Delteil, and Ta Quang Buu meet secretly, as soon as possible, at a place and time selected by the French.

The four men met that evening in a villa on the outskirts of

21 Cmd. 9186, p. 165.   22 *Ibid.*, p. 167.   23 *Ibid.*, p. 168.
24 L&D, p. 211.

Geneva. Ta Quang Buu was reported to have unfolded a map of Indochina, pointed to northern Vietnam, and said it was necessary for the Vietminh to have a state, a capital for their state, and a port for their capital,[25] and the state he envisaged would comprise territories in Tonkin and northern Annam down to the region of Hué (about 16° 30′ N. lat.). The division he contemplated was only temporary, he emphasized, until general elections had been held in Vietnam, after which the country would be unified. When asked by the French what territorial compensations they would be offered for their abandonment of Tonkin, Ta Quang Buu gave no answer. Before the meeting ended, he stressed the need for secrecy and indicated that he preferred bilateral talks to the "inconveniences" of the larger political conference. Ta Quang Buu impressed the French officers with his impatience to reach an agreement.

At about 4 a.m. on 11 June, Delteil and de Brébisson reported the substance of their conversations to Chauvel and to Frédéric-Dupont, who had replaced Marc Jacquet as minister for the Associated States. Frédéric-Dupont, believing the Vietminh proposals made at the secret military discussions the evening before could save the Laniel government, returned by train to Paris.[26] He and Laniel agreed they should convene a special meeting of the Council of Ministers to discuss whether the government ought not try to cut off Assembly debate on the basis of the "imminence of success" at Geneva. Bidault, meanwhile, having arrived in Geneva at daybreak on the 11th, was informed of recent developments by Chauvel. The Foreign Minister telephoned Laniel and apparently expressed his feeling that the Vietminh proposals did not represent anything more than "interesting" proposals. In any case, Laniel did *not* call a Council of Ministers meeting or attempt to stop the Assembly debate.

The press duly noted the arrival in Paris of Frédéric-Dupont, and rumors of new proposals from the Vietminh soon began to circulate in Paris.[27] A United Press dispatch reported that the Vietminh had come forth with a wholly new proposal and that an agreement had been reached that allocated a regroupment zone to the Vietminh in Tonkin.[28] Hanoi and Haiphong were excepted, this report said, and were to be used by the Franco-Vietnamese forces for regroupment. This evoked a categorical and public denial by Hoang Van Hoan in Geneva; the reports of an agreement, he said, were entirely without foundation.[29] This was technically true, of course, since no agreement had been reached, and Ta Quang Buu had not pro-

[25] L&D, p. 212.   [26] L&D, pp. 207-208.
[27] T/L, 12 June 1954; NYT, 12 June 1954.
[28] Le Monde, 12 June 1954.   [29] Ibid., 13 June 1954.

posed that Hanoi or Haiphong be used as assembly areas for the French.

Neither rumors nor the arguments by the Premier stilled the debate, and on Saturday, 12 June, Laniel lost a vote of confidence, 306 to 293. An absolute majority had not voted against his government, but the vote was sufficient to persuade Laniel to tender his resignation, which was accepted by President Coty on the 13th.[30] The vote, of course, was occasioned by the Indochina debate, but the right-wing (Gaullist) critics of even the government's policy of lukewarm support for EDC were included in the opposition. Forty-five of the seventy-five Gaullists voted against the Premier, as well as thirty-three of the seventy-six Radical Socialist deputies, twelve of the twenty-four Social Union deputies, and the Communists and the Socialists.[31] Bidault, at Geneva, received the news soon after the vote was enrolled, indicated that he would remain there until his successor could take over the direction of the French delegation, and declared his opposition to adjournment of the conference.

[V]

Molotov and Eden had a private meeting on 12 June at which, Eisenhower related, the latter "proposed to see Molotov once more and then break from the conference meanwhile recommending that Laos and Cambodia put their case before the United Nations."[32] According to Eisenhower, he and his advisors agreed to break off "major participation" in the conference having received news of the fall of the Laniel government. This decision was compatible with the President's message to Bedell Smith on the 19th, proposing a reduction in "stature" of the American delegation instead of withdrawal from the conference. According to Eden, however, Bedell Smith showed him a telegram from the President on 15 June, instructing the American delegate to do what he could to end the conference as rapidly as possible,[33] but Eden opposed breaking off negotiations at this point.

To resolve this difference we must, of course, wait for release of the

---

[30] *JO*, 13 June 1954, p. 2983 (sess. of 12 June). Three hundred fourteen votes were required to compel Laniel to resign but only 306 votes were enrolled against his government. Technically, therefore, the Premier need not have resigned (article 49 of the Constitution of the Fourth French Republic). Under the prevailing conditions, the President could accept the Premier's resignation if it were tendered. After consultations with President Coty, the Premier resigned and the President accepted the resignation. Laniel believed his position was untenable in view of the fact that his cabinet was divided on his Indochina policy.

[31] *JO*, 13 June 1954, pp. 2988-2989 (sess. of 12 June).

[32] DDE, p. 365.

[33] E, p. 144.

relevant correspondence, but it is possible that Eden misconstrued the Eisenhower telegram, which *may* have proposed a reduction in the stature of the American delegation rather than its complete withdrawal. Eisenhower's appreciation of the British Foreign Secretary's position may have been due to faulty intelligence from Geneva. It was reported that, on the 14th, Eden proposed *suspension* of the Indochina talks until the secret military conversations between the French and the Vietminh had been concluded.[34] In light of developments on 15 and 16 June, Eden may have forgotten that he had threatened the Communists with an end of negotiations. The reader should recall that, on the 15th, Britain joined fifteen other states in bringing the Korean Conference to an end.

[VI]

Let us return now to Saturday, 12 June, when the French officers, Delteil and de Brébisson, met again with Colonel Ha Van Lau and Ta Quang Buu. The Vietminh representatives did not seem overly concerned about Frédéric-Dupont's breach of secrecy in his disclosure of the proposals of the 10th; on the contrary, they seemed pleased that the French had not refused, out of hand, to consider such proposals.[35] The French set two conditions to their acceptance of *a* solution but not necessarily *the* solution envisaged by Ta Quang Buu:

1. An official declaration by the Vietminh of its intention to refrain from interfering in Laotian and Cambodian affairs, and the eventual withdrawal of Vietminh forces from Laos and Cambodia.

2. The retreat of Franco-Vietnamese forces from the delta would be effected only if Vietminh forces were withdrawn north of Porte D'Annam (18° N. lat.).

General Delteil also asked Ta Quang Buu if he had meant Haiphong when, on 10 June, he spoke of the need for a port for the capital of the DRVN. He also inquired into the disposal of French economic interests in Tonkin by the Vietminh and whether the religious liberties of Roman Catholics, particularly in the Phat Diem and Bui Chu regions, would be respected. Ta Quang Buu assured Delteil his government would seek a solution that conformed to the "honor of the belligerents" and one in which French economic and cultural interests would be respected. At a third meeting, on 13 June, Ta Quang Buu made three important points. (1) Haiphong was the port of which he had spoken on the 10th. (2) The partition envisaged by the DRVN was temporary, and only an expedient by means

[34] *T/L*, 15 June 1954; *Econ.*, 19 June 1954, p. 986.
[35] L&D, p. 213.

of which hostilities might be brought to an end. In other words, it was not to be regarded as a definitive political solution, which would come only with the reunification of Vietnam after general elections. (3) French insistence upon a declaration of noninterference in Laos and Cambodia could only mean an end to the conversations.[36]

By these "secret" and significant conversations of 10, 12, and 13 June, which represented an elaboration of Pham Van Dong's proposals of 25 May, the Vietminh sought a large zone (Ta Quang Buu called it a "state") comprising all Tonkin, and Hanoi and Haiphong, and Annam as far south as Hué. In this region the DRVN would have indisputable authority, but this solution was only temporary, the Vietminh spokesman emphasized on 10 June and again on the 13th. Elections were to be held, and these would provide for the legal reunification of Vietnam. Ta Quang Buu's behavior seems to have been characterized by a sense of urgency, as if he were in a hurry to secure a commitment from the French as soon as possible. Chauvel, through de Brébisson, suggested the need for exploratory conversations. This was accepted a day later, and the first meeting of the officers occurred that very same day. Ta Quang Buu also stressed the need for secrecy and the fact that the best solution to the Vietnam problem could be achieved by direct contact between the French and the Vietminh.

The DRVN delegates must have followed the debate in the National Assembly very closely; they knew the Laniel government was *in extremis*. When de Brébisson proposed discussions to elucidate Pham's proposals, the Vietminh seized on this immediately. Now, when the government of the obdurate Bidault was in danger of collapsing, they might obtain French agreement to discuss a solution directly with them, and, secondly, they might secure the very best terms for a settlement. The impending governmental crisis in Paris accomplished something the Dien Bien Phu wounded and five weeks of negotiations at Geneva had not: the acceptance by the French of the need to *consider* partition, even to the extent of a complete withdrawal from the delta, and the willingness of the French to deal at arm's length with the Vietminh. Thus, it is not surprising that Bidault might have wanted to put a damper on Frédéric-Dupont's mission in Paris. Apart from Vietminh sincerity or reasonableness, he probably understood that the Vietminh were taking advantage of the French domestic situation, and he stubbornly refused to bargain under such conditions.

Could the DRVN delegation have wanted to keep these meetings so secret that the Russians and Chinese would not know about them?

[36] L&D, pp. 214-215.

This was not beyond the realm of possibility, at least initially, but after Frédéric-Dupont's trip to Paris and the leaks to the press, the other Communist delegations may have become somewhat curious! A Vietminh spokesman publicly denied that "new proposals" had been made by his government. Yet, despite this breach of Ta Quang Buu's injunction of secrecy, the Vietminh did not seem disturbed. They met with the French officers again on 12 and 13 June and pursued their proposals with haste.

The Soviets, however, could not be opposed to direct Franco-Vietminh dealings; and Molotov had suggested such talks to Bidault on two separate occasions in May. Nonetheless, the Vietminh delegation may have acted independently of the Soviets and Chinese. If so, it seems unlikely that the Communist delegations would not be informed of developments after the 10th. The Soviets' knowledge, however, is a moot point (at least at present) that I have raised to suggest that the Vietminh were not slavishly subservient to either the Chinese or the Soviets. American officials had often said the Indochinese War and the Geneva Conference were largely French affairs; correspondingly, the Soviets might have regarded the war as primarily a Vietminh affair. If the Vietminh, assisted diplomatically by their Soviet and Chinese mentors on the periphery of the conversations, could extract a favorable agreement from the French, one that could subsequently be presented to the conference as the only reasonable solution, so much the better. Thus it seems likely that the injunction of secrecy was designed not to keep the Vietminh's allies in ignorance but to prevent obstruction by the SVN Vietnamese. The conversations on the evening of the 10th, conducted by four of the six members of the military commission for Vietnam, were not attended by Colonel Le Van Kim, who represented the SVN. His absence, in my opinion, was deliberate: Ta Quang Buu, knowing the French commitment to avoid partition even as an interim solution, wanted to keep SVN officials in ignorance of his proposals. Accordingly, the Vietnamese nationalist allies of France could not hinder agreement between the French and the Vietminh by appealing to the French to honor their commitment to the SVN.

A few other remarks are in order. First, the sense of urgency the Vietminh apparently displayed could be attributed to their desire to secure the best possible solution during the political debacle in Paris. Their concern to secure an agreement directly with the French, outside the framework of the larger political conference, may have represented their distrust of those negotiations. Third parties, whether the United States or even the DRVN's Communist allies, might, in the view of the Vietminh, only lessen its chances of securing a favorable diplomatic settlement of the war. In other words, the DRVN would have the greatest freedom of action in dealing directly with the French. At the same time, this would of course be a fillip to the Vietminh claim to speak for all the Vietnamese people.

Ta Quang Buu's response to the French proposal for the Vietminh withdrawal from Laos and Cambodia demonstrated Vietminh reluctance to lose the opportunity to act as sponsor and protector of the Pathet Lao and Khmer Issarak. In each of these movements Vietminh influence was decisive. The Communists had maintained that there had been no invasion of Laos and Cambodia, that the "liberation governments" embodied the aspirations of the peoples of those states. The Vietminh spokesmen probably felt they could not now accept a declaration implying that some of their troops were in Laos and Cambodia, and illegally as well.

[V I I]

On Monday, 13 June, Molotov and Eden met together. Afterward the conference met again, in restricted session, and Molotov agreed to the principle that a neutral nations' supervisory commission need make only *major* decisions by unanimous vote.[37] This, however, was hardly a concession inasmuch as his conception of "major" was vague and could be construed as applying to the greater part of the decisions such a commission might make. Molotov also proposed that India be made permanent chairman of the supervisory commission and, in the event of an equal division of votes, the Indian representative would have a "casting vote." The purport of this proposal was not clear: Did Molotov mean India would vote twice? In any case, it does not seem to have been regarded as a significant development. At the end of the session Eden proposed suspension of the conference until the secret military talks had ended.

At a plenary session of the Korean Conference the next day, the sixteen non-Communist states broke off further discussions on the Korean question and declared that it would serve no useful purpose to continue talks as long as the Communist delegations rejected the two fundamental propositions upon which a political settlement must be based: genuinely free elections throughout Korea and recognition of the authority and competence of the United Nations.

It was also announced that Prime Minister Churchill and Foreign Secretary Eden had accepted an invitation of several weeks' standing to go to Washington for talks with the President; the visit was scheduled for the weekend beginning Friday, 25 June.[38] At his news conference on the 15th, Dulles said the meeting had no agenda and grew

[37] *Econ.*, 19 June 1954, p. 986.
[38] *DSB*, 28 June 1954, p. 989 (press release of 15 June).

out of no emergency. The invitation had not been accepted before this, he said, because it was not convenient for Eden to come to the United States while the Geneva Conference was in progress. "It looks now as though the Geneva Conference either will be terminated or recessed or perhaps reduced to a lower level of negotiation, so that it now seems a convenient time to have the sort of informal get-together which has been in our minds for some time."[39] Dulles said the United States had not given up its view that the situation in Southeast Asia would be improved by the creation of a collective defense system. He hoped the forthcoming talks might allow progress to be made on this project. "There seems to be some indication that the British feel that the possibilities of Geneva have been exhausted and that the result is sufficiently barren so that alternatives should now be considered."[40]

Bedell Smith announced that he would be leaving Geneva at the end of the week; and it was rumored that the remaining ministers would leave at about the same time.

These events seem to have had a shock effect upon the Communists. On the evening of the 15th Molotov visited Eden and made concessions on the composition and function of the supervisory commission. On Wednesday, 16 June, Chou En-lai visited Eden and told him that "he thought he could persuade the Vietminh to withdraw [from Laos and Cambodia]."[41] China was willing to recognize the royal governments of these two states, Chou stated, provided no American bases were established on their territories. Eden notified Bidault of these developments and advised him to meet privately with the Chinese Premier. Bidault accepted Eden's advice and spoke with Chou on the 17th. The two ministers agreed that two additional military staff groups would meet in Geneva to arrange for a cessation of hostilities in Laos and Cambodia. Chauvel worked up a formal proposal and pursued the matter after Bidault left for Paris on the 17th.

Meanwhile, at a restricted session on 16 June, Molotov had proposed that Indonesia be made the fifth member of the neutral nations' supervisory commission, with India, Pakistan, Czechoslovakia, and Poland, or, in the alternative, that a three-member commission be established of representatives from India, Indonesia, and Poland.[42] This was a significant concession since the Communist states would not be able to prevent commission decisions by an adverse vote. Laos and Cambodia were also discussed at this session. Significantly, Pham Van Dong and Chou admitted there were Vietminh

[39] *Ibid.*, p. 990.   [40] *Ibid.*   [41] E, p. 145.
[42] *Econ.*, 19 June 1954, p. 986.

"volunteers" in these states,[43] but they did not admit that Laos or Cambodia had been invaded by the Vietminh. Eden, as we have seen, stated that Chou actually spoke about a Vietminh withdrawal —or, more accurately, about persuading the Vietminh to withdraw.[44] Finally, and significantly, Molotov returned to his position of 14 May, admitting the priority of a military solution over political questions.

On Friday, 18 June, the conference again met in restricted session. Walter Robertson, American Assistant Secretary of State, sitting in for Bedell Smith, who was in Berne, made what Eden called a "violent and wholly unexpected attack on the Chinese proposals."[45] Robertson's speech did not seem to prevent progress, however. The delegates agreed upon a proposal and communiqué, drafted by Chauvel the next day, that provided for two sets of meetings in Geneva between representatives of the French *and* the Vietminh military commands to discuss the cessation of hostilities in Laos and Cambodia. The first question was the withdrawal of all "foreign armed forces" and "foreign military personnel" from the territories of these states. The military commissions were instructed to report back to the conference within twenty-one days.[46]

Thus within the course of two to four days in the sixth week of the Indochina Conference, the diplomatic logjam had been broken by concessions from the Soviets and the Chinese. The supervisory commission, fated to be ineffective by virtue of the principle of unanimity, was saved by Molotov's consent to place the two Communist states (Poland and Czechoslovakia) in a minority relative to the three non-Communist (but "nonaligned") states (India, Pakistan, and Indonesia). Vietminh "volunteers" were to be withdrawn from Laos and Cambodia, and *Vietminh* staff officers were to represent the Pathet Lao and Khmer Issarak "governments" on the military commissions established on the 19th.[47] Chou En-lai even offered to have his government recognize the royal governments of Laos and Cambodia—conditioned, however, upon the neutralization of these states. The offer may also have been conditioned upon the establishment of satisfactory relations between the royal governments and the "liberation" movements.

Eden now had every reason to be optimistic. With these major obstacles removed, he was convinced that the Communists indeed wanted a peaceful solution. Moreover, he was encouraged by the reports from the military commission for Vietnam, where, as we have

[43] *T/L*, 21 June 1954.   [44] E, p. 145.
[45] *Ibid.*; *NYT*, 19 June 1954.   [46] *Econ.*, 26 June 1954.
[47] Thus it appeared that the Chinese delegation would no longer press for inviting the Pathet Lao and Khmer Issarak to the conference.

seen, the Vietminh had definitely committed itself to a temporary partition of Vietnam as the most effective means of ending hostilities and dealing with the manifold problems of an armistice. As this was in full agreement with Eden's conceptions of the form a cease-fire should take, he could look optimistically to the time the conference would reconvene to receive the reports of the military commissions. France, as of 17 June, had a new Premier, Pierre Mendès-France, who—there was every reason to believe—would accept partition. Since Mendès-France had imposed a thirty-day deadline upon French efforts to obtain an honorable cease-fire, Eden could also expect that he and Bidault's replacement at Geneva would be able to expedite a settlement. Whether this could be done depended upon two unknown quantities: the position of the Communist delegations on the many issues that still required resolution and the attitude and policies of the United States, whose administration still officially opposed partition.

[VIII]

On the evening of 13 June—the same day he accepted Laniel's resignation—President René Coty asked Pierre Mendès-France to form a new government. Mendès-France at first declined, but at a second meeting with the President, on the morning of the 14th, he accepted and was officially designated Coty's choice as the new Premier.[48] The candidate had now to be approved by the National Assembly, and this was very much in doubt; the vote would be taken Thursday, 17 June. In the meantime, the Premier-designate assiduously sought information about the military situation in Indochina and the state of negotiations at Geneva. On 14 and 15 June he met with French staff officers and was apprised of the weaknesses of the French expeditionary corps in the Red River delta, weaknesses that might result in a shattering defeat within a month. On the 16th he learned of the Eden-Chou conversations at which the Chinese Premier had accepted the necessity of withdrawing "foreign troops" from Laos and Cambodia. Mendès-France also was briefed on the state of the secret Delteil–Ta Quang Buu talks. The trend of negotiations at Geneva convinced him that the major elements of a settlement based on partition had already been tabled and that as the new Premier he would have to pursue a cease-fire with sufficient determination and flexibility to ensure that the conference did not again become bogged down. The military situation in Tonkin, moreover, persuaded him of the pressing need for a quick cease-fire, before conditions deteriorated even further.

[48] L&D, p. 222.

Mendès-France decided he must set himself a deadline: if within a month's time he had not succeeded in obtaining an honorable cease-fire, he would resign. A dramatic offer of this kind might just rally the National Assembly behind him, and he might prove those parliamentary experts wrong who had predicted that he could not win the Assembly's support.

On 17 June Mendès-France addressed the deputies. A compromise peace in Indochina was required by the facts of the situation, he said. France need not, however, accept conditions for peace that were contrary to her interests. She still had material and moral resources in the Far East; she still had the support of her allies; and she still had her heroic armed forces. Thus a peace wholly acceptable to France was possible, and he would do his utmost to realize this possibility. However, he would allow himself and his government four weeks (until 20 July) to obtain a satisfactory settlement, after which, if he failed to achieve peace, he would resign.[49]

The Assembly gave Mendès-France 310 votes, enough to make him Premier. However, because he refused to accept the 99 affirmative Communist votes,[50] a second vote had to be taken. This was enrolled, after debate, at 2 a.m. on the 18th and, to the surprise of the experts and the deputies alike, Mendès-France received 419 votes.[51] The Fourth Republic had her sixteenth Premier.

On Saturday, 19 June, Mendès-France formed his cabinet. He would be his own Foreign Minister; Guy La Chambre was named minister for the Associated States; and General J. P. Koenig, a Gaullist, was appointed Minister of Defense, replacing René Pleven.[52] (Koenig was notable for his opposition to EDC.) Because Socialists and the Popular Republicans (M.R.P.) refused to accept cabinet posts, the government, with its Radical Socialist and Gaullist ministers, was somewhat *right* of center. The Premier himself was *left* of center making an interesting contrast.

Jean Chauvel was to remain at the head of the French delegation at Geneva until such time as the Premier might arrive to take charge of the negotiations. There were few personnel changes in the delegation, in any case. General Delteil and Colonel de Brébisson were instructed to continue their secret talks with the Vietminh.

---

[49] *JO*, 18 June 1954, pp. 2992-2994 (sess. of 17 June). Mendès-France fixed the deadline in these words: "*Je me presenterai devant vous avant le 20 juillet et je vous rendrai compte des resultats obtenus. Si aucune solution satisfaisante n'a pu aboutir à cette date, vous serez libérés du contrat qui nous aura liés et mon gouvernement remettra sa démission à M. le Président de la République*" (p. 2993). An English translation of this speech appears in *Docs., 1954*, pp. 72-78.

[50] *JO*, 18 June 1954, p. 3003.

[51] *Ibid.*, pp. 3007, 3037-3038. One hundred forty-seven deputies abstained. See *Le Monde*, 19 June 1954.

[52] *NYT*, 20 June 1954.

Undersecretary of State Walter Bedell Smith (left) arrives in Geneva to replace Mr. Dulles as head of the U.S. Delegation. Accompanying him is U. Alexis Johnson, U.S. Ambassador to Czechoslovakia. 1 May 1954.

Secretary of State John Foster Dulles studies official papers in his car after a late afternoon session of the Berlin Conference. 1 February 1954.

Pham Van Dong (left), Deputy Premier and Foreign Minister of the DRVN arrives in Geneva. At the airport to greet him were Andrei Gromyko, Soviet Deputy Foreign Minister (behind Pham Van Dong); V. Molochkov, Soviet Minister to Switzerland (right foreground); and Chou En-lai, Premier of the CPR (behind Molochkov). 4 May 1954.

Anthony Eden, British Foreign Secretary, has a friendly talk with Chou En-lai at the CPR villa in Geneva. 27 May 1954.

Premier Chou En-lai confers informally with his negotiating team at the CPR villa in Geneva. 5 June 1954.

Secretary of State Dulles, British Prime Minister Winston Churchill, President Dwight Eisenhower, and Foreign Secretary Anthony Eden pose for pictures on the White House lawn during Anglo-American talks. 25 June 1954.

French Premier Pierre Mendès-France talks with Pham Van Dong and the Premier's aides. 20 July 1954. An agreement to partition Vietnam at the 17th parallel was made a few hours later.

Ta Quang Buu, Deputy Defense Minister of the DRVN, signs the Vietnam cease-fire agreement, Palais des Nations, Geneva. 21 July 1954.

President Eisenhower sent a cordial letter to President Coty on the 18th that, nonetheless, betrayed some of the apprehension Washington felt over the governmental crisis in France and the policies the new Premier might adopt. The letter read in part:

In Indo-China our nation has long shown its deep concern by heavy financial and material aid which continues. The proposals for a united defense which we submitted to Monsieur Laniel represented on our part a momentous and grave decision. Nothing has happened here to change the attitude thus expressed, even though the lapse of time and the events which have come to pass have, of course, created a new situation. But I assure you that we shall be ready in the same spirit to open new discussion as the forthcoming French Government may deem it opportune.[53]

[I X]

On 20 June Eden and Bedell Smith left Geneva; Molotov planned to leave shortly; and Chou En-lai intended to engage in some peripatetic diplomacy while the senior diplomats were away from Geneva and the conference was suspended. The conference continued after 20 June, but only in this sense: the military commissions continued to meet, and lesser ranking diplomats attended desultory and meaningless sessions of the political conference.[54] U. Alexis Johnson, the American ambassador to Prague, who headed the American delegation, later recorded that he was not certain of his duties and had no explicit instructions.[55]

On their way from Geneva, Eden and Bedell Smith stopped in Paris and met Mendès-France, who assured them he would do nothing to weaken the Western alliance. From his two official visitors the Premier obtained an expression of interest in the recent Vietminh démarche and its offer of partition. Mendès-France, for his part, promised that he would not accept a cease-fire in Indochina that amounted to a surrender to the Vietminh. He told Bedell Smith that he planned to meet Premier Chou En-lai in the near future, even though this might have an adverse affect upon American public opinion.[56] We have seen that Bidault met with Chou on 17 June, but this meeting was not publicized. The new Premier, however, was the object of American apprehension and even mistrust, and a meeting with Chou could only heighten these sentiments.

Eden promised to return to Geneva well before the 20 July dead-

[53] *DSB*, 28 June 1954, p. 991.
[54] L&D, p. 226.
[55] OHP statement of U. Alexis Johnson.
[56] DDE, p. 366.

line Mendès-France had set for concluding a peace settlement. Bedell Smith made no commitment,[57] merely remarking that Alexis Johnson was in Geneva and would provide an adequate American "presence" during any future negotiations. This was clearly an indication that Washington had decided to "reduce the stature" of the American delegation at Geneva; and Mendès-France was disturbed by the implications of this decision for his efforts to obtain a settlement.

One of the principal reasons for official American mistrust of the new Premier was his record of favoring direct negotiations with the Vietminh to bring the Indochinese War to an end. His dramatic gesture, setting himself a deadline of 20 July to obtain a cease-fire, was disapproved by many American policymakers. French and American critics asserted that this tactic would encourage the Communists to make excessive demands; Senator Knowland said it played into their hands.[58] Certainly, the Communists might delay coming to an agreement until the last days of the period Mendès-France had allotted himself, and the Premier, eager to obtain a settlement, might make concessions that, in a more leisurely conference atmosphere, he would not make.

But Mendès-France believed he had sound reasons for establishing the 20 July deadline. His talks with French military advisors on 14 and 15 June had pointed up the weakness of the delta defenses and the possibility of a catastrophic defeat. Reinforcements, he concluded, must be sent to Tonkin unless an armistice was quickly agreed upon. Although recent developments at Geneva held the possibility of peace, no French Premier could ignore the dangers confronting the French Union forces in Tonkin nor the chance that there would not be an armistice. He would therefore allow the Communists thirty days to demonstrate to the world that they sincerely desired peace, during which time the Vietminh could not stage a major military offensive against the delta—Mendès-France hypothesized—without compromising their protestations for peace. At the same time, the French Union forces, incapable of taking the offensive, could regroup and consolidate their defenses. Moreover, if an accord was not reached within the thirty-day period, Mendès-France must request the Assembly to send reinforcements if the security of the French Union forces was to be assured. This would take time, however, and the French could use the thirty-day period for preparing these moves.

The Premier disclosed his reasons for establishing the deadline in

[57] E, p. 146.
[58] NYT, 20 June 1954.

a speech to the Assembly on 22 July;[59] an earlier explanation, he said, would have revealed to the Communist adversary the precariousness of the French military position. This was certainly true, but the Premier's speech on 22 July seemed more like an after-the-fact rationalization. His setting a deadline on 17 June was primarily a dramatic political gesture for winning the support of the National Assembly, which otherwise might have withheld such support, and the gesture succeeded: Mendès-France became Premier, winning an astounding 419 votes. But the theories he later offered were questionable at best.

The Vietminh negotiators delayed, pressing the French for concessions that might be granted if the Mendès-France government became sufficiently desperate as the 20 July deadline approached. In addition, there was not even a quasi-truce in the delta. The Vietminh pressed local attacks and won local victories; the French Union forces withdrew according to plans that had been laid down by Laniel and his National Defense Committee in early June. No massive Vietminh offensive materialized, yet General Giap maintained enough pressure in the delta to keep French officials in a state of almost constant apprehension. Finally, the decision to ask the Assembly to send reinforcements was not made until late June. On 17 June Mendès-France would certainly not have wanted to suggest the possibility of a call-up of reserves in the event of failure at Geneva. He could not estimate how the Assembly would have reacted to such a proposal; indeed, he might not have become Premier if he had proposed such a step on the 17th. It was not until 7 July that Mendès-France told the deputies of his plan to submit—on 20 July, with his resignation—a formal proposal for the dispatch of reinforcements to Indochina.[60] But he would do this simultaneously with submission of his resignation, after his mission to achieve peace in Indochina had failed.

Mendès-France's deadline had the additional effect of making it very difficult for Eisenhower, Churchill, Dulles, and Eden—scheduled to meet in Washington on 25 June—to agree to plans that might frustrate the Premier's attempts to secure a cease-fire. It is, of course, highly unlikely that the British would have agreed to such plans, but the fact that the French Premier had given himself thirty days was sufficient reason for all parties to wait until the end of the period. The nonaligned nations certainly believed that the Western allies should not make any unconciliatory moves at least until 20 July. Mendès-France was not the Premier when the Anglo-American talks had been announced on 15 June (talks to which the French had *not* been invited), but his deadline of 20 July put France in the position of

[59] *JO*, 23 July 1954, pp. 3533-3535 (sess. of 22 July).
[60] *JO*, 8 July 1954, pp. 3265-3267 (sess. of 7 July).

controlling, to some extent, the decisions the British and Americans might make relative to Indochina. At the very least it was a constraint upon Anglo-American freedom of decision on Southeast Asia matters. Its most direct effect, no doubt, was to postpone collective defense pact discussions for another month. We might legitimately ask whether the Communists might not have realized this as well and concluded that American intervention or Anglo-American agreement on collective action was improbable until after 20 July; hence they could safely pursue a dilatory course at Geneva.

Although the advantages and disadvantages of the French Premier's deadline will no doubt continue to be debated, an additional factor should not be ignored. The thirty-day period was not really long enough to allow the diplomats to consider several aspects of the settlement that needed thorough reflection. The history of the Geneva Conference reveals that the Communists caused delays; the ministers did not reopen serious negotiations until one week before Mendès-France's deadline. The military commissions had drafted substantially complete texts of a settlement, but there were several major issues and a host of minor issues that could be resolved only by the ministers themselves. On 21 July Mendès-France got his agreement for a cessation of hostilities in Laos, Cambodia, and Vietnam, for which the French, and perhaps the peoples of the world, could be thankful. But the world did not get a settlement and relevant documents that were as soundly drafted as they might have been had there been no deadline.

Chapter 16

DIPLOMATIC INTERLUDE

[I]

While the French governmental crisis held the headlines in the European and the American press, other events of importance were occurring. On 16 June Prince Buu Loc resigned, and Emperor Bao Dai named Ngo Dinh Diem the new Premier of the SVN. Diem was an ardent Vietnamese nationalist, an anti-Communist, a Roman Catholic, and a person not noted for Francophile sentiments, and Bao Dai was reported to have said he hoped Diem's appointment would please Washington.[1] We do not know what, if any, pressures were exerted by the Administration officials upon Bao Dai during this period, but Diem's appointment was unusual. Diem had at one time urged Bao Dai to abdicate; hence the Emperor's relations with Diem were cool. We might speculate that Bao Dai was willing to risk appointing Diem to comply with American "suggestions," and thereby guarantee American support for himself and his regime. Diem's appointment, moreover, was a measure of the extent to which French influence upon the Emperor had declined. French officials in Indochina had for many years prevented the accession to Premier of anyone who was an ardent Vietnamese nationalist, and those who became troublesome or uncompliant were soon asked to resign. In any event, Diem's nationalism and his reputation for incorruptibility held promise that, if given time, he might become what his predecessors had failed to be under French "guidance": a genuinely popular and effective Premier.[2]

The new French Premier was evidently concerned about Diem's attitude toward the Geneva negotiations. Mr. Eisenhower wrote that Mendès-France made one request of Bedell Smith at their meeting on 20 June: "that we use our influence with . . . Ngo Dinh Diem . . . to prevent him from needlessly obstructing any honorable truce which the French might reach with the Vietminh."[3] Eisenhower did not mention the under secretary's reaction, nor even his own attitude toward Diem, but Mendès-France no doubt correctly guessed that

[1] *NYT*, 15 June 1954.

[2] At the time of his appointment Diem had little, if any, following and few supporters, but this was true of almost every non-Vietminh Vietnamese. French policy prevented the rise of a "charismatic" or popular Vietnamese political figure—other than Ho Chi Minh, a nationalist and a Communist rebel against French dominion.

[3] DDE, p. 366.

Diem would oppose both partition and direct negotiations with the Vietminh.

When Prince Buu Loc resigned on the 16th he declared, according to a *London Times* report, that he had fulfilled his duties: he had *concluded* the two treaties of independence and association with France.[4] Emperor Bao Dai, in accepting the resignation, also used "concluded" in his reference to the two treaties, which the reader will recall were merely *initialed* by Laniel and Prince Buu Loc on 4 June. What did this choice of words indicate? Had the prince and the Emperor been advised that the ceremony at the Hôtel Matignon had given the SVN sovereignty and independence, or were they simply using the term imprecisely? We do not know. But Diem, the new Premier, would always maintain that the SVN was fully sovereign, from a time before he became Premier until there could be no question that his government possessed all the attributes of an autonomous *de facto* sovereign state.

[II]

The day after the White House announced the visit of Prime Minister Churchill, President Eisenhower told a press conference, on 16 June, that his forthcoming meeting with the British leader had the purpose of cementing the tie between Britain and the United States. There was no international question, he continued, that the two heads of state would not talk about, and the British had accepted his long-standing invitation because they felt that "possibilities" at Geneva had now been exhausted.[5] For the week or two preceding this press conference, the lack of progress at Geneva might well have persuaded analysts that Dulles had been right. Indeed the secretary had said, on the 15th, that he had never expected the Geneva Conference to be "productive of anything good."[6]

Thus for a brief period after 15 June the President and Mr. Dulles may have believed that now the British would consent to a conference on a Southeast Asia collective defense pact. This was corroborated by a letter Churchill sent to Eisenhower a few days after the investiture of Mendès-France. The President had asked the Prime Minister for his opinion about the new French Premier, his pledges to end the Indochinese War, and the like, and in his reply Churchill had criticized the French for fighting the Indochinese War with

---

[4] *T/L*, 17 June 1954.

[5] *NYT*, 17 June 1954.

[6] Indeed, Dulles remarked that by the time Churchill and Eden arrived, the Geneva Conference would be terminated or recessed, or would have reached a new phase or been reduced to a lower level of negotiations. *DSB*, 28 June 1954, p. 990.

"untrustworthy local troops." After eight years of war, Churchill said, "Mendès-France had decided to get out on the best terms he could secure," and he was inclined to believe that Mendès-France was right. Churchill still opposed the use of either British or American troops, "except as a 'rescue' operation." Then, according to Eisenhower's account, Churchill said the Communists should be prevented from establishing a base in the Pacific area and he "recommended a SEATO (Southeast Asia Treaty Organization), corresponding to NATO," with wide Asian support. The President was delighted with this response to his administration's "earlier suggestion."[7]

On the 16th and 17th of June, however, Premier Chou En-lai and Molotov made the concessions that revitalized the conference. The announcement of the Anglo-American talks and the issuance of the declaration that the non-Communist delegations were breaking off the Korean negotiations might have persuaded the Soviets and the Chinese that the Indochina Conference might also be permanently adjourned. A solution to the Indochina debacle now seemed possible. Eden's impatience was assuaged and his faith in the Geneva negotiations reconfirmed. Before the 16th, Eden may have had to agree reluctantly with the American Secretary of State that the conference would not be productive. But after 16 June the concessions had changed the situation completely, and Eden's theories might be "right." Not only had the Communists been unwilling to see the conference break up, the Vietminh appeared to have accepted, in principle, the solution Eden himself favored, that is, partition for Vietnam and separate consideration of the problems connected with the Laotian and Cambodian hostilities (the withdrawal of "foreign" forces).

After his return to London, Eden reported to the House of Commons on 23 June and described the limited success the British had achieved in establishing different "treatment" for Laos and Cambodia. British efforts, he maintained, had enabled armistice talks to begin in each of the three Associated States. The British had restrained the West from precipitate action and he himself had acted as an intermediary between the United States and China at the risk of being called a "Municheer." Eden once more asserted the familiar British policy of awaiting the outcome of negotiations before acting upon plans for a NATO-type organization for Southeast Asia.[8] These remarks were warmly applauded by the MPs. On the other hand, the Foreign Secretary's sober words of warning were not well received, a phenomenon that distressed the editors of the *Economist*, who regarded the attitude of Parliament as bordering on complacency.[9] But Eden was cautiously optimistic:

> I think there is a chance—I do not put it higher than that—there is a chance that, with continued patience, these long and difficult negotiations will produce an acceptable result. Any agreement reached must, of course, do more than simply bring the fighting to an end, urgent though it is. It must pay regard to the wishes of the peoples of Indo-China and to the legitimate rights of France. Such an agreement, if we can get it, will provide a basis upon which to build the security of South-East Asia.[10]

In one passage of his report to the House of Commons, Eden dwelt upon security in Southeast Asia:

> I hope that we shall be able to agree to an international guarantee of any settlement that may emerge from Geneva. I also hope that it will be possible to agree on some system of South-East Asian defense to guard against aggression. *In other words, we could have a reciprocal arrangement in which both sides take part, such as Locarno.* We could also have a defensive alliance such as NATO in Europe and, let me add, such as the existing Chinese-Soviet Treaty provides for the Far East so far as the Communist powers are concerned.[11]

His address to Commons led Harold Macmillan to acclaim Eden as the Prime Minister's political heir, but his reference to Locarno-type guarantees evoked a wave of criticism in the United States. In the Locarno treaties of October 1925, Germany and France and Germany and Belgium had accepted their existing common frontiers and had agreed not to commit aggression against one another. The signatories, which included Great Britain and Italy, in addition to the three states immediately concerned, "guaranteed" the frontiers in the sense of agreeing to come to the assistance of the victim of an act of aggression. With respect to an Indochina settlement, Eden later wrote that he had contemplated "a reciprocal defensive arrangement in which each member gives guarantees."[12]

In the United States "Locarno" seems not to have stirred memories of the short era of "good feeling" in the twenties, which the Locarno pacts helped create, but of the thirties, when Hitler made his great territorial gains. Locarno was also unjustifiably associated with the

[9] *Econ.*, 19 June 1954.
[10] E, p. 147.
[11] *H. C. Debates*, 5th Series, Vol. 529, emphasis added; *NYT*, 27 June 1954. Both Clement Attlee and Aneurin Bevan pledged Labour support for Eden's policies at Geneva.
[12] E, p. 150.

Munich conference and a policy of appeasement, which it was said Britain now wanted to follow in Asia. Because the Locarno treaties created the conditions for the admission of Germany to the League of Nations, it was felt that a new Locarno might pave the way for Communist China's admission to the United Nations.[13] Administration officials, including officials of the State Department, used none of these arguments against Locarno-type guarantees, but it was quite clear that the idea was coldly received. An argument over the exchange of advance copies of Eden's speech to the House of Commons occasioned some bad feeling. The official Washington position was that Eden should have broached such an important suggestion with the administration.[14] The British could not understand this view: Eden did not believe he was introducing any new ideas; he had often spoken of guaranteeing the Geneva settlement, and had simply done so again on 23 June.

In the exchange of views, other arguments were offered against the idea of Locarno-type guarantees.

1. The idea contemplated guarantees from Communist powers. These would be merely "paper pledges" of peace since the postwar era provided abundant evidence that Communist states would not keep their word.

2. Locarno-type guarantees did not deal with the problem of indirect aggression and subversion, which could, and would, make a mockery of a guaranteed frontier.

3. A mere guarantee would imply that the United States and Britain were not willing to take the more positive step of sending troops to Southeast Asia. In other words, it could not be an effective deterrent, and might invite aggression, direct or indirect.

4. Entering into reciprocal arrangements with the C.P.R. would constitute formal recognition and imply the willingness of the guarantors to permit Communist China's admission to the U.N.

5. An influential segment of American opinion was neither aware of the administration's acceptance of partition nor prepared to acquiesce in such a settlement, and Eden's suggestion implied that a line would be drawn in Indochina and guaranteed. Most American officials would not espouse an arrangement that placed millions of Indochinese under Communist rule; it amounted to accepting, then guaranteeing, Communist conquests.

In addition to these arguments against Locarno-type guarantees, the American press suggested that Eden had made his speech to please the Labour Party or India, that he had again made a declara-

---

[13] Coral Bell, *Survey of International Affairs, 1954* (London: Oxford University Press, 1957), p. 58.
[14] *NYT*, 25, 26 June 1954.

tion of independence on behalf of British foreign policy, and that British independence had given support to neo-isolationist sentiment in the United States.[15] Several congressmen even moved to amend the Mutual Security Act through a provision to withhold funds from any country that agreed to guarantee Communist-conquered territories in Asia.[16] This move was eventually defeated, but it demonstrated the intensity of feeling evoked by Eden's suggestion of Locarno-type guarantees for Indochina. The reaction was not confined to two or three days after the delivery of Eden's report but continued throughout the Churchill visit, and after. Opinion was somewhat mollified by the Prime Minister's long-standing popularity in the United States and his good humor, but expressions of concern continued well into July.

In terms of the alleged novelty of a guarantee, the British, it seems to me, have the weight of facts on their side. On several occasions Eden, as well as Bidault, had suggested that the Geneva settlement be guaranteed; whether by the Geneva powers, the Colombo powers, the United Nations, or others was a matter to be arranged once the conference had agreed upon the essentials of a cease-fire. Thus guarantees were no new idea, but "Locarno" in the Eden speech of 23 June produced a furor in the United States that truly baffled the British. Eisenhower himself later said the press response at that time was "exaggerated."[17]

Eden wanted a guarantee of the frontier created by a partition of Vietnam; he did not want the writ of the Vietminh to run throughout Vietnam, nor did he expect the Vietminh to be defeated or acquiesce in a decision that denied them territory. Thus the guaranteed frontier would not be the Sino-Vietnamese border on the one hand nor the Thai-Vietnamese or Laotian-Cambodian-Vietnamese border on the other. The conference must partition Vietnam and then guarantee the demarcation line. Did Eden regard this line as temporary? It seems not. He spoke of guarding against aggression and, as an example, gave a Locarno-type guarantee of a settlement that determined the frontier. Both he and Churchill, ultimately concerned about Malaya, favored partition because it would create a buffer state (usually a permanent entity) between Thailand (which bordered on Malaya) and the Communist states of the DRVN and the C.P.R. The Prime Minister, in his letter to the President in mid-June, indicated that he wanted to prevent the Communists from establishing a "firm base in

[15] NYT, 25 June 1954; Christian Science Monitor, 24 June 1954.
[16] U.S. Congressional Record, 82d Congress, 2d sess., 30 June 1954, p. 8892.
[17] DDE, p. 368.

the Pacific Area."[18] Finally, it must be remembered that the Locarno treaties, which Eden had in mind, guaranteed frontiers that had been fixed by the Versailles treaty, frontiers that, in 1925, *all* the signatories regarded as permanent. Hence, though the Vietminh had accepted partition on a temporary basis, arguments can be made that Eden wanted a guarantee for a Vietnam partitioned upon a basis other than one that allowed regroupment of troops and the eventual communization of all Vietnam.[19]

The selection of guarantors was very important, of course. As the Soviet Union and China would not agree to a U.N. guarantee, two other alternatives were a guarantee by the conference itself or by the Colombo powers. By mid-June it was evident that the United States would not guarantee an accord that transferred territories to a Communist state. If this had been in doubt before Eden's speech to the House of Commons on 23 June, there could have been no doubt of it afterward; the furor over "Locarno" provided the answer.[20] There might still be a guarantee by the conference, however, without United States participation, but the substantiality and effectiveness of such a guarantee was at least open to doubt. As for a Colombo powers guarantee, a negative answer was provided at the end of June; it was not an explicit no but it was, as we shall see, a no nevertheless.

[III]

Walter Bedell Smith, having returned to Washington from Geneva and Paris, delivered a Geneva Conference progress report to twenty-nine congressional leaders on 29 June. He told the congressmen that the administration now accepted the probability that Premier Mendès-France would partition Indochina, but Laos and Cambodia, official opinion held, could be saved. The United States planned no armed intervention and no general increase in American military strength.[21] It was not certain whether the Under Secretary of State would return to Geneva; first, because of the administration's decision to reduce the stature of the American delegation at Geneva; second, because Bedell Smith was in ill health. As it turned out, Bedell Smith returned to Geneva in July to continue what almost all non-Communist commentators regarded as extremely competent diplomacy. This was Bedell Smith's last mission. He resigned from his post as Under Secretary of State in October for reason of health.

[18] DDE, p. 366.
[19] See *Econ.*, 3 July 1954, pp. 41-42.
[20] According to Eden, Secretary Dulles told him there was little chance of a U.S. guarantee. E, p. 148.
[21] DDE, p. 366; *NYT*, 24 June 1954.

[IV]

Churchill and Eden arrived in Washington on 25 June. The Prime Minister, in his inimitable way, selected an apt phrase to describe the purpose of his visit and its relation to the Anglo-American disagreements of the preceding three months: "I have come . . . to talk over a few family matters and to make sure there are no misunderstandings." The "family matters" the Prime Minister had in mind included Indochina and Southeast Asia, thermonuclear weapons, and European affairs generally. Alternatives to EDC would almost certainly be discussed. The two heads of state realized that one of the reasons for the unpopularity of the Laniel-Bidault policies among French deputies of the left and right had been the government's support, however lukewarm, of the EDC. There were also signs that the Germans were becoming impatient. Chancellor Adenauer on 20 June had declared that the German people could not wait indefinitely for full sovereignty;[22] and on 23 June Dulles stated that Germany would formally be given sovereign status if the EDC treaty was not ratified soon. On the 25th, sources in Washington disclosed that Dulles had set midsummer as the deadline for ratification.[23]

On 25 June, the day the British party arrived, EDC and the exchange of information on nuclear weapons were the principal topics of discussion.[24] On Saturday, the 26th, the four statesmen turned to Indochina. As Eden viewed his purpose in visiting Washington, his task

> was to persuade the United States Government at least to give the French a chance of reaching a settlement at Geneva within the next few weeks. This implied that there must not be, before the Conference was over, any publicized meeting to plan and proclaim an anti-communist alliance in South-East Asia. We should make it plain once more that we could not commit outselves to any form of "united action" in the area, before the results of Geneva were known.[25]

We have seen that Dulles's statements at his news conference on 15 June could have been construed as indicating he believed the British were at last ready to begin discussions on a collective defense arrangement in Asia. But that was before the Communist concessions of the 16th and 17th, and the secretary's reflections on the changed aspect of the Geneva Conference are not available. Eden later wrote that Dulles seemed willing to countenance partition of Vietnam (which he was) and agreed with the Foreign Secretary that

[22] NYT, 24 June 1954.   [23] NYT, 26 June 1954.
[24] See Bell, op. cit., p. 59.   [25] E, p. 148.

nothing short of armed intervention could redress the situation in Indochina.[26] *Full Circle* reinforces this writer's conclusion that Eden contemplated permanent partition. Speaking of Dulles, Eden wrote:

[He] stressed that partition would only be effective if the French could be persuaded to abandon their stranglehold on the Vietnamese economy. Otherwise, the non-communist regime would be vulnerable to subversion from within. I accepted the force of this.[27]

The conclusion is also supported by provisions of the most important document to emerge from the meeting, a confidential seven-point joint position paper declaring what Eden called "the minimum terms which the United States and the United Kingdom would feel able to accept" in a negotiated settlement at Geneva. On 29 June, Churchill and Eisenhower approved the text of this joint paper and transmitted it to the French government and to the American and the British delegations at Geneva. This document stated the willingness of both governments to respect an armistice agreement on Indochina that

1. Preserves the integrity and independence of Laos and Cambodia and assures the withdrawal of Vietminh forces therefrom.

2. Preserves at least the southern half of Vietnam, and if possible an enclave in the delta; in this connection we would be unwilling to see the line of division of responsibility drawn further south than a line running generally west from Dong Hoi [about 17° 30' N. lat.].

3. Does not impose on Laos, Cambodia, *or retained Vietnam any restrictions materially impairing their capacity to maintain stable non-Communist regimes*; and especially restrictions impairing their right to maintain adequate forces for internal security, to import arms and to employ foreign advisors.

4. *Does not contain political provisions which would risk loss of the retained area to Communist control.*

5. Does not exclude the possibility of the ultimate reunification of Vietnam by peaceful means.

6. Provides for the peaceful and humane transfer, under international supervision, of those people desiring to be moved from one zone to another of Vietnam; and

7. Provides effective machinery for international supervision of the agreement.[28]

The italicized portions of points 3 and 4, when read with point 5, envisage permanent partition insofar as neither government was will-

[26] *NYT*, 2 July 1954.   [27] E, p. 148.
[28] E, p. 149 (emphasis added). See also DDE, p. 368.

ing, in principle, to accept the communization of the non-Communist portion of Vietnam. Point 5, read alone, declared an Anglo-American willingness to accept reunification, and hence implied that partition would be temporary. But the governments (point 4) did not want a settlement that might risk the loss of the retained area in Vietnam. If Korea was an indication of what the Geneva diplomats must expect, it was clear that the Communists would not permit the loss of an area retained by their protégé. Hence permanent partition was implicit in the policy outlined in this document.[29]

On 26 June, the French government had instructed Bonnet to inform Dulles and Eden of Chauvel's intention to contact Pham Van Dong in Geneva for direct discussion of questions relating to a cease-fire. Bonnet also expressed Premier Mendès-France's hope that he would have the support of France's American and British allies in undertaking to negotiate an honorable settlement at Geneva. Three days later, the French were informed of the contents of the seven-point joint position paper, which evoked satisfaction and approval in Paris because it appeared that the Eisenhower administration had officially come around to the view that partition was a probable solution.[30] Mendès-France might reasonably have concluded that the seven points represented Anglo-American acquiescence and support for the policies he would pursue at Geneva.

On 28 June the Prime Minister held a press conference in Washington at which he urged the United States to allow the Soviet Union to pursue the prospect of material well-being and declared his faith in coexistence with the Communist powers. He advised his audience that his government and the Eisenhower administration would immediately press discussions affecting Southeast Asia "whether or not an agreement is reached on Indo-China."[31] This announcement was confirmed in one of the two communiqués issued by the four statesmen:

> We discussed South-East Asia and, in part, examined the situation which would arise from the conclusion of an agreement on Indo-

[29] As Mr. Eisenhower wrote in commenting upon the position paper: "If partition of Vietnam were to become a fact, approximately half of that country *must* remain non-Communist, south of the 18th Parallel." DDE, p. 368 (emphasis added).

[30] L&D, p. 244. But according to the *NYT* (15 July 1954), it was Premier Mendès-France who sent a detailed statement to Washington during the Eisenhower-Churchill talks. These points were redrafted, and reportedly emerged as the "seven points." Eisenhower and Dulles thought the seven points should be regarded as the minimally acceptable conditions of a settlement. The Prime Minister and Mr. Eden "merely wished to state a 'hope' that the French would settle for nothing less" (DDE, p, 368). Eisenhower did not say how this difference of views was resolved, but see Chapter 17 below.

[31] *NYT*, 29 June 1954.

China. We also considered the situation which would follow from failure to reach such an agreement.

We will press forward with plans for collective defense to meet either eventuality.

We are both convinced that if at Geneva the French Government is confronted with demands which prevent an acceptable agreement regarding Indo-China, the international situation will be seriously aggravated.[32]

Eden wrote that a study group had been set up to prepare the way for SEATO.[33] The Prime Minister's remarks, the language of the communiqué, and the foundation of a SEATO study group seemed to signify final plans for diplomatic action, that is, the immediate scheduling of discussions on SEATO. However, apart from preliminary Anglo-American joint study-group talks in July, no multilateral discussions on the establishment of SEATO were held until after the negotiations at Geneva ended on 21 July. Records of the study-group proceedings are not yet available, but, whether or not the talks made significant progress, Dulles presumably was happy to have obtained British agreement on the need to begin preliminary multilateral planning on even a limited basis. On Wednesday, 30 June, after a one-day meeting of the ANZUS powers in Washington, a communiqué was issued in which the Australian and New Zealand representatives endorsed the administration's plans for the defense of Southeast Asia. They agreed that plans for SEATO should be "pressed forward" and that "immediate action" was required to bring about SEATO's early realization.[34]

This conference also produced a second communiqué, which came to be known as the Potomac Declaration. It vowed support by the British and American governments for the United Nations and for a regional organization to preserve the peace in Southeast Asia. It then declared:

We uphold the principle of self-government and will earnestly strive by every peaceful means to secure the independence of all countries whose peoples desire and are capable of sustaining an independent existence. We welcome the processes of development, where still needed, that lead to that goal. *As regards formerly sov-*

[32] *DSB*, 12 July 1954, p. 49. With respect to Western European affairs, the communiqué stated in part: "It is our conviction that further delay in the entry into force of the E.D.C. and Bonn Treaties would damage the solidarity of the Atlantic nations."

[33] *E*, p. 149. This was confirmed by implication by the Prime Minister in his 12 July speech to the House of Commons (see n. 38 below).

[34] *DSB*, 30 June 1954, p. 50.

*ereign states now in bondage, we will not be party to any arrange-
ment or treaty which would confirm or prolong their unwilling
subordination.* In the case of nations now divided against their
will, we shall continue to seek to achieve unity through free elections supervised by the United Nations to insure they are conducted fairly.[35]

No reference was made to Eden's Locarno concept in either communiqué, and this caused some disappointment in Great Britain. It
was understood there, however, that Eden would continue to work
for guarantees after his return to Geneva. The italicized portion of
the communiqué was at least indirectly relevant to the Geneva proceedings; it was, as the *New York Times* wrote, formal recognition
that while the West might have to acquiesce in Communist expansion, it would not sanctify it.[36] This certainly did not represent
British policy at the time.

Subsequently, in a speech in the House of Commons on 12 July,
Churchill stated that British ideas on the guarantee of any settlement
that might be reached at Geneva had been explained to the Americans and were now better understood.

> It is hoped that should an acceptable settlement be reached on the
> Indo-China problem, means may be found of getting the countries
> which participated at the Conference to underwrite it. We hope,
> too, that other countries with interest in the area might also sub-
> scribe to such an undertaking. This was the basis on which the idea
> was put to the Americans and it is one of the problems to be exam-
> ined in Washington by the Anglo–United States Study Group
> set up as the result of our talks.[37]

With regard to the defense of Southeast Asia, the Prime Minister
declared that the allies had to plan "not only for the contingency of
a negotiated settlement but for other eventualities less agreeable." He
continued:

> The arrangements for collective defence in Southeast Asia will
> proceed whether or not agreement is reached at Geneva, though
> their nature will depend on the result of the Conference. The con-
> cept of a collective defence system is not incompatible with the
> settlement we hope for at Geneva. . . . There is no doubt that
> the Foreign Secretary's care and zeal in bringing the five Asian
> Colombo powers prominently into the situation is fully appreciated
> now by the United States Government. Their association would be

[35] *DSB*, 12 July 1954, p. 49 (emphasis added).
[36] *NYT*, 28 June 1954.   [37] *Docs., 1954*, p. 69.

and is regarded as important and welcome. All I say on the subject today is that there is no intention of presenting cut-and-dried formulas on a "take it or leave it" basis to potential Asian members.[38]

The French, as we have seen, welcomed the Anglo-American seven points. Within two days, however, they sought clarification of the meaning of "respect" in the phrase the United States and the United Kingdom would "respect an armistice agreement on Indo-China," which adhered to the seven points listed in the position paper. An unidentified American official in Paris is reported to have said: "This term means that we would not oppose a settlement conforming to the 'seven points.' It does not mean that we would be disposed to guarantee such a settlement."[39] This statement, it seems to the writer, was an accurate assessment of the official American view. It was in agreement with several of Dulles's public statements about a possibly undesirable settlement of the Indochinese War, and it conformed to the more recent Potomac Declaration. It is therefore surprising that, a few days later, Bedell Smith would have told Bonnet that "respect" meant *recognize* and that any accord that conformed to the seven points would have the value of a settlement in the eyes of the administration.[40] If the under secretary said this, he apparently was unaware of the implications of "recognize" and the legal niceties of a policy of disassociating one's government from a treaty or situation of which it disapproved. We know that Mendès-France was disappointed by the refusal of the United States to "associate" itself with the settlements of 21 July, and perhaps his disappointment derived from Bedell Smith's explanation of "respect" in late June. There was much other evidence, however, to show that the administration would follow the course it eventually followed, but Mendès-France may simply have failed to get "the word." (This may not have been the Premier's fault, in view of the many voices "speaking for" the administration.)

The Churchill-Eden visit to Washington did much to reassure policy- and opinion-makers of Britain and the United States that, in spite of past disagreements, the areas of agreement were substantial. But another incident showed the divergent approaches. Drew Middleton reported from London that many British regarded the administration's China policy as the main impediment to peace in Asia.[41] Then, toward the end of the Eisenhower-Churchill talks, it was rumored that the Prime Minister and Mr. Eden believed the admission of

[38] *Ibid.*, pp. 69-70. [39] L&D, pp. 245-246.
[40] But this is what Lacouture and Devillers reported (L&D, p. 246).
[41] *NYT*, 27 June 1954.

China to the U.N. was inevitable.[42] Senators Knowland and Lyndon Johnson, the Senate majority and minority leaders, declared that the United States must leave the U.N. if China were admitted, and they had substantial senatorial support for their opinions. Knowland went even further. If China were admitted to the U.N., he would resign his Senate leadership "so that without embarrassment to any of my colleagues or to the Administration I can devote my full efforts in the Senate and throughout the country to terminate United States membership in that organization and our financial support to it."[43]

Knowland's concern at that particular moment no doubt derived from the belief that the administration, in his view, had bowed for too long to British desires in matters affecting East Asia. He was determined to prevent American acquiescence in Britain's approach to relations with the Communist Chinese, and therefore had decided to take a stand on the issue of a seat for the C.P.R. in the U.N. In addition, Knowland may have been anxious about what the administration might promise the French in order to obtain a more satisfactory cease-fire at Geneva. He was almost certainly aware of the suggestion, made as early as February, that China might be willing to pressure the Vietminh to accept a less favorable settlement if concessions were made, concessions only the United States could make. Thus Knowland's speech of 1 July could be understood as a measure of his uncertainty over the direction of America's East Asia policy and his fear that the administration might make a deal with the Chinese.

The President commented upon the U.N. issue at his press conference on 6 July. In the present situation, he said, he was "completely and unalterably opposed" to the C.P.R.'s admission to the U.N. unless (!) Communist China established a record of good faith and capacity to discharge its international obligations. Advancing the cause of peace by getting out of the U.N., the President added, would have to be decided when and if the C.P.R. gained a U.N. seat: repudiation of solemn treaty obligations by the United States could be done only after the most careful deliberation.[44] During the course of that week both Eisenhower and Dulles deprecated withdrawal from the U.N. On the 8th, Dulles said: "I don't think there is going to be any United States withdrawal from the United Nations or any occasion for it"; he added that the United States would invoke the veto to prevent China's admission. By the weekend, unofficial sources re-

[42] *NYT*, 3 July 1954.
[43] *NYT*, 2 July 1954.
[44] *NYT*, 7 July 1954. Senator Herbert Lehman (Dem., N.Y.) remarked that Senator Lyndon Johnson did not speak for all Democrats when he said the U.S. must withdraw from the United Nations if the C.P.R. were admitted. *NYT*, 11 July 1954.

ported that the Prime Minister had assured the administration the British government did not intend to promote China's case and might even encourage postponement of the question when it arose in autumn.[45] This assurance was made explicit by the Prime Minister on 12 July in an address to the House of Commons.[46]

Senator Knowland's dramatic promise to resign his Senate leadership over the question of a U.N. seat for the C.P.R. came during another of the many Indochina debates in the Senate. By 1 July the Senate leaders knew that the administration would acquiesce in a partition of Vietnam; Bedell Smith, of course, had informed them of this decision on 23 June.[47] In late June the French began planned withdrawals (Operation Auvergne) in various areas of the Red River delta, designed to consolidate the delta's defense perimeter. But the State Department still believed it was a public demonstration of weakness.

Knowland's Senate speech on 1 July represented the frustration the activists must have been experiencing at this time. "As we meet here today," Knowland said,

> our ally, France, in a thinly disguised surrender, is being required to permit ten million Vietnamese in the Red River delta and northern Vietnam to pass under Communist control. The net result of these developments will be a Communist victory in Asia of no mean proportions.[48]

Citing Chinese aggression in Korea and American troop losses, Knowland complained that the U.N. had not prevented the spread of communism and he vowed to resist the C.P.R.'s admission to the U.N. Many senators could not agree with Senator Knowland's views on the U.N., but a large proportion of them shared his apprehension,

[45] *NYT*, 11 July 1954.

[46] The possibility of the C.P.R.'s admission to the U.N., the Prime Minister said, was mentioned during the recent talks with the President and Secretary of State, but "it played no noticeable part in our discussions, and was not an immediate issue. It cannot in any way be raised for some time and if it should be raised, which is by no means certain, we shall undoubtedly have a different situation to face than any which now exists. . . . [Although] Her Majesty's Government still believes that the Central People's Government should represent China in the United Nations, they certainly do not consider that this is the moment for the matter to be reconsidered." *Docs.*, *1954*, pp. 70-71.

[47] It is interesting that the Under Secretary of State, not Dulles, told the senators of the decision to acquiesce in partition. Perhaps Secretary Dulles purposely avoided the task of breaking such news to some of his senatorial critics, who might wish to saddle him with the blame for the likely outcome of the Geneva Conference.

[48] *NYT*, 2 July 1954. Senator Knowland also pointedly asked whether "nations which have been conditioned to not risking in Vietnam be prepared to risk in Cambodia, Laos, Thailand, Burma, Malaya, India, Pakistan, Formosa, Japan, Indonesia, the Philippines, Australia and New Zealand?"

even distrust, of the French and their handling of the Indochinese War and the Geneva negotiations, and they expressed disappointment over the almost certain division of Vietnam. Senate opinion, in large part, accounted for the administration's policy of disassociating the United States from any arrangement or treaty that allocated territories and peoples to a Communist Vietminh regime.

[V]

Mendès-France informed Chauvel of his desire to establish early contact with Pham Van Dong, but the ambassador advised the Premier against such a step; he suggested, instead, that he meet with Chou En-lai, who had expressed interest in meeting the new French Premier.[49] The meeting was arranged for the afternoon of Wednesday, 23 June, at the French embassy in Berne, and the Premiers exchanged views for two and one-half hours and covered a number of topics vital to an Indochina settlement. Chou confirmed the priority of the military over the political aspects of a settlement.[50] Generally associating himself with the Vietminh proposals, he expressed his support for "large zones of regroupment," to which Mendès-France replied that the location of a demarcation line between the zones dominated all other questions.[51] The French Premier added that the Vietminh demanded a line farther south than the circumstances warranted. Chou said the military commission would have to reach agreement *within three weeks*, after which the foreign ministers could return to Geneva. (A date three weeks from the day of the Chou–Mendès-France meeting would fall on 14 July, six days before the expiration of the French Premier's self-imposed period for obtaining a settlement.) Mendès-France, well aware of the effects of a delay of this length, told Chou that three weeks must be considered the "maximum," but Chou's reply is not known. As it turned out, the foreign ministers did not return to Geneva until 12 July, and were not prepared to discuss the substance of the reports of the military commission until the 14th.

Mr. Eisenhower subsequently wrote that he had been informed Chou "recognized the existence of the state of Vietnam, which he had not done before. . . . He professed a desire to see the two states become unified by direct negotiations at a later time and gave no objection to Mendès-France's assertion that general elections could not be held in the near future."[52] It is not clear what Eisenhower meant by his statement on Chou's recognition of the state of Vietnam; the C.P.R., after all, had recognized the DRVN in early 1950.

[49] L&D, p. 230.   [50] DDE, p. 369.
[51] L&D, p. 232.   [52] DDE, p. 369.

According to one account, the Chinese Premier professed a desire to see the two Vietnamese delegations establish contact, Mendès-France merely noted that formidable political and psychological obstacles prevented the nationalist Vietnamese from taking such a step. He could assure Chou, however, that he would promote direct Franco-Vietminh negotiations.[53]

Premier Chou apparently took the position that Vietnam must *eventually* be unified by general elections, but it is not certain that either he or Mendès-France discussed specific dates. In private, Pham Van Dong had earlier suggested a six-month period between a cease-fire and elections.[54] There were few illusions among the French and the other non-Communist experts that so short a delay could result in anything but a Vietminh electoral victory.[55] It was estimated that if elections could be delayed a year or more, the Diem regime might have an opportunity to stabilize the southern portion of Vietnam, win popular support, and become an effective competitor of Ho Chi Minh and his political allies.

On the matter of a settlement in Laos and Cambodia, Chou again showed a willingness to have the hostilities in those states disjoined from the question of hostilities in Vietnam. He also offered to recognize the royal governments of Laos and Cambodia and adhere to a policy of nonintervention in the internal affairs of these states. He conditioned such a policy upon (1) guarantees that would prevent other states from transforming Laos and Cambodia into bases for aggression and (2) recognition by the royal governments of the movements of national resistance (i.e. the Pathet Lao and Khmer Issarak). In the case of the Pathet Lao, Chou said, the conference must set up regroupment zones for its forces. After an armistice, the Vietminh who presently were on Laotian and Cambodian territory would be withdrawn.[56]

[53] L&D, p. 232.

[54] L&D, p. 228.

[55] *NYT*, 24 June 1954. Eisenhower later wrote: "I have never talked or corresponded with a person knowledgeable in Indochinese affairs who did not agree that had elections been held as of the time of the fighting, possibly 80 per cent of the population would have voted for the Communist Ho Chi Minh as their leader rather than Chief of State Bao Dai." DDE, p. 372.

[56] *NYT*, 24 June 1954. On the 24th, the day after his meeting with the Chinese Premier, Mendès-France responded to a number of interpellations from the deputies on the composition of his government. In his principal remarks, he reaffirmed his intention to resign if he did not obtain peace in Indochina by 20 July. "*Si, dans trente jours, je le répète, la paix ou plutôt un règlement temporaire, un cessez-le-feu, n'était pas obtenu, j'affirme que je laisserai à mes successeurs une situation meilleure que celle que j'ai trouvée.*" *JO*, 25 June 1954, p. 3048 (sess. of 24 June) (emphasis added).

With respect to the EDC, the Premier announced he had proposed a plan that was destined to bring about a rapprochement between its supporters and op-

On Thursday, 24 June, Mendès-France met with three of his advisors to set a course for his Indochina policy.[57] The Premier, General Ely, Jean Chauvel, Guy La Chambre, minister for the Associated States, and Alexandre Parodi, secretary general of the Quai d'Orsay, formed an executive group that made six important decisions:

1. The government would seek a solution based upon a provisional partition of Vietnam. Belligerent forces would be regrouped into zones, defined by a single demarcation line, in the vicinity of Porte d'Annam (about 18° N. lat.).[58] Such a line was reasonably defensible.

2. Since the conference had agreed in principle that a military solution had priority over the resolution of political questions, the French would consider elections a political question and seek to have the cease-fire agreement omit specifying a date for elections.

3. Haiphong should be retained under French control as long as possible to permit evacuation of French Union troops by sea if regroupment procedures required such a step.

4. To avoid a military catastrophe in the delta and strengthen the French bargaining position at Geneva (and retain even the partial allegiance of SVN troops), the government must take steps to protect the French expeditionary force. Although recognizing the difficulties he would have with the National Assembly, Mendès-France nonetheless agreed to *consider* sending reinforcements to Indochina. He would raise the question at the meeting of the National Defense Committee on the 28th.[59]

5. Chauvel and his colleagues would expedite negotiations with their Vietminh counterparts at Geneva.

6. The French negotiators would seek to neutralize the Roman Catholic bishoprics of Phat Diem and Bui Chu, in the southern region of the Red River delta.

Before adjourning, the executive group decided to apprise Washington of the decisions it had made. It is highly probable that both President Eisenhower and Prime Minister Churchill were aware of these decisions when they met on the 25th, several days *before* their advisors had completed preparation of the seven-point position paper (whose contents were described earlier in this chapter).

---

ponents. He had appointed a committee of two (General Koenig and Bourgès-Manoury) to conciliate the factions and realize a compromise plan. He promised the Assembly he would not adopt a policy of *"marchandage planétaire"*; that is, he would not bargain EDC's rejection for peace in Indochina. The Assembly accepted the composition of the Mendès-France government by a vote of 433 to 23. *JO*, 25 June 1954, pp. 3050, 3085-3086.

[57] My account is based on Ely, pp. 173-183, and L&D, pp. 233-235.

[58] In a telegram to Bidault on 13 June, General Ely had indicated that partition was a desirable solution. Ely, p. 167.   [59] DDE, p. 360.

La Chambre raised the question of informing the Diem government of these decisions and the substance of the Premier's conversations with Chou the day before. SVN officials, he said, were concerned that the French were not interested in their opinions. Mendès-France gave an oblique but negative reply: It was necessary that French officials proceed quickly, he said.[60]

[60] In late June the regime of Jacobo Arbenz Guzman, in Guatemala, was overthrown by a force of Guatemalan soldiers led by Carlos Castillo Armas. Because the Arbenz regime was believed to be controlled by the Guatemalan Labor Party, a Communist organization, the administration had become alarmed at the possibility that a Communist government might become established in the Western Hemisphere, and hence the Castillo Armas coup was welcomed in official U.S. circles. In contrast to Indochina, the threat of communism had been met and expunged (for the time being) from what was regarded as a vital area, and this had been accomplished quickly, without the need for agonizing decisions or U.S. troops, at little cost, and with the assistance and sympathy of compliant allies (Honduras and Nicaragua). Moreover, no major Communist power posed the danger of confrontation. The administration made the most of the Guatemalan coup, not for the benefit of the European allies or the Organization of American States (among both groups there were doubts about the wisdom of U.S. policy) but for the benefit of the activists in the GOP and for the general public, who were disappointed with the cautious Indochina policy of the President and Secretary Dulles.

Chapter 17

MOBILE DIPLOMACY

[I]

Premier Chou En-lai left Geneva on 25 June;[1] returning to Peking, he stopped off in New Delhi for three days and in Rangoon for two days. In the Indian capital, where he was cordially received by Prime Minister Nehru, he discussed the problems of Asia and particularly the prospects for peace in Southeast Asia. On the 27th, Chou held a press conference and asserted: "Revolution cannot be exported, and at the same time outside interference with the expressed will of the people should not be permitted."[2] In a communiqué issued on the 28th, Nehru and Chou referred to the Sino-Indian agreement on Tibet of 29 April and reaffirmed the Five Principles of Peaceful Coexistence. Recognizing different social and political systems in Asia and the world, the Prime Ministers declared:

> If . . . the above-mentioned principles are accepted and acted upon, and there is no interference by any one country with another, these differences should not come in the way of peace or create conflicts. . . .
>
> . . . In particular, the Prime Ministers hoped that these principles would be applied to the solution of problems in Indochina where a political settlement should aim at the creation of free, democratic, unified and independent states which should not be used for aggressive purposes or be subjected to foreign intervention.[3]

The emphasis upon unified and independent states in Indochina could be understood to mean Nehru had agreed that the partition of Vietnam was to be temporary. The phrase to the effect that the states of Indochina "should not be used for aggressive purposes" was generally taken to mean that both Prime Ministers opposed the establishment of American bases in Southeast Asia. The communiqué went on to state that the adoption of the Five Principles would help create "an area of peace" that could be gradually enlarged. Finally, the friendship between China and India "would help the cause of world peace and the peaceful development of their respective countries as well as other countries of Asia."[4]

[1] On 21 June the Chinese Premier had invited the delegates of the DRVN, Laos, and Cambodia to a private meeting. *Econ.*, 26 June 1954.

[2] *Hindu*, 28 June 1954, quoted in Coral Bell, *Survey of International Affairs, 1954* (London: Oxford University Press, 1957), p. 60.

[3] *Docs., 1954*, pp. 278-280 (quotation on p. 279).

[4] *Ibid.*, p. 280.

The meeting between the Prime Ministers and the language of the communiqué gave rise to a variety of comments, usually critical or anxious, in Western newspapers. The question was raised whether Nehru and Chou had not agreed to combine their efforts to keep India, Burma, and the other Colombo powers out of an American sponsored SEATO. It was reported that the Chinese Premier had asked Nehru to sign a Sino-Indian nonaggression pact, which the other Colombo powers and Asian states would then be invited to sign, but Nehru seems to have declined.[5] He was said to prefer that China unilaterally declare it would respect the territorial integrity of the Southeast Asian states.[6] The Chinese Premier, as we have seen, publicly declared that revolution could not be exported; he then asserted the right of the people of any state to select their system of government without interference from another state.

Did Nehru and Chou tacitly agree that neither India nor China would contribute forces to repel aggression against a third Asian country? An article in the *New York Times* of 2 July suggested that they had, and that this was the "death knell" of both the SEATO concept and Eden's suggestion for Locarno-type guarantees in Indochina. India, obviously, would not have joined a SEATO, but Nehru's opposition to the creation of a collective defense alliance for Southeast Asia prior to and during the Geneva Conference did not prevent SEATO's coming into existence in September. Its only Asian members, however, were Pakistan, Thailand, and the Philippines. To what extent Nehru exercised his influence to persuade the policymakers of Ceylon, Burma, and Indonesia to remain aloof from SEATO is unknown. Thus, although the Chou-Nehru communiqué and the policy it represented did not prevent SEATO's establishment, Chou's diplomacy in June may have contributed to making the prospect of SEATO less attractive to other Asian states than it might otherwise have been.

The Chou-Nehru communiqué repeatedly underlined the efficacy of the Five Principles for the maintenance of peace in Southeast Asia and elsewhere, and implied that both India and China preferred a nebulous declaration of principle to the more substantial commitment of Locarno-type guarantees for negotiated settlements. This conclusion is supported by statements in the *Hindustan Times*, the official organ of the Congress Party, commending the Five Principles. The author of these comments went on to criticize Dulles's idea for a SEATO; it would divide Asia into rival political blocs, he said, as Europe was divided, and thus make conflict inevitable. The concept

[5] *NYT*, 29 June 1954.
[6] Bell, *op. cit.*, p. 60 (n. 4).

of Locarno-type guarantees did not have this disadvantage, but they required each signatory to come to the aid of another signatory that had been attacked. The Five Principles entailed no obligation of this sort; aggression could be dealt with under the provisions of the United Nations Charter.[7]

On 28 June, Premier Chou En-lai arrived in Rangoon for talks with Prime Minister U Nu, and a communiqué similar in tone and content to the Sino-Indian communiqué was issued by Chou and U Nu on the 29th. It made reference to the Five Principles and proclaimed their efficacy for establishing the sense of security and mutual trust that was necessary for peaceful coexistence. In view of their border dispute with the C.P.R., the Burmese were no doubt reassured by the sentiments expressed in the communiqué

> The Prime Ministers reaffirmed that the peoples of every nation have the right to select their own system of government and way of life without interference on the part of any other nation. Revolution is not for export; similarly, outside interference in the expressed will of the people of any nation cannot be tolerated.[8]

From Rangoon, Chou traveled to the China-Tonkin frontier, where he met with Ho Chi Minh. The two men "had a full exchange of views on the Geneva Conference with respect to the question of the restoration of peace in Indo-China and related questions." After these talks, Chou departed for Peking, on 5 July.[9]

[II]

Returning to Geneva with firm decisions from Premier Mendès-France and his small executive group, Chauvel met with Pham Van Dong on 25 June. The DRVN minister's attitude was reasonably encouraging; he thought a settlement, in its major aspects, could be worked out in about ten days.[10] On the 26th, the "subcommittee" of the Vietnamese military commission—General Delteil, Ta Quang Buu, Colonel de Brébisson, and Colonel Ha Van Lau—met again, but an SVN military representative was pointedly excluded. Fifteen days before, Ta Quang Buu, in response to a French inquiry, had elaborated upon the kind of cease-fire his government wanted: a temporary division of Vietnam into two major zones, with the de-

---

[7] According to the *Overseas Hindustan Times* of 29 July 1954, Nehru had written a letter to the Prime Minister of Ceylon, Sir John Kotelawala, in which he expressly opposed Locarno-type guarantees for the Geneva settlements. See also *T/L*, 29 June 1954.

[8] *Docs., 1954*, pp. 280-281 (quotation on p. 281).

[9] *People's China*, 16 July 1954, p. 38; *T/L*, 7 July 1954.

[10] The following account is based on L&D, pp. 237-242.

marcation line at about 16° 30′ north latitude (in the region of Hué) and the cities of Hanoi and Haiphong within the zone controlled by the DRVN. The subcommittee had met several times, the last time on 22 June, but now Delteil had explicit instructions from his government, the new Mendès-France government, to explore and to settle the details of a cease-fire. The Vietminh representatives, instead of showing the impatience for agreement they had demonstrated at the earlier meetings, began to stall. Ta Quang Buu asked Delteil why Mendès-France could not come to Geneva and treat with Pham Van Dong, as the French Premier had done when he met Chou En-lai in Berne on the 23d.

On 28 June the Vietminh representatives demanded that the demarcation line be set slightly north of the 13th parallel. When the French officers stated that an 18th parallel line was a fundamental condition for a cease-fire, Ta Quang Buu argued that the Vietminh had controlled Qui Nhon (13° 45′ N. lat.) and Faifo (about 16° N. lat.) since the beginning of the war. Neither the French nor the Vietminh moved from their negotiating positions when the group met again the next day; then Buu made another demand. Earlier, at the meeting on 13 June, he had conceded that the French would need time to evacuate their troops from the delta after a cease-fire; no time period was specified, but the French wanted at least six months. Now, on the 29th, Ta Quang Buu insisted that the last French troops must leave Haiphong no later than three months after a cease-fire, and he was reported to have reduced this allowance to two months at a session held several days later. Speaking as the representatives of the Pathet Lao, the Vietminh members of the group demanded that the Pathet Lao be assigned regroupment areas in northeastern and southern Laos (the Bolovens plateau region), where the Pathet Lao would exercise the same authority the DRVN exercised in its zone north of the 13th parallel. Moreover, the Vietminh wanted authorization to station its troops in southern Laos for an unspecified period after the French had withdrawn their troops.

These demands for a demarcation line at the 13th parallel would do more than put the Vietminh 250 miles farther south, well into southern Annam; Laos, on the east, would border entirely upon the DRVN and have no common border with the "retained," non-Communist portion of Vietnam. In addition, the DRVN would share a portion of the Cambodian frontier. With Vietminh troops in southern Laos and along the northeastern frontier of Cambodia, the DRVN would be in a strong position to "influence" the Cambodian government. If the Pathet Lao were given quasi-sovereign powers in its regroupment areas in northeastern and southern Laos and the DRVN were given the right to station troops in Laos, the Royal Government of Laos might find itself unable to resist the demands of a Pathet Lao–Vietminh combination.

The French refused to bow to the Vietminh demands and the Vietminh delegates refused to modify them. The talks remained stalemated until after the ministers returned to Geneva, in the second week of July. Why had the Vietminh, having impressed the French as eager to secure agreement in early June, become such hard bargainers? There are four hypotheses for this change.

1. The longer the Vietminh held out, the more pressed the Mendès-France government would feel, particularly as the deadline date of 20 July approached. By mid-July the French government might be willing to pay a higher price for a cease-fire merely to survive. Mendès-France seems to have believed that this was a reason for the adversary's intransigence. In a letter to Chauvel of 2 July, the Premier wrote: "It is evident that our interlocutors are speculating on the 20 July expiration date. They think we are pressed. We are, but not to the point of accepting anything (the 13th parallel, for example)."[11]

2. The military situation in the Red River delta demonstrated the weakness of the French position. The Vietminh staged no major offensives, but in local engagements and scattered guerrilla actions it maintained fairly continuous pressure upon the French expeditionary corps. In late June the French high command ordered Operation Auvergne to begin: withdrawal of the corps from advanced positions in the delta to more easily defensible lines. The withdrawal especially affected the southern portion of the defense perimeter, from which 50,000 troops were evacuated and an equal number of civilians. The Catholic bishoprics of Phat Diem and Bui Chu also were abandoned, as was the key communications center of Ninh Binh, some 35 miles south of Hanoi.[12] The withdrawals were conducted pursuant to a decision reached by the National Defense Committee in mid-May, but apparently Mendès-France was not fully apprised of the timing or extent of the withdrawals.[13]

Operation Auvergne had two effects. No matter how necessary, the withdrawal was a confession of weakness, which would encourage the Vietminh diplomats to make greater demands of the French; and these movements of French Union troops confirmed the opinion, held by many in the United States, that the Mendès-France government wanted peace at any price. Point 2 of the "seven points" required the French to retain an enclave in the delta if this was possible, and—although few knew of the seven points—official Washington expected the French to retain the delta cities. Operation Auvergne convinced

[11] Quoted in L&D at p. 242.
[12] DDE, p. 369; Ely, pp. 183ff.
[13] L&D, p. 240.

many highly placed administration officials and congressmen that the French were not even willing to try to hold on to Hanoi and Haiphong, that these withdrawals were the prelude to complete evacuation. Senator Knowland's Senate speech of 1 July criticized the French retreat and the handing over of 2 million Vietnamese to Communist control.[14]

3. In negotiating directly with the Vietminh outside the ministerial conference (now virtually suspended), the French did not have the support of allies. Also, in the absence of the Soviets and the Chinese, the Vietminh was not subject to the restraint a great-power ally might have had upon its policies. Thus the Vietminh, in the context of the Delteil–Ta Quang Buu meetings, could attempt to take full advantage of the French, its only constraints being those it might unilaterally impose upon itself. The policymakers of the DRVN, therefore, primarily concerned with securing an independent and unified Vietnam, may have been aware of the desire of the C.P.R. to assume the role of peace-maker in Asia and of the Soviet Union to promote a détente—or of either state to avoid a confrontation and perhaps even a war with the United States—but the Vietminh would minimize these (and other) factors and give them much less weight in its calculations than its most pressing problem: bringing its war for independence to a successful conclusion. In a larger political conference the Soviets and the Chinese—in other words—would have limited the Vietminh's freedom of decision because, as great powers, they would have to consider not only the Indochinese situation but the global situation as well. The Vietminh could discount the importance of nuclear weapons (either by design or, perhaps, from ignorance), but the Soviet Union and the C.P.R. could not. The American threat of massive retaliation was much more credible to the Soviets and the Chinese than to the Vietminh. Nor was Ho Chi Minh particularly interested in persuading the Colombo powers of his peaceful intentions, but the Chinese certainly were, and they might not have wanted the belligerence of their small ally to the south attributed to them. Thus these (and other) factors might have persuaded the large Communist powers to press the Vietminh to modify its demands. But such pressures could be operative only when the Russian and Chinese diplomats returned to Geneva, when the conference itself would become much more viable than it had been after 23 June.

4. Finally, it is not beyond the realm of possibility that the Vietminh believed the French and American critics of Premier Mendès-

---

[14] The State Department issued a report stating the French government had not fully informed the United States of troop withdrawals; this was indignantly denied in Paris. *NYT*, 10 July 1954.

France. If indeed he was willing to make peace at any price, Ta Quang Buu would naturally raise the price for his government's agreement to a cease-fire. The United States, moreover, had indicated that it was reducing the stature of its delegation at Geneva. American officials had, on several occasions, insisted that both the conduct of the Indochinese War and the negotiations at Geneva were French affairs. If this meant that the United States was, in effect, withdrawing its support for French efforts, the Mendès-France government might feel so isolated that it would meet very stringent demands for a settlement.

In accordance with General Ely's recommendation at a meeting of the National Defense Committee on Monday, 28 June, Mendès-France raised the question of sending reinforcements to Indochina. The committee concluded that, should it be necessary to continue the war, reinforcements would be required, but they could not come entirely from the regular army; reserve units, with conscripts, would have to be sent. The Premier waited ten days before telling the Assembly the conclusions of the defense committee. In that period, as we have seen, the bilateral military talks in Geneva remained deadlocked. On 7 July Mendès-France told the Assembly that "reasons to hope for a favorable and honorable outcome are present," but he warned that he might have to ask the deputies to authorize sending conscripts to Indochina.[15] Before he resigned he would submit a bill embodying such an authorization to the Assembly. It was hoped that this gesture would provide evidence of a determination to continue the war rather than accept an unsatisfactory cease-fire agreement.

[III]

On 4 July, Franco-Vietminh military talks began at Trunggia, in the Tonkin delta.[16] These talks had been authorized by the Geneva Conference resolution of 29 May, along with the military staff talks at Geneva (the latter had begun much earlier, on 2 June). The Trunggia talks, it was anticipated, would provide the draftsmen of the cease-fire documents with technical information that would be necessary for their work at Geneva. On the 6th and 7th, the military commissions on Laos and Cambodia began to function.[17] Shortly afterward, the ministers themselves arrived in Geneva. Molotov returned on the 8th, Mendès-France on the 10th, and Eden and Chou

[15] JO, 8 July 1954, p. 3266 (sess. of 7 July).

[16] DDE, p. 369; NYT, 6 July 1954. On 7 July the SEATO joint study group held the first of a series of meetings in Washington.

[17] Econ., 17 July 1954. The French and Vietminh members of the Trunggia commission agreed to a prisoner of war exchange on 14 July.

on the 12th. The French Premier dined with Molotov on the day of his arrival, and the next day he met Pham Van Dong. Not much has been revealed of the substance of these conversations, but Mendès-France commented afterward that Pham Van Dong gave him the impression the Vietminh wanted a settlement with an early date for elections.[18] The Vietminh position, however, had not changed substantially since 26 June, at least not sufficiently to be acceptable to the new Premier.[19]

But with four of the five great-power ministers in Geneva, the question of greatest interest was whether Dulles (or Bedell Smith) would return to head the American delegation. Alexis Johnson had remained in Geneva after Bedell Smith's departure on 23 June, his instructions gave him no discretionary power or freedom of decision; all matters had to be referred to Washington.[20] During the period the principal ministers were away, the delegations merely marked time;[21] hence Johnson's limitations posed no substantive difficulties for negotiations generally or non-Communist bargaining tactics in particular. But the conference was about to come alive again, and the presence of an American representative with a rank approximately equivalent to that of the other great-power ministers was important to France and Britain. At his 8 July press conference, Dulles announced that he had no plans to return to Geneva, nor did Bedell Smith; U. Alexis Johnson would attend the conference as an "observer" for the United States. The attitude of the administration was described on 11 July by Thruston B. Morton, Assistant Secretary of State for Congressional Relations:

> [We] have no way of knowing whether a settlement can be reached and, if one is reached, whether or not it will be acceptable. . . . However, this much can be safely said. The United States will not become a party to any agreement which smacks of appeasement. Nor will be acknowledge the legitimacy of Communist control of any segment of South-East Asia any more than we recognized the Communist control of North Korea.[22]

The fact that domestic political pressures made Dulles reluctant to upgrade the American delegation and the fact that Congress distrusted French policy, particularly Mendès-France's Indochina policy, did not lessen the consequences of this kind of disassociation. The French government regarded this as a blow to its efforts to maintain a semblance of negotiating strength within a "united front" of non-Communist delegations. The absence of a minister of the stature of

[18] *NYT*, 11, 12 July 1954.   [19] L&D, p. 256.
[20] OHP statement of U. Alexis Johnson.
[21] DDE, p. 369.   [22] *DSB*, 11 July 1954, p. 121.

the Secretary of State or the Under Secretary of State would make it very difficult to obtain a satisfactory settlement, in the opinion of the Premier, and this was an opinion the British government wholly shared.[23]

The President, aware of the sentiments of America's British and French allies, asked Dulles to draft a message to Mendès-France explaining the administration's "reasons for preferring to avoid full diplomatic participation in a conference the results of which we could not approve." Dulles was instructed to send a copy of the message to Eden. As Eisenhower wrote:

> If the British and French replied in a clear and firm manner so that we could go along with their positions, then I said either Foster or Bedell should go back. Foster drafted the memo, and read it to me about 6:30 p.m., and it was dispatched that night [10 July].[24]

On 11 July Ambassador Dillon flew to Geneva and for two hours conferred with the French Premier, to whom he gave the Dulles letter.[25] The message seems to have contained a statement of American misgiving that the French could not, or would not, obtain a settlement that conformed to the seven points. Mendès-France remonstrated with Dillon.[26] It is Mr. Eisenhower's recollection that Mendès-France requested that Dulles fly to Geneva for talks with Eden and himself,[27] and on 12 July the President and Dulles acceded to his request. Dulles would go to Europe—not to Geneva but to Paris. The Premier agreed to this, and a meeting between the Big Three ministers was set for Tuesday afternoon, 13 July, at the United States embassy. A brief announcement of this meeting was made to the press on the 12th.[28]

The decision that Dulles would fly to Paris for talks with Mendès-France, and the subsequent decision to send Bedell Smith to Geneva, may have been made a bit easier for the administration by a speech Prime Minister Churchill made to the House of Commons on 12 July. The decision that Dulles should fly to Europe was made before the Prime Minister's speech, but the decision to ask Bedell Smith to return to Geneva was not made until late on the 13th; hence it is possible that the speech was one of the factors that influenced both President Eisenhower and Secretary Dulles. Expressing astonishment at Senator Knowland's remarks about the possibility of the C.P.R.'s admission to the U.N., and "still more that these reports seem to be

[23] *NYT*, 9, 11 July 1954; E, p. 156.   [24] DDE, p. 369.
[25] *NYT*, 12 July 1954.   [26] L&D, p. 247.
[27] DDE, pp. 369-370. But the *New York Times* of 13 July 1954 reported that Mendès-France had made the request for Dulles to attend through Alexis Johnson.
[28] *NYT*, 13 July 1954.

in some way or other linked with our visit [to the U.S.] as if we came over for such a purpose," Churchill declared that, although the China–United Nation problem was mentioned, "it played no noticeable part in our discussions, and was not an immediate issue. It cannot in any way be raised for some time and if it should be raised, which is by no means certain, we shall undoubtedly have a different situation to face than any which now exists."[29] These words of assurance from the Prime Minister, who had won the trust of many Americans over the years, scotched rumors that Britain was asking the United States to make concessions to China so that the French could obtain a satisfactory settlement in Indochina. Dulles could less easily be described as an "appeaser" should he—or Bedell Smith—lend his presence to the Geneva negotiations.

On the 8th, the *New York Times* correspondent in Geneva reported that the French had relinquished Bidault's idea for a guaranteed settlement.[30] In view of the position of the United States, it was said, France would not press for a guarantee. The British, however, had not given up their hope for a guarantee, and Churchill, in his Commons speech of 12 July, stated that he had explained British ideas for a guarantee to the Americans. "It is hoped that should an acceptable settlement be reached on the Indo-China problem, means may be found of getting the countries which participated at the Conference to underwrite it."[31]

The Secretary of State issued a statement before his departure for Paris, late on 12 July.

[My] trip to Paris is without prejudice to the previously expressed position that neither I nor Under Secretary Smith have at the present time any plans for going to Geneva, where the United States is presently maintaining contact with developments through Ambassador U. Alexis Johnson and his associates.

My trip does show, I hope, that I wish to leave no stone unturned in seeking to find the course which will best serve the traditional friendship and cooperation of France and the United States. . . .

We also attach great value to preserving the united front of France, Great Britain, and the United States which during this postwar period has so importantly served all three of us in our dealings with the Communists.[32]

On the morning of Tuesday, 13 July, Pham Van Dong visited Mendès-France before the latter flew to Paris to meet Mr. Dulles. The Vietminh minister was upset and asked the Premier not to leave

[29] *Docs., 1954*, pp. 65-72 (quotation on p. 70).
[30] *NYT*, 9 July 1954.   [31] *Docs., 1954*, p. 69.   [32] *DSB*, 12 July 1954, p. 123.

Geneva, after which he offered the French a demarcation line at the 16th parallel.[33] The cities of Hué and Tourane, however, would lie in the zone assigned to the DRVN, as would colonial route 9, connecting Savannakhet, in Laos, with the Annam coastal plain, and this route was the only direct access from Laos to the sea. When Mendès-France, dissatisfied with the offer, directed Dong's attention to these facts, the Vietminh minister remarked that his government would grant the Laotian government the right to use route 9. Mendès-France reminded Pham Van Dong that the Berlin experience did not recommend such an arrangement.[34]

Thus the announcement of a meeting of the Big Three ministers in Paris seems not to have been without effect. It is not clear how the Communist delegations interpreted Dulles's trip to Paris or his pre-departure statement. Until 12 July the Vietminh could reasonably have expected the United States to wash its hands of the Geneva Conference and its settlement,[35] but now the American Secretary of State was coming to Europe—not to Geneva, but to Paris. What schemes might he now have in mind? If a flight to Paris had a symbolic meaning for the GOP right wing, in that Dulles still sought to disassociate the United States from a conference that must result in the communization of part of Vietnam, his flight could have been construed by the Communists as symbolic of a new American effort to hinder or subvert the Geneva negotiations. Pham Van Dong's reaction and concession demonstrated Vietminh concern that Dulles might try to persuade Mendès-France to break off the negotiations; he might even offer the French token reinforcements for the defense of the delta. Neither the Vietminh, nor the Soviets or Chinese, could know what was afoot. Pham Van Dong's concession was a measure of the extent to which he anticipated a settlement favorable for the DRVN *and* the extent to which the Big Three meeting might result in action that would deny his government that settlement.

We do not know the details of Molotov's or Chou's reaction to the announcement of the Paris meeting, but Tass carried a report that betrayed apprehension. The Soviet delegation, it said, was confident that the United States would not succeed in hampering the negotiations, and it accused Dulles of being afraid to express his views openly at the conference. Chou visited Mendès-France on the 13th, shortly before the latter saw Pham Van Dong, and he was reported to have launched a tirade against American "war-mongers," but Mendès-

---

[33] Ely, p. 203. This has been confirmed independently of Ely by a person I am not at liberty to identify.

[34] L&D, p. 258.

[35] This is not to say that the United States would wash its hands of Indochina.

France reminded the Chinese premier that the United States and France were allies.[36] In another account, Chou appeared more équable. He asked the French Premier why he could not demonstrate his good will by accepting the line the Vietminh had demanded, to which Mendès-France answered that no line other than the 18th parallel offered the same advantages. The Vietminh controlled areas between the 13th and 16th parallels, he told Chou, but the French controlled areas between the 16th and 18th parallels.[37] If the French were to accept a line at the 16th parallel, the Vietminh would receive areas held by the Franco-Vietnamese forces. It is conceivable that Mendès-France, with his emphasis on the 16th parallel, unintentionally *told* Chou what the DRVN must concede. On leaving Mendès-France, Chou suggested that the belligerents take several steps to meet each other, but, he added, this did not mean each must take the same number of steps. More than an hour later, Pham Van Dong made his concession, offering a demarcation line at the 16th parallel. It is conceivable that the Chinese (and the Soviets) were apprehensive about Dulles's trip and pressed the DRVN delegation to accept a line at the 16th parallel, 150 miles north of the line it had demanded on 26 June. If Pham Van Dong had evinced distress or anxiety when he met with Mendès-France, it may have been due to some rather firm words from the Chinese and the Soviets.

[IV]

Later in the day, on 13 July, the Secretary of State met the French Premier at the American embassy in Paris and, after dinner, joined by Eden at the Matignon, the three ministers discussed the negotiations at Geneva. Mendès-France, who sought to persuade Dulles that he did not intend to depart from the seven points, argued that "at no point had his position diverged from the minimum terms which had been defined" by the British and American leaders two weeks earlier in Washington.[38] Dulles said it would be better to have an American delegation of middle rank at Geneva, and to keep the Communists ignorant of American intentions. He said he wanted the Communists to think that there were no misunderstandings among the Western allies, which was one reason he had come to Paris.

Mendès-France insisted that the presence of a high-ranking Ameri-

---

[36] The accounts of the Chou–Mendès-France meeting and the Tass comment are reported in the *NYT*, 14 July 1954.

[37] L&D, p. 257. It was confirmed, independently of this source, that the Chinese and DRVN Premiers appeared to be considerably worried by the Dulles trip.

[38] E, p. 156. This account of the ministers' meeting in Paris is based upon E, pp. 156-157; DDE, p. 370; L&D, pp. 248-251; and other sources I am not at liberty to identify.

can delegate at Geneva might mean the difference between an honorable settlement and no settlement at all. In the latter case, the war would continue and the Vietminh might stage a large offensive before French reinforcements arrived, which could well be disastrous. He told Dulles of the concession Pham Van Dong had made that morning, after learning of the Paris meeting, and that Dulles's or Bedell Smith's presence at Geneva would strengthen the impression of Western unity and enable the Premier to obtain additional concessions. According to Eden's recollection, Dulles said that if France was compelled to depart from the seven points,

> the United States would then have to dissociate herself from the resulting agreement. He said that even if the settlement adhered to the seven points faithfully, the United States still could not guarantee it. American public opinion would never tolerate "guaranteeing the subjection of millions of Vietnamese to Communist rule." Dulles concluded by saying that he did not want to put himself in the position of having to say no in public. To this Mendès-France replied that the United States would not escape the dilemma by refusing to appear at Geneva. Since they were already represented at the Conference, they would have to make a decision in any case.[39]

Mendès-France reemphasized the point that Dulles's suspicions about his departing from the seven points were unjustified. He wanted Dulles to come to Geneva precisely because he believed he could better secure the minimum acceptable terms embodied in those points if Dulles were there. The French Premier showed Dulles a map of Indochina and pointed first to the line the Vietminh demanded, the 16th parallel, near Faifo; then to the line the French wanted, near the 18th parallel. Dulles asked if he didn't have the map upside down—were the French demanding a line north of the line mentioned in point 2 of the seven points (i.e. a line running west from Dong Hoi at about 17° 30′ N. lat.)? Mendès-France said yes and added that, in certain respects, the French approach was more demanding than the Anglo-American approach.

That evening Dulles informed the President the matter of the partition line was not yet settled but was proceeding favorably. The Vietminh, he said, had agreed to withdraw its forces from Laos and Cambodia and to recognize the royal governments of these states. Although it was not certain, the Vietminh appeared to have withdrawn its demand for authorization to station troops in eastern Laos. On the morning of the 14th, Dulles met with Eden and told him

[39] E, p. 156.

that Bedell Smith would return to Geneva if his health permitted. The two ministers agreed to exchange a joint position paper with Mendès-France that embodied the seven points, and hence would be a mutual recognition by the Big Three ministers of the terms of a minimally acceptable settlement. It was agreed that one document would be prepared, setting forth the American and French views, and Eden would express his general agreement with these views in a separate document.

After this meeting Eden and Dulles went to the Quai d'Orsay and informed Mendès-France of their desire to have the Premier sign a position paper, and the Premier agreed. Dulles told the President the "French and British attitudes seemed firm enough,"[40] and Bedell Smith was instructed to return to Geneva. A tripartite communiqué, issued on the 14th, declared that it would

> serve the interest of France and of the Associated States, and of the peace and freedom of the area, if the United States, without departing from the principles which Mr. Dulles expressed, were once again to be represented at Geneva at the ministerial level.[41]

Accordingly, Bedell Smith would be requested to return to Geneva "at an early date."

A confidential Franco-American declaration was signed in the early afternoon of the 14th, having been drafted in the frenetic atmosphere of the American embassy that morning. It stated that

> the United States, while recognizing the right of those directly concerned to accept conditions other than the seven points . . . is ready to *respect* conditions [of a settlement] corresponding to these seven points. . . .[But] it is not necessary to ask the United States . . . to respect conditions, which . . . [in the opinion of the United States government] differ sensibly from those designated above. The United States will publicly disassociate itself [from conditions it regarded as differing from the seven points].[42]

According to Eden's account, Dulles stated that the United States could not *guarantee* a settlement that conformed to the seven points, and it would disassociate itself from a settlement that did not *conform* to these points.

What would the official American position be were Mendès-France to obtain a settlement that fully met the conditions imposed by the position paper of 29 June? Eden implied, and the Franco-American position paper stated, that the United States would *respect* such a

---

[40] DDE, p. 370.   [41] *Docs., 1954*, p. 282.
[42] L&D, p. 250 (emphasis added).

settlement ("respect"—the word that had been used in the original Anglo-American joint position paper). Did this mean "respect" in the sense that a party assumed positive obligations under the terms of the settlement, or did it mean passive admission of the facts of a situation, perhaps coupled with a commitment not to use force to change the situation after a settlement had been achieved and a cease-fire realized? Eden and Mendès-France understood "respect" in the first sense; and perhaps Dulles gave them grounds for such an understanding, perhaps Bedell Smith. In any event, both the President and Mr. Dulles understood the term in the second sense. This divergence, one of many that materialized during the Indochina crisis, produced disappointment among the British and French delegations and evoked criticism at the conclusion of the conference. Then, as we shall see, Smith was instructed to inform the Geneva Conference participants that the United States would not use force to disturb the agreements and the final declaration, of which it merely "took note." The ambiguous word was not used at the end of the conference, but the sense of the American declaration of 21 July was that the United States would respect the agreements in the passive sense mentioned above.

Upon returning to Washington, Dulles issued a statement to the press describing the purpose of his flight to Paris and the results of his meeting with Mendès-France and Eden.

> The United States has been concerned to find a way whereby it could help France, Viet-Nam, Laos, and Cambodia find acceptable settlements without in any way prejudicing basic principles to which the United States must adhere if it is to be true to itself, and if the captive and endangered peoples of the world are to feel that the United States really believes in liberty.[43]

Bedell Smith would be asked to return to Geneva, Dulles said, but

> this is on the understanding, to which both the French and British Ministers expressly agreed, that renewed participation by the United States at the ministerial level will be without departing from the U.S. principles which I have described. . . .

> I believe that we have found a *formula* for constructive allied unity which will have a beneficial effect on the Geneva Conference. And it carries no danger that the United States will abandon its principles.[44]

Dulles did not say what this "formula" was but he undoubtedly meant the seven points, now embodied in a joint Franco-American position

[43] *Docs., 1954*, p. 283.   [44] *Ibid.* (emphasis added).

paper. There were grounds, at that time, for believing such a paper existed, but its contents were not publicly known.

The Paris meeting had beneficial effects upon Franco-American relations insofar as Dulles or Mendès-France determined those relations; each impressed the other favorably. Dulles was pleasantly surprised by the other man's toughness, abilities as an advocate and negotiator, and apparent *un*willingness to accept peace at any price. He would seek what Dulles could regard as a satisfactory settlement— in the sense that, although partition would be accepted, the non-Communist portion of Vietnam would have an adequate base for development and survival. Mendès-France, who felt that his political enemies in France and in Washington had succeeded in creating a false impression of his character and politics, seems to have relieved Dulles of some of these prejudices during their two-day meeting.[45] The incident of the "upside down map" was revealing: Dulles could not at first believe that Mendès-France would demand more than the minimal conditions of the seven points. The anti-French coterie in the State Department had perhaps prejudiced him in that respect, but Dulles now understood that the map was "right side up."

It appears that Dulles also made a favorable impression upon Mendès-France with his suppleness and realism, which were not revealed in the secretary's speeches and public remarks. Dulles, no mean advocate himself, persuaded the French Premier of the reasonableness of his government's policies.[46] The United States must not recognize Communist conquests, but this did not exclude safeguarding the continued existence of the SVN; also, the administration was not asking the French to continue fighting, and would not veto the French truce terms. Dulles sent a warm letter to Mendès-France a few days after the Paris meeting in which he declared that the friends of France were with the Premier. Dulles said he was happy they had found a way by which the United States could support him at Geneva *without violating America's principles and without the risk of a misunderstanding.*[47] Could the Secretary of State nevertheless have left Paris not completely satisfied that Mendès-France understood the rationale of his policy? Dulles's choice of words at least raises the suspicion that this was so.

On 13 July Pham Van Dong conferred for the first time with the head of the SVN delegation, Tran Van Do, whom Ngo Dinh Diem

[45] *NYT*, 14, 15 July 1954.
[46] *NYT*, 16 July 1954.
[47] L&D, pp. 250-251, where the letter from Dulles and Mendès-France is quoted. An especially interesting sentence reads: "*Et je suis heureux que nous avons trouvé une voie par laquelle,* sans violation je l'espère de nos principes *et sans risque de mésentente ulterieure, nous pourrons manifester clairement à Genève le soutien que nous vous apportons*" (emphasis added).

had named to replace Nguyen Quoc Dinh as Foreign Minister, and the Vietminh minister proposed consultations in preparation for national elections that would be held no later than six months after the cease-fire. Needless to say, Do made no commitment.[48] A day or two later, Do sent a note to Mendès-France protesting the latter's failure to inform the Vietnamese of the details of the Paris meeting;[49] his note also expressed the SVN's opposition to partition and its support of U.N. supervision of elections. The French simply denied the basis for Do's protest: General Ely, they said, had informed Diem; President Coty informed Bao Dai; and Mendès-France informed Tran Van Do. There is a record of Tran Van Do's having seen Mendès-France on the 12th and Eden on the morning of the 13th, before either had gone to Paris,[50] and it is quite possible that Do and Mendès-France met on the 14th or 15th, before Do sent his note of protest, but Do complained throughout the last week of the conference that he was being ignored by the French delegation. (It was reported that an SVN nationalist, Tran Van Chuong, saw Dulles in Paris on the 14th,[51] and told the secretary of his government's opposition to the abandonment of Hanoi and Haiphong and the Roman Catholic areas of Phat Diem and Bui Chu. Interestingly enough, he did not condemn partition *per se*; he merely opposed acceding to the Vietminh demand for partition at the 13th parallel.)

On 4 July Bao Dai had been informed of the Franco-Vietminh talks between Chauvel and Pham Van Dong—no less than twenty-five days after the secret Delteil–Ta Quang Buu talks had started and eight days after the Chauvel-Dong talks had begun on an official basis (official in the sense that a French Premier had authorized such direct dealings). Bao Dai was apprised of the Franco-Vietminh conversations and the fact that the Mendès-France government intended to base a settlement upon partition, which the Emperor almost certainly knew from unofficial sources. The French informed the Emperor not because the SVN, as an interested state, was entitled to know of the talks but because the French wanted to secure the Emperor's "cooperation." The French, in short, did not want the Emperor or his government to cause trouble. If the Vietminh had continued to show the eagerness for a settlement it had shown in early June, the SVN might never have been officially informed. When Guy La Chambre, minister for the Associated States, told Mendès-

---

[48] *NYT*, 14 July 1954.
[49] *NYT*, 18 July 1954; *Manchester Guardian*, 19 July 1954.
[50] *NYT*, 14 July 1954.
[51] *NYT*, 16 July 1954. Killed by the editor, the clipping appears in the Private Papers of John Foster Dulles (File 1v. A).

France of Diem's grievances, the French Premier brushed them aside with a comment that speed was of the essence.[52] With the Vietminh turned recalcitrant negotiator after 26 June and a settlement on the "knife edge" (as Eden said), the French wanted to be sure neither the Emperor, Diem, nor Diem's ministers stood in the way of a settlement. Thus Maurice Dejean, former High Commissioner for Indochina, visited Bao Dai at Cannes on 4 July. Dejean reported that he accepted the news of an inevitable partition with composure but insisted upon guarantees for the southern, non-Communist area of Vietnam.[53]

Whatever Bao Dai may have known, however much he may have accepted partition, Ngo Dinh Diem, in Saigon, had a different appreciation of the situation. He was angered by the French withdrawal in the delta and the abandonment of the Catholic bishoprics of Phat Diem and Bui Chu. Diem, a Roman Catholic, disapproved withdrawals that put thousands of his co-religionists under Vietminh control, but he was adamant about partition. He would not accept such a solution, regardless of the alternatives. He espoused wholeheartedly—without reservation—the declaration of 24 April of Prince Buu Loc's government: Neither the chief of state nor the government of the State of Vietnam "will consider themselves bound by decisions which are contrary to the independence and the unity of their nation."[54]

[V]

In his investiture speech of 17 June, Mendès-France had deplored the division of opinion the EDC treaty had caused and he promised to introduce "definite proposals" in the National Assembly before the summer recess, scheduled for mid-August. The Premier was not an outright opponent of EDC, nor was he a supporter of the defense community scheme. He approved of economic integration, but did not believe that military integration would be accepted by the French public. When Laniel left office he had told Mendès-France that he had canvassed parliament and there was not a majority in favor of EDC, but, he added, postponing the question of ratification would disturb the allies. In addition to the constraints under which Laniel and Bidault had labored (the need for Soviet *and* American support at Geneva and hence the need to avoid approving or rejecting the EDC treaty), Mendès-France labored under the constraint that his cabinet, largely a Radical-Gaullist cabinet, was opposed to EDC.

[52] L&D, p. 235.   [53] L&D, p. 241.
[54] See Chapter 13 above and L&D, p. 107.

Indeed, his Defense Minister, General Koenig, was one of its leading opponents.[55]

When Molotov raised the question of EDC at his meeting with Mendès-France on 10 July, the Premier said he would not discuss the subject with the Soviet minister until after the Geneva Conference. At the Paris meeting of the Big Three ministers, when Dulles raised the question, Mendès-France (one report related) persuaded the Secretary of State that the EDC treaty would not be approved by the Assembly in its present form. Dulles was surprised to learn this, and angered that his advisors had given him a false appreciation of the situation.[56] While there may be some basis for this report, we should remember that London had concluded, no later than June, that the French would *not* ratify the treaty, and London had tried to make the State Department understand this fact.[57] It is difficult to believe that Dulles was entirely unaware of the Foreign Office's estimates of EDC's chances. On 13 June, Mendès-France asked Secretary Dulles not to "mix" Indochina and the EDC nor mention EDC in the communiqué, and Dulles had understood and agreed. This does not mean that Mendès-France did not tell the secretary the EDC treaty could not receive enough support for ratification in the Assembly, but it implies that little was said on the matter. In fact, Dulles may have retained some hope of success. His treatment of Mendès-France after EDC's rejection by the Assembly in August seems to show that he may have believed, even after mid-July, that with effort, or by amending the treaty in minor respects, Mendès-France could win support for the treaty.

Eisenhower later wrote that Mendès-France had told Bedell Smith in late June that (1) he supported European unity "in every field"; (2) he would defer Assembly action until after 20 July (the date he had set as his deadline for securing a cease-fire in Indochina); (3) he could then "obtain ratification by a large majority" (!) because his reputation would be enhanced by his having made peace in Indochina; and (4) he might consider amending the treaty *after* its ratification.[58] Certainly this unequivocal expression of confidence in EDC's ratification tended to persuade Dulles there was still a chance of success. Mendès-France later claimed that French officials had not told the Americans the truth about EDC's probable fate, but Mr. Eisenhower has given credible evidence that, in June, Mendès-France himself told Bedell Smith that EDC would be ratified if he succeeded at Geneva.

Did the Premier forget, "conveniently" or otherwise, that he had

[55] Some of the facts in this section are based upon statements by sources I am not at liberty to identify.
[56] *Le Monde*, 17 July 1954.   [57] *NYT*, 16 June 1954.   [58] DDE, p. 401.

made such a statement? Did he change his mind before he saw Dulles in Paris? Did he explain to Dulles on 13 or 14 July how poor EDC's chances were? These questions are important because they touch upon Mendès-France as a negotiator. Later, after EDC had been rejected by the Assembly, he was accused of having made a deal with Molotov: peace in Indochina and his political survival in exchange for nonratification of EDC. Moreover, he was regarded as having been less than candid with his American ally about EDC's prospects and his own intentions with respect to the treaty. I shall not attempt to take up these matters until somewhat later,[59] but the reader should remember that the bases for such sentiments toward Mendès-France are closely related to events and the Premier's words and actions in early July.

IN MY OPINION, Mendès-France did not change his mind about EDC's chances. In early June he believed the treaty could not be ratified unless it was amended in some particulars; hence on 17 June he told the Assembly that, in an effort to reconcile opposing views, he would introduce proposals that would enable France "to obtain the over-all national support indispensable to any European defense project."[60] At the end of July, René Massigli, the French ambassador in London, told Eden that Mendès-France proposed to discuss amendments to the EDC treaty with the other signatories because he was convinced it could not obtain a majority in the Assembly in its present form.[61] If Bedell Smith had told President Eisenhower, on or about 23 June, that Mendès-France would secure EDC's ratification, we may conclude either that the Premier misled Bedell Smith, that the Under Secretary of State misunderstood Mendès-France's assertions, or that Mr. Eisenhower misunderstood Bedell Smith. Eisenhower is definite on one point: Mendès-France said he would first secure ratification; then, after France was committed, he would seek to amend the treaty.

My own conclusion is as follows. Mendès-France was anxious to persuade Bedell Smith to return to Geneva; if he had an American presence at Geneva, and the Americans could prevent Diem from "needlessly obstructing any honorable truce,"[62] he could secure peace. With enhanced prestige, he told Bedell Smith, he would get the EDC treaty through the Assembly, but he said nothing of amending the treaty before its ratification, and pointedly asserted that he would submit such proposals *after* France was committed. In spite of his

[59] See Chapter 20 below.
[60] *JO*, 18 June 1954, p. 2993 (sess. of 17 June); *Docs., 1954*, p. 76.
[61] E, p. 165.
[62] DDE, p. 366 (quotation on p. 401).

opinions on the poor chances for even an *unamended* EDC treaty, Mendès-France made these statements to Bedell Smith because he knew that if he told the American what he really believed, he might not secure the administration's promise to send a senior diplomat to Geneva. He may very well have believed that the American reaction to the unpleasant truth about EDC's probable rejection would be to mistrust the Premier's motives, to doubt that he really wanted the EDC, and to conclude that if the French Assembly was not willing to support the American plan for German rearmament, the United States ought not support the Premier's Geneva efforts—which, in any case, would result in a settlement just barely acceptable to the Eisenhower administration.

When Dulles met Mendès-France in Paris on 13 July, the Premier still had to persuade either the secretary or the under secretary to return to Geneva, and, as the matter of EDC arose once again, he persuaded Dulles not to "mix" Indochina and the EDC. Whatever the French Premier told Dulles, the latter left Paris still thinking the EDC treaty, with proper leadership, could be put through the French parliament if Mendès-France obtained an Indochina armistice.[63] In my view, Mendès-France may have told Dulles that EDC's chances were poor, but he did not undertake to persuade him of this in the way he persuaded him of the desirability, even necessity, of asking Bedell Smith or Dulles to take part in the Geneva Conference. He did not, in other words, state that he *could not* procure a majority vote in the Assembly for the treaty. To do so might very well have ruined his efforts to secure Dulles's return to Geneva. Because Mendès-France believed the secretary had been prejudiced against him by his French and American critics, he would not provoke Dulles's suspicion of his attitudes toward EDC by telling him the treaty could not or would not be ratified. He skirted the issue. He would worry himself and his Allies about the EDC after the 20 July deadline, now only a week away.

As INDICATED earlier, the principal concern of the British and American governments after June was the adverse effect a French rejection of EDC might have upon West German public opinion, and particularly upon Konrad Adenauer's political position. The Prime Minister and the President, after discussing West German sovereignty at their Washington meeting, issued a communiqué on 28 June declaring that the two chiefs of state "agreed that the German Federal Republic should take its place as an equal partner in the community of Western nations, where it can make its proper contributions to the defense of

[63] *NYT*, 15 July, 18 August 1954.

the free world."[64] They also declared that "further delay in the entry into force of the EDC and Bonn Treaties would damage the solidarity of the Atlantic nations." Under the Bonn treaty of 26 May 1952, the German Federal Republic was not to regain full sovereignty until the EDC treaty came into force,[65] and for this reason the Adenauer government was eager to see France ratify the EDC. In his address to the House of Commons on 12 July, Churchill recognized the patience Adenauer had shown "during the last few years when we have all been hoping, almost from month to month, that the French Government would ratify [the Bonn and EDC treaties]."[66] Eisenhower and Churchill agreed to push for granting full sovereignty to West Germany in the event France failed to ratify the EDC treaty,[67] and on 4 July an Anglo-American committee of representatives of the State Department and the Foreign Office met in London to discuss the future course of their policies respecting West Germany. In a letter to Alexander Wiley, chairman of the Senate Foreign Relations Committee, Dulles wrote that this joint committee had recommended, in the event the French National Assembly failed to ratify EDC or adjourned without taking action, "the French Government should, as a first step, be asked to join with the United States, the United Kingdom and the Federal Republic in bringing the Bonn conventions into force in the absence of the Treaty."[68]

By late July it was apparent that the administration was determined to push ahead with German rearmament. Although a French rejection of EDC would postpone German rearmament for a time, other arrangements—alternatives to the defense community—would be made by Britain and the United States. In the fall, if necessary, both houses of Congress would be recalled in order to grant Germany full sovereign powers after an alternative to EDC had been negotiated. This also seems to have been the substance of Dulles's report to the Senate Foreign Relations Committee on his return from Paris.[69] Senator Wiley, it is interesting to note, defended the administration's decision to ask Bedell Smith to return to Geneva by asserting that the refusal to do this would have offended the French thereby hurting the chances of EDC and weakening NATO!

An impatient Congress, however, had taken steps that, in effect, threatened France (and Italy) with sanctions should it fail to ratify the EDC treaty. Insofar as these steps were viewed as a threat by the Assembly's deputies, it is doubtful that they improved EDC's

[64] *Docs.*, *1954*, p. 62.
[65] The occupation regime also would end at this time.
[66] *Docs.*, *1954*, p. 69.   [67] *NYT*, 15 July 1954.
[68] *Docs.*, *1954*, pp. 104-106 (quotation on p. 105).
[69] *NYT*, 16, 17 July 1954.

chances. Nevertheless, in the Mutual Security Act of 1954, Congress included the Richards amendment, carried over from the 1953 act of that name. The effect of this provision would be to withhold half the appropriated aid from countries that failed to ratify the EDC treaty.[70] On 10 July the Senate Foreign Relations Committee voted to halt military aid to France and Italy as of 31 December if, by that time, these countries had not ratified EDC *or* an acceptable alternative.[71] Dulles and General Gruenther appealed to the Senate to soften the measure so as not to include aid funds in "the pipeline." Gruenther said NATO would be endangered if such funds were cut off, and the Senate complied: Nonratifying countries would be denied aid programmed for fiscal years 1954 and 1955.[72] Senator Knowland, however, indicated he would continue the fight against aid to France if EDC was not ratified. On the matter of EDC and the status of West Germany, on 30 July the Senate approved a resolution declaring it was the "sense of the Senate that the President, if he judges that future developments make this desirable and in the national interest, should take such steps as he deems appropriate and as are consistent with United States constitutional processes to restore sovereignty to Germany and to enable her to contribute to the maintenance of international peace and security."[73]

Two other Mutual Security Act amendments, unrelated to EDC, reflected the temper of Congress at the time.

1. Military assistance to countries "committed by treaty to maintain Communist rule over any defined territory in Asia" was to be withheld. This provision, which would deny aid to countries participating in Locarno-type guarantees of an Indochina settlement, introduced during the furor over Eden's "Locarno" proposal of 23 June. The Prime Minister did not allay congressional concern on his Washington visit, and the amendment was retained. It remained part of the Mutual Security Act of 1954 as approved by the Congress on 26 August.[74]

2. A proviso to the same act, introduced by Senator Knowland, also became law. In the event the C.P.R. was seated in the United Nations, the President was to inform Congress of the implications of this action and its potential effects upon American foreign relations, including United States membership in the U.N.[75] Knowland had

---

[70] The amendment was named for James P. Richards, a Democratic representative from South Carolina. For accounts of the efforts to attach the amendment to the Mutual Security Act of 1954, see *NYT*, 15, 17 June 1954.

[71] *NYT*, 11 July 1954.　　[72] *NYT*, 13 July 1954.　　[73] *Docs., 1954*, p. 106.

[74] Public Law 665, 83d Congress, sec. 121.

[75] *Ibid.*, sec. 101. The House unanimously adopted a resolution opposing the admission of the C.P.R. to the U.N. (H. Res. 627, 15 July).

asked for a more rigorous provision, but this was blocked by the firm insistence of the President.

The mood of Congress was antagonistic to the policies of America's NATO allies, which did not bode well for the future of that alliance. There was a dangerous resurgence of "going it alone" sentiment, particularly among right-wing Republicans. This trend was ultimately reversed by a circumspect President and Secretary of State, considerably assisted by the Democrats and the GOP moderates.

Chapter 18

THE DEADLINE

[I]

In the last hectic week at Geneva, most of the negotiations were conducted by the heads of the delegations in private meetings (Eden, for example, probably attended five meetings a day);[1] and the total number of such meetings between the heads of the nine delegations—and Krishna Menon—may have been as high as fifteen, possibly twenty, in the course of one day. No records are available for most of these conferences and, of course, no minutes were prepared, except in the form of memoranda, which are not yet available to the historian. Information on conference activities, therefore, must be based largely upon the recollections of the diplomats involved and upon the accounts of news correspondents.

Eden has recorded that an immense number of political and military draft agreements had accumulated by mid-July,[2] products of the delegations' working groups and the military commission for Vietnam, which by this time had prepared a skeleton cease-fire agreement. Similar agreements for Laos and Cambodia had not yet been drafted by the military commissions for those states; they were not ready until the very last day of the conference, and were completed only after a truly immense effort by the staffs of the commissions and the French, DRVN, Laotian, and Cambodian delegations. Apart from the principal issues, which had still to be resolved, the conference participants had the not insignificant task of reconciling the accumulated drafts and agreeing upon language that was satisfactory both to the signatories and the nonsignatory delegations.

On Wednesday, 14 July, Eden returned to Geneva from his Paris meeting with Dulles and Mendès-France. He visited Molotov almost immediately and reassured him that nothing had been agreed upon in Paris by the Big Three ministers that would in any way interfere with the proceedings at Geneva.[3] We do not know if the Foreign Secretary pointed to the omission in the Paris communiqué of any mention of a Southeast Asia treaty organization, but certainly China —and to a lesser extent the Soviet Union—was concerned lest the Associated States be persuaded to join SEATO and subsequently

[1] E, p. 157; *Econ.*, 17 July 1954.
[2] E, p. 157.
[3] *NYT*, 15 July 1954.

agree to the establishment of American bases on their territories. An assurance that the three Western foreign ministers had not made commitments that would obstruct the conference could be taken to mean that Britain and France, at least, did not feel they were precluded from bargaining about the neutralization of Laos and Cambodia.

On Thursday evening, 15 July, Premier Mendès-France, having arrived in Geneva that afternoon, dined with Molotov, after which they conferred privately for more than three hours. The Soviet minister appears to have been amicable, but made no move toward the French positions on the major issues that separated France and the DRVN.[4] The two ministers met again on the 16th and 17th, and Eden also was present. They discussed a French draft of a cease-fire agreement Chauvel had distributed on the 12th, and compared it with a draft submitted by the Soviets the day before. There appear to have been substantial areas of disagreement. The following outline of primary issues will indicate where the parties stood as of Saturday, 17 July, three days before the French Premier's self-imposed deadline.

The demarcation line. The French demanded the 18th parallel; the DRVN, supported by the C.P.R. and the Soviet Union, demanded the 16th parallel. Molotov argued that the 16th parallel had historical significance because in 1945 it had delimited the Nationalist Chinese and the British zones of control subsequent to the Japanese surrender. He also pointed out that, since partition would be temporary, there was no reason for the French to remain obdurate on this point; after all, the DRVN delegate had compromised: he had agreed to accept the 16th parallel after first demanding, with some justification, the 13th. (Between the 16th and 18th parallels were the cities of Hué, Tourane, and Dong Hoi; colonial route 9, connecting Savannakhet and the Annam coastal plain; and colonial route 1, running along the coast. Acceptance by one belligerent of the line demanded by the other would mean the loss of these cities and an important highway and segment of another highway.)

A delta enclave. Molotov rejected, in principle, the retention by either belligerent party of enclaves in the zone of the other.[5] Premier Mendès-France, by the 17th, was resigned to the loss of the Red River delta and the cities of Hanoi and Haiphong.[6] The United States was not pleased by this development but the French had no alternative; their defense of the delta was near collapse.

---

[4] L&D, pp. 261-262; Marquis Childs, *The Ragged Edge* (New York: Doubleday, 1955), p. 179.   [5] *NYT*, 18 July 1954.

[6] The *New York Times* of 11 July 1954 reported that Mendès-France was prepared to negotiate on the future status of Hanoi and Haiphong; on 14 July the same newspaper reported that the Premier had resigned himself to the loss of these cities.

French troop withdrawals from the delta. Mendès-France wanted twelve months for this but the DRVN demanded withdrawal within three months. Molotov insisted on no more than six months.

Elections in Vietnam. Mendès-France had agreed to all-Vietnamese elections when he met Chou En-lai at Berne on 23 June—although this of course was a "political issue," which, according to a procedural agreement of May, should have been considered only after the military problems had been resolved. Molotov and Premier Chou had reversed themselves on this procedural agreement in the second week of June, during the National Assembly debate that resulted in the fall of the Laniel government. The new French Premier must have felt compelled to accept elections, which Ta Quang Buu had demanded in his secret talk with General Delteil and Colonel de Brébisson on 10 June. Such acceptance was an admission that partition was to be temporary—at least that is what the DRVN delegation understood. The reader should recall, however, that Mendès-France had accepted the seven points, point 4 of which implied permanent partition.

The French insisted that the conference should not at that time decide upon an election date. Pham Van Dong wanted elections six months after a cease-fire, Molotov at the end of 1955—in sixteen months.[7]

Composition of the international supervisory commission (ISC). Eden's proposal for an ISC made up of the Colombo powers was still tabled, as was Molotov's proposal for a commission composed of representatives of India, Pakistan, Indonesia, Czechoslovakia, and Poland—or, alternatively, Poland, India, and Indonesia. It appears that the United States, France, and the other non-Communist delegations, except Britain, preferred some form of United Nations supervision. The United States delegation was not enthusiastic over an ISC composed of one (or two) Communist representative and two (or three) Asian "neutralist" states. On 18 July Chou proposed (or perhaps accepted a proposal for) an ISC consisting of India, Canada, and Poland.[8] Thus a Western state, a Communist state, and a nonaligned state were to be represented on the ISC. (This was, perhaps, the antecedent of Khrushchev's *troika* proposal for reorganizing the office of the U.N. Secretary General: the West, the Communist powers, and the nonaligned states would be equally represented.) Mendès-France and Eden favored this kind of ISC, but Dulles, informed by Bonnet of the proposal, criticized it.[9] He pre-

---

[7] It is interesting to note that the *New York Times* (18 July 1954) suggested that, as in Korea, all-Vietnamese elections might never materialize.

[8] E, p. 159.

[9] L&D, p. 264.

ferred to see an ISC of truly neutral nations; and a Communist state, he is reported to have said, could be neutral.[10]

Mode of ISC: decision-making. Mendès-France conditioned his acceptance of an ISC made up of India, Canada, and Poland upon the Communist delegations' dropping their insistence upon the rule of unanimity, which would have given any of the three commission members a veto over decisions. Molotov's proposal for unanimity only on "major" decisions was still tabled; but, as indicated earlier, his notion of a major decision was so broad as to render his proposal almost equivalent to a blanket insistence upon unanimity. Part of Dulles's dissatisfaction with an ISC having a Polish representative reflected his assumption that the rule of unanimity would be adopted by the conference.

ISC duties and procedures of operation. These items had been considered by the staffs of the delegations and the only major disagreement was over the relationship between the ISC and the joint mixed commissions (composed of French Union and Vietminh representatives). The DRVN wanted the mixed commissions to be independent of the ISC; the French, supported by the British and Americans, envisaged ISC control over the mixed commissions.

A Cease-fire guarantee. The United States would not guarantee a cease-fire, and there is evidence that India and Burma also would refuse to do this, both Colombo powers preferring to commit themselves to the Five Principles of Coexistence. Eden, at this date, appears to have given up on his schemes for guarantees, particularly a Locarno-type guarantee. He spoke in more general (and nebulous) terms of Australia, New Zealand, and the Colombo powers' "associating" themselves with a settlement, and over the weekend of 17/18 July the Foreign Secretary wrote to the governments of these seven states. "If we reached a settlement," he wrote later, "I asked them to *associate* themselves with it *in some form* as soon as possible."[11] If the settlement failed, Eden hoped the seven countries would join with France, Great Britain, the United States, and various Asian states in a collective defense of the area.

Mendès-France's views on a guarantee are not clear, but very probably he preferred to have a settlement guaranteed. He might even have believed that the United States would eventually come around

[10] If agreement could be reached on the composition of an ISC for Vietnam, the conference would have to invite the states so chosen to assume supervisory responsibilities, and these states would have to accept the invitations. As it turned out, the governments of the states selected by the conference to provide ISC commissioners and inspectors (Canada, India, and Poland) were willing to assume the obligations imposed by the cease-fire agreements and hence accepted the invitations.

[11] E, p. 159 (emphasis added).

to Eden's views, although Dulles and the President had explicitly stated that the United States could not guarantee a settlement that resulted in the communization of millions of Vietnamese.

On the 16th, Molotov had insisted there could be no truce without United States "approval," and he continued to press for American approval of the entire settlement until the last day of the conference.[12] Chou also demanded a United States guarantee for the truce, but it was understood that Mendès-France told him this was not possible.[13] If this was true, the French Premier *did* understand that the United States could not formally guarantee the settlement; but he might have continued to feel that the administration would decide to "associate" the United States, in an informal way, with the agreements of the settlement.

Protection of personal private property and French commercial interests in the DRVN zone.   These matters were still being discussed. The French had demanded guarantees for the Roman Catholic bishoprics of Phat Diem and Bui Chu, but the DRVN, having occupied these towns during the French withdrawal in early July, resisted their demands.

Laos and Cambodia.   In June Premier Chou, and subsequently the DRVN delegation, had agreed that all "foreign troops" should be withdrawn from Laos and Cambodia. In late June and early July, however, the DRVN demanded privileges for the Pathet Lao, which would have meant a partition of Laos similar to that of Vietnam. Eden, as well as Mendès-France, resisted this demand. As for Cambodia, the DRVN demanded various military and political rights for the Khmer Issarak. The Cambodian delegation consistently adhered to its May position: surrender by the rebels, amnesty, and their integration into the body politic of Cambodia.

The French gained the DRVN's recognition of their right to maintain two bases in Laos—one at Seno-Savannakhet, another at a location still to be determined in the Mekong River valley—which they had obtained under the Franco-Laotian treaty of October 1953. The contingents necessary to garrison these bases were excepted from the provision for the general withdrawal of foreign troops from Laotian territory. It is possible that Chou agreed to this exception because he believed a French presence in Laos was a form of insurance against an American presence.[14]

Neutralization of Laos, Cambodia, and the southern zone of Vietnam.   Molotov and Chou En-lai were opposed to the establishment of military bases on Laotian and Cambodian territory (with the

[12] *NYT*, 18 July 1954; DDE, p. 370.
[13] *NYT*, 20 July 1954.
[14] Suggested by a source I am not at liberty to identify; see also E, p. 157.

exception of the two French bases noted above). Also, they demanded assurances that neither state would participate in a military alliance, particularly in SEATO. Evidently these same prohibitions applied to the southern zone of Vietnam.

On the 17th the Chinese Premier had visited Eden and expressed his concern about the Paris tripartite talks. He asserted that the Big Three meant to split Southeast Asia in two by means of an anti-Communist alliance, and he insisted that the three Associated States be "independent, sovereign and neutral." Eden had responded:

> I could reassure him on some of this. I said that there was nothing new about the proposed defensive agreement in South-East Asia, which I had myself been advocating for years. It would merely form a counterpart to the Soviet-Chinese alliance, and I added that so far as I knew there was no intention that the Associated States should be members.[15]

Unless Dulles had changed his mind and had so informed Eden, the last sentence can be questioned. Throughout April and May secretary Dulles had sought to have the states of Laos and Cambodia incorporated in a regional security organization.

Although the reports are conflicting, it seems that the Secretary of State had not changed his mind. In one account, Dulles, on 19 July, was reported to have denounced the neutralization of Laos and Cambodia to Henri Bonnet as inadmissible and contrary to point 3 of the seven points.[16] In another account, perhaps reflecting an administration decision after Dulles's denunciation to Bonnet, it was reported that the United States would probably acquiesce in neutralization since SEATO could provide protection for the Associated States even though they were not members of the projected alliance.[17] The same account stated that the administration viewed the question of military bases and troops as more important than membership or nonmembership in a regional alliance, and, since the United States, in any event, would not be associated with the settlement, the problem would not be insurmountable!

It is possible that Eden spoke only for himself, or for Mendès-France as well, when he reassured Chou En-lai of the nonmembership of the Associated States in SEATO. Both Eden and Mendès-France sought to ease the Chinese Premier's worries over a United States presence in Southeast Asia. But Chou seems to have demanded a guarantee of noninvolvement from Washington as well.[18] It is not clear how Eden responded to this demand.

[15] E, p. 158.   [16] L&D, p. 264.   [17] NYT, 20 July 1954.
[18] NYT, 18 July 1954.

[II]

On the 17th Bedell Smith, looking somewhat haggard from his illness, returned to Geneva. On the 18th, a Sunday, Bedell Smith and Molotov made conciliatory speeches during a restricted session of the conference.[19] There was apprehension for a time among the French and British delegations because Molotov had requested this restricted session. It was believed he might break off negotiations, denounce the non-Communist delegations, or make unacceptable demands of them. But he did none of these, and Mendès-France and Eden were greatly relieved.

Tran Van Do, head of the SVN delegation, repeated some of the protests in his note to the French government of the day before. He informed the conference that his government opposed partition and he condemned the abandonment by the French high command of thousands of Vietnamese in the Red River delta during Operation Auvergne. In Saigon, Diem told Donald Heath, the American ambassador, that he intended to denounce the settlement made at Geneva and would not recognize the duties and obligations assumed by France for the State of Vietnam. He asked Heath if the United States would support him.[20] Heath's response is not known, but on 17 August President Eisenhower directed that aid to the Associated States be given directly to these states rather than through the French government.[21]

On the 19th, Pham Van Dong spoke to several newspaper correspondents, declared that the conference had already reached substantial agreement on a number of issues, and said he was optimistic about the possibilities for a settlement.[22] His attitude seems to have reflected the attitude of the Communist states generally. On the preceding day Radio Peking had announced that a settlement was imminent; Tass announced, on the 19th, that a settlement had been achieved.[23] But the major issues that divided the participants still had to be resolved, and Mendès-France had only twenty-four hours to bring this about. Apart from drafting the agreements the conference must eventually adopt, the only progress that week had been the acceptance of a proposal for an ISC made up of India, Canada, and Poland and some relatively minor concessions by the DRVN delegation on the regroupment zone for the Pathet Lao.

Secretary Dulles appeared before the Senate Appropriations Com-

---

[19] *Econ.*, 24 July 1954, p. 296.
[20] L&D, p. 264.
[21] DDE, p. 371.
[22] *NYT*, 20 July 1954.
[23] *NYT*, 11 July 1954, quoting a Reuters dispatch.

mittee on 19 July and told the senators about the seven points and the administration's projected approach to the Geneva settlement. The United States would not sign an Indochina peace arrangement, he said; on the other hand, it would not do anything to upset a reasonable settlement.[24] Bedell Smith at the same time informed Eden that the United States government would not associate itself with a conference communiqué or declaration.[25]

[III]

The documents embodying the settlement would comprise three cease-fire agreements (one for each of the three Associated States) and a conference declaration, drafts of which the Communist and non-Communist delegations began to exchange on the 19th.[26]

On Tuesday, the 20th, apparently aware that the United States would acquiesce in a neutralization of Laos and Cambodia, Mendès-France attempted to reach an agreement with Chou En-lai on these states that would be satisfactory to both Premiers. Mendès-France insisted upon the complete independence of Laos and Cambodia, Chou upon preventing their joining SEATO. A restriction of the kind the Chinese Premier wanted was a limitation upon the sovereign right of the royal governments to join alliances, but such restrictions were not unknown in history, although the governments of Laos and Cambodia, and their supporters, might object to them. In any case, the two Premiers agreed that the three Associated States were not to become members of an alliance that did not conform to the provisions of the United Nations Charter.[27]

On the afternoon of the 20th the heads of five delegations principally concerned with the Vietnamese cease-fire met at the French villa: Eden, Molotov, Chou En-lai, Mendès-France, and Pham Van Dong. (Bedell Smith and Tran Van Do were absent.) At this meeting the Soviet minister proposed the 17th parallel as the line of demarcation between the zones, which Eden and Mendès-France accepted, although this proposal was about 30 minutes' latitude south of the line (running west from Dong Hoi at about 17° 30′ N. lat.) specified in point 2 of the seven points.[28]

The group then turned to the question of a date for general elections in Vietnam. Mendès-France stated his preference for fixing no date at all and Pham Van Dong again insisted that elections be

---

[24] *NYT*, 20 July 1954.   [25] E, pp. 159-160.   [26] *NYT*, 20 July 1954.
[27] L&D, p. 266.
[28] General Ely had been informed by the Premier of the progress of the negotiations and had advised him on the location of a demarcation line. When told that the diplomats had agreed on the 17th parallel, Ely admitted this was a militarily possible solution. Ely, p. 167.

held six months after the cease-fire. The French and British had agreed among themselves that at least eighteen months would be required to permit the Diem government to bring stability to the southern zone and give that government some chance of winning an election. After the restatement of the French and DRVN positions, however, Molotov proposed a delay of two years (!), and Eden and Mendès-France accepted the proposal at once. The group then broke up, after agreeing to a final plenary session at 9 p.m., which a short time later was postponed until 11 p.m.

Although Eden was very pleased by the developments at the villa that afternoon and Mendès-France was more relieved than pleased —there would indeed be a cease-fire in Indochina; the Geneva Conference would not fail—an incident occurred that threatened to upset the understandings and agreements that were soon to eventuate in the formal settlements. Sam Sary, a member of the Cambodian delegation, notified the conference that he would not sign the cease-fire agreement or any of the other documents produced by the military commission for Cambodia or the technical staffs of the delegations. Molotov's first reaction was that the Americans had instigated this Cambodian decision in order to prevent agreement. The group that had met earlier at the French villa gathered at the British villa at about 8:30 p.m. Sam Sary was present but Bedell Smith had sent a representative to attend in his place.[29]

Sam Sary said he would not sign the agreements because they limited the freedom of the Cambodian government to decide whether or not it would join an alliance; moreover, the agreements limited Cambodia's right to request military assistance from the United States or any other country. Limitations such as these, Sam Sary said, were unacceptable restrictions upon Cambodia's newly won independence. The Cambodian minister also expressed concern for the future of his country, which he said might become an object of Communist expansionism, and he wanted to reserve the right to ask the United States to establish bases on Cambodian territory.

The great-power ministers argued with Sam Sary to no avail. The American diplomat assured him the SEATO pact, then being prepared, would give Cambodia some assurance against Communist aggression, but Sam Sary persisted. Mendès-France's midnight deadline passed; and shortly after 2 a.m. the Cambodian minister announced that he had seventeen other demands! Molotov thereupon announced that he would acquiesce in the first demand: Cambodia would be permitted to request foreign military assistance in the event its security was threatened. Mendès-France then entered the

[29] E, p. 159; L&D, p. 271.

lists: What you have accorded Cambodia, he said, you must also recognize for Laos; that would be simple justice. Molotov assented.

Thus the last obstruction was overcome and the final plenary session was rescheduled for the 21st in the early afternoon (the Cambodian cease-fire agreement would be signed shortly before the session convened). Meanwhile, nothing would prevent the signing of the Vietnamese and the Laotian cease-fire agreements, which was done shortly before 3 a.m. by Ta Quang Buu for the DRVN and by General Henri Delteil for the French Union high command.[30] Officially, the Indochinese War was over on 21 July, but it was not the kind of war to be ended simply by a conference or a governmental fiat; it would take time to notify all the irregular and guerrilla units in places remote from the command centers of the Vietminh. In Cambodia, the cease-fire was to become finally effective at 8 a.m. Peking mean time (PMT) on 23 July; in Laos, at 8 a.m. PMT on 6 August. Vietnam was divided into three sectors for cease-fire purposes: in northern Vietnam hostilities were to cease on 27 July, in central Vietnam on 1 August, and in southern Vietnam on 11 August —at 8 a.m. PMT in all sectors.

[I V]

When the delegates of the nine states participating in the Geneva Conference gathered for the last time in the Palais des Nations, three cease-fire agreements had been signed: the Vietnamese and the Laotian agreements, by General Delteil and Ta Quang Buu, and the Cambodian agreement by Ta Quang Buu and General Nhiek Tioulong, commander in chief of the Khmer national armed forces. All three agreements were to go into force at midnight, Geneva time, on 22 July.

The conference also had before it a final declaration and six unilateral declarations, two each from France, Laos, and Cambodia. Although Bedell Smith had informed Eden of the United States decision not to associate itself with the final declaration, Mendès-France was disappointed by the decision.[31] The French Premier had evidently concluded that the agreement between Dulles and him-

[30] Although the Laotian and Vietnamese cease-fire agreements were signed at about 3 a.m. on 21 July, they were officially dated midnight (Geneva time) 20 July. See article 47 of the Vietnamese agreement and article 41 of the Laotian agreement.

[31] OHP statements of U. Alexis Johnson and a person I am not at liberty to identify. An administration official has said: "[At] the very last we refused to join in the final declaration of the Conference. Mendès-France felt very put out by this. I don't say there was any breach of faith there at all. I think it was made clear to Mendès-France what our role would be, but he was very, very much hoping that he could get us to join in the final declaration."

self upon the substance of the Paris joint position paper (which incorporated the seven points) meant the United States would formally recognize the cease-fire agreements and the provisions of a final conference declaration.

The misunderstanding seems to have involved the use of the ambiguous word "respect."[32] If the settlement satisfied the seven points, did the American consent to "respect" the agreements mean a guarantee of some kind of positive support for them or did it mean the United States would refrain from interfering with the implementation of their terms? The public statements of both President Eisenhower and Secretary Dulles should have relieved Mendès-France of any illusion about the official American position, but apparently they did not. Eden did not feel the American position was reasonable; Dulles, he said, "had been at least as responsible as ourselves for calling the Geneva Conference."[33] Both Eden and Mendès-France were worried lest the Soviets or the Chinese, who had demanded that the United States formally adopt the Geneva settlements, create difficulties at the final session because of the American position. Eden sought out Molotov before the final plenary session and they agreed that the problem of signatures could be eliminated. The heading of the final declaration would merely list the participating countries:[34]

> Final Declaration of the Geneva Conference on the problem of restoring peace in Indo-China, in which the representatives of Cambodia, the Democratic Republic of Viet Nam, France, Laos, the People's Republic of China, the State of Viet Nam, the Union of Soviet Socialist Republics, the United Kingdom and the United States of America took part.[35]

[V]

Eden, chairman of the eighth and last plenary session, proposed that the Geneva Conference "take note" of the agreements embodied in the documents he then proceeded to list: the separate cease-fire agreements for Vietnam, Laos, and Cambodia, and the unilateral declarations of the governments of Laos, Cambodia, and France. He noted that it had been agreed among the parties not to publish any of the agreements pending further agreement among them. "The reason for this, I must explain to my colleagues, is that these Armistice

---

[32] See Chapter 16 above.   [33] E, p. 160.   [34] *Ibid.*

[35] *Docs., 1954*, p. 311. The texts of the final declaration and the unilateral declarations appear in *Docs., 1954*, pp. 311-314, and in *Further Documents relating to the Discussion of Indo-China at the Geneva Conference*, Misc. No. 20 (1954), Cmd. 9239 (London: Her Majesty's Stationery Office, 1965), pp. 9-11, 40-42, hereafter referred to as Cmd. 9239. The texts of the cease-fire agreements, the final declaration and the unilateral declarations are reprinted in the Appendix.

terms come into force at different dates. And it is desired that they should not be made public until they have come into force."[36]

The chairman then asked the principal delegates "to express themselves upon" the final declaration of the Conference and he named each delegate in turn.

Mendès-France: "Mr. Chairman, the French Delegation approves the terms of this Declaration."

Phoui Sananikone (Laos): "The Delegation of Laos has no observations to make on this text."

Chou En-lai: "We agree."

Molotov: "The Soviet Delegation agrees."[37]

Tep Phan, the Cambodian delegate, called the conference's attention to a document he said was missing from those listed by the chairman, which contained a declaration by the Cambodian government reserving its legitimate rights and interests in certain regions of the southern zone of Vietnam, which he termed "Cambodian lands in South Viet Nam." Calling attention to paragraphs 7, 11, and 12 of the final declaration, Tep Phan stated: "Cambodia has no intention of interfering in the internal affairs of the State of Viet Nam and associates herself fully with the principle of respect for its integrity, provided certain adjustments and regularisations be arrived at with regard to the borders between this State and Cambodia, borders which so far have been fixed by a mere unilateral act of France."[38] Eden said the allegedly missing document had just reached him and hence he had not inscribed it on the agenda; but he did not think it was the task of the conference to deal with controversies over the frontiers between Cambodia and Vietnam.

Eden then called upon Pham Van Dong to make a statement. The DRVN minister did not address himself to the final declaration but to the remarks of Tep Phan. Dong merely expressed his reservations with regard to Tep Phan's statement "in the interests of good relations and understanding between our two countries."[39]

Taking note of the Cambodian and DRVN statements, Eden turned to Bedell Smith, who noted that he had told his colleagues on 18 July that the United States was not prepared to join in the declaration as submitted. He then made his government's position a matter of record by reading this unilateral declaration to the conference:

> The Government of the United States being resolved to devote its efforts to the strengthening of peace in accordance with the principles and purposes of the United Nations

[36] Cmd. 9239, p. 5.
[37] The preceding statements appear in Cmd. 9239, p. 5.
[38] *Ibid.*, p. 6.
[39] *Ibid.*

Takes Note of the Agreements concluded at Geneva on July 20 and 21, 1954, between (*a*) the Franco-Laotian Command and the Command of the People's Army of Vietnam; (*b*) the Royal Khmer Army Command and the Command of the People's Army of Vietnam; (*c*) the Franco-Vietnamese Command and the Command of the People's Army of Vietnam, and of paragraphs 1 to 12 of the Declaration presented to the Geneva Conference on July 21, 1954.

The Government of the United States of America

Declares with regard to the aforesaid Agreements and paragraphs that (i) it will refrain from the threat or the use of force to disturb them, in accordance with Article 2 (Section 4) of the Charter of the United Nations dealing with the obligation of Members to refrain in their international relations from the threat or use of force; and (ii) it would view any renewal of the aggression in violation of the aforesaid Agreements with grave concern and as seriously threatening international peace and security.

In connection with the statement in the Declaration concerning free elections in Vietnam, my Government wishes to make clear its position which it has expressed in a Declaration made in Washington on June 29, 1954, as follows:

"In the case of nations now divided against their will, we shall continue to seek to achieve unity through free elections, supervised by the United Nations to ensure that they are conducted fairly."

With respect to the statement made by the Representative of the State of Vietnam, the United States reiterates its traditional position that peoples are entitled to determine their own future and that it will not join in an arrangement which would hinder this. Nothing in its declaration just made is intended to or does indicate any departure from this traditional position.

We share the hope that the agreements will permit Cambodia, Laos and Vietnam to play their part in full independence and sovereignty, in the peaceful community of nations, and will enable the peoples of that area to determine their own future.[40]

The conference, Eden said, "will . . . wish to take note" of this statement. He then called on Tran Van Do, head of the SVN delegation, who asked to have the final declaration (paragraph 10) amended to incorporate the following text.

The Conference takes note of the Declaration of the Government of the State of Viet Nam undertaking: to make and support every effort to re-establish a real and lasting peace in Viet Nam; not to

[40] *Ibid.*, pp. 6-7; *Docs., 1954*, pp. 316-317.

use force to resist procedures for carrying the cease-fire into effect, in spite of the objections and reservations that the State of Viet Nam has expressed, especially in its final statement.[41] [The statement to which Tran Van Do apparently referred was a protest against what he called the summary rejection of an SVN proposal for an armistice without a partition of Vietnam.]

It protests solemnly: (*a*) the hasty conclusion of the armistice agreement, contracted only by the high authority of France and the Vietminh notwithstanding the fact that the French High Command controls the Vietnamese troops only through a delegation of authority by the Chief of State of Viet-Nam, and especially notwithstanding the fact that many clauses of this agreement are of such a nature as gravely to compromise the political future of the Vietnamese people; (*b*) the fact that this armistice agreement abandons to the Vietminh territories, many of which are still in possession of Vietnamese troops and thus essential to the defense of Viet-Nam in opposing a larger expansion of Communism and virtually deprives Viet-Nam of the imprescriptible right to organize its defense otherwise than by the maintenance of a foreign army on its territory; (*c*) the fact that the French High Command has arrogated to itself without preliminary agreement with the delegation of the State of Viet-Nam the right to fix the date of future elections, notwithstanding that a matter of a clearly political character is concerned.[42]

Tran Van Do concluded by reserving for his government "complete freedom of action to guarantee the sacred right of the Vietnamese people to territorial unity, national independence and freedom." The declaration did not say that the SVN would not recognize various elements of the settlement, but such a construction could be placed upon it; and the subsequent official attitudes and actions of the Diem government show that this was the construction the Diem government adopted. It was, as we have seen, a continuation of the policy enunciated by Prince Buu Loc in the spring.

The chairman suggested that the conference take note of the SVN declaration.[43] Since there were no apparent objections to this procedure, Eden then proposed that the co-chairmen (himself and Molotov) address telegrams to the governments of India, Canada, and Poland asking them to undertake supervisory armistice duties as members of the ISC. The conference agreed. Eden also informed the delegates that he and Molotov would jointly prepare a proposal for their consideration on the operation costs of the ISC. Since there was no objection to this procedure, Eden expressed his thanks to

[41] Cmd. 9239, p. 7.   [42] *Docs., 1954*, pp. 315-316.   [43] Cmd. 9239, pp. 7-8.

the town of Geneva and to the Swiss government. Bedell Smith and Molotov made brief parting comments. Tran Van Do made a last, futile attempt to amend the declaration, but Eden declared the conference could not now amend the final act, "which is the statement of the Conference as a whole, but the Declaration of the Representative of the State of Viet Nam will be taken note of."[44] Eden then adjourned the conference.

[VI]

The documents of the Geneva Conference, loosely referred to as the Geneva Accords of 1954, are analyzed in detail in Part III, but at this point I should like to outline the principal terms of the settlements and some of their effects. (The reader should bear in mind that, for brevity, a host of legal and political problems is passed over.)

VIETNAM

1. A provisional line of demarcation between the northern and southern "regroupment zones" was established at about the 17th parallel—more accurately, at the Song Ben Hat (River). (1)[45]

2. Although orders for an immediate cease-fire would be immediately transmitted to all units in Vietnam, formal cease-fire dates were established: 27 July for northern Vietnam, 1 August for central Vietnam, and 11 August for southern Vietnam. (11)

3. The military high commands of the PAVN and the French Union forces were required to complete their troop withdrawals from the zone of the opposite party within 300 days after the cease-fire. (15)

4. These results of the partition should be noted:

a. French troops were required to withdraw entirely from the Red River delta. They had to withdraw from Hanoi and its defense perimeter within 80 days of the cease-fire and from Haiphong within 300 days.

b. Population estimates vary, but from 10.5 to 12 million persons would come under the jurisdiction and control of the DRVN in the north and from 9.5 to 11 million persons would come under the jurisdiction and control of the authorities of the south.[46]

5. General, all-Vietnamese elections were to be held in July 1956, after consultations between representatives of the DRVN and the

---

[44] *Ibid.*, p. 9.

[45] The numerals or state names listed in parentheses refer to the articles (or chapters) of the cease-fire agreements for the particular states. *FD*, followed by a number, refers to the final declaration and the numbered paragraph therein.

[46] *NYT*, 30 July 1954; *T/L*, 26 July 1954. B. B. Fall, "The Cease-Fire in Indo-China—An Appraisal," *Far Eastern Survey* (October, 1954).

SVN or France, and were to begin on 20 July 1955. (FD 7; see also article 14 of the cease-fire agreement.)

6. Civilians in one zone were to be permitted to move to the other zone until troop movements were completed, that is, within 300 days. (14c)

7. Subject to detailed regulations, the introduction into Vietnam of troops or other military persons and arms, munitions, aircraft, and ordnance was prohibited. The establishment of new military bases, under the control of France or the DRVN or a foreign state, was prohibited. (16 to 18)

8. France and the DRVN undertook to ensure that the zones assigned to them did not adhere to any military alliance and would not be used for the resumption of hostilities. (19)

9. An ISC would be established for Vietnam, another for Laos, and another for Cambodia. In all three commissions an Indian representative would be chairman, and Poland and Canada also would be represented. The duties of the ISCs were spelled out in the separate cease-fire agreements for each of the three Indochinese states. Generally they comprised supervision of the armistice and the troop withdrawals and investigation of alleged violations of the agreements. (Vietnam, chap. VI; Cambodia, chap. IV; Laos, chap. VI)

10. Provision was made for the establishment of joint commissions, made up—in the case of Vietnam—of representatives of France and the DRVN. The tasks of these joint commissions related to military and technical matters involving the armistice and the regroupment of troops. (Vietnam, chap. VI; Cambodia, chap. IV; Laos, chap. VI)

11. Decisions or recommendations of an ISC pertaining to violations or threats of violations that might lead to the resumption of hostilities had to be unanimous. Amendments to the cease-fire agreements, recommended by an ISC, to the Geneva powers, had to be made on a unanimous basis. All other recommendations or decisions were to be based upon a majority vote. (Vietnam, 41-43; Cambodia, 20-21; Laos, 34-35)

12. The ISC had the right to *inform* the members of the Geneva Conference in the event a party refused to put an ISC recommendation into effect. This provision (Vietnam, 44) and paragraph 13 of the final declaration (under which the members of the conference agreed to consult one another on matters referred to them by the ISC) institutionalized the conference and its co-chairmen and gave these quasi-institutions continuing duties with respect to the settlements pertaining to each of the three Indochinese states. (See also Cambodia, 22, and Laos, 36.)

13. None of the three cease-fire agreements was guaranteed by one

or by several conference participants. The final declaration, in thirteen paragraphs, stated that the conference "takes note" of the agreements. The delegates did not sign the declaration; they merely expressed their agreement or associated themselves with the declaration. The exceptions to this procedure were as follows.

a. The United States delegate made a declaration that took note of the cease-fire agreements and paragraphs 1 through 12 (but not paragraph 13) of the final declaration, and stated that the United States would not use force to disturb them. In effect, this declaration was a formal refusal to associate the United States with the Geneva agreements and declarations.

b. The SVN delegate did not agree to or formally associate his government with the final declaration; he issued a formal protest that declared the SVN government reserved complete freedom of action to guarantee the rights of the Vietnamese people to national unity, independence, and freedom.

c. The DRVN delegate did not address himself to the final declaration when he made his concluding statement; he simply expressed reservations about the Cambodian claim to territories in southern Vietnam.

After the conference ended, none of the delegates formally submitted the final declaration to their governments for ratification.

CAMBODIA

1. The cease-fire in Cambodia was to become formally effective no later than 7 August, although it would be ordered immediately. (1, 2, 3)

2. All foreign armed forces, including those of France and the DRVN, were required to be withdrawn from Cambodia within ninety days of the coming into force of the cease-fire agreement. (4)

3. Khmer resistance forces were to be demobilized within thirty days, but, subject to the declaration quoted earlier, they were to be integrated into the national community without reprisals, or discrimination against their constitutional rights as individuals. The final declaration noted that national elections would be held in 1955 and the demobilized forces would be free to participate in them. (5, 6; FD 3)

4. By its declaration, the Cambodian government stated that

a. It would not enter a military alliance that was not in conformity with the principles of the United Nations Charter;

b. It would not permit the establishment of military bases by a foreign power *"as long as its security is not threatened"*;

c. Between the date of the cease-fire and the date of the final settlement of political problems, it would not solicit foreign aid in war matériel, personnel, or instructors *"except* for the purpose of the *effective defense of the territory."* (7; FD 4, 5)

5. The provisions relating to the ISC and the joint commissions were similar to those in the Vietnam agreement (described above).

L A O S

1. A cease-fire in Laos, although ordered immediately, would become effective no later than 6 August. (1, 2, 5)

2. Withdrawal of military forces was to be accomplished within 120 days after the agreement came into force. "Vietnamese People's Volunteers" were to be withdrawn from Laos, except for those who had settled in Laos "before hostilities," and the latter were to be the subject of a special convention. The French were permitted to provide military personnel for training units of the Royal Laotian Army, but the strength of these training cadres must not exceed 1,500 officers and noncommissioned officers. The French were also permitted to maintain two military bases, one at Seno-Savannakhet and the other at a still to be determined location in the Mekong River valley. The strength of the effectives maintained at these bases was not to exceed 3,500 men. (4, 6, 8)

3. The Laotian government obligated itself not to permit the introduction of arms and munitions into its country, except a "specified quantity of armaments in categories specified as necessary for the defense of Laos." It also obligated itself, by its declaration, not to permit the establishment of military bases upon its territory nor join a military alliance, subject to the same exceptions governing Cambodia (Cambodia, 4). (7, 9; FD 4)

4. Pending a political settlement, units of the Pathet Lao "shall move into the Provinces of Phongsaly and Sam-Neua." The status of the Pathet Lao was otherwise left undetermined (14). The government of Laos, however, declared that all citizens would be integrated into the national community without discrimination. The government would "promulgate measures to provide for special representation in the Royal Administration of the provinces of Phong Saly and Sam Neua during the interval between cessation of hostilities and the general elections of the interests of Laotian nationals who did not support the Royal forces during hostilities." The final declaration took note of the Laotian declaration and the fact that elections were to be held in 1955. (FD 3)

5. The provisions relating to the ISC and the joint commissions were similar to those in the Vietnam agreement (described above).

Chapter 19

REACTIONS TO THE SETTLEMENTS

[I]

The reaction of the American public to the Geneva settlements was largely one of indifference. Opinion had been alerted in April by the administration's warnings of possible intervention in Indochina, and the public remarks of such "interventionists" as Admiral Radford, Vice President Nixon, and Walter Robertson (Assistant Secretary of State for Far Eastern Affairs) were sometimes construed as following an official policy of preparing the American people for a more active military commitment to save Southeast Asia from communism. Rumors of intervention continued to circulate about Washington during May and June but, invariably, other news stories, such as the Army-McCarthy hearings and the Guatemalan insurrection, were given greater prominence in the American press. By mid-July the American people were little concerned with the vagaries of the Geneva negotiations: intervention, it seemed, was not imminent and Indochina had become just another name in the series of cold war trouble spots. The settlements of late July brought peace, but peace in Southeast Asia was not welcomed with feelings of relief, as it was in France and Britain, nor was it regarded as a major defeat for "free-world democracy," except by some members of the GOP conservative wing. The Indochina settlement, in short, was of secondary importance in the opinion of most of the American public and a large segment of the press.

A small segment of the public, however, was worried about the significance and implications of the Geneva settlements. Senator Knowland called Geneva one of the great Communist victories of the decade.[1] Newspapers such as the *Christian Science Monitor* and the *New York Herald Tribune*, both of which had followed events in Indochina rather closely, called the settlements of setback for the non-Communist West.[2] Generally, State Department opinion agreed with this assessment.[3] American diplomats felt that the Vietnamese cease-fire agreement augured trouble for the non-Communist government of southern Vietnam in establishing a viable anti-Communist regime in Saigon and in developing good relations between the Diem government and the French army, both of which, at least ostensibly, had

---

[1] *NYT*, 22 July 1954.
[2] *Christian Science Monitor*, 21 July 1954; *NYHT*, 23 July 1954.
[3] *NYT*, 24 July 1954.

obligations under the cease-fire agreement. The Vietnamese government, it was reported, had advised American diplomats in Saigon that it would be powerless to resist Communist expansion, militarily or politically.

The official administration view was set forth by the President, Secretary of State Dulles, Under Secretary of State Bedell Smith, and Secretary of Defense Wilson the week after the conference ended. At his press conference on 21 July, President Eisenhower said he was glad the agreements had put an end to the bloodshed in Indochina. Describing the American position with respect to the agreements, he emphasized that the United States "has not itself been a party to or bound by the decisions taken by the Conference."[4] He added that it was "our hope that [the conference] will lead to the establishment of peace consistent with the rights and needs of the countries concerned. The agreement contains features which we do not like, but a great deal depends on how they work in practice." The President also said that the government was pursuing discussions with other states with a view to organizing a collective defense in Southeast Asia against further "direct or indirect Communist aggression in that general area." The United States also was requesting the governments of Cambodia and Laos to accede to the appointment of a resident American ambassador or minister in the capitals of these states, and the embassy in Saigon would be maintained.[5]

To a correspondent's question whether there were elements of appeasement in the Geneva settlement, Eisenhower replied:

> This agreement . . . was not what we would have liked to have had. But I don't know, if I were put up against it at this moment [whether I would be able] to find an alternative, to say what I would or could do. [Since I] . . . had no better plan, I am not going to criticize what they [at Geneva] had done.[6]

The statement of Secretary Dulles on 23 July was more detailed and more didactic than the President's.

> The Geneva negotiations reflected the military developments in Indochina. After nearly eight years of war, the forces of the French Union had lost control of nearly one-half of Vietnam, their hold on the balance was precarious, and the French people did not desire to prolong the war.

---

[4] *Docs., 1954*, p. 317.
[5] *Ibid.*, p. 318. The editor, P. V. Curl, also noted that on 18 August the Senate confirmed the appointments of Robert McClintock as ambassador to Cambodia and Charles W. Yost as minister to Laos.
[6] *NYT*, 23 July 1954.

These basic facts inevitably dominated the Indochina phase of the Geneva conference and led to settlements which, as President Eisenhower said, contain many features which we do not like.[7]

The United States, Dulles continued, because it was "... neither a belligerent in Indochina nor subject to compulsions that applied to others, ... did not become a party to the conference results." The results were merely noted, with a statement that—in accordance with the U.N. Charter—the United States would not use force to overthrow the settlements. Dulles cited two lessons the "free nations concerned" should have learned and that should be kept in mind to prevent "the loss in northern Vietnam from leading to the extension of communism throughout Southeast Asia and the Southwest Pacific."

1. Resistance to communism needed popular support: people should feel they were defending their own national institutions, and therefore should have genuine national independence.

Dulles noted that independence was already a fact in Laos and Cambodia, and had been demonstrated at Geneva, notably by the government of Cambodia. He also referred to Premier Mendès-France's instructions to French representatives in Vietnam to complete precise projects for the transfer of authority to the SVN government by 30 July, which would "give reality to the independence which France had promised."

2. Arrangements for collective defense must be made in advance of aggression, and now was a practical time to bring a SEATO into being. "In this connection we should bear in mind that the problem is not merely one of deterring open armed aggression, but of preventing Communist subversion which, taking advantage of economic dislocations and social injustice, might weaken and finally overthrow the non-Communist governments."[8]

Upon returning to Washington on 23 July, Bedell Smith repeated an expression Eden had used after the closing session of the Geneva Conference: The cease-fire agreements were "the best which we could have possibly obtained under the circumstances. It is well to remember that diplomacy has rarely been able to gain at the conference table what cannot be gained or held on the battlefield."[9] About a week later, the Under Secretary of State appeared on the national television networks and repeated this sentiment. Like Secretary Dulles, Bedell Smith emphasized the point that the settlement

---

[7] *DSB*, 2 August 1954, p. 163.
[8] *Ibid.*, p. 164.
[9] *NYT*, 24 July 1954. Bedell Smith felt that Munich was a "damned poor term" to apply to the Geneva Conference.

reflected a local military situation; and he said the United States did not accept the truce lines as permanent political solutions.[10]

Secretary of Defense Wilson, who had been a rather consistent opponent of a policy of American intervention in Indochina, called the Geneva settlements "the best answer at the moment." The Indochinese War, he said, was a revolution, not just a war between Communist and anti-Communist forces, and the nature of the aggression in Indochina made it very difficult to deal with. There had been oversights and errors in the "free world" assessment of the Indochina Communist problem, he said, and he generally minimized the role American armed force could have played in Indochina.[11]

Although the public statements of the President and the Secretary of State did not appear to reflect the alarm of Senator Knowland or the *Herald Tribune*, their private feelings were probably best expressed by Walter Robertson on 30 July in a speech to the American Legion of Virginia: "It would be an understatement to say that we do not like the terms of the cease-fire agreement just concluded."[12] Indeed, General J. Lawton Collins got the impression that Dulles, Alexis Johnson, Robertson, and others were pessimistic about the SVN's chances for survival. Dulles, Collins later recalled, told him: "Frankly, Collins, I think our chances of saving the situation there are not more than one in ten."[13] Another high level official reported that he was "disillusioned" by the attitude of the State Department that Laos was "about to go down the drain."[14] Bedell Smith believed two provinces (Phong Saly and Sam Neua) would be lost, but he was somewhat optimistic about the future of the rest of Laos. General Collins said that, after Dulles had traveled to Laos and Vietnam in early 1955, the secretary remarked that the chances for the SVN's survival had improved to fifty-fifty; and Dulles, he said, was pleased with Ngo Dinh Diem.

Apart from his press conference statement (briefly described above), President Eisenhower's more interesting remarks about the conference's results appeared later. He referred to the Vietnam cease-fire agreement as that "terrible agreement at Geneva"[15] (well after insurgent activity in South Vietnam had been renewed). In his *Mandate for Change*, he noted the "element of tragedy in an agreement that put great numbers of people under Communist domination."

[10] *DSB*, 1 August 1954, pp. 192-193.
[11] *NYT*, 21 July 1954.
[12] *DSB*, 30 July 1954, p. 259.
[13] OHP statement of General J. Lawton Collins.
[14] From a source I am not at liberty to identify.
[15] OHP statement of Dwight D. Eisenhower.

[But] By and large, the settlement obtained by the French Union at Geneva in 1954 was the best it could get under the circumstances. It ended a bloody war and a serious drain on France's resources. More important, it saw the beginning of development of better understanding between the Western powers and the nations of Southeast Asia. It paved the way for a system of true cooperation between both in the never-ending struggle to stem the tide of Communist expansionism.[16]

Washington was soon distracted by another, though related, episode: President Syngman Rhee's visit to the United States (from 26 through 30 July), his talks with President Eisenhower, and especially his speech to a joint session of Congress on 28 July. In that speech Rhee asserted that the failure of the Geneva Conference to bring about the unification of Korea had rendered the Korean armistice agreement invalid. He urged both the unification of Korea by force and the overthrow of the Communist regime in China. With American air and naval support for South Korean and Nationalist Chinese troops, the C.P.R. government could be destroyed, without the need for United States ground troops. If the Soviet Union intervened, the war must be carried to Soviet production centers by the U.S. Air Force. These centers must be destroyed before the Russians had produced enough bombers and hydrogen bombs to be able to launch a surprise attack. Rhee warned that Soviet and Chinese talk of peace might lull the United States into a "sleep of death."[17]

Congressional reaction to the speech was less than enthusiastic. Although the Korean President had merely developed the arguments of some extreme American activists to their logical conclusion—renewal of the Korean War, the overthrow of the Peking regime, and a better-now-than-later attitude toward a war with the Soviet Union[18]— Congress did not like what it heard. Not only was there more than substantial opposition to a resumption of hostilities in Korea, the congressmen had a singular distaste for the open and frank advocacy of thermonuclear destruction of Chinese and Soviet production centers by an allied leader who was a guest of the government and speaking in that government's chambers. On 3 August Dulles told a news conference that, in his view, the failure of the Geneva Conference to bring

16 DDE, pp. 374-375. As for the number of Vietnamese "put . . . under Communist domination," it is Bernard Fall's estimate that, after partition, the SVN government controlled about the same number of people it controlled before partition, which is to say the DRVN exercised *de facto* control over about 12 million Vietnamese, whom some American accounts described as having been *transferred* to Communist control. See B. B. Fall, *Viet-Nam Witness: 1953-66* (New York: Praeger, 1966), pp. 51-68.
17 *NYT*, 29 July 1954.
18 *Econ.*, 21 August 1954.

about the unification of Korea on an acceptable basis had not invalidated the armistice arrangement. The Communists had not violated the agreement of July 1953, and hence there was no justification for a resumption of hostilities.[19]

President Rhee doubtlessly found President Eisenhower politely unsympathetic to his theories. (On 21 July Eisenhower had said the United States had no intention of making an aggressive move to free North Korea.) The Rhee-Eisenhower communiqué of 30 July stated simply that the Republic of Korea and the United States would "move forward, in accordance with the Charter of the United Nations and the resolutions of the General Assembly on Korea, to achieve a unified, democratic, and independent Korea."[20] But Rhee was dissatisfied with what he called American timidity and myopia in the Far East,[21] and a number of disputes roiled American-Korean relations during the summer and early fall.[22]

By 17 November, however, the principal disagreements were liquidated and the two governments exchanged the instruments of ratification of the U.S.–R.O.K. mutual defense treaty (to which the Senate had consented on 26 January). In an agreed minute, initialed by the ambassadors of the two allies at Seoul, the United States promised up to $700 million for aid and assistance in strengthening the Korea armed forces. A paragraph of the minute declared that the United States agreed "in the event of an unprovoked attack upon the Republic of Korea, to employ, in accordance with its constitutional processes, its military power against the aggressor."[23] These steps reassured Seoul. The Rhee government could reasonably conclude—as no doubt the governments of the great powers had concluded—that hostilities would not be renewed. In September the British government had announced a reduction in the strength of Commonwealth forces in Korea, and in the same month Peking announced a reduction of seven divisions in its forces assigned to Korea.

[I I]

Premier Mendès-France appeared before the National Assembly on 22 July to explain what he had accomplished at Geneva and to seek a vote of approval for the Geneva agreements. He received such a vote on 23 July by a significant majority: 462 votes for and 13 votes

[19] *NYT*, 4 August 1954.
[20] *DSB*, 9 August 1954, p. 197; *Docs.*, *1954*, p. 344.
[21] *NYT*, 22 August 1954.
[22] See R. P. Stebbins, *The United States in World Affairs, 1954* (New York: Harper & Row, 1956), p. 275; Coral Bell, *Survey of International Affairs, 1954* (London: Oxford University Press, 1957), p. 282.
[23] *Docs., 1954*, pp. 344-347 (quotation on p. 346).

against, with 140 abstentions.[24] The size of the victory was only one indication of the relief felt by the French that the Indochinese War was at an end. However, at least among the Assembly deputies, the feeling of relief was mixed with regret and discouragement over the military defeats in Indochina, both actual and prospective; over what must surely be a loss of influence in Southeast Asia; over the now problematical future of the French Union; and over the decline in French prestige, of which the Geneva settlements were both a sign and a symptom. Mendès-France's words to the National Assembly were memorable: "I do not have any illusions and I do not want anyone to have any illusions about the contents of the agreements. The texts are sometimes cruel because they consecrate facts which are cruel."[25]

The Premier then described his approach to the negotiations at Geneva and related the history of the negotiations from shortly before the time he assumed the role of Foreign Minister until the cease-fire agreements were signed. At the time of his investiture speech he had imposed a time limit of thirty days because "it was necessary for preparation in France of the dispatch of reinforcements and it had to be used as a formal notice to our adversaries to give proof of their will for peace."[26] As for the future, Mendès-France noted that Laos had asked for the continuance of the Franco-Laotian treaty of October 1953. "As for the Vietnam Expeditionary Corps regrouped in the south, it will be maintained at its present level. It will have complete liberty of movement." But he had accepted the necessity for the withdrawal of the French expeditionary corps "when interested Governments ask it."[27]

As for the political situation in Vietnam,

> the government has given instructions to the High Commissioner in Indochina to submit to Vietnamese authorities, between now and 31 July, precise plans for the transfer of competences still retained by France, . . . [plans] which will consecrate in administrative reality the independence which France has engaged herself to recognize and which have just been solemnly reaffirmed in the Final Act of the Geneva Conference. . . .

> Indeed, the agreements have established in Vietnam a situation which, as I have already said, has a provisional character. . . . [But] Vietnam can now look forward to a prompt economic restoration which alone will render possible the social progress which

[24] JO, 24 July 1954, pp. 3588-3589, 3619-3620 (sess. of 23 July).
[25] JO, 23 July 1954, p. 3533 (sess. of 22 July).
[26] Ibid.
[27] Ibid., p. 3535.

its leaders have adopted for their program. [Vietnam], like Cambodia and Laos, can in this regard rely upon France's assistance. A program of economic and technical assistance is in preparation. Its execution must not be delayed.[28]

Finally, Mendès-France asserted that he had tightened the "links of friendship and alliance with the United States" in spite of the fact that the end of the hostilities in Indochina constituted a "difficult hurdle for the Western Alliance."[29]

The Geneva settlements were not exempt from criticism in the National Assembly, and Georges Bidault criticized the Premier for what amounted to abandonment of the Associated States to the Communists. Indochina, Bidault said, had been neutralized by the agreements without adequate guarantees for their security.[30] Mendès-France responded by pointing out that the expeditionary corps was to remain in Indochina. Both Bidault and Frédéric-Dupont argued that Mendès-France had obtained terms no better than the Laniel government had obtained from the Communists by early June.[31] Whatever the criticisms, the Assembly approved the settlements with what appears to have been sober acceptance of the overriding necessities of the situation in Indochina at the time.[32]

[III]

At the conclusion of the Geneva Conference, Eden looked upon the settlements as the best France could have obtained under the circumstances,[33] and he maintained this view in his memoirs, written some six years later. Although the results were not entirely satisfactory, an eight-year war had been halted and international tension had been reduced "at a point of instant danger to world peace." He was gratified that his "faith in the negotiations had to some extent been justified and that we had managed to stop the fighting on acceptable terms," although he knew the Indochina problem had not been completely resolved.[34]

The Prime Minister congratulated the Foreign Secretary on the "success that has rewarded your patient, persevering skill,"[35] and Eden was generally praised in the British press and in the House of Commons. The Labour Party, however, was more enthusiastic than

[28] *Ibid.*

[29] *Ibid.*, p. 3536; *JO*, 24 July 1954, p. 3583 (sess. of 23 July).

[30] *JO*, 24 July 1954, pp. 3577-3579 (sess. of 23 July).

[31] For Frédéric-Dupont's speech, see *JO*, 23 July 1954, pp. 3540-3543 sess. of 22 July).

[32] See General Ely's assessment of the political situation in France after the cessation of hostilities in Ely, Chapter XI.

[33] E, p. 160.   [34] E, p. 161.   [35] *NYT*, 23 July 1954.

the secretary's own party about the results at Geneva, although sentiment among Tory MPs, while recognizing that the settlements amounted to a French defeat at the hands of a Communist-inspired movement, was generally appreciative of Eden's efforts and achievements. British official and unofficial opinion was equally relieved that a local war that could have led to a Soviet-American confrontation and possibly a thermonuclear war had been averted. Other, more sober, assessments of the conference emphasized that it had not been a victory for Mendès-France or Eden, nor for the spirit of reason, nor for those who had faith in negotiations as such; the agreements acknowledged a defeat. The agreements also were acknowledged a defeat by the editors of the *Economist*.

> There had been a long story of French bungling and the position was past redemption. No one had an alternative course to suggest —not even the Americans, unless they were willing to send a large army. M. Mendès-France and Mr. Eden were right to make the best they could of a bad job, and they did it skillfully. But no one should be under any delusion that it was anything but a very bad job. Geneva was about as much a victory in the diplomatic field as Dunkirk in the military.[36]

India welcomed the Geneva settlements without reservation. The Colombo powers, through Sir John Kotelewala, the Prime Minister of Ceylon, expressed their "deep satisfaction" with the agreements and pledged their "firm support."[37] The Indian government accepted the invitation to act as chairman of the international supervisory commissions for Vietnam, Laos, and Cambodia.

[IV]

The Soviet and the Chinese press hailed the Geneva agreements. Malenkov declared that Geneva convincingly demonstrated that Socialists could give proof of their peaceful intentions.[38] The C.P.R. was even more lavish in its praise, and Premier Chou En-lai termed the conference a tremendous success. Peace had been restored in Indochina, he noted, and world tensions had been reduced. The settlement showed that international disputes could be resolved through negotiations, provided the countries concerned were sincerely anxious for peace. He emphasized facts of obvious importance to Peking; namely, foreign military bases would not be allowed in Indochina and adherence to military alliances had been proscribed.

[36] *Econ.*, 31 July 1954, p. 342.   [37] E, p. 162.
[38] *NYT*, 25 July 1954.

The Delegation of the People's Republic of China fully endorses and supports these agreements and declares its willingness to join with the nations concerned in insuring the thorough implementation of these agreements.[39]

Chou then urged that the governments of Asia adopt the Five Principles of Peaceful Coexistence as a guide to their foreign policies.

A *People's Daily* (Peking) editorial on 22 July echoed Chou's sentiments.

When the people of the world take the cause of peace into their own hands, the forces of peace become invincible. The convening of the Geneva Conference and the arrival at agreement on the Indo-China question are clear proof that these forces are irresistible.

The editorial then accused the American delegation of having opposed the reasonable proposals of other delegations, of having sought to widen differences, and of having created obstacles to a settlement. But despite its intrigue and scheming, the efforts of the United States did not succeed, it said; the conference had arrived at an honorable settlement.

[All] the countries concerned must guarantee the implementation of the agreements and the *attainment of democracy and unification by the countries of Indo-China.* They must stand guard against any plot to undermine peace in Indo-China. (Emphasis added.)

The *People's Daily* then announced the C.P.R.'s approval and support of the Geneva agreements and pledged that China would strive with all "peace-loving peoples and states of the world for [their] thorough implementation." As an indication of the importance Peking placed upon Geneva and China's role at the conference, the *Daily* underscored China's great-power status:

For the first time as one of the Big Powers, the People's Republic of China joined the other major powers in negotiating on vital international problems and made a contribution of its own that won acclaim of wide sections of public opinion. The international status of the People's Republic of China as one of the big world powers has gained universal recognition. Its international prestige has been greatly enhanced.

The Vietnamese leaders, however, Vietminh and SVN, were not satisfied. The *New York Times* reported that the DRVN delegation at Geneva had declared it could have won all of Tonkin and most of Annam, Cochin China, Laos, and Cambodia within a year if the

[39] Supplement to *People's China* (Peking), 1 August 1954.

war had continued; however, the Chinese and the Soviets had forced it to acquiesce in the settlement.[40] Citing *Le Monde* (6 March), the *Survey of International Affairs, 1954* said:

> [There] was canvassed in France the possibility of what was called, by wildly optimistic analogy, "the Markos solution," that is, the hope that China might be induced by threats or promises to drop Mr. Ho Chi Minh, as Russia had dropped General Markos in Greece. . . . In as far as Mr. Ho Chi Minh was to get a good deal less, in the immediate future, than he might have militarily hoped for, the faint, almost unrecognizable, ghost of "the Markos solution" may be said to have hovered over the final settlement.[41]

Although Pham Van Dong did not formally accede to the final declaration, at least on the record, he and his government held that *France* was bound by the terms of the cease-fire agreement for Vietnam. The partition of Vietnam was to be temporary and elections were to be held in July 1956. In the view of the DRVN, France—if not the other Geneva Conference participants as well—was obligated to fulfill those provisions of the cease-fire agreement and the final declaration that would bring about the unification of Vietnam. It probably felt, in view of the public declarations of its Chinese ally, that it could rely upon Peking for support for its policy of achieving "democracy and unification" in Indochina.

Shortly after the end of the conference, Ho Chi Minh issued this appeal:

> The Geneva Conference has come to an end. It is a great victory for our diplomacy. . . .

> At this conference, the struggle of our delegation and the assistance given by the delegations of the Soviet Union and China have ended in a great victory for us: The French Government has recognized the independence, sovereignty, unity, and territorial integrity of our country. . . .[42]

> In order to re-establish peace, the first step to take is that the armed forces of both parties should cease fire.

[40] *NYT*, 25 July 1954.

[41] Bell, *op. cit.*, pp. 71-72.

[42] By unilateral declaration the French government stated that, in connection with the reestablishment of peace in Indochina, it would "proceed from the principle of respect for the independence and sovereignty, the unity and territorial integrity of Cambodia, Laos, and Viet-Nam" (*Docs., 1954*, p. 314). The declaration did not touch upon the crucial question: With which government of the presumably independent Vietnam (the DRVN or SVN) would the French government deal? At the time of the Geneva agreements, the French had formally recognized only the State of Vietnam of which Bao Dai was chief of state.

The regroupment in two regions is a temporary measure; it is a traditional step for the implementation of the armistice and restoration of peace, and paves the way for national reunification through general elections. Regroupment in regions is in no way a partition of our country, neither is it an administrative division.

. . . [A] number of regions formerly liberated by us will now be temporarily occupied by the French troops before they leave for France.

This is a necessity; North, Central, and South Viet-Nam are territories of ours. Our country will certainly be unified, our entire people will surely be liberated. . . .

Our compatriots in the South were the first to wage the war of Resistance. . . . I am confident that they will place national interests above local interests or permanent interests above temporary interests, and join their efforts with the entire people in strengthening peace, achieving unity, independence, and democracy all over the country.[43]

The last paragraph suggests that Premier Ho may have been very much concerned about the reaction of Vietminh cadres and forces in the south, many of which could not have been pleased with the outcome of the Geneva Conference or the assignment of the territories south of the demarcation line to the French high command. But for Ho, the watchword was "unity":

In order to carry the day, our people, armymen, and cadres from North to South must unite closely. They must be one in thought and deed. . . .

I call on all our compatriots . . . to follow strictly the lines and policies laid down by the Party and Government.

With respect to the Geneva agreements, the DRVN leader stated:

We are resolved to abide by the agreements entered into with the French Government. At the same time, we demand that the French Government correctly implement the agreements they have signed with us.

THE GOVERNMENT of Ngo Dinh Diem, and its supporters in Saigon, were as emphatic as the Vietminh in their desire for the unification of Vietnam. The Vietminh had been willing to accept temporary *de facto* partition for purposes of a cease-fire and troop regroupment,

[43] Ho Chi Minh, *On Revolution*, ed. B. B. Fall (New York: Praeger, 1967), pp. 271-273.

but the SVN leaders opposed even this. They would have preferred —however unrealistically in terms of the conditions existing in July—assembly and disarming of troops in many small regroupment areas throughout Indochina, together with control measures that, in effect, would have denied substantial political advantages to the Vietminh. In the last hours of the Geneva Conference, Tran Van Do had announced that his government would reserve its freedom of action and would regard itself bound by the terms of the cease-fire and the final declaration only in limited respects.[44]

This show of defiance was not necessarily coupled with optimism for the future, however. The SVN delegation had been virtually ignored by the French throughout late June and July; its efforts to forestall partition had failed; Tran Van Do's attempt to amend the Geneva documents had been dismissed.[45] The SVN, moreover, understood as well as the French government that the cease-fire agreements represented a military defeat for the forces of the French Union and that the settlement was symbolic of the decline, if not the imminent collapse, of French influence and prestige in Indochina. The future of the SVN must have appeared bleak to the non-Communist nationalists in the weeks after the conference adjourned. Their adversaries, who would soon occupy Hanoi and Haiphong, were disciplined and well organized and had victories over the French to their credit; the government and political parties of the south had no victories and were undisciplined and disorganized. Ngo Dinh Diem would need time, and would have to use that time wisely. He would also need freedom from French controls.

After the Geneva settlement the SVN perfected its functional independence and quickly came to exercise the prerogatives of sovereign authority free of French interference, more so than any predecessor government (except, of course, the Vietminh). The SVN leaders would need, and would obtain, the financial, political, and moral support of the only other state besides itself that had refused to be encumbered by the terms of the Geneva final declaration: the United States. This was indeed a trump card, but—whatever the agreements or understandings between Diem and the American ambassador in Saigon, Donald Heath, and whatever promises of assistance had been made to the SVN by the administration before August 1954— the majority of politically astute non-Communist Vietnamese regarded the Geneva settlements a defeat for the French and the destruction

[44] *Docs., 1954*, pp. 315-316; *Relazioni internazionali*, Series 2, 18, No. 31 (31 July 1954): 926. (These statements are analyzed in Chapter 23 below.) Tran Van Do resigned as Foreign Minister after the conference (*Econ.*, 24 July 1954), but Diem asked him to continue in this post, which he did.

[45] Cmd. 9239, pp. 7-9.

of their hopes for a unified, non-Communist Vietnam. Unaware, in July, of what they might hope for from the United States or other Western powers, most of the SVN leaders had received a blow to their morale that signified an inauspicious beginning for the exercise of their newly won independence.[46]

[V]

At his news conference on 21 July, President Eisenhower announced that the United States was pursuing the organization of a collective defense system for Southeast Asia.[47] (The Anglo-American study group, which had met in Washington for the first time on 7 July, produced very general agreement upon the shape of the projected alliance by the end of the month. On the 23d, Dulles stated that the new treaty organization would not have a unified command or organized forces similar to those of NATO because the prospective signatories did not share a common heritage or common purposes; in fact, they had many conflicting purposes, only some of which could be reconciled by a collective defense organization. Nor was it clear, as yet, whether Cambodia, Laos, and the SVN would become members of the alliance, although they would be included within the area the alliance would protect.[48] It was understood that Britain opposed the inclusion of the three Indochinese states because of understandings between Eden and Chou and because of the terms of the Geneva final declaration paragraph 5, which the British believed obligated the Indochinese states to refrain from joining a military alliance,[49] but these obligations were not understood to prevent a guarantee of their neutrality.

Ever since Dulles had officially proclaimed the concept of united action (in his Overseas Press Club speech on 29 March), the idea of a NATO-like organization had been studied within the State Department. As we have seen, "united action" came to mean a collective defense—or SEATO, as the organization came to be called—and by the time the Indochinese War ended it was assumed that SEATO would have three principal objects: (1) to deter or to meet direct Communist aggression in the area, particularly Communist Chinese aggression; (2) to strengthen the states of Southeast Asia, particularly in respect of their internal security, in order to prevent subversion; and (3) as a corollary to 1 and 2, to foster economic development and eliminate actual and potential factors leading to instability.[50]

By mid-August it was agreed that the prospective members of

[46] *NYT*, 24 July 1954.
[48] *NYT*, 23, 24, 25 July 1954.
[50] *NYT*, 1 August 1954.
[47] *Docs., 1954*, p. 318.
[49] Bell, *op. cit.*, p. 75.

SEATO would meet in Manila on 6 September to discuss and, presumably, sign the treaty that would bring the alliance into being.[51] Although there had been speculation to the contrary, Hong Kong and Taiwan would not be included within the area of SEATO's protection, and only one of the Colombo powers, Pakistan, had agreed to join SEATO. The Secretary of State had no illusions that India, Burma, or Indonesia would agree to participate in a collective defense, but he had accepted Eden's policy of inviting all the Colombo powers to join. On 30 July, Eden had sent messages of invitation to the Prime Ministers of the five states, explaining the need for SEATO and that their "participation [at the meeting] would do much to determine the nature and policies of the projected organization."[52] John Kotelawala, the Prime Minister of Ceylon, who proposed that the Colombo powers meet in Rangoon to consider SEATO or other alternatives, was interested, India and Indonesia opposed the proposal and subsequently with Burma and Ceylon declined Eden's invitation.[53] Participation in SEATO, Nehru believed, would run counter to the declared policy of neutrality and nonalignment of the Colombo powers.

The foreign ministers of Australia, France, New Zealand, Pakistan, the Philippines, Thailand, Great Britain, and the United States met in Manila from the 6th through the 8th of September. However, the absence of Asian states (other than Thailand, the Philippines, and Pakistan) and the exclusion of Taiwan and Hong Kong would make SEATO considerably less extensive and comprehensive than had been anticipated in some quarters; and the participation of the Western powers tended to produce suspicion, resentment, and criticism among the nonaligned states of Asia. This adverse Asian reaction would have been stronger than it was had it not been for two factors.

First, there was participation by three Asian states, and the proclamation of the Pacific Charter, signed concurrently with the SEATO treaty, reinforced sentiments with which the Colombo powers were heartily in agreement. In the first operative paragraph of the charter the signatories declared that

> In accordance with the provisions of the United Nations Charter, they uphold the principles of equal rights and self-determination of peoples and they will earnestly strive by every peaceful means to promote self-government and to secure the independence of all countries whose people desire it and are able to undertake its responsibilities.[54]

Second, SEATO's powers were considerably limited by the unwillingness of the United States (represented in Manila by Dulles,

[51] *NYT*, 11, 13 August 1954.   [52] E, pp. 161-162.
[53] *NYT*, 8 August 1954.   [54] *Docs.*, 1954, p. 318.

Senator H. Alexander Smith [Rep., N.J.], and Senator Mike Mansfield [Dem., Mont.]) to make firm commitments, formally and in advance, against the aggression SEATO was expected to deter. Such reticence had been signaled by Dulles at his press conference on 23 July, when he had said SEATO could not be like NATO, and a few weeks later it had been revealed that the ANZUS treaty would serve as a model for the SEATO treaty rather than the NATO treaty, in which the commitments of the signatory states were more definite and far-reaching. At the opening session of the SEATO conference, on 6 September, Dulles told the delegates that SEATO's purpose was to warn possible aggressors that "an attack upon the treaty area would occasion a reaction so united, so strong, and so well placed that the aggressor would lose more than it could hope to gain." This could be accomplished by "mobile striking power, plus a strategically placed reserve."[55] The American strategy underlying SEATO, at least at its inception, would be the strategy of the New Look; and no American troop units would be earmarked for SEATO assignment. In addition, there would be no integrated military command, which disappointed some of the delegations at Manila, particularly those of Australia and the Philippines.

The heart of the SEATO treaty, in terms of the obligations of the signatories in the event of an attack, was article IV, paragraph 1, which should be compared with article 5 of the NATO treaty.[56]

SEATO Treaty	*NATO Treaty*
Art. IV (1). Each party recognizes that aggression by means of armed attack in the treaty area against any of the Parties or against any State or territory which the Parties by unanimous agreement may hereafter designate, would endanger its own peace and safety, and agrees that it will in that event act to meet the common danger in accordance with its constitutional processes. . . .	Art. V. The Parties agree that an armed attack against one or more of them in Europe or North America shall be considered an attack against them all; and consequently they agree that, if such an armed attack occurs, each of them, in exercise of the right of individual or collective self-defense recognized by Article 51 of the Charter of the United Nations, will assist the Party or Parties so attacked by taking forthwith, individually or in concert with the other parties, such action as it deems necessary, including the use of armed force, to restore and maintain the security of the North Atlantic area.

[55] *DSB*, 20 September 1954, pp. 391-392.

[56] For the text of the SEATO treaty, see *Docs., 1954*, pp. 319-322; for the text of the NATO treaty, see *Treaties and Other International Acts* (Series 1964); Raymond Dennett and R. K. Turner (eds.), *Documents on American Foreign Relations* (Princeton: Princeton University Press, 1950), XI: 612-615. For analyses of the treaty, see, for example, E. D. Hawkins, in Falk, pp. 168-173; Wolfgang Friedmann, in *ibid.*, p. 300; R. A. Falk, *ibid.*, pp. 388-391; Chatham House Study

Whereas the NATO treaty covers a reasonably well-defined geographical area (Europe and North America, and the areas stipulated in article VI), the SEATO treaty refers to a "treaty area," which is defined in article VIII as the "*general area* of Southeast Asia, including also the entire territories of the Asian parties, and the *general area* of the Southwest Pacific not including the Pacific area north of 21 degrees, 30 minutes, north latitude." The area covered was somewhat indefinite, but Hong Kong and Taiwan were definitely excluded.

The provision in the SEATO treaty whereby the parties might designate states or territories that would come under SEATO "protection" had no analogue in the NATO treaty, and was, as we have seen, a result of understandings at the Geneva Conference affecting the nonparticipation of Laos, Cambodia, and Vietnam in military alliances. A protocol that was concluded at the same time as the SEATO treaty declared that the parties "unanimously designate for the purpose of Article IV the States of Cambodia and Laos and the free territory under the jurisdiction of the State of Vietnam." Krishna Menon criticized the protocol as a serious breach of the Geneva agreements, and Prime Minister Nehru regarded the Treaty, in its entirety, "most unfortunate" and likely to be productive of tensions in the area, thereby reversing the "trend of conciliation" set at Geneva.[57] Later in September the Indian Prime Minister, recalling the "old days" when "great powers" had spheres of influence in Asia, told the House of the People:

> It seems to me, this particular Manila Treaty is looking dangerously in this direction of spheres of influence to be exercised by powerful countries; because, ultimately it is big and powerful countries that will decide and not the two or three weak and small Asian countries that may be allied to them.[58]

The SEATO treaty phrase, "endanger its own peace and safety," is much less forceful than the NATO treaty statement that an attack on one party "shall be considered an attack against them all"; the

---

Group, *Collective Defence in South East Asia* (London: Royal Institute of International Affairs, 1956), pp. 8-14; the brief by the Legal Advisor of the State Department, "The Legality of United States Participation in the Defense of Viet Nam" (4 March 1966), in *American Journal of International Law* 60 (1966): 565, 573-575, 579-580; J. N. Moore and J. L. Underwood, "The Lawfulness of United States Assistance to the Republic of Viet Nam," *Duquesne University Law Review*, 5 (1966-67): 305-308; Lawyers' Committee on American Policy towards Vietnam, *Vietnam and International Law* (Flanders, N. J.: O'Hare Books, 1967), pp. 67-70; and "Memorandum of Law of the Lawyers' Committee," reproduced in the *Congressional Record* (23 September 1965), pp. 5-6.

[57] Bell, *op. cit.*, p. 80, citing *l'Humanité* of 8 September 1954.
[58] George Modelski (ed.), *SEATO: Six Studies* (Melbourne: F. W. Cheshire, 1962), p. 205.

NATO treaty explicitly requires the signatories to regard an attack upon another signatory as a *casus belli*. Whether the signatories must *declare* war or respond in another way is dealt with in the succeeding clause, but each signatory is obligated to consider an attack on another signatory as an attack upon itself. In the SEATO treaty, however, an attack upon one treaty state is to be regarded merely as an act dangerous to "the peace and safety" of each signatory.

By article V of the NATO treaty, an attack upon one of the parties obligates each of the other parties to assist the victim by "such action it deems necessary, including the use of armed force." By article IV of the SEATO treaty, an act of aggression upon a treaty state obligates the parties to "act to meet the common danger in accordance with [their] constitutional processes." While the SEATO clause is less definite than the NATO clause, the NATO treaty's Article V should be read with the Vandenberg Resolution, which conditions United States' participation in NATO and its response to attacks on the NATO area upon the observance of the constitutional processes of the United States, including the constitutional provision pursuant to which Congress declares war.[59] In law, then, the response of the United States to attack upon either the NATO or the SEATO treaty areas may be quite similar, for in both cases the United States, again by law, is obligated to act, but only in accordance with its constitutional processes. In fact, however there are two differences:

1. The United States did not contemplate assignment of its armed forces to SEATO, as it did for NATO. In the former case, as Secretary Dulles said, reliance would be upon a highly mobile strategic reserve. An attack upon a NATO area, where American troops are stationed, would more likely be regarded by Congress as a cause for war than an attack upon Asian areas, where there would be no American troops and hence no American casualties.

2. Inasmuch as thermonuclear weapons could be delivered within minutes, there may be no time to consult Congress, in which case the President of the United States, acting pursuant to the phrase of NATO article V that an attack upon one is an attack upon all, might order instant and massive retaliation without waiting for a declaration of war by Congress. The reader will recall that much of the debate over massive retaliation centered on this point.[60] Yet, thermonuclear war confined to the SEATO treaty area seemed unlikely in 1954.

The United States delegation appended an understanding to the

[59] Department of State, *American Foreign Policy: 1950-55*, Publication No. 6446 (Washington, D.C.: 1957), I: 819-820.

[60] See Senate Foreign Relations Committee, *Report on SEATO* (25 January 1955), in *ibid.*, pp. 929-945.

SEATO treaty that American recognition of "aggression by means of armed attack" (article IV) would be construed to mean "communist aggression," but the United States would consult with the other parties in the event of other forms of aggression.[61] The rationale behind this understanding seems to have been the fear that Pakistan, a SEATO treaty signatory, might—with some color of authority—claim that the SEATO powers should take action in the continuing Indian-Pakistani dispute over Kashmir. Pakistan's usual charge of Indian aggression in Kashmir might occasion a SEATO involvement, to which the United States was resolutely opposed.

BECAUSE INSURGENT operations in the Indochinese War had convinced statesmen who were interested in a collective defense system for Southeast Asia of the need for formal recognition of and response to subversion, as distinct from overt aggression, the SEATO treaty contained such a provision in article IV, paragraph 2:

> If, in the opinion of any of the Parties, the inviolability of the integrity of the territory, or the sovereignty or political independence of any party in the treaty area or of any other State or territory to which the provisions of paragraph 1 of this Article [i.e. article IV] from time to time apply is threatened in any way other than by armed attack or is affected or threatened by any fact or situation which might endanger the peace of the area, the Parties shall consult immediately in order to agree on the measures which should be taken for the common defense.

The terms of this paragraph can become operative upon notification by one of the parties to the others that, *in its opinion*, at least one of the conditions for operability had been satisfied. These conditions, which are considered inviolable, are a signatory's territory, its sovereignty, and its political independence.

The states covered by this provision, "any Party in the treaty area," are Australia, New Zealand, the Philippines, Thailand, and Pakistan (the reader should consult article VIII for the definition of the treaty area). By virtue of the protocol to the treaty, Laos, Cambodia, and the "free territory under the jurisdiction of the State of Vietnam" also were covered.

The threatening actions, or merely threats, against which the states in the treaty area are protected are broadly described: a state may be "*affected* or threatened by any *fact* or *situation* which might endanger the peace of the area."

The breadth of these clauses reflects the great difficulty the draftsmen had in characterizing subversion and indirect aggression. Even

[61] *Docs., 1954*, p. 322.

the U.N. International Law Commission had insurmountable difficulties in attempting to define aggression,[62] and defining the particular
form of the potential threat in Southeast Asia for formal treaty purposes probably was a great deal more difficult than the task undertaken by the U.N. Nevertheless, the "if" clause of paragraph 2
granted wide license for the signatories to claim that at least one
of the preconditions for action had been fulfilled. Given the fulfillment of any precondition, what action would be taken?

The action was simply *consultation* among the parties "in order to
agree on measures which should be taken for the common defense"—
the only obligation under article IV (2) was to *consult* in order to
agree on measures for defense. There are no descriptions of the measures that might be taken; and the parties are limited in only one
respect in determining what measures should be taken: article IV (3)
states that *no action on the territory* of any designated state or territory (i.e. Laos, Cambodia, and the "free territory under the jurisdiction of the State of Vietnam") "shall be taken except at the invitation
or with the consent of the government concerned." No effort was
made to spell out the kind of agreement that is necessary among the
parties before one or before several of them can take measures "for
the common defense." Should the agreement be based upon a unanimous or upon a majority vote of the parties to the SEATO treaty?
What would be the effects of acquiescence—or of outright opposition
—by one or more parties to the proposed measures? The answers to
such questions were certainly no clearer in 1954 than in the 1960s.
Subsequently a "committee of security experts," composed of members of the national police forces and intelligence services of the
parties, was established[63] and given the task of identifying, assessing,
and exchanging information on the nature and extent of Communist
subversion in the treaty area. But still there has been no real clarification of the nature of acts that would bring article IV (2) into operation. The provision remains controversial.

If SEATO members such as Australia, the Philippines, and Thailand, who were particularly concerned about security, did not get
a precise American military commitment, the Asian members did not
get specific promises of American economic aid. Although administration officials (Secretaries Dulles and Wilson, for example) had
underlined the importance of economic development in the Southeast
Asia states in order to render them more resistant to communism, the
United States delegation and the British and Australian delegations were prepared to agree to no more than the very general, un-

[62] Julius Stone, *Aggression and World Order* (Berkeley: University of California
Press, 1958).
[63] Modelski, *op. cit.*, p. 32.

specific wording of article III, under which the parties undertook to "cooperate with one another in the further development of economic measures, including technical assistance, designed . . . to promote economic progress and social well-being."

But perhaps it was not so much American as British reluctance that prevented SEATO from becoming a better instrument for economic assistance in its early days. At his press conference on 24 August, Dulles had suggested that SEATO might be based upon two treaties, one economic, the other military.[64] Presumably the economic treaty would have spelled out, at least in greater detail, how economic and technical assistance would be administered by the SEATO secretariat. Britain, it was understood, opposed a broadly conceived economic development scheme that might duplicate or conflict with the functions of the Colombo Plan. In addition, SEATO's Asian membership was too limited for the treaty organization to be a useful agency for the distribution and administration of aid.[65]

AFTER RETURNING to the United States from Manila, Mr. Dulles delivered an address on nationwide radio and television, on 15 September, in which he briefly explained the objects of SEATO and the terms of the SEATO treaty. Referring to the separate protocol, which "extends the Treaty benefits to Cambodia and Laos and the free territory of Viet-Nam," the secretary said:

> The Indochina armistice created obstacles to these three countries' becoming actual parties to the treaty at the present time. The treaty will, however, to the extent that is practicable, throw a mantle of protection over these young nations.

> This Manila Pact represents a considerable accomplishment. I would have been glad if it had come earlier. But it is definitely better now than never.[66]

Dulles directed assurances to two audiences: first, to budget-conscious officials and congressmen and, more generally, to the supporters of the New Look in the United States, and second, to the nonaligned, post-colonial states. To the first audience, he declared that the treaty would not require the government to make material changes in its military plans. The possibility of creating a joint military force was discussed at Manila, Dulles said, but

> I explained that the United States' responsibilities were so vast and so far-flung that we believed that we would serve best, not by earmarking forces for particular areas of the Far East, but by devel-

[64] *NYT*, 25 August 1954.   [65] Modelski, *op. cit.*, pp. 38, 136.
[66] *DSB*, 27 September 1954, pp. 431-433 (quotation on p. 432).

oping the deterrent of mobile striking power, plus strategically placed reserves. . . . [American military plans] already call for our maintaining at all times powerful naval and air forces in the Western Pacific capable of striking at any aggressor by means and at places of our choosing. The deterrent power we thus create can protect many as effectively as it protects one.[67]

The Secretary of State did not, however, explain how naval and air forces would deter the subversion against which the parties might take measures under article IV (2) of the SEATO treaty. China—but not necessarily other national insurgents—*might* be deterred. It was doubtful whether the mobile strategic reserves envisaged under the New Look were capable of meeting extensive insurgent operations in Southeast Asia. But, as we have seen, the administration had declared that American policy would rely upon local troops rather than American combat troops.

Dulles then assured the nonaligned states that whatever measures might be taken against threats and subversive activity, they would "never involve intervention in the purely internal affairs of another state." Later in the address he said:

> The Manila Pact is directed against no government, against no nation, and against no people. It is directed only against aggression. The fact that the Communists find that objectionable is tragically revealing of their ambitions.[68]

These assertions were, in part, a response to condemnations of SEATO by the Soviet Union and the C.P.R. and in part to criticisms from nonaligned statesmen. Krishna Menon, as we have seen, called the protocol a violation of the Geneva agreements and SEATO a "modern version of a Protectorate." SEATO, in his words, was "an organization of some imperial powers and some other powers who may have interest in it to join together in order to protect a territory which they say may be in danger. We are part of that territory and we say we do not want to be protected by this organization."[69]

Subsequently, on 1 February 1955, the Senate consented to ratification of the SEATO treaty by a vote of 82 to 1 and the President ratified it on 4 February 1955. Thailand had been the first member state to ratify the treaty and deposit its ratification with the government of the Philippines, on 2 December 1954. The treaty came into force 19 February 1955, when all of the remaining signatories had deposited their instruments of ratification at Manila.

[67] *Ibid.*
[68] *Ibid.*, p. 433.
[69] Quoted in Modelski, *op. cit.*, p. 65.

Three of the SEATO treaty signatories, France, Britain, and the United States, which had been participants in the Geneva Conference, together with the other SEATO states, had in effect, by virtue of the protocol to the treaty, guaranteed the Geneva agreements in this respect: overt aggression under article IV (1) of the treaty or any threat of the kind specified in article IV (2) against Laos, Cambodia, or the "free territory" of Vietnam would obligate the SEATO parties to respond either by consultations or by action in accordance with their constitutional processes. For the United States, however, only "communist aggression" gave rise to obligations under the treaty. The administration had refused to agree to proposals at Geneva for a guarantee of the Indochinese settlements in which the United States might be associated, as a joint guarantor, with either the Soviet Union or the C.P.R. In SEATO, the United States assumed the role of a joint guarantor, but only with non-Communist states and only against Communist aggression. It had made no commitment guaranteeing any terms of the Geneva agreements. However, inasmuch as SEATO represented the instrument by means of which the United States would respond to renewed Communist aggression in Southeast Asia, including aggression against any of the three protocol states, the Southeast Asia Treaty Organization was a particular kind of guarantee of the Geneva agreements.

Chapter 20

THE FRENCH REJECT EDC

[I]

Upon his return from Geneva, Mendès-France learned that a special panel he had appointed in June, composed of Bourgès-Manoury (a pro-EDC Radical) and Minister of Defense Koenig (anti-EDC) had not succeeded in reconciling opposing views on the EDC treaty, and from 11 through 13 August the Premier presented his own proposals. He intended to ask the EDC signatories to accept various changes in the treaty, he told his cabinet;[1] but the changes the Premier submitted would—if adopted—profoundly affect the European Defense Community. Specifically, Mendès-France proposed:

1. To suspend, for eight years, the operation of the supranational provision, and, more specifically, to suspend those supranational decisions of the board of commissioners that, in the opinion of any signatory, affected the vital interests of its state (such suspension, however, would be subject to mediation);

2. To grant every signatory the right to withdraw from the EDC if either the United States or Britain withdrew its troops from continental Europe or if Germany were unified;

3. To limit the troops integrated in the European army to those stationed in particular zones (principally on German Federal Republic territory);

4. To reserve for the armed forces of each signatory, for four years, the right to consider and grant promotions in military rank; but this provision would apply only to states that already had an army. (Because West Germany would be the only EDC member that did not have an army, only the Federal Republic would lose jurisdiction over military promotions.)[2]

Before submitting these rather drastic proposals to his cabinet, Mendès-France had attempted, unsuccessfully, to effect a compromise among the conflicting points of view by offering to amend the treaty in a few, comparatively minor particulars. The only chance for the treaty's success in the Assembly, he had concluded, was by way of amendments that vitiated the principles of supranationality and national equality upon which the Treaty of Paris was based. Despite such proposals, Koenig and two other Gaullists resigned from

[1] *NYT*, 15, 16 August 1954.
[2] *NYT*, 23 August 1954. As submitted in Brussels, the Premier's proposals appeared in the form of a draft protocol. *Docs., 1954*, pp. 90-100.

the government. Then, on 19 August, the Premier went to Brussels to confer with the EDC signatories and British and American representatives, but there his proposals were received with open hostility. The other signatories refused to countenance such a drastic alteration in the EDC concept. At the very least, it was believed, adoption of the Mendès-France proposals would require the signatories to resubmit the treaty to their parliaments for ratification.

The Brussels Conference seems to have been unpleasant for all the participants. Many of France's allies felt that Mendès-France's proposals were another ploy in a long series of French demands for concessions or special conditions, or another tactic for delaying EDC's ratification. But now the allies would brook no delay, and the Premier later recalled that he was sure his fellow delegates believed he was acting in bad faith. For example, David K. E. Bruce, the American delegate, was still convinced there was a majority in the National Assembly for an unamended EDC treaty, while the Premier insisted the treaty could not get through the Assembly. Dulles cabled Mendès-France, urging him to make concessions and modify his demands, but the Premier refused to alter the substance of his proposed amendments.[3] In the opinion of many delegates at Brussels, he appeared stubborn, even disagreeable, and Paul Henri Spaak of Belgium tried to conciliate the French, with only partial success.

Mendès-France's difficulties, in fact, were not only with the allied delegations but even with the French integrationists, such as Robert Schuman, who bitterly opposed the approach adopted by the Premier. Both Schuman and André Philip made their views public and declared the Premier's "compromise" unacceptable.[4] All this put the Premier in an awkward position and perhaps accounts, in part, for his obduracy. He had been attacked by the anti-EDC Gaullists for his position on EDC, even after the formulation of his "compromise"; now he was attacked by the pro-EDC M.R.P. He therefore made a decision he apparently did not care to make, because he had to resign himself to the defeat of his compromise plan. He would submit the unamended treaty to the Assembly but he would not advocate its ratification; he would not make its ratification a matter of confidence.[5]

The Brussels Conference adjourned on 22 August in complete disagreement, with the delegates exchanging recriminations. The communiqué announced that the delegates, despite "long discussion of the changes which, according to the French Government, should be made in the Treaty of Paris, . . . were not able to reach agree-

[3] NYT, 23 August 1954.
[4] Daniel Lerner and Raymond Aron (eds.), France Defeats EDC (New York: Praeger, 1957), p. 160.
[5] NYT, 25 August 1954; E, p. 166.

ment."[6] The communiqué then listed the aims of the six governments, which it said had remained unchanged: contributing to the unification of Germany while avoiding its neutralization, furthering European cooperation, and working out a political and economic formula for European integration.[7]

Mendés-France returned to Paris and made a complete report of the Brussels negotiations to the cabinet and parliamentary commissions, giving his ministers the impression that he believed the treaty would be defeated. On 26 August the Premier stated that he would favor German rearmament but not the form of rearmament contemplated in the treaty. He would ask the National Assembly to vote on the unamended treaty but he would not recommend its approval, nor would he make the issue a matter of confidence, which might entail his resignation.[8] Realizing that rejection of the treaty was almost certain, EDC proponents prepared a motion to adjourn debate and to instruct the government to resume negotiations with the other EDC treaty signatories. EDC opponents, however, countered with a motion to pass on to other business, which had priority over the motion to adjourn, and the Assembly took up the procedural question, which masked the question of substance.[9] On 30 August the deputies voted to pass on to other business: 319 votes for, 264 votes against, 43 abstentions.[10] The French National Assembly had in effect rejected EDC. Three ministers immediately resigned from the cabinet (Bourgès-Manoury, Hughes, and Petit) but the Mendès-France government survived.

Dulles termed the EDC rejection a "shattering blow" to American policy, and there were similar reactions throughout Europe. Fortunately, however, NATO statesmen maintained a proper perspective on EDC's defeat in France, and the Secretary of State decided not to interrupt preparations for the Manila Conference. Just before his departure for the Philippines, Dulles warned against "any abrupt or ill-considered action" by Congress or administration officials that might tend to aggravate relations between France and the NATO powers.[11] Eden took the initiative in finding a practical and workable solution, advocating proposals the British Foreign Office had developed and was developing, together with the willing cooperation of

[6] *Docs., 1954*, p. 89.

[7] Concurrently with the communiqué, the signatories of the EDC treaty (but not the French government) published a declaration interpreting the EDC treaty. *Docs., 1954*, pp. 100-104.

[8] Lerner and Aron, *op. cit.*, p. 161. Also see Stanley Hoffman's cogent analysis, "The Postmortems," in Lerner and Aron, pp. 165-196.

[9] *NYT*, 31 August 1954.

[10] *JO*, 31 August 1954, pp. 4471, 4473-4474 (sess. of 30 August).

[11] R. P. Stebbins, *The United States in World Affairs, 1954* (New York: Harper & Row, 1956), p. 151.

Dulles, Mendès-France, Adenauer, and other Western leaders. These efforts by the end of the year, resulted in the establishment of the Western European Union.[12] The Federal Republic of Germany, which became fully sovereign, would participate on a basis of equality in a European collective security scheme, and its right to rearm would be subject to limitations in which the Bonn government acquiesced.

THE DRAMATIC story of EDC's defeat, which its supporters called the "Crime of August 30,"[13] and the equally dramatic efforts of Western diplomats, particularly British diplomats, to salvage the situation might well be the subject of an extensive independent study, but they detain us here because the issue of EDC was intimately related to the issue of Indochina, both within the policymaking apparatus of France, Britain, the United States, and even the Soviet Union, and between the leading participants in the Geneva Conference. We have seen the ways in which the EDC project and incidental questions were connected with the various issues raised, at one time or another, at Geneva. Only one question remains that requires attention: Did Premier Mendès-France make a deal with the Soviet Foreign Minister—the defeat of EDC in exchange for concessions that would permit an acceptable Geneva settlement by his deadline date of 20 July? Had the Premier engaged in the kind of "global bargaining" Bidault had rejected in February?[14] There is no evidence that Mendès-France made such a deal, but evidence of this sort certainly would not have been made public. I propose, therefore, to examine the circumstantial evidence and the arguments for and against the hypothesis of a Geneva–EDC deal.

1. In his investiture speech, the Premier had indicated he would soon submit proposals on EDC, implying that he would support an amended treaty. Except for his talk with Bedell Smith on 23 June, at which he said he could get the treaty through the Assembly if he achieved a success at Geneva, he had insisted that the treaty must be amended. He instructed Massigli to tell Eden that an unamended treaty could not get through the Assembly, and he warned Dulles, on 14 July, that the EDC did not have a majority, but apparently he did not convince the Secretary of State. That he failed to do so can be attributed either to Dulles's unwillingness to accept the Premier's assessment or to the Premier's prudence in not trying to convince the secretary of an unpleasant truth. According to Mr. Eisenhower's account, the Premier gave other officials the impression

[12] E, pp. 168 ff.
[13] Lerner and Aron, op. cit., p. 162.
[14] NYT, 24 February 1954.

that he would seek to amend the treaty *after* its ratification. In any case, Mendès-France said he would submit amendments to the EDC, and he made such statements long before he met Molotov. Indeed, French deputies and diplomats believed the Premier intended to suggest amendments. If the United States government was surprised by Mendès-France's move in merely proposing amendments, there had been a failure in communication between Paris and Washington, and this failure can be attributed to one or several causes.

a. The Premier deliberately misled the United States.

b. The pro-EDC forces (M.R.P. deputies, for example), which monopolized the communications channels to the American government and the American press, consistently took an unjustifiably optimistic view of the chances of an unamended treaty. The supporters of the EDC in the United States wanted to hear good news and listened only to the "inside information" from their M.R.P. sources.

c. The warnings from the Premier or from those in France who were skeptical of EDC's chances were dismissed by the State Department and other administration officials as the opinion of those who either opposed EDC or were not prepared to support it. Such attitudes might have been favored by the anti-French bias that had been generated during the Indochina crisis of the preceding months. Among the European integrationists in the executive branch in Washington, there was a continuing mistrust of French tactics and delays vis-à-vis the EDC.

d. It is possible that some administration officials were not surprised by the Premier's decision to attempt to amend the treaty. (The reader should distinguish the procedural decision to pursue a policy of amending EDC from the *substance* of the proposed amendments; some individuals were disturbed merely because Mendès-France sought to amend the treaty; many more were shocked by the content of his proposed amendments.) Privately, American officials may have expected amendments but could not announce their expectations, which might have produced sentiment in Paris for further delays and more amendments.

In my opinion, the Premier did not deliberately mislead the United States when he suggested amendments to the EDC treaty. Although he may not have been entirely candid with Bedell Smith, his public statements should have apprised American officials of his probable tactics in handling the EDC matter in Paris. I doubt that all administration officials were surprised by the Premier's decision to propose amendments. Unquestionably, there was a lack of understanding and irritation, surprise, and even confusion in Washington, but this, in my view, was a result of bad intelligence. The M.R.P. deputies, most

of whom supported the EDC, had been in control of the Quai d'Orsay
for a long time and had well-established contacts with American
officials and correspondents, but there were no M.R.P. ministers in
the Mendès-France government. Moreover, most M.R.P. members of
the Assembly distinctly opposed the Premier and distrusted his
position on EDC. Thus, in August, as M.R.P. deputies or spokesmen
were still the principal sources of opinion and intelligence for the
administration and the American press, it is not surprising that such
reports were somewhat inaccurate and biased. Inasmuch as the
Premier had indicated he would seek to amend the treaty before he
had even met Molotov, the mere fact that he suggested amendments
in August neither proves nor disproves the hypothesis of a deal between Molotov and Mendès-France.

2. The substance or content of the amendments Mendès-France
proposed at Brussels shocked the allies and the EDC supporters,
which, if adopted, would have destroyed EDC's central concept of
supranationality and required the signatories to treat West Germany
on a basis other than complete equality. The signatories, moreover,
would have had to resubmit the treaty to their parliaments for
ratification. The drastic nature of the proposed amendments, therefore, seems to provide some basis for the assertion that Mendès-France
had made a deal with the Soviets, this being his way of fulfilling his
end of the bargain. This is, of course, a possibility. Although the
Premier may have warned both Dulles and Eden that an unamended
treaty could not win in the French Assembly, he may not have told
them the nature of the amendments he had in mind. Certainly
Britain was not prepared to support the Premier's proposals.[15] Prime
Minister Churchill and Mr. Eden urged him to accept the EDC treaty
with the Spaak "interpretations" and get this version through the
Assembly. The delegations of the signatories were quite disturbed
by the Premier's attitude at Brussels.

But Mendès-France sought to conciliate the pro-EDC and anti-
EDC factions *in France* by means of his proposals, and hoped the
allies would understand. Perhaps he should have understood that
he would meet opposition at Brussels—that for the pro-EDC allies
(except possibly Italy) his proposals were the crowning exasperation
of a long series of exasperations. Whether or not his assessment of
the allies' reaction was realistic, he seems to have felt his proposals
deserved more sympathetic consideration than they received. His
personal attitudes toward the EDC, which are important for understanding his expectations at Brussels, his irritation with his allies, and
his subsequent decision to remain neutral during the Assembly de-

[15] E, pp. 166-167.

bate, derive from the fact that Mendès-France was neither an opponent nor an avid supporter of EDC; he believed West Germany must soon regain full sovereignty, and would inevitably rearm, but he hoped to attach limitations upon the privilege of rearmament. He had some faith in the efficacy of European integration, particularly in several economic sectors, but he was not enthusiastic for military integration. In short, Mendès-France, aware that EDC was a divisive issue in French politics, felt (justifiably in my opinion) that it was not worth the bitterness, the quarrels, and the governmental instability it produced.

Raymond Aron has said that not since the Dreyfus affair had France been riven by such a controversy,[16] and a great deal can be said for the argument that France's allies—particularly the United States—should not have pressed for the EDC when they could see what this was doing within France. EDC generated disunity within the Western alliance and gave rise to permanent resentments. If Mendès-France, as reported, said that France had been dragged through the mud at Brussels[17]—and allowance is made for the fact that this was only one of many bitter statements to which the Brussels Conference gave rise—it represented the Premier's feelings. The allies did not appreciate the difficulty of his position, nor the merit of his reservations about EDC's efficacy, nor the merit of *some* of the arguments of the anti-EDC forces.

The amendments the French Premier submitted to his cabinet in mid-August, and at Brussels one week later, *could* have been the by-product of a deal with Molotov, but they *could* have been the work of a politician-statesman seeking to conciliate the pro-EDC and anti-EDC forces in France. Though none too enthusiastic about EDC, Mendès-France understood that its rejection might do irreparable harm to the Western alliance, and whatever his views on the desirability of working for a détente with the Soviet Union, he certainly did not believe a weakened West was prerequisite for a détente. I am inclined to believe that Mendès-France's reactions to the Brussels Conference genuinely reflected his belief that his proposals were not drastic nor designed to bring about EDC's rejection. This, of course, is opinion; but the only definite conclusion we can draw from the Premier's proposed amendments is that they support either the hypothesis of a Molotov–Mendès-France deal or the contrary hypothesis, that no such deal had been made.

3. Although Premier Mendès-France agreed to submit an unamended treaty to the National Assembly for debate, his government would

---

[16] Lerner and Aron, *op. cit.*, p. 10.
[17] *NYT*, 25 August 1954.

remain neutral; he did not make the vote on the EDC a matter of confidence. But, had he made the issue a vote of confidence—it might be argued—it was quite possible that some of the deputies who had, in effect, voted against EDC might have felt constrained to vote for the treaty rather than see the Mendès-France government fall. Because the Premier had won acclaim after having negotiated a cease-fire in Indochina, EDC might not have been defeated if he had placed his personal prestige on the line. It would be well, however, not to exaggerate the Premier's popularity. He had achieved peace in Indo-china, but not a peace based upon victory.

As he himself had said, parts of the Geneva agreements were "cruel," and many deputies believed he need not have agreed to the trans-ference to the DRVN of Hanoi and Haiphong nor to the neutraliza-tion of Laos and Cambodia. Because it was relatively easy for a Premier to expend his political capital in the Fourth Republic, al-though most EDC supporters in the United States would not ap-preciate this fact of political life, Mendès-France may well have felt that he should not risk whatever good will he had won from his Geneva "success." Nor was he such a strong supporter of EDC to be-lieve it was worth jeopardizing his government. Moreover, there were many precedents for governmental neutrality on controversial questions, which had been a successful technique for sustaining vari-ous governments. René Pleven, for example, when he had been Pre-mier (1950-1951 and 1951-1952), maintained neutrality on the issues of electoral reform and state subsidies for church schools, and his government had survived votes on these questions.[18] In the Fourth Republic it was the mediator who was most successful, and we should not condemn the Premier for using this tactic to secure his own and his government's political future.

The French Premier may not have provided the strong pro-EDC leadership the Eisenhower administration would have liked to have seen, but this does not mean Mendès-France had made a deal with Molotov to refrain from giving the treaty the support that France's allies thought it deserved. Other tenable hypotheses support the French government's neutrality on 30 August.

4. Although the significant concessions of the Communist delega-tions at Geneva after the ministers returned in early June were made by Molotov or at Molotov's behest

a. Moving the demarcation line north from the 13th to the 17th parallel,

---

[18] P. M. Williams, *Politics in Post-War France* (2d ed.; London: Longmans, Green, 1958), p. 190.

b. Agreement upon all-Vietnamese elections two years from the date of the cease-fire,

c. Granting the governments of Cambodia and Laos the right to call for foreign military assistance if their security was threatened,

d. Agreement upon the composition of the ISC and to exceptions in the rule of unanimity,

these concessions are entirely compatible with explanations other than that of a deal with the French Premier.

The leaders of the Soviet Union may very well have wanted to end the Indochinese War, particularly if it held risk of a confrontation between the United States and themselves. Moreover, the settlement was based upon the victory of the Communist DRVN. Although the Vietminh settled for less than it might have expected (barring United States intervention), it could have been persuaded that the partition of Vietnam was temporary, and all available evidence suggests that, in fact, it believed this. The Vietminh may even have expected support from the Soviet Union in executing the provisions of the Geneva agreements that would ensure the unification of Vietnam.

It is undoubtedly true that European questions, particularly European collective security, German rearmament and unification, and Soviet relations with the NATO allies, were given greater weight than Soviet-Vietminh relations in the strategic thinking of the Soviet leaders. They would, presumably, attach greater importance to the defeat of EDC than to the unification of Vietnam under DRVN control. But callousness toward the values and interests of a small ally, which is typical of most great powers, did not mean Molotov succeeded in closing a deal with Mendès-France. The Soviet Foreign Minister bought a favorable peace settlement at Geneva with Vietminh currency, but it is unlikely that he bought a defeat of EDC with the same currency.

5. It has been suggested that Molotov knew the EDC treaty was *in articulo mortis* and hence need not have entered into an agreement with the French Premier to bring about a result that was, in any event, inevitable.[19] But this is not necessarily true. The Kremlin leaders, it seems to me, had to accept the *possibility* of an EDC victory; they could not assume that French rejection of the treaty was inevitable. Anti-EDC propaganda from the Soviet Union intensified through August, and on 24 July and 4 August the Soviet Union had dispatched notes to the Western governments requesting an all-

[19] Coral Bell, *Survey of International Affairs, 1954* (London: Oxford University Press, 1957), p. 72.

European conference on collective security.[20] This démarche was widely regarded as an attempt to undermine the position of EDC's supporters within France. Even if we assume that the Soviet leaders
sincerely wanted a détente, and that the prospect of a unified and
rearmed Germany profoundly disturbed them, their notes of July and
August nevertheless appeared aimed at securing EDC's defeat. The
fact that their motives for seeking this goal may seem somewhat justified from the point of view of a dispassionate Western analyst in the
late 1960s does not alter the fact that they wanted EDC rejected and
sought to influence French political processes to accomplish this goal.
That they went to great lengths during the month of August suggests
that they believed EDC still had a chance of success. That Soviet propaganda was so intense in August, *after* an alleged Molotov–Mendès-
France deal, suggests:

 a. There was no deal;

 b. Soviet leaders had no faith in Mendès-France's word or no
confidence in his ability to secure the defeat of EDC (Why, then,
would Molotov have made such a deal in the first place?); or

 c. The Soviet propaganda and the proposals for a European conference were meant to assist the French Premier in his efforts to
secure EDC's rejection by the National Assembly.

 In determining which of these alternatives applied, we should note
that, until September, the French Communists refrained from attack-
ing the Premier. Of course, the leaders of the French Communists
might have assumed that by remaining silent they would, in the end,
contribute to EDC's defeat. Overt verbal attacks upon the Premier
or the treaty might have caused those deputies who were anti-Communist and either anti-EDC or merely antipathetic to EDC to
abstain on the vote, or even to vote for the treaty because of their
anti-Communist sentiments.

 6. Like Eden, the French Premier believed that European and American relations with the Soviet Union could be improved. In August,
Mendès-France had declared that the Geneva settlements represented a breach in the "wall of distrust" between East and West.[21]
The Soviet notes of late July and early August appealed to those in
France who favored negotiations with the Soviet Union and to those
who favored delaying action on the EDC. The *New York Times*
reported that Mendès-France felt some Assembly members wanted

---

[20] *Further Correspondence between Her Majesty's Government in the United
Kingdom and the Soviet Union regarding Collective Security*, Misc. No. 26 (1954),
Cmd. 9281 (London: Her Majesty's Stationery Office, 1954), pp. 2-7; *DSB*, 20
September 1954, pp. 398-401; *Docs., 1954*, pp. 241-245.
[21] *NYT*, 7 August 1954.

another attempt to work with the Soviets (such as that at Geneva) before France committed herself to EDC.[22]

Could the Premier have decided in July that, by agreeing to a deal with Molotov, he would get assistance in securing an acceptable Indochina settlement, and that this arrangement would persuade the Russians of his good intentions and his willingness to believe their professions of détente? The Premier's action from October through December, when he worked closely with European diplomats in fashioning over a dozen documents establishing the Western European Union, granting West Germany sovereignty and the right (subject to limitation) to rearm, settling the Saar question, and admitting West Germany to NATO make it difficult to accept an affirmative answer to this question. In December he secured the ratification of these documents in the National Assembly, in some cases by making the issues votes of confidence. The Soviets sustained their efforts to prevent the success of these complex but fruitful Western negotiations. Mendès-France, however, significantly contributed to frustrating these efforts while continuing to profess his desire for an easing of East-West tensions; and he was consistent in his plans to achieve an important place for France in the councils of the West. He could not fulfill his designs and, among other things, oppose the British plan for the Western European Union. Although the WEU did not have the EDC's potential for supranational development, it was nevertheless a remarkable achievement as a collective defense effort, particularly after the dark September days when pessimism among the NATO leaders was pervasive.

Mendès-France supported the WEU project, and managed to obtain what he regarded as firm British and American commitments to maintain troops in Europe. This would counterbalance West German influence in the union. He also saw to it that German rearmament and remilitarization was limited, and he obtained a reasonably favorable settlement of the Saar question. There was a period in December, after the Assembly voted down a crucial protocol for the revision of the Brussels treaty, which created the WEU, when the prestige of France appeared to have suffered a severe blow. But the Premier put the fate of his government in the balance, and during the last days of December, with successive votes of confidence, the most important products of the late autumn negotiations were ratified by the Assembly. The Brussels treaty was ratified by a vote of 287 to 260, subject to an unwritten agreement that, along with the execution of provisions of the treaty, the government would make an effort to reach a *modus vivendi* with the Communist states.[23]

[22] *NYT*, 18 August 1954.
[23] Stebbins, *op. cit.*, p. 180.

The December debates in the Assembly showed how deeply the Premier had alienated the M.R.P. by his August proposals to amend the EDC and his subsequent actions during the EDC debate: in mid-December two-thirds of the M.R.P. voted against the Brussels treaty's protocol to show its resentment toward Mendès-France. It would have been strange if the Premier had made a deal with Molotov in July and his M.R.P. enemies had not heard of it and almost immediately used it to destroy the Premier. Conversely, Mendès-France would certainly have understood that were he to make a deal with the Russians and news of the deal were leaked, his political career might well be ended. Moreover, in view of the current anti-Communist state of American public and official opinion, news of such a deal would do irreparable harm to Franco-American relations. It seems to me that Mendès-France would not have taken such risks, even though an honorable peace in Indochina was prerequisite for the survival of his government.

Post-Geneva events, in my opinion, lend themselves to explanations or interpretations other than the hypothesis of a deal between Molotov and Mendès-France. Stated simply, the best hypothesis is that Mendès-France was a politician and did not want his government to fall because of an issue for which he had little enthusiasm. But the Premier was also a statesman; he understood that EDC had divided French opinion and had embittered relations among deputies of the Assembly. He did not feel that an unamended treaty was worth the dissension it had caused; hence he proposed rather drastic amendments. Even then, he did not satisfy the R.P.F. (the Gaullists), and he alienated the M.R.P. If the Brussels conferees had agreed to his amendments, he probably would have made the treaty a question of confidence at the end of the debate. But they had not agreed, and thereby, the Premier seems to have felt, they had shown little appreciation of his difficulties and the political situation in France. He therefore felt justified in remaining neutral when the crucial vote was taken, although his tactics won him the enmity of the M.R.P.

In February 1955 the pro-EDC forces voted with the opposition in the vote on France's North African policy, which caused the fall of the Mendès-France government. But such political enemies, who nursed long-standing resentment against what they regarded as the opportunistic chicanery of the Premier, would have exploited news of a Molotov–Mendès-France deal much earlier. They did not—perhaps because they had not heard of such a deal. But the M.R.P. had many sources of information at the Quai d'Orsay, which it had dominated for many years, and it would be most surprising if some M.R.P. deputies had not been told of the deal, had such a deal been made. This would have been particularly true of the Mendès-France government, which was constantly troubled with "leaks" during the summer of 1954.

It is my conclusion that Premier Mendès-France made no deal with Molotov for the defeat of the EDC treaty. The reader will appreciate that this conclusion is based upon inferences from circumstantial evidence, but—for the present—the contrary conclusion, which asserts the existence of such a deal, must also be based upon that kind of reasoning and that kind of evidence.

PART III

The Geneva Agreements: Analysis and Implementation

Chapter 21

THE VIETNAM CEASE-FIRE AGREEMENT

[I]

The Agreement on the Cessation of Hostilities in Vietnam came into force at midnight, Geneva time, on 22 July 1954 (47),[1] having been signed two days earlier by Brigadier General Henri Delteil for the commander in chief of the French Union forces in Indochina and by Ta Quang Buu for the commander in chief of the People's Army of Vietnam. The document comprised six chapters, forty-seven articles, and an annex that delineated the boundaries of the provisional assembly areas and the location of the provisional military demarcation line and the demilitarized zone. The conference's final declaration "took note" of the terms of the cease-fire agreement. (For a fuller understanding of the Geneva settlement on Vietnam, appropriate paragraphs of the final declaration should be read along with the agreement.)

The final declaration was not signed; and neither the SVN nor the United States delegation associated their governments with its terms. The SVN delegation lodged a formal protest against various elements of the settlement, and the United States government, through Bedell Smith, issued a rather elaborate declaration of its views on the principal documents produced at the conference.[2] The heads of the Laotian, Cambodian, and DRVN delegations did not expressly associate themselves with the final declaration. Thus five of the nine delegations at the Geneva Conference did not expressly or unreservedly commit their governments to the terms of the final declaration. Eden, however, formally associated the British government with the text of the declaration; Mendès-France approved its terms; Chou En-lai and Molotov "agreed" to it. Thus ministers of four of the five great powers verbally approved the declaration, although the responses of Chou and Molotov were as ambiguous as they were terse.

At the outset, then, we are confronted with important questions about the binding effect of the two principal documents that embodied the Vietnamese settlement negotiated at Geneva. How, and in exactly what ways, were the signatories of the cease-fire agreement bound? How, and in what ways, were the conference participants

---

[1] The numbers in parentheses refer to the article numbers of the cease-fire agreement for Vietnam; *FD*, followed by a numeral, designates paragraphs of the final declaration.

[2] A record of the final plenary session appears in Cmd. 9239, Misc. No. 20 (1954), *Further Documents relating to the Discussion of Indo-China at the Geneva Conference* (London: Her Majesty's Stationery Office, 1965), pp. 5-9.

obligated to act under the terms of the final declaration and the supplementary declarations or statements? Both questions are obviously related since the declaration and the agreement on the cessation of hostilities are related. Another question of vital importance is the juridical status of the final declaration. Was it an "unsigned treaty," whose terms the conference participants were obligated to observe, or was it merely a "minute" of the conference? I shall put off dealing with these questions until I have had an opportunity to analyze the terms of the documents in greater detail.

Paragraph 6 of the final declaration read, in part: "The Conference recognizes that the essential purpose of the agreement relating to Viet Nam is to settle military questions with a view to ending hostilities." Fulfillment of the essentially military purpose of the settlement was the primary responsibility of the signatories of the cease-fire agreement, namely, the commanders in chief of the PAVN and the French Union forces in Indochina. The terms of the agreement applied generally to the armed forces of both parties (24), although the commanders were directly responsible for executing the provisions of the agreement (27).

With respect to the military aspects of the settlement, the duties of the commanders in chief were of obvious importance and were detailed in the cease-fire agreement. Thus the commanders were required to "order and enforce the complete cessation of all hostilities in Viet Nam by all armed forces under their control" (10). They were also responsible for ensuring that persons under their command who violated the cease-fire agreement would be suitably punished (22), and they were to take "all steps and make all arrangements necessary to ensure full compliance with all the provisions of the present Agreement by all elements and military personnel under their command" (27).

The armistice was to be simultaneous throughout Vietnam (11), although, because of the time required to transmit cease-fire orders to the lowest echelons of combatants, the final effective date varied according to region. Thus a complete cease-fire would be in effect in northern Vietnam by 27 July, in central Vietnam by 1 August, and in southern Vietnam by 11 August. After the cease-fire became effective in northern Vietnam, the parties, through their commanders in chief, undertook not to engage in large-scale offensive action in any part of Indochina. Air forces based in northern Vietnam were not to be committed outside that sector (this provision affected only the French, of course, since the DRVN had no air force).

After the cease-fire, the forces of the belligerents were to regroup in two principal regroupment zones, which were divided by a demarcation line at about the 17th parallel. This military demarcation line was provisional (1)[3]; but the forces of the PAVN were to regroup north of the line after their withdrawal from areas they controlled south of the line, and the French Union forces were to regroup south of the line. An Annex to the agreement and an attached reference map located the line precisely. A demilitarized zone, not wider than 5 kilometers, was established on each side of the demarcation line (1). This strip of territory would act as a buffer zone between the regroupment zones, assisting in preventing incidents that might lead to a resumption of hostilities. Military forces, supplies, and equipment were to be withdrawn from the demilitarized zone within twenty-five days after the entry into force of the cease-fire agreement (5).

Civil administration and relief in the zones on either side of the demarcation line were made the responsibility of the commanders in chief of the parties of the respective regroupment zones (8), and the commanders in chief would determine the number of persons who were to be permitted to enter the demilitarized zone for administrative purposes. No persons, however, military or civilian, were to be permitted to enter the demilitarized zone except those who were concerned with relief work and the conduct of civil administration, and those who had been specifically authorized to enter by the Joint Commission for Vietnam (7). Article 6 forbade any person to cross the demarcation line unless authorized to do so by the joint commission.

The regroupment of belligerent forces into their respective zones was regulated by fairly detailed provisions. The disengagement of the combatants, withdrawals, and transfer of all military forces, together with their equipment and supplies, were to be completed within 300 days (2, 15 [a]).[4] The parties undertook to inform each other of their plans for movement from one regroupment zone to the other within 25 days of the agreement's entry into force (11). Regroupment would be accomplished by the successive withdrawal of troop echelons from predetermined sectors, the location and bounds of which were set forth in the annex to the agreement (15 [b]). French Union forces were required to withdraw from the Hanoi defense perimeter within 80 days and from the Haiphong perimeter within 300 days; the PAVN from the Plaine des Joncs provisional assembly area within 100 days and the Pointe Camau assembly

---

[3] The final declaration, in paragraph 6, stated that the conference recognized the military demarcation line is provisional and "should not in any way be interpreted as constituting a political or territorial boundary."

[4] After the cease-fire became effective in a particular sector of Vietnam, the belligerent parties were allotted fifteen days to disengage their forces and move them into provisional assembly areas prior to their scheduled withdrawal into either of the two regroupment zones (15[f]1).

area within 200 days. Withdrawal of the PAVN from central Vietnam would be made in three stages, the first within 80 days, the last within 300 days (15 [f]2). Other technical details, including the establishment and delimitation of provisional assembly areas and the formulation of procedures for the disengagement of troops, their concentration in assembly areas, and their subsequent withdrawal, were either described in article 15 or in the annex or left to the determination of the Trunggia Military Commission (and its successor, the Joint Commission for Vietnam) (12 [b], 15 [f]1; see also 12 [b]1).

The French and the Vietminh high commands undertook to permit no hostile acts during withdrawals and regroupment,[5] nor would they take any "step whatsoever which might hamper such withdrawals and transfers." More positively, they agreed to assist each other to this end, as far as this was possible (15 [c]), and to permit (1) no destruction or sabotage of public property, (2) no injuries to the life and property of the civilian population, and (3) no interference in local civil administration (15 [d]). In this connection, it should be noted that paragraph 8 of the final declaration stated that the provisions of the cease-fire agreements (the three separate cease-fire agreements, for Vietnam, Laos, and Cambodia), which were intended to ensure the protection of individuals and property, "must be most strictly applied."

The signatories also agreed to remove or neutralize mines, booby traps, and like devices within the number of days determined by the Trunggia Military Commission, or, in the alternative, to mark clearly the areas that might be mined (12 [a]). Article 13 authorized the Trunggia commission to establish air corridors for French military transport aircraft between the principal French zone south of the demarcation line and the provisional assembly areas assigned to French Union forces in northern Vietnam. Finally, the signatories agreed that the "armed forces of each party shall respect the demilitarized zone and the territory under the military control of the other party, and shall commit no act and undertake no operation against the other party and shall not engage in blockade of any kind in Viet Nam" (24).

Chapter IV of the cease-fire agreement related to the liberation and repatriation of prisoners of war and a category of individuals designated "civilian internees," the latter defined as "persons who, having in any way contributed to the political and armed struggle between the two parties, have been arrested for that reason and have

[5] The agreement prohibited stationing troops of one party within 1,500 meters of the provisional assembly areas of the other party (15[f]). During a withdrawal of the forces of one party through the territory of the other party, the latter was required to withdraw its forces 3 kilometers from each side of the route (12[b]2).

been kept in detention by either party during the period of hostilities" (21 [b]). All prisoners of war and civilian internees captured since the beginning of hostilities in Vietnam "during military operations or in any other circumstances of war and in any part of the territory of Viet Nam" were to be liberated within thirty days of the effective cease-fire date in each of the three theaters of operation defined in article 11. They were to be surrendered to the appropriate authorities of the other party, who would assist them in proceeding "to their country of origin, place of habitual residence or the zone of their choice" (21 [c]). Paragraph 9 of the final declaration enjoined the "competent representative authorities of the Northern and Southern zones of Viet Nam" to refrain from individual or collective reprisals against persons who might have collaborated, in any way, with one of the parties during the war. This provision applied not only to "civilian internees" but, presumably, to all noninterned persons against whom charges might conceivably be brought subsequent to the cessation of hostilities.

Civil administration in each of the two major regrouping zones was placed under the control of the party whose forces were to be regrouped there (14 [a]). Thus the commander in chief of the PAVN had control of civil administration in northern Vietnam and the commander in chief of the French Union forces had control of civil administration in southern Vietnam. Territories controlled by one party but subject to transfer to the other party were to be administered by the former until its troops had been withdrawn according to the terms of article 15. The delta cities were the subject of a special provision: "The transfer of the civil administration of Hanoi and Haiphong to the authorities of the Democratic Republic of Viet Nam shall be completed within the respective time-limits laid down in Article 15 for military movements" (14 [b]) (i.e. eighty days for Hanoi and 300 days for Haiphong).

Civilians who might wish to leave a district controlled by one party and reside in the regroupment zone assigned to the other party were to be permitted to do so; moreover, the authorities of a particular district were supposed to help civilians who had opted to leave (14 [d]). The final declaration had something to say on this point, though in an awkward fashion: "The *provisions of the agreements* on the cessation of hostilities . . . *must*, in particular, allow everyone in Viet Nam to decide freely in which zone he wishes to live" (para. 8; emphasis added). The parties to the agreement also undertook to refrain from reprisals or discrimination against persons or organizations because of their activities during the war; they were also to guarantee their "democratic liberties" (14 [c]). Paragraph 9 of the final declaration stated that the competent authorities of the zones of Vietnam "must not permit" reprisals against alleged collaborators.

Article 14, the *only* provision of the cease-fire agreement that refers to general elections, does so in a rather oblique way: "Pending the general elections which will bring about the unification of Viet Nam, the conduct of civil administration in each regrouping zone shall be in the hands of the party whose forces are to be regrouped there in virtue of the present Agreement." Thus the agreement implied that elections would be held, but nowhere did it say they *shall* be held. Such mandatory language appeared in the final declaration, however. The reader should recall that, by virtue of paragraph 6 of the declaration, the Geneva Conference recognized that the essential purpose of the Vietnamese cease-fire was to settle *military* questions with the view to ending hostilities. Moreover, this same provision stated that the conference recognized that the military demarcation line was provisional and was not to be interpreted as constituting a political or territorial boundary. According to paragraph 7, general elections "shall be held in July 1956, under the supervision of an international commission composed of representatives of the Member States of the International Supervisory Commission, referred to in the agreement on the cessation of hostilities." Moreover, consultations in preparation for the elections were to be held between "competent representative authorities of the two zones from July 20, 1955, onwards."

Paragraph 7 of the final declaration is very significant. During the conference France and her allies had insisted upon the primacy and priority of a military resolution of the Indochinese conflict; in mid-May Molotov conceded that priority status, but reneged on the concession on 8 June. After Mendès-France became Premier, the Soviet minister again agreed that the Geneva Conference concentrate primarily upon the task of seeking a military settlement, postponing the resolution of political problems until after a cease-fire had been effected. From the time (in early June) that it became clear the DRVN government was prepared to accept partition, the members of its delegation, during meetings of the military commission and at the political conference itself, continually emphasized the provisional nature of the regroupment zones and the temporary character of the partition. Both Molotov and Chou En-lai *seem* to have espoused this position as well, although the statements of the Soviet minister were somewhat ambiguous. Because the conference had generally agreed, by late June, that the settlement in Vietnam would take the form of partition, the question of all-Vietnamese elections reflected the concern of most of the delegations with the problem of the relative permanence or impermanence of the partition.

Although we cannot be sure exactly when Mendès-France accepted the principle that elections should unify Vietnam, he had probably done this as early as 23 June, about the time he met Chou En-lai at Berne. If this was the case, the French Premier, the principal non-Communist bargainer at Geneva, returned to the negotiating table after having agreed that the military settlement he would seek must be supplemented with the understanding that elections would be held after the cease-fire came into effect. Indeed, during July the conference participants (at least those ostensibly working toward a settlement) did not discuss whether all-Vietnamese elections were to be held but whether the formal documents embodying the settlement negotiated at Geneva should be explicit about the elections. Mendès-France preferred that the conference documents remain silent on the matter, but it was agreed, on 20 July, that two years should elapse between the cease-fire and the elections. Molotov had suggested this interim period, and Eden and Mendès-France were quite pleased by the proposal. In any event, the primarily military settlement contained a major element of a political nature. Anticipating a political settlement of the problems generated during the Indochinese War, the final declaration unequivocally stated that general elections were to be held in July 1956. The cease-fire agreement, as we have noted, recorded this understanding in an indirect fashion: Article 1 speaks of the provisional nature of the demarcation line and article 14 of the conduct of civil administration pending general elections that would bring about the unification of Vietnam.

The final declaration, however, embodied—in very explicit fashion —the *understanding* of Eden, Molotov, Chou En-lai, Mendès-France, and Pham Van Dong on the date of elections. Since the DRVN minister demanded elections within six months, and the Vietminh had the upper hand militarily in Tonkin, Pham Van Dong could not have been happy with his two great-power allies. He could either acquiesce in Molotov's proposal for elections after two years or reject it. Because the latter would not only win him the displeasure of his Soviet ally but possibly stall the conference, precipitate a governmental crises in France, and lead to a continuation and possible widening of the war, Pham Van Dong acquiesced. But he did not formally associate his government with the final declaration which leads to a rather curious state of affairs: One of the belligerent parties did not expressly consent to the terms of a major document for settling the war in which it was involved.

In paragraph 7 the conference declared that "so far as Viet Nam is concerned, the settlement of political problems, effected on the basis of respect for the principles of independence, unity and territorial integrity, shall permit the Vietnamese people to enjoy the

fundamental freedoms, guaranteed by democratic institutions established as a result of free general elections by secret ballot." Because
the Geneva settlement did not settle the political problems, this portion of paragraph 7 was not immediately operative; it was prospective. It spoke of the principles that should guide those who, in
the future, would seek a political settlement for Vietnam. "The settlement of political problems," it read, "shall permit the Vietnamese
people to enjoy the fundamental freedoms." The principles upon
which such a settlement would be based were fourfold: respect for
the territorial integrity of Vietnam, its independence, its unity, and
the freedom of the Vietnamese peoples as guaranteed by democratic institutions established through free elections by secret ballot.
Both the SVN and the DRVN delegations would agree that future
negotiators, whether participants of a reconvened Geneva Conference
or the Vietnamese themselves, must be guided by the first, second,
and third principles. As for the fourth principle, Communist and
non-Communist negotiators would very likely agree upon the need
for "democratic institutions" as a guarantee for the fundamental
freedoms of the Vietnamese but would undoubtedly understand
"democratic" in a very different sense.

In any event, the statement of general principles in paragraph 7 of
the final declaration is followed by a more definite requirement. "In
order to ensure that sufficient progress in the restoration of peace has
been made, and that all the necessary conditions obtain for free
expression of the national will, general elections shall be held in July
1956." Perhaps this statement was offered only as an explanation for
putting off elections for two years; but the language raises questions.
How would general elections show that "necessary conditions obtain
for free expression of the national will" when free elections, as such,
would constitute the expression of the national will? How could free
elections show that "sufficient progress" had been made in the restoration of peace? Should not progress toward peace be a precondition for free general elections? What if competent representative
authorities from the northern and southern zones of Vietnam could
not agree on procedures for elections by July 1956? If discussions
on the unification of Korea at the United Nations, Panmunjom, and
Geneva were any indication, the chances of agreement between
parties—one of whom might refuse to be put in a minority status in
any government, provisional or permanent—were definitely poor. I
do not mean to imply that agreement on election procedures would
be impossible and that the Geneva participants should have realized
this. The diplomats *might* have felt that, by mid-1955, Vietnamese
leaders might be disposed to attempt to settle Vietnamese problems
themselves. However, one Vietnamese faction might refuse to permit

the other faction to gain an advantage from election procedures, and the Korean experience should have served as a warning of the probable outcome of the consultations prescribed in paragraph 7.

Neither the cease-fire agreement nor the final declaration elaborated upon the effects of stalemate during the prospective consultations. The only guidelines offered the consulting authorities were the very general principles of independence, unity, territorial integrity, and democratic institutions created through free elections by secret ballot. Neither document dealt with the kind of problems that ultimately arose: the refusal of one party to consult about, and subsequently participate in, elections. Granted it was primarily a military settlement, and the conference draftsmen could not spend time drafting an acceptable outline of election procedures, and granted that an agreement upon election procedures, or upon sanctions for refusal to comply, or upon the rights of one party to appeal to the conference probably could not have been achieved within the French Premier's self-imposed deadline; nevertheless, some conferees—in their more sober moments must have realized the very great difficulties would arise in attempting to unify Vietnam. It is possible that some of the diplomats at Geneva realized that Vietnam would remain divided—not for two years, but semi-permanently— in the same way Korea has remained divided. Victor Bator suggests that the Western ministers probably understood that the demarcation line would not be temporary but would take on permanent reality as a political boundary between two bitterly antagonistic states;[6] and probably the Geneva delegations anticipated this outcome. Although paragraph 6 of the final declaration emphasized that the line "should not in any way be interpreted as constituting a political or territorial boundary," the SVN delegation protested partition and the DRVN delegates never tired of reminding their interlocutors that partition was merely a temporary, interim solution.[7]

Given the express statement in paragraph 7, was there an obligation to hold elections, and who was obligated to act pursuant to this provision? Let us be clear about a point that was mentioned earlier: the French government was *not* obligated to promote the consultations of 1955, nor was it obligated to see that elections were held in 1956 *under the terms of the agreement on the cessation of hostilities,* for that document contained no mandatory or prescriptive provisions for consultations or elections. The cease-fire agreement *implied*

---

[6] "Geneva, 1954: The Broken Mold," *Reporter,* 30 June 1966, pp. 15-18.

[7] Molotov, who had demonstrated skill, toughness, and canniness in past conferences and who had a reputation for a "realistic" approach to world political problems, must not have been sanguine about the prospects for Vietnam's unification.

that elections leading to the unification of Vietnam would be held, but there was *no* obligation pertaining to general elections because there was *no* provision that required them. Moreover, the agreement did not specify when elections would be held, what procedures would be followed, and when preliminary consultations would begin. If we refer only to the cease-fire agreement, and no other document, we might conclude that all-Vietnamese elections were merely to be hoped for.

The final declaration, as we have seen, was more explicit. According to its terms, general elections were scheduled for a definite date, but with respect to the contents of this declaration, we may fairly inquire whether it bound the French government to promote the scheduling of consultations and the holding of general elections on the specified dates. Further, were any of the other participant states at the Geneva Conference bound by paragraph 7 of the declaration? If so, what states were obligated, and in what ways? Having posed these rather crucial questions, I should like to put off answering them until I have analyzed the remaining provisions of the documents relating to the cease-fire in Vietnam and determined what other obligations might have been created pursuant to such provisions.

[I I]

The cease-fire agreement prohibited the introduction into Vietnam of troop reinforcements and additional military personnel (16), subject to one principal qualification, rotation, which was defined as the replacement of units no larger than battalion size by other units of the same echelon (16 [a–e]). Article 20, which specified points of entry for rotation personnel in each of the two major regroupment zones, would presumably make inspection by the joint commission and the ISC and its inspection teams somewhat easier.

Effective from the date of entry into force of the cease-fire agreement, the establishment of new military bases in Vietnam was prohibited (18). In addition, it was stipulated that "no military base under the control of a foreign state may be established in the regrouping zone of either party; the two parties shall ensure that the zones assigned to them do not adhere to any military alliance and are not used for the resumption of hostilities or to further an aggressive policy" (19).

Finally—completing the provisions that sought to demilitarize Vietnam—article 17 prohibited the introduction into Vietnam of "all types of arms, munitions and other war material, such as combat aircraft, naval craft, pieces of ordnance, jet engines . . . jet weapons and armored vehicles" (17 [a]), and unassembled parts of war matériel, arms, and munitions of all types that would subsequently be assembled (17 [d]). The parties to the agreement were permitted to replace, on a piece-for-piece basis, arms and munitions that had been destroyed, damaged, worn out, or used up after the cessation of hostilities (17 [b]). However, the introduction of arms and munitions for replacement purposes would be subject to inspection at specified points of entry (17 [c, e, f], 20).

In paragraphs 4 and 5 of the final declaration the conference merely *took note* of the clauses in the cease-fire agreement prohibiting the introduction into Vietnam of foreign troops, military personnel, and arms and munitions; the establishment of military bases in Vietnam under foreign control; and the membership of either party in "any military alliance." The French government unilaterally declared its readiness to withdraw its troops from the territory of Cambodia, Laos, and Vietnam "at the request of the Governments concerned" and within a period that would be fixed by agreement between the parties.[8] The conference took note of this declaration (FD 10).

The cease-fire agreement established organs for the supervision of the various activities prescribed and prohibited by its terms. Responsibility for the execution of the agreement rested with the parties (28) but an international commission, more specifically an "international supervisory commission" or ISC, was established at the time of the cease-fire to provide for control and supervision (29, 44).[9] In addition, the agreement provided for setting up a joint commission, composed of an equal number of representatives of the commanders of the two parties, whose task was to facilitate execution of those provisions of the cease-fire agreement concerning the joint action of the parties (30, 31). Article 33 specified, in more explicit terms, the activities the joint commission would supervise:

1. A simultaneous and general cease-fire affecting all regular and irregular armed forces of the two parties;

2. Regroupment of the armed forces of the two parties;

3. Observance of the demarcation lines between the regrouping zones and of the demilitarized sectors; and

4. Generally helping the parties execute the provisions of the agreement, ensuring liaison between them, and endeavoring to solve disputes and questions that might arise.

The joint commission, chaired by a president with the rank of general, was to set up a number of joint groups, composed of an equal number of officers from the commands of both parties (32). These

---

[8] The French declarations appear in Cmd. 9239, *op. cit.*, p. 42.

[9] The ISC for Vietnam was instructed to act in close cooperation with the ISCs for Cambodia and Laos, established pursuant to the terms of the cease-fire agreements for those states (45).

joint groups, to be located on the provisional demarcation line, would carry out the tasks assigned to them by the joint commission under the grant of authority of article 33. The commission and its groups would have complete freedom of movement within the demilitarized zone (9). They could regulate the number of civil police who might enter that zone and determine whether the police should be armed. No one was to carry arms within the demilitarized zone without the specific authorization of the joint commission (8). The commanders of the forces of the two parties were instructed to give full protection and all possible assistance to the joint commission and its joint groups (25).[10] The parties, moreover, were to notify both the joint commission and the ISC of the arrivals and departures of all personnel (presumably military personnel) (16 [f]) and shipments to or from Vietnam of war matériel, arms, and munitions (17 [e]).

The ISC was to be composed of representatives of Canada, India, and Poland and presided over by the representative of India (34). The terms of responsibility of the ISC were broadly drawn; no attempt was made to allocate competences or duties between the ISC and the joint commission where such competences overlapped. Thus article 36, which granted the ISC responsibility for the execution of the provisions of the agreement, should be read with article 33, granting responsibilities in a similar fashion to the joint commission. Article 36 reads in part:

[The ISC] shall fulfil the tasks of control, observation, inspection and investigation connected with the application of the provisions of the agreement on the cessation of hostilities, and it shall in particular:—

(a) Control the movement of the armed forces of the two parties, effected within the framework of the regroupment plan.

(b) Supervise the demarcation lines between the regrouping areas, and also the demilitarized zones.

(c) Control the operations of releasing prisoners of war and civilian internees.

(d) Supervise at ports and airfields as well as along all frontiers of Viet Nam the execution of the provisions of the agreement on the cessation of hostilities, regulating the introduction into the country of armed forces, military personnel and of all kinds of armies, munitions and war material.

Thus the responsibilities of the ISC under subparagraphs a, b, and d of article 36 were similar to those of the joint commission under

[10] Costs incurred by the operations of the ISC and its inspection teams and the joint commission and its joint groups were to be shared equally between the two parties (26).

article 33. The responsibilities or competences of the two commissions differed in this respect, however: the joint commission supervised execution of provisions concerning joint actions of the two parties (30); the ISC supervised the execution of almost all provisions relating to the cease-fire, whether or not requiring joint action by the parties. The ISC, however, had no control over the joint commission. Thus the arguments of the Communist delegations at Geneva had prevailed on this particular point since they had insisted upon the autonomy of the two commissions: neither commission was formally subordinate to the other; and the ISC had no authority to direct the joint commission to perform any action or consider any question. Under the terms of article 40, if the members of the joint commission were unable to reach an agreement "on the interpretation to be given some provision or on the appraisal of a fact," the ISC was to be informed of the disputed question. But it could merely recommend a solution to the parties and notify the joint commission of its recommendation. The joint commission was in no way obligated to adopt an ISC recommendation or perform according to its terms.

The ISC was instructed to establish both fixed and mobile inspection teams, composed of an equal number of military officers appointed by and representing India, Canada, and Poland (35). The fixed teams were to be located at points specified in article 20, the points of entry for rotation personnel and shipments of war matériel, arms, and munitions. The mobile inspection teams would be assigned "zones of action" by the parent ISC, which were to include the demilitarized zone and "regions bordering the land and sea frontiers of Viet Nam"(35). Within their assigned zones of action the mobile teams were to have the right to move freely. The parties to the agreement were to ensure that the teams received "from the local civil and military authorities all facilities they may require for the fulfilment of their tasks (provision of personnel, placing at their disposal documents needed for supervision, summoning witnesses necessary for holding enquiries, ensuring the security and freedom of movement of the inspection teams, etc.)" (35; see also 9 and 25, pursuant to which the commanders of the forces of the two parties were to afford protection to the ISC and its inspection teams). The parties were also to provide the inspection teams "with modern means of transport, observation and communication as they may require" (35). Like the joint commission, the ISC was to be notified by the parties of the arrival and departure of personnel and war matériel (16 [f], 17 [e]). The inspection teams at the points of entry (20) were authorized to supervise and to inspect the rotation of units or groups of personnel, the arrival and departure of individual personnel

(16 [g]), and to supervise the transshipment of authorized replacements of war matériel (17 [f]).[11]

The inspection teams, fixed or mobile, were to report the results of their investigations or observations to the ISC jointly—or separately if the members of the team disagreed with each other over the substance of particular conclusions (38). The teams would also inform the ISC of their inability to settle an incident and of their disagreement over an appraisal of a situation that might or might not constitute a violation or a threat of violation (presumably of the provisions of the cease-fire agreement [39]).[12] The ISC must then study the team report and inform the parties of "measures which should be taken for the settlement of the incident, ending of the violation or removal of the threat of violation" (39). The ISC could not compel the parties to comply with its recommendations; it could merely tell the parties what ought to be done.

The voting procedures of the ISC were substantially in accord with the Communist proposals at the Geneva Conference, particularly those by Molotov on 16 June. The following matters required a unanimous decision on the part of the ISC members.

1. Questions concerning the refusal by the armed forces of one party to effect the movements provided for in the regroupment plan (42 [a]);

2. Questions concerning violations by the armed forces of one of the parties of the regrouping zones, territorial waters, or air space of the other party (42[b]); and

3. Recommendations concerning amendments and additions to the provisions of the cease-fire agreement to ensure its more effective execution (41).

All other recommendations were to be adopted by majority vote (41), but article 42, though it dealt with ISC matters that required unanimous consent, could be more broadly construed. It read: "When dealing with questions concerning violations, or threats of violations, which might lead to a resumption of hostilities, [42(a and b); i.e. points 1 and 2 above], the decisions of the International Commis-

---

[11] Reports by the parties to the ISC and the joint commission on the arrival and departure of military personnel had to be made two days in advance; while movement of troops into or out of Vietnam was in progress, daily reports were required (16[f]). The parties also were obligated to submit reports on all incoming shipments of war matériel (for replacement purposes) to the ISC and the joint commission. These reports "shall indicate the use made of the items so replaced" (17[e]).

[12] I use "presumably" because article 39 does not state *what* might be violated: "If any one inspection team is unable to settle an incident or considers that there is *a violation or a threat of a serious violation*, the International Commission shall be informed" (emphasis added). But violation of what—the cease-fire agreement, the final declaration, the norms of international law?

sion must be unanimous." If a question were within the scope of points 1 and 2 (above) but concerned violations or threats of violations that might lead to a resumption of hostilities, it could be argued that one or more members of the ISC could demand that a resultant recommendation be approved by a unanimous decision. One might predict, therefore, that on all crucial questions (i.e. questions concerning matters that could lead to a resumption of hostilities) the ISC would be divided.

Whether the decision on a particular question was to be adopted on the basis of a majority or a unanimous vote, the ISC, in any case, had no power of enforcement. If either the French or the DRVN high command (the "parties") violated or threatened to violate the agreement, a unanimous decision of the ISC might persuade the culpable party to change his policies, but, apart from the force of this "moral suasion" the agreement contained no explicit provision for constraining either party. However, three factors of constraint operated independently of the terms of the cease-fire agreement:

1. As either party could resume hostilities, the other party might regard resumption as highly undesirable and therefore alter its policies. However, because the French government and National Assembly had persuaded all observers that it wanted an end to the war once and for all, France would have been most unwilling to resume hostilities even under the most embarrassing circumstances.

2. After early September, SEATO might have deterred a resumption of hostilities by the Vietminh. Southern Vietnam was "protected" by virtue of the protocol to the SEATO treaty, and article IV of that treaty encompassed both direct and indirect aggression against the protocol states.

3. Finally, although the United States did not associate itself with the final declaration, the declaration Bedell Smith had read into the record took note of the cease-fire agreement for Vietnam and paragraphs 1 through 12 of the final declaration, and stated that "any renewal of the aggression in violation of the aforesaid Agreements" would be viewed with "grave concern" and as "seriously threatening international peace and security." This declaration may have restrained the parties to some extent; involvement of the United States in Southeast Asia was regarded by a substantial proportion of French officials as undesirable, as must have been true of DRVN officials as well.

Thus a unanimous decision by the ISC respecting a violation or threat of violation of the agreement might have persuaded the culpable party to adhere to ISC recommendations, but it was unlikely that the ISC would unanimously agree on any recommendation of importance—more particularly, any recommendation of the kind specified in articles 41 and 42. The experience of the Military

Armistice Commission for Korea and the Korean Neutral Nations' Supervisory Commission showed quite clearly that, on all crucial questions, the Communist and the non-Communist delegates did not agree; unanimity was simply not possible. The ISC experience need not have been identical to that of the Korean commissions, but the reports of the ISC after 1955 reveal the inability of the Canadian and Polish members to agree with each other on most matters of substance.

The only course open to the ISC in the event its recommendations were unheeded was to report the refusal of one or both parties to comply to the members of the Geneva Conference (43). If the ISC could not agree on questions requiring unanimity (41, 42), the members of the ISC would submit a majority report and one or more minority reports to the conference; and whenever the activity of the ISC or its inspection teams was hindered, the ISC would inform the conference of the facts of such hindrance. The members of the conference—at least those who had associated themselves with the final declaration—agreed to consult with one another on all questions that might be referred to them by the ISC "in order to study such measures as may prove necessary to ensure that the agreements on the cessation of hostilities in Cambodia, Laos and Viet Nam are respected" (FD 13). The actions and recommendations of the conference members were not specified and would presumably be determined at the time the members reconvened.

The United States government took note of paragraphs 1 to 12 of the final declaration but not paragraph 13, presumably because the Eisenhower administration, under the circumstances then prevailing in Washington, must refuse to consult with the Chinese Communist regime on any question whatever. The effect of the United States declaration at the final plenary session of the conference was to reserve that government's freedom of action while making public its position on a number of questions—among others, the future of Vietnam and the possible resumption of hostilities. But the effect or intent of the omission to take note of paragraph 13 of the final declaration is not clear. It can of course be argued that it was a refusal to consult by implication; or it may have been meant further to reserve the freedom of action of the administration (if such was possible); or it may merely have been a device for suspending decision until a crisis occurred in Indochina that would reconvene the Geneva Conference. If this happened, the United States would determine, at that time, whether it would consult with the other members of the conference. In view of the fact that the Kennedy administration participated in the Geneva Conference on the Laotian question (1961–1962) and *signed* the protocol to the declaration on the neutrality of Laos—

along with the C.P.R.—the omission of paragraph 13 in the United States declaration may now be only a historical curiosity.

The French government issued two unilateral declarations at the final plenary session of the conference, the first relating to its readiness to withdraw its troops from Cambodia, Laos, and Vietnam, and the second stating that "the French Government will proceed from the principle of respect for the independence and sovereignty, the unity and territorial integrity of Cambodia, Laos and Viet Nam" in the settlement of all problems connected with the reestablishment and consolidation of peace in Indochina. The conference took note of this declaration (FD 11) and made a statement quite similar to it: "In their relations with Cambodia, Laos and Viet Nam, each member of the Geneva Conference undertakes to respect the sovereignty, the independence, the unity and the territorial integrity of the above-mentioned States, *and to refrain from any interference in their internal affairs*" (emphasis added).

The final provision of special interest in the cease-fire agreement, article 27, stated that the signatories (i.e. the French Union and the PAVN high commands) "and *their successors in their functions* shall be responsible for ensuring the observance and enforcement of the terms and provisions (of the agreement)."[13] Who were the "successors in their functions"? In attempting to construe article 27, it is helpful to compare its language with that of the Korean armistice agreement's section 17, which reads: "Responsibility for compliance with and enforcement of the terms and provisions of this armistice agreement is that of the signatories hereto and *their successors in command*."[14] The Korean agreement was signed by Lt. General William K. Harrison, Jr., senior delegate for the United Nations, and General Nam Il, senior delegate for the Korean People's Army and the Chinese People's Volunteers, and subsequently by General Mark W. Clark, commander in chief of the U.N. command, Marshal Kim Il Sung, supreme commander of the KPA, and P'eng Teh-huai, commander of the CPV.

The expression "successors in command" is relatively unambiguous: whoever succeeded General Clark as commander in chief of the U.N. command and Marshal Kim as supreme commander of the

---

[13] Article 27 also provided that the commanders in chief of the armed forces of the two parties must "take all steps and make all arrangements necessary to ensure full compliance with all the provisions of the present Agreement by all elements and military personnel under their command.

"The procedures laid down in the present Agreement shall, whenever necessary, be studied by the Commanders of the two parties and, if necessary, defined more specifically by the Joint Commission."

[14] The Korean armistice agreement, 27 July 1953, *T.I.A.S.* No. 2782 4 U.S.T. 234 (1953); *DSB*, 3 August 1953, p. 134 (emphasis added).

KPA would be a successor in command. Similarly, the French and Vietminh military officers who might succeed Generals Ely and Giap as commanders in chief, respectively, of the French Union forces and PAVN would be successors in command, but who might Ely's and Giap's "successors in function" be? Insofar as "function" could be construed as the functions of a commander in chief, "successors in function" *could* be equivalent to the corresponding expression in the Korean armistice agreement. This interpretation is reinforced by paragraph 6 of the final declaration, wherein the conference recognized that "the essential purpose" of the cease-fire agreement was "to settle military questions with a view to ending hostilities." Thus, presumably, "functions" would be essentially military functions, and these, it could be argued, would be carried out by Generals Ely and Giap and their "successors in command."

But France had unilaterally declared its willingness to withdraw its troops from Vietnam at the request of the government concerned. The French government, moreover, had recognized the State of Vietnam (in 1950), Bao Dai as chief of state of the SVN, and the government of Ngo Dinh Diem as the duly constituted government of the SVN. General Ely, in August 1954, reiterated his government's official stand: the SVN was the state of the Vietnamese people and the government of Ngo Dinh Diem, in theory, represented that people.[15] Therefore, if either Bao Dai or Diem asked the French to withdraw their troops and the French government complied with this request, who would be the "successors in function" of the French commander in chief? Would it be the commander of the army of the State of Vietnam, or Diem himself? This question is of very great importance. In the first place, the French Union high command (through General Delteil) agreed, in article 14 of the agreement, that "pending the general elections which will bring about the unification of Viet Nam, the conduct of civil administration in each regrouping zone shall be in the hands of the party whose forces are to be regrouped there." This article did not impose upon the French an obligation to hold elections, but it declared that civil administration in southern Vietnam would be vested in the French high command and (by article 27) its "successors in function." If the French left, who—if anyone—would administer the southern regroupment zone?

The cease-fire agreement, moreover, contained a number of provisions that imposed rather protracted or extended duties upon the signatories. For example, the PAVN had up to 300 days to withdraw from Quang Ngai and Binh Dinh provinces and up to 200 days to withdraw from the Pointe Camau provisional assembly area, and such

[15] *Le Monde*, 31 August 1954; Ely, 238-249, particularly 239 and 241-242.

withdrawals and concomitant troop assembly and transfer procedures required the performance of certain acts by both of the former belligerents (see article 15). If the French left before the expiration of the troop withdrawal period, the PAVN would confront the army of the SVN, and in 1954 there could be no doubt of the outcome if such a confrontation led to an outbreak of hostilities. Thus there remained the possibility that if the French removed their troops from southern Vietnam and dissolved their high command in compliance with a request of the Diem government, a situation would be created that would not be conducive to peace in Vietnam.[16]

The problem of the construction of "successors in function" in article 27 relates to another, more fundamental problem: the status of the government of the SVN. At Geneva, Tran Van Do tried to have his government's declaration entered into the record, which Eden refused to permit, but this did not affect the significance and effect of Do's declaration and protest; his government reserved its freedom of action. If we assume *arguendo* that the SVN was sovereign and the Diem government was its duly constituted government, it had the right to take the position expressed in the Tran Van Do's protest. It could refuse to recognize the terms and provisions of the final declaration and the cease-fire agreement. It could refuse to accept, in particular, article 14 of the agreement, which vested civil administration in the southern zone "in the hands" of the French high command, and it could refuse to accept a construction of article 27 that made the commander of the army of the SVN (or the Diem government itself) the "successors in function" of the French high command.

In one respect the problem of successors of the French command is academic. The French completed the withdrawal of their troops from southern Vietnam in April 1956 and the French commander, General Jacquot (a successor in both function and command of General Ely), dissolved the French high command; the PAVN troop withdrawals from the south also were complete by that time. Other institutions and procedures that were based upon terms of the cease-fire agreement were expected and in fact continued to be operative; for example, the ISC and joint commission continued to function. However, they did so at the sufferance of the government of the RVN, which, though hostile to the idea of dealing with the government of the DRVN, agreed to respect certain provisions of the cease-fire agreement that would reduce the chances of a resumption of hostilities.[17]

[16] There were other duties of a continuing nature, for example, cooperation with the ISC (25, 27, 35) and the prohibitions on troop reinforcements, new bases, and the introduction of arms and munitions (Chap. III).

[17] The RVN government, in addition, did not approve the ISC and its Polish

But what were the effects of the provisions that banned the introduction of troops and armaments, prohibited adherence to military alliances and the establishment of new bases in southern Vietnam, and vested civil administration in a party that was no longer in Vietnam? It is my opinion that the government of the SVN, not being a party to the cease-fire agreement, was free to accept or reject any of its provisions. Even if the French and the DRVN signatories meant the term "successors in function" to include the DRVN or the SVN successors of the French high command, they could not create and impose obligations of this sort upon the government of the SVN. These conclusions are, without doubt, controversial, but I will attempt to justify them in succeeding chapters. Also, I have been discussing the obligations imposed pursuant to the cease-fire agreement, not the final declaration, and will consider the significance of this latter document in the next chapter.

Communist representative. Nor was the Diem regime pleased with India's representation on the commission; India had not recognized the SVN, and India's policies in Asia were regarded as pro-Communist.

Chapter 22

THE FINAL DECLARATION AND
THE VIETNAM SETTLEMENT

[I]

COLLECTIVE OBLIGATIONS

In Chapter 21 it was asserted that the agreement on the cessation of hostilities gave rise to no obligation to hold general elections in Vietnam, but if such an obligation was created by any of the documents produced at Geneva, it was the final declaration that did so, particularly paragraph 7, stating that "general elections shall be held in July 1956." It is of course true that the agreement speaks of the demarcation line as "provisional" and, in article 14, vested civil administration in the parties "pending the general elections which will bring about the unification of Viet Nam." Admittedly, the delegates of the DRVN and their government in Tonkin understood that elections were to be held in 1956, and perhaps the French government understood this as well; so let us assume there was such an understanding between the signatories of the cease-fire agreement. Nevertheless, the absence of language in the agreement explicitly requiring elections must mean that the agreement, in and of itself, cannot be regarded as the source of any obligations for preparing and scheduling general elections in Vietnam.

The final declaration, however, is quite another matter, and in this chapter we will consider the legal consequences of this document. In analyzing the provisions of the declaration we shall have occasion to discuss the positions of the governments of the United States and the State of Vietnam, both of which explicitly refused to approve the declaration and reserved their positions in rather specific ways. In the case of the SVN, we shall have to consider in greater detail (in Chapter 23) what obligations, if any, were imposed upon the government of that state by the final declaration and by the cease-fire agreement. In this way we shall return to the questions discussed at the end of the preceding chapter, particularly the right or prerogative of the Diem government to accept or reject any of the terms of the settlement.

Nine of the thirteen paragraphs of the final declaration begin with the words "The Conference takes note," "The Conference recognizes," or "The Conference expresses [or] declares."[1] But to what

---

[1] The reader is referred to the Appendix for the text of the final declaration.

extent were the conference participants bound *collectively* by a declaration that purports to speak for the entire group of states that gathered in Geneva in mid-1954? In the absence of the consent, either written or verbal, of *all* nine participants, the final declaration created no *collective* conference obligations. The title of the document certainly does not alter its legal consequences. The reader will recall that Eden and Molotov agreed upon the form and wording of the title as a means to mollify the Chinese delegation, which might have objected to the United States' refusal to *sign* the declaration. The title reads: "Final Declaration of the Geneva Conference on the problem of restoring peace in Indo-China, in which the representatives of [the nine participating states] took part." The title merely announced that the representatives of nine states *took part* in a conference at Geneva. It must be emphasized that in the absence of the consent, written or verbal, of *all* the conference participants, the declaration imposed no *collective* obligations, whatever the form of the title. To be completely accurate, I should say that unless *all* the participating states consented to the terms of the declaration and bound themselves thereto according to the procedures required by their respective constitutions, the operative terms of the declaration were not binding upon *all* the participants of the Geneva Conference.[2]

Did the nine conference participants give their consent? Some did so only verbally, others not at all. None of the heads of delegations subscribed to the declaration by *signing* it, and much has been made of the fact that the declaration was not signed. Lacouture says that a new form of international cold-war agreement was created thereby; others have argued whether an unsigned treaty can create obligations among the states that negotiated the treaty. The answer, of course,

---

[2] For the necessity of consent in order for a treaty to be binding upon the parties thereto, see Hersch Lauterpacht, *International Law, a Treatise by L. Oppenheim* (8th ed.; London: Longmans, Green, 1958), I: 890; C. C. Hyde, *International Law, Chiefly as Interpreted and Applied by the United States* (2d rev. ed.; Boston: Little, Brown, 1945), II: 489, 493; Paul Fauchille, *Traité de Droit International Public* (8th ed.; Paris: Librairie Rousseau & Cie., 1926), I: 297-298; Paul Guggenheim, *Traité de Droit International Public* (Geneva: Librairie de l'Université and Georg & Cie., S.A., 1953), 1: 56-57; Wilhelm Wengler, *Völkerrecht* (Berlin: Springer, 1964), 1: 210ff.; Alfred Verdross, *Völkerrecht* (4th ed.; Vienna: Springer, 1959), p. 110.

The reader should understand that I am not, at this point, considering whether *some* parties were bound by the terms of the final declaration but, rather, whether *all* the parties were bound. The language of the declaration purports to speak of the conference as a collectivity and implies that all participants of the conference were obligated by the operative provisions of the final declaration. But for *all* the participants to have been bound, *all* of them must have consented to be bound. Thus the question presently under consideration is simply Did *all* the participants consent to be bound by the terms of the final declaration?

is that *under certain circumstances* an unsigned treaty can become law between the parties.[3] But this is not really the point: to be bound by the terms of a treaty a state must "consent" to its terms,[4] which is usually done by means of the signature of the chief executive, plenipotentiary, or authorized representative of the executive. Subsequent to signature, ratification procedures may result in either the formal acceptance of the treaty or its rejection. In the latter case the signature does not operate to bind the state, because—according to the constitutional processes of the signatory—it has not consented to the treaty; it is not bound thereby until and unless the entire process of signature plus ratification is completed.[5]

Although a state may also consent to be bound by an oral declaration, verbal adherence may or may not suffice to bind a state to the terms of a treaty, depending upon the state's constitutional requirements. In any event, consent to the terms of a treaty may be given in writing or orally. It is possible, in either case, for a state to become bound thereby.

It is equally clear, however, that a state may withhold its consent or explicitly refuse to adhere to a treaty its representatives had discussed, negotiated, and perhaps even drafted. In the absence of consent, a treaty can impose no new or additional obligations upon a state. Competence to consent to be bound by a treaty or to refuse to consent is an attribute of the state as a sovereign and independent entity. (If the reader is unhappy about a norm that permits a state unilaterally to determine how and to what extent it will be bound by treaty obligations, he may find solace in the knowledge that he is in the company of a large and estimable group of jurists and political philosophers that has grown in number over the centuries.)

The rule that states must consent to be bound must be refined in one particular: a state may give its consent expressly—that is, in writing or verbally—at the time treaty negotiations are concluded or it may consent by the conduct or behavior of its authoritative policymakers. In other words, a state may give its consent impliedly.[6] Since, however, there are limits for inferring consent from

---

[3] See Lauterpacht, *op. cit.*, p. 898; *Status of Eastern Greenland, P.C.I.J.*, Series A/B, No. 53 (1933); Harvard Research in International Law, Part III: "Law of Treaties," *Supplement to the American Journal of International Law*, 29 (October 1935): 689-691, 722-739; Fauchille, *op. cit.*, p. 297; Guggenheim, *op. cit.*, pp. 62-64; Verdross, *op. cit.*, p. 100.

[4] See the authorities cited in n. 2 above.

[5] Lauterpacht, *op. cit.*, pp. 908-910; Hyde, *op. cit.*, p. 516; C. G. Fenwick, *International Law* (2d. ed.; New York: Appleton-Century, 1934), pp. 334-335; Harvard Research in International Law, *op. cit.*, pp. 769-778, 763-769; Fauchille, *op. cit.*, pp. 317-328; Verdross, *op. cit.*, pp. 106-107; Georges Scelle, *Cours de Droit International Public* (Paris: Domat-Montchrétien, 1948), p. 619.

[6] Mere tacit acquiescence in a treaty's terms does not suffice to bind a state,

the behavior of a state, we must turn from our abstract legal analysis to the facts of the Geneva negotiations and settlement.

All nine heads of the delegations at Geneva, as a collective body, did not *expressly* consent to their states' being bound by the terms and provisions of the final declaration. Thus, although the declaration purports to speak for the conference, it is at most officious and misleading; it is at least only one of many public documents that relies upon a fiction to disguise fundamental disagreements between negotiators.

[II]

OBLIGATIONS OF INTERESTED STATES

At this point let us turn from the collective obligations of the conference under the final declaration to the individual obligations of each conference participant.

GREAT BRITAIN

Eden, who made the most formal and unequivocal verbal statement in associating the British government with the provisions of the final declaration, said "On behalf of Her Majesty's Government in the United Kingdom, I associate myself with the final Declaration of this Conference."[7] A statement such as this could effectively bind the British government: it could be construed as a formal expression of consent. The fact that it was made orally rather than in writing would not alter the legal consequences, either in terms of international law or the constitutional law of the United Kingdom. But there is, of course, the question of the meaning of "associate"; what does it mean to say that the British government has "associated" itself with the final declaration? Did Eden, in fact, effectively express his government's consent to be bound? Since successive British governments since 1954 have regarded themselves obligated, in some ways, to the terms of the declaration, the question is perhaps academic. In other circumstances "associate" might have produced problems of interpretation, but in view of Britain's relative disinterest in Indochina and the relatively few and uncostly obligations that might be incurred pursuant to the terms of the declaration, Eden's verbal association with that document has, as yet, created no problems of interpretation.

On the assumption that Eden's statement effectively bound the

---

however (Lauterpacht, *op. cit.*, p. 898). The state's policymakers must conduct state business in such a way that its consent to be bound can be reasonably inferred from that conduct.

[7] Cmd. 9239, p. 5.

British government, what obligations did that government incur? If the reader will refer to the text of the declaration in the Appendix, he will note that in paragraphs 1, 4, 5, 10, and 11 the conference *took note* of the various documents related to the settlement for Vietnam, namely, the cease-fire agreement and the two unilateral declarations of the French government. The phrase "takes note" imposed no obligations upon the British government (nor upon any of the other governments participating in the conference for that matter); it merely registered recognition that certain events had transpired, and no more. It did not incorporate by reference the terms of the cease-fire agreement or the unilateral declarations. It was not intended to, nor did it, create legal obligations.[8]

Paragraph 2 of the final declaration, which expressed the satisfaction of the conference at the ending of hostilities, could not have the effect of imposing an additional obligation upon the British government. Paragraphs 6 through 9 express the conference's *understanding* of the meaning of the terms of the cease-fire agreement and its general intent. Thus the conference recognized that the essential purpose of the cease-fire agreement was to settle military questions in order to end hostilities and that the demarcation line was provisional and "should not in any way be interpreted as constituting a political or territorial boundary" (FD 6).

Paragraphs 7 through 9 use almost mandatory language: representative authorities of the northern and southern zones of Vietnam "must not permit" reprisals against collaborators (FD 9); provisions of the cease-fire agreement designed to protect individuals and property "must be most strictly applied" and "must . . . allow everyone in Viet Nam to decide freely in which zone he wishes to live" (FD 8); settlement of political problems relative to Vietnam (at an unspecified time in the future) "shall permit the Vietnamese people to enjoy the fundamental freedoms, guaranteed by democratic institutions established as a result of free general elections by secret ballot" (FD 7); consultations concerning these elections between representatives of the two zones "will be held" from 20 July 1955 onward (FD 7).

Whatever the effect of this mandatory language, it did not impose

[8] When the language of a treaty indicates that the parties thereto meant only to formulate general statements of principle or policy, no legal obligations are created. "Intention of the parties" is a question of fact, to be decided in each case (Lauterpacht, *op. cit.*, p. 900), but in the case of the final declaration it is impossible to determine what the parties intended. For example, Great Britain, the Soviet Union, and the C.P.R. did not intend to obligate themselves to see that all-Vietnamese elections were held, although they seem to have intended that the competent representative authorities in the northern and southern regroupment zones schedule elections; but what if the latter authorities should disagree or refuse to cooperate with each other?

positive obligations upon Britain. In fact, one will search in vain for obligations that might have been incurred by Great Britain under the language of paragraphs 1 through 11. Only in the last two paragraphs, 12 and 13, did the British government accept positive obligations: it would consult with other members of the conference on any question referred to the conference by the ISC (FD 13); and it would respect the sovereignty, independence, unity, and territorial integrity of Vietnam and refrain from interference in its internal affairs (FD 12).

In addition to these obligations, Eden's consent in April to serve with Molotov as co-chairman of the conference has led his successors voluntarily to assume the obligation as one of the permanent co-chairmen of the conference.

The Soviet Union and the C.P.R.

We may apply the same analysis to the consent of the governments of the Soviet Union and the C.P.R. This assumes that Molotov's terse remark, "The Soviet Delegation agrees," and Chou's "We agree" were expressions of consent.[9] Since neither the Soviet government nor Peking has, as yet, directly challenged the binding effect of the final declaration, I will not inquire into the effect of the Chinese and the Soviet minister's "comments" upon that declaration, except to note that they are ambiguous. In any case, the only obligations incurred by the Soviet Union or the C.P.R. are those of paragraphs 12 and 13, and are similar to Great Britain's.[10]

Cambodia and Laos

With respect to the Vietnamese cease-fire, the governments of Laos and Cambodia incurred no greater obligations than the governments of Britain, China, and the Soviet Union. Laos, it may be argued, incurred no obligations at all relative to Vietnam. At the final plenary session Phoui Sananikone had "no observations to make" on the text of the declaration[11] and made no on-the-record remarks that could be construed as a consent to its terms. We must conclude, I think, that the Laotian government did not *expressly* consent to be bound at the conference. As for Cambodia, Tep Phan declared that "Cambodia has no intention of interfering in the internal affairs of the State of Viet Nam and associates herself fully with the principle of respect . . ." for the integrity of the State of Vietnam. But his promise of respect for these principles was expressly conditioned upon regu-

[9] Cmd. 9239, p. 5.
[10] Like Great Britain, the Soviet Union could also be said to have consented to provide a co-chairman for the quasi-institutionalized Geneva Conference.
[11] Cmd. 9239, p. 5.

larization of the Cambodian-Vietnamese border;[12] in fact, the Cambodian diplomat expressly reserved his government's claim to "Cambodian lands in South Viet Nam." Other than these remarks, Tep Phan made no undertaking on behalf of his government to consult with members of the conference on questions referred to it by the ISC (FD 13) nor did he express himself on the unity or independence of Vietnam (FD 12). Cambodia's "consent," therefore, was partial and qualified.

THE UNITED STATES

The response of the United States government was given in the declaration made by Bedell Smith at the last session on 21 July.[13] Taking note of the cease-fire agreement for Vietnam and paragraphs 1 through 12 of the final declaration, the Bedell Smith declaration *obligated* the United States in these respects:

1. The United States would refrain from the threat or use of force to disturb the cease-fire agreement and paragraphs 1 through 12 of the final declaration "in accordance with Article 2 (Section 4) of the Charter of the United Nations dealing with the obligations of Members to refrain in their international relations from the threat or use of force." The declaration then read: "[The United States government] would view any renewal of the aggression in violation of the aforesaid Agreements with grave concern and as seriously threatening international peace and security." This statement did not obligate the United States to act or to refrain from acting; it was merely an expression of an attitude.

2. Incorporated by reference in the Bedell Smith declaration was a paragraph of the joint Anglo-American communiqué of 29 June: "In the case of nations now divided against their will, we shall continue to seek to achieve unity through free elections, supervised by the United Nations to ensure that they are conducted fairly."[14] Thus the United States government unilaterally undertook to make continuing efforts to unify Vietnam by means of elections that were (*a*) free and (*b*) supervised by the United Nations (*not* by the ISC or by representatives of members of the ISC as specified in paragraph 7 of the Final Declaration).

3. In rather vague terms, the American declaration stated that the United States government would "not join in an arrangement which would hinder" fulfillment of the principle that "peoples are entitled to determine their own future."

The declaration made by Bedell Smith at Geneva should be read with other official statements emanating from Washington. The

---

[12] *Ibid.*, p. 6.   [13] *Ibid.*, pp. 6-7.   [14] *Docs., 1954*, p. 64.

President, at his press conference of 21 July, declared that the United States was "not itself a party to or bound by the decisions taken by the Conference."[15] Also, in the Pacific Charter, signed at Manila on 8 September, the United States reaffirmed the statement in the Bedell Smith declaration respecting fulfillment of the principle of self-determination of peoples:

> [In] accordance with the provisions of the United Nations Charter, they [i.e., the signatories of the Pacific Charter] uphold the principles of equal rights and self-determination of peoples and they will earnestly strive by every peaceful means to promote self-government and to secure the independence of all countries whose people desire it and are able to undertake its responsibilities.[16]

Subsequently, on two separate occasions in late 1954, the United States and the French governments held official talks in Washington. On 29 September both governments reaffirmed their intention "to support the complete independence of Cambodia, Laos, and Viet-Nam. Both France and the United States will continue to assist Cambodia, Laos and Viet-Nam in their efforts to safeguard their freedom and independence and to advance the welfare of their peoples."[17] France was prepared to retain units of its expeditionary corps in Indochina "in agreement with the government concerned, within the limits permitted under the Geneva agreements and to an extent to be determined." It was further agreed that economic aid would be channeled directly to the states concerned, which merely recognized a decision the administration made in August to aid the Saigon, Vientiane, and Phnom Penh governments directly rather than through French channels.[18] On the occasion of Premier Mendès-France's visit to the United States in late November and after discussions with Mr. Dulles and the President, a joint communiqué was issued that reaffirmed the understandings of the French and American governments embodied in the communiqué of 29 September (quoted above).[19]

The official declarations at Geneva and afterward must be understood as having been supplemented by the terms of the Southeast Asia Collective Defense Treaty, which was signed on 8 September and which entered into force on 19 February 1955. This treaty has been considered in some detail above and I will not repeat that analysis here, except to note the following. Laos, Cambodia, and the "free territory under the jurisdiction of the State of Vietnam" were designated, by a separate protocol, as states that were covered by the provisions of article IV. No action would be taken on the territories of

[15] *Ibid.*, p. 317.   [16] *Ibid.*, p. 318.   [17] *Ibid.*, p. 365.
[18] DDE, p. 371. See *DSB*, 11 October 1954, p. 534.
[19] *Docs., 1954*, p. 79.

these designated states "except at the invitation or with the consent of the government concerned."[20] And the designation by the SEATO signatories of Laos and Cambodia was not a violation *per se* of the Laotian or Cambodian cease-fire agreements because the governments of these states must first consent to SEATO action on their territories, and they were, in principle, entitled to give that consent if their security should be threatened. (See the unilateral declarations of the governments of Laos and Cambodia [FD 5 and article 7 of the Cambodian cease-fire agreement]. There was, however, no provision in the Laotian cease-fire agreement equivalent to article 7 of the Cambodian agreement.) Neither Laos nor Cambodia adhered to SEATO; hence there was no violation of the cease-fire agreements. Whether consent to accepting foreign military assistance pursuant to the SEATO treaty, either in troops or matériel, constituted a violation of the agreements was a question that would have to be determined at the time either Laos or Cambodia gave such consent. And, even then, we must recognize that it might be difficult to contest a determination by the governments of these states that they must request SEATO assistance *because their security was threatened.*[21]

With respect to United States obligations vis-à-vis the Geneva settlement for Vietnam, we may conclude that the government of the United States, except in the particulars noted above, did not consent to be bound by the terms of the final declaration or the cease-fire agreement. It was, moreover, free to withhold such consent. The decision to withhold its consent and the expression of its official position in the Bedell Smith declaration constituted no violation of other international obligations of the United States, as, for example, those in the United Nations Charter.

The United States government voluntarily assumed obligations to refrain from the threat or the use of force to upset the agreement or paragraphs 1 through 12 of the final declaration, to continue to seek to achieve Vietnamese unity through free elections supervised by the U.N., and to refuse to enter an arrangement that hindered the self-determination of peoples. The declaration to refrain from the threat or use of force was qualified in two respects. It made reference to article 2 (4) of the United Nations Charter, according to which the members of the U.N. agreed to "refrain in their international relations from the threat or use of force against the territorial integrity or political independence of any state." This broad declaratory article must, of course, be read with other relevant articles of the U.N.

[20] *Ibid.*, p. 321.
[21] Could the SEATO protocol be termed a violation of the documents relating to the Vietnam cease-fire? See Chapter 27 below.

Charter, particularly article 51, which states in part: "Nothing in the present Charter shall impair the inherent right of individual or collective self-defense if an armed attack occurs against a Member of the United Nations, until the Security Council has taken measures necessary to maintain international peace and security." Secondly, the Bedell Smith declaration also warned that the United States government would view "any renewal of the aggression in violation of the aforesaid Agreements with grave concern and as seriously threatening international peace and security." It does not indicate what action the United States might take if there were a renewal of aggression, but this statement was certainly reinforced by the provisions of the SEATO treaty some seven weeks later, particularly article IV thereof, which provided for various responses by the SEATO signatories in the event of a direct or indirect armed attack against states within the "Treaty area" or upon the states of Laos, Cambodia, or "free" Vietnam.

The United States did not agree to consult with other members of the Geneva Conference on questions referred by the ISC, although nothing precluded a future agreement to consult. Indeed, in 1961 and 1962 the United States met with the members of the conference on the Laotian question, and will very likely consult with these same states again within the quasi-institutional framework established at Geneva in 1954. Apart from the terms of the Bedell Smith declaration, the so-called Potomac Declaration of 29 June, and the Manila Charter of 8 September, the United States government did *not* agree, pursuant to paragraph 12 of the final declaration, to respect the sovereignty, independence, unity, and territorial integrity of Laos, Cambodia, and Vietnam, nor did it agree to refrain from interfering in the internal affairs of these states. The reader, of course, must be aware that the Potomac and the Bedell Smith declarations committed the United States, in principle, to the unity of Vietnam by means of free elections under U.N. supervision. Moreover, the Manila Charter and the Bedell Smith declaration reiterated the "traditional position" of the United States government in supporting the principle of self-determination of peoples. Also, the latter declaration explicitly expressed the hope that "the agreement will permit Cambodia, Laos and Viet Nam to play their part in full independence and sovereignty, in the peaceful community of nations."

Having taken note of paragraphs 1 through 12 of the final declaration, the United States was in a position similar to Britain, the C.P.R., and the Soviet Union in this respect: no positive obligations were incurred under those paragraphs. The statement in paragraph 7 to the effect that elections "shall be held in July 1956, under the supervision [of the ISC]," must be regarded, in respect of the United States, as having been superseded by the terms of the Bedell Smith declaration, which indicated that the United States would continue to seek the unification of Vietnam "through free elections, *supervised by the United Nations.*"

The United States did *not* commit itself *not* to send troops or military personnel or arms and munitions to Vietnam (FD 4), nor did it commit itself to refrain from establishing bases in the southern regroupment zone (FD 5). In fact, were the government of the SVN to consent, the United States, *and Britain and France as well,* might, in theory, act to respond to an armed attack against southern Vietnam (SEATO treaty art. IV and protocol) by sending troops and arms, and perhaps even by establishing bases there. This was entirely consistent with the commitment of the Bedell Smith declaration to refrain from the threat or use of force "to disturb" the agreement, which was limited or circumscribed by the reservation pertaining to "any renewal of aggression." In that case, viewing such renewal with grave concern and as a threat to international peace and security, the United States would be free to respond according to the provisions of the SEATO treaty, and might respond by military means within the territories of the protocol states, provided the governments of Laos, Cambodia, or the State of Vietnam consented to this.

With respect to the statements of principle and fact in paragraphs 6 through 11 of the final declaration, the legal effect (if any) of the United States' "taking note" thereof is difficult to assess. Certainly the United States agreed that the Geneva settlement was a military rather than a political solution (see FD 6); it has never denied that the military demarcation line was provisional; and its statements in support of unity for Vietnam may be understood as emphasizing these facts. Of course, Dulles and others might have surmised that the division of Vietnam would be as "temporary" as the division of Korea or Germany, but the official American position has consistently recognized the theoretically provisional nature of such divisions.

[III]

OBLIGATIONS OF SIGNATORY STATES

France

Let us now consider the obligations incurred by the principal states in the Vietnam settlement: France, the Democratic Republic of Vietnam, and the State of Vietnam, upon which the execution of the provisions of the cease-fire agreement and the final declaration devolved. At the last plenary session of the conference Mendès-France stated that the "French Delegation approves the terms of this [the final] Declaration."[22] Having given his verbal approval, the Premier returned to Paris, where he formally notified the National Assembly of the terms of the Indochina settlement, and the Indochina policy of the Premier was debated in the Assembly on 22 and 23 July. The resolution with which the government formally associated itself was that of Deputies Delbos and Valabrègue, which ultimately won the approval of the Assembly. It read in part:

> The National Assembly . . . records with satisfaction the cessation of hostilities in Indochina, due, in large part, to the decisive action of the President of the Council; . . . affirms . . . its willingness to protect, within the bounds of the French Union and within the limits of the agreements concluded (*dans le cadre de l'Union française et des accords conclus*), the French and the Indochinese peoples friendly to France, who intend to remain faithful to the work of emancipation which it constantly pursues; asks the Government to continue, in necessary agreement with our allies, a policy of peace among all peoples.[23]

During the debate three other resolutions were offered, and the language of one of them (presented by Deputies de Chambrun, Meunier, and others) is particularly interesting. It read in part:

> The National Assembly approves the declarations of the President of the Council and invites the Government: 1. to apply the Geneva agreements with the same will to peace which attended their conclusion so that the state of war will be followed as rapidly as possible by cooperation in all areas between the French people and a unified and independent Vietnamese people.[24]

The language of the de Chambrun resolution responds positively to the fact of a settlement; that is, it *approved* the declarations of the Premier and invited his government to apply the Geneva agreements in a certain way.

The Delbos-Valabrègue resolution, on the other hand, is very vague; it "records" the fact of the cease-fire (but not the cease-fire agreement or the final declaration!) and, in elevated prose, affirms the willingness of the Assembly to protect certain peoples within the bounds of the French Union and the agreements concluded. Mendès-France accepted this resolution because, he said, he could not accept a resolution that did not approve his actions at Geneva. Thus, it is possible to argue that the Delbos-Valabrègue resolution was not a ratification

[22] Cmd. 9239, p. 5.
[23] *JO*, pp. 3584-3589, 3614-3620 (sess. of 23 July).
[24] *Ibid.*, p. 3584.

of the cease-fire agreement, the final declaration, or the unilateral declarations.

Let us assume, however, that passage of the resolution by the Assembly on 23 July constituted ratification.[25] In effect, then, the Assembly confirmed the signature of General Delteil and accepted the fact that the French Union high command was bound by the terms of the cease-fire agreement. It also confirmed, in effect, the two declarations of the French government issued by its delegation at Geneva on 21 July. What, then, was the French government obligated to do?

1. It agreed to adhere to the principles of respect for the independence, sovereignty, unity, and territorial integrity of Cambodia, Laos, and Vietnam (its unilateral declaration referring to FD 11).

2. It agreed to withdraw its troops from Indochina at the request of the governments concerned, except where, by agreement between the parties, a certain number of French troops were to remain at specified points for a specified time (its unilateral declaration referring to FD 10).

3. The French also agreed to adhere to the technical procedures for the cease-fire and troop withdrawal and the transfer and regroupment of troops according to chapters I, II, and V of the cease-fire agreement, insofar as these procedures affected French troops and French Union troops under the authority of the French high command (see art. 27) and insofar as they did not violate the principles of respect for the independence and sovereignty of Vietnam.

4. The French government agreed to conduct the civil administration of the southern regroupment zone "pending the general elections which will bring about the unification of Viet Nam" (14[a]). But how compatible with the principle of respect for the sovereignty of Vietnam was this provision of the agreement? Vietnam's sovereignty could only mean that a Vietnamese government must be permitted to exercise sovereign authority in Vietnam; in other words, it must be permitted to conduct civil administration in Vietnamese territories.

At the time of the cease-fire agreement, France recognized only one

[25] The reader should be aware of another legal problem, whose consequence would have been to relieve France of all formal obligations pursuant to the Geneva agreements. Article 27 of the Constitution of the Fourth French Republic (1946) stated: "Treaties relating to . . . peace treaties . . . , those which concern the personal status and the property rights of French citizens abroad . . . and those which carry with them the cession, exchange or acquisition of territory, are final only after having been ratified by a law." It could be cogently argued that the Geneva agreements came within the terms of this article and hence had to be ratified by a law duly promulgated by the National Assembly. But the National Assembly merely approved Mendès-France's Indochina *policy* and a law of the kind envisaged by article 27 was never passed. Thus the binding effect of the Geneva agreements upon the Mendès-France government or its successors was at least questionable.

government of Vietnam, the State of Vietnam, of which Bao Dai was the chief of state and Ngo Dinh Diem the Premier, and recognition of the Bao Dai regime was reaffirmed by the French in August. Even if French signature of the agreement with that of DRVN minister Ta Quang Buu and the establishment of a French mission in Hanoi to which delegate general Jean Sainteny was dispatched both constituted implied recognition of the DRVN, the more explicit and formal recognition of the Bao Dai-Diem regime as *the* government of Vietnam committed France, by virtue of the unilateral declaration, to respect the sovereignty of the only "Vietnam" it formally recognized—that is, the State of Vietnam. This meant that the conduct of civil administration must be vested in the hands of the Diem government as expeditiously as possible after Diem demanded that this be done. It also meant that French troops must be withdrawn, should Diem request such a step, since the French had committed themselves to a withdrawal if they were requested to do so by the government concerned.

5. The French government also agreed to refrain from reprisals and to permit persons to leave the areas under its control (14[*c-d*]).

6. By the provisions of articles 16 and 17, the French government agreed to refrain from introducing troops, military personnel, and arms and munitions into Vietnam.

7. Articles 18 and 19 of the agreement can be construed as a promise by the French not to establish new military bases in Vietnam, and also as a commitment not to arrange for the establishment of such bases by their allies. The parties to the agreement were to ensure that the "zones assigned to them do not adhere to any military alliance and are not used for the resumption of hostilities to further an aggressive policy" (19). But to what extent could France ensure that the guarantees of article 19 were fulfilled if it would withdraw its army from Vietnam upon the request of the government concerned? Lacking an army and economic pressure (which after the summer or fall of 1954 only the United States was in a position to exert), the French government would not have the *means* to fulfill article 19.

8. Pursuant to article 21, the French government agreed to liberate prisoners of war and "civilian internees" (21 *b*) within thirty days.

9. Finally, under chapter VI of the cease-fire agreement, the French government agreed to provide military officers for service on the joint commission, to cooperate with the ISC and the joint commission, and to permit the ISC to move freely in the southern regroupment zone and within the demilitarized zone south of the demarcation line. It further agreed to provide facilities, transportation,

and communications for the ISC and its inspection teams (35). Insofar as permission for the ISC to operate on territories in southern Vietnam was within the competence of the French government to grant, it could fulfill the provisions of chapter VI. However, were it to abide by its declaration to respect the sovereignty and independence of the State of Vietnam,[26] it could not compel the SVN government to permit the ISC to function: this was an obligation that the SVN government must voluntarily assume.

Pursuant to paragraph 12 of the final declaration, the French government undertook (in its unilateral declarations) to respect the sovereignty, independence, unity, and territorial integrity of Vietnam, and also to refrain from interference in the internal affairs of that state (a commitment not expressly enunciated in the unilateral declarations). However, paragraphs 1 to 6 and 8 to 11 created no obligations in addition to those created by the terms of the cease-fire agreement. French approval of paragraph 7 of the final declaration meant that the French government believed any future political settlement in Vietnam "shall permit the Vietnamese people to enjoy the fundamental freedoms guaranteed by democratic institutions established as a result of free general elections by secret ballot." Was France obligated by this language to do anything at all? The same mandatory language was used in subsequent sentences: "General elections shall be held in July 1956, under the supervision [of the ISC]"; "consultations will be held . . . from July 20, 1955, onwards." Was France obligated to see that consultations and elections were held? If either the SVN or the DRVN governments refused to consult or cooperate with each other in planning and holding elections, what was France obligated to do? Paradoxically, anything France chose to do would constitute interference in the internal affairs of the SVN or the DRVN (FD 12) or infringement of the sovereignty of either governmental entity.

It might be argued that, since the DRVN consented to elections, its subsequent refusal to hold them would justify intervention by France, but what of the government of the SVN, which had reserved its position on the cease-fire agreement and on the final declaration? How would interference or possible intervention comport with the sovereignty of the SVN, which France had formally recognized? As a practical matter, France would not be in a position to persuade the SVN to hold elections for several reasons.

[26] The unilateral declaration, as indicated above, stated that the French government would respect the sovereignty of Vietnam—not the State of Vietnam nor the Democratic Republic of Vietnam. Since, however, France had already formally recognized the State of Vietnam as sovereign in Vietnam, the unilateral declaration could be said to have bound the French government to respect the sovereignty and independence of the State of Vietnam.

1. The French government had committed itself to withdrawing its troops at the request of the governments concerned. If Diem or his successors asked for the withdrawal of French troops, and France complied, she would be in no position to compel the SVN government to accept elections. I believe it is also safe to say that neither the French government nor the French people were prepared to use force in 1954, 1955, or 1956 to compel either the DRVN or the SVN governments to accept elections.

2. In view of statements made by Premier Mendès-France in 1954 and the debates in the National Assembly at the time, it was clear the French did not intend to resort to the use of force to ensure that the provisions of the declaration were executed, unless vital French security and national interests were affected. Consultations in 1955 and elections in 1956 were not of such importance as to require the French to resort to force, even if they had been able to do so.

3. In any future Vietnamese political settlement in which France might be involved, the French government would be guided by the principles of Vietnamese unity, territorial integrity, sovereignty, and independence, and would show due regard for the fact that in July 1954 it believed elections *ought* to be held in July 1956.

4. Finally, the French government was obligated to assist the ISC and the representatives of the member states of the ISC in promoting peace in Indochina, in bringing about conditions that would enable the elections to be scheduled, and to cooperate with the ISC members in the elections' supervisory tasks.

Other than such consultative, remonstrative, and advisory duties, France was under no obligation to see that elections were held pursuant to paragraph 7 of the final declaration. Having fulfilled its duties under the cease-fire agreement, the unilateral declarations, and the final declaration—*as described above*—France could not be accused of violating any provisions of these documents if either the SVN or the DRVN refused to consult in 1955 or to schedule elections in 1956. Although it may be academic, it should be explicitly stated that France was not responsible, under the provisions of chapter III of the cease-fire agreement, for the introduction of troops, arms, or munitions into Vietnam nor for the establishment of military bases upon the territory of southern Vietnam after 1956. I do not necessarily mean to imply that *any* state was so responsible, in the sense that the introduction of training personnel and combat troops of the United States and others constituted a violation of chapter III of the cease-fire agreement or of the final declaration; I wish only, at this point, to make the negative statement that France was not responsible.

The DRVN

It is fairly safe to assume, although Ta Quang Buu signed the cease-fire agreement on behalf of the commander in chief of the PAVN, that the DRVN government ratified the agreement. Subsequent policy statements, and the adherence of the PAVN and the DRVN to the terms of the cease-fire, could be taken to mean that DRVN officials regarded the agreement as obligatory. During the first two years after the cease-fire, the DRVN frequently contested the interpretation of provisions of the agreement and, more frequently, disagreed with the French and with members of the ISC inspection teams on the facts of particular incidents. Generally, however, the official behavior of the DRVN could be construed as implying ratification of the agreement and willingness to act as the "successors in function" of the PAVN high command (art. 27).

If we assume ratification, the DRVN government was obligated to the terms of the cease-fire agreement in much the same way as the French government. Officials of the DRVN had to adhere to the procedures for implementing the cease-fire and for the assembly, withdrawal, and regroupment of troops. They had to respect the demilitarized zone and cooperate with the joint commission and the ISC, as required by article 25 and 35. They had to refrain from reprisals against persons and organizations, and permit civilians residing in their zone to emigrate (14[c and d]). Article 14 (a) presented no real problem of interpretation (as it did for the French in the southern regroupment zone): civil administration in the northern regroupment zone would be in the hands of the high command of the PAVN and its civilian directors, the officials of the DRVN government.

The DRVN also was obligated to refrain from importing arms, ordnance, and munitions into areas under its jurisdiction (17[a]), except for post-hostilities replacement of damaged or worn-out arms and munitions (17[b]). Although, presumably, the troops or military personnel of allies could not be invited into northern Vietnam (16), no limitation was placed upon the size of the PAVN. After the cessation of hostilities the DRVN could expand its army to a level determined only by the available quantity of arms and military supplies. Additional arms and supplies, except for replacements, could not be accepted without violating article 17 of the cease-fire agreement. According to articles 18 and 19, the DRVN would establish no new military bases in the northern zone nor allow any bases to be established there by a foreign power; nor could the DRVN adhere to a military alliance or otherwise permit its zone to be used for an aggressive policy. Also, it should be noted that neither the DRVN nor France was formally obligated to abide by the recommendations concerning disputes, violations, and threats of violations the ISC submitted to them pursuant to articles 39 and 40.

The fact that Pham Van Dong did not express approval or disapproval of the final declaration is a further indication of the informality that attended the final session of the Geneva Conference. Thus Dong could not be said to have given his government's express consent to obligations under the declaration. Nevertheless, the post-Geneva conduct of the DRVN government, particularly in its efforts to arrange for consultations with the SVN government in 1955 and to schedule elections in 1956, can be construed as implied consent. This conclusion cannot be drawn with full certainty, but I will assume, *arguendo*, that the DRVN government was bound by the *operative* provisions of the final declaration. It was obligated, therefore, to consult with the other members of the conference on questions the ISC referred to the conference in order to study measures necessary to ensure that the cease-fire agreements for Vietnam, Cambodia, and Laos were respected (FD 13). It was further obligated to respect the sovereignty, independence, unity, and territorial integrity of Cambodia and Laos and to refrain from interfering in their internal affairs (FD 12).

This, however, did not prevent the DRVN from assisting the Pathet Lao in 1955 and 1956 nor dispatching PAVN troops across the Laotian border in late 1958; nor has it hindered DRVN use of territory in Laos and Cambodia for supporting insurgency in southern Vietnam in the years after 1959. There are some who believe the DRVN was justified in its interference in the internal affairs of Laos and its nonrespect for the territorial integrity of Cambodia and Laos because of the refusal of the SVN to agree to elections in 1956. But this does not explain the DRVN's support of the Pathet Lao in 1955 and 1956. It may be, after all, that we were mistaken in assuming the DRVN impliedly consented to the terms of the final declaration. Or it may be that the DRVN selected the provisions it would regard as binding on itself, on France, on the government of the SVN, and on the other conference participants, and chose to ignore other provisions.

Because the DRVN was obligated to perform many of the acts of which the conference took note in the final declaration (by virtue of related provisions in the cease-fire agreement), we need not discuss them again, except for paragraph 7, which asserted that general elections were to be held in July 1956. Whether or not the DRVN was bound by the operative provisions of the declaration, the Hanoi government in 1955 and 1956 unsuccessfully sought to arrange for consultations and for elections; and, given the assumptions of the DRVN leaders and the Vietminh military victories in the spring of 1954, it was perhaps justified in its irritation with the conference participants' unwillingness to compel the SVN to cooperate. Although we do not know Hanoi's attitude toward the Soviet Union or the C.P.R. in 1956, the U.S.S.R. tried to reconvene the Geneva Conference in that year but its efforts were not fruitful. Perhaps Hanoi expected more forceful insistence upon elections, and may have felt that Molotov had made too many concessions to France in 1954 to obtain the peace in Indochina the Malenkov regime desired. These concessions, largely at Vietminh expense and easy for Molotov to have made, had led to the blind alley in which the DRVN officials found themselves in 1956. We know, at any rate, that Hanoi was angry with the French, who it believed were obligated to see that the SVN government complied with paragraph 7 of the final declaration.

But paragraph 7 qualified the bald statement that "general elections shall be held in July 1956." For one thing, the elections were to be supervised by an international commission composed of representatives of the ISC member state, and the DRVN did not always cooperate fully with the ISC, as was required by articles 25 and 35 of the cease-fire agreement. Would the DRVN have cooperated with the election supervisory commission in 1956? The question, obviously, cannot be answered, but it is worth pondering.

Paragraph 7 also stated that the settlement of political problems in Vietnam "shall permit the Vietnamese people to enjoy the fundamental freedoms, guaranteed by democratic institutions established as a result of free general elections by secret ballot." Would the DRVN have agreed to elections by secret ballot, to free elections, and to the establishment of democratic institutions? SVN and United States officials answered these questions in the negative, and Saigon concluded it was pointless even to consult with Hanoi about elections that could not possibly be free to establish institutions that could not possibly be "democratic." Whether the SVN was legally justified in refusing to cooperate in planning and holding elections is a question we must still consider, but the reader should be aware of the very great difficulties attendant upon the meaning of "free" and "democratic." Experience in Korea and Eastern Europe showed that Communist and non-Communist governments understood these terms in very different senses.

Chapter 23

THE VIETNAMESE STATE AND
THE GENEVA AGREEMENTS

[I]

In this chapter we will examine the legal and political responsibilities of the State of Vietnam under the Geneva settlements of July 1954. In order to assess such responsibilities, it is necessary to determine whether the French government or the French high command, on the one hand, or the other Geneva powers, on the other, could encumber the SVN with the duties ostensibly imposed by the Geneva agreements. This question, in turn, depends upon the juridical status of the SVN (and, indirectly, upon the juridical status of the DRVN) in 1954 and subsequent years. In the arguments that follow I am not concerned with definitively answering the question whether the SVN was ever a sovereign state; rather, I will approach the subject in this way. First, I will assume the SVN was sovereign on 21 July 1954; then I will assume the SVN became sovereign only after the Geneva Conference ended; and finally I will assume the SVN was never sovereign *in law*. I will examine the legal consequences of each assumption and attempt to draw some conclusions about SVN and DRVN obligations.

A. The SVN Sovereign in July, 1954

Let us first assume that on 21 July the SVN was a fully sovereign state and its government duly constituted. What, then, was its position? To answer this question we must refer to three documents and to the text of a proposed amendment to the final declaration the SVN delegation issued in the last days of the conference. Document 1 was a proposal for a cease-fire, without the partition of Vietnam, and a contingency paper dated 20 July. Document 2 was a protest, dated 21 July.[1]

In document 1 Tran Van Do pointed out that the military cease-fire agreement between the French and the Vietminh high commands endangered the future of the State of Vietnam. It would lead, he said, to an abandonment of territories, peoples, and public and civil services. Do averred that the "delegation of power which the French High Command had received from the Chief of State of the State of

---

[1] Documents 1, 2, and 3 appear in *Relazioni internazionali*, Series 2, 17, No. 31 (31 July 1954): 926; document 3 also appears in *Docs., 1954*, pp. 315-316.

Vietnam insofar as it concerned Vietnamese troops" did not entail, for the SVN, consequences as serious as partition and the loss of territories and peoples. The delegation of the State of Vietnam, Do said, regretted that it *could not subscribe* to a solution that brought about partition and reduced the SVN's capacity to resist Communist expansion.

In document 2 the SVN delegation noted that the settlement the conference was about to accept meant a preliminary or provisional division of Vietnam, which could not fail to produce the very same effects in Vietnam that were exemplified by Germany, Austria, and Korea. A solution of this kind would be disastrous for the people of Vietnam and for the peace of the world. Tran Van Do then reiterated his government's proposals, which comprised these elements:

1. A cease-fire at the present positions of all military units;

2. Regroupment of troops into two assigned zones as limited in area as possible;

3. Disarmament of irregulars;

4. After a period of stabilization, disarmament of Vietminh troops and immediate withdrawal of foreign troops; and

5. United Nations control of the cease-fire, regroupment, disarmament, withdrawal, and administration of the entire country, and general elections as soon as the U.N. had established order and security throughout Vietnam.

During the final plenary session, the Vietnamese minister sought to have paragraph 10 of the final declaration amended by the following text:

> The Conference takes note of the Declaration of the Government of the State of Viet Nam undertaking:
>
> to make and support every effort to re-establish a real and lasting peace in Viet Nam;
>
> not to use force to resist the procedures for carrying the cease-fire into effect, in spite of the objections and reservations that the State of Viet Nam has expressed, especially in its final statement.[2]

Presumably, the conference informally took note of this SVN text.[3]

Document 3, the "final statement" of the SVN delegation (referred to in the text of the proposed amendment to paragraph 10), protested the "summary rejection" of the SVN cease-fire proposal, the abandonment of territories to the Vietminh (thus making defense against Communist expansion virtually impossible), and the many clauses of the agreement that gravely compromised the political future of the Vietnamese people. It also protested "the hasty conclusion of the

[2] Cmd. 9239, p. 7.
[3] *Ibid.*, pp. 7-8.

armistice agreement, contracted only by the high authority of France and the Vietminh notwithstanding the fact that the French High Command controls the Vietnamese troops only through a delegation of authority by the Chief of State of Viet-Nam," and "the fact that the French High Command has arrogated to itself without preliminary agreement with the delegation of the State of Viet-Nam the right to fix the date of future elections, notwithstanding that a matter of a clearly political character is concerned." Also, the protest of the SVN requested the conference to take note of these protests and of the fact that "it reserves to itself complete freedom of action to guarantee the sacred right of the Vietnamese people to territorial unity, national independence and freedom."

Did the conference take note of this protest or merely take note of the text of the SVN amendment to paragraph 10 of the final declaration—or both? Eden's suggestion that the conference take note of the SVN declaration was informal and imprecise in its terms, and the language in the proposed amendment did not appear in either document 1 or document 2. The question arises: To what declaration did the proposed amendment refer? This question had no easy answer, but in my opinion it is safe to assume that documents 1, 2, and 3, and the proposed amendment offer sufficient evidence to assess the official SVN position with respect to the Geneva settlement. These documents and texts can be construed as follows.[4]

1. The high command of the army of the SVN and the government of the State of Vietnam were not bound by the terms of the cease-fire agreement. They were not, moreover, "successors in function" of the signatories (pursuant to art. 27). The French high command, *according to the theory of the SVN delegation*, maintained command over the troops of the SVN through a grant or delegation of authority from the Vietnamese chief of state, but the French high command could not bind the SVN to the terms of an arrangement as significant as the cease-fire agreement without the preliminary consent of the duly constituted authorities of that state. Such consent had not been obtained, and in any case would not have been given.

2. Notwithstanding the fact that the SVN incurred no obligations pursuant to the cease-fire agreement, the SVN government undertook not to use force to resist procedures for carrying the cease-fire into effect, despite its protests and reservations. It would, moreover, support every effort to reestablish peace in Vietnam. Presumably, then,

---

[4] The reader should remember that in part A of this chapter we are assuming, *arguendo*, that on 21 July 1954 the SVN was a duly constituted government of a sovereign state. The enumeration that follows is largely an interpretation of the point of view of the SVN government, not the author's conclusions with respect to the SVN's obligations.

the SVN high command would adhere to the cease-fire provisions of the agreement (11) and Vietnamese troops would cooperate with French Union troops during withdrawal, reassembly, and regroupment (5, 12, 15), which would include evacuation of SVN troops from the Red River delta and from the cities of Hanoi and Haiphong (14[b], 15). Because the tasks of the ISC and the joint commission were intimately connected with the procedures whereby a cease-fire would be made effective, the SVN government would either have to cooperate with these commissions or at least tolerate their activities within the southern regroupment zone (i.e. within territories subject to SVN jurisdiction). Undoubtedly, the undertaking not to use force to resist the cease-fire procedures carried an obligation not to interfere with the operations of the ISC or the joint commission. Whether it also carried an obligation to cooperate in the fashion envisaged in article 35 may be doubted. Like France and the DRVN, the SVN was not required to execute recommendations of the ISC made pursuant to articles 39 or 40.

3. The partition of Vietnam was provisional and the demarcation line was not meant to be a political boundary. The SVN delegation, however, expressed its concern that Vietnam would remain divided, as had Korea, Germany, and Austria.

4. The SVN delegation protested the French high command's arrogation of the right to fix a date for elections without the preliminary agreement of the Vietnamese government. This was particularly serious, in the view of the SVN, because the cease-fire agreement was meant to bring about a military, not a political settlement in Vietnam, and elections were strictly a political matter. According to this view, article 14(a), which vested the civil administration of the southern regroupment zone in the hands of the French high command (or the French government), was also a political solution. One would therefore expect the SVN to demand that the French turn over control of civil administration to the Vietnamese rather quickly, long before July 1956, the date fixed in the final declaration for all-Vietnamese elections. In fact, the Mendès-France government took steps to this end only one week after the close of the Geneva Conference and, in accordance with its unilateral declarations, eventually gave the Vietnamese in the south complete functional authority over the administration of their own civil and military affairs. Thus the SVN did not regard article 14(a) as binding; in fact, this article was a dead letter before the end of 1954.

5. Articles 16 and 17 prohibited the introduction into Vietnam of troop reinforcements, additional military personnel, arms, munitions, combat aircraft, and ordnance, but the SVN did not consent to be bound by these articles. The same can be said of articles 18 and 19,

prohibiting the establishment of new military bases or military bases under the control of a foreign state and adherence of the SVN to a military alliance. Because Tran Van Do expressed his government's fears that the terms of the cease-fire agreement would reduce the SVN's ability to resist Communist expansion, it could be expected that the Diem government would do what it could to improve its defensive capabilities. Even within the terms of article 16, the SVN was free to expand its army until it reached the limits of its ability to train, equip, and supply its troops and cadres. Article 17 prohibited the importation of arms and munitions, but the SVN, if it was not bound by that article, was free to import prohibited war matériel from the state that was most concerned with Communist expansion in Southeast Asia, namely, the United States.

We should remember, however, that Do sought to introduce an amendment to paragraph 10 of the final declaration that presumably represented the official position of the SVN government. This proposed amendment referred to an SVN declaration, of which the conference rather informally took note, in which the State of Vietnam undertook to "make and support every effort to re-establish a real and lasting peace in Viet-Nam." One might cogently argue that such an undertaking obligated the SVN to accept the prohibitions of articles 16 through 19, and the argument is particularly strong in the case of article 19, wherein the parties were to ensure that the zones assigned to them were not "used for the resumption of hostilities or to further an aggressive policy." The SVN's obligation to support peace efforts in Vietnam would certainly include assumption of the responsibility to see that the southern regroupment zone, under its jurisdiction, was not used in a manner proscribed by article 19. But we cannot, of course, press the argument too far; the obligations, if such there were, were self-imposed. The exigencies of self-defense, both in law and in practice, would force the SVN to take steps to meet a threat to its security and certainly a threat to its existence.[5]

6. Let us turn now to the familiar paragraph 7 of the final declaration. The SVN government indicated its willingness to have all-Vietnamese elections *after stability and order had returned to the country,* but when would this be? The SVN response would have been: we cannot say, but the United Nations should be given the task of verify-

---

[5] It might be possible to argue that the SVN was bound to observe articles 16-19, pertaining to the neutralization of Vietnam, because the SVN was the successor of France and a treaty of neutralization is "dispositive"; that is, it imposes obligations upon states that have seceded from or have become independent of a parent state. D. G. Partan, in Falk (pp. 210-212), in effect makes such an argument, but compare D. P. O'Connell, *The Law of State Succession* (Cambridge: The Syndics of Cambridge University Press, 1956), pp. 49-50, and see the discussion in n. 13 below.

ing the conditions of stability and order. The SVN, moreover, wanted the U.N. to supervise elections rather than an ISC that had a Communist representative and was chaired by an Indian representative (whose government had not been as friendly to the aspirations of the SVN—the Indians might call them "pretensions"—as the latter government would like). Thus the SVN position on elections differed from the substance of paragraph 7 in these respects: it did not want to fix a date for elections; it preferred to condition their date upon U.N.-verified conditions of stability and order; and the elections must be supervised by the U.N. Apart from these vital differences, moreover, the SVN challenged the right of the French high command to fix the date for elections. But perhaps it is incorrect to say that the French high command fixed the date inasmuch as this was agreed upon at one of the last private meetings between Eden, Molotov, Chou En-lai, Pham Van Dong, and Mendès-France (neither Bedell Smith nor Tran Van Do was present, however). Thus, while it is correct to say that elections had been fixed without the preliminary consent of the SVN (which in any case would not have been given), it would be more accurate to say that the diplomats who attended a restricted, private meeting agreed among themselves when the elections should be held.[6] Although the draftsmen of the final declaration chose to use language that implied a consensus, the declaration that the *conference* had agreed that elections should be held in July 1956 was as much based upon a fiction, as was the protest of the SVN delegation.

Thus the SVN government most certainly did not give its consent to paragraph 7. Nor would its official behavior subsequent to the Geneva Conference justify a conslusion that, in some way, the SVN had *impliedly* consented to the terms of paragraph 7. On the assumption that the State of Vietnam was fully sovereign in July 1954 and its government was duly constituted, the SVN incurred no obligation to comply with the mandatory language: "General elections shall be held in July 1956."

7. In his protest of 21 July, Tran Van Do reserved to the SVN government "complete freedom of action to guarantee the sacred right of the Vietnamese people to territorial unity, national independence and freedom." Such a reservation could license almost any action, including the use of force, but the SVN government and its army were in no condition to employ force in 1954. The reservation should be read with the text of Do's proposed amendment, which stated that the SVN government would not "use force to resist the procedures

---

[6] Pham Van Dong rather unhappily acquiesced in the July 1956 date. He had asked for setting an election date six months after the cease-fire.

for carrying the cease-fire into effect, in spite of its objections and reservations."

B. The SVN Sovereign after July 1954

The two treaties of independence and association between the SVN and France, *initialed* by Prince Buu Loc and Premier Laniel on 4 June, had not been ratified by the time the Geneva Conference ended; thus the sovereign status of the SVN was juridically unclear. It might therefore be argued that the SVN was not sovereign at all, and the arguments that have been raised against the legal status of the SVN in 1954 might be buttressed with evidence of its lack of functional independence. Not until after the cease-fire did France complete the transfer of real control of governmental agencies to the Vietnamese.[7] On 21 July, critics would assert, the SVN not only was not sovereign in law, it was not sovereign in fact.

Indeed, the SVN's functional independence had not been perfected by the time the conference ended and even its juridical independence was under a cloud. The 4 June treaties had merely been authenticated, not ratified—and were never formally ratified. It was probably the unilateral declaration of the French government on 21 July that perfected the juridical independence of the SVN, stating that, in the settlement of all problems connected with the reestablishment and consolidation of peace in Vietnam, the French government would "proceed from the principle of respect for the independence and sovereignty, the unity and territorial integrity of . . . Viet Nam." The declaration speaks only of Vietnam, not the SVN, but neither does it speak of the DRVN; hence we are left the task of interpretation. Both before and after the Geneva settlement, France formally recognized the State of Vietnam of which Bao Dai was the chief of state, that is, the SVN. But since 1950 the United States, Great Britain, and more than thirty other states (many of them allies of France) had recognized and established formal diplomatic relations with the SVN. Thus there is some basis for arguing that the French government meant the SVN when it used the designation "Viet Nam" in its declaration.

It is not difficult, however, to find defects in the *sovereign status* of Vietnam, whether we assert on the one hand that the SVN government or, on the other hand, that the DRVN government was the duly constituted government of that state. Certainly the Vietminh enjoyed functional independence in areas controlled by its forces, but this was a consequence of the fact that the Vietminh was in rebellion

---

[7] General Ely has briefly described the process by which SVN authorities assumed control of civil and military functions (Ely, pp. 259-264).

against France. In areas controlled by French Union forces, the Vietnamese only slowly and laboriously won *some* measure of functional independence up to the time the Geneva Conference adjourned. If degree of functional independence were the basis for regarding either the DRVN or the SVN sovereign, the DRVN was the sovereign entity, but determination on this basis puts a premium on insurgency.

Insurgents who are able to control territory for an extended length of time can claim to be sovereign, and can claim to speak for the people of the country, and can contest the legitimacy of the incumbent government. Most third-party governments are reluctant to recognize insurgent regimes, at least early in a civil or internal war, and even are slow to recognize a state of belligerency between insurgents and an incumbent government.[8] Functional independence *alone* is not generally accepted as a basis for extending recognition to insurgents. The political interests of states may dictate otherwise, as when states of a particular ideological orientation recognize insurgent movements of similar orientation, but governments generally take the position that—although the exercise of functional independence may show a capacity for waging civil war effectively, and hence capability for controlling some areas of a country—it does not necessarily show that insurgents represent the people (if we assume these governments accept self-determination of peoples as the legitimating principle) or that the insurgents are otherwise entitled, in law, to exercise sovereignty over *all* the territory of the state. Governments usually are loath to endanger relations with their allies or antagonize other friendly governments by extending recognition or otherwise attributing sovereign or quasi-sovereign status to insurgent movements within the borders of allied or friendly governments.

Let us assume, however, that on 21 July the government of Ngo Dinh Diem did not legitimately exercise the powers of a government of a sovereign state, that the SVN government was not *the* duly constituted government of Vietnam. What consequences follow from this state of affairs, particularly in respect of the cease-fire agreement, the final declaration, and the unilateral French declarations?

1. The various documents, proposals, and protests of the SVN delegation would simply be the inconsequential mutterings of an entity that was a participant of the Geneva Conference, an entity that had

---

[8] In this connection, see R. A. Falk, "Janus Tormented: The International Law of Internal War" and George Modelski, "The International Relations of Internal War," in J. N. Rosenau (ed.), *International Aspects of Civil Strife* (Princeton: Princeton University Press, 1964). See also the essays by K. W. Deutsch, A. C. Janos, and William Kornhauser in Harry Eckstein (ed.), *Internal War* (New York: The Free Press of Glencoe, 1964).

no standing to protest or otherwise speak for or on behalf of the Vietnamese people.

2. For the purposes of a military settlement, the French high
command, and ultimately the French government, would be responsible for performing the actions that would bring about a cessation
of hostilities. The army of the SVN was subordinate to the high command of the French Union and hence would be bound by the orders
of that command and the obligations it incurred. (Let us assume that
the grant of authority from Bao Dai to the French, attaching state of
Vietnam troops to the French command structure, was a mere for-
mality elicited by the French from a compliant puppet.)

3. The French high command would be bound by the provisions
of the cease-fire agreement, as indicated in Chapter 21. The commander in chief of the French Union forces in Indochina (General
Ely) was to order and to enforce a complete cease-fire in Vietnam by
armed forces *under his control* (10). SVN forces were under his control; hence General Ely was responsible for ensuring that they adhered to the technical procedures for a cease-fire (see chapter II of
the agreement). The French high command also was responsible for
ensuring that no troops, military personnel, arms, munitions, and
ordnance were introduced into Vietnam (16, 17), that no new military bases were established (18, 19), and that the southern regroupment zone did not adhere to a military alliance and was not used for
the resumption of hostilities or to further an aggressive policy (19).
The conduct of civil administration in the southern zone would be
vested in the French high command (14[a]).

4. Under article 27, the commander of the French Union forces
was to take all steps and make all arrangements necessary to ensure
full compliance with "all the provisions" of the agreement "by all elements and military personnel under" his command. Units of the
SVN army were elements under the command of the French high
command; hence the commander's responsibility under article 27 extended to them.

Also, according to article 27, "the signatories of the present Agreement and their successors in their functions shall be responsible
for ensuring the observance and enforcement of the terms and provisions thereof." Clearly, then, a French military officer who succeeded General Ely would be bound by article 27, but would an
SVN officer be bound as well? If we ignore the fact that the agreement was signed on behalf of the French high command *as* the
French high command, it would have been most extraordinary for an
SVN officer to have formally succeeded General Ely or his French
successors. If on 21 July, however, the SVN government and its army
were completely subordinate to the French government and the

French Union high command, one could argue that SVN officers and officials, insofar as they exercised the *functions* of the French command, were bound by article 27 and, by virtue of that article, by the provisions of the entire cease-fire agreement.

5. If the SVN was not the sovereign entity in the southern regroupment zone on 21 July, I think we must assume that France was sovereign. If the SVN was not sovereign—according to our assumption—the French government, presumably, had not yet perfected the independence of the Vietnamese people in the southern regroupment zone and France, in effect, remained sovereign by virtue of her colonial rule, dating from the nineteenth century.

If, as could be argued, France had not perfected the independence of the Vietnamese people in the northern regroupment zone—any more than in the southern zone—who was the sovereign entity in the northern zone? This question is important for a number of reasons, only one of which I will consider at this point. In a unilateral declaration of 21 July the French government stated that, for the settlement of all problems connected with the reestablishment and consolidation of peace in Vietnam, it would proceed "from the principle of respect for the independence and sovereignty, the unity and territorial integrity of . . . Viet Nam." What entity was the legatee of a French bequest of sovereignty and was to assume the role of the sovereign in Vietnam: the DRVN, the SVN, or some other entity? What entity could insist, on behalf of the "Viet Nam" of the French declaration, that France must fulfill the terms of that declaration and proceed from respect for the principles of independence, sovereignty, unity, and territorial integrity? What "concerned" government could request the French to withdraw their troops from Vietnam pursuant to the terms of their second unilateral declaration? No one can contest the fact that on 21 July, and afterward, the DRVN exercised functional sovereign authority in much (and eventually all) of the northern regroupment zone;[9] that it did so was a result of the PAVN's successes in the war with France and, subsequently, of the terms of the cease-fire agreement pursuant to which the French Union army relinquished control of territories north of the demarcation line to the DRVN. Nevertheless, despite the DRVN's control of territories and people in the north, the French did not formally recognize the DRVN after July 1954; they maintained formal diplomatic relations with the SVN, whose functional independence the French government expeditiously perfected throughout the remainder of 1954 and in 1955. Thus whatever the terms of the cease-fire agreement, the

[9] The Soviet Union and the C.P.R. had of course recognized the juridical sovereign authority of the DRVN since 1950, just as the United States, Britain, and France had recognized the SVN in that same year.

effect of France's policy after Geneva was to perfect the *functional* independence of a second Vietnamese government. The withdrawal of French troops and the dissolution of the French high command in April 1956 was but the final act in this process.

An independent observer's analysis of the Vietnamese polity might run as follows. In July 1954 there were, in the *legal theory* of the powers, two Vietnamese governments: the SVN, recognized by non-Communist states, and the DRVN, recognized by Communist states. In terms of the working attributes of sovereignty, two governmental, entities *in fact* controlled the territory and peoples in Vietnam: the DRVN and France. For the sake of argument in this part of our discussion (part B), I have asked the reader to assume that the SVN was not a duly constituted government in July 1954 and its state (of which Bao Dai was chief of state) was not a sovereign state. This assumption may have been valid in July 1954, but it was not correct in 1955 or 1956, when the government of Ngo Dinh Diem possessed the attributes of a government of a sovereign state. By April 1956, at the very latest, there were not only *in legal theory* two sovereign entities in Vietnam (the DRVN and the RVN),[10] there were *in fact* two Vietnamese governmental entities that functioned as sovereign, independent states.

It should be understood that in 1956, *in legal theory* Vietnam was not permanently divided and the demarcation line was still provisional; the great powers and the DRVN and RVN governments insisted upon this proposition. In theory, Vietnam was not politically divided and the Vietnamese people were a unit. In fact, Vietnam was partitioned, but this was understood to be a provisional partition only, for purposes of effectuating a cease-fire and a regroupment of troops. In fact, two governments functioned in Vietnam in 1956, but what was the *theory* of the situation in April 1956? An all-Vietnam political settlement would permit the establishment of a single government that would represent the people of Vietnam within a unified Vietnamese state, but prior to such a settlement, what was the legal status of the DRVN and the SVN (or its juridical successor, the RVN)? The formal recognition of these governments by the Communist and non-Communist powers, respectively, was in effect an assertion that one *or* the other represented *all* the Vietnamese people. In this case

[10] The phrase, "in legal theory," should be understood to mean that Communist legal theory allowed for another, wholly different entity. For the so-called objective observer, this makes two sovereign entities. The reader should also be aware of the fact that on 26 October 1955, the SVN became the RVN. (See Chapter 24.) When events prior to 26 October 1955 are considered, I have referred to the Vietnamese administration south of the demarcation line as the SVN. When considering events after 26 October 1955, I refer to the administration in southern Vietnam as the RVN.

theory, whether Communist or non-Communist, was hardly commensurate with the facts. The identity of the governmental entity that was to represent the Vietnamese people was as yet undetermined, and at this writing remains undetermined. Nor is this theory compatible with the theory expressed by spokesmen for the United States, France, Britain, the Soviet Union, and the C.P.R. during the Geneva Conference, namely, the principle of self-determination of peoples, to which an all-Vietnamese political settlement should comply (see paragraphs 6 and 7 of the final declaration and, in the case of the United States, the Potomac Declaration and the Bedell Smith declaration).

It therefore seems to this writer that in 1955 and 1956, after the RVN government had achieved functional independence, the legal status of both the RVN and the DRVN government was this: each was a provisional government, pending resolution of the status of each in a political settlement that would be based upon all-Vietnamese elections. I have said nothing of the character of the political settlement or the elections, nor of the procedures according to which elections might be conducted; I have said merely that a viable *theory* of the status of the RVN and the DRVN in *1955 and 1956* would hold that these governmental entities were provisional until elections would resolve the question of who would represent and speak for the Vietnamese people. This theory is compatible with the facts as they stood in 1955 and 1956 because the powers, great and small, *in principle* recognized that elections must form the basis of a political settlement in Vietnam. These powers included the United States, Great Britain, the Soviet Union, the Chinese People's Republic, France, the DRVN, and the SVN—not to mention other interested states, including India and the other Colombo powers.

Let us return to the question posed earlier: What entity would be the beneficiary of the French government's declared intention to respect the sovereignty and independence of Vietnam? In certain ways, both the RVN and the DRVN. French policy in 1955 and 1956, though inconsistent, could be represented as an attempt to "live with" both Vietnamese regimes until a political settlement was reached through general elections that brought about the unification of Vietnam. Indeed, in 1954 it seemed as if the French government had determined to treat both the SVN and the DRVN as *provisionally* sovereign in their respective zones. France, while perfecting the independence of the Vietnamese in the south by turning over greater control of the government to the SVN, maintained a consulate in Hanoi and dispatched a special mission to the DRVN to negotiate on subjects relating to future relations between France and the DRVN. Formally, however, the French continued to recognize only the SVN, of which

Bao Dai was chief of state. The policy of perfecting the SVN's independence made it the prime beneficiary of French policy; however, the French government never denied the principle that elections must bring about Vietnam's unification.[11]

The process of transferring the governmental agencies in the southern regroupment zone to SVN control did not comport with article 14(a) of the cease-fire agreement, which vested the conduct of civil administration in the hands of the French high command "pending the general elections which will bring about the unification of Viet Nam." Of course, the alternative to fulfilling the promise of independence for the Vietnamese *in the south* was to resist the demands of SVN officials (and other Vietnamese) for greater Vietnamese control of the civil administration. Retaining control *until* general elections were held would have enabled the French strictly to comply with the terms of article 14(a); but was this a viable alternative? It would not have been proper for the French to have resisted the demands of the Vietnamese in the south, particularly in view of their unilateral declarations at Geneva. Hence the policy the French followed in southern Vietnam could hardly be called a violation of 14(a)—how could a policy of "emancipation" be regarded a violation of the cease-fire agreement? Also, it is doubtful that the French could have resisted such demands in light of the political situation in Paris; a decision by the Mendès-France government to resist the demands for autonomy by SVN officials would have met strong opposition from parties of the center and the right. Finally, we can be fairly certain the United States pressed the French to perfect the SVN's independence, which the administration had urged throughout the winter and spring; and after Geneva it was the proclaimed policy of the United States to make the SVN (and its juridical successor, the RVN) a bulwark against communism. A most important element in this policy was a fully autonomous SVN that was completely free of all restraints that might be interpreted by sensitive Vietnamese or sensitive Asians as remnants of colonialism.

7. Given our assumption that on 21 July the SVN government did not exercise the powers of a duly constituted government of a sovereign state, what was the effect of paragraph 7 of the final declaration? Who was obligated to act, and in what way? The first requirement of action, according to paragraph 7, was consultations on elections between the "competent representative authorities of the two zones" on and after 20 July 1955. It is indisputable that the

[11] Yet one may ponder the political (and legal) implications of France's joining SEATO. The Mendès-France government, after all, had consented to the protocol to the SEATO treaty, bringing the "free territory under the jurisdiction of the State of Vietnam" within the provisions of article IV.

DRVN government could have legitimately appointed "competent representative authorities" from the northern regroupment zone, but who would have provided them from the southern zone? To the extent that civil administration in the south was vested in the French high command (14[a]), one could argue that the French high command would delegate representative authority to persons it designated; and in view of Mendès-France's approval of the final declaration, one might even maintain that the French government was required to designate representatives for consultations. Although we cannot be sure that the draftsmen of paragraph 7 meant the French high command or its designees by the ambiguous phrase "competent representative authorities," by July 1955 the government of Ngo Dinh Diem had assumed virtually complete control of southern Vietnam's civil administration. The government that (in our hypothesis in part B) did not have the authority characteristic of an independent government of a sovereign state on 21 July 1954, had such authority by July 1955. There can be little doubt of the RVN's sovereign attributes in April 1956, after the last French troops had withdrawn from Vietnam, and few would contest the assertion that the French had relinquished control in the south to the RVN long before that time. The French program of emancipation in the south removed all doubt concerning the status of prospective SVN (later, RVN) designees as "competent representative authorities." By July 1955, in fact and in theory, the Diem government had the authority to appoint representatives to consult with DRVN representatives.

The next step in the procedures outlined in paragraph 7 of the final declaration was general elections, which were to be held in July 1956 under ISC supervision. According to the language of the declaration, the elections were to be "free general elections by secret ballot" and were designed to establish "democratic institutions" that would enable the Vietnamese people to "enjoy the fundamental freedoms." Moreover, execution of the provision for elections, and other provisions of the agreement and declaration as well, would create a "necessary basis for the achievement in the near future of a political settlement in Vietnam" (FD 6 and 7). Was the French or the SVN government obligated under the mandatory language of paragraph 7?

a. Irrespective of the status of the SVN in July 1954, by July 1956 the RVN government (successor of the SVN) exercised sovereign authority in the southern regroupment zone; that is, RVN control of the agencies of the government, army, and bureaucracy was virtually complete by the month of the scheduled elections. According to the legal theory upon which France, the United States, Great Britain, and more than two dozen other states based their foreign policy, the

Diem government was the duly constituted government of a sovereign state. As the government of a sovereign state, the Diem regime was free to assume or to refuse to assume any obligations imposed by the terms of the final declaration.[12] If, on 21 July, Mendès-France accepted obligations on behalf of France's SVN wards in respect of elections, the juridical and functional successors of France in the southern zone (i.e. the SVN) could disavow these obligations. Although international legal authorities are divided on the extent to which successor states are bound by obligations incurred by parent or predecessor states, recent authorities are in substantial agreement that, on treaty provisions governing internal political matters (as opposed to external commercial, economic, or cultural questions), the successor state is not obligated. This is certainly true of political arrangements that might affect the structure or form of the government of the successor state and of political questions whose resolution might affect the pattern of competition among rival political groups for offices and authority.[13] And this international legal

[12] On the freedom of states to assume or refuse to assume obligations under treaties to which they are not parties or to which they may become parties at some future time, see the authorities in n. 2 of Chapter 22.

[13] O'Connell, *op. cit.*, pp. 211-213, 267; see also J. M. Jones, "State Succession in the Matter of Treaties," *1947 British Yearbook of International Law*, pp. 366-372. On problems involving the law of state succession, the facts are of vital importance, so much so that it is almost impossible to make uncontroversial generalizations (see Ian Brownlie, *Principles of Public International Law* [London: Oxford University Press, 1966], p. 635, and *Free Zones of Upper Savoy and the District of Gex*, P.C.I.J. Reports, Series A/B, No. 46 [1932], pp. 156-158). It might be argued that the SVN was bound by paragraph 7 of the declaration as a successor of France because, it is said, the treaty obligations of a state are not affected by any change in the state's governmental organization or its constitutional system (Harvard Research in International Law, art. 24 of "Draft Convention on the Law of Treaties," *American Journal of International Law Supplement*, 29 [1935]: 1044, and the comment on pp. 1044-1055). This rule certainly has some force where external or foreign commercial obligations are involved (R. W. G. de Muralt, *The Problem of State Succession with Regard to Treaties* [The Hague: W. P. Van Stockum, 1954], pp. 129-130), but there are exceptions; for example, when violent revolutions or upheavals so upset an existing political regime that old treaties are no longer compatible with the new order (*Law of Treaties*, pp. 1051-1052).

Although the SVN did not come into being through violent revolution, the attaining of independence by that former colony could be regarded as a change so significant that *some* obligations of the parent state would not survive. Jurists and statesmen of the post-colonial states would certainly insist that treaties affecting the internal structure and functioning of their governments would cease to have obligatory force. O'Connell has termed treaties that affect the public or administrative law of a successor state "personal treaties" (*op. cit.*, pp. 211 ff.), and obligations under such treaties are extinguished in cases of total secession (p. 275). Again, "A State which begins its life by breaking off from an older international person does so, speaking generally, unencumbered by treaty provisions, and with unfettered freedom to enter into whatever international agreements it considers appropriate" (*ibid.*, p. 32). See also C. C. Hyde, *International Law, Chiefly as Interpreted and Applied by the United States* (2d ed.; Boston: Little, Brown, 1954), II: 1538-1541. Attainment of independence, moreover, constitutes such a fundamental

rule is corroborated by the facts of state practice after the Second
World War. Thus the SVN (later the RVN) when it succeeded
France as the sovereign authority in the southern regroupment
zone, was legally free to disavow any political obligations France had

change of status that the government of a post-colonial state might have the right
to terminate treaty obligations if it desired to do so; see, for example, the International Law Commission's draft article 44(2) in *United Nations Yearbook of the
I.L.C.* (1963), p. 207; and *American Journal of International Law,* 58 (1964),
pp. 283-284: "When a fundamental change has occurred with regard to a fact or
situation existing at the time when the treaty was entered into, it may be invoked
as a ground for terminating or withdrawing from the treaty if: (*a*) the existence
of that fact or situation constituted an essential basis of the consent of the parties
to the treaty; and (*b*) the effect of the change is to transform in an essential respect the character of the obligations undertaken in the treaty." For examples of
the actual practice of succeeding states in the recent past, see M. M. Whiteman,
Digest of International Law (Washington, D.C.: U.S. Government Printing Office,
1963), pp. 936-1002.

It is interesting to note that the following provision was included in the Franco-
Laotian Treaty of Friendship and Association of 22 October 1953: "The French
Republic recognizes and declares that the Kingdom of Laos is a fully independent
and sovereign State. Consequently, it shall replace the French Republic in all rights
and obligations resulting from any international treaties or special agreements
entered into by the French Republic on behalf of the Kingdom of Laos or French
Indochina prior to the present agreement" (Whiteman, *op. cit.,* p. 978). There
was no equivalent provision in the Franco-Vietnamese treaties initialed on 4 June
1954, and the absence of a devolution clause in any of the documents relating
to Vietnamese independence makes resolution of the succession problem more
difficult.

Was the government of the SVN bound as a successor state to respect articles
16-19 of the cease-fire agreement, articles that had in effect neutralized, or sought
to neutralize, Vietnam? O'Connell (*op. cit.,* p. 49) has written: "Treaties which
create real rights are described as 'dispositive.' Their legal effect is to impress on
a territory a status which is intended to be permanent, and which is independent
of the personality of the State exercising sovereignty. The most important of such
treaties are those which provide for the neutralization or demilitarization of a
region, or in which rights of way over territory or rights of navigation on national
waterways are accorded to a neighboring State. 'Dispositive Treaties,' asserted the
Swiss Government in its counter-memorial in the case of the *Free Zones of Upper
Savoy,* 'transfer or create a real right. And real rights in international law are
those which are attached to a territory, and which essentially *valent erga omnes.*'"
O'Connell (p. 57) also quotes Sir Arnold McNair's dissenting opinion in *The
International Status of South West Africa* (Advisory Opinion, *I.C.J. Reports*
[1950], pp. 153-154): "From time to time, it happens that a group of great Powers, or a large number of States both great and small, assume a power to create
by a multipartite treaty some new international regime or status, which soon
acquires a degree of acceptance and durability extending beyond the limits of the
actual contracting parties, and giving it objective existence. This power is used
when some public interest is involved, and its exercise often occurs in the course
of the peace settlement at the end of a great war."

In determining the applicability of these precepts for the facts of the Geneva
settlement for Vietnam, the author submits these observations for consideration:

1. The treaty that "neutralized" Vietnam was a bilateral treaty between the
French high command and the DRVN high command; it was not a multipartite
treaty.

2. Because the final declaration (paragraphs 4 and 5) merely "took note" of
articles 16-19 of the cease-fire agreement, we find no positive, mandatory "law-

assumed on its behalf. This is certainly true of the political obligation to hold elections.

b. If one insists that the SVN was never a legitimate entity and
had no standing to accept or to refuse to accept the obligations
imposed by the unambiguous language of paragraph 7 of the final
declaration, we must resolve the question upon whom paragraph 7
imposed positive responsibilities? If the answer is France, we must
recognize that the French government was neither willing nor able
—in the summer of 1955 or thereafter—to see to it that consultations
or elections were held. According to this point of view, France
violated article 14(*a*) of the cease-fire agreement and paragraphs 6
and 7 of the final declaration. For the reasons discussed in the preceding two chapters, the author cannot accept this view, which
ignores the very profound ambiguities in the relevant Geneva documents and the facts and consequences of the political evolution of
the SVN regime in the southern zone.

If the reader insists that, in spite of the nonsovereign, illegitimate
status of the SVN (later, RVN), this governmental entity was bound
to consult with the DRVN in 1955 and obligated to agree to
schedule elections in 1956, the theory behind his position would
seem to be that the RVN was continuously subordinate to the French
until the summer of 1956 (and perhaps afterward). Holding such
status, the RVN would therefore be bound to perform in the same
way the French were bound; that is, to fulfill the terms of the final
declaration, which Mendès-France approved in July 1954 and to
which he committed France. But this theory, unfortunately for its
adherents, does not comport with the facts; the SVN did not remain
subordinate to the French government, nor was the SVN regarded

---

making" language that unambiguously evinces the intent of the great powers or
"a large number of States both great and small" to create a new international
regime or status for Vietnam. Given the absence of real consensus at Geneva, we
cannot infer an intent to legislate on the part of the Geneva powers. The reader
should compare the 1954 Geneva settlement with other peace settlements, for
example, the Geneva settlement of the Laotian question in 1962. The latter agreements formally neutralized Laos, and all the governments participating in the
conference formally obligated themselves to accept the status "legislated" for Laos.

3. The "public interest" (as McNair expressed it) was probably served by
articles 16-19 inasmuch as these provisions were insurance against a resumption
of hostilities.

4. Whether Vietnam was effectively neutralized or neutralized "in effect," no dispositive treaty could abrogate either the SVN's or the DRVN's right to defend itself
against direct or indirect aggression. (Whether or not there was such aggression
against the SVN after 1956 is a question of fact that, in this study, I prefer to
avoid.) Thus if the SVN were the victim of aggression, it could—in law—call upon
its allies to supply arms and munitions; it could consent to the establishment of
Vietnamese or foreign military bases; and it could consent to the dispatch of the
troops of its allies. Compare D. G. Partan's analysis in Falk, pp. 210-212.

subordinate by any of the states with whom it had diplomatic relations.

A more viable theory, in the author's opinion, was offered above: both the SVN and the DRVN were quasi-sovereign in their respective zones by 1955. Although "quasi-sovereign" masks a host of difficulties, it nevertheless indicates that neither the SVN nor the DRVN was truly legitimate, according to the principle of self-determination, and neither entity could be legitimated until a political settlement, based upon all-Vietnamese elections, was achieved.[14] Within their respective zones, however, the DRVN and SVN (later, the RVN) governments exercised functional sovereignty in 1955 and 1956; that is, each governmental entity controlled the civil service, bureaucracy, police, and armed forces, and each entity had brought a modicum of order, at least temporarily, to the areas under its jurisdiction.

The Geneva settlement for Vietnam may or may not have been the best possible outcome under the circumstances, but the final declaration was not addressed to the vital questions: Who was obligated to consult and to cooperate in holding elections? How could the conference participants ensure that the principles of independence, unity, and territorial integrity were respected? Which participants would attempt to achieve a political settlement for Vietnam in the "near future"? With the failure of the Korea phase of the Geneva Conference so recent, how would the states concerned ensure that elections in Vietnam were free and by secret ballot? How would they—how could they—agree upon the procedures for such elections? If Vietnamese leaders and Vietnamese leaders alone were to seek a political settlement, how would the conference regulate the settlement procedures? What would the conferees do if the Vietnamese disagreed among themselves on matters of vital importance for the completion of procedures leading to the unification of Vietnam?

It may have been expecting too much of the statesmen at the Geneva Conference to say they should have dealt with all of these problems; but in view of the lack of consensus among the conferees and the ambiguities and incompleteness of the final declaration, it does no justice to the complexities of the Vietnamese situation, either in fact or legal theory, to speak glibly of "violations" of the "Geneva Accords." The term "accords" implies a consensus that simply did not exist with respect to a variety of basic issues and the notion of violated agreements implies that someone was responsible for the

[14] The author has not assumed the necessity or desirability of a political settlement in Vietnam based upon the principle of national self-determination; however, the Geneva conferees achieved consensus on at least this point: the eventual settlement could be legitimated only by proper application of the principle of self-determination.

performance of certain acts. With respect to the elections, it is this author's opinion that France was not responsible under the terms of paragraph 7. Whether the SVN became sovereign on 21 July 1954 or at a later date prior to July 1956, it was free to refuse to be bound by the terms of the final declaration. If, as we assumed in part A, the SVN government was duly constituted and could legitimately exercise the rights and assume the obligations of the government of a sovereign state, it could not be said to have violated the cease-fire agreement and the final declaration, whose terms it had protested. If, as we assumed in part B, the SVN was not sovereign on 21 July 1954, by 1955 it had come to exercise the attributes of sovereignty and it continued to have formal recognition of legitimacy from a number of other states. Whenever the SVN coupled its legal with its functional independence (i.e. when its government assumed control of civil administration in the southern zone), it could be argued that it had then become a successor state of France, duly sovereign and free to disavow whatever *political* obligations (if any) France had incurred on its behalf.

C. The SVN Never Sovereign

Finally, the third alternative (also discussed in part B) was that the SVN was never sovereign and hence had not the competence legitimately to refuse to fulfill the terms of paragraph 7 of the final declaration. To assume that the SVN was never in any sense sovereign, in July 1955 or later, is as untenable as assuming that the SVN's sovereignty was in every sense complete in July 1954. In each case the facts contradict the assumptions. The theory, moreover, has this difficulty: if the SVN was bound by the final declaration, it was bound by virtue of the French Premier's approval and the National Assembly's awkwardly worded resolution supporting the Premier's achievements at Geneva. France, the theory holds—and through France the SVN (and later, the RVN)—was obligated to consult with the DRVN in July 1955 and afterward and to cooperate in planning, scheduling, and executing all-Vietnamese elections in July 1956. Whatever lacunae existed in France's responsibility under the cease-fire agreement, the unilateral declarations, and the final declaration must necessarily have affected the SVN's responsibilities since the SVN could be assumed to have been similarly bound (according to the theory) only as an entity subservient to France and therefore only to the extent that France was bound. A good argument can be made that the final declaration, read with the declarations to withdraw troops from Vietnam and to respect the sovereignty and independence of Vietnam, did not require France to perform any acts pursuant to paragraphs 6 and 7 of the declaration; that is to say, France could and did relieve itself of direct responsibility for the all-Vietnamese elections by perfecting the sovereignty of the SVN and withdrawing all its troops from Vietnam. If the French had no obligations vis-à-vis elections, then, according to the theory, neither did the governmental entity subordinate to France, the SVN.

A final point on the theory of the permanently nonsovereign status of the SVN is that in 1955 and 1956 the DRVN government urged *the SVN government* to appoint representatives for election consultations and to hold elections at the time scheduled in the final declaration, thus recognizing that the cooperation of the SVN would be necessary to effect implementation of election procedures. These direct communications with the Saigon government obviously did not constitute recognition of the SVN as *the* sovereign government in the southern regroupment zone, but they show that the DRVN leadership appreciated that SVN officials would have to acquiesce in elections, that France had abandoned its position of influence over Vietnamese affairs, and that the SVN, for all practical purposes, was the primary political authority in the south.

[II]

Thus, whether sovereign in 1954, 1955, or 1956, the SVN government (and its successor, the RVN government) could refuse to be bound by the political provisions of the final declaration when it achieved sovereign status, and in doing this violated no rules of customary international or treaty law.[15] It is possible to maintain that Diem's refusal to consult with DRVN representatives was hardly commensurate with Tran Van Do's proposed amendment to paragraph 10 of the final declaration, according to which the SVN undertook "to make and support every effort to re-establish a real and lasting peace in Viet Nam." The Diem government refused to deal with the Communist DRVN regime or cooperate with Hanoi in planning for elections because elections in the northern zone, Diem argued, could not be free and because the DRVN would not permit the es-

---

[15] See Lawyers' Committee on American Policy towards Vietnam, *Vietnam and International Law* (Flanders, N.J.: O'Hare Books, 1967), pp. 45-48, for opposite conclusions. Also, compare the reasoning of the Lawyers' Committee paper with my own in this chapter and in Chapters 22 and 24. The stand of the Lawyers' Committee is, in large part, a brief that was composed to rebut the assertions and conclusions of another brief, a memorandum of the Legal Advisor of the State Department, "The Legality of United States Participation in the Defense of Vietnam," of 4 March 1966 (in *American Journal of International Law*, 60 [1966]: 565 ff. Both documents should be read as one would read briefs in adversary proceedings: with profound skepticism. For the refusal of the SVN (and later the RVN) to implement the election provisions of the final declaration and the justification for that refusal, see the legal advisor's memorandum in *ibid.*, pp. 577-578.

tablishment of genuinely democratic institutions. In view of the Korean experience and the DRVN's conduct of its internal affairs in 1955 and 1956, there was perhaps some basis for the SVN Premier's sentiments. It was unlikely that the DRVN would have agreed to United Nations supervision of the elections, which both the SVN and the United States wanted.

Agreeing to consultations, however, would not have been a commitment to hold elections. Moreover, the preliminary talks could have strengthened Diem's image in Asia, particularly if DRVN demands proved excessive or confirmed the Premier's suspicions that the DRVN Communists were likely to be as intransigent as the Korean Communists had been in their dealings with the South Koreans. In that event Diem could have broken off consultations, maintaining that he had made efforts to promote a lasting peace in Vietnam, based upon free elections, but these efforts had failed.

On the other hand, Hanoi might have been willing to make an effort to obtain Diem's agreement upon election procedures by making concessions, which could have been embarrassing for Diem. Consultations between the Vietnamese rivals could have disturbed the delicate political equilibrium in the south and lost Diem the support of many of his anti-Vietminh and anti-Communist political allies among the elites of the south. But this is conjecture. In any event, Premier Diem chose not to follow the policy some of the Geneva participants had outlined in the final declaration; he chose, instead, to refrain from all dealings and all official contact with the DRVN.

[III]

Let us briefly review the results of our analysis to this point.

1. If on 21 July 1954 the SVN was the duly constituted government of a sovereign state, it was free to withhold its consent to be bound by any of the provisions of the several Geneva documents—unless its subsequent conduct could be construed as implied consent. Between July 1954 and July 1956, however, the SVN government (after October 1955, the RVN government) adhered to policies fully consonant with the position outlined in documents 1, 2, and 3, analyzed at the beginning of this chapter, and such conduct offers no grounds for an objective observer to conclude that the SVN impliedly gave its consent to be bound by the Geneva agreements to any greater extent than was stated in these documents.[16]

[16] Could the SVN, although completely independent and sovereign, be bound by the terms of both the cease-fire agreement and the final declaration as the third-party beneficiary of the Geneva settlement for Vietnam? Such a theory would hold that, although the SVN was not a party to the settlement, it directly benefited therefrom and was estopped to deny that various obligations accom-

2. If on 21 July 1954 the SVN was not the duly constituted government of a sovereign state, or the SVN was not sovereign but became such before July 1956, the SVN (or later, the RVN) government was free at whatever time it came to exercise sovereign authority to refuse to be bound by the Geneva agreements—unless obligations were im-

---

panied the enjoyment of the peace and functional independence that followed upon the Geneva settlement. The general rule, however, states that treaties that purport to impose obligations upon third parties are null and void, at least to the extent of the obligations so imposed. See I.L.C. draft article 58 in *U.N. Yearbook of the I.L.C.* (1963) and article 18(*a*) in Harvard Research in International Law (*op. cit.* n. 13 above). Generally speaking, international law does not recognize a third-party-beneficiary theory of this sort (Hersh Lauterpacht, *Oppenheim's International Law* [8th ed.; London: Longmans, Green, 1958], p. 894, and P.C.I.J. reports: *Certain German Interests in Polish Upper Silesia*, Series A, No. 7 [1926], pp. 27 ff., and *Factory at Chorzow*, Series A, No. 17 [1928], pp. 43 ff.). There are, however, exceptions to the rule (see R. F. Roxburgh, *International Conventions and Third States* [London: Longmans, Green, 1917], Chapter 7), but none was relevant to the facts of the Vietnamese situation in 1954. Lauterpacht (*op. cit.*, p. 928) has written: "The rule that treaties cannot validly impose obligations upon States which are not parties to them follows clearly from the sovereignty of States and from the resulting principle that International Law does not as yet recognize anything in the nature of a legislative process by which rules of law are imposed upon a dissenting minority of States. However, in proportion as international society is transformed into an integrated community, a departure from the accepted principle becomes unavoidable, in particular in the sphere of preservation of international peace and security."

But the Geneva agreements were hardly the international legislative product of a more integrated international community; they were not even the legislative product of the nine delegations at Geneva. Was the regime established for Vietnam objective, creating rights and duties for third-party states in the same way, say, that a demilitarized regime was established for the Aaland Islands? The Committee of Jurists on the Aaland Islands question (*League of Nations Official Journal*, Special Supplement No. 3 [October, 1920], p. 18), commented: "[By] reason of the objective nature of the settlement of the Aaland Islands question by the Treaty of 1856, Sweden [in this case the third party] may, as a Power directly interested, insist upon compliance with the provisions of this Treaty in so far as the contracting parties [France, Great Britain, and Russia] have not cancelled it. This is all the more true owing to the fact that Sweden has always made use of it and it has never been called in question by the signatory Powers."

1. This decision of the Committee of Jurists can be cited in support of the proposition that the treaty of 1856 created a *right* for the benefit of Sweden, not an *obligation* Sweden might be called upon to perform. And the same can be said of the *Swiss Free Zones* case (n. 13 above). The rule according to which third-party states may be affected by the terms of a treaty is less well settled in the case of obligations as opposed to rights (Harvard Research in International Law, *op. cit.*, pp. 919-920, 924 ff.).

2. At least one commentator (F. de Visscher) was troubled by the task of reconciling the opinion of the jurists in the Aaland Islands case with established principles of international law that hold that treaties bind only the parties (*ibid.*, p. 928).

3. In my opinion the situation in Vietnam in 1954 does not offer facts that constitute an exception to the well-established rule that treaties may not impose obligations upon states that are not parties thereto. This is true, *a fortiori*, where as in the case of the Geneva settlement, not even the obligations of the nonsignatory conference participants are clear.

posed upon the SVN as the successor of France. The legal rule according to which obligations are held to survive state succession does not, however, extend to so-called internal political arrangements, such as those contemplated in paragraph 7 of the final declaration. Moreover, even if the SVN were regarded obligated as the successor of France, it could be bound only to the extent that the French government was bound. Succession does not, in and of itself, create new obligations. Thus if we assume that the SVN was bound as much as France was bound, we must ask how and in what way France was bound. Having examined this problem in preceding chapters, we have seen the serious formal difficulties involved in assigning the French government any responsibilities in Indochina, and in Vietnam in particular, beyond the implementation of a cease-fire, the nonintroduction into Indochina of arms and military personnel, agreement to consult with other Geneva Conference participants, and recognition of the unity, independence, sovereignty, and territorial integrity of Vietnam.

3. If on 21 July 1954 the SVN was not the duly constituted government of a sovereign state, and became such only after July 1956 —or has never become such—the SVN was bound by the Geneva agreements to the same extent that France was bound. But, as we have seen, France's obligations with respect to the political aspects of the Geneva settlement were not at all clear; hence the SVN's obligations were equally ambiguous.

4. In discussing the sovereign status of the SVN and the DRVN we have distinguished between sovereignty in fact (functional sovereignty) and juridical sovereignty (sovereignty in legal theory), which should help clarify discourse on a rather complicated and controversial question. The results of our analysis can be schematized in the following fashion.

STATUS OF THE TWO VIETNAMS

The State of Vietnam

Juridical Sovereignty	Functional Sovereignty
(Early July 1954)	
The Treaties of 4 June had been initialed but had not been signed or ratified. The juridical sovereignty of the SVN was therefore in doubt. Yet France, the U.S., the U.K., and other states had established formal diplomatic relations with the SVN.	For all practical purposes, the French government (and the French high command) controlled the governmental and military apparatus in Vietnam. It would be very difficult to attribute functional sovereignty to the SVN in early July 1954.

STATUS OF THE TWO VIETNAMS

The State of Vietnam

Juridical Sovereignty   *Functional Sovereignty*

(After 21 July 1954)

It is possible to argue that the French unilateral declaration of 21 July established the juridical sovereignty of the SVN (i.e. when coupled with statements of French officials after July). But the unilateral declaration was ambiguous; hence even after 21 July the juridical sovereignty of the SVN was not wholly clear.

By 21 July the functional sovereignty of the SVN had not changed. But after late July and August the French government began to perfect the functional independence of the SVN.

(In July 1956)

The treaties of 4 June 1954 had neither been signed nor ratified. The meaning of the French government's unilateral declaration had not been clarified, except to the extent that successive French governments regarded the SVN government as the legal government of Vietnam. One could argue, however, that the juridical sovereignty of the RVN in southern Vietnam was less ambiguous in 1956 than before because of the continued formal recognition of the RVN by more than thirty states.

By July 1956 the RVN exercised *de facto* sovereign authority in Vietnam south of the demarcation line. The Saigon government controlled the governmental apparatus, the police, and the army; the RVN had a population, territory, government, and capacity to enter into relations with other states.

The Democratic Republic of Vietnam

(Early July 1954)

The juridical status of the DRVN was in doubt in spite of the fact that France had concluded a treaty with a "Republic of Vietnam" in 1946 (Ho Chi Minh was one of the signers).[17] However, its grant of independence was incomplete, and one could say that ultimately the Franco-Vietminh war was fought over this issue. However, the C.P.R, the U.S.S.R., and other Communist states had recognized the DRVN.

In areas of Tonkin controlled by the PAVN, the DRVN *probably* exercised functional sovereignty. It would be more difficult to describe the DRVN's authority over Vietminh-held areas in the south.

[17] This agreement read in part: "The French Government recognizes the Republic of Vietnam as a free state, having its Government, its Parliament, its army, and its finances and forming part of the Indochinese Federation and the French Union" (*Bulletin Hebdomadaire*, No. 67 [18 March 1946], in H. R. Isaacs, *New Cycle in Asia* [New York: American Institute for Pacific Affairs, 1947], p. 169). The agreement did not recognize the independence or sovereignty of the "Republic of Vietnam." Moreover, this republic formed part of the French Union; hence the grant, whatever its form or content, was conditioned by French law respecting this union. The agreement of 1946 was signed in Hanoi by Jean Sainteny for France, by Ho Chi Minh for the Vietminh, and by Vu Hong Khanh for the Viet

STATUS OF THE TWO VIETNAMS

The Democratic Republic of Vietnam

Juridical Sovereignty	*Functional Sovereignty*
(After 21 July 1954)	
Communist-bloc states argued that the unilateral declaration of the French had formally perfected the sovereignty of the DRVN, but that declaration was ambiguous; France did not formally recognize the DRVN. The French had, however, co-signed a military agreement with the DRVN representative. This probably gave *some* status to the DRVN, but such status was unclear.	The functional sovereign status of the DRVN did not, of course, change immediately on the date of the Geneva agreements.
(In July 1956)	
The juridical sovereignty of the DRVN in northern Vietnam was perhaps less ambiguous in 1956 than before as a result of its continued formal recognition by Communist states.	By 1956 the DRVN had perfected its authority and control over all Vietnam territories north of the demarcation line. It had a population, territory, government, and capacity to enter into relations with other states.

5. Neither the SVN (and its successor, the RVN) nor the DRVN has ever exercised functional sovereignty throughout Vietnam. In July 1954 the DRVN probably could be regarded as *de facto* sovereign in areas controlled by the Vietminh in Tonkin while the French, *not* the SVN, exercised functional sovereignty in non-Vietminh-held areas. (The reader will appreciate that even this is a simplification: certain areas of Vietnam were controlled neither by the French nor the DRVN Vietminh but by various non-Annamese tribes and Vietminh insurgents in the south whose links with the DRVN were tenuous.) By 1956 the RVN and the DRVN were *de facto* sovereign in their respective zones south and north of the demarcation line.[18]

Nam Quoc Dan Dang (the VNQDD or Vietnam Nationalist Party) (E. J. Hammer, *The Struggle for Indochina, 1940-1955* [Stanford: Stanford University Press, 1954], pp. 153 ff. and 82-84). It is a mistake to identify the "Republic of Vietnam," named in the 1946 agreement, with the DRVN or the SVN, all of which were juridically distinct. In view of the differences between the French and the Vietnamese after 1946, the identity of the "Republic of Vietnam" is not entirely clear. Moreover, the VNQDD was as much a party to the 1946 agreement as the Vietminh and was entitled to whatever rights and benefits that agreement purported to establish.

[18] This conclusion is in accord with the essays by E. D. Hawkins (in Falk, pp. 165, 173-177) and J. N. Moore (pp 239-241). See also B. S. N. Murti, *Vietnam Divided* (Bombay: Asia Publishing House, 1964), pp. v, 176; and J. N. Moore and J. L. Underwood, "The Lawfulness of United States Assistance to the Republic of Viet Nam," *Duquesne University Law Review*, 5 (1966/1967): 241-247. For a contrary point of view, see Quincy Wright in Falk (pp. 277-278) and W. Standard, "United States Intervention in Vietnam Is Not Legal," *American Bar Association Journal*, 52 (1966): p. 627 at 630. R. A. Falk takes the position that the

The juridical sovereign status of the RVN and the DRVN is unclear. Paragraph 6 of the final declaration, upon which there was a consensus, provided for a military settlement only; a political settlement would come at some future time. If we agree that a political settlement in Vietnam should be based upon the principle of national self-determination—and all the Geneva conferees seemed to agree upon this point—I think we must conclude that in 1956 (and at least up to the time of this writing) neither the RVN nor the DRVN could be regarded as legitimate governments of Vietnam. As there has been no all-Vietnamese political settlement, neither government can be said to be the product of the self-determination of the Vietnamese people.

6. National self-determination as the supreme legitimating principle of a Vietnamese settlement must be regarded as an ideal. Implementation of elections by means of which the Vietnamese people would determine their polity would have given rise to a host of difficult problems in 1955 and 1956, and will be attended by similar difficulties in any future settlement.[19] The United States, the RVN, Great Britain, and other states have never accepted the Hanoi regime's claim to be the legitimate government of the Vietnamese state and nation. Correspondingly, the Soviet Union, the C.P.R., the DRVN, and other states do not accept the RVN's claim to legitimacy. However, despite conflicting claims and the unsatisfied ideal of self-determination, the governments of Hanoi and Saigon have been "going concerns" since 1954. It is beyond doubt that the DRVN has continuously exercised *de facto* sovereignty north of the demarcation line since that time.[20] After 1954, and certainly no later than 1956, the SVN government (or its successor, the RVN government) has been *de facto* sovereign in south Vietnam, until insurgent operations began to intensify in 1959, after which various areas in the south ceased to be controlled by Saigon.

Given the fact that (1) at the time consultations between "competent representative authorities" were scheduled by the final declaration the SVN and DRVN regimes were operating political en-

---

SVN evolved as a *de facto* political entity "despite the contrary intentions of the Geneva Settlement" (Falk, p. 460 [and p. 370]). See also D. G. Partan, "Legal Aspects of the Vietnam Conflict," *ibid.*, pp. 216-218; and Lawyers' Committee on American Policy towards Vietnam, *Vietnam and International Law* (Flanders, N.J.: O'Hare Books, 1967), pp. 38-39.

[19] For the problems involved in the practical application of the principle of national self-determination, see Alfred Cobban, *National Self-Determination* (Chicago: University of Chicago Press, 1944); Rupert Emerson, *From Empire to Nation* (Boston: Beacon Press, 1960), pp. 295-359; *idem, Self-Determination Revisited in the Era of Decolonization*. Occasional Papers in International Affairs, No. 9, December 1964 (Cambridge: Harvard University Center for International Affairs, 1964); R. F. Randle, "From National Self-Determination to National Self-Development," *Journal of the History of Ideas* (forthcoming: Jan. 1970).

[20] The French retained control of Haiphong for 300 days after the cease-fire.

tities in their respective zones and (2) that two generally antagonistic groups of states chose formally to recognize only one of the two
Vietnamese governments, we will make greater progress in our search
for clarification of the issues by looking at the situation as it was
rather than by assessing the situation against the unrealized ideal of
national self-determination. The RVN and the DRVN, as "going
concerns," have exercised functional sovereignty in their respective
zones. This state of affairs has been regarded as sufficient by the
foreign ministries of many states, both Communist and non-Communist, for qualifying either the RVN or the DRVN as sovereign
in fact and in law. However, it is possible to argue that, without a
final political settlement, the two Vietnams are only provisionally
sovereign in law (i.e. quasi-sovereign).

7. Could a provisionally sovereign entity, such as the RVN, refuse
to consult for the purpose of planning elections? Could it have
refused to cooperate with the DRVN in holding elections in 1956,
despite the language of paragraph 7 of the final declaration? To answer these questions we would have to elucidate the incidents and
attributes of quasi-sovereignty, and perhaps even reexamine the concept of sovereignty and its place in international legal theory. Without general agreement upon the nature of quasi-sovereignty, we cannot with any degree of certainty assert that the SVN had the absolute right to refuse to assume obligations under paragraph 7 of the
conference declaration. But neither can we deny that the RVN had
that right. Hence we cannot speak with any certainty of the RVN's
violating the Geneva agreements in view of the position taken by
that government in documents 1, 2, and 3 and by virtue of its subsequent conduct. That the United States, Great Britain, and other
states believed the Saigon regime could refuse to assume the obligations of the Geneva agreements must count for something, at least in
the sense that formal relationships were established among themselves
vis-à-vis the RVN. Within this important grouping of states the
RVN was treated as the sovereign successor of France in South Vietnam with the competence to determine its relations with the DRVN.[21]
According to this view the Diem government was not obligated
to consult or to schedule elections pursuant to paragraph 7 of the final
declaration; nor was it bound to any greater extent than that revealed
in Tran Van Do's protest and declaration and Premier Diem's
declarations.

---

[21] The determination by the U.S., the U.K., and other states that the SVN was
not obligated under the terms of paragraph 7 of the declaration was not, of course,
conclusive upon other states (e.g. Communist-bloc or nonaligned states).

Chapter 24

THE IMPLEMENTATION OF THE SETTLEMENT IN VIETNAM

[I]

The ISC for Vietnam was established in Hanoi on 11 August 1954. Fixed and mobile inspection teams, composed of an equal number of officers from each ISC delegation (India, Canada, Poland), were installed both north and south of the demarcation line beginning in September (35).[1] The commission assigned two mobile teams to a skeleton headquarters in Saigon, paid occasional visits to that southern capital city, and planned formally to move its headquarters there in August 1955. After long and apparently arduous negotiations, the Republic of Vietnam (the SVN became a republic on 26 October 1955) consented to the establishment of ISC headquarters in Saigon in November 1956 but the latter did not start functioning there officially until 1958.

Contact between the signatories of the cease-fire agreement and the ISC and its inspection teams was maintained through liaison missions in Hanoi and liaison officers appointed to each team. The Joint Commission for Vietnam also was set up in early August, with headquarters first at Phu Lo and then on the outskirts of Haiduong. The French Union and the PAVN high commands appointed delegations to serve on the joint Commission and its subcommissions at Quynh Khe (DRVN), Quang Tri (SVN), and Phung Hiep (SVN). The ISC for Vietnam—and the ISC for Laos and Cambodia as well —created a secretariat for intracommission organization and service work, but the secretariat for the Vietnam ISC was the most elaborate and developed of the three. Pursuant to provisions of the three cease-fire agreements, the secretariats were required to "act in close cooperation."[2] To this end, the first of a series of secretariat conferences was held in Hanoi in early November.

---

[1] *First and Second Interim Reports of the International Commission for Supervision and Control in Vietnam*, Vietnam No. 1 (1955), Cmd. 9461 (London: Her Majesty's Stationery Office, 1955), p. 10 (hereafter referred to as VN 1 & 2). In this, as in the preceding chapter, the Vietnamese administration south of the provisional demarcation line is referred to as the SVN when events prior to 26 October 1955 are discussed. On and after 26 October 1955, when the Republic of Vietnam was proclaimed, the Vietnamese administration south of the demarcation line is referred to as the RVN.

[2] See article 45 of the Vietnam cease-fire agreement, article 24 of the Cambodian agreement, and article 38 of the Laotian agreement.

Although a number of clashes between the people of various areas and the armed forces of the French high command were reported to the ISC during the crucial months immediately after the cease-fire, the commission was able to declare that the cease-fire had become effective and that there had been no violations of chapter I or articles 10 and 11 of the Geneva agreement.[3] Some delay was encountered, however, in establishing mobile inspection teams for supervising the demarcation line and the demilitarized zone. As late as April 1955 the commission had to rely upon its fixed teams at Dong Hoi (SVN) and Tourane (DRVN) for implementing its supervisory mandate in the DMZ (36[b]). Happily, the ISC reported no delays in the regroupment of the former belligerents into the areas assigned pursuant to article 15(f) (1) and the annex to the cease-fire agreement. The mechanics of the orderly transfer of military authority were somewhat more complicated, of course. Upon the advice of the ISC, a plan and protocol were adopted by the PAVN and the French forces for the transfer of the Hanoi perimeter sector by sector. Under the observation of five of the commission's mobile teams, Hanoi and its defense perimeter was transferred to PAVN officers and DRVN officials between 6 and 10 October.[4] The same plan was successfully applied to the Haiduong perimeter on 31 October.

Greater problems were encountered during the transfer of administrative and essential public services in Hanoi. Complaints that French authorities and businessmen were dismantling and removing equipment were registered but the ISC was able to persuade the parties to sign another technical protocol for minimizing such activities insofar as they were being carried out by government officers. But essential services, such as water supply, electricity, and transport, were operated by private concerns that indicated they were unwilling to continue the management of the services after 8 October, although DRVN authorities had stated that they were willing to treat the service contracts as valid.[5] An ISC interim report described how the question was ultimately resolved.

[3] VN 1 & 2, pp. 12-13.

[4] According to the *NYT* (30 October 1954), the Vietminh army was greeted with genuine fervor by the people of Hanoi.

[5] In July, Pham Van Dong wrote to Mendès-France assuring him that the rights of French persons having property in the northern zone would be respected, that businessmen might continue their activities, and in fact should be encouraged to do so (*Le Monde*, 25, 26 July 1954). Well after the transfer of Hanoi to the DRVN, Jean Sainteny, the French delegate general to the DRVN worked out an agreement with Pham Van Dong that purported to regulate cultural and economic matters between the French and DRVN governments. The agreement provided that French businessmen would not suffer discrimination and that profits might be transferred to the franc zone. *Le Monde*, 11, 12 December 1954.

After discussions with the two parties, the International Commission proposed the following measures to ensure that there was no break in essential services:

(*a*) All essential equipment for the running of these installations should be left behind.

(*b*) Sufficient supply of coal for two months and spare-parts and other equipment for two years should be left behind.

(*c*) Although the Management of these firms would pass on to the Democratic Republic authorities, technicians and specialised personnel should be induced to remain, provided the Democratic Republic authorities would give necessary guarantees in respect of their persons and property.

(*d*) Specialised personnel of the Democratic Republic could be invited to Hanoi so as to effect the change-over of these services gradually before the date of evacuation.

(*e*) All the above proposals were acted on by both parties and just as in the case of military withdrawals and transfers, the transfer of civil and administrative services, public buildings and public offices, and essential public services were carried out successfully by the two parties. No break occurred in any of these services in spite of the difficult circumstances in which they were transferred.[6]

The commission drew the parties' attention to the exemplary, peaceful, and orderly transfer of Hanoi and Haiduong, which "showed that orderly transfer could only take place if the two parties co-operated in the process and, well in advance of the dead-line, held joint discussions and agreed upon an integrated plan of withdrawal and transfer."[7]

By the end of October the PAVN had withdrawn from the Ham Tan, Xuyen Moc, Quang Ngai, and Plaine des Joncs assembly areas without incident, under observation (except in the Plaine des Joncs) by mobile teams of the ISC. Withdrawals from the Pointe Camau assembly area were completed by 7 February 1955.[8] A dispute arose between the parties over the withdrawal of PAVN troops, which were required to be removed in three stages from the central Vietnam provisional assembly area (15 [2]). A protocol for withdrawal of troops was eventually concluded, however, and further withdrawals took place, without incident, by 31 October. The third and last contingent of PAVN troops was due to be removed from central Vietnam by 19 May 1955, 300 days from the date of entry into force of the cease-fire agreement; at the same time, the Haiphong perimeter was due to be transferred from the French high command to the DRVN. After reviewing various documents and proposals from both parties

[6] VN 1 & 2, p. 16   [7] *Ibid.*   [8] *Ibid.,* p. 45.

concerning these last important transfers of territory, and after reviewing a number of complaints and countercomplaints, the ISC prepared and submitted to the two high commands a series of suggestions for the orderly transfer of public services.[9] Troop withdrawals began on 22 April 1955 and were completed before the expiration of the 300-day period; and the commission reported that "public properties and the essential services were handed over intact and in running order."[10]

A dispute between the parties arose quite early over the implementation of article 21, relating to prisoners of war and "civilian internees." The disagreements generally involved disparities in the number of prisoners that either party was prepared to release and the number of prisoners either party believed the other party held. Under ISC prodding, prisoner exchange began on 14 August, with the commission's lending its suggestions and good offices in the manifold controversies that arose. By 9 September, at the end of the time limit set in article 21 (*a*), the prisoner exchange stood as follows:[11]

	FUF	DRVN-PAVN
French figures	65,477	11,706
DRVN figures	65,465	11,882

The commission, on 4 November, requested the parties to supply it with consolidated statements listing the number of prisoners of war and civilian internees released and the number still detained. The parties replied that they had fulfilled their obligations under article 21 and were no longer detaining any prisoners. Claims and counterclaims kept the dispute over article 21 alive, which led the ISC to declare: "The atmosphere between the parties in the solution of complicated cases of prisoners of war, civilian internees, and 'ralliés' and deserters is not as co-operative as envisaged in the general scheme of the Agreement."[12] After November 1954 the commission was almost continuously beset with varying claims of the parties respecting alleged violations of article 21 and the illegal detaining of civilian internees and other prisoners who, according to the claims, ought to have been released.

A series of minor clashes between French Union forces (or French civil and military police) and groups of people in south and central Vietnam (in the SVN) precipitated a procedural dispute between

---

[9] *Ibid.*, pp. 51-52.
[10] *Fourth Interim Report of the International Commission for Supervision and Control in Vietnam*, Vietnam No. 3 (1955), Cmd. 9654 (London: Her Majesty's Stationery Office, 1955), p. 6 (hereafter referred to as VN 4). See also Ely, pp. 214-218.
[11] VN 1 & 2, p. 18. *FUF* means French Union Forces.
[12] *Ibid.*, p. 46. See also Ely, pp. 213-214.

the parties but did not otherwise threaten to lead to a resumption of hostilities. The DRVN wanted investigations conducted by a joint team from the joint commission and a team from the ISC; the French wanted a team composed only of representatives of the ISC. The ISC finally suggested a solution that was ultimately accepted by the parties: investigations would be carried out by ISC teams assisted by representatives of the parties. The latter would not, however, "participate in the appraisal of the facts and in the preparation of the report."[13] The commission also created an *ad hoc* committee of legal experts, subsequent to its investigations, and reserved its decision and recommendations pending review of reports by this committee. No further indication of the outcome of this review appeared in the commission's interim reports.

These incidents, and others that were subsumed by the ISC under the political or civil arrangements of article 14, were believed to have occurred because the French high command had failed to establish effective "civil military administration in areas taken over by them in Central and South Vietnam."[14] This happened because, in the view of the ISC, civil administrators did not always accompany military forces; hence an administrative vacuum occurred in certain areas. In situations of this kind, incidents that resulted in the denial of "democratic freedoms" (14 [c]) and injury to life and property were bound to occur.[15] The commission suggested that the parties plan their withdrawals and transfers in accordance with provisions of the cease-fire agreement, presumably article 14 (b), which stated:

> Steps shall be taken to ensure that there is no break in the transfer of responsibilities. For this purpose, adequate notice shall be given by the withdrawing party to the other party, which shall make the necessary arrangements, in particular by sending administrative and police detachments to prepare for the assumption of administrative responsibility.

The relatively successful transfer of Hanoi and Haiduong was suggested as an example to the parties for the conduct of future withdrawals.

[II]

The implementation of the "political" terms of the cease-fire agreement was less felicitous than the implementation of its military terms.

---

[13] *Ibid.*, p. 27.

[14] *Ibid.*, p. 29.

[15] The militia of the Hoa Hao and other sects often moved into areas evacuated by the PAVN before French forces could arrive. The commanders of these militias were "war lords" in the areas they controlled, governing independently of French or SVN mandates.

This was evident in the first interim report of the ISC and in every report thereafter. Under the rubric "political," I include article 14 (c), freedom from reprisals and discrimination; article 14 (d), freedom of movement from one major zone to the other; and articles 16 through 19, prohibiting the introduction of new military equipment, personnel, and bases into Vietnam.

A. ARTICLES 14(c) AND 14(d)

In view of the many complaints and petitions received by the ISC relating to alleged violations of articles 14(c) and 14(d), the commission established a "committee on freedoms" on 19 October. The committee had the task of controlling and supervising the action taken by the parties pursuant to these articles and was authorized to recommend principles and procedures for their implementation to the ISC.[16]

Under article 14 (c) the complaints of the DRVN authorities usually alleged that, in areas under the jurisdiction of the French high command, reprisals and illegal detention of former resistance members were occurring on a large scale.[17] The French authorities usually denied the charges, counterclaiming that the DRVN was interfering in civil and military administration in areas under French control through a wide network of sympathizers and cadres. The ISC investigated many of these charges and, pending formal recommendations on specific cases, asked the parties to observe the spirit of article 14 (c) by refraining from detention, arrest, or prosecution of persons solely on the grounds of their holding particular political opinions. It also appealed to the parties to approach their problems in a practical spirit, not in a narrow formalistic manner, and it gently criticized the French high command for its failure to ensure that no administrative hiatus occurred in central and south Vietnam (south of the demarcation line) after the withdrawal of PAVN forces but before the arrival of French military authorities.[18]

After the spring of 1955 the ISC continued to receive complaints alleging violations of article 14 (c). Some of these complaints were investigated, and most of them were forwarded to the high commands for comment and remedial action.[19] But, increasingly, a new factor af-

[16] VN 1 & 2, pp. 21, 37-38.

[17] *Third Interim Report of the International Commission for Supervision and Control in Vietnam,* Vietnam No. 2 (1955), Cmd. 9499 (London: Her Majesty's Stationery Office, 1955), p. 9 (hereafter referred to as VN 3).

[18] VN 1 & 2, pp. 22, 29.

[19] See *Fifth Interim Report of the International Commission for Supervision and Control in Vietnam,* Vietnam No. 1 (1956), Cmd. 9706 (London: Her Majesty's Stationery Office, 1956), p. 8 (hereafter referred to as VN 5), and *Sixth Interim Report of the International Commission for Supervision and Control in Vietnam,* Vietnam No. 1 (1957), Cmd. 31 (London: Her Majesty's Stationery Office, 1957), p. 10 (hereafter referred to as VN 6).

fected the performance of both the ISC and the French high command: the growing autonomy of the government of the State of Vietnam (after 26 October 1955, the RVN) in the southern regroupment zone. The problem was stated succinctly in the commission's fourth interim report (for the period 11 April to 10 August 1955):

> The declared opposition of the Government of the State of Vietnam to the Geneva Agreement makes it obvious that the French High Command is not in a position to enforce execution of its undertaking under Article 14 (c) to refrain from reprisals and discrimination against persons or organisations on account of their activities during the hostilities or to guarantee their democratic liberties. The French High Command is also finding it more and more difficult to carry out its obligation, under Article 25, to assist and cooperate fully with the Commission in the investigation of complaints alleging violation of Article 14 (c) and the prompt execution of the Commission's recommendation after investigations are completed.[20]

The same complaint was registered by the ISC in its fifth interim report (for the period 11 August to 10 December 1955), and, by the time the sixth interim report (11 December 1955 to 31 July 1956) was prepared, the commission was unable to send investigatory teams into south Vietnam.[21] It was unable to obtain the concurrence of the French high command and, more importantly, the permission of the government of the Republic of Vietnam. The latter insisted that security conditions in particular areas rendered investigations impossible (the commission often disputed this) or laid down conditions unacceptable to the ISC.[22]

The Canadian delegation did not fully accept the rather unsympathetic Indian-Polish assessment of SVN (and later, RVN) culpability in frustrating ISC functions. In the fourth interim report the Canadian delegate entered an amendment to the majority view, which declared that commission difficulties were

> largely due to the fact that with the completion of the regroupment of forces with which the French High Command and the P.A.V.N. High Command, as military commands, were directly concerned, the Commission has become increasingly concerned with

[20] VN 4, p. 10. The ISC had noted difficulties in the implementation of article 14(c) as early as the second interim report (late 1954); see VN 1 & 2, p. 50. See also VN 5, p. 8.

[21] VN 6, pp. 13, 27.

[22] *Seventh Interim Report of the International Commission for Supervision and Control in Vietnam*, Vietnam No. 2 (1957), Cmd. 335 (London: Her Majesty's Stationery Office, 1957), p. 9 (hereafter referred to as VN 7).

matters . . . which in South Vietnam are not, for constitutional and administrative reasons, the direct responsibility of the French High Command, although the French High Command continues to be responsible to the Commission under the Agreement.

. . . The situation in connexion with these matters has been affected by the fact that the authorities in South Vietnam directly concerned with them are responsible to the Government of the State of Vietnam and not to the French High Command, and by the fact that the Government of the State of Vietnam is not a signatory to the Cease-Fire Agreement, and does not at present regard itself as bound by its terms. Hence the French High Command despite its best efforts to co-operate fully with the Commission cannot, without the co-operation of the Government of the State of Vietnam, fully implement its obligations under Article 25 of the Cease-Fire Agreement. This situation, which is now under review by the parties directly concerned, has an adverse effect on the work of the Commission and the implementation of the Cease-Fire Agreement.[23]

Certainly the task of implementing article 14(c) in the south was made especially difficult by the fact that the Hoa Hao, Cao Dai, and Binh Xuyen sects began to challenge the authority of the Diem regime as early as the fall of 1954. The sects had their own militia, by means of which they assured control of areas of southern Vietnam they had no intention of relinquishing to the central government in Saigon. Virtual civil war broke out in March 1955 and continued intermittently until October. Diem emerged victorious, and much strengthened from this contest with the sects, but the unstable situation was hardly conducive to the development of the democratic liberties envisaged by article 14(c).[24]

The Republic of Vietnam was proclaimed on 26 October 1955, Emperor Bao Dai having been dethroned in June, ostensibly by the action of the imperial family. On 11 January 1956, Diem, now President of the RVN, promulgated General Order No. 6, giving special powers to the government to detain or deport persons for reasons of public security. The PAVN high command complained that this ordinance violated article 14(c). In March the ISC communicated its views to the French high command (*not* to the RVN government):

[23] VN 4, pp. 24-25.
[24] Diem's opposition to the sects was undoubtedly strengthened by United States support. On 3 November General J. Lawton Collins, special ambassador to Vietnam, declared that the United States would "aid only an army loyal to the South Vietnam government." He added that the United States would not recognize a government established by force. *NYHT*, 5 November 1954.

[No] law, regulation or order in either of the two zones could, in any way, supersede the obligations which the two parties have undertaken under the provisions of Article 14(c). . . . [The] Commission expected that any action taken under General Order No. 6 would be taken with due regard to the provisions of Article 14(c) and if complaints were brought to the notice of the Commission regarding the application of this decree or any other law, regulation or order in either of the two zones, . . . the Commission would take steps to satisfy itself that there had been no reprisals or discrimination against persons on account of their activities during the hostilities and that their democratic liberties had not been infringed.[25]

This was a rather extraordinary view to take in light of the role and competence of the ISC and the attitudes of the governments of the DRVN and the RVN. It is not difficult to understand why the commission was unable to perform according to its conception of its competence. The RVN government refused to consent to the presence of ISC teams, whose purpose was to investigate PAVN complaints of reprisals and discrimination due to the application of General Order No. 6.[26]

According to figures reported by the ISC for the period ending 5 May 1955, about 890,000 persons moved from the northern to the southern zone. In the same period, about 2,600 persons moved from the southern to the northern zone.[27] Beginning in September 1954, the ISC received complaints from the French high command (and the SVN) alleging that obstacles were being put in the way of the free movement of evacuees, in violation of article 14(d). Often the DRVN countercharged that many people in the northern zone were being induced to move south by undue pressures of French officials and Roman Catholic priests.[28] The commission reminded the parties that, under article 14(d), they must not merely permit civilians to move from one zone to another according to their choice but should assist in such movements. In October an ISC mobile team, acting pursuant to a French complaint of hindrances to the movement of evacuees from Phat Diem, undertook an investigation and found that 10,000 evacuees in that area were unable to leave the district owing to the cumbersomeness of DRVN administrative procedures. The ISC committee on freedoms persuaded DRVN authorities to adopt new procedures and the bulk of the evacuees was transferred within ten days. However, complaints from the French high command continued to be registered with the commission.

[25] VN 6, pp. 12-13.
[27] VN 4, p. 30; Ely, pp. 218-230.
[26] VN 7, pp. 9-10.
[28] VN 1 & 2, p. 22.

Restrictions upon the internal movements of civilians from province to province and a complex permit system were the particular matters against which the French complaints were directed. Under increasing pressures, the ISC emphatically declared that it would not "be a party to any panicky and unorganized exodus of refugees, [but] held that the administrative processes should not be so clumsy, slow and complex as in effect to defeat the provisions of Article 14(*d*)."[29] Because there was a time limit upon the movement of civilians (300 days from the entry into force of the agreement), the commission instructed the committee on freedoms to review thoroughly the problems arising under article 14(*d*) with the view of substantially fulfilling the desires of civilians to change their residence before the expiration of the time limit.[30] During the period of the third interim report (11 February to 10 April 1955), a large volume of complaints continued to come in, and investigations by mobile teams in various districts of the DRVN led the ISC to conclude that implementation of article 14(*d*) would continue to be unsatisfactory

> unless administrative arrangements and the provision of transport facilities are urgently improved. . . . [In] light of the progress made in the implementation of this Article so far, it is not possible to state at this stage that Article 14(*d*) will be implemented in full within the time-limit laid down.[31]

At the urging of the ISC, the parties agreed on an extension to 20 July of the period prescribed for change of residence between zones.[32] In this period, between 18 May and 20 July, complaints from both French and PAVN authorities continued to come in, and the mobile teams of the ISC continued to investigate the new as well as the old charges. In the summary of movements and investigations under article 14(*d*) in the commission's fourth interim report, the differing appreciations of the Canadian delegation, on the one hand, and the Indian and Polish delegations, on the other, were clearly evident. The substance of the report of the latter two delegations—in this instance the majority report—was as follows.[33]

1. In spite of hostile demonstrations staged against ISC teams in refugee camps in south Vietnam (i.e., the SVN) the teams reported there was no foundation for the PAVN's allegation that thousands of persons were victims of systematic propaganda antagonistic to the

[29] *Ibid.*, pp. 23, 29.
[30] *Ibid.*, pp. 52-54.
[31] VN 3, p 9.
[32] The British government had proposed a time extension to the Soviet government, which subsequently intimated that the DRVN was amenable to an extension. VN 3, p. 3.
[33] VN 4, p. 12.

DRVN. The ISC denied that there were substantial numbers of persons in the south who wished to move to the northern zone.[34]

2. The volume of demand for permits to move south was huge, as was the strain upon the transportation facilities of the DRVN; nevertheless the teams were obstructed and delayed "in several cases by narrowness of local officials and in a few cases by organized social groups who were hostile to those who wanted to go and live [in the southern zone]."[35] Most of the hindrances were overcome, but not without great strain upon commission personnel and delay in the implementation of article 14(d).

3. Authorities in both zones had overly complicated administrative procedures for processing evacuees.

4. Religious, social, and "local" influences were used by the authorities of both parties either to persuade persons to change their zones of residence or to dissuade them from doing so.

5. Short of a nation-wide census to ascertain each individual's choice of zone of residence and following this up by executive action to implement this choice, the Commission could not satisfy itself that everyone in Vietnam who wanted to change the zone of his residence had done so before 18th May, 1955. Nevertheless, the Indian and Polish delegations believed they could conclude: "It was obvious that by 18th May the bulk of the persons who wanted to change the zone of their residence had succeeded in doing so."[36]

6. During the extension period an additional 4,700 persons went from north to south, bringing the total number to about 893,000, according to commission figures. Another 1,700 moved from south to north, for a total of about 4,300. According to the Indian and Polish delegations, "it was obvious that the increase in the number of persons who wanted to move from the south to go and live in the [northern zone] during the period of the extension up to 20 July was due to fear of reprisals or discrimination in view of the anti-Geneva Agreement and anti-Communist propaganda taken up by the State of Vietnam during June and July."[37]

7. In view of the firm stand of the SVN against the Geneva agree-

---

[34] On 3 August Diem had exhorted the people living north of the demarcation line to rally to the SVN; he later requested, and received United States assistance in the massive evacuation (*Le Monde*, 4 August 1954). In a "somewhat impetuous fashion" at the beginning of July, during Operation Auvergne, the apostolic vicars of Phat Diem and Bui Chu had started an evacuation movement that—according to Donald Lancaster in *The Emancipation of French Indochina* ([London: Oxford University Press, 1961], pp. 343-344)—was encouraged by Diem, the Vietnamese Catholic hierarchy, and the local authorities; but the Vatican and the Paris Foreign Mission Society instructed missionaries to remain at their posts in the north. It was subsequently estimated that, of all persons who moved from north to south, 75 to 95 percent were Roman Catholic.

[35] VN 4, pp. 12-14.   [36] *Ibid.*   [37] *Ibid.*

ment and the strained relations between the parties, there would have been no chance to secure an extension for movements of persons who may have failed to exercise their choice before 20 July 1955.

The Canadian delegation offered an amendment, dealing with the implementation of article 14(*d*), to portions of the fourth interim report. This amendment asserted that

1. Persons who wished to exercise their option to move to the south were not being permitted to do so, and in some cases were prevented from doing so. "Soldiers, political cadres and local militia were frequently stationed in the houses of the Catholic population with instructions to prevent them from leaving their homes in order to contact the teams."[38] Would-be evacuees were frequently molested, or grouped in areas from which ISC teams were excluded; local clergy were intimidated and subject to imprisonment.

2. In the opinion of the Canadian delegation, the obstructions were no "mere social manifestation but an organized plan. While it has been impossible for the Commission to prove that these measures were organised as a matter of policy by the authority in control of the North, owing to the frequency and the common features of this form of obstruction in all provinces investigated there would seem to be little doubt that these obstructions and hindrances had been deliberately planned."[39]

3. There were no serious problems connected with the movement of persons from the southern zone to the northern zone until the end of the 300-day period, after which there were two demonstrations by would-be refugees in Saigon. Arrangements were soon made to move these persons to the northern zone.

4. It was not possible to say whether all persons who wished to move from one zone to the other had been able to move. The commission had the duty to see to it that all persons who *expressed their desire to move before 20 July* or had been prevented from exercising their right to choose their zone of residence should be permitted to change zones *after* 20 July.[40]

After the expiration of the period for the movement of persons between zones the ISC pursued its investigation of "residual" cases; that is, cases of persons who had applied for or had received permits to move before 20 July but had not moved by that date.[41] The Canadians' ambitious desire to allow all persons who wanted to move before 20 July could not be implemented. Although the commission discussed the question with the high commands, there was no substantial movement of civilians between zones after 20 July 1955.

[38] *Ibid.*, p. 19.   [39] *Ibid.*   [40] *Ibid.*, p. 22.
[41] "Residual case" is defined in greater detail in VN 4, p. 14.

B. Articles 16 through 19

As early as August 1954 the ISC had difficulties carrying out its supervisory duties pursuant to articles 16–19 because the parties failed to notify the commission of movements of war matériel and the rotation of troops. In many instances the parties insisted that the movements were internal, and French authorities argued that supervision of internal movements was beyond the competence of the ISC. The commission, however, instructed its teams to check all exports and imports of war matériel and military personnel, whether or not the local authorities gave notice.[42] Two specific complaints submitted by the PAVN high command, alleging violation of article 17 by French authorities through the unloading of war matériel from two ships, were investigated by ISC teams and found not to be violations.[43] Otherwise, the principal problem of the commission in 1954 and 1955, under these articles, was the location of the fixed inspection teams on the Vietnamese-Chinese and Vietnamese-Cambodian frontiers.[44] The French authorities charged that the DRVN had increased its military strength by illegally and covertly importing arms and munitions from the C.P.R.[45] but the ISC found no evidence of such activity. However, French officials remained skeptical: if the French high command had not been able to detect and prevent such shipments before the cease-fire, how could the ISC, with very limited capabilities, detect movements at night across the largely inaccessible Chinese-Vietnamese border?[46]

Increasingly after mid-1955 the ISC received complaints from the PAVN that United States military missions were landing in the SVN (later, the RVN). The commission informed the French high command that notification should be given by both parties of visits of foreign military missions.[47] When the Saigon fixed team reported that U.S. Navy planes were visiting Saigon airport regularly without advance notification, the French liaison mission was informed that advance forecasts of military aircraft arrivals should be given to the commission. In early 1956, when the ISC sought to carry out reconnaissance of uncontrolled airfields in both zones, permission of the DRVN and RVN authorities was given in some but not all cases, and apparently with great reluctance.[48] Reconnaissance of offshore islands also was inadequate. RVN authorities imposed restrictions upon the movements of commission teams and insisted upon twenty-

[42] VN 1 & 2, p. 25.   [43] VN 4, p. 11.   [44] VN 3, p. 48.
[45] *NYT*, 30 December 1954.
[46] Frédéric-Dupont, *Mission de la France en Asie* (Paris: Editions France-Empire, 1956), p. 206.
[47] VN 5, p. 11.   [48] VN 6, p. 20.

four to forty-eight hours' notice of a team's request for access to a particular area. In early 1956 the DRVN government obtained the withdrawal of a mobile team from its assigned zone in the Chinese-Vietnamese border,[49] leaving a wide area of the frontier without ISC supervision.

The commission's Saigon team continued to report arrivals of U.S. military aircraft, military personnel, and war matériel. In response, the French high command informed the ISC that the U.S. military personnel were in transit or were replacements for the U.S. Military Assistance Advisory Group (MAAG) and that the Vietnamese military personnel were returning from training courses outside the country. After remonstrances by the ISC, the situation improved somewhat, to the extent that the French command notified the commission of arrivals and departures of aircraft and personnel. In early 1956 the French asked the ISC to grant permission for the entry of 350 U.S. military personnel as part of a temporary equipment recovery mission (TERM). The commission delayed decision for about two months but the American soldiers and officers arrived in late May, confronting the ISC with a *fait accompli*.[50] Although the RVN granted the commissioners permission to inspect TERM installations, the ISC apparently was more interested in receiving reports from the RVN government than accepting the offer of the RVN to permit ISC inspection of TERM facilities. Reports from the RVN on TERM were not forthcoming.[51] After accusations by the PAVN that the U.S. MAAG constituted an alliance in contravention of article 19, the RVN informed the commission that MAAG had been in Vietnam since 1950, with no change in its status, structure, or activities, and hence did not constitute a violation of the Geneva agreement. The RVN did not reply to an ISC request for comments upon DRVN charges that two other technical missions in the southern zone had come into existence and also constituted violations of the cease-fire agreement.

Thus from 1954 to 1957, and particularly after mid-1956, the function of the ISC in supervising compliance with articles 16–19 was seriously curtailed—so seriously, in fact, that one would be justified in concluding that the provisions were rapidly becoming dead letters and the ISC an ineffectual instrument for ensuring that the northern and southern zones would remain demilitarized. Certainly part of the problem was the fact that SVN (later, RVN) officials, throughout 1955, were becoming increasingly self-confident. The ISC itself admitted that questions "dealing with enforcement of obligations undertaken by the High Commands on behalf of the civil

[49] This was the team assigned to Phuc Hoa. VN 7, p. 13.
[50] VN 6, p. 25.
[51] VN 7, pp. 16-17.

administrations in their zones naturally involved a restriction on the sovereignty claimed by the civil administrations in the zones of both High Commands." In the south, therefore, "the independent attitude of the Government of the State of Vietnam, which controlled the civil administration and which had not signed the Geneva Agreement, made the obstructions and difficulties progressively more serious and the French High Command could not take adequate remedial action." Yet, even in the northern zone, "delay, obstruction and grudging co-operation were the main features in respect of investigations undertaken by the Commission . . . in respect of Article 14(d), Article 21 and surveys in respect of reconnaissance of border areas to decide action required under Article 36(d)."[52]

This situation caused the ISC, in mid-1955, to reconsider its role in Vietnam, but its self-examination resulted in a difference of opinion between the Canadian delegation and the Indian and Polish delegations. The latter reported that the ISC had been informed by the SVN that it would "give full protection and practical co-operation to the Commission as an International Peace Commission but will not make a formal or public declaration to that effect in view of the position taken by it with reference to the Geneva Agreement and the Final Declaration."[53] Since the activities of the ISC in the discharge of its responsibilities resulted in an infringement of the sovereignty of both the DRVN and the SVN, the commission could not carry on in the face of the declared opposition of the SVN, even though the latter had agreed to cooperate on an *ad hoc* basis. In the opinion of the Indian and Polish delegations, an *ad hoc* arrangement was outside the Geneva agreement and "naturally amounts to revocation of the Agreement and the Commission cannot be party to any such arrangement." According to the Canadian delegation, the SVN, while giving informal assurances of full protection and co-operation to the ISC as an international peace commission, was not formally engaged or obligated in respect of ISC functions. However, the ISC felt this *ad hoc* arrangement was unsatisfactory and expressed the hope that "the parties directly concerned will be able to work out more durable and dependable arrangements which would place the Commission in a more favourable position to carry out its functions."[54]

The Polish and Indian delegations believed that the ISC's tasks might continue indefinitely inasmuch as the commission, according to article 14(a), had been entrusted with duties pending the unification of Vietnam. Until such unification was effected, civil administrative arrangements in the zones were provisional. The commission,

[52] VN 4, pp. 15-16.   [53] *Ibid.*, p. 17.   [54] *Ibid.*, p. 25.

the fourth interim report averred, could wind up its activities only after political problems arising from the regrouping south and north of the provisional demarcation line had been settled.[55] Because of the opposition of the SVN, however, the provisional political problems might never be resolved. As a result of the increasing ineffectiveness of the French high command (according to the appreciation of the Indian and Polish delegations), ISC activities could continue only under "extremely trying conditions. . . . It cannot, however, continue to function with any effectiveness unless the difficulties mentioned . . . above . . . are resolved satisfactorily by the Co-Chairmen and the Geneva Powers at a very early date." In the Canadian view, however, the ISC *would continue its activities to the extent made possible by the cooperation of the French high command, the SVN, and the DRVN.*[56] In short, the Canadian delegation seemed (in spite of the somewhat contradictory language quoted in the preceding paragraph) to be advocating *ad hoc* arrangements with the SVN government, whose attitudes toward the ISC would be crucial after mid-1955. *Ad hoc* arrangements would at least permit the ISC to function in reasonable amity with the functionally sovereign government south of the demarcation line. The Indian and Polish delegations asked the co-chairmen and the "Geneva Powers" to attempt to resolve the difficulties in implementing the political provisions of the cease-fire agreement,[57] but in 1956 these problems became more acute with the liquidation of the French high command in late April and the suspension of joint commission functions in May.[58] After April there was no legal successor to the French signatory under the cease-fire agreement.

In one other respect, the government of the RVN unequivocally indicated its attitude toward the Geneva settlement: in 1955 the SVN (later, RVN) had refused to consult with the authorities of the DRVN for the purpose of discussing all-Vietnamese elections; and in July 1956 the RVN refused to hold such elections.[59] On 30 March

---

[55] VN 4, p. 17.   [56] *Ibid.*, p. 25.
[57] VN 5, p. 15; VN 6, pp. 30-33.
[58] On 6 April 1956 the RVN government issued a statement that declared French and Vietnamese officials had fixed a timetable for the withdrawal of the French expeditionary corps. This had been done at the request of the RVN in order to protect its sovereignty. "[In] the interests of peace the Republic of Vietnam considers that it cannot accept the presence on its territory of any foreign troops nor the granting of any military base. It does not, moreover, see the necessity of joining any military alliance." Though not recognizing the provisions of the Geneva agreement, the RVN would continue to extend "effective co-operation" to the ISC as an organization working for peace. Noble Frankland (ed.), *Documents on International Affairs, 1956* (London: Oxford University Press, 1959), pp. 720-721.
[59] In June 1955, Pham Van Dong declared that the DRVN was prepared to send delegates to a consultative conference to discuss elections. On 16 July, in a

1956 the Foreign Ministry of the Soviet Union addressed a note to the British ambassador in Moscow accusing RVN authorities of sabotaging Vietnamese national unification. The note demanded full implementation of the Geneva agreement and called for a new conference on Indochina with the participation of the powers that had attended the Geneva Conference of 1954, together with the three supervisory powers. The Soviet government, the note concluded, would not object to preliminary talks between the co-chairmen. In reply, in a note of 5 April, the British accepted the latter proposal; and in a second note, dated 9 April, the British challenged the substantive arguments raised in the Soviet note. The RVN, the note declared, was not obligated to hold elections in 1956, although the British government had hoped the RVN would do so, and in fact had advised that government to do so. In response to the charge that RVN authorities were preparing cadres for a campaign in the north, thus resuming hostilities, the British note stated:

[In July 1954] the forces at the disposal of the French Union High Command in Vietnam amounted to approximately 350,000 men. Since then over 100,000 French troops have been withdrawn and

radio broadcast, Diem declared that the SVN was not bound by the Geneva agreements, and although he was willing to have partition ended by free elections, he demanded that the leaders of the DRVN give proof of their readiness to place national interests above Communist interests (Lancaster, *op. cit.*, p. 370). Dong then sent notes to the ISC and the French and SVN governments demanding the convening of a consultative conference. Diem, on 9 August, retorted that conditions of freedom must be assured in the north before elections could be held. On 28 June, Secretary of State Dulles had stated: "We are not afraid at all of elections [in Vietnam], provided they are held under conditions of genuine freedom which the Geneva armistice agreement calls for. If those conditions can be provided we would be in favor of elections, because we believe that they would bring about the unification of the country under free government auspices" (*DSB*, 11 July 1955, p. 50). Then, on 30 August, Dulles declared that conditions in the DRVN ruled out the possibility of free elections (*NYHT*, 31 August 1955). On 21 September, Diem issued a statement: "[There] can be no question of a conference, even less of negotiations [with DRVN authorities]" (*T/L*, 22 September 1955). In August, Dong appealed to the co-chairmen, asking them to take measures to implement the Geneva agreements; and in November he again asked Molotov to urge Britain to cooperate in seeing that the Geneva agreements were respected. These demarches proved ineffectual (Lancaster, *op. cit.*, p. 372). In March 1958, when the Hanoi government again asked the RVN authorities to establish normal relations, Saigon asserted that the DRVN was to blame for the existing state of affairs; however, if the authorities in the north satisfied five preconditions, normal relations might be established. (1) Let all Vietnamese who desired to do so emigrate to the southern zone; (2) Reduce the strength of the PAVN to the same level as that of the ARVN (Army of the Republic of Vietnam); (3) Refrain from all acts of sabotage and terrorism in the south; (4) Cease requiring that residents of the north write favorably of local conditions in their letters to friends and relatives in the south; and (5) Allow all persons to work in freedom to improve their standard of living. Hanoi did not accept these preconditions. Geoffrey Barraclough, *Survey of International Affairs, 1956-1958* (London: Oxford University Press, 1962), pp. 420-421.

there will soon be none left, while the Vietnamese army itself has been reduced by 20,000 men. In North Vietnam, however, there has been no such reduction in military strength. . . . On the contrary, the Vietminh army has been so greatly strengthened by the embodiment and re-equipment of irregular forces that, instead of the seven Vietminh divisions in existence in July, 1954, there are now no less than twenty. This striking contrast between massive military expansion in the North and the withdrawal and reduction of military forces in the South speaks for itself.[60]

Soviet Deputy Foreign Minister Andrei Gromyko and Lord Reading met in London in late April and early May 1956, discussed problems relating to Laos and Vietnam, and at the conclusion of their talks addressed separate notes to the French government, the ISC, and identical notes to the governments of the RVN and the DRVN. In the latter notes the co-chairmen declared that they attached great importance to the maintenance of the cease-fire under the supervision of the ISC. They strongly urged the DRVN and RVN authorities "to make every effort to implement the Geneva Agreements on Vietnam, to prevent any future violation of the military provisions of these agreements and also to ensure the implementation of the political provisions and principles embodied in the Final Declaration."[61] The co-chairmen asked the two governments to transmit their views on the time required for beginning consultations on all-Vietnamese elections and the time required for holding these elections as a means for unifying Vietnam.

To the ISC and the governments of the two Vietnams, the co-chairmen conveyed their concern that the dissolution of the French high command would increase the commission's difficulties; however, they were "confident that the authorities in both parts of Vietnam will show effective co-operation and that these difficulties will in practice be removed." The co-chairmen asked the French government to use

[60] *Vietnam and the Geneva Agreements*, Vietnam No. 2 (1956), Cmd. 9763 (London: Her Majesty's Stationery Office, 1956), pp. 8-9 (hereafter referred to as Cmd. 9763). Earlier, in December 1955, the British government sought to make clear its conception of the British Foreign Secretary's role as co-chairman of the Geneva Conference. "There is no reference in the Agreements on the Cessation of Hostilities in Cambodia, Laos, and Vietnam or in the Final Declaration . . . to the Co-Chairmen as such or to any special responsibilities devolving upon Her Majesty's Government and the Soviet Government by virtue of the fact that Sir Anthony Eden and Mr. Molotov had acted as chairmen at alternate sessions of the Geneva Conference. . . . In the view of Her Majesty's Government their obligations and responsibilities and those of the Soviet Government are neither more nor less than those of the other Powers adhering to the Final Declaration. . . . For reasons of practical convenience, however, it has become customary for Her Majesty's Government and the Soviet Government to act as a channel of communication [between the ISC and the Geneva powers]." VN 4, p. 3.

[61] Cmd. 9763, p. 10.

its good offices in solving the practical problems associated with the implementation of the cease-fire agreement and, further, they invited the French to discuss the matter with the government of the RVN. It was significant that the Soviet and British ministers did not call for a new conference on Indochina.[62]

Acknowledging the co-chairmen's statement, the ISC declared that it would persevere in its efforts to maintain peace in Vietnam and would continue to deal with the parties "on the basis of the *status quo* until arrangements . . . envisaged in the Co-Chairmen's message to the French Government 'are put into effect.'"[63] Discussions between the French High Commissioner and the RVN officials were concluded at the end of July. On 15 August the French liaison mission to the ISC was dissolved and a *"mission chargée des relations avec la C.I.C.,"* a liaison mission to the ISC was established by the Saigon government to facilitate dealings between the ISC and the RVN. Although this ended what the ISC called the *"status quo* requested by the Co-Chairmen," the commission on 14 September advised the co-chairmen that it would deal with the liaison body created by the RVN.[64]

In establishing the liaison mission, the RVN reiterated the April 1956 declaration of Diem (now RVN President) that its government was prepared to offer effective cooperation to the commission but was not prepared to assume responsibility for the implementation of the Geneva agreements in Vietnam. In late August the DRVN government transmitted a letter to the ISC denouncing the arrangements that had been made between France and the "Southern Administration" for the withdrawal of the French high command. It insisted that the Geneva agreements be fully implemented by the parties and that, as a signatory, France was responsible for execution of the agreements until it had made "arrangements for handing over *responsibilities under the Agreements* to the Republic of Vietnam."[65]

[62] The co-chairmen agreed that they would consult together and discuss measures to ensure the implementation of the cease-fire agreement, including the proposal to convene a new conference (Cmd. 9763, p. 11). In reply to the ISC note, the French government declared that it would contribute to upholding the Geneva agreement and was ready to use its good offices for that purpose. It was to be understood, the reply said, that the French government could not accept any new responsibilities, and its good offices were given only so long as the RVN offered its cooperation (Frankland, *op.cit.,* p. 723). For the RVN's reply, see *ibid.,* pp. 723-724; for the DRVN's reply, pp. 726-728.

[63] VN 6, p. 32. The co-chairmen had not used the expression "status quo"; rather, they expressed the hope that the ISC "will persevere in their efforts to maintain and strengthen peace in Vietnam on the bases of the fulfillment of the Geneva Agreements on Vietnam." Cmd. 9763, p. 11.

[64] VN 7, p. 5.

[65] *Ibid.,* p. 23 (emphasis added).

[III]

[There] has been no consultation between the two Parties with a
view to holding free nation-wide elections for the unification of the
country, and to resolving the political problems and thus facilitat-
ing an early termination of the activities of the Commission and
the fulfillment of its tasks. The Commission is confident that this
important problem is engaging the attention of the Co-Chairmen
and the Members of the Geneva Conference.[66]

Thus conclude the eighth, ninth, tenth, and eleventh interim reports
of the ISC, which covered the period May 1957 to February 1961.
During that period the ISC sought to implement the Geneva agreement as the commissioners, even more frequently in disagreement,
understood its terms. The task was of course very difficult, and
doomed to failure, because the RVN did not regard itself bound by
the terms of either the agreement or the final declaration, and it refused to deal with the DRVN upon any terms, precluding for the
period under study (and for the foreseeable future) the political
settlement suggested by some of the powers at Geneva. The cooperation of the RVN and the DRVN was frequently grudging at
best, and sometimes was refused outright. The authorities of both
Vietnams lay petitions, claims, and counterclaims before the commission, whose activities each party so often hindered. Nor did the
co-chairmen act upon the problems posed by the continued division
of Vietnam, the actions (or lack of action), of a non-obligated party
(i.e., the RVN) to the cease-fire agreement, or what the ISC called
"violations" of the Geneva agreement. In July 1960, in fact, the co-
chairmen recommended reductions in the commission's personnel
in order to achieve "certain economies," and this was done in the face
of the ISC's deteriorating financial situation.[67]

Did the co-chairmen recognize that, after 1956, they were confronted with a wholly new situation, a situation not envisaged by the
Geneva agreement and hence one with which the ISC was simply not
competent to deal? It seems that this question must be answered
in the affirmative—that this was the implication of the co-chairmen's
message to the ISC, the RVN, and the DRVN. Certainly the ISC
would remain in Vietnam after 1956: a useful device for restraining

[66] *Eighth Interim Report of the International Commission for Supervision and
Control in Vietnam*, Vietnam No. 1 (1958), Cmd. 509 (London: Her Majesty's
Stationery Office, 1958), p. 15 (hereafter referred to as VN 8).

[67] *Eleventh Interim Report of the International Commission for Supervision and
Control in Vietnam*, Vietnam No. 1 (1961), Cmd. 1551 (London: Her Majesty's
Stationery Office, 1961), pp. 5, 27 (hereafter referred to as VN 11). With no
possibility of a political settlement in sight, the ISC would continue functioning
indefinitely. It may have been this prospect that prompted the co-chairmen to
urge economies in the commission's operations.

the Vietnamese authorities in both zones, it seemed to be the symbol of the Geneva conference in respect of the fundamental matter on which there was consensus; namely, that open hostilities should not be resumed. But by 1960 it was evident that the political situation was deteriorating, that incidents of a new conflict had occurred and were occurring, and in such circumstances the ISC was powerless to prevent them.

The history of Vietnam after 1954, and the origins of the so-called Second Vietnamese War, will require careful research at some future time, when more documents and personal memoirs are available. In this section I will merely bring to a close the story of the functioning of the ISC for Vietnam as an institution established by the Geneva agreement of 1954.

In April 1957 the commission notified the co-chairmen that it had not been able to supervise the implementation of article 14(c), the guarantee of democratic freedoms, because it had not received the assistance and cooperation of the RVN.[68] RVN authorities had not even replied to ISC inquiries in the "majority of pending cases referred to it alleging reprisal or discrimination," and concurrence for the deployment of inspection teams had been refused. The co-chairmen did not formally and substantively reply to this notification. In the eighth interim report (1 May 1957 to 30 April 1958) the commission reported no change in the attitude of the RVN authorities, who refused to recognize the obligatory force of article 14(c) in the south.[69] Although the ISC indicated that the RVN government was cooperating by supplying documents concerning "civilian internees" (21), the commission was impelled to inform the members of the Geneva Conference (43) that the RVN had not implemented its recommendations and had hindered supervision of the implementation of article 14(c).[70] In this report, and in the eleventh interim report (1 February 1960 to 28 February 1961), the ISC concluded—with the Canadian delegation dissenting on one finding—that the RVN had not afforded the commission the assistance and cooperation required by article 25. The RVN government, however, did not regard itself bound by article 25.[71]

In 1959, when the PAVN high command complained that the passage of Law 10/59 by the National Assembly of the RVN had violated article 14(c), the ISC reaffirmed its 1956 determination that no law could be passed in either zone that could supersede the "obligations which the two Parties have undertaken" under that provision.[72]

[68] VN 7, p. 29.   [69] VN 8, p. 13.   [70] *Ibid.*, p. 7.   [71] VN 11, pp. 8-9.
[72] *Tenth Interim Report of the International Commission for Supervision and Control in Vietnam*, Vietnam No. 1 (1960), Cmd. 1040 (London: Her Majesty's Stationery Office, 1960), pp. 11-12 (hereafter referred to as VN 10).

The difficulty, however, was that the RVN (at that time the SVN) had not been a party to the Geneva agreement, no matter what the ISC said. In 1960, in its eleventh interim report (1 February 1960 to 28 February 1961), the commission decided that Law 10/59 did not contain a provision that would discriminate against or subject to reprisal persons who came within the terms of article 14(*c*).[73] The Polish delegation dissented. In May 1960 the PAVN high command informed the ISC that its decision was unacceptable, and Prime Minister Pham Van Dong addressed a letter to the co-chairmen calling for reconsideration and repeal of the commission's decision. The commission subsequently dispatched a letter to Dong defending its position. The letter stated that, although either party might address a letter to the co-chairmen, the Geneva agreement contained no provision for an appeal to the co-chairmen against the decision of the ISC. Again, the Polish delegation dissented.

In 1959, despite its stand on article 14(*c*), the government of the RVN expressed its concern to the ISC over the problem of subversion in southern Vietnam,[74] but the Polish delegation emphatically opposed even mentioning the fact that complaints of subversion had been made. "[The] Polish Delegation finds that the above-mentioned complaints should be considered as communications concerning cases beyond the scope of the Geneva Agreement. Such communications cannot be referred to in the Interim Report."[75] In 1960 the RVN made additional complaints of subversion, and the ISC and its legal committee studied both the new and the old complaints. The Indian and Canadian delegations expressed the view that the ISC could not divest itself of its responsibility to investigate any act "alleged to be abetted by one Party against the other which may be detrimental to the peace" in Vietnam—even though subversion, as such, was not mentioned in the Geneva agreement.[76] Nevertheless, on 11 December 1961 the PAVN liaison mission to the ISC declared that it would "resolutely reject all decisions taken by the International Commission relating to the so-called 'subversive activities' in South Viet-Nam, a question which has no relevance to the Geneva Agreement."[77] It would, moreover, reject all requests for comments.[78]

---

[73] VN 11, p. 9.   [74] VN 10, p. 13.   [75] *Ibid.*, p. 26.   [76] VN 11, p. 14.

[77] *Special Report to the Co-Chairmen of the Geneva Conference on Indo-China,* Vietnam No. 1 (1962), Cmd. 1755 (London: Her Majesty's Stationery Office, 1962), p. 5 (hereafter referred to as *SR*).

[78] D. C. Watt, *Survey of International Affairs, 1961* (London: Oxford University Press, 1965), p. 351. After 1958, the government of the RVN was increasingly concerned with the terror campaign waged against its provincial and district officials and its civil servants, a campaign which it attributed to DRVN cadres operating in the south. In 1959, forty to fifty Vietnamese were murdered each month in the south; by 1961 these figures had reached 500 per month, and open

The reader will recall that the joint commission ceased to function in May 1956; then, in April 1958, the French mission to the joint commission was withdrawn, and despite the remonstrances of the ISC, the decision on withdrawal was declared irrevocable.[79] Because the demilitarized zone had been placed under the supervisory competence of the joint commission pursuant to chapter I of the cease-fire agreement, a serious lacuna existed in the control regime for Vietnam. Who would issue permits to persons who wished to enter the demilitarized zone (see articles 7-9)? Who would ensure that the demilitarized zone retained its buffer-zone character (see article 1)? The RVN refused to assume the role of successor to the French high command on the joint commission, although the ISC and the PAVN high command apparently desired this. Saigon, in its view providing for Vietnamese citizens in the DMZ south of the demarcation line, authorized the chief of Quang Tri province to issue permits to persons either ordered to enter or desiring to enter the zone. The ISC did not regard this arrangement as "appropriate"[80] but the situation remained unchanged, and the problems created by the nonexistence of the joint commission remained unresolved.[81]

Under the articles enjoining the introduction of arms and troops into Vietnam and the establishment of military alliances or new bases, the commission continued to make investigations and reconnaissances whenever it was permitted to do so, subject to the restrictions the governments of the RVN and the DRVN imposed. When the PAVN high command lodged a complaint that a military alliance had materialized between the RVN and the SEATO signatories and that the RVN had sent representatives to a SEATO meeting in March 1958, in violation of the cease-fire agreement, the government of the RVN asserted that the sending of observers and military personnel to foreign countries and on missions abroad was an internal question

---

clashes between the armed forces of the RVN and the so-called Vietcong had also occurred.

The term "Vietcong" is used to describe insurgent forces in Vietnam, but its usage and definitions are controversial; Douglas Pike, *Viet Cong* (Cambridge, Mass.: The M.I.T. Press, 1966), page facing p. 1.

[79] *Ninth Interim Report of the International Commission for Supervision and Control in Vietnam*, Vietnam No. 1 (1959), Cmd. 726 (London: Her Majesty's Stationery Office, 1959), p. 7 (hereafter referred to as VN 9).

[80] VN 10, p. 6.

[81] VN 11, p. 6. See Chapter 25 for a discussion of the border dispute between Cambodia and the RVN. The ISC for Cambodia forwarded complaints of the Royal Cambodian government to the ISC for Vietnam; and in one case it forwarded the report of an *ad hoc* investigating team that verified that armed forces of the RVN had violated the Cambodian frontier in Stung Treng province (VN 9, p. 5). The RVN government denied the competence of the ISC to consider border conflicts and rejected the conclusions of the *ad hoc* team of the Cambodian ISC (VN 10, p. 5). See also VN 7, p. 5; VN 8, pp. 5-6; VN 11, p. 5.

that "falls under the sovereignty of the [RVN]" and in no way concerned the Geneva agreement.[82] The presence of the United States' temporary equipment recovery mission (TERM) also was a constant concern of the ISC, which impliedly criticized the RVN for failing to supply adequate information about TERM's activities, and then expressed the hope that the mission would be withdrawn by 1959 or 1960. The RVN government notified the commission in January 1961 that TERM had been disbanded and about a fourth of its personnel had been transferred to the U.S. Military Assistance Advisory Group (MAAG), the remainder having left Vietnam. The Polish delegation associated itself with the view of the delegation of the PAVN high command that all the TERM personnel had been transferred to MAAG and that this constituted a violation of articles 16 and 25. In this connection, the PAVN also alleged that there had been an increase in the number of U.S. military personnel in South Vietnam. The ISC noted that, according to its records, 2,002 U.S. military personnel arrived in the RVN between January 1956 and December 1957 and, in the same period, 1,243 had left; thus arrivals exceeded departures by 759.[83] The matter was still under commission consideration in 1961.

By 1960 the situation had markedly deteriorated. The RVN complained that the DRVN had committed open and direct aggression through Laos against the provinces of Kontum and Pleiku in October 1960. Although the Indian and Canadian delegations insisted it was within the ISC's competence to investigate allegations of aggression of this kind, the Polish delegation did not participate in the voting because, in its view, the RVN complaint did not constitute a *prima facie* case, and in any case was groundless.[84] The PAVN high command averred that the commission could not even ask for comments. By mid-1962 the ISC, having apprised itself of the facts of the military situation in Vietnam, prepared a *Special Report to the Co-Chairmen of the Geneva Conference on Indo-China.*[85] This document, essentially a majority report, was the product of the Indian and Canadian delegations (the Polish delegation disagreed with the majority's conclusions). Following upon RVN allegations of subversion committed by the DRVN and a second charge of aggression in Kontum and Pleiku provinces in September 1961, the commission instructed its legal committee to examine the allegations and the evidence in support thereof, and the committee made the following findings (the Polish delegation dissenting), findings that a commission majority accepted.

[82] VN 10, p. 18; VN 7, pp. 16-17; VN 8, p. 11.
[83] VN 9, p. 13; VN 10, p. 19; VN 11, pp. 17-18.
[84] VN 11, p. 23.   [85] SR, *op.cit.*

1. In specific cases there was evidence to show, beyond a reasonable doubt, that armed and unarmed personnel, arms, and supplies had been sent from the northern zone to the southern zone "with the object of supporting, organizing and carrying out hostile activities, including armed attacks, directed against the Armed Forces and Administration of the Zone in the South. These acts are in violation of Articles 10, 19, 24, and 27 [of the cease-fire agreement]."[86]

2. The PAVN had allowed the "Zone in the North to be used for inciting, encouraging and supporting hostile activities in the Zone in the South, aimed at the overthrow of the Administration in the South."

3. The commission's teams had observed the continuous arrival of war matériel in southern Vietnam (i.e., the RVN) but, since the teams were denied the right of control and inspection, the quantity and nature of the war matériel could not be determined. Several violations of articles 17 and 25 were recorded against the RVN.[87]

4. The establishment of a U.S. military assistance advisory command and MAAG's continued existence in southern Vietnam resulted in the introduction of a large number of U.S. military personnel, in violation of article 16.

5. Although there was no formal alliance between the United States and the RVN, the military assistance command and MAAG amounted to a "factual military alliance," prohibited by article 19.[88]

In making findings 3, 4, and 5, the commission took under advisement a letter from the RVN government, dated 9 December 1961, declaring that the RVN had exercised its inherent right of self-defense against acts of aggression committed by the DRVN when it requested United States military assistance. Nevertheless, the Indian and Canadian delegations recommended that the Geneva co-chairmen take

[86] *SR*, p. 7.
[87] *SR*, p. 8
[88] *SR*, p. 10. In 1961 the concern of the United States for the continued existence and viability of the RVN became much greater. Vice President Lyndon B. Johnson visited Saigon in May and described the situation in the south as one of the "utmost gravity." An economic mission, headed by Eugene A. Staley, was dispatched to the RVN in mid-June. On his return, Staley recommended a 15 percent increase in the strength of the ARVN and reorganization of the economic and social structures of the villages to form "agrovilles" and "strategic hamlets." In October, President John F. Kennedy sent still another mission to Saigon, under General Maxwell Taylor. He also called General James Van Fleet from retirement to assist the U.S. Army in establishing a counterinsurgency training program for the RVN. In November it was announced that the dispatch of technicians and equipment deliveries would be stepped up. In December the State Department released a "white paper," *A Threat to the Peace*, documenting U.S.-RVN allegations of DRVN-sponsored subversion, sabotage, and terror in the south. D. C. Watt, *op. cit.*, pp. 349-361, and Committee on Foreign Relations, *Background Information relating to Southeast Asia and Vietnam*, March 1966 (Washington, D.C.: U.S. Government Printing Office, 1966), pp. 84-92.

remedial action to ensure that the "parties" (*a*) respect the zones of the other party; (*b*) strictly observe articles 16–19 in respect of the ban on the import of war matériel and the introduction of military personnel; (*c*) commit no hostile acts against the other; (*d*) do not allow the zones assigned to them to adhere to a military alliance; and (*e*) cooperate with the ISC in fulfillment of its tasks of supervision and control. The majority delegations made no recommendations respecting a political settlement in Vietnam, consultations between the authorities of the RVN and the DRVN, or the holding of elections.[89]

The Polish delegation, in a separate statement addressed to the co-chairmen, reiterated its challenge of the competence of the commission to consider allegations of subversion. The Poles also asserted that there was no evidence to substantiate the charges of aggression committed by the DRVN and that the activities of the RVN and the United States constituted a flagrant violation of the Geneva agreement and threatened the peace of Southeast Asia. The Polish delegation accused the majority delegations of ignoring the RVN's violation of article 14(*c*) by the latter's "persecution of former resistance members followed by the persecution of all democratic elements which is certainly one of the most important causes of the widespread movement against the Government of the Republic of Viet-Nam."[90] Another cause of the anti-RVN movement, according to the Polish statement, was the refusal of the RVN to act upon reunifying Vietnam, in spite of the repeated proposals made by the DRVN and the efforts of the ISC to facilitate negotiations between the parties. The statement concluded with a request that the co-chairmen see that United States forces withdraw from Vietnam, that the U.S. military assistance command be dissolved, and that article 14(*c*) be observed by the RVN.

After the *Special Report*, the ISC issued no more interim reports, and for all practical purposes ceased to function in an investigatory role in Vietnam.[91]

[89] *SR*, p. 11.

[90] *SR*, pp. 21-22.

[91] The ISC issued two more special reports in 1965. In the first of these, *Special Report to the Co-Chairmen of the Geneva Conference on Indo-China* (Vietnam No. 1 [1965], Cmd. 2609 [London: Her Majesty's Stationery Office, 1965]), the Indian and Polish delegations called the attention of the co-chairmen to the grave situation resulting from the decision of the United States and the RVN to take military action against military installations in the DRVN in February 1965. The ISC requested the co-chairmen to issue an immediate appeal to "all concerned with a view to reducing tension" (p. 5). The Canadian delegation issued a separate statement dealing with the "intensification of the aggressive policy of the Government of North Vietnam" and concluded that the DRVN's activity was a direct and grave violation of the Geneva agreement (presumably article 24): "The cessation of hostile activities by North Vietnam is a prerequisite to the resto-

ration of peace in Vietnam as foreseen by the participants in the Geneva Conference of 1954" (pp. 14-15).

The second report, *Special Report to the Co-Chairmen of the Geneva Conference on Indo-China* (Vietnam No. 2 [1965], Cmd. 2634 [London: Her Majesty's Stationery Office, 1965]), noted that the DRVN government had asked the ISC to withdraw all its fixed teams, and the commission reluctantly complied (p. 6). In a separate statement, the Polish delegation declared that the ISC teams were in direct physical danger in areas under attack by U.S. aircraft; hence the DRVN had asked that they be withdrawn.

The British government sought to reconvene the Geneva Conference in 1965, but the Soviet Union took the position that it would be inappropriate to call a conference so long as the United States was committing aggression in Indochina. The mission of the British special representative, Patrick Gordon Walker, who sought to obtain the views of the supervisory powers and the members of the Geneva Conference on the situation in Vietnam, was similarly unsuccessful; the governments of the C.P.R. and the DRVN refused to receive him. See *Recent Exchanges Concerning Attempts to Promote a Negotiated Settlement of the Conflict in Viet-Nam*, Vietnam No. 3 (1965), Cmd. 2756 (London: Her Majesty's Stationery Office, 1965), pp. 19, 27-28, 34, 37, 41, 57, 59, 69, 71, 86-87.

Chapter 25

THE SETTLEMENT FOR CAMBODIA

[I]

The Agreement on the Cessation of Hostilities in Cambodia, simpler than its Vietnamese or Laotian analogue, ultimately was made possible by Premier Chou En-lai's proposal in mid-June to persuade the Vietminh to withdraw its troops from Cambodia and Laos in exchange for an agreement neutralizing these countries. After this major concession, representatives of the PAVN and the Khmer national armed forces met together (as members of the Military Commission for Cambodia) to work out the technical details of a cease-fire. To the extent that the Khmer Issarak was a considerably weaker insurgent movement than the Pathet Lao, and certainly much weaker than the Vietminh, a settlement that embodied requirements for the withdrawal of PAVN units boded well for the Royal Government of Cambodia. Moreover, the fact that the provisional demarcation line in Vietnam was near the 17th parallel, hence some 200 miles north of the northern frontier of Cambodia, meant that Cambodia and the DRVN would not share a common border. The regime that might again decide to assist the Khmer Issarak insurgents could do so only by infiltrating through Laos or southern Vietnam, a more difficult undertaking for the DRVN than assisting the Pathet Lao, for example, which was grouped just across the Laos-DRVN frontier.

The Cambodian settlement required these basic elements: a cease-fire, accompanied by regroupment and withdrawal of foreign armed forces; assembling and disarming the Khmer Issarak and a determination respecting the future of those who had fought in its name; provisions for the demilitarization of Cambodia; and provisions for the supervision of the terms of the cease-fire and concomitant troop movements. The cease-fire agreement was structured in the order of the elements listed above. Chapter I related to the cease-fire, ordered for 8 A.M., Peking mean time, on 23 July (1),[1] it would become fully effective no later than 8 A.M. (PMT) on 7 August (2[a]). The fifteen-day interval was established to allow time for transmitting cease-fire orders to the lowest echelons of the armed forces of the belligerent parties in all the combat areas of Cambodia. The parties undertook not to engage in "any large-scale operation" before the cease-fire became effective(3[c]).

---

[1] As in the preceding chapters the numbers in parentheses refer to the article numbers of the cease-fire agreement (in this chapter the Cambodian agreement) in Cmd. 9239, which comprises the Appendix.

The Cambodian agreement was signed by General Nhiek Tioulong for the commander in chief of the Khmer national armed forces and by Ta Quang Buu for the commander in chief of the Khmer resistance forces and the "Commander-in-Chief of the Vietnamese Military Units."[2] The reader should note this latter expression: Ta Quang Buu did not sign this document on behalf of the commander in chief of the People's Army of Vietnam, as in the case of the Vietnamese and Laotian cease-fire agreements, but on behalf of the commander in chief of the Vietnamese military units in Cambodia. This constituted an admission of the presence of PAVN units in Cambodia during hostilities, a fact the DRVN, C.P.R., and Soviet delegations had denied until mid-June. Even afterward, the Communist delegations always spoke of the withdrawal of "foreign forces" from Cambodia and Laos, never publicly admitting that Vietminh (as well as French) troops were implied by that expression. Although in the Delteil–Ta Quang Buu talks of late June the DRVN minister refused to admit the presence of Vietminh troops in the interior Associated States, in July the DRVN leaders apparently were persuaded that, if an Indochinese cease-fire was to be achieved, Vietminh units must be withdrawn from Cambodia and Laos and, of course, some mention (albeit discreet mention) of a Vietminh presence must be made.

Chapter II of the cease-fire agreement concerned procedures for the withdrawal of "Foreign Armed Forces and Foreign Military Personnel." According to article 4(1), these procedures applied to

(a) the armed forces and military combatant personnel of the French Union;

(b) the combatant formations of all types which have entered the territory of Cambodia from other countries or regions of the peninsula;

(c) all the foreign elements (or Cambodians not natives of Cambodia) in the military formations of any kind or holding supervisory functions in all political or military, administrative, economic, financial or social bodies, having worked in liaison with the Viet Nam military units.

The withdrawals were to be completed within ninety days of the entry into force of the agreement, that is, no later than ninety days after 23 July (4[2]). The commanders in chief, who were responsible for the execution of the agreement (10, 31) and who undertook to punish violators (26), also agreed *not* to permit any hostile actions during withdrawals (4[3]), including the destruction or sabotage of public property and attacks upon the life or property of the civilian

[2] Cmd. 9239, p. 18.

population (4[4]). Further, the commanders undertook not to permit interference with local civil administration. Responsibility for the execution of these and other provisions, as in the Vietnam cease-fire agreement, devolved upon the "signatories . . . and their successors in their functions"—a phrase we shall have to return to shortly.

Within thirty days after the cease-fire order had been published, the parties "undertake that . . . the Khmer Resistance Forces shall be demobilized on the spot; simultaneously, the troops of the Royal Khmer Army shall abstain from taking any hostile action against the Khmer Resistance Forces" (chapter III, article 5). The demobilized Khmer Issarak would be treated in accordance with the declaration of the Cambodian delegation, the text of which was incorporated *in toto* in article 6 of the cease-fire agreement. In this declaration, the Royal Government of Cambodia resolved to take the measures necessary to integrate all citizens into the national community and to guarantee them enjoyment of the rights and freedoms provided in the constitution.[3] Article 6 also declared that no reprisals would be taken against the Khmer Issarak nationals or their families and that these nationals were entitled to the same constitutional guarantees for their persons, their "democratic freedoms," and their property as other Cambodians. Prisoners of war and civilian internees captured in Cambodia during the period of hostilities, whatever their nationality, were to be "liberated" after entry into force of the agreement (8[a])[4] Foreign prisoners of war, captured by either party, were to be liberated by surrender to the authorities of the other party, who would then "give them all possible assistance in proceeding to the destination of their choice" (8[c]).

An international supervisory commission, with headquarters at Phnom Penh, was established for Cambodia (11). Composed of representatives of Canada, India, and Poland and presided over by the Indian representative, this ISC would function in much the same fashion as the ISC for Vietnam. Fixed and mobile teams were to be set up by the ISC, and the mobile teams were to have zones of action on the land and sea frontiers of Cambodia. The mobile teams were to be permitted to move freely within the limits of their assigned zones, and local civil and military authorities were to furnish them whatever facilities were required for the fulfillment of their tasks (12).[5]

[3] *Ibid.*, p. 40.

[4] "Civilian internees" was understood to mean all persons who, having in any way contributed to the political and armed struggle between the two parties have been arrested for that reason or kept in detention by either party during the period of hostilities" (8[b]). See article 21(b) of the Vietnamese cease-fire agreement.

[5] "Facilities" might include provision of personnel, access to the documents needed for supervision, summoning of witnesses for inquiries, security and freedom of movement of the inspection teams, etc. (12).

The ISC was generally responsible for supervising execution of the provisions of the cease-fire agreement, with these duties in particular: (1) controlling the withdrawal of foreign forces; (2) ensuring that the frontiers of Cambodia were respected; (3) controlling the release of prisoners of war and civilian internees; and (4) supervising, at ports, airfields, and the Cambodian frontier, "the application of the Cambodian declaration concerning the introduction into Cambodia of military personnel and war materials on grounds of foreign assistance" (13).

In a unilateral declaration at Geneva on 20 July, the Cambodian delegation had stated:

> The Royal Government of Cambodia, is resolved never to take part in an aggressive policy and never to permit the territory of Cambodia to be utilized in the service of such a policy.
>
> The Royal Government of Cambodia will not join in any agreement with other States, if this agreement carries for Cambodia the obligation to enter into a military alliance not in conformity with the principles of the Charter of the United Nations, or as long as its security is not threatened, the obligation to establish bases on Cambodian territory for the military forces of foreign Powers.
>
> The Royal Government of Cambodia is resolved to settle its international disputes by peaceful means, in such a manner as not to endanger peace, international security and justice.
>
> During the period which will elapse between the date of the cessation of hostilities in Viet Nam and that of the final settlement of political problems in this country, the Royal Government of Cambodia will not solicit foreign aid in war material, personnel or instructors except for the purpose of the effective defence of the territory.[6]

Accordingly, the second and the fourth paragraph of this declaration were incorporated in article 7 of the cease-fire agreement, and the self-imposed commitment of the fourth paragraph, not to solicit foreign aid (except for defense purposes), empowered the ISC to supervise such abstention under article 13.

Quite obviously, the Cambodian government, as the government of an independent state, must decide what materials were necessary for "effective defence," but its independent determination might conflict with the assessments and conclusions of the commissioners and the ISC inspection teams. Certainly the crucial question, what was necessary for the effective defense of Cambodia, had a variety of answers. Since neither the ISC nor the quasi-institutionalized conference to which the ISC reported instances of a party's refusal to put its recommendations into effect (22) had enforcement power, the

[6] Cmd. 9239, p. 41.

Cambodian government was not obligated to accept an ISC determination on this question, nor could it be compelled to do so. Moreower, since the "regime" established for Indochina was so informal, the government of Cambodia would have fairly broad discretion in determining when the defense of the state required the solicitation of foreign troops or military assistance. Sam Sary, it will be recalled, delayed the conference settlements for several hours on 20 July by demanding recognition of Cambodia's sovereign right to take whatever steps were necessary to protect its territories and peoples. His stand, which unnerved the great-power delegations, was a reflection of the determination of his government to insist that it be accorded all the rights and privileges of a fully sovereign state. It was only one of many instances history provides of a new state jealously guarding the rights that independence has brought it.

In any event, in cases of violation or threats of serious violation, whether with respect to the importation of arms and military personnel or *other* provisions of the agreement, the inspection teams were to inform the ISC of their findings. The ISC, in turn, would make recommendations to the parties (18). These recommendations, when they concerned violations or threats of violations that might lead to a resumption of hostilities, had to be adopted by a unanimous vote of the ISC. Article 21 specified two rather important categories of violations that came within the unanimity provision: (1) refusal by foreign armed forces to effect the movements established in the withdrawal plan and (2) a violation or threat of violation of Cambodia's integrity by foreign armed forces. All other questions were to be adopted by majority vote.[7]

Refusal by one party to put an ISC recommendation into effect could be reported to the members of the Geneva Conference by the other, aggrieved party or by the ISC itself. The latter would also report all cases where its work was being hindered (22). When the ISC could not reach unanimity, as required by article 21, it would transmit a majority report and one or more minority reports to the members of the conference.

The cease-fire agreement also established a joint commission that was composed of an equal number of representatives provided by each command of the signatories (14, 15). The competence of the joint commission was complementary to (if potentially competitive with) that of the ISC. The former was empowered "to facilitate the implementation of the clauses relating to the withdrawal of foreign forces . . . [and] the clauses . . . on the cessation of hostilities relating

---

[7] The decision of the ISC to reduce its activities (25), and recommendations for amendments to the cease-fire agreement (20) had to be adopted unanimously by the ISC delegates.

to the simultaneous and general cease-fire in Cambodia for all regular and irregular armed forces of the two parties" (5, 6, 14). More particularly, the joint commission was authorized to assist the parties in execution of the terms of the agreement, to ensure liaison between the parties, and to attempt to settle disputes that might arise between them, to the extent the disputes were connected with the implementation of the agreement (29, 14). The commission could also establish joint groups, some of which could be sent to supervise the movements of regular, irregular and foreign armed forces (14).[8]

The commanders (i.e., those on whose behalf the agreement was signed) undertook to afford full protection and all possible assistance and cooperation to the ISC, its inspection teams, and the joint commission in the performance of their functions (28). Article 24 required the ISC for Cambodia to work in close cooperation with the ISCs for Vietnam and Laos, whose coordination of functions would be accomplished by the secretaries general of the three commissions.

[II]

The Cambodian cease-fire agreement purported to obligate, in some respects, five distinct parties: the commander in chief of the People's Army of Vietnam, the commander in chief of the Khmer national armed forces, the commander in chief of the Khmer Issarak, the French high command (4[1] [a]), and the Royal Government of Cambodia. Yet the agreement was signed only by General Nhiek Tioulong, a general in the Khmer national armed forces, for the commander of those forces, and by Ta Quang Buu, a minister of the DRVN. How were the nonsigning parties obligated pursuant to this agreement?

1. Article 4(1) (a) stated that the withdrawal procedures applied to the armed forces and military combatant personnel of the French Union. Formidable legal problems were avoided by the concurrent proclamation of two unilateral declarations by the French government,[9] the first declaring the readiness of the French to withdraw their troops from the territory of Cambodia at the request of the government concerned (i.e. the Royal Governmemt of Cambodia) and the second indicating that the French government would proceed on the principles of respect for the independence, sovereignty, unity, and territorial integrity of Cambodia for settling all problems connected with the reestablishment of peace in Cambodia. The French government would fulfill the pledges of its unilateral declarations by with-

---

[8] Costs for the operation of the joint commission were to be shared equally by the two parties (30).

[9] Cmd. 9239, p. 42.

drawing its forces from Cambodia in accordance with the relevant provisions of the cease-fire agreement.

2. Of the concessions made by the Communist delegations in June, the most curious was the agreement to drop the demand for representation of the Khmer Issarak and the Pathet Lao. Thenceforward the DRVN delegation "represented" these movements on the military commissions for Cambodia and Laos and at the political conference itself.

We may well wonder what the leaders of the two insurgent groups thought of this arrangement; in the case of the Cambodian cease-fire, it was agreed that the Khmer Issarak should be demobilized on the spot! Even with the guarantees of their civil rights in article 6, the insurgents may have been displeased with the DRVN's arrogation of the right to speak on their behalf. Many insisted, however, that the Khmer Issarak was a creature of the Vietminh and without its support would have collapsed. This may indeed have been the case, and therefore the DRVN delegation could speak for the Khmer resistance forces because they were controlled by the Vietminh.

But this explanation is not *entirely* accurate; Son Ngoc Thanh, one of the principal Khmer Issarak leaders, was not completely controlled by the Vietminh. Moreover, in view of the fact that Son Ngoc Minh, president of the Khmer resistance "government," appealed for the observance of the settlement in late July,[10] it is not impossible that the Khmer Issarak freely consented to Vietminh representation in June and to the terms of the cease-fire agreement relating to demobilization. Also, Khmer Issarak leaders never challenged the obligatory force of the agreement, and their conduct after July evinced an intent to adhere to its terms. In the early autumn the delegation that represented the Khmer Issarak and Vietnamese (PAVN) units on the joint commission informed the members of the delegation of the Royal Government of Cambodia that "the latter were free to deal according to the normal laws of the country with any bands masquerading as Khmer Resistance Forces."[11]

3. The Royal Government of Cambodia had a number of important and continuing duties under the cease-fire agreement, but did General Nhiek Tioulong's signature, on behalf of the commander in chief of the Khmer national armed forces, effectively bind the Cambodian government? It appeared that it did, but formal evidence in support of this conclusion came many months after the agreement

[10] Coral Bell, *Survey of International Affairs, 1954* (London: Oxford University Press, 1957), p. 93.

[11] *First Progress Report of the International Commission for Supervision and Control in Cambodia for the Period Ending December 31, 1954*, Cambodia No. 1 (1955), Cmd. 9458 (London: Her Majesty's Stationery Office, 1955), p. 5 (hereafter referred to as Cmd. 9458 [No. 1]).

was signed. Thirteen days after signing an agreement with the United States for direct military aid (on 16 May 1955),[12] the Royal Government issued a communiqué that declared:

> The Royal Government intends scrupulously and always to respect the terms of the Geneva Agreement concerning it, as well as the undertakings taken in its name at the Asian-African Conference at Bandung by its delegation led by His Royal Highness Upayuvareach Norodom Sihanouk; the Government renews hereby its approval of the declaration made by him concerning the neutrality of Cambodia.
>
> But our countrymen undoubtedly understand that although neutral a nation must defend itself and must have the means to defend its integrity and its independence.
>
> In so far as the aid of friendly nations is given to Cambodia without infringement of her sovereignty or of her neutrality, the Government considers that this aid must be accepted in order to save our compatriots from heavier sacrifices for the maintenance of indispensable national armed forces.[13]

With the demobilization of the Khmer Issarak and the withdrawal of Vietminh military units, there was but one government in Cambodia, and no insurgent movement challenged its legitimacy. It is not altogether clear when Cambodia became an independent state, but presumably the Geneva cease-fire agreement, together with the French declarations, were the instruments by which it achieved independence. Unlike the case of the Vietnam cease-fire agreement, a Cambodian officer (not a French officer) signed the Cambodian agreement. Thus there could be less difficulty in interpreting the phrase, in article 31, that the signatories and "their successors in their functions shall be responsible for the observance and enforcement of the terms and provisions [of the agreement]." By its public statements and its conduct subsequent to 21 July, the Cambodian government indicated that it regarded itself bound by the agreement.

4. The principal duties of the parties to the cease-fire agreement were military in nature; hence the high command of the PAVN had the authority to agree to and carry out withdrawals and related duties. The DRVN, *per se*, was not a party to the agreement and did not regard itself a successor in function of the commander of the Vietminh units in Cambodia. It remained, of course, a party very

---

[12] TIAS 3240, 16 May 1955; 6 U.S.T. 995-1006 (1955).

[13] *Third Interim Report of the International Commission for Supervision and Control in Cambodia for the Period April 1 to July 28, 1955*, Cambodia No. 3 (1955), Cmd. 9579 (London: Her Majesty's Stationery Office, 1955), pp. 16-17 (hereafter referred to as Cmd. 9579 [No. 3]).

much interested in the continued adherence of the Cambodian government to its declarations on the neutral character of the Cambodian state (witness Vo Nguyen Giap's protest to the Cambodian ISC over the conclusion of the military-aid agreement between Cambodia and the United States).[14] After the cease-fire, the withdrawal and demobilization provisions of the agreement, for all practical purposes, had been executed by November or December and the Cambodian government and the high command of the Cambodian national armed forces continued to be the parties most directly responsible for performance of the required tasks under the cease-fire agreement. The DRVN (and the PAVN) had no duties or obligations under the agreement after the withdrawals had been completed.

[III]

In the final declaration, the Geneva Conference "took note" of the Cambodian declaration (1) indicating an intention to permit all citizens to take their place in the national community with full civil rights (FD 3), (2) resolving not to request military aid "except for the purpose of the effective defence of their territory" (FD 4), and (3) renouncing the right to enter into "any agreement with other states if this agreement includes the obligation to participate in a military alliance not in conformity with the principles of the Charter of the United Nations . . . or, so long as [its] security is not threatened, the obligation to establish bases on Cambodian . . . territory for the military forces of foreign Powers" (FD 5). Paragraph 9 declared that the authorities of Cambodia "must not permit any individual or collective reprisals against persons who have collaborated in any way with one of the parties during the war, or against members of such persons' families." The conference also took note of the two French declarations (discussed earlier), and the participants agreed to consult one another on any question referred to them by the ISC (for Cambodia as well as for Vietnam and Laos) (FD 10, 11, 13). In their relations with Cambodia, the states of the Geneva Conference undertook to respect sovereignty, independence, unity, and territorial integrity and to refrain from interference in its internal affairs (FD 12).

In attempting to assess the obligations of the participants of the Geneva Conference we are confronted, even in the case of Cambodia and Laos, with the task of interpreting the expression "takes note of." There is no reason to believe that these words had any legal significance beyond their *prima facie* meaning. The expressions "Conference" or "members of the Conference," moreover, should be understood in the context of the events and stated positions of the dele-

[14] *Ibid.*, pp. 17-19.

gates at Geneva. Most of the great-power participants agreed, in principle, to consult one another on questions referred to them by the ISC (FD 13), but the United States and the SVN had not so agreed, and the official position of the DRVN and the Laotian delegation on this and other matters remained unclear. In the case of the Cambodian settlement, the lack of consensus has not been productive of political controversy because, given the agreement of the PAVN to withdraw from Cambodia, settlement procedures were considerably simplified. After the demobilization of the Khmer Issarak, there was only one government in Cambodia, and it had declared it would respect the cease-fire agreement and make every effort to remain neutral in cold-war conflicts within Indochina and beyond.

The final declaration, nevertheless, sought to impose an obligation of a political nature upon Cambodia. Paragraph 3 noted the declaration proclaiming the Royal Government's intention to permit all citizens to take their place in the national community, in particular by participating in general elections; and these elections, in conformity with the constitution of Cambodia, "shall take place in the course of the year 1955, by secret ballot and in conditions of respect for fundamental freedoms." General elections were indeed held in 1955, but the political situation prior to these elections is of sufficient interest to require detailed attention. The circumstances are interesting because they reveal the kind of relations that had been established between the Cambodian government and the ISC.

On 24 January the government of Penn Nouth resigned and was succeeded by an "elections government," under Leng Ngeth, which announced that general elections would be held on 17 April. Before that date, however, a referendum would be held, from 7 to 9 February, to seek the verdict of the Cambodian electorate on the "Royal Mission"—specifically, on the question: Has the Royal Mission been accomplished to the satisfaction of our people? The voting, by *open* ballot, resulted in an affirmative response of 99.8 percent.[15] The ISC decided that the referendum did not fall within its competence, because it was extraconstitutional, and, in any case, had not been envisaged by the cease-fire agreement and the final declaration.[16]

On 19 February, King Norodom Sihanouk called the members of the ISC and the diplomatic corps to his palace and declared that, because of the internal political situation and popular demonstrations (in his favor), he intended to amend the 1947 constitution and insti-

[15] This account is based upon the *Second Progress Report of the International Commission for Supervision and Control in Cambodia for the Period January 1 to March 31, 1955*, Cambodia No. 2 (1955), Cmd. 9534 (London: Her Majesty's Stationery Office, 1955) (hereafter referred to as Cmd. 9534 [No. 2]).
[16] *Ibid.*, p. 12.

tute a project for political reform. The April general elections would be postponed until June, at the latest, and a second referendum—to determine the will of the electorate—would be held. The ISC's reaction was interesting:

> The Commission . . . was not concerned with the merits of the reform project. It was bound only to examine the scheme for one aspect, namely, whether any of the changes proposed were or were not in conformity with the international obligations undertaken by the Cambodian Government at Geneva. The main questions to be decided: in view of the reference made to the Cambodian Constitution in Article 6 of the Geneva Agreement and in Point 3 of the Final Declaration . . . , are major changes in the existing Constitution permissible till the first elections after Geneva are held? Will not such changes alter the terms on which the two parties at Geneva agreed to a political settlement? If such changes are permissible, should such amendments be made in accordance with the procedure laid down in the Constitution or not? Are any of the proposed changes discriminatory against the former residents in terms of Article 6?[17]

Before taking a position, the ISC decided to wait until it had received an official text of the reform-project proposals.

Then, on 26 February, the ISC asked for an audience with the King to obtain clarification of various aspects of the proposals. On the 28th, King Sihanouk informed the commission that general elections would be held on the basis of the 1947 constitution, and the ISC dropped its request for an audience with the King. Then, on 2 March, the King dramatically announced his abdication in favor of his parents, King Norodom Suramarit Kossaman and Queen Kossaman. In his abdication message the King referred to his reform subject in these terms:

> [The] reforms did not please certain politicians, certain personalities of the State, and certain intellectuals and privileged people who have the bad habit of using their intelligence and their influence to oppress the poor and the ignorant. These people have sustained all sorts of manifestations against me. They have put themselves "en rapport" with foreigners to attack me on the fallacious pretext that I was sabotaging certain articles of the Geneva Agreements.[18]

On 15 March the Cambodian government announced that it was abandoning its plans for a second referendum, and apparently aban-

[17] *Ibid.*, p. 14.   [18] *Ibid.*, p. 37, but see also p. 40

the settlement for cambodia

doning the reform projects as well, at least for the time being. General elections were scheduled for 11 September 1955.

The ISC came under attack in the Saigon press (and elsewhere) for interfering in the internal affairs of Cambodia, for opposing the reform proposals, and for being responsible for King Sihanouk's abdication. However, it is probably more accurate to regard the abdication as a political gesture undertaken by the King in order to engage more freely in popular and party politics:[19] in fact, after his abdication the former King, now Prince, Sihanouk, organized his own political party, the Popular Socialist Community.[20] As for interference in Cambodian internal affairs, it was certain that, although the ISC took no official, collective stand on the reform projects and the postponement of elections, the "Commissioners had doubts on the compatibility of some aspects of the reform project with the international commitments given by the Cambodian Government at Geneva."[21] It was evident, however, that unidentified commissioners had discussed the matter with the Cambodian government. In the words of the ISC itself,

Any informal suggestions that were made by the Commissioners in their individual capacity were meant to persuade the Government, before it took any final decisions, to examine quietly and carefully the problem whether or not the Royal reforms were compatible with the international obligations undertaken by Cambodia at the Geneva Conference.[22]

In mid-March the commission wrote to Prime Minister Leng Ngeth in an attempt to correct "the false impressions created by such misleading stories" as had appeared in the foreign press. Interestingly, the Prime Minister did not deny that the ISC had interfered in the internal affairs of Cambodia; rather obliquely, he declared that "neither His Majesty Norodom Sihanouk nor His Majesty Norodom Suramarit nor the Royal Government have in their messages, speeches and public declarations ever mentioned the International Commission."[23] The ISC also asserted that it had never received a complaint from the Royal Government about its activities.

In mid-March Prince Sihanouk visited New Delhi, where he told the press that the ISC had been fulfilling its task satisfactorily." I have no observations to make regarding its activities," he said. "The main

[19] *Christian Science Monitor*, 2 March 1955.
[20] This was the Sangkum Ryaster Niyum, or simply the Sangkum.
[21] Cmd. 9534 (No. 2), pp. 14-15.
[22] *Ibid.*, p. 15.
[23] *Ibid.*, p. 16.

part of its job is finished with the evacuation from Cambodia of foreign troops. It now has only to assist at elections which are to be held in September."[24] Both Prince Sihanouk and Prime Minister Nehru joined in declaring that the Geneva agreements ought to be fully implemented.[25]

The ISC performed no major functions until the election campaign began in earnest, in August 1955, although it issued an interim report in July that collected the documents and correspondence relating to the Cambodian-American military assistance agreement of 16 May.[26] During the campaign, the commission's conclusion on the nature of its functions and performance was as follows: "Our approach can be shortly described as one of general observation and not supervision."[27] But the royal government was apprehensive of ISC activity and insisted, during meetings with the commissioners, that elections were an internal matter. The ISC may have convinced the Prime Minister that it had no intention of interfering in Cambodian affairs, but the Popular Socialist Community, Prince Sihanouks' party, was not so persuaded, and implied that the commission was exceeding its powers. The opposition parties, on the other hand, principally the Democratic Party and the Pracheachun or People's Party (supported by former Khmer Issarak leaders), wanted the ISC to become more deeply involved in the elections under what they regarded as the commission's broad powers.

The ISC's conception of its obligations under the cease-fire agreement entailed more than observation; although the commissioners, their staff, and inspection teams behaved with admirable circumspection, the ISC believed it was obligated to become involved in Cambodian affairs. In the fourth interim report it defined its responsibilities as follows.

(i) It had to examine the Electoral Laws to make sure that they . . . safeguard secrecy of ballot.

(ii) It had to study the application of the laws of the country in regard to democratic freedoms so as to understand the scope of Article 6 [of the cease-fire agreement].

(iii) It had to satisfy itself that there was no discrimination against the former members of the Khmer Resistance Forces. It followed from this obligation regarding non-discrimination that the Commission had to keep itself informed of the conduct of the electoral campaign, the nature of the electoral practices in the

---

[24] *Ibid.*　　　[25] *Ibid.*, p. 39.　　　[26] Cmd. 9578 (No. 3).
[27] *Fourth Interim Report on the International Commission for Supervision and Control in Cambodia for the Period April 1 to September 30, 1955*, Cambodia No. 1 (1956), Cmd. 9671 (London: Her Majesty's Stationery Office, 1956), p. 9 (hereafter referred to as Cmd. 9671 [No. 4]).

country, the liberties enjoyed by the participating citizens, etc., in order to assess the rights of the former members of the Khmer Resistance Forces towards whom it had a special responsibility.[28]

The commission, in applying such principles, gathered information during the campaign, met with the Prime Minister at least once a week, brought petitions and complaints to the attention of the government, and "intervened with the Government if there was any major issue of possible discrimination against the former members of the Khmer Resistance Forces, as in the case of the Pracheachun Party."[29] In June, for example, An-Meang, a former member of the Khmer Issarak, complained to the ISC that the Royal Government had refused to register the Pracheachun Party. The commission brought the complaint to the attention of the Prime Minister, arguing that if registration was refused, charges of violation of article 6 of the cease-fire agreement would surely be made and the validity of the elections questioned.

> [The] Prime Minister agreed that he would take steps to expedite the registration of the party. However, he wanted the party to affirm its adherence to constitutional forms of activity. Although strictly such a guarantee was not called for from reintegrated citizens, the Commission advised the Pracheachun to give such an assurance.
>
> The matter was satisfactorily settled and the Pracheachun was registered in time to nominate thirty-five candidates for the elections.[30]

The Pracheachun, the Democratic Party, and other opposition parties complained that they could not conduct an effective campaign because of official pressure and because the government applied the penal code in cases of *lèse-majesté*. In fact, the Cambodian government had warned all parties that arrests and prosecution could be expected if candidates attacked the sovereign or members of the royal family (of which Prince Sihanouk, of course, was a member) and if they defamed the Royal Government or incited disorder.[31] Certain forms of criticism of the Cambodian-American aid agreement also were prohibited.[32] The ISC's remonstrations were courte-

---

[28] *Ibid.*, pp. 8-9.   [29] *Ibid.*, p. 9.

[30] *Ibid.*, p. 11.

[31] *Ibid.*, p. 12. Criticism of Prince Sihanouk as the Supreme Counsellor of the Sangkum was allowed, but disparaging remarks directed against him as prince or ex-King would be punished.

[32] "If a person said that the American treaty was not in the interests of the country, no action would be taken. But if that person said, for example, that the Government had 'sold the country to the United States' and spread false reports

ously but firmly parried by the Prime Minister, who was reported to have said the Cambodian judiciary was well trained and independent and could be expected to do justice and allow "good faith" criticism.[33]

As the elections approached the situation grew tense. The ISC found evidence that armed bands were engaging in anti-government propaganda in Stung Treng province (but no evidence of Vietminh support of these bands).[34] The Prime Minister, Leng Ngeth, told the ISC commissioners that the Pracheachun and Democratic parties were out to subvert the regime. Nevertheless, elections were held on schedule, and the ISC was reasonably sure that secrecy had been preserved. The Popular Socialist Community received 83 percent of the votes, winning all ninety-one seats in the National Assembly; the Democratic Party received 12 percent of the vote, the Pracheachun Party 4 percent, and five other parties about 1 percent. Seventy-five percent of the registered electors voted. While the result was not wholly unexpected in view of Prince Sihanouk's great popularity, the elections were criticized both in Cambodia and abroad. The ISC concluded, however, that the settlement foreseen under article 6 of the cease-fire agreement had been completed.

> The conclusion of the general elections is the culmination of the process of reintegration of the former members of the Khmer Resistance Forces into the national community envisaged in Article 6 of the Geneva Agreement. Certain cases pending with the Government, based on petitions by the ex–K.R.F. and investigations by our Teams, will be followed up, but no new major cases, necessitating the Commission's intervention, are expected. The Commission is confident that no reprisals will be taken against the former members of the Khmer Resistance Forces and that the policy of broad national reconciliation will be followed.[35]

[IV]

Irrespective of legal problems relating to the effect of paragraph 3 of the final declaration, which stated that Cambodian elections "shall take place in the course of the year 1955," and irrespective of the fact that the head of the Cambodian delegation at Geneva, Tep Phan, did not address himself to the question whether or not his government approved the final declaration, elections were held in September 1955. It is perhaps a moot point whether the final declaration

---

that 20,000 American troops would be stationed in Cambodia, he would be prosecuted." *Ibid.*, p. 12.

[33] *Ibid.*, p. 13.
[34] *Ibid.*, p. 16.
[35] *Ibid.*, p. 24 (and p. 17).

obligated the Cambodian government in any way, but its obligation under the terms of the cease-fire agreement, insofar as they related to the prospective elections (under article 6, for example, and the unilateral declaration incorporated therein) was important. Article 6 stated that the "situation" of the demobilized Khmer Issarak would be decided according to the Cambodian declaration wherein the Royal Government had declared itself "resolved to take the necessary measures to integrate all citizens, without discrimination, into the national community and to guarantee them the enjoyment of rights and freedoms for which the Constitution of the Kingdom provides." Further, it declared that "all Cambodian citizens may freely participate as electors or candidates in general elections by secret ballot." We have seen that King Sihanouk, heartened by his success in the early February 1955 referendum, postponed elections and offered reform proposals, which would be the subject of a second referendum, when the people would decide whether elections should be held under the new or the old constitution. More importantly, the people would decide on the form of the new constitution, not the National Assembly, which at that time was constitutionally empowered to make such changes. The Assembly had been dissolved, the King explained, but, because all laws were the expression of the people's will, the people could decide on their new constitution.[36]

According to the King's reform-project proposals, the new constitution would provide for provincial assemblies, direct election of mayors of communes, and a National Assembly whose delegates would be elected by the communes' mayors (not directly by the people). It was clear that the King would have substantial control over the National Assembly and that it would be largely an instrument in his hands, more so than under the old constitution. Thus, under the new constitution, a centralized monarchical government would rule the newly independent state. The King would repeat the process that had proved so effective in Europe in the last century: he would harness popular sentiment to his person, at the same time limiting the authority of the political party leaders, the political oligarchs, and the National Assembly.

The King also proposed residential qualifications for provincial assembly and National Assembly candidates (who would have to stand as individuals, not as party representatives): candidates, according to the reform proposals, must have resided in their constituencies for three years. This provision, of course, would have prevented most of the demobilized Khmer Issarak supporters from standing as candidates, and it was this proposal that disturbed the ISC com-

[36] Cmd. 9534 (No. 2), p. 14.

missioners. The residence qualification could be said to deprive various Cambodian citizens (i.e. ex-Khmer Issarak supporters) of their right freely to participate "as electors or candidates in general elections," as required by article 6 of the cease-fire agreement.

Although King Sihanouk told the people he had pledged to hold elections in 1955, he told the diplomatic corps and the ISC, on 19 February, that the people would determine whether these elections would be held under the new or the old constitution.[37] Under the old constitution, residential requirements would not disqualify former resistance members, as would happen under the new constitution. Yet, on 28 February, two days after its request for an audience, King Sihanouk informed the ISC that elections would be held under the *old* constitution. Then, on 2 March, to the surprise of even his closest advisors, the King abdicated. Because the elections were to be held under a constitution that permitted party politics to play an important role, he would put himself in a strong position for playing party politics and by this means eventually achieve his goal of a centralized government. The elections, moreover, would be delayed until September, allowing the King (now Prince Sihanouk) more time to organize his party and his campaign. Thus the King's dramatic abdication was a calculated political step, taken because of the internal political situation in Cambodia, as the ISC later stated in its second progress report.[38]

But we cannot leave the explanation at this. What persuaded King Sihanouk that he could not (perhaps should not) accomplish his goals by his reform-project proposals? Several kinds of pressures were exerted against him after 19 February 1955, pressures from

1. Political party leaders and other Cambodians with a vested interest in the constitutional *status quo* that in some ways limited the King's powers;

2. Former Khmer Issarak leaders who feared the consequences of the changes, which would both limit their civil rights and their right to stand as candidates of a "people's party" in general elections;

3. Diplomats in Phnom Penh who thought the reform program and its referendum was unconstitutional or would prejudice the rights or opportunities of former Khmer Issarak forces, with whom they sympathized; and

4. The members of the ISC, who individually urged the Cambodian government "to examine quietly and carefully the problem whether or not the Royal reforms were compatible with the international obligations undertaken by Cambodia at the Geneva Conference."[39]

However cautious, the behavior of the commissioners was extra-

[37] *Ibid.*, p. 13.   [38] *Ibid.*, p. 15.   [39] *Ibid.*

ordinary in two respects. First, their suggestions to the government, quite conservative in nature, tended to support the domestic forces that opposed constitutional (or extraconstitutional) changes. The ISC urged calm reflection, and warned that the reforms *might* violate the Geneva agreement. That the unofficial ISC position was useful to King Sihanouk's opponents can be seen in a very revealing sentence in his abdication speech: "[The critics of the reform proposals] have put themselves 'en rapport' with foreigners to attack me on the fallacious pretext that I was sabotaging certain articles of the Geneva Agreement."[40]

Second, their suggestions implied that the ISC was competent to pass upon internal political matters of the very greatest significance for a Cambodian government. The ISC asked: "Are major changes permissible till the first elections after Geneva are held?" "If such changes are permissible, should such amendments be made in accordance with the procedure laid down in the Constitution?"[41] It is no wonder that the Saigon press, sensitive to infringements of the southern Vietnam government's prerogatives by the ISC for Vietnam, criticized the Cambodian ISC for what it regarded as assumption of a political competence it did not have.

The imaginative King Sihanouk had found an alternative way for controlling the political affairs of Cambodia, at the same time preventing a clash between himself and the ISC. The King was flexible; and with evidence from the first referendum of overwhelming popular support, he decided to abdicate and enter the party lists against the Democratic Party and the Pracheachun. By abandoning his reform project, he would avoid being blamed for a violation of the Geneva Agreement, however ill-founded such allegations. His government's legitimacy, he may have felt, would have been compromised by charges that he violated Cambodia's international obligations, and newly independent Cambodia should develop a reputation for strict adherence to international obligations. Had the commissioners been less circumspect in fulfilling their political mandate, as they saw it, or had the King faced the possibility of frustration of his political ambitions, the ISC would have found the Royal Government increasingly less cooperative, whatever the Geneva agreements for Cambodia meant or required. Even during the elections the press of the Popular Socialist Community (Prince Sihanouk's party) accused the ISC of interfering in Cambodia's internal affairs.

My own conclusions from a review of the political scene in Cambodia in 1955 are rather prosaic, perhaps, but should be stated: the elections were held, as "required" by paragraph 3 of the final declara-

[40] *Ibid.*, p. 37.   [41] *Ibid.*, p. 14.

tion, but the political settlement may not have been brought about in such a way that Prince Sihanouk, Nehru, and others could proclaim that Cambodia had fulfilled the "obligations" incurred at Geneva. Under different conditions—evidence of internal or external threats to the state, a challenge to the monarchy as an institution, or the like—the elections might have been postponed indefinitely or conducted in an obviously contrived fashion. The ISC's conduct, in fact, constituted interference in Cambodia's affairs; and the *prima facie* success of the fulfillment of Cambodia's article 6 obligations was based upon several all-important factors: the PAVN had withdrawn, the Khmer Issarak had been demobilized, and King (later Prince) Sihanouk was a popular figure. In short, the Cambodian state was a reasonably healthy polity: no powerful group challenged the legitimacy of the Royal Government's rule over the traditional territories and peoples of Cambodia.

[V]

ISC supervision of the cease-fire procedures (i.e. the military aspects of the settlement) went relatively smoothly in the three or four months after the Geneva Conference, but several matters are worth noting.

1. Demobilization of the Khmer Issarak forces was carried out unilaterally without ISC supervison.[42] The ISC began to function on 11 August and the joint commission on 20 August, but by that time, demobilization had almost been completed. The Royal Government was convinced that all the Khmer Issarak forces had not been demobilized, that many retained their arms or had hidden them in caches, and that armed bands continued to roam about the country. Reintegration of the Khmer Issarak into the Cambodian community, according to the government, posed a serious problem because proper registration procedures had not been followed. But ISC investigations did not bear out the fears and suspicions of the Cambodian government. The commission decried the mutual suspicions and their effect upon the reintegration of former resistance personnel under the terms of article 6 of the cease-fire agreement.[43] In the fourth interim report (3 October 1955), the commissioners wrote:

> With the completion of general elections in Cambodia, a general political settlement may be said to have been achieved. The Commission's responsibility with regard to political matters concerning former resistants may, therefore, be regarded as having been concluded.[44]

[42] Cmd. 9458 (No. 1), p. 5.   [43] Cmd. 9534 (No. 2), p. 5.
[44] Cmd. 9671 (No. 4), p. 7.

The ISC continued to received petitions and complaints, but in its sixth interim report (8 July 1958) the ISC concluded that the royal government had "fulfilled its obligations in respect of re-integration of the former members of the Khmer Resistance Forces under Article 6 of the Cease-fire Agreement."[45]

2. French troops, for the most part, had been withdrawn from Cambodia before 11 August[46] but evacuation of the Vietminh military units did not begin until 12 October. By the 18th, ISC officer-delegates had verified the withdrawal of 2,384 Vietminh from Cambodian territory. The Royal Government held that some Vietminh remained in Cambodia, having merged with the local population, but the ISC could find no evidence of this—nor of armed Vietminh units. The commission investigated other related charges of the Cambodian government; but it concluded that no substantial number of former Vietminh soldiers or irregulars remained in Cambodia.

3. Until the time of its seventh interim report, 28 July 1959,[47] the ISC reported no violations of the cease-fire agreement's ban on the introduction of arms, munitions, ordnance, and military personnel, the establishment of military bases, or the formation of provocative alliances. Subsequent to the Cambodian-American military aid agreement of 16 May 1955, the Royal Government, on 29 May, declared its intention to remain neutral and to fulfill its obligations under the Geneva agreement, and the ISC continued to monitor the shipments of supplies from the United States to Cambodia. In its fifth interim report (15 April 1957), the ISC noted that it had received "good cooperation" from the Royal Government.[48] It had examined documents relating to the quantities of military supplies received and was "of the unanimous opinion that the figures submitted by the Royal Government are not in excess of its effective defence requirements."[49] Subsequently, the commission reported no new developments under the heading of arms shipments.

4. Border incidents were of almost continuous ISC concern from

[45] *Sixth Interim Report of the International Commission for Supervision and Control in Cambodia for the Period January 1, 1957 to December 31, 1957*, Cambodia No. 1 (1958), Cmd. 526 (London: Her Majesty's Stationery Office, 1958), p. 6 (hereafter referred to as Cmd. 526 [No. 6]).

[46] Cmd. 9458 (No. 1), p. 6.

[47] *Seventh Interim Report of the International Commission for Supervision and Control in Cambodia for the Period January 1, 1958 to December 31, 1958*, Cambodia No. 1 (1959), Cmd. 887 (London: Her Majesty's Stationery Office, 1959) (hereafter referred to as Cmd. 887 [No. 7]).

[48] *Fifth Interim Report of the International Commission for Supervision and Control in Cambodia for the Period October 1, 1955 to December 31, 1956*, Cambodia No. 1 (1957), Cmd. 253 (London: Her Majesty's Stationery Office, 1957), p. 21 (hereafter referred to as Cmd. 253 [No. 5]).

[49] *Ibid.*

1954 to 1959, and in August 1955, on three separate occasions, unidentified bands of irregulars opened fire upon Voeunsai in Stung Treng province. The ISC sent an investigation team that, despite the Royal Government's allegations to the contrary, found no evidence of Vietminh involvement, but it found evidence inculpating certain Cambodian anti-government (ex–Khmer Issarak) forces.[50] With respect to alleged border violations by armed forces of the SVN (later, RVN), the ISC took the position that only direct talks between Vietnamese and Cambodian authorities could bring about a settlement.[51] Official complaints, however, were forwarded to the ISC for Vietnam for comment. In 1956 the two Indochinese governments held talks, but such incidents continued to occur.[52]

In May 1957 a border raid gave rise to a major dispute among members of the ISC on the competence of the commission under its Geneva mandate. As an *ad hoc* team of the ISC described the incident,

> on May 2, 1957, eighteen Vietnamese [RVN] Military personnel raided the Cambodian villages of Samrong and Bathu, approximately 2 1/2 kilometers from the Vietnam-Cambodian border using fire arms and injuring persons and damaging property; one raider was killed and seven others were taken as prisoners including a Lieutenant who explained that the raid was carried out under the orders of his Battalion Commander; he stated that he was not sure of the frontier limits.[53]

In considering the report of the *ad hoc* team, the Canadian delegate declared that the ISC was not competent to deal with border incidents that involved the government of the RVN. The Indian delegate took the view, concurred in by the Polish delegate, that the ISC was competent to deal with all reports and complaints of aggression or threats of aggression against Cambodian territory.[54] Over the opposition of the Canadian delegate, a majority report on the border raid was forwarded to the co-chairmen of the Geneva Conference, along with the minority report of the Canadian delegate, but the co-chairmen made no reply.[55]

A similar dispute arose in June 1958, after an alleged violation by RVN forces of the Cambodian frontier in Stung Treng province. In this instance the Canadian objected even to sending an *ad hoc* investigating team to the province, but he was outvoted, and the investigating team confirmed that RVN forces had violated the frontier. The Canadian delegate confirmed the accuracy of the facts but, as forces of the RVN were involved, he insisted this put the matter outside the competence of the ISC. He was again outvoted, and,

[50] Cmd. 9671 (No. 4), pp. 18-20.   [51] Cmd. 9534 (No. 2), p. 8.
[52] Cmd. 253 (No. 5), p. 20.   [53] Cmd. 526 (No. 6), p. 7.
[54] *Ibid.*, p. 25.   [55] *Ibid.*, p. 7.

pursuant to article 21 of the cease-fire agreement, majority and minority reports were sent to the co-chairmen.[56]

The Canadian delegate's theory was that the ISC for Cambodia, created by and empowered to act according to an agreement signed on behalf of the high commands of Cambodia and the DRVN, could deal only with acts of aggression or threats of aggression by the DRVN against Cambodia (or Cambodia against the DRVN), and not with acts committed by the RVN, a nonsignatory. The Indian delegate, however, regarded the ISC mandate as more broadly drawn; that is, he believed the commission was competent to deal with *any* act of aggression against Cambodia.[57]

Though controversial, it seems to me that the Canadian view was the more valid. After a complaint of the Royal Government of Cambodia that Thai forces had violated its frontier and that the buildup of Thai troops and facilities across the Khmero-Thai frontier constituted a threat of aggression against Cambodia, the ISC voted *against* sending an investigating team to the area. The Canadian delegate was joined by the Indian delegate (the Polish delegate *supported* a resolution for investigation), and their vote was based upon the view that the ISC had no competence to investigate matters involving the government of Thailand.[58] It was not evident, on the face of the ISC report, why the Indian delegate made a distinction between incidents involving Thai forces and those involving RVN forces; however, it seems that he believed the Geneva agreements constituted an international security regime for Vietnam, Cambodia, and Laos—but not for Thailand. The Indian delegate to the ISC, as well as the Indian government, was not troubled by the fact that the RVN did not accept this concept of an international regime in Indochina.

5. The ISC began to reduce its staff and its activities after the September 1955 elections; from a force of 307, the ISC staff was reduced to 76 by 1 January 1959.[59] After 1958 the activity of the ISC for Cambodia, up to the time of this writing, has been of negligible significance.

[56] Cmd. 887 (No. 7), pp. 19-22.

[57] Article 13 of the cease-fire agreement stated that the ISC "shall be responsible for supervising the execution by the parties of the provisions of the present Agreement . . . and shall in particular: (*a*) control the withdrawal of foreign forces . . . and see that frontiers are respected. . . ."

Article 21 stated that the decisions of the ISC must be unanimous on questions concerning" violation or threat of violation of the country's integrity by foreign armed forces." The Indian delegate construed these provisions broadly, as authorizing the inquiry into acts committed by forces of the SVN within Cambodian territory. The Canadian delegate regarded the competence of the ISC limited, as indicated in the text. He might have argued that the term "foreign armed forces," as used in chapter II of the agreement, meant either French or DRVN forces.

[58] Cmd. 887 (No. 7), pp. 22-24.

[59] Cmd. 9671 (No. 4), pp. 24-25; Cmd. 887 (No. 7), pp. 7-8.

Chapter 26

THE SETTLEMENT FOR LAOS

[I]

The Agreement on the Cessation of Hostilities in Laos was signed by General Henri Delteil for the commander in chief of the French Union forces in Indochina and by Ta Quang Buu for the commanders in chief of the PAVN and the "fighting units" of the Pathet Lao. The commanders were to order a cease-fire throughout Laos (1), which was to become effective no later than 8 a.m., Peking mean time, 6 August, by which time the cease-fire orders would have been transmitted to all units of the fighting forces in Laos (2).

Immediately after the cease-fire, the belligerents were to disengage and assemble in areas assigned to them by the Joint Commission for Laos (11, 12).[1] This movement was to be completed within fifteen days, after which the French forces and the Vietnamese "people's volunteer" forces (VPV) would withdraw from Laos on routes and according to schedules fixed by the joint commission (13, 4[b] [c]). Withdrawal of all foreign forces was to be completed within 120 days (4[a]).

The introduction of troop reinforcements or other types of military personnel and the establishment of new military bases on Laotian territory were prohibited, although the French command would be permitted to leave cadres behind, not to exceed 1,500 officers and noncommissioned officers, for training the Laotian national army (6, 7). In addition, the French were to be allowed to maintain two bases, one at Seno, the other in the Mekong valley, and the troops at these bases were to number no more than 3,500 (8). Article 9 of the cease-fire agreement prohibited the introduction into Laos of armaments, munitions, and military equipment of all kinds, "with the exception of a specified quantity of armaments in categories specified as necessary for the defence of Laos." On 21 July the Royal Government of Laos had issued a declaration stating it would never pursue a policy of aggression nor permit Laotian territory to be used in furtherance of such a policy, and that it would settle its international disputes by peaceful means.

[1] The joint commission, made up of an equal number of representatives of the "Commands of the parties concerned" (29), was empowered to fix the site and the boundaries of five provisional assembly areas for the reception of VPV forces, five such areas for the French forces in Laos, and twelve provisional assembly areas, one in each province, for the reception of fighting units of the Pathet Lao (12).

The Royal Government of Laos will never join in any agreement with other States if this agreement includes the obligation for the Royal Government of Laos to participate in a military alliance not in conformity with the principles of the Charter of the United Nations or with the principles of the agreement on the cessation of hostilities or, unless its security is threatened, the obligation to establish bases on Laotian territory for military forces of foreign Powers. . . .

During the period between the cessation of hostilities in Viet Nam and the final settlement of that country's political problems, the Royal Government of Laos will not request foreign aid, whether in war material, in personnel or in instructors, except for the purpose of its effective territorial defence and to the extent defined by the agreement on the cessation of hostilities.[2]

As in the case of Cambodia, the question arises Who would determine the "specified quantity of armaments in categories specified as necessary for the defence of Laos" (9)? The Laotian declaration certainly did not answer this question. It purported to permit aid for effective territorial defense "to the extent defined by the [cease-fire agreement]," other than granting the French high command the right to maintain two bases and training cadres, the agreement was silent on the size of the requisite defense forces. Presumably the government of Laos, as the government of a sovereign state, would have the right to make that determination, its conception of the adequacy of a defense force might be very different from an equivalent assessment by its neighboring states or the ISC for Laos.

As in the case of Vietnam and Cambodia, paragraph 4 of the final declaration took note of the Laotian resolution not to request foreign aid, except for the purpose of an effective defense and to the extent defined by the cease-fire agreement (this exception concerned the contingents of French forces that were to remain in Laos). Paragraph 5 took note of the declaration of the Laotian government that it would not join an agreement with other states if this included the obligation to participate in an alliance not in conformity with the U.N. Charter. The legal effect of these provisions was problematical, particularly since the head of the Laotian delegation at Geneva, Phoui Sananikone, had neither rejected nor approved the terms of the final declaration; he had made no observation whatever.

The fighting units of the Pathet Lao were to assemble in provisional assembly areas (one in each of the twelve provinces) and move to the provinces of Phong Saly and Sam Neua, in northern and north-

___
[2] Cmd. 9239, pp. 41-42.

eastern Laos, on the Lao-DRVN frontier (12, 14). Movement of the Pathet Lao forces through an established corridor to these two provinces was to be completed within 120 days of the entry into force of the agreement. Pending a political settlement, the Pathet Lao would remain in Phong Saly and Sam Neua. The parties undertook to refrain from reprisals and from discriminating against persons or organizations for their activities during the hostilities. They also undertook to guarantee the democratic freedoms of such persons (15). But, as neither the Laotian government nor the high command of the Pathet Lao signed the cease-fire agreement, how were they obligated pursuant to its terms?

1. We may presume that the Pathet Lao leaders consented to representation at the Geneva Conference by the DRVN delegation (they may even have consented to the terms of the settlement), but we do not know what agreements, if any, were reached between the Pathet Lao and the Vietminh. The Laotian insurgents were more numerous and relatively more important than the Khmer Issarak in Cambodia, and, not having collectively agreed to demobilization, they could (and would) continue to play a vital role in internal Laotian politics. Beyond the provisions for concentrating the Pathet Lao in Phong Saly and Sam Neua, the cease-fire agreement was silent on the status of the former insurgents: it simply ordered them to northeastern Laos and made no attempt to delineate their relationship with the Royal Government of Laos, or their obligations (if any) under the terms of the cease-fire agreement. Article 14 merely stated that "pending a political settlement," the Pathet Lao "shall move" into Phong Saly and Sam Neua. We might assume that some of the Geneva delegates believed the political settlement for Laos would have to be worked out through a series of Pathet Lao–Royal Laotian Government conversations, followed ultimately by general elections; hence it would be left to the Laotians themselves to establish guidelines for their interrelations. On the other hand, this assumption might not be correct: perhaps the draftsmen were so rushed during the last hectic week at Geneva that they simply produced an inadequate text for article 14 or, realizing its inadequacies, submitted the article in its imperfect form rather than provoke an inevitable series of disputes that might delay the conclusion of an armistice in Laos.

2. The Royal Government of Laos unilaterally undertook to allow all Laotian citizens to participate freely as electors or candidates in general elections by secret ballot. It also "resolved to take the necessary measures to integrate all citizens, without discrimination, into the national community and to guarantee them the enjoyment of the rights and freedoms for which the Constitution of the Kingdom provides." It also announced that it would "promulgate measures

to provide for special representation in the Royal Administration of the provinces of Phang Saly [*sic*] and Sam Neua during the interval between the cessation of hostilities and the general elections of the interests of Laotian nationals who did not support the Royal forces during hostilities."[3] It remained to be seen how the Laotian government would implement this declaration, particularly since the Pathet Lao would survive as a political force and hence as a continuing challenge to the government. Rules for the Pathet Lao's conduct, other than for its movement into specified areas, were not set forth in the cease-fire agreement, but its conduct after the settlement would surely have an effect upon the Royal Government's performance of its unilateral pledges. Complete intransigence by either Laotian rival, and perhaps even minor disagreements, would surely lead to a resumption of hostilities inasmuch as the military forces of both the government and the insurgents would continue in being. The latter would not, after all, be "assimilated" in the Laotian body politic, in the way the Khmer resistance forces had been assimilated. It was possible, of course, that the Pathet Lao and the Royal Government would negotiate their differences, but the Geneva agreement offered neither guarantees that they would do this nor guidelines for such negotiations—nor for third-party states who might have an interest in the outcome.

Paragraph 3 of the final declaration took note of the Laotian declaration on the reintegration of citizens into the national community and the statement that all citizens would be permitted to participate in the "next general elections, which, in conformity with the constitution of each of these countries, shall take place in the course of the year 1955, by secret ballot and in conditions of respect for fundamental freedoms." Negotiations between the Laotian rivals took place throughout most of 1955, and elections were held in December 1955, but the final political settlement for Laos, envisaged in the final declaration, was not achieved until more than two years later. The Pathet Lao and the Royal Government of Laos simply could not agree upon important preliminary political arrangements. Here was another instance of the draftsmen of the declaration having presumed to speak for parties that did not consent to the terms they sought to impose. More importantly, the "Conference" chose not to anticipate the probable "realities" of political conditions in Laos after the cease-fire; that is, the *de facto* division of Laos that tended to preserve, and even reinforce, the differences between the factions and to discourage the compromises prerequisite to a political settlement. Indeed, the situation invited the intervention of the DRVN in Laotian internal affairs.

[3] *Ibid.*, p. 41.

As in the Vietnamese and Cambodian agreements, responsibility for the implementation of the Laotian cease-fire agreement rested with the commanders in chief of the parties and their "successors in their functions" (22, 17). Who were the successors in functions of the signatories?

1. After the anticipated withdrawal of PAVN units from Laos, the Pathet Lao would be the sole insurgent faction. But Ta Quang Buu had signed the cease-fire agreement on behalf of the commanders in chief of the Pathet Lao and the PAVN, and if we assume he had been authorized to do this, then after PAVN withdrawal the commander of the insurgents was the sole successor in function of the joint obligors. (i.e. the commanders of both the PAVN and Pathet Lao).

2. The French high command was bound by the terms of the Laotian cease-fire agreement during the withdrawal of the French Union forces and afterward, as long as French forces remained in Laos, as they were entitled to do under articles 6 and 8. Whether the Royal Government was, in law, the successor in function of the commander in chief of the French Union forces may be doubted. Inasmuch as Laos had become independent in October 1953, the French government or the French high command could not obligate the Laotian government without its consent. Furthermore, because the Royal Government had addressed itself to the Geneva settlements through two declarations, its consent to assume obligations would have to be contained in those declarations. In the first declaration, however, the Laotian government pledged not to join alliances not in conformity with the U.N. Charter and not to request foreign aid except for its territorial defense, and in the second declaration it promised to integrate all citizens into the national community, to guarantee citizens' rights, and to promulgate measures for the special representation of the Pathet Lao before general elections were held. Therefore, beyond the pledges in these declarations, the Laotian government could not be said to have consented to the provision which purported to name it a "successor in function" of the French high command.

What, then, were the consequences of this state of affairs? There were no untoward consequences in the implementation of the military provisions of the cease-fire agreement, because the Laotian government cooperated with the French high command. However, we can single out two problem areas (among others) that the reader should keep in mind in the subsequent analysis.

a. The cease-fire agreement was held to apply to "all the armed forces of either party." Further, "the armed forces of each party shall respect the territory under the military control of the other party, and engage in no hostile acts against the other party" (19). This provision bound the French, the DRVN, and the Pathet Lao military commanders (and their forces), but did it also bind the Royal Government of Laos? Was the latter obligated to "respect" the territories in Phong Saly and Sam Neua occupied and militarily controlled by the Pathet Lao? The Geneva documents provide no answer to these questions. Certainly the declaration in which the Laotian government resolved to settle its *international* disputes by peaceful means could be construed as a pledge to respect the territory of the DRVN, but it would be stretching a point to say the declaration applied to Phong Saly and Sam Neua, part of the Laotian state, whose unity and integrity most of the Geneva powers had agreed to respect.

b. A regime of supervision and control, similar to the regimes established under the Vietnamese and Cambodian cease-fire agreements, was established under chapter VI of the Laotian agreement (24–39, 2(*b*), 3(*b*), 4(*f*) and (*g*), 20, 21, 23). An ISC, with headquarters in Vientiane, was constituted with representatives of Canada, India, and Poland (25, 37), and a joint commission also was established (28). Because the provisions relating to the competence and functioning of the Laotian commissions were almost identical to those of the commissions for Vietnam and Cambodia, they will not be analyzed here. We should note, however, that the signatories undertook to cooperate with the ISC and its inspection teams in the performance of their duties (26). The duties of the ISC, moreover, were set forth in general terms in article 27.

Broadly responsible for supervising the parties' execution of the provisions of the cease-fire agreement, the ISC was to

> fulfil the functions of control, observations, inspection and investigation, connected with the implementation of the provisions of the Agreement on the cessation of hostilities, and shall in particular:—
>
> (*a*) control the withdrawal of foreign forces in accordance with the provisions of the Agreement on the cessation of hostilities and see that frontiers are respected;
>
> (*b*) control the release of prisoners of war and civilian internees;
>
> (*c*) supervise, at ports and airfields and along the frontiers of Laos, the implementation of the provisions regulating the introduction into Laos of military personnel and war materials;
>
> (*d*) supervise the implementation of the clauses of the Agreement on the cessation of hostilities relating to rotation of personnel and to supplies for French Union security forces maintained in Laos.

Although the ISC would require the cooperation of the Royal Government of Laos, which had not explicitly consented to ISC operations on its national territories, this ostensible legal defect did not produce serious problems inasmuch as the Laotian government generally facilitated ISC functioning. As we shall see, difficulties for the ISC arose from other sources: the Laotian terrain, lack of cooperation by the Pathet Lao, and the inadequacy and incompleteness of the Geneva settlement for Laos in respect to the standing and obligations of the Pathet Lao and the nature of the Lao–Pathet Lao relationship.[4]

[I I]

The ISC for Laos was formed by 11 August and the joint commission about the same time. While both commissions debated the technical details of disengagement, regroupment, and withdrawal of forces, the former belligerents proceeded to implement the terms of the cease-fire agreement, without supervision by the ISC. However, in the words of the commission, "Neither party . . . gave to the other or to the International Commission precise information regarding the movement of its troops sufficiently in advance as to make supervision effective."[5] By 19 November the French had substantially completed the evacuation of their troops (except those they were authorized to maintain in Laos under articles 6 and 8), and the DRVN completed its evacuation by 22 November. Supervision had been impeded by lack of cooperation, bad weather, inadequate communication and transportation facilities, the difficult terrain of Laos, and the ISC's inability to distinguish Vietnamese and Pathet Lao units. Thus the commission could not be absolutely certain the Vietnamese had fully withdrawn from Laos, particularly since it had to "rely . . . on the assurances given by the two parties that they have completely withdrawn their forces in accordance with the terms of the Geneva Agreement."[6]

After the ostensible completion of troop disengagement and with-

[4] Another difficulty arose when the DRVN began to supply arms to the Pathet Lao. (If the allegations of the Royal Government of Laos were true, the DRVN also sent political cadres and military personnel into Phong Saly and Sam Neua.)
Article 16, almost identical to article 8 of the Cambodia agreement and article 21 of the Vietnam agreement, governed the liberation and repatriation of prisoners of war and "civilian internees." As it turned out, neither the Royal Government nor the VPV-Pathet Lao parties adhered to the provisions of the Geneva agreement (see the *First Interim Report of the International Commission for Supervision and Control in Laos*, Laos No. 1 [1955], Cmd. 9445 [London: Her Majesty's Stationery Office, 1955], pp. 18-26, [hereafter referred to as as Cmd. 9445 (Laos No. 1)]). It is perhaps academic to ask whether the Royal Government was obligated pursuant to the terms of article 16.
[5] Cmd. 9445 (Laos No. 1), p. 11.
[6] *Ibid.*, p. 15. The chief of the VPV-Pathet Lao delegation to the joint commission made the following declaration: "I solemnly declare that the High Command of the Vietnamese People's Volunteer Army has decided to withdraw completely all the forces of the Vietnamese People's Volunteers from Laos to Vietnam in conformity with the date [19 November] provided for in the Geneva Agreement." *Ibid.*, p. 16.

drawals on 22 November, the Royal Government pushed for the dissolution of the joint commission. On 14 January 1955 the Franco-Laotian delegation to the joint commission announced their wish for its immediate dissolution, and in late January they unilaterally withdrew. The Franco-Laotian delegation had demanded that the joint commission,

> containing "a military foreign body," should be disbanded and that the Vietnamese People's Volunteers and French Union Delegations should cease to function in Laos in a Liaison Mission or in any other capacity. They suggested that the International Commission could be aided in its task by a Joint Royal Laotian/"Pathet Lao" Mission with Headquarters in Vientiane.[7]

The sensitivity of the Royal Government to the "military foreign body," that is, the delegation of the Vietnamese people's volunteers, was noteworthy. The VPV chief delegate agreed to the formation of a Lao-Pathet Lao liaison mission with the ISC, but maintained that it would not be "sufficiently qualified to represent both the Vietnamese People's Volunteers High Command and the High Command of the Fighting Units of 'Pathet Lao.'" As one of the parties to the Geneva agreement, the VPV delegation wanted to continue to function until the agreement had been fully implemented. In spite of the Vietnamese arguments, however, the joint commission ceased to function on 15 February.

The inability of the Laotian ISC to function in its supervisory role can be seen quite clearly in the matter of forced recruitment. In late August and early September 1954, the Royal Government had complained that the Vietnamese and Pathet Lao had forcibly recruited and indoctrinated Laotian citizens in areas controlled by their forces. After denials and counterarguments, ISC teams conducted a rudimentary investigation, which revealed little or nothing. The ISC concluded:

> [The] investigation carried out . . . was rendered difficult by its inability to check the withdrawal of all Vietnamese People's Volunteers/"Pathet Lao" troops out of Laos or to check entry of "Pathet Lao" troops into Phong Saly and Sam Neua, due to lack of or insufficient withdrawals and routes of withdrawal, due to inadequate transport facilities, and, lastly, due to weather conditions in Laos, which during the monsoon months were most unpredictable. In spite of all these difficulties, it will be evident that the

[7] *Second Interim Report of the International Commission for Supervision and Control in Laos*, Laos No. 2, Cmd. 9630 (London: Her Majesty's Stationery Office, 1955), p. 8 (hereafter referred to as Cmd. 9630 [Laos No. 2]).

International Commission carried out spot investigation through random selection among the troops practically throughout the whole country.[8]

It was also evident that the ISC teams had not answered the question of forced recruiting.[9]

The Commission was not unaware of the poor quality of its supervisory and investigatory work, but physical difficulties were only part of the problem. More serious, in the view of the ISC, "were the difficulties that arose out of the vagueness of some of the provisions of the Geneva Agreement."[10] The problems that resulted from this vagueness were compounded by mutual suspicion and mistrust, which was nowhere more evident than in the regroupment and movement of Pathet Lao forces and their concentration in Phong Saly and Sam Neua. Article 14 had merely stated that the fighting units of the Pathet Lao were to move to these provinces pending a political settlement. The first problem to arise was the size of the Pathet Lao assembly areas within Phong Saly and Sam Neua.

The French and the Laotians asserted that on or before 6 August 1954, the date of the cease-fire, the western areas of these provinces had been under the control of French Union "Special Commandos," and the Vietnamese people's volunteer–Pathet Lao party on the joint commission refused to recognize such control, except to the extent that the commandos ("pirates" as they called them) had been paradropped into various areas in violation of the cease-fire agreement. Otherwise, the Vietminh–Pathet Lao representatives argued, their forces had control of the entire area comprising Phong Saly and Sam Neua. They also argued that the term "provinces" (in article 14's expression "the fighting units of 'Pathet Lao' . . . shall move into the Provinces of Phong Saly and Sam-Neua") meant that the Pathet Lao would station themselves throughout the provinces, not merely in limited areas thereof. An agreement on 30 August, which fixed the number and extent of the provisional assembly areas in Laos, did not extend to Phong Saly and Sam Neua; hence the controversy remained unresolved. The ISC took the position that it should "abstain from making too rigid a recommendation and aim particu-

[8] Cmd. 9445 (Laos No. 1), p. 31.

[9] See *ibid.*, pp. 53-57, for a tabulation of VPV-Pathet Lao withdrawals. According to the table, the ISC checked the withdrawal of about 5,000 VPV troops. Because withdrawals started before the ISC teams were emplaced and they did not (and could not) check all withdrawals, we may safely assume that more than 5,000 VPV troops were in Laos as of the date of the cease-fire. See *ibid.*, pp. 58-60, for a tabulation of French Union troop withdrawals. The ISC counted approximately 3,000 Pathet Lao troops who were moving or preparing to move to Phong Saly and Sam Neua provinces.

[10] *Ibid.*, p. 51.

larly at summoning the two parties to reconcile their points of view."[11] It recommended, however, that the joint commission examine the question of Pathet Lao "reception sites" and investigate the allegation that Laotian national army units were in control of areas of the provinces.

On 18 September the Laotian Minister of Defense, Kou Voravong, was assassinated, possibly in retaliation for the government's arrest of former insurgents.[12] The Prime Minister, Prince Souvanna Phouma resigned; and one month later, Katay Sasorith formed a government that was to last until February 1956. Meanwhile throughout September and October 1954, the parties exchanged arguments and proposals on the status of the Pathet Lao in Phong Saly and Sam Neua, the ISC lent its good offices in an effort to reconcile the opposing views. On 4 November, at a meeting of the ISC and the joint commission at Vientiane, the representative of the Pathet Lao declared that "the 'Pathet Lao' forces recognize the Royal Government and that in principle the administration of 'Pathet Lao' in the two provinces of Sam Neua and Phong Saly is classified under the Supreme Authority of the Royal Government."[13] In a resolution on 3 December, the ISC urged representatives of the Pathet Lao and the Royal Government to examine means for attaining a political settlement and reestablishment of the Royal Administration in Phong Saly and Sam Neua.[14] In early January, representatives of the Laotian rivals met at Plaine des Jarres and established a "consultative political conference." On 18 January 1955 they issued a declaration recognizing the necessity of collaborating for the implementation of the Geneva agreement and the maintenance of the unity and complete independence of Laos.[15] Then, on 9 March, they agreed not to permit the recurrence of hostile acts and skirmishes which had marred the Laotian cease-fire since its inception.[16] The ISC, which had not received official notification of the Plaine des Jarres negotiations or the declarations, asserted that "in the absence of this information it was unable to evaluate the political situation and offer such advice and suggestions as might, in its opinion, help the Parties to come to a settlement. The Commission, therefore, requested that it be kept regularly informed of the progress of the work of the Conference."[17]

The amity of the rivals was short-lived, however. Military clashes continued to occur. In early April the Royal Government alleged that political talks were making no progress because the Pathet Lao

[11] *Ibid.*, p. 43.
[12] *NYT*, 20 September 1954. See also Donald Lancaster, *The Emancipation of French Indochina* (London: Oxford University Press, 1961), p. 402.
[13] Cmd. 9445 (Laos No. 1), p. 76.   [14] *Ibid.*, p. 46.
[15] Cmd. 9630 (Laos No. 2), p. 9.   [16] *Ibid.*, pp. 34-35.
[17] *Ibid.*, p. 9.

". . . considered themselves still under the authority of the Vietminh High Command, and as having conquered the provinces of Phong Saly and Sam Neua." The Pathet Lao, in turn, accused the government of conspiring with the United States. On 25 April the Laotian government withdrew from the Plaine des Jarres conference. On the same day, at the Bandung Conference, Pham Van Dong told Prime Minister Katay, Nehru, and Chou En-lai that the DRVN considered the settlement in Laos "a question of internal order which the royal government of Laos and the Pathet Lao are entirely free to solve in the best way possible."[18] Katay and Pham Van Dong agreed that their two governments should develop harmony and good neighborly relations within the framework of the Five Principles of Peaceful Coexistence.

The Royal Government remained suspicious, however, that the DRVN not only supported the aspirations of the Pathet Lao but had dispatched, and was dispatching, arms and cadres into Phong Saly and Sam Neua, and it asked the ISC what measures the commission proposed to take to insure against these activities.[19] In July, the government explicitly requested the ISC to supervise the DRVN's introduction of personnel and war equipment into the two provinces.[20] On 26 July the commission replied by letter to the Laotian Prime Minister, declaring that the Pathet Lao was denied the right to import arms; hence the question of "their consulting the International Commission in advance or submitting data does not arise." If the ISC had reason to believe the Pathet Lao was importing arms, the letter continued, it would be incumbent upon the commission "to investigate with a view to bringing abuses to an end." The letter concluded rather weakly, in the fashion typical of the Laotian ISC: "You will appreciate that the International Commission is physically unable to control the entire northern boundary with regard to general allegations of illicit imports and in order to detect such imports of arms, the International Commission has to depend on sufficiently specfic information received either from its teams or from the aggrieved party."[21] This led the Canadian delegation to observe that the only

[18] Geoffrey Barraclough and R. F. Wall, *Survey of International Affairs, 1955-1956* (London: Oxford University Press, 1960), p. 20.

[19] Cmd. 9630 (Laos No. 2), p. 26.

[20] *Ibid.*, p. 27. At about this time the Royal Government of Laos furnished the ISC with an estimate of war matériel it considered necessary for the defense of Laos in 1955. By an exchange of notes in July, the United States and the Royal Government of Laos concluded an assistance agreement "to further the economic cooperation objectives of [the Economic Cooperation Agreement of 9 September 1951 between the U.S. and Laos] and to promote the effective defense of the Kingdom of Laos." TIAS 3664, 6 and 8 July 1955.

[21] *Third Interim Report of the International Commission for Supervision and*

procedure for determining whether the Pathet Lao was importing arms was upon complaint by the Royal Government of Laos *after* the alleged acts had occurred. Moreover, the investigations could not be conclusive because of the lack of helicopters and Pathet Lao liaison officers.[22]

The Royal Government of Laos had scheduled general elections for 28 August 1955, but in early June the Pathet Lao denounced the elections as illegal and demanded that the government return to a political conference to organize elections that conformed to the spirit of the Geneva agreement and the final declaration. On 7 June the Royal Government announced that because the royal administration had not been reestablished in Phong Saly and Sam Neua, it would not be possible to organize elections in those provinces in accordance with Laotian electoral law.[23] However, on 10 June a joint session of the National Assembly postponed elections until 25 December 1955. Then, four days later, the ISC addressed a letter to the Royal Government reiterating its hope that talks between the Laotian parties would be resumed without delay and pursued until a political settlement was reached. The letter also stated:

> The Geneva Agreement in Laos does not make any specific mention of the establishment of the Royal Administration in any part of Laos, but the right of the Royal Government to the actual administration of the two provinces may be deduced from the recognition by the Geneva Powers of the unity of Laos and the sovereignty of the Royal Government over the entire country. This has never been disputed and has been recognized in principle by the Fighting Units of "Pathet Lao" in their Declaration of 4th November, 1954.

> The Commission realises, however, that in view of the conditions prevailing in the provinces of Phong Saly and Sam Neua it would be difficult to establish the Royal Administration in these provinces effectively without the political settlement envisaged in Article 14 of the Agreement. It is presumed that whatever arrangement may be arrived at between the Parties will conform to the basic pattern of the Geneva Agreement.[24]

When talks began again in Vientiane, on 15 July 1955, agenda item 9, general elections, was the occasion for lengthy discussions. The Pathet Lao representatives demanded that the electoral law be amended to conform to the post-hostilities situation in Laos and be

---

Control in Laos, Laos No. 1 (1957), Cmd. 314 (London: Her Majesty's Stationery Office, 1957), p. 94 (hereafter referred to as Cmd. 314 [Laos No. 3]).
[22] *Ibid.,* p. 28.   [23] Cmd. 9630 (Laos No. 2), p. 11.
[24] *Ibid.,* pp. 17-18.

made more democratic, in conformity with the Geneva agreement. The Royal Government insisted that the electoral law did not discriminate against the Pathet Lao, that special provisions need not be provided for them, and that amendments could be made only by the action of the National Assembly.[25] The government finally agreed to modify the election procedures in some particulars, but it refused to accept mixed Lao–Pathet Lao election-control commissions and it rejected the proposal that full and effective restoration of the royal administration in Phong Saly and Sam Neua should be considered only *after* the elections. Talks on agenda item 2, the establishment of the royal administration in the two northern provinces, plodded on until 5 September, when they were suspended, despite the exhortations of the ISC.

Prime Minister Katay and Prince Souphanouvong, the leader of the Pathet Lao, met in Rangoon from 9 to 13 October and again agreed to halt hostile actions against each other's forces. The only other achievement of this meeting, apart from the resolution of several minor procedural questions, was the agreement to hold a third set of talks in Vientiane. These talks began at the end of October but ended in deadlock, and general elections were held on 25 December, without the participation of the Pathet Lao, which regarded them illegal and invalid. The Canadian delegation to the ISC believed the elections were in conformity with the Laotian constitution, which *required* that elections be held in 1955. The Canadians also felt that the elections were not contrary to the Geneva agreement and that the Royal Government had done all that could be expected to secure the cooperation of the Pathet Lao. The Polish delegation argued that the elections were not in conformity with the Geneva agreement and that the ISC had not played a role in the elections nor issued a report dealing with them. The latter allegation was certainly true; in the words of the ISC report: "The Commission was not asked to play any part in the elections and it did not adopt any official attitude towards them."[26] Finally, the Indian delegation took the view that the Royal Government could hold elections whenever it pleased, but, since no political settlement had been reached with the Pathet Lao, the elections did not conform to the Geneva agreement.

This divergence of ISC opinion on the legality of the December elections was characteristic of the views of the commission's delegations throughout 1955. When, in early May 1955, the Canadian delegate introduced a draft resolution to guide the Laotian parties in their negotiations toward a political settlement, the Polish delegate ob-

[25] Cmd. 314 (Laos No. 3), pp. 6-8.
[26] *Ibid.*, p. 9.

jected.[27] Establishment of the royal administration in Phong Saly or Sam Neua, he insisted—as well as the more general question of a political settlement—did not come within the scope or competence of the ISC, and interference by the commission in these matters would extend its powers beyond the limits set by the Geneva agreement. The commission, according to the Polish delegate, could only offer its good offices, which had to be acceptable to both parties. This conception of the Laotian ISC's competence contrasted dramatically with the conception of the Polish delegation to the Cambodian ISC, where the Polish delegation tended to support the demands of the former Khmer Issarak and the Pracheachun for *wider* ISC powers. The Canadian delegate agreed to indefinite postponement of discussion of his proposed draft resolution; instead, he again raised the question of the jurisdiction of the Royal Government in Phong Saly and Sam Neua.

The second interim report of the ISC in Laos is a bit more explicit (and candid) than its first interim report with respect to the conflicting views of the status of the rivals in the two northern provinces. The second report reads in part:

> The Commission had decided *by majority vote* that some Royal troops existed in the two northern provinces before and at the time of the cease-fire of 6 August, 1954. . . . The fact is that, before the cease-fire, the military situation in these two provinces was extremely fluid and that neither of the High Commands knew precisely where their men were, and if they did know, they were not prepared to disclose the details. After the Commission's pronouncement, that the Royal forces did, in fact, exist in the northern provinces prior to 6th August, 1954, it was claimed by the "Pathet Lao" that they had no right to be there and that they should, therefore, withdraw. The Commission decided that in the face of these two conflicting interpretations of the Geneva Agreement, *there was no possibility of either the Commission agreeing on a common interpretation* or both the Parties accepting it. Yet the incidents and clashes continued and it was obvious that if they were to be prevented, some solution, without affecting the legal claims and liabilities of the Parties, had to be found. Various solutions were examined by the Commission, but it became increasingly evident that, without both sides agreeing to such a solution, no effective work could be done or the declaration by the Parties made on 9th March, 1955, implemented.[28]

[27] Cmd. 9630 (Laos No. 2), p. 11.
[28] *Ibid.*, p. 13 (emphasis added).

Differences of opinion among the ISC delegates appeared on a number of other issues:

1. The Polish delegation argued that since unanimity on the meaning of article 14 was not possible, the ISC should not discuss it. The Canadian delegation argued that recognition of the sovereignty of Laos at Geneva implied the right of effective administration in Phong Saly and Sam Neua and that article 14 merely provided for military regroupment of the Pathet Lao in those provinces. It did not establish a political regime for the insurgents in the Northeast. The Indian delegation believed that, unless agreement between the Laotian rivals was possible, legal interpretation of article 14 by the ISC would serve no useful purpose, but discussion of that article, at a suitable time, should proceed. "In the circumstances the Commission has not yet given its own interpretation of Article 14."

2. As for the control of some areas of Phong Saly and Sam Neua provinces by commandos of the French Union forces, the Polish delegation challenged the authenticity and accuracy of the documentary evidence of the military committee of the ISC (the documents having been supplied by the French liaison mission). The Canadian and Indian delegations believed the evidence was valid and that it substantiated the claim of the Laotian government that its forces (as a part of the French Union force) were in control of portions of the two provinces.

3. When a relatively large armed clash occurred at Nong Khang, the Polish delegation could not ignore the fact that two hostile forces were confronting each other in Sam Neua.[29] The Poles, nevertheless, asserted that the presence of Franco-Laotian troops in the province was a violation of article 14 of the Geneva agreement, according to which the Pathet Lao had been assigned the *totality* of the two northern provinces.

4. The Indian delegation, having little desire to engage in polemics over the meaning of article 14, proposed to remove the possibility of future hostilities by the demarcation of areas under the control of the rival Laotian forces, with the understanding that their positions would not be strengthened. The Polish delegation objected to this on the grounds that it would restrict the rights of the Pathet Lao under article 14! Although, eventually, the Polish delegation appeared willing to allow a provisional demarcation and the creation of a no-man's-land around these areas, it voted against an ISC resolution of 20 April 1955 instructing the ISC military committee to determine the areas controlled by the rivals. The Pathet Lao also rejected the resolution, despite the fact that it contained a clause which held that

[29] *Ibid.,* p. 14.

any determination by the military committee would be without prejudice to the rights of the parties under article 14.

Although the Polish delegation recognized, in principle, the right
of the Royal Government to reestablish its administration in the two
provinces, reestablishment should come about, the Poles argued,
only through a direct agreement between the Lao–Pathet Lao parties.
Moreover, they believed the ISC should restrict its activities to ex-
horting the rivals to meet to discuss a settlement. The commission
might offer its good offices (which the rivals would be free to accept
or reject), but that was all. In effect, the Indian delegation accepted
the Polish view that the ISC had very limited competence; to do
otherwise, the Indian delegation believed, would be to urge the Royal
Government to use force to impose its administration in Phong Saly
and Sam Neua, which would lead to a civil war, an eventuality the
Indians wished to avoid.

From April through December 1955 the military committee of the
ISC, in consultation with representatives of the Laotian rivals, sought
a cease-fire agreement for Phong Saly and Sam Neua, based upon
the separation of the hostile forces. In December 1955, after a long
series of consultations, the Indian and Polish delegations reached
agreement upon the terms of a resolution effecting a demarcation and
a separation of forces in Sam Neua. The Canadian delegation opposed
the resolution—among other reasons—because it feared this ISC
action might tend to formalize the *de facto* partition of Laos. Commission action on the resolution was deferred because of later political
developments.

5. In December 1955 the Canadian delegation offered a resolution
for restoring the royal administration in Phong Saly and Sam Neua,
in the belief this would help stabilize the situation there. The
Polish delegation objected: ISC competence, it argued, was limited
to the maintenance of a cease-fire; it was not empowered to solve
Laotian political problems, which in any event had been referred to
the co-chairmen, and no action should be considered until the co-
chairmen had made their views known. A modified resolution was
adopted by majority vote, on 7 January 1956, recommending reestablishment without delay of the royal administration in the provinces, concurrently with the measures necessary to ensure the integration of the Pathet Lao without discrimination.[30] The Polish delegation opposed the resolution but abstained during the voting. The
co-chairmen, Selwyn Lloyd and Molotov, were notified of the ISC
action and the views of the three delegations.[31]

[30] Cmd. 314 (Laos No. 3), pp. 9, 47-48.
[31] *Ibid.*, pp. 49-50.

[III]

In February 1956 the government of Prime Minister Katay Sasorith lost its parliamentary support and was replaced, in March, by a government headed by Prince Souvanna Phouma. The prince declared that his policy would be to settle the "Pathet Lao problem" and achieve a "general reconciliation through patriotism and loyalty." "No effort shall be spared," he said, "so that negotiations with the adverse party [may] be crowned by the loyal reconciliation longed for by all."[32] After an exchange of letters between Prince Souvanna Phouma and Prince Souphanouvong, and after the usual delays, talks between the princes began in Vientiane on 1 August. The ISC, although it did not attend these talks, provided forces to ensure the security of Prince Souphanouvong. Joint declarations, issued on 5 and 10 August, reported that progress had been made. Laos, it was agreed, would base its foreign policy upon Nehru's "five principles"; it would "keep good relations with all countries, in particular, *with neighbouring countries*"; and it would not adhere to a military alliance nor allow any country to establish military bases in Laos (apart from those permitted by the Geneva agreement).[33] An effective cease-fire was to be negotiated by a mixed military committee and the democratic liberties of all citizens would be fully guaranteed. General elections, by free and secret ballot, would be held, with the understanding that the Pathet Lao political front (the Neo Lao Hak Xat) and other Pathet Lao organizations would be free to engage in political activities throughout Laos. Subsequent to these elections a "national union government," with Pathet Lao participation, would be formed. The provinces of Phong Saly and Sam Neua would (finally) come under royal administration, and would be reorganized and governed in the national pattern. A mixed political committee was established to formulate detailed plans for implementing these "Vientiane agreements," as they came to be known.[34]

In August, Prime Minister Souvanna Phouma went to Peking and Hanoi, where he announced that his policy for Laos was "peace and neutrality." A Lao-Vietnamese statement, issued by the Prime Minister and Pham Van Dong, declared that future relations between the two countries would be governed by the Five Principles of Peaceful Coexistence.[35] On 31 October 1956, the mixed military committee con-

[32] *Ibid.*, p. 53.

[33] *Ibid.*, pp. 54-57 (emphasis added).

[34] On 24 September 1956 the ISC adopting a resolution that took note of the Vientiane declarations, stated that the commission considered the declarations formed "a suitable basis for final agreement in respect of all outstanding matters in conformity with the Geneva Agreement." *Ibid.*, p. 57.

[35] Lancaster, *op. cit.*, p. 404.

cluded a cease-fire agreement, and on 2 November the mixed political committee signed an agreement for the establishment of diplomatic relations with neighboring countries with the least possible delay. Supplementary accords were signed in December 1956, and a note-worthy feature of this agreement (of 28 December) was the royal government's consent to form a coalition government with the Pathet Lao *before* the supplementary elections.[36]

> In order to enable co-operation between the two Parties to achieve National unity and facilitate the settlement of the pending questions, the two Princes are agreed on the expansion of the present Government before the holding of the general supplementary elections. The coalition government, to which the Pathet Lao Forces will be adequately represented, will thus constitute a symbol of the national reconciliation on the basis of a proper policy aiming at building up a pacific, democratic, united, independent and prosperous Laos. The coalition government will have to receive the confidence of the National Assembly in accordance with the Constitution.
>
> Once the coalition government is formed, the Pathet Lao Forces will function as a political organization named "Neo Lao Haksat" which will undertake its activities according to law like all other political parties.[37]

The Laotian parties, which officially notified the ISC of the progress they had made, requested the commission to apprise the Geneva co-chairmen that—as soon as supplementary elections were held—the settlement envisaged by article 14 of the Geneva agreement would have been realized. But difficulties again arose, although the Laotian National Assembly had amended the electoral law to conform to the provisions of a Lao–Pathet Lao agreement of February 1957.[38] The ISC again urged the parties to continue their negotiations "with the utmost vigour,"[39] but a political crisis on 31 May 1957 resulted in the resignation of Prince Souvanna Phouma's government. The crisis lasted until 9 August, during which time Katay Sasorith tried twice—unsuccessfully—to form a new government, and a third attempt by another party leader also failed. Finally, Prince Souvanna succeeded in forming a government that was approved by the National Assembly.

In mid-September, having received two letters and a resolution from the ISC (during the summer) asking it to consider the im-

[36] Cmd. 314 (Laos No. 3), pp. 57-66.
[37] *Ibid.*, p. 67.
[38] The proposed text of the new electoral law appears in *ibid.*, pp. 68-76.
[39] *Ibid.*, pp. 12-13.

portance of implementing the agreements necessary for a final settlement, the Royal Government declared itself ready to accept the ISC's exhortatory resolution. Prince Souphanouvong expressed satisfaction that the ministerial crisis had been resolved by the re-investiture of Prince Souvanna Phouma and said he hoped the policies of reconciliation would continue. On 25 September, talks between the princes again were started in Vientiane. Pursuant to a second set of Vientiane agreements, produced in November 1957, Prince Souvanna formed a provisional national union government with two former members of the Pathet Lao.[40] This government was approved by the National Assembly on 18 November—the same day the Neo Lao Hak Xat, the Pathet Lao united-front organization, began its activities throughout Laos. Supplementary elections for twenty new Assembly seats were scheduled for 4 May 1958. In early December the provinces of Phong Saly and Sam Neua were officially handed over to the Royal Government.[41] At a special ceremony at Plaine des Jarres on 18 February, 1,500 Pathet Lao troops were integrated into the Royal Laotian Army. More than 4,000 other troops, reported to have been demobilized, took up residence in Phong Saly and Sam Neua.

Elections were held on 4 May, as scheduled. The Neo Lao Hak Xat and an allied party won thirteen of the twenty supplementary seats, but Prince Souphanouvong registered a number of complaints, during the campaign and afterward, alleging discrimination and fraud. The Prime Minister replied that investigations would be conducted but that only the Laotian courts, the National Assembly, and the Ministry of the Interior were competent to deal with these matters, not the ISC. In fact, on 20 March 1958 the Prime Minister informed the ISC that his government had decided it would ask the commission to withdraw as of the date of elections, since these elections constituted the final act in the implementation of the Geneva agreement.[42] The prince also sent copies of his letter to the governments of the three supervisory powers (India, Canada, and Poland) and to the Geneva co-chairmen, requesting that the latter apprise the supervisory states of their views. Although the ISC reduced its activities and withdrew a number of teams before the elections, its activity had not been liquidated by 8 May, when the commis-

[40] Prince Souphanouvong had the portfolio of the Minister of Plans, Reconstruction and Urbanism; Phoumi Vongvichit was the Minister of Culture and Fine Arts.

[41] *Fourth Interim Report of the International Commission for Supervision and Control in Laos*, Laos No. 1 (1958), Cmd. 541 (London: Her Majesty's Stationery Office, 1958), p. 13.

[42] *Ibid.*, pp. 75-76.

sioners discussed the matter of ISC withdrawal. The Canadian delegation wished to terminate the ISC's activities immediately on the grounds that, with the supplementary elections, a political settlement for Laos had been achieved. The Polish and Indian delegations insisted, however, that the ISC could withdraw only after the elections had been validated in the National Assembly.[43] Article 39 required unanimity for reducing ISC activity, and, because of the division of opinion among the commissioners, no action was taken. The Royal Government pressed for withdrawal, however; and on 13 May asked to be informed of the measures being taken to withdraw the commission's teams. On 15 May the Prime Minister stated that elections had been duly held and that any questions concerning the validity of the elections in any of the provinces would be settled according to Laotian law by the National Assembly.

The Canadian delegation persisted in arguing that the ISC's functions were at an end; the Polish delegation argued that, regardless of the fulfillment of the terms of article 14, other provisions of the Geneva agreement and various pledges of the Royal Government of Laos undertaken at Geneva were unfulfilled. And "(these) obligations would . . . exist for the Royal Government until the *final political settlement in Vietnam*"![44] The Indian delegation took a somewhat similar view: the government of Laos was still bound by commitments undertaken at Geneva; moreover, the PAVN, a party to the cease-fire agreement, did not accept the Laotian request to dissolve the ISC. Therefore, the proposal for dissolution "was bound to have serious repercussions on the working of the Geneva Agreement in all Indochina, introduce discord and disharmony in the workings of the Laos Commission and, if followed by unilateral withdrawal, might have serious consequences for peace in Indochina."[45]

On 22 May the Royal Government made still another request for the termination of ISC activities; and on the 31st, apparently to reassure the governments of the supervisory powers, Prime Minister Souvanna Phouma advised the ISC chairman that his government intended to continue to uphold the engagements undertaken at Geneva in July 1954.[46] On 19 July, over the opposition of the Polish delegation, the commission voted to adjourn *sine die*, but reconvene if necessary, in accordance with normal procedures. Thus the ISC did not dissolve itself or in any way alter its legal status. The decision to adjourn was a procedural one, which, in the opinion of the Indian and Canadian delegations, did not require a unanimous vote.

[43] *Ibid.*, p. 15.
[45] *Ibid.*
[44] *Ibid.*, p. 16 (emphasis added).
[46] *Ibid.*, p. 121.

Chapter 27

THE SPIRIT OF GENEVA

[I]

Although the expression "Geneva Accords" has become part of the vocabulary of historians and statesmen, it is doubly misleading. First, it implies a meeting of minds or an accord between the diplomats at Geneva, a consensus of the conference delegates upon military and political arrangements for the three Indochinese states; second, it implies that the documents that embodied the settlements for Cambodia, Laos, and Vietnam were sufficiently similar in form, content, and obligatory force to be subsumed under a label of this sort. The Geneva accords, of course, comprised a number of very different documents: six unilateral declarations, three cease-fire agreements, a final declaration, and the minutes of the last plenary session of the conference. Only in the case of the cease-fire agreements can we speak of accords having been reached, in the sense that each was a bilateral agreement between the relevant military high commands committing the parties to perform a number of acts designed to bring about a cease-fire and a disengagement, withdrawal, and regroupment of their armed forces. The final declaration was an accord only for the states that consented to observe its terms. Not all the participating states so consented, and even those that approved its provisions did so in a legally ambiguous fashion. Moreover, the language of most of the Geneva documents was unclear in rather crucial respects, implying the absence of a consensus.[1]

It has often been suggested that some or all of the conference participants "should adhere to the spirit of the Geneva Accords,"

---

[1] On the general problem of ambiguity, J. N. Moore has observed: "[The] Geneva Accords themselves reflect a highly ambiguous settlement and conceal a number of fundamental problems with which the Conference—perhaps intentionally—did not come to grips" (Falk, p. 256, and pp. 262, 304). See also R. A. Falk, *ibid.*, p. 369. I am in general disagreement with Falk's conclusions (in Falk, pp. 463-464); however, this is not the place to discuss the many points raised by the adversaries about the wider question of the legality of United States involvement in Vietnam after 1965 (see Falk, *passim*). It is this writer's opinion that Moore's essay, "The Lawfulness of Military Assistance to the Republic of Viet-Nam" (Falk, pp. 237ff.), and Falk's essay, "International Law and the United States' Role in the Viet Nam War" (Falk, pp. 362ff.), are two examples of sound legal research and creative jurisprudence—with, however, diametrically opposed points of view. The reader who will take the trouble to compare my Chapters 21-24 and 27 with the essays by Moore and Falk will find that I am closer to Moore's position and in general agreement with him and Underwood (*op. cit.*) to the extent their writings deal with the Geneva agreements of 1954.

that the states concerned "should return to the Geneva Agreements." What can these suggestions mean? One scholar, Victor Bator, has categorically asserted: "A 'return' to Geneva of 1954 would mean as many things as there were parties to it, as would immediately become clear when the assorted representatives reached the conference table."[2] In the article in which this statement appeared, Bator argued that each state-participant and its delegation had different, even discordant, reasons for wanting peace in Indochina in 1954 and that, beyond the written documents, there were several tacit understandings among the powers that conflicted with the written provisions; indeed, that there were serious ambiguities and contradictions even in the documents themselves. Although admitting the force of many of Mr. Bator's arguments, we ought not peremptorily dismiss the notion that there also were matters upon which the conference participants agreed, and it would be a useful exercise to attempt to determine what these matters were.

Perhaps they were so insignificant that Bator's conclusions are wholly tenable—perhaps a conference consensus was so completely lacking that reference to the Geneva accords at some future time would be vain and fruitless and would tend to hamper rather than expedite negotiations. On the other hand, such an investigation may show that there was (and remains) some substance to the concept of a "spirit of Geneva"—that it would be possible to "return" to the Geneva agreements, in the sense of relying upon them for the settlement of military and political problems. It is, of course, impossible to go back to the Geneva of 1954, just as it is impossible to go back to the San Francisco of 1945 and the Locarno of 1925: people, governments, and states have changed, and many other events also have altered the character of the relations between the states concerned. Nevertheless, the principles and procedures upon which the Geneva diplomats achieved consensus may provide a framework for future discussions.

In the preceding chapters we have studied the various Geneva documents rather closely. We know fairly well what the documents *purported* to do (although the reader might wish to reread the final declaration, the cease-fire agreements, and their analyses in Chapters 21, 22, 25, and 26). But what the documents purported to accomplish, what the participants wanted them to accomplish, and the legal effect the documents actually had are quite different things. Let us examine the elements of the settlements and determine whether and to what extent the delegations achieved consensus of a sort that would enable us to conclude that a particular provi-

[2] Victor Bator, "Geneva, 1954: The Broken Mold," *Reporter*, 30 June 1966.

sion was the product of the conference as a whole and not merely a part thereof. It is only those matters upon which all the Geneva powers agreed, expressly or tacitly, that we should consider as reflecting or comprising the content of a "spirit of Geneva."

A. MILITARY ASPECTS

1. The cease-fire agreements

The four powers that assented to the final declaration—that is, Britain, France, the Soviet Union, and the C.P.R.—welcomed the ending of hostilities (FD 1, 2, 6). Both the United States and SVN delegations tacitly agreed upon a cease-fire, the former through the Bedell Smith declaration that "any renewal of the aggression" would be viewed "with grave concern,"[3] and both the U.S. and the SVN by means of statements that they would not use force to disturb the military settlements or resist procedures for carrying them into effect. The terms of the unilateral declarations of the Laotian and Cambodian governments can easily be construed as agreement upon a cease-fire, both within their own states and within the territories of their Indochinese neighbors. The DRVN did not formally approve the final declaration, but Ta Quang Buu signed the Vietnam cease-fire agreement, in which articles 10 and 11 stipulated that the signatories agreed upon a cease-fire. He also signed the Laotian cease-fire agreement, and tacitly agreed to the principle of a simultaneous cease-fire throughout Indochina.

It is my conclusion, therefore, that there was a conference consensus upon a cessation of hostilities in each of the three Indochinese states. Some states accepted the cease-fire unreservedly; others accepted it tacitly, in the form of a promise not to resist its implementation. Although the policymakers of the governments concerned probably had their own unique reasons for wanting a cease-fire, and we should not ignore those reasons or fail to appreciate that subsequent events could change them substantially, it is meaningful to speak of a conference consensus on a cease-fire.

2. Execution of the technical military procedures relating to the cease-fire (disengagement, assembly, withdrawal, regroupment, etc.)

Certainly the signatories of the three cease-fire agreements consented to the procedures for implementing the cessation of hostilities within the territories of the respective states. The delegations that explicitly consented to the final declaration (France, Britain, the Soviet Union, and the C.P.R.) could also be said to have agreed to these technical procedures (see FD 2 and 6); and what we know of the negotiations during the last week of the conference reinforces this

---

[3] Cmd. 9239, pp. 6-7.

conclusion. The SVN, however, protested regroupment procedures that resulted in a partition of Vietnam and placing Vietnamese territories under the jurisdiction and control of the Communist Vietminh. The United States delegation did not formally address itself to these matters; the Bedell Smith declaration simply "took note" of the cease-fire agreements. However, Tran Van Do and Bedell Smith declared that their governments would refrain from the use or threat of force to disturb the military aspects of the settlements; and these declarations could be construed as at least tacit acquiescence in the technical procedures.

I conclude, therefore, that it is also meaningful to speak of a conference consensus on such procedures, provided we understand that we are referring only to military matters for the effective implementation of the cease-fire and not to civil or political matters.

3. Supervision of the implementation of the cease-fire (establishment and operation of the international supervisory commissions)

Apart from the signatories of the cease-fire agreements, who agreed to cooperate with and assist the ISCs, the other Geneva powers (the U.K., the U.S.S.R., the C.P.R., the U.S., and the SVN) did not explicitly refer to the commissions' status or operations. We could, however, restate the earlier arguments (above) to find a consensus on the regime of the ISCs in Indochina, again with the understanding that we are concerned only with supervision of the military aspects of the settlement, as opposed to the civil or political aspects. Subsequently, the SVN government agreed to cooperate with the Vietnamese ISC as an international peace commission, although SVN officials repeatedly declared that they were not bound by the cease-fire agreement.

4. The "neutralization" of Indochina (i.e. the provisions of the cease-fire agreements and the final declaration prohibiting the introduction of troops, other military personnel, and arms and munitions into the three Indochinese states and the provisions enjoining the establishment of new military bases and military alliances)

The heads of the British, French, Chinese, and Soviet delegations, in agreeing to the final declaration, "took note" of the clauses in the cease-fire agreements "neutralizing" the Indochinese states. The Laotian and Cambodian governments agreed, by unilateral declarations, not to seek foreign aid, in war matériel or personnel, except for the purpose of "effective defence." This exception was noted in the final declaration (FD 4). There was no analogous exception respecting Vietnam, and the prohibition purported to be more absolute. Paragraph 5 of the final declaration "took note" of the prohibition against military alliances and foreign military bases. Laos and Cambodia were again excepted, to the extent that such bases would be permitted if the security of these states was threatened.

Thus Britain, France, the Soviet Union, the C.P.R., the DRVN, Cambodia, and Laos ostensibly agreed upon prohibiting the introduction of arms and troops into the Indochinese states and the establishment of military bases and formation of military alliances. The government of the United States reserved its position, however; and the Bedell Smith declaration simply did not address itself to "neutralization." But the Anglo-American joint position paper of late June 1954, in which Prime Minister Churchill acquiesced, declared there should be nothing in the prospective Geneva settlements that would materially impair the capacity of the governments of Laos, Cambodia, and "retained Vietnam" to maintain stable non-Communist regimes.[4] It would be a fair interpretation of the Bedell Smith declaration to say that the "renewal of aggression" that would be viewed "with grave concern" meant "Communist aggression and would call for positive steps to strengthen the governments of Laos, Cambodia, and "retained Vietnam." This conclusion is valid for two reasons. First, statements by Dulles and the President in July indicated that they believed the Indochinese governments should and would retain the right to take measures in their self-defense, irrespective of the language of the Geneva settlements. Second, the SEATO treaty, concluded 8 September 1954 and signed by Britain, France, and the United States (among others), provided the basis for active assistance by the SEATO signatories for the defense of Cambodia, Laos, and southern Vietnam upon the consent of the governments of these states.

The SVN government, moreover, refused to subscribe to the Geneva settlement since it reduced the SVN's capacity to resist Communist expansion.[5] Tran Van Do reserved complete freedom of action for his government to guarantee the rights of the Vietnamese people to independence and freedom.

Clearly, there was no consensus among the conference participants on the "neutralization" of Indochina. Neither the United States nor the SVN could seriously object to the neutralization of Laos and Cambodia, however, since the governments of both states had the right to call upon foreign powers for assistance in defense of their territories. This was the substance of the exception (a "loophole"

---

[4] See Chapter 16.

[5] In a paper dated 20 July (referred to as document 1 in Chapter 23 above), the SVN delegation made this statement: "The absolute prohibition against the importation of new armaments into Vietnam after the armistice would only constitute an advantage for the Vietminh inasmuch as no control could effectively prevent them from receiving arms across the lengthy Chinese frontier." The SVN, Do concluded, could not accept the loss of vital territories and population *and* give up the right to organize an effective defense. See *Relazioni internazionali*, Series 2, 17, No. 31 (31 July 1954): p. 926.

perhaps) that Sam Sary had won for the Cambodian government and that he and Mendès-France had won for the Laotian government. As we have seen, there was no such exception in the Vietnamese settlement, but could we not—by implication—incorporate an exception in the Vietnamese agreement similar to that expressed in the Cambodian and Laotian agreements? Could a government of Vietnam take the steps it deemed necessary for the effective defense of its territories, which might include requesting and accepting foreign military assistance? Probably it could not, since the ostensible theory of the final declaration was that Vietnam was a single state that in two years' time, would have a single government. In the interim, the indeterminate legal status of the "administrations" in the two regroupment zones would make it difficult for all the Geneva powers to admit that either Vietnam administrative authority had the right to defend its zone against incursions of the forces of the other zone. That is to say, the American and British governments (and possibly the Mendès-France government) might take the position that the French high command, and subsequently the SVN, could indeed take steps prohibited by the Vietnam cease-fire agreement to defend itself against the DRVN. But certainly the C.P.R., the Soviet Union, and the DRVN would not admit such a right.

If the cease-fire agreement and the final declaration had provided that, pending a political settlement, the authorities in each "neutralized" zone of Vietnam retained their right of self-defense, not only against foreign states but against each other, obviously, then, we could find a consensus. But the documents do not permit this construction; and to construe them in this fashion would constitute a substantial revision of their content.[6]

B. POLITICAL ASPECTS

1. *General principles of a political settlement for the Indochinese states*

The delegations of Great Britain, the Soviet Union, France, and the C.P.R. explicitly undertook to respect the sovereignty, independence, unity, and territorial integrity of Cambodia, Laos, and Vietnam and to refrain from interference in their internal affairs (FD 12). A French unilateral declaration repeated these undertakings. The United States

---

[6] The reader should be clear on this point: I am not arguing that there is no basis for inferring that either the SVN or the DRVN had the right of self-defense against the other; I am saying there was no consensus or agreement on the question (as there was no consensus on the more general question of neutralization). This was the case, because of the problematical status of the SVN and the DRVN (Do provisional "administrations" have the right of self-defense?), the absence of provisions spelling out the rights and duties of the "administrations" toward each other, and the failure to anticipate that the SVN and not France would likely assume control of the "administration" south of the demarcation line.

delegation, in a unilateral declaration, expressed the "hope that the agreement will permit Cambodia, Laos and Viet Nam to play their part in full independence and sovereignty, in the peaceful community of nations."[7] The United States, the Bedell Smith declaration stated, would continue to seek to achieve the unity of "nations divided against their will" by means of free elections under U.N. supervision. The hope was expressed that the Geneva settlements would enable the peoples of Indochina to determine their own future. This declaration, read with the Potomac Declaration (29 June 1954) and the Pacific Charter (8 September), constituted an undertaking by the United States similar to that of the other great powers at Geneva.

The small powers—Cambodia, Laos, the DRVN, and the SVN—unquestionably claimed the full attributes of sovereignty and independence. The protest of the SVN on 21 July was an explicit assertion of this claim, as was Ho Chi Minh's appeal to the Vietnamese peoples of 22 July.[8] But did these states also undertake to respect the sovereignty of each other?

a. The Cambodian government (generally) undertook to settle its international disputes by peaceful means and not to adhere to an aggressive policy. Specifically, it declared that although it had no intention of interfering in the internal affairs of the "State of Viet-Nam" and it fully associated itself with the principle of respect for territorial integrity, certain adjustments and regularizations of the Khmero-Vietnamese border, fixed by the unilateral act of France, would have to be made.[9] The Cambodian government made no statement with respect to Laos.

b. The Laotian government, in its unilateral declaration, also undertook to settle its international disputes peacefully and not to pursue aggressive policies. The Laotian delegation made no reference to either Cambodia or Vietnam.[10]

c. Neither the DRVN nor the SVN government explicitly assumed obligations vis-à-vis Laos and Cambodia, nor, obviously, did either government agree to respect the sovereignty, independence, and territorial integrity of the other or to refrain from interference in the other's internal affairs.[11] According to the theories of the DRVN and SVN (and all the great powers), Vietnam, as a *whole* or as a *unit*, was independent and sovereign.

[7] Cmd. 9239, p. 7.

[8] The SVN protest appears in *Docs., 1954*, pp. 315-316; the DRVN Premier's appeal appears in Ho Chi Minh, *On Revolution*, ed. B. B. Fall (New York: Praeger, 1967), pp. 271-273.

[9] Cmd. 9239, p. 6.

[10] But see article 19 of the Laotian cease-fire agreement, which could be construed as an undertaking by the Royal Government of Laos to respect the territory under DRVN control (as well as territory militarily controlled by the Pathet Lao).

[11] In order to fulfill the military objectives of the Vietnamese cease-fire agree-

The great powers, but not the lesser powers, reached a consensus at Geneva on the general principles of a settlement for Cambodia, Laos, and Vietnam. Of course, each of the lesser powers would demand that all other states (including the other lesser powers) respect its independence, sovereignty, unity and territorial integrity.

2. Basis for a political settlement for Vietnam

The powers that assented to the final declaration agreed that a political settlement for Vietnam was to be based upon "free general elections by secret ballot" (FD 7). And the United States delegate separately declared that free elections were essential to bring about the unification of Vietnam. Even the SVN delegate agreed, in principle, upon the necessity for general elections. Although Pham Van Dong made no explicit remarks on the matter at the last plenary session, it was clear that he (and his government) also accepted elections as the basis for a political settlement. But neither Laos nor Cambodia commented upon the nature of a political settlement for Vietnam.

Thus apart from the minor exceptions of the Laotian and Cambodian representatives, who in any event accepted the principle of general elections as the basis for a settlement in their countries, the conference achieved consensus in agreeing that "free general elections" were a necessary basis for a Vietnamese political settlement. Disagreement over the precise nature of *free* elections was to be mitigated to some extent by supervision, however. All the delegations concurred in the need for supervised elections; but the United States and the SVN delegations insisted upon the desirability of United Nations supervision; France, the Soviet Union, the C.P.R., and Britain agreed upon supervision by an international supervisory commission composed of representatives of Canada, India, and Poland and chaired by the Indian representative.[12] The DRVN tacitly accepted this latter form of supervision. Thus there was a lack of consensus among the conference participants over the instrumentality for supervising elections in Vietnam.

3. The time by which the political settlement for Vietnam was to be achieved

Paragraph 6 of the final declaration stated: "The Conference expresses its conviction that the execution of the provisions set out

ment, the PAVN high command had agreed to respect the "territory under the military control" of the French high command (article 24).

[12] Eden agreed to supervision by the ISC for Vietnam, even though he and Prime Minister Churchill, in June, had associated themselves with the Potomac Declaration, which in general terms advocated free elections, supervised by the United Nations, for all divided nations.

in the present declaration and in the agreement on the cessation of hostilities creates the necessary basis for the achievement *in the near future* of a political settlement in Viet Nam" (emphasis added). This, of course, presupposed execution of the terms of paragraph 7, which declared that "general elections shall be held in July, 1956," after preliminary consultations between competent representative authorities of the two zones on and after 20 July 1955. Presumably, the political settlement "in the near future" would wait on the outcome of the elections. The great powers (other than the United States) and the DRVN assented to this "timetable" in July 1954. The Bedell Smith declaration merely took note of paragraphs 6 and 7 of the final declaration.

It is impossible, in my view, to find in this declaration an intent to commit the United States formally to any schedule for a political settlement generally or, more specifically, to commit the United States to a timetable for elections. In fact, the Eisenhower administration wished to reserve its freedom of action, as was made clear by the statements of the President, Secretary Dulles, and Bedell Smith in the first two weeks after the end of the conference. The position of the SVN delegation was similar to that of the United States: noncommitment to precise dates for elections and preliminary consultations. Finally, it should be noted that neither the Laotian nor the Cambodian delegations addressed itself to this problem. It is thus impossible to find a conference consensus on the time when a Vietnamese political settlement would be achieved.[13]

4. The political settlements for Cambodia and Laos

The Royal Governments of Cambodia and Laos agreed to hold elections as the basis for the political settlements affecting their polities, and Britain, France, the Soviet Union, and the C.P.R. concurred. The United States delegation expressed the hope that the "agreement" would permit the peoples of Laos and Cambodia to determine their future, and, because American officials often coupled self-determination and elections, we can fairly presume that the Eisenhower administration agreed upon the desirability of elections in Laos and Cambodia. However, we cannot find U.S. agreement upon certain particulars, namely, elections *in 1955* and the mode of election supervision. Neither the SVN nor the DRVN addressed itself to the question of a Cambodian or Laotian political settlement.

[13] The conferees achieved a negative consensus on the appropriateness of applying the principle of national self-determination concurrently with their recognition of the independence and sovereignty of Vietnam. In effect, they decided that application of the principle was *not* appropriate in view of the conditions *then* existing in Vietnam. However, the principle would be applied at some later time.

Thus, among the states that were concerned with the problems of Cambodia and Laos (and this group comprised all the great powers), there was a consensus that the political settlements for those two states should take the form of free general elections.

5. Consultations among the Geneva participants

Although the British, French, Soviet, and C.P.R. delegations agreed to consult one another on questions referred to them by the ISCs (FD 13), the Bedell Smith declaration failed even to take note of this provision of the final declaration. This, in effect, was a tacit refusal to be bound to consult on an institutionalized basis with the C.P.R. The delegations of the SVN, DRVN, Cambodia, and Laos did not indicate whether they were willing to consult. There was, therefore, no consensus on consultations.

6. Obligations relative to the peoples of Cambodia, Laos, and Vietnam

This heading would include the duties of obligated states to protect the property of citizens; to prevent reprisals; to integrate former insurgents, prisoners of war, and civilian internees in the bodies politic of Cambodia, Laos, and Vietnam; to guarantee the civil rights of the Indochinese peoples, particularly by allowing all persons to participate in general elections, either as candidates or electors; to permit movement of persons between zones (in the case of Vietnam); and generally to protect the "democratic liberties" and "fundamental freedoms" (FD 3, 7) of all peoples.

The Cambodian and Laotian high commands and their governments undertook no commitments (i.e. civil rights–type commitments) in territories under the jurisdiction of the other, nor did they undertake commitments in respect of peoples in territories in either regroupment zone of Vietnam. The PAVN high command, on the other hand, was obligated to fulfill certain terms of the agreements in both Laos and Cambodia. However, with the withdrawal of its units from these two countries, performance devolved principally upon the governments concerned and the high commands of the Khmer Issarak and Pathet Lao, neither of which was represented at Geneva. The PAVN and its government were obligated to perform according to the terms of articles 9, 14, 21, and 36 of the Vietnam cease-fire agreement in *both* zones in Vietnam. The French high command was bound to perform in respect of Laos and Vietnam only as long as French troops remained in either country. Upon the withdrawal of French troops, French obligations (with respect to the civil rights of peoples) would cease. After withdrawal, neither the French high command nor the French government could properly insist upon performing duties that had become matters of domestic concern for the governments of Vietnam and Laos; that is, the French could not "interfere" and at the same time fulfill their promise to respect the sovereignty and independence of these states.

Paragraphs 8 and 9 of the final declaration, upon which the head delegates of Great Britain, France, the C.P.R., and the Soviet Union agreed, declared that the authorities in Cambodia, Laos, and the northern and southern zones of Vietnam *"must not permit* any individual or collective reprisals against persons who have collaborated with one of the parties" and *must ensure* that provisions of the cease-fire agreements intended to protect individuals and property were "most strictly applied." As rather stronger language than the phrase "take note of" that the draftsmen of the final declaration usually employed, this can be taken to mean that four of the five great powers (the United States excepted) ostensibly agreed upon the need to guarantee civil rights, at least according to each party's understanding of such rights.

The United States and the SVN simply did not address themselves substantively to the states' obligations to the peoples of Indochina.[14] Nevertheless, United States officials often expressed themselves, during and after the conference, on the rights of the Indochinese peoples, and official papers, such as the Pacific Charter and the U.N. Charter, could be construed as indicating that the United States, in principle, concurred in the desirability of protecting the "fundamental freedoms" of the Indochinese peoples. Moreover, it is possible to assess the official American attitude on such matters as reprisals, the integration of insurgents, and the processing of prisoners of war and civilian internees. Very likely these were regarded as within the domestic jurisdiction of the states concerned. It does not do injury to the facts or the official United States position to find a verbal consensus among the five great powers on the principles of respect for civil, personal, and property rights and the democratic liberties of the peoples of Indochina. Among the small powers, the DRVN, Cambodian, and Laotian governments also accepted these principles for their own states. The SVN delegation, in its protest at the last plenary session, reserved the right to protect the "freedom" of the Vietnamese people. Thus, even in this instance, there was an agreement in principle.

We may summarize the results of the preceding analysis as follows.[15]

[14] The SVN delegation insisted upon guaranteeing the rights of persons to move from the northern to the southern regroupment zones.

[15] The preceding survey and the table that follows do not purport to cover every subject discussed at Geneva and every provision of the Geneva documents. They touch upon the major problems, however, which is sufficient for our purposes in this chapter.

Was There a Consensus?

A. Military Aspects	Great-Power Consensus	Conference Consensus
1. Cease-fire?	Yes	Yes
2. Execution of technical military procedures, including the withdrawal of foreign troops and the belligerent forces?[16]	Yes, with the tacit approval of the U.S.	Yes, with the tacit approval of the U.S. and the SVN.
3. Supervision by ISC of military provisions?	Express approval by the signatories of the cease-fire agreements; tacit approval by the others.	
4. "Neutralization": a. Cambodia and Laos?	Yes, we can interpret U.S. policy statements from July through September 1954 as acquiescence in "neutralization," provided the governments retained a capacity for effective self-defense (which the relevant Geneva agreements ostensibly provided).	The SVN did not address itself to this question.
b. Vietnam?	No. In the case of Vietnam there were no exceptions to the right of either zone authority to defend itself against attack (particularly against the other). The U.S. did not associate itself with the Vietnam "neutralization" provisions. Moreover, the administration regarded the SVN's right of self-defense as essential.	The SVN did not concur. The governments of Cambodia and Laos did not address themselves to this question.
B. Political Aspects	Great-Power Consensus	Conference Consensus
1. On general principles: respect for the sovereignty, independence, and territorial integrity of Cambodia, Laos, and Vietnam, and refraining from interfering in their internal affairs?	Yes, with the understanding that all parties regarded Vietnam, in theory, as a unitary state.	The small powers did not address themselves to the rights of the other but claimed such rights for themselves.

[16] I have been unable to determine the official position of the United States government on the assignment of the Laotian provinces of Phong Saly and Sam Neua to the Pathet Lao.

B. Political Aspects	Great-Power Consensus	Conference Consensus
2. Political settlement for Vietnam:		
a. Free, general elections?	Yes	Same as B1 above.
b. Supervision?	Yes on the principle of supervision, no on supervision by the ISC.	
3. Vietnam elections in July 1956?	No; the U.S. reserved its position.	No; the U.S. and the SVN reserved their positions.
4. Political settlements in Laos and Cambodia?	Yes on elections, no on details of the elections (the U.S. did not address itself to the details).	The small powers did not address themselves to the political settlements for each other.
5. Consultation among the Geneva participants?	No	No
6. Obligations to the peoples of Laos, Cambodia, and Vietnam?	It is possible to conclude that all the participants agreed, in principle, to respect the democratic liberties and fundamental freedoms of the Indochinese peoples. There was, however, no consensus on specifics.[17]	

A "spirit of Geneva" is meaningful, I submit, only if we define it as referring to matters upon which the conference participants achieved consensus. This definition could be stretched a bit further, to comprise those questions upon which the five great powers concurred, and perhaps could also include the principle that formed the very basis of the conference: the desirability of negotiating to restore peace in Indochina.[18]

There are, however, at least two objections to this definition of the "spirit of Geneva": (a) it means a good deal more than the mere sum of those matters on which there was consensus or (b) it means much less. In the former case, it might be argued that the Geneva settlements were holistic: they represented a will to peace, reciprocal feelings of mutual benefit and good will, and were an exemplification of the Five Principles of Peaceful Coexistence that should color all the future relations of states concerned with the political problems of Indochina. In the latter case, arguing that the consensus represented much less than what the words of the agreements purported to say, the putative critic might hold that crucial words in the agreements ("free elections," "democratic institutions," "fundamental freedoms," etc.) were understood in very different senses by the participants—that the reasons for the participating powers' agreeing to the elements of the ostensible consensus were as varied as their assess-

---

[17] No provisions were made for enforcement or sanctions in the civil rights category (or any other category, for that matter).
[18] See the Berlin Conference communiqué of 18 February in *FMM*, p. 217.

ments of their own national interests. What was important, the critic might argue, was the extent to which the real interests of the participating states were compatible with each other. If the interests of the United States, relative to Southeast Asia—as understood by the administration's policymakers—were incompatible with the interests of Great Britain, or the C.P.R., or the DRVN—as these interests were understood by their respective governments—it would be meaningless and even misleading to speak of a consensus.

Knowledge of the positions of the Geneva powers during the negotiations ought to convince us that little can be said for the proposition that the "spirit of Geneva" represented something *more* than a consensus, *more* than the agreement in principle upon the matters set out in tabular form above. The Geneva powers were not moved by an altruistic will to peace; rather, they were moved by conflicting self-interests. Because there was strong disagreement over many matters of importance and the Geneva conferees deliberately avoided broaching certain matters, it can serve no useful purpose to insist that the Geneva documents accomplished *more* than they purported to accomplish—or even *all* they purported to accomplish. If there was an atmosphere of mediation and conciliation at Geneva, it was merely sufficient to enable the participants to produce a settlement by Mendès-France's deadline. If there was a desire for peaceful coexistence, it was surely inchoate, and would have to be cultivated with great care by the states concerned.

The other view—that "real" consensus was minimal or nonexistent—in effect denies that the Geneva documents had any value whatever. It asserts that, except in the rare instances when diplomats have achieved a complete meeting of minds, it is impossible to express an imperfect agreement in writing. In short, it holds that a treaty is a mere memorandum that is only *evidence* of an agreement, and the evidence is rebuttable on grounds that the express declarations, the words, do not denote what the negotiators really meant when they used them. If we were to accept this view, the process according to which states reach agreement would become even more complicated and unreliable than it presently is. Fortunately, we can steer between these extreme criticisms and say that the expressions "Geneva accords" and "spirit of Geneva" mean those elements of the settlements for Cambodia, Laos, and Vietnam that were embodied in the several conference documents upon which at least the *great powers* achieved consensus.

The large-scale resumption of hostilities in Vietnam in the sixties and the involvement of the United States in the "Second Indochinese War," have highlighted the inadequacies of the Geneva agreements of 1954. But it will be in the current movement toward a settlement of that war and the resolution of post-war problems that the diplomats of the antagonistic parties and other interested states must find some common basis for agreement. Here, a careful study of not only the inadequacies of the 1954 agreements, but the adequacies as well—the items upon which there was a consensus—will be essential. If "returning to the Geneva agreements" means that the negotiators who seek to solve the problems in Southeast Asia are to use the "accords" as their point of departure, those negotiators may want to note the following elements of the Geneva settlements of 1954.[19]

1. The agreement, in principle, to negotiate in order to restore peace in Cambodia, Laos, and Vietnam and to attempt to solve the military and political problems related to the on-going hostilities.

2. The cessation of hostilities, the elaboration of procedures for the implementation of a cease-fire, the execution of these procedures, and effective supervision of their implementation by an international supervisory commission (possibly a revitalized ISC but probably not a U.N. body). Perhaps the most important elements of a cease-fire agreement are the withdrawal of foreign troops and the regroupment of the indigenous belligerent forces.

3. The neutralization of Indochina, but neutralization that allows the governments of Cambodia and Laos to call upon foreign powers for military assistance in the exercise of their right of self-defense, should this become necessary. Neutralization includes the following: (a) prohibitions on the importation of specified kinds and quantities of arms and munitions, (b) prohibitions on the entry of foreign military personnel, (c) prohibitions on the establishment of foreign military bases, and (d) agreement not to join military alliances

[19] The Laotian civil war eventuated in a second Geneva Conference in 1961 and 1962 (see section III below). The documents produced at this conference (a declaration on the neutrality of Laos and a protocol to this declaration) will probably have to be consulted, along with the 1954 Geneva documents, in the future elaboration of a peace settlement for Indochina. Secretary of State Dean Rusk and Adlai Stevenson, U.S. Permanent Representative to the U.N., believed peace should be achieved in Vietnam on the basis of the Geneva agreements of 1954 *and* 1962 (*DSB*, 11 May 1964, pp. 733-736 [Rusk]; *DSB*, 24 August 1964, pp. 272-274 [Stevenson]; *DSB*, 15 May 1965, pp. 362-371 [Rusk]). The State Department report, *Aggression from the North* (dated 27 February 1965), asserted that Hanoi's program of "armed aggression" was "directly contrary to the Geneva accords of 1954 and of 1962 to which North Viet-Nam is a party" (see *Background Information Relating to Southeast Asia and Vietnam* [2d rev. ed.], Committee on Foreign Relations, U.S. Senate, March 1966, p. 197, and *DSB*, 22 March 1965, pp. 404-425). A State Department memorandum, dated 8 March 1965 and titled *Legal Basis for United States Actions against North Viet-Nam*, reiterated this charge (in *Background Information*, p. 202). A State Department press release, dated 7 January 1966 and setting forth the official U.S. position on Vietnam, declared: "The Geneva Agreements of 1954 and 1962 are an adequate basis for peace in Southeast Asia" (*ibid.*, p. 262).

not in conformity with the United Nations Charter. It should again be emphasized that the Geneva powers did not achieve consensus on the right of either the SVN or the DRVN to defend their territories; nor did the powers address themselves to the problem of limiting the effective strength of the armed forces of the Indochinese states; nor did they weigh the likelihood of civil war in Laos or Vietnam or consider appropriate third-power responses to such civil wars.

The elements of a consensus also comprised:

4. Agreement upon the necessity for a political settlement for the Indochinese states, based upon the principles of sovereignty and independence, respect for their territorial integrity, and the undertaking of third parties to refrain from interfering in the internal affairs of Cambodia, Laos, and Vietnam (with the understanding that the same principles must govern the interrelations of the Indochinese states as well). Each of the three Indochinese states was to be regarded as a unitary state. In the legal theories of all the Geneva powers there was only one Vietnam.

5. Agreement that a political settlement for Cambodia, Laos, and Vietnam must eventually be based upon general elections supervised by a non-Indochinese supervisory organ.

6. Finally, the agreement that it was necessary to guarantee various civil and political liberties of the peoples of Indochina. (The Geneva powers, which did not agree upon the precise nature or details for implementing these guarantees, also differed in their interpretations of the terms they used in these very guarantees.)

[II]

The SEATO treaty was not a violation of the Geneva agreements; nor did it run counter to the "spirit of Geneva," as that expression has been defined above. The protocol to the treaty extended the protection of article 4, relating to the response of the signatories to direct and indirect aggression against treaty-area states, to Cambodia, Laos, and the "free territory under the jurisdiction of the State of Vietnam." However, the competence of the SEATO parties to act within the territories of the protocol states was contingent upon the invitation and consent of the governments of these states. A violation of the Geneva agreements through the buildup of SEATO forces could arise only if the protocol states consented to such a buildup. The governments of Cambodia and Laos, in any case, were permitted to take the steps necessary to ensure the effective defense of their territories. Presumably this included the right to call upon any individual state or collectivity of states, including SEATO, for military assistance. Moreover, Cambodia, Laos, and the SVN were not signatories of the SEATO treaty. Thus the Laos and Saigon governments had not formally entered the alliance, and the question whether the SEATO treaty conformed to the principles of the United Nations did not arise. (Cambodia and Laos had obligated themselves not to enter a military alliance not in conformity with the U.N. Charter.)

The SVN government, which had reserved to itself the right to take all steps necessary to defend the territories under its jurisdiction, assumed no specific obligations with respect to entering military alliances, other than the obligation—unilaterally assumed—not to resist procedures for the implementation of the cease-fire. The SVN did not join SEATO; however, it was gratuitously covered by the terms of the protocol. The question of a violation of the Vietnam cease-fire agreement could arise only if the SVN became a member, in law or fact, of the SEATO alliance or consented to SEATO military assistance. However, in view of the position of the SVN, and the United States, it was meaningless to speak of a violation of an agreement the SVN regarded as completely ineffective in denying it the right of self-defense.

Did the SEATO treaty look toward the perpetuation of the division of Vietnam? If it did, it could be said to violate the principle of respect for the unity of Vietnam, upon which all the great powers concurred. But the SEATO treaty was directed against aggression (in the view of the United States government, Communist aggression). It did not seek to elaborate political principles affecting the internal or foreign affairs of Vietnam. The SEATO treaty, at least on its face, did not preclude the unification of Vietnam by peaceful means—that is, by means that did not require resort to overt force, or subversion, or threats to the peace defined in article 4(2). If we read the treaty with the seven-point Anglo-American position paper, we must conclude that the policy of the two powers was to do nothing that would impair the ability of a non-Communist government to maintain itself south of the demarcation line for an indefinite period of time. In spite of British and French approval of the final declaration, the governments of both these states joined the United States and the other SEATO parties in extending SEATO protection to the SVN. This, coupled with the maintenance of formal diplomatic relations with the SVN, tended to perpetuate the partition of Vietnam, inasmuch as the SVN subsequently refused to normalize its relations with the DRVN.

But the SEATO treaty did not formally foster a division of Vietnam; reunification by peaceful means was not, and is not, precluded by its terms. If United States' Southeast Asia policy in July 1954 could be said to have rested, in principle, upon the proposition that Vietnam must not be unified under the aegis of a Communist-dominated government, then United States acceptance of the principle of respect for Vietnamese unity would have been qualified in a very important way—but I believe it is incorrect to say that United States policy was so qualified. Many officials appeared to take this position, but, as far as I can determine, it was not the policy of the President and his Secretary of State. It would be more correct to say that the United States was not prepared to accept the unification of Vietnam *by force*. In this sense, SEATO was the organizational form of that determination; and in this sense it was fully commensurate with Bedell Smith's declaration and the final declaration, insofar as the latter projected the peaceful unification of Vietnam.

[III]

An international conference on the settlement of the Laotian question met intermittently in Geneva from May 1961 to July 1962. This conference could be regarded as a reconvened Geneva Conference inasmuch as it functioned within the institutional framework established in 1954. Delegates of the Geneva powers, joined by representatives from the ISC supervisory powers (Canada, India, and Poland) and representatives of Burma and Thailand, sought to end the civil war in Laos, a war in which the United States and the Soviet Union had become indirectly involved in support of opposing factions. The course of the Laotian war was complicated by the fact that three parties more or less challenged the right of each other to rule Laos: the Pathet Lao, led by Prince Souphanouvong; the faction on the right, headed by Phoumi Nosavan and Prince Boun Oum; and the party of the center, led by Prince Souvanna Phouma. We need not describe the intricacies of the factional rivalries in Laos or the diplomacy of intervention of the third states; the history of the conflict has been dealt with elsewhere.[20] What must concern us here, however briefly, is the substance of the settlement embodied in the documents executed by the conference participants on 23 July 1962. If we are fully to appreciate the essential nature of the 1954 settlements, we should view them as partially supplemented by the 1962 agreements, certainly insofar as they affected Laos, and also to the extent that the relationships of third states were altered in consequence. I submit that we should look upon the Geneva agreements of 1954 and 1962 as—together—embodying settlements for Indo-

[20] A. J. Dommen, *Conflict in Laos* (New York: Praeger, 1964); S. N. Champassak, *Storm over Laos* (New York: Praeger, 1961); R. H. Fifield and C. H. Schaaf, *The Lower Mekong* (Princeton: Van Nostrand, 1963); A. M. Halpern and H. B. Fredman, *Communist Strategy in Laos* (Santa Monica: Rand Corp., 1960).

china. In speaking of the "spirit of Geneva" or "returning to the Geneva accords," in the sense of relying upon past settlements as precedents for the future, we must analyse the form and content of the 1962 documents to determine how they supplemented the earlier agreements and we must understand the ways in which they changed the power political configuration in Southeast Asia.

In June 1961, having been urged by the Geneva powers to meet separately, apart from the Geneva conference, the three princes who led the Laotian factions conferred in Zurich and agreed upon a political program. The substance of their agreement, as contained in a joint communiqué issued on 21 June 1961, was as follows:

(1) A provisional government of national union, comprising representatives of the three parties, would be formed. Its primary task would be to implement a policy of peace and neutrality, based upon the five principles of peaceful coexistence.

(2) The provisional government would, in respect of its internal policy, execute a cease-fire agreement, realize the unification of the armed forces of the three parties in a single National Army, guarantee democratic liberties to all people and insure the unity, neutrality, independence and sovereignty of Laos.

(3) With regard to external policy, the provisional government would respect all treaties and agreements signed in conformity with the interests of the Laotian people (including the 1954 Geneva Agreements). Further, it would refuse to permit all foreign interference in Laotian internal affairs; it would demand the withdrawal of all foreign troops; and it would refuse to participate in any military alliance and would, moreover, refuse to recognize the protection of any military alliance.[21]

After another year of negotiations between the three factions and the other Geneva powers, the Royal Government of Laos issued a "statement of neutrality" on 9 July 1962 in which Souphanouvong, Boun Oum, and Souvanna Phouma all concurred. Elements of the joint communiqué of 1961 were incorporated in it, and it explicitly declared that the Royal Government of Laos would

not enter into any military alliance or into any agreement, whether military or otherwise, which is inconsistent with the neutrality of the Kingdom of Laos; it will not allow the establishment of any foreign military base on Laotian territory, nor allow any country to use Laotian territory for military purposes or for the purposes of

[21] *International Conference on the Settlement of the Laotian Question*, Laos No. 1 (1962), Cmd. 1828 (London: Her Majesty's Stationery Office, 1962), pp. 13-15 (hereafter referred to as *Laos Conf.*).

interference in the internal affairs of other countries, nor recognize the protection of any alliance or military coalition, *including SEATO*.[22]

Representatives of the thirteen Geneva powers (not including Laos) agreed to a declaration on the neutrality of Laos on 23 July 1962. The signatories welcomed the "statement of neutrality" of the Royal Government and declared they would recognize and respect Laotian sovereignty. They appealed to "all other States" to respect the sovereignty, independence, neutrality, unity, and territorial integrity of Laos and to refrain from any action inconsistent with the principles of the declaration. The parties undertook six commitments.

1. They would commit no act that, directly or indirectly, might impair the sovereignty of Laos.

2. They would not resort to the use or threat of force or other measures that might impair the peace of Laos.

3. They would not attach political conditions to any assistance they might offer or that Laos might seek.

4. They would not bring Laos into a military alliance or any other agreement inconsistent with Laotian neutrality, and they would respect the wish of the Royal Government not to recognize the protection of any alliance or military coalition, including SEATO.

5. They would not use Laotian territory for intervening in the internal affairs of other countries, or use the territory of any country, including their own, for interfering in Laotian affairs.

6. They would not introduce foreign troops or military personnel into Laos, nor would they establish foreign military bases, strong points, or installations of any kind.

At this point we should note the respects in which the joint communiqué, the statement of neutrality, and the declaration on the neutrality of Laos were commensurate with the essential elements of consensus in the 1954 agreements. First, all parties agreed upon a cease-fire; in fact, the United States had successfully demanded a cessation of hostilities as a precondition of its participation in the conference. Second, the details of the cease-fire and its implementation by the Laotian factions were left to the Laotians and regarded by the conference participants as one of several "internal" problems they would not explicitly legislate. The thirteen powers could be said to have tacitly concurred in the technical military procedures through which a cease-fire would be realized. Third, the neutralization of Laos was agreed upon, in a fashion more explicit and less legally ambiguous than in the 1954 agreement. The commitment of the great powers and the RVN, the DRVN, and others to the principle

---

[22] *Laos Conf.*, p. 16 (emphasis added).

of Laotian neutrality was unequivocal. Fourth, the signatories undertook to consult jointly with the Royal Government of Laos and among themselves to consider measures they might take in the event of a violation or threat of violation of the sovereignty, independence, neutrality, unity, or territorial integrity of Laos. Finally, the conference achieved consensus upon the general principles of a settlement (i.e. the points enumerated in the preceding sentence).

In accepting the principle of the unity of Laos, the powers not only agreed to regard Laos as a unitary state in legal theory, they tacitly refused to apply the partition solution. And they did not mention a political settlement, regarding this as an "internal" matter. Obviously, it would be a mistake to ignore the extent to which Laotian politics affected the negotiations at Geneva. Nevertheless, the legal basis of the framework for a political settlement was left for the three princes to discuss in their talks in Zurich and Vientiane. The great-power patrons of the Laotian factions were very much the interested bystanders, and disagreements over political questions in part accounted for the fact that negotiations continued for another year after the issuance of the joint communiqué. A crucially important political aspect of the arrangement made by the three princes was the decision to permit representatives from each of the three parties in the provisional national union government to veto policies they did not approve.

The thirteen powers, together with Laos, agreed to the supervision of Laotian neutrality by the International Supervisory Commission for Laos, established by the 1954 agreement. Supervisory procedures and related regulations were embodied in a protocol to the declaration on the neutrality of Laos, which all conference participants duly signed. The protocol also contained unequivocal provisions prohibiting the introduction into Laos of arms, munitions, and war matériel, foreign regular and irregular troops, and all other military personnel (articles 4, 5, 6).[23] Three provisions, relating to the operation of the ISC in Laos, were of particular interest:

1. Foreign troops were to withdraw only along routes determined by the Royal Government in consultation with the ISC. Articles 2, 3, and 10 of the protocol were designed to ensure the commission's supervision, or at least observation, of all troop movements.

2. Article 9 stated:

The Commission shall, with the concurrence of the Royal Government of Laos, supervise and control the cease-fire in Laos.

---

[23] Article 6 contained the usual exception that arms, munitions, and war matériel could be imported in "such quantities . . . as the Royal Government of Laos may consider necessary for the national defense of Laos."

The Commission shall exercise these functions in full cooperation with the Royal Government of Laos and within the framework of the Cease-Fire Agreement or cease-fire arrangements made by the three political forces in Laos, or the Royal Government of Laos. It is understood that responsibility for the execution of the cease-fire shall rest with the three parties concerned and with the Royal Government of Laos after its formation.

As this article indicated, the ISC's duties would be determined to a great extent by the terms of the cease-fire the three Laotian factions worked out, not by the conference. The factions, in turn, would be responsible for implementing the cease-fire agreement they had formulated.

3. The costs of the ISC's operations were assessed against all the conference participants, according to the formula of article 18. This arrangement was a considerable improvement over article 21 of the Laotian agreement of 1954, according to which costs were to be shared equally by "the parties" (i.e. the French high command and the high commands of the PAVN and the fighting units of the Pathet Lao). Although informal financial arrangements were elaborated by the co-chairmen and the supervisory powers between 1954 and 1956, serious problems had arisen.[24]

The documents of the 1962 settlement, fully conformable to the "spirit of Geneva" in respect to the *military* aspects of the settlement, were more soundly based than the 1954 documents. The conference participants committed themselves, explicitly and unambiguously, to the terms of the declaration and the protocol, and this included the United States as well. Kennedy administration officials were unhappy with the regime for Laos, and particularly with the provisions for the Laotian government's nonrecognition of SEATO protection, but they finally came around to the view that, if there was to be a settlement at all, it would have to be based upon the kind of settlement that was eventually embodied in the documents. Furthermore, all the interested or "concerned" parties were at the conference and all were signatories of the declaration and the protocol: the great powers, the ISC supervisory powers, the two Vietnams, and three neighbors of Laos (Cambodia, Thailand, and Burma). The lengthy, often bitter negotiations between the three Laotian factions, which had resulted in the political agreements that provided the basis for the neutralization agreements of the larger conference, were

---

[24] *Third Interim Report of the International Commission for Supervision and Control in Laos*, Laos No. 1 (1957), Cmd. 314 (London: Her Majesty's Stationery Office, 1957), pp. 38-40; *Fourth Interim Report of the International Commission for Supervision and Control in Laos*, Laos No. 1 (1958), Cmd. 541 (London: Her Majesty's Stationery Office, 1958), pp. 23-24.

equally important. Thus all the parties that might be obligated in a settlement were present and in a position to consent to be obligated.

It is especially significant that the ISC for Laos was not endowed with new competence in the 1962 settlement. Because of its demonstrated impotence after July 1954, one might have expected a broadening of ISC powers or a clarification of its role, but, this was not done. At Geneva, the Communist delegations opposed a stronger or more "rationalized" ISC, and their views prevailed even in 1962.[25] Whether this was a "victory" at the expense of the United States and its allies will be argued for some time. Still, experience with international supervision under the auspices of the United Nations or supervision by other international commissions, might have impelled the delegations to realize that they should not be overly ambitious in their plans for a revitalized ISC for Laos.[26]

With respect to the political aspects of the settlement, there was a major difference between the achievements of the two conferences.[27] At the first conference an attempt was made to adumbrate the basic elements of a political settlement and to include guarantees of the democratic freedoms of the Indochinese peoples in the agreements. At the second conference, however, the declaration and protocol, for all practical purposes, were devoid of provisions that might effect an internal arrangement in Laos or obligate the Royal Government of Laos to perform certain actions for the benefit either of its citizens or the other two factions. Indeed, these matters were regarded *as* internal, to be settled by the Laotians themselves. The second Geneva Conference, in theory, was concerned only with the international aspects of the Laotian question. Although this formula might have been the only one according to which the conferees could have achieved a settlement, one must recognize that problems connected with a civil or internal war in which great powers have become involved are not exclusively (or inherently) "internal." This was particularly true of Laos, where the settlement was to be based upon neutralization, because this solution invariably requires arrangements that affect, if not directly interfere with, matters that have been traditionally regarded as strictly within the domestic jurisdiction of a state. In fact, it could even be argued that neutrality should be safeguarded by any "means that appear necessary in the circumstances of the case."[28]

---

[25] George Modelski, *The International Conference on the Settlement of the Laotian Question, 1961-1962* (Canberra: Australian National University, 1962), pp. 29-30. This is a short but excellent analysis of the conference's diplomacy.

[26] *Ibid.*, p. 34.

[27] The settlements were similar insofar as the conferees agreed upon the general principles of a settlement: respect for its sovereignty, independence, unity, and territorial integrity, and noninterference in the internal affairs of Laos.

[28] Modelski, *op. cit.*, p. 23. See also Modelski's discussion of the various alterna-

Nevertheless, the conference participants chose to adopt the fiction that they were not providing a regime that would affect internal Laotian affairs. The principle of neutrality and the neutralization procedures were defined as external matters; hence the declaration and protocol were largely devoted to elaborating the principle and procedures for such implementation. A political settlement and democratic or civil rights guarantees for Laotian citizens and parties were "internal," and the multilateral conference documents were silent on the general questions.

---

tive *kinds* of neutralization the delegations sought to achieve (pp. 25-28). See also C. E. Black *et al., Neutralization and World Politics* (Princeton: Princeton University Press, 1968).

Chapter 28

AN ACCOUNTING

[I]

Given the weaknesses of the French position in Indochina and the instability and division of opinion within the French government, it is difficult to envisage settlements substantially different from those that were agreed upon in Geneva in July 1954. This is all the more true because of Mendès-France's self-imposed time limit. It was not that the French Premier gave up anything he might have insisted upon under other circumstances—he proved to be a shrewd and hard bargainer—it was the fact that the DRVN delegation caused delays and the business of the conference did not begin in earnest until a week before the deadline. It was under the almost frantic conditions of this last week that the Geneva documents took their final form. In this final chapter we will assess the extent to which each state-participant in the conference could be said to have gained or lost something from the Geneva agreements. We will then conclude with a review of the weaknesses of the Geneva documents and the Geneva settlements.

[II]

To ascertain the "gains" and "losses" of each state-participant at the conference, one would have to know the policies of those states; and one would have to estimate, in a very qualitative fashion, the extent to which the settlements did or did not fulfill the posited policy aims of the various states. There are, of course, major difficulties in attempting this sort of analysis. In the first place, even now we cannot be absolutely certain of the Indochina policies of the Western powers in 1954, and we know even less about the aims of the C.P.R. and the Soviet Union at that time. Secondly, policies are not static, they undergo constant revision in response to the impact of events and personalities; hence the standard against which we seek to measure gains and losses is a shifting one. This was certainly true of events in Indochina during the period of this study: the goals of the governments' policymakers were continually revised, and in the case of France and the SVN, even the governments changed. Thirdly, there is no absolutely valid qualitative, much less quantitative, measure for the gains accruing from a sequence of events a particular state's policies may have affected or effected. An outcome that might have been regarded as beneficial in 1954 might be viewed as disadvantageous in 1960 or the year 2000.

In the commentary that follows we will restrict ourselves to an assessment of gains or losses from the point of view of an observer in late 1954 who had the information we now possess. We will discuss the relative success of different policies only in very general terms, and we will have to make some tentative but perhaps rather controversial assumptions about the nature of these policies—assumptions that must, of necessity, rest upon conjecture and incomplete evidence.

THE CHINESE PEOPLE'S REPUBLIC

Perhaps the Chinese gained most at the Geneva Conference. Even the C.P.R.'s mere presence at the conference was no mean achievement in view of the youthfulness of the Peking regime and the standing refusal of the United States and others to recognize its legitimacy. Not only was the C.P.R. ably represented by Chou En-lai and his staff, it was evident to all that the Premier played an important, even a crucial role in the negotiations. The C.P.R., in appearance as well as fact, was a great power.

Peace had been restored in Indochina without the intervention of the United States; indeed, the "neutralization" of Cambodia, Laos, and Vietnam and the presence of French training cadres in Laos seemed to provide an assurance that the United States could not become involved there for a time. Besides, peace was not unwelcome: the conflicts in Vietnam and Laos were not far distant from the major cities of southern China. Further, United States intervention—had the war gone on—might have called for defensive counterintervention by the C.P.R. Peace in Indochina—the kind of peace achieved at Geneva—secured the area on China's southern borders. Peking could continue to concentrate almost entirely upon problems of internal development and reconstruction. Also, the part played by Premier Chou at Geneva supported the image of the C.P.R. as a "peace-maker" in Asia, an image the Chinese leaders sought to cultivate in 1954. Even the settlement was ideal, for the C.P.R. incurred no formal, positive commitments; that is, the Chinese were obligated to do no more than consult with the other Geneva powers in the event violations or threats of violations were reported by the ISCs. The settlements had not been guaranteed; hence the C.P.R. shared no duties with the other powers to act collectively to preserve them.

Inasmuch as the Geneva agreements represented, at least for the foreseeable future, the end of French influence in Southeast Asia, after 1954 or 1955 the newly independent governments of Indochina

would undoubtedly be more amenable to closer relations with the
C.P.R. Moreover, a Communist insurgent force had won the right
to administer Tonkin and Annam south to about the 17th parallel.
The Vietminh had not been given control over all of Vietnam, but
this was no loss for the C.P.R. It is entirely possible that the Chinese
leaders were not kindly disposed to Ho Chi Minh's potential pan-
Indochinese aspirations, and they may not have wanted a strongly
nationalistic and united Vietnam on their southern frontier. But, this
is speculation. In any event, Peking had supported the Vietminh,
with material assistance and by diplomatic means; obeisance to
fraternal Socialist unity had been observed. If, as was more likely,
the Chinese desired a united and Communist Vietnam, but a Vietnam manageable by Peking, they could look forward to Ho's anticipated electoral success in 1956. Meanwhile they could direct their
diplomacy toward improved inter-Asian relations, aimed indirectly at
preventing United States interference. The C.P.R., therefore, would
profit from a temporary equilibrium in Indochina.

As for the "costs" of the settlements, the Vietminh and the Pathet
Lao may have been displeased because the C.P.R.'s compromises
could be said to have denied the insurgents some of the rewards due
them from their actual and anticipated victories in the colonial war.
But this setback was relatively slight and could be overcome by further economic assistance and ideological support. And the Pathet
Lao, although it was not accorded representation at the conference,
had been assigned two provinces for regroupment and might hope
eventually to exercise some influence upon the Royal Government.
It might be suggested that Peking did fail to link its acquiescence in
a settlement for Indochina with concessions from the West respecting
the status of Taiwan, entry into the U.N., the lifting of trade embargoes, and diplomatic recognition by the United States. Could
not this failure be termed a "cost" sustained by the Peking regime?
I think not—although we know little about Chinese expectations during the period under study. There is no evidence that at Geneva
Premier Chou En-lai sought to do more than very effectively demonstrate to the world China's role as a great power and the need for
consultations with the C.P.R. in the settlement of any East Asian
problem. While the Communist Chinese leaders may have been disappointed with the communiqué of the Berlin conference, and the fact
that they were not formally accorded a place as one of the "convening powers" of the Geneva conference, they probably did not expect
to secure significant concessions from the United States. This is not
to say that the C.P.R. did not regard American policy as a galling
insult, but merely that the Communist Chinese leaders, after their
initial irritation with the Berlin communiqué, probably did not ex-

pect the Geneva conference *per se* to effect a change in United States policy and a solution of the Taiwan problem. Geneva offered the Chinese the means for playing the role of a great power, whether or not the United States recognized the C.P.R. Thus, I think we must say that the C.P.R. delegations' participation, performance, and the achievements at Geneva constituted a "gain" of a very high order.

THE SOVIET UNION

Soviet leaders also could be pleased with the fact that a new Communist and nationalist Vietnamese regime had been established in Southeast Asia without intensification or internationalization of the Franco-Vietminh war—without, in other words, a confrontation with the United States. They too had supported the Vietminh and espoused its claims, although Soviet military assistance had been substantially less than that of the Chinese. Soviet support, however, could be—and was—represented as exemplary Socialist solidarity. If there were disagreements among the Chinese, Soviet, and DRVN policymakers before Geneva, and among their delegations at the conference, they were certainly much less evident than the disagreements of the Western powers. The Soviets, moreover, had sponsored the C.P.R.'s "debut"; and in one sense they were more interested in promoting improved Sino-Soviet relations than in supporting Vietminh aspirations at Geneva.

The Malenkov faction, in my opinion, welcomed the cease-fire in Indochina. A peripheral conflict that might be the occasion for a much larger war—even a catastrophic war—had been resolved. "Peaceful coexistence" was shown to be possible. Indeed, the international situation might even permit the diversion of Soviet resources to sectors of the economy other than defense.

The European theater was of much greater interest to the Soviets in 1954 and the defeat of the EDC treaty by France was a paramount policy aim at the time. That the Indochina debacle had removed many pro-EDC ministers from the political scene with the accession of Mendès-France to the post of Premier could be greeted only with enthusiasm in the Kremlin. And the disarray in the Western alliance must also have been comforting. The possibilities this offered for lessening United States influence in Europe were undoubtedly discussed as much as (if not more than) the Indochinese War. In fact, it is no exaggeration to say that the Soviet leaders regarded the Indochinese War as secondary to their European concerns and as a means for indirectly promoting their interests in Europe.

Vietminh demands for the control of most of Vietnam had not been satisfied—and it was Molotov, even more than Chou En-lai, who had made the concessions that placed their Vietnamese allies in a less advantageous position. We do not know to what extent the DRVN leaders were angered by Soviet policy, nor whether they had expected more sympathetic support from the C.P.R. and the Soviet Union or were persuaded that, under the circumstances, their great-power allies felt they had to compromise. Perhaps, because the DRVN was such a small, such a new state, the attitudes of the Vietminh leaders did not matter. But disenchantment with the Soviets could result in Vietminh reluctance to accept Soviet advice in arranging political affairs at some future time. Later, the lessened ability of the Soviets to influence Hanoi, either in absolute terms or relative to the C.P.R. may have been a by-product of disappointments the Vietminh felt at Geneva. In this sense, it was a "cost" incurred by the Soviet Union.

In addition to Molotov's agreement to consult with the other Geneva powers, the Soviet Foreign Minister had assumed the duties of co-chairman of the conference. This was largely a procedural task, however, with no obligation to enforce the provisions of the Geneva agreements or otherwise to act collectively to preserve the political equilibrium in Indochina.

India

Though not one of the Geneva powers, India was so directly interested in Indochina, and so directly involved in the Geneva Conference through the embassy of Krishna Menon, that a few brief comments about India's gains from the settlements are in order.

The cease-fire had brought peace to Indochina, the preeminent goal of India's East and Southeast Asia policy throughout 1954. Also, the settlements would ultimately result in the complete expulsion of the French colonial regimes, another result welcome to the New Delhi government, which was avowedly anti-colonial. Further, the entrance of the C.P.R. into the ranks of the great powers at Geneva was the occasion for improved Sino-Indian and Sino-Burmese relations, based upon the Five Principles of Peaceful Coexistence. Neither these principles nor the Geneva settlements, moreover, obligated the Indian government to act as a guarantor of Asian peace. Apart from the duties assumed in connection with staffing the ISCs, India would not be called upon to expend money or men for any state's defense other than her own. To the extent that states adhered to the Five Principles, there would be no need for commitments for collective security or collective defense in Asia; nor would the Geneva powers have to concern themselves with the implementation of the Geneva agreements. In 1954 the Indian government believed in the efficacy of appeals to the good will of the statesmen and diplomats of the world.

Through the mechanism of the supervisory regimes in Cambodia, Laos, and Vietnam, India obtained an institutional means for influencing events in Indochina in a way that supplemented the traditional diplomatic means. It was in India's interest to see that the Geneva agreements were implemented and that relations between China, India, and the states of Southeast Asia were improved. The Indian delegation on the ISCs could contribute to these policy aims by a broad interpretation of ISC competence, by remonstrating with the governments of Cambodia, Laos, and the two Vietnams, and by promoting a consensus among the delegations of the three supervisory powers whenever this was possible.

GREAT BRITAIN

For the British government, the greatest achievement of the Geneva Conference was the ending of a war that threatened to provoke open intervention by the United States and the C.P.R. and might ultimately lead to a thermonuclear holocaust. Eden's role in the elaboration of the settlements was crucial: he was the intermediary between the recalcitrant parties. He thought of himself as the "honest broker," seeking a middle ground upon which a cease-fire could be based. The Foreign Secretary, though no doubt motivated by the highest principles, also was motivated by practical political principles that could secure not only his political survival but his political future as the heir of Sir Winston Churchill. The Geneva Conference had shown that Eden was a peace-maker, and an independent peace-maker at that: British diplomacy prior to and during the conference was not dominated by the White House and the State Department. The Geneva negotiations had also proved that the British valued the Commonwealth and were responsive to Indian opinion. Moreover, Britain had not become associated with French colonialism in Indochina. A policy of "negotiations first," it was hoped, could achieve the cease-fire that would relieve the government of the agonizing decision on whether or not to intervene collectively in Indochina to prevent its control by a Communist insurgent movement—a movement, however, that was rather embarrassingly nationalist and anti-colonialist.

Negotiations would permit the Foreign Office to assess the sincerity of the Soviet regime's professed desire for peaceful coexistence more adequately—at least this was how the British policy of negotiations at Geneva was advertised to various U.S. officials in the spring of 1954. This rationale, in my view, was a fictitious or thinly disguised explanation of Britain's real reasons, which were based upon British national interests: the profound reluctance of the Churchill government to become involved in Indochina—for convincing economic and military reasons, and for reasons of domestic and Commonwealth politics as well. If Geneva were to fail, only then would the crucial decisions be made; but not until then. In the end, the conference eventuated in the cease-fire that brought Great Britain the benefits of a peaceful settlement.

There were certain costs, however. British policy antagonized both the French and the Americans, and, though the Western alliance seemed to be in fair condition by the year's end, it had been in a perilous state on several occasions earlier in 1954. And the personal antipathy that arose between Dulles and Eden would have untoward consequences during the Suez crisis of 1956.[1] The settlements, moreover, papered over the military weakness of France (some would say a French defeat): the DRVN, established in Hanoi, would govern Tonkin and northern Annam according to the same Communist principles that had motivated the Malayan insurgents against whom the British had been fighting for six years. However nonideological British foreign policy might be, this situation had to have been a subject of official concern. Indeed, this attitude was reflected in Eden's desire, in the early stages of the conference, to establish southern Vietnam, Laos, and Cambodia as "buffers" against "communist expansion." We see it again in the Anglo-American position paper of late June and in the agreement to establish and to join SEATO in September. It was hoped that the governments of newly independent Cambodia and Laos and the "administration" in southern Vietnam would evolve into stable, secure, and viable instruments of the popular will. If and when elections were held, the non-Communist governments might fare well in their contests with the Vietminh and the Pathet Lao.

The British, therefore, could look upon the Geneva settlements with a measure of satisfaction and relief, but no doubt this was tempered by a small but rather gritty measure of apprehension. The benefits of the cease-fire were readily appreciated in Great Britain, but there were sober warnings as well. The editors of the *Economist* declared in the 24 July 1954 issue:

> Relief is justifiable; relaxation is not. Already the Communist propaganda machine throughout the world has swung into action with the arguments that Geneva has shown that negotiation can solve all problems, that China and Russia have satisfied all demands for proof of their peaceful intent, and that the time has come to scrap all the free nations' plans for joint defence through the European Defense Community, Nato, or a South East Asian pact. . . .

[1] See Victor Bator, *Diplomatic Tragedy* (Dobbs Ferry, N.Y.: Oceana, 1965).

The Geneva agreement will encourage the already strong desire for relaxation among free nations. But, as on so many earlier occasions, it must be realized that this would be a one-sided relaxation.[2]

THE UNITED STATES

By the time the Geneva Conference ended, most Americans who were still concerned with events in Indochina were skeptical that the United States had gained anything from the settlements; nevertheless, there were some rather important benefits. The United States had not intervened in the Indochinese War, and hence there would be no war in a congressional election year. Moreover, the fiscally conservative principles the Eisenhower administration followed would not be violated. The New Look defense strategy could be implemented and the nation's conventional war capability, which must certainly have been expanded in the event of intervention, could be reduced. The United States had not decisively assisted the French, who in the eyes of many Asian leaders were waging a colonial war in Indochina. Hence United States policy could not as easily be pictured as imperialistic or colonialist by its critics.

But what could be termed the United States' losses were more evident in July 1954 than its benefits or gains. Even the more prudent policymakers (Dulles, Wilson, and the President) were obviously disquieted and not solely because the activists regarded the establishment of the DRVN in northern Vietnam as the greatest defeat for United States foreign policy since the "loss" of China. The Vietminh, having won a great victory at Dien Bien Phu, appeared to be well on its way to gaining other victories in the Red River delta when it agreed to a cease-fire. Although France must suffer the consequences of its military losses, the fact that French losses were gains for a Communist insurgent force meant that the United States' policy of "free world" containment of Communist expansion had at least symbolically failed in this instance. A state that would certainly ally itself closely with the C.P.R. and the Soviet Union had become established in Indochina. In Laos, the Pathet Lao would regroup in Phong Saly and Sam Neua; but there also—as in southern Vietnam, with the incipient conflicts between the government and the sects—the political situation was unstable. Administration officials could hardly be sanguine about the future of non-Communist governments in the

[2] *Econ.*, 24 July 1954, p. 260. One week later the editors were quite blunt in their assessment of what was accomplished at Geneva: "The agreements reached last week were not a victory either for the West, or for the spirit of reason, or for M. Mendès-France, or for Mr. Eden. They were the acknowledgement of a defeat." *Ibid.*, 31 July 1954, p. 342.

SVN and Laos. At best, the Geneva settlements put a stop to a war in which French weaknesses were all too evident. They had won a respite for the non-Communist governments of Indochina, and in time these governments might become viable non-Communist regimes, but in mid-1954 this was only a hope.

United States officials were also displeased with the "neutralization" provisions in the Vietnamese cease-fire agreement. These provisions, it was believed, denied the SVN the capacity to defend itself, but did not establish adequate control measures against the DRVN's importation of arms from the C.P.R. However, the official attitude of the SVN and the United States toward the settlements implied that, if necessary, military assistance would be provided. The protocol of the SEATO treaty established the apparatus by which United States assistance or intervention could be legally justified.

Another cost generated by the Indochina debacle was the strain upon the Atlantic Alliance during the Indochina crisis and the Geneva Conference. Yet one could hardly attribute any resulting disunity to the settlements *per se* inasmuch as most of the disagreements arose well before the conference ended (between the Berlin Conference and the Dulles trip to Paris on 13 July). By mid-July the policymakers of Britain, France, and the United States had reconciled their policies and, in general, knew the form the Indochina settlement would assume—although there appeared to be a last-minute misunderstanding over the decision of the Eisenhower administration not to associate the United States government with the final declaration. In any case, the EDC caused a much greater crisis and more permanent damage to the Western alliance than the Geneva settlements.

A final consideration is the success or failure of Dulles's policy of deterrence by threats of serious consequences in the event all of Vietnam or Indochina was communized. This was a *damage-limiting* policy, and in my view rather effective. Besides backing up the extraordinarily weak bargaining position of the French, it provided incentive for a settlement more acceptable to France and the West before the real battle for the delta began and before the security of the French expeditionary force became endangered.

Certainly not all the concessions made by the Soviet and Chinese ministers were attributable to American threats, but Dulles's policy, his attempt to line up allies for a Southeast Asia collective defense organization—and the evident American disinterest in the Geneva Conference—could have persuaded the Communist delegations that Dulles might prefer to have the conference end in a stalemate. In this eventuality, the Vietminh might have to face the armed forces of the United States, Great Britain, and other powers. Of course the Vietminh—and perhaps the Chinese and the Soviets—might regard this as unlikely, but it could not be dismissed out of hand; intervention would appear possible to the Communists. Hence Eden's threat to break off conversations in mid-June was implicitly underscored by the Dulles policy of "noising off," and the threat to break off negotiations had dramatic results. Especially in the last week of the conference, the Soviets may have been persuaded by that frequently uttered proposition: "If the Communists won't make peace with Mendès-France, they won't make peace with anyone." If the French Premier had resigned on 21 July, this would surely have meant the end of the conference, in turn opening the way for possible intervention.

Thus the Dulles' policy, reinforced by the comments and prophecies of Senator Knowland, Admiral Radford, Walter Robertson, and others, formed a backdrop for the Geneva negotiations. The reluctance of the United States to officiate at the demise of French interests in Southeast Asia made it appear that administration officials might be persuaded to withdraw from the conference and follow an independent, interventionist policy if the Communists were too intransigent and demanded all of Vietnam. In this sense, Western negotiations at Geneva pivoted on "the fulcrum of American power."[3]

FRANCE

France was the principal loser at Geneva. Cambodia, Laos, and Vietnam became independent and did not associate themselves in a French Union. Symbolically, Dien Bien Phu was a major defeat for French military units, which would be withdrawn from Cambodia and Vietnam, portending France's incapacity to influence the policies of the governments of her former colonies, at least for the immediate future. With the great cities of Hanoi and Haiphong to be handed over to the DRVN within three months after the settlement, the prospects for French commercial and financial interests were dim, not because the DRVN would precipitately expropriate French property but because most French investors and businessmen in Tonkin suspected they would do so—if not immediately, within a year or two. Perhaps Mendès-France could eventually establish a *modus vivendi* with both Vietnamese governments for future economic and cultural relations; then again, this might prove impossible. Ngo Dinh Diem and many other non-Communist nationalists in the SVN were anti-French and had already turned to the United States for financial and political support. In the north, China or the Soviet Union would very likely become the primary influence and source of assistance.

[3] *Ibid.*, 24 July 1954, p. 260. The phrase was applied to Eden's diplomacy at Geneva.

The ending of the bloodshed in Indochina, particularly since it was accomplished with skill and dignity by Mendès-France, Jean Chauvel, and their associates, was certainly a gain. The settlement as the French Premier had said, was "cruel," but it was nonetheless honorable—in the sense that it was accepted as honorable by most of the deputies and by the French public. With the ending of the war, there was no longer a need to call up the reserves or send more men to ensure the security of the expeditionary force. The French government could now turn to problems closer to the *métropole*: to European affairs in particular and to colonial problems it now had the resources and capability adequately to manage—such as the maintenance of order in Tunisia and Algeria!

THE SMALL STATES

The independence of Cambodia and Laos was recognized by all the major powers represented at Geneva—certainly a most important gain for the governments and peoples of these two states. Cambodia, moreover, was placed in an advantageous position and given the opportunity of becoming a truly sovereign, viable state, for all foreign armed forces would be withdrawn and all insurgents demobilized. Some French troops would remain in Laos, of course, but this was not unwelcome. All Vietminh troops in Laos, and French troops in excess of those permitted to remain, would be evacuated, but the Pathet Lao forces would not be demobilized. The latter would regroup and move to Phong Saly and Sam Neua, their very existence constituting a challenge to the sovereignty of the Royal Government of Laos.

Cambodia and Laos, both subject to various neutralization provisions, each unilaterally undertook to respect the terms that forbade importation of arms, establishment of foreign military bases, acceptance of foreign military personnel, and adherence to alliances not in conformity with the U.N. Charter. Yet both states could accept assistance for the defense of their territories, a major exception to their ostensibly neutral status. Cambodia's borders with Vietnam had not been definitively established, elections had been scheduled for 1955, and an ISC for Cambodia had been established (which would interfere in Cambodian internal affairs), but these were minor burdens in comparison with the advantages of independence and the recognition of that independence by the five great powers. The Royal Government of Laos was in a much less enviable position, mainly because the Pathet Lao had been assigned territories, which, in its continued possession, amounted to a *de facto* partition of Laos. Thus the Geneva settlement brought independence to Laos but not unity.

The Vietminh delegation played a leading role at the Geneva Conference, with the C.P.R. and the Soviet Union "running interference." Eventually, however, the French dealt directly with the Vietminh, such dealings being the key to the honorable cease-fire Mendès-France sought. Thus the DRVN delegation was accorded significant status at the conference in recognition of the strength and success of its army. The status of the DRVN was also somewhat enhanced by the shabby treatment accorded the SVN delegation. French troops would be withdrawn from the northern zone in due course and the Vietminh could complete its transformation from an insurgent force to administrators of an unquestionably sovereign socialist state. The purported neutralization of Vietnam favored the DRVN vis-à-vis the SVN even if the C.P.R. had not thereafter illegally provided the former with arms and munitions. (Neutralization favored the DRVN so long as the Saigon regime received no external assistance).

Vietnam had not been united under the DRVN in 1954. If Pham Van Dong's proposals of late May were any indication, the Vietminh leaders did not expect to achieve that goal immediately, but no doubt they expected to be awarded more territory, and probably they were disappointed with Molotov's proposal to have elections two years (rather than six months) after the cease-fire. They could have anticipated an electoral success in early 1955; they could be somewhat less certain of the outcome of elections in July 1956, simply because this was two years away. They may even have suspected that the two-year, temporary partition might become a permanent partition. Because the areas whose control was denied the DRVN offered easy access to Cambodia as well as Laos, a not insignificant geopolitical cost was incurred by the DRVN. Finally, we might ask how the Vietminh cadres in the south reacted to the concessions made by Pham Van Dong. Their disappointment—if any—could result in the diminished influence of the northern regime upon its friends in the south.

The SVN government could be grateful for two consequences of the Indochinese War: the support and assistance of the United States (although this was an indirect result of the conference) and Vietnam's complete independence (although it had not been determined who would govern the newly independent state). At the conference. Tran Van Do and his associates were virtually ignored by the French, and no one ever seriously considered their rather unrealistic proposals. The neutralization provisions of the cease-fire agreement did not favor the SVN, and the documents themselves did not even mention the SVN. It was implicit in the terms that were used that France spoke for the SVN as an adult might speak for a minor or a ward, and because the SVN's protests could have prevented a settlement by the French Premier's deadline, they were more or less politely but firmly ignored. Thus, although the Geneva Conference could not be said to have ended advantageously for the SVN, the cease-fire agreement gave Diem a valuable respite, at least two years, within which time his administration might become more secure and the SVN relatively stable. Apparently, however, this advantage was appreciated neither by the SVN nor the United States, both of which were initially pessimistic about the Diem regime's ability to survive.

[III]

Weaknesses of the Settlements

1. Although a number of rather explicit provisions purported to effect the neutralization of Indochina, there were no prohibitions upon the buildup of local forces. Theoretically, the governments of Cambodia, Laos, the SVN, and the DRVN could increase the strength of their armed forces without limit. Actually, there was a practical limitation in that weapons and munitions to equip larger forces would not be available if the Geneva powers adhered to the prohibitions of the cease-fire agreements. On the other hand, any of the Indochinese governments could undoubtedly find ways to augment its forces if it had a mind to do so; and weapons that had been damaged or had worn out during the hostilities could be replaced. Governments that had not participated in the Geneva Conference, and the Geneva participants that chose to ignore the terms of the final declaration and the cease-fire agreements, could supply the Indochinese governments with arms. Within a year, then, the latter could be in a position to wage a rather effective local war, a war in which the non-Indochinese states would find it difficult not to interfere.

Adherence to the prohibition against the importation of arms, munitions, and war matériel would maintain only a weak SVN army relative to the PAVN, particularly after the withdrawal of the French military units. This state of affairs, which could not have pleased Diem, may account for the Saigon government's fears that establishment of even the most informal contacts with the DRVN would put the latter in a position to exploit the SVN's weaker military capabilities.

2. The ISCs were not given the means or competence adequately to observe, let alone control and supervise, the introduction of arms, munitions, and military personnel across the land and sea frontiers of the Indochinese states. Although the cease-fire agreements purported to endow the ISCs with powers, not enough attention was paid to the practical difficulties their inspection teams might encounter—for example, difficulties of movement and communication,

resulting in part from a lack of cooperation or the inability of the governments to cooperate and in part from the rugged terrain and bad weather. Had there been a modicum of mutual confidence or a serious intent by the Geneva powers to abide by the terms of the agreements and declarations, the ISCs could have performed their duties adequately, even if not completely effectively. But the lack of good will among some of the states invited them to take advantage of omissions and ambiguities in the Geneva documents. The instability, actual or potential, that resulted from a long and bitter war induced the Indochinese governments to hedge their estimates of the forces and matériel required for internal security and self-defense, and sensitive about their newly won independence, they mistrusted the international commissions that operated within their borders. Eventually this mistrust was transformed into noncooperation and deliberately imposed restrictions upon ISC operations.

The cessation of hostilities in Laos increasingly took on the appearance of a temporary truce pending an expected renewal of conflict between Pathet Lao and Royal Government troops. In Vietnam, SVN and DRVN officials persuaded themselves there was only one Vietnam and that their governments must speak for the whole Vietnamese nation. For a time, Ho Chi Minh and his associates may have believed that elections in 1956 would result in a victory for the DRVN, yet he (and Diem) strengthened his armed forces in anticipation of a conflict between the two Vietnamese governments. Whether arms and munitions were clandestinely introduced into Laos and into the DRVN across the Chinese frontiers could not be proved with certainty until the late 1950s; presumably, however, such introduction had occurred. As for the SVN, the ISC for Vietnam was prevented from inspecting various airfields and dock areas where the introduction of weapons could have occurred—and is known to have occurred during the late 1950s and early 1960s. (One day, perhaps, we shall know exactly when the DRVN and the SVN began to import weapons and in what quantities.) In any event, the ISCs for Laos and Vietnam were incapable of keeping adequate account of the importation of arms and the movement of troops, ships, and aircraft.

3. The settlements did not eliminate the insecurity felt by the Laotian and Cambodian governments, and particularly by the SVN government. Under the circumstances, it would have been unrealistic to expect the great powers to attempt to provide a regime that would make the incumbent Indochinese governments secure. In the case of Vietnam, it would probably have been impossible to guarantee either the SVN or DRVN, for in theory there was only one Vietnam with two temporary administrations functioning within its borders. Although the British Foreign Office had been thinking in terms of

Locarno-type guarantees in June 1954, the reaction of its American ally precluded its pursuing this concept. It was doubtful, moreover, whether France, the C.P.R., or the Soviet Union would have agreed to guarantees; and without great-power guarantees the settlements were fragile, neither offering incentives for compliance nor imposing sanctions for noncompliance. In this situation, the new governments of Indochina would inevitably lack confidence and a sense of security.

It would be most difficult, if not impossible, to determine whether the governments of the "two Vietnams" were more authoritarian than they might have been under conditions of greater security. Certainly the Diem regime's fear of subversion was directly responsible for its attitude toward article 14(c) of the cease-fire agreement; that is, the provision that guaranteed civil liberties and forbade reprisals or discrimination against persons because of their activities during hostilities. Diem and his officials frequently cited threats of civil war, instigated by the sects, and subversion by Communists in extenuation of measures the ISC and the DRVN regarded as violations of 14(c).

4. The movement of 900,000 Vietnamese from the north to the south did not portend well for the stability of Vietnam. There were problems in resettling the northern refugees in the south, in a different cultural and religious milieu. There were, for example, the fears and antipathies of the refugees toward the DRVN regime, fears that reinforced Diem's sentiments and his determination neither to deal with the DRVN nor comply with provisions of the Geneva agreements that might result in his sharing or losing political authority south of the demarcation line.

The evacuation procedures adopted by the DRVN were cumbersome and dilatory, although this was due in part to a shortage of DRVN civil servants. Nevertheless, the movement south of so many thousands of people was an embarrassment to the Hanoi regime. If the allegations of the ISC's Canadian delegation were correct—that the DRVN deliberately hindered the movement of persons entitled to change their place of residence under article 14(d) of the Vietnamese cease-fire agreement—it was almost surely because the mass movements belied the DRVN's claim to speak for all the Vietnamese and because so many of the persons who emigrated were civil servants and skilled laborers whose services would be needed in the construction of a newly independent state in the north.

5. It was not really clear who among the parties or institutions created at Geneva had the right to interpret the various documents embodying the settlements for the three Indochinese states. This caused an acute problem in Laos, where the ISC explicitly claimed the right of interpretation and construction—a claim that was recognized by neither the Pathet Lao nor the Royal Government of Laos.

But at no time subsequent to the Laotian ISC's assertion of this claim did any of the Geneva powers attempt to clarify the question. According to the cease-fire agreements, if the joint commissions were "unable to reach an agreement on the interpretation of a provision or on the appraisal of a fact," the ISCs were to be informed and their recommendations were to be sent directly to the parties. What was not entirely clear, however, was the right of the ISCs to render an interpretation without the reference of a question to them from the joint commissions. And what would happen after the joint commissions ceased to function? Of course, amendments or additions to the agreements could be made by the *unanimous* vote of any of the ISCs, but where interpretation did not amount to an amendment, the problem remained. Moreover, in the case of interpretations that constituted amendments, the question of the right to interpret the agreements became intertwined with the more general and refractory question of the voting principle according to which the ISCs functioned, namely, the principle of unanimity.

6. The ISCs, ultimately, had no competence to sanction the parties; they could recommend procedures and solutions to disputes but they could not impose their will. In instances of violations or threats of violation the ISCs had no powers of enforcement, merely instructions to inform the members of the Geneva Conference of such instances. To the reader familiar with international organizations in the twentieth century, this incapacity of the ISCs to enforce decisions or recommendations was neither unique nor extraordinary. In the absence of guarantees by the Geneva powers, however, there were few incentives to comply, other than (*a*) the influence the supervisory powers chose to exert to see that the institutions for which they provided delegates were able to function adequately or (*b*) whatever unreliable and uneven pressure the Geneva powers might informally exert.[4] In the latter case, however, other factors (cold war competition, hegemonic tensions, promotion of political, economic, or ideological interests) would far outweigh the rationale by which one or several of the powers would remonstrate with their Indochinese ally to adhere to the terms of the agreements or adopt an ISC recommendation. Hence it was not surprising that the ISCs in Laos and Vietnam became increasingly impotent. Not only did these organizations lack control over the parties and events, the Geneva powers displayed a notable lack of interest in the supervisory regimes and

[4] The deterrent effect of the SEATO guarantees should not be discounted, but SEATO provided a rather special kind of "incentive," directed as it was (at least in the American view) against a Communist threat. Moreover, the organization was not established within the framework of the Geneva agreements.

an unwillingness to exert even a minimal amount of influence in an effort to back up the meager competence of the ISCs.

7. Because the supervisory capacity of the ISCs was so limited and their capacity to control the procedures requisite to the implementation of the settlements was nonexistent, the principle of unanimity did not have the obstructive effects we might expect. On matters of consequence, where the parties refused to implement a recommendation, the ISCs were merely empowered to inform the members of the Geneva Conference. In the event of disagreement among the delegates to the commissions, minority and majority reports were to be forwarded to the members, who would then be apprised of all views on a particular question. At the level on which the ISCs dealt with the parties, however, a nonunanimous recommendation would be respected disproportionately less, and as the Canadian view became increasingly identified with the non-Communist approach to Southeast Asia problems and the Polish view identified with the Communist outlook, the effectiveness of the ISCs lessened. In short, whatever may have been the hope of the Indian government, the ISCs had become cold war victims.

The principle of unanimity, though obviously not responsible for the ISCs' ineffectiveness, tended to reinforce the pre-conceived attitudes or perceptions of the antagonists toward future Vietnamese and Laotian disputes. The Geneva Conference of 1961-1962 did not change the rule of unanimity, and the competence of the Laotian ISC was not appreciably enlarged. Some would say these were wise decisions: adopting a majority principle would have been quixotic, and an illusory change at best. Nonetheless, the ISCs were limited even in their capacity to render persuasive recommendations. It is not surprising that the ISCs for Laos and Vietnam were institutional symbols of the inadequacy and incompleteness of the Geneva Conferences of 1954 and 1961–1962.

8. Demobilization, regroupment, disarmament, and withdrawal were often accomplished without adequate ISC supervision. This was due to the decision of the commanders of the insurgent forces (and their supporters) in each of the three states to comply with the procedural military terms of the cease-fire before the ISCs had established their headquarters and posted their inspection teams. But this unsupervised compliance fostered a sense of insecurity in the governments of Cambodia, Laos, and the SVN, which believed that arms had been hidden away, that insurgent cadres had demobilized without registering, and that many regular and irregular Vietminh troops had not completely withdrawn. Investigations were conducted by the Cambodian ISC but produced no evidence to support these

suspicions, which served to reassure the Royal Government of Cambodia to some extent. In Vietnam, however, the Diem government was never satisfied that all persons who bore allegiance to the Vietminh had either emigrated to the north or, if they remained in the south, had severed their connections with local clandestine anti-Diem organizations. Perhaps, under conditions of civil war against the sects, the SVN government could not be reassured; perhaps it simply chose to believe the worst.

9. Neither the co-chairmen nor the Geneva powers displayed great interest in the functioning of the ISCs after the conference adjourned in July 1954. The British Foreign Office's view of its Foreign Secretary's limited procedural duties as one of the co-chairmen was undoubtedly correct. Eden, in accepting the task of chairing the conference—along with Molotov—had assumed no obligations for his government beyond those of the other Geneva powers—in addition, of course, to the procedural duties of acting as a "clearing agent" for communications with the ISCs. After the time for the elections "scheduled" in the final declaration had passed, the British and Soviet governments expressed the hope that hostilities would not be renewed and that both the DRVN and the RVN would implement the political provisions of the agreement and the declaration. Beyond this, however, nothing was done to resolve the differences between the RVN and the DRVN. The other powers displayed no interest in promoting the political settlement projected for Vietnam in 1954, and cared even less about the supervisory regime of the ISCs. In fact, the co-chairmen asked the Vietnamese ISC to effect economies in its operation. The great powers might give lip service to the "Geneva Accords," but by 1956 it was clear, even to the Hanoi government, that they were prepared to see the ISCs drastically reduce, perhaps even cease, their operations. More importantly, they appeared willing to acquiesce in the existence of two Vietnams and two regimes in Laos while publicly professing that there was only one Vietnam and only one Laos.

10. The ISC delegations developed a strong sense of their institutional importance in the first year of their operations. This phenomenon, particularly noticeable in the Indian delegations, reflected the Indian government's view of the importance of the Geneva settlements. It also reflected another important element: ISC regimes allowed India to exercise a benign influence in Southeast Asia, pleasantly lacking in costly obligations. Coupled with the sense of mission of the ISC delegations was a tendency to exaggerate the legal status and competence of the ISCs relative to the governments of the Indochinese states. In view of the circumstances and the limited mandate of the ISCs, and ultimately the lack of support for the com-

missions by the great powers, the attitude of the ISCs might impress some observers as officious, as examples of "institutional sovereignty." We have seen that the Cambodia ISC intervened in Cambodian politics in 1954 and 1955; it is also noteworthy that the Vietnam ISC refused to deal with the RVN government on a basis acceptable to the latter. Although the RVN government had declared it was not bound by the terms of the cease-fire agreement, it offered to deal with the ISC on an *ad hoc* basis as an international peace commission, but the ISC chose the alternative of reduced contacts with the RVN and the latter's grudging cooperation rather than attempt to work on an *ad hoc* basis. The commission (particularly the Indian delegation) argued that it had been created by the fiat of the Geneva Conference and exercised supervisory jurisdiction, however limited, over the RVN, a theory the Saigon government would not accept. Such insistence by the ISC for Vietnam was unrealistic and unwise.

11. The factor of nonobligated parties was a most serious weakness of the Geneva settlement. The SVN was not an obligated party, nor for that matter was the United States—except to the extent that, by their unilateral declarations, they could be said to have assumed limited duties. Although there was no consensus among the Geneva powers on many matters, the language of the final declaration clearly implied a non-existent broad consensus.

12. Because the vagueness and ambiguity of the provisions of the settlement documents has already been considered, in some detail, we need not review them here. The weaknesses of the documents will be evident to the careful analyst who will undoubtedly raise the following questions for which, unfortunately, the Geneva agreements provided no answers—or, at most, inadequate answers.

a. What was the status of the Pathet Lao in Phong Saly and Sam Neua pursuant to article 14 of the Laotian cease-fire agreement? When would these provinces become subject to the jurisdiction and control of the Royal Laotian Government? What rights did that government have in Phong Saly and Sam Neua prior to a political settlement? What rights, if any, did the Pathet Lao have under the unilateral Laotian declaration according to which measures would be promulgated to provide for special representation of the former insurgents in the royal administration? What were the Pathet Lao's rights under article 19? Who were the "successors in function" of the signatories of the agreement under article 22? Under what circumstances would the security of Laos be threatened, thus permitting the Royal Government to invite the establishment of foreign military bases?

b. Under the Cambodian and Laotian cease-fire agreements and the unilateral declarations of the governments of these states, what quantity of war matériel could be imported for the "effective defence" of national territory? Did Cambodia and Laos retain an "inherent right of individual or collective self-defense" (article 51 of the U.N. Charter), and if so, was this right limited in any way?

c. What was the legal effect of article 14(*a*) of the Vietnam cease-fire agreement? Who were the successors in function of the signatories pursuant to article 27? Had the French government sought to bind the SVN by this expression? Was the high command of the army of the SVN bound by article 24?

d. When France, in its unilateral declaration, undertook to respect the independence and sovereignty of "Vietnam," and when, in paragraph 12 of the final declaration, the Geneva powers that assented thereto undertook a similar obligation, which government (or administration) of the theoretically unitary state of Vietnam was to be regarded as the bearer of Vietnamese sovereignty?

e. What did the draftsmen intend to achieve by the provisions in the final declaration pursuant to which the conference "took note" of other documents or events? In paragraphs 7 and 9, who were the "competent representative authorities" in the two zones of Vietnam? What was the meaning and legal effect of *each statement* in paragraph 7? (What are "fundamental freedoms"? What was the effect of the mandatory "shall permit," "shall be held"? How would elections ensure that sufficient progress had been made in the restoration of peace?) What was the effect, if any, of the title of the final declaration?

13. The settlement for Vietnam was perhaps most pernicious *if,* by the ostensible agreement of the heads of the delegations and the sweeping language of the final declaration, it led the Vietminh and the attentive publics of the world to believe that the military *and* political aspects of the settlement rested upon a consensus of the Geneva powers, a consensus, that—supposedly—had been effectively translated into the obligations the declaration and agreements purported to impose. If the Vietminh leaders believed that SVN objections and disavowals were worthless and that the United States government would support the performance of the political provisions of the settlement, and if they believed that the French government would deal only with the DRVN and see that the Vietnamese in the south did not prevent execution of the political agreements, then the Vietminh leaders had been misled. They failed to appreciate the incompleteness of the settlements, the unwillingness of even their Soviet and Chinese allies fully to support their aspirations, and France's inability to influence compliance or performance with the terms of the agreements and the declaration. If the Geneva agreements had generated great expectations among the Vietminh leaders, later events must produce disillusionment and bitterness. Indeed, it appears this happened after the French withdrew in April 1956, after July had passed with-

out all-Vietnamese elections, and after the co-chairmen and the Geneva powers served notice that they were unwilling to do anything more than *urge* compliance upon the SVN. It is my view that the Geneva agreements did not effect a political settlement. To the extent that it was believed they had accomplished this, disillusionment and disappointment would be profound.

Of course, the merits of the settlements should not be ignored or denigrated. Peace had been restored to Indochina, at least temporarily. Procedures for the regroupment and withdrawal of the hostile forces had been established. Independence from colonial rule for Cambodia, Laos, and divided Vietnam had been formally and collectively recognized.

The *basis* for a political settlement had been laid in three respects: a supervisory regime of international commissions was established; the neutrality of the three Indochinese states had been adumbrated; and the governments of the C.P.R., the Soviet Union, Britain, France, and India heralded the settlement as an instance of "peaceful co-existence." Only the future could determine whether these were positive factors and whether a political settlement that would be meaningful to the Vietnamese and Laotians could be achieved. Probably the crucial factor was the political settlement: if the intensity of the conflicts of interests between the great powers could be gradually lessened and if the nebulous principles of the *Panch Shila* were to find fulfillment in the liquidation of other disputes between East and West, the inadequate bases for Indochina's neutralization and the limitations upon the competence of the ISCs could be remedied either by *ad hoc* agreements or by reconvening the Geneva Conference. But these were rather big "ifs" in 1954.

The Geneva Conference was not to be the first thaw in the cold war. The noble sentiments of the unilateral declarations and the final declaration appear, in retrospect, to have been weaknesses rather than strengths: the elements of the settlement that were likely to produce disagreement were glossed over too easily. Perhaps this was the price of a cease-fire by the Mendès-France deadline of 20 July 1954; or perhaps it was simply the price of a cease-fire for Indochina.

Appendix

DOCUMENTS PERTAINING TO
THE SETTLEMENT OF
THE INDOCHINESE WAR[1]

DOCUMENT 1

Final Declaration of the Geneva Conference on the problem of restoring peace in Indo-China, in which the representatives of Cambodia, the Democratic Republic of Viet Nam, France, Laos, the People's Republic of China, the State of Viet Nam, the Union of Soviet Socialist Republics, the United Kingdom and the United States of America took part.

July 21, 1954

1. The Conference takes note of the agreements ending hostilities in Cambodia, Laos and Viet Nam and organising international control and the supervision of the execution of the provisions of these agreements.

2. The Conference expresses satisfaction at the ending of hostilities in Cambodia, Laos and Viet Nam; the Conference expresses its conviction that the execution of the provisions set out in the present declaration and in the agreements on the cessation of hostilities will permit Cambodia, Laos and Viet Nam henceforth to play their part, in full independence and sovereignty, in the peaceful community of nations.[2]

3. The Conference takes note of the declarations made by the Governments of Cambodia and of Laos of their intention to adopt measures permitting all citizens to take their place in the national community, in particular by participating in the next general elec-

---

[1] The documents collected in this Appendix are reprinted from Cmd. 9239. (The maps and annex to the agreement on the cessation of hostilities in Vietnam are omitted.) All footnotes are the author's.

[2] Paragraphs 1 and 2 refer to (*a*) chapter I, articles 3, 7-9; chapter II, articles 12-15; chapter III, articles 16-17; and chapter V, articles 23, 25-27 of the Agreement on the Cessation of Hostilities in Vietnam (referred to herein as Vietnam and reproduced as Document 4 below); (*b*) chapter IV; chapter V, articles 28-30; and chapter II, articles 5-6 of the Agreement on the Cessation of Hostilities in Cambodia (referred to herein as Cambodia and reproduced as Document 2 below); (*c*) chapter I, articles 3-4; chapter III, articles 12-13; chapter V, articles 18, 20-21; and chapter VI of the Agreement on the Cessation of Hostilities in Laos (referred to herein as Laos and reproduced as Document 3 below).

tions, which, in conformity with the constitution of each of these countries, shall take place in the course of the year 1955, by secret ballot and in conditions of respect for fundamental freedoms.[3]

4. The Conference takes note of the clauses in the agreement on the cessation of hostilities in Viet Nam prohibiting the introduction into Viet Nam of foreign troops and military personnel as well as of all kinds of arms and munitions. The Conference also takes note of the declarations made by the Governments of Cambodia and Laos of their resolution not to request foreign aid, whether in war material, in personnel or in instructors, except for the purpose of the effective defence of their territory and, in the case of Laos, to the extent defined by the agreements on the cessation of hostilities in Laos.

5. The Conference takes note of the clauses in the agreement on the cessation of hostilities in Viet Nam to the effect that no military base under the control of a foreign State may be established in the regrouping zones of the two parties, the latter having the obligation to see that the zones allotted to them shall not constitute part of any military alliance and shall not be utilised for the resumption of hostilities or in the service of an aggressive policy. The Conference also takes note of the declarations of the Governments of Cambodia and Laos to the effect that they will not join in any agreement with other States if this agreement includes the obligation to participate in a military alliance not in conformity with the principles of the Charter of the United Nations or, in the case of Laos, with the principles of the agreement on the cessation of hostilities in Laos or, so long as their security is not threatened, the obligation to establish bases on Cambodian or Laotian territory for the military forces of foreign Powers.[4]

6. The Conference recognises that the essential purpose of the agreement relating to Viet Nam is to settle military questions with a view to ending hostilities and that the military demarcation line is provisional and should not in any way be interpreted as constituting a political or territorial boundary. The Conference expresses its conviction that the execution of the provisions set out in the present declaration and in the agreement on the cessation of hostilities creates the necessary basis for the achievement in the near future of a political settlement in Viet Nam.

7. The Conference declares that, so far as Viet Nam is concerned, the settlement of political problems, effected on the basis of respect for the principles of independence, unity and territorial integrity,

[3] See Documents 5 and 6 (below) and Cambodia, articles 6, 8, 13; and Laos, articles 16-17.
[4] See Vietnam, chapter III, articles 18-19, and chapter VI, article 36; Documents 7-8 (below); Cambodia, articles 7 and 13; and Laos, chapter II, and chapter VI, article 27.

shall permit the Vietnamese people to enjoy the fundamental freedoms, guaranteed by democratic institutions established as a result of free general elections by secret ballot. In order to ensure that sufficient progress in the restoration of peace has been made, and that all the necessary conditions obtain for free expression of the national will, general elections shall be held in July 1956, under the supervision of an international commission composed of representatives of the Member States of the International Supervisory Commission, referred to in the agreement on the cessation of hostilities. Consultations will be held on this subject between the competent representative authorities of the two zones from July 20, 1955, onwards.[5]

8. The provisions of the agreements on the cessation of hostilities intended to ensure the protection of individuals and of property must be most strictly applied and must, in particular, allow everyone in Viet Nam to decide freely in which zone he wishes to live.[6]

9. The competent representative authorities of the Northern and Southern zones of Viet Nam, as well as the authorities of Laos and Cambodia, must not permit any individual or collective reprisals against persons who have collaborated in any way with one of the parties during the war, or against members of such persons' families.[7]

10. The Conference takes note of the declaration of the Government of the French Republic to the effect that it is ready to withdraw its troops from the territory of Cambodia, Laos and Viet Nam, at the request of the Governments concerned and within periods which shall be fixed by agreement between the parties except in the cases where, by agreement between the two parties, a certain number of French troops shall remain at specified points and for a specified time.[8]

11. The Conference takes note of the declaration of the French Government to the effect that for the settlement of all the problems connected with the re-establishment and consolidation of peace in Cambodia, Laos and Viet Nam, the French Government will proceed from the principle of respect for the independence and sovereignty, unity and territorial integrity of Cambodia, Laos and Viet Nam.[9]

12. In their relations with Cambodia, Laos and Viet Nam, each member of the Geneva Conference undertakes to respect the sovereignty, the independence, the unity and the territorial integrity of the above-mentioned States, and to refrain from any interference in their internal affairs.

[5] Vietnam, articles 1 and 14.
[6] Vietnam, articles 14 (c) and 14 (d) (and articles 9, 21, 36); Cambodia, articles 6 and 8; Laos, articles 14-16.
[7] Vietnam, article 14 (c); Cambodia, articles 5-6; Laos, articles 15.
[8] See Document 9 (below); Vietnam, articles 15-17; Cambodia, articles 4-6, 14; Laos, articles 4, 6, 8, 13, 19, 27-28.
[9] See Document 10 below.

13. The members of the Conference agree to consult one another on any question which may be referred to them by the International Supervisory Commission, in order to study such measures as may prove necessary to ensure that the agreements on the cessation of hostilities in Cambodia, Laos and Viet Nam are respected.[10]

DOCUMENT 2

Agreement on the Cessation of Hostilities in Cambodia

July 20, 1954

CHAPTER I

Principles and Conditions Governing Execution of the Cease-Fire

Article 1

As from twenty-third July, 1954, at 0800 hours (Peking mean time) complete cessation of all hostilities throughout Cambodia shall be ordered and enforced by the Commanders of the Armed Forces of the two parties for all troops and personnel of the land, naval and air forces under their control.

Article 2

In conformity with the principle of a simultaneous cease-fire throughout Indo-China, there shall be a simultaneous cessation of hostilities throughout Cambodia, in all the combat areas and for all the forces of the two parties.

To obviate any mistake or misunderstanding and to ensure that both the ending of hostilities and all other operations arising from cessation of hostilities are in fact simultaneous,

(a) due allowance being made for the time actually required for transmission of the cease-fire order down to the lowest échelons of the combatant forces of both sides, the two parties are agreed that the complete and simultaneous cease-fire throughout the territory of Cambodia shall become effective at 8 hours (local time) on August 7, 1954. It is agreed that Peking mean time shall be taken as local time.

(b) Each side shall comply strictly with the time-table jointly agreed upon between the parties for the execution of all operations connected with the cessation of hostilities.

[10] Vietnam, articles 40-43; Cambodia, articles 18-22; Laos, articles 21-36.

Article 3

All operations and movements connected with the execution of the cessation of hostilities must be carried out in a safe and orderly fashion.

(*a*) Within a number of days to be determined by the Commanders of both sides, after the cease-fire has been achieved, each party shall be responsible for removing and neutralising mines, booby traps, explosives and any other dangerous devices placed by it. Should it be impossible to complete removal and neutralisation before departure, the party concerned will mark the spot by placing visible signs. Sites thus cleared of mines and any other obstacles to the free movement of the personnel of the International Commission and the Joint Commission shall be notified to the latter by the local military Commanders.

(*b*) Any incidents that may arise between the forces of the two sides and may result from mistakes or misunderstandings shall be settled on the spot so as to restrict their scope.

(*c*) During the days immediately preceding the cease-fire each party undertakes not to engage in any large-scale operation between the time when the Agreement on the cessation of hostilities is signed at Geneva and the time when the cease-fire comes into effect.

Chapter II

Procedure for the Withdrawal of the Foreign Armed Forces and Foreign Military Personnel from the Territory of Cambodia

Article 4

1. The withdrawal outside the territory of Cambodia shall apply to—

(*a*) the armed forces and military combatant personnel of the French Union;

(*b*) the combatant formations of all types which have entered the territory of Cambodia from other countries or regions of the peninsula;

(*c*) all the foreign elements (or Cambodians not natives of Cambodia) in the military formations of any kind or holding supervisory functions in all political or military, administrative, economic, financial or social bodies, having worked in liaison with the Viet Nam military units.

2. The withdrawals of the forces and elements referred to in the foregoing paragraphs and their military supplies and materials must be completed within 90 days reckoning from the entry into force of the present Agreement.

3. The two parties shall guarantee that the withdrawals of all the forces will be effected in accordance with the purposes of the Agreement, and that they will not permit any hostile action or take any action likely to create difficulties for such withdrawals. They shall assist one another as far as possible.

4. While the withdrawals are proceeding, the two parties shall not permit any destruction or sabotage of public property or any attack on the life or property of the civilian population. They shall not permit any interference with the local civil administration.

5. The Joint Commission and the International Supervisory Commission shall supervise the execution of measures to ensure the safety of the forces during withdrawal.

6. The Joint Commission in Cambodia shall determine the detailed procedures for the withdrawals of the forces on the basis of the above-mentioned principles.

CHAPTER III

Other Questions

A.—THE KHMER ARMED FORCES, NATIVES OF CAMBODIA

Article 5

The two parties shall undertake that within thirty days after the cease-fire order has been proclaimed, the Khmer Resistance Forces shall be demobilised on the spot; simultaneously, the troops of the Royal Khmer Army shall abstain from taking any hostile action against the Khmer Resistance Forces.

Article 6

The situation of these nationals shall be decided in the light of the Declaration made by the Delegation of Cambodia at the Geneva Conference, reading as follows:—

"The Royal Government of Cambodia,

In the desire to ensure harmony and agreement among the peoples of the Kingdom,

Declares itself resolved to take the necessary measures to integrate all citizens, without discrimination, into the national community and to guarantee them the enjoyment of the rights and freedoms for which the Constitution of the Kingdom provides;

Affirms that all Cambodian citizens may freely participate as electors or candidates in general elections by secret ballot."

No reprisals shall be taken against the said nationals or their families, each national being entitled to the enjoyment, without any discrimination as compared with other nationals, of all constitutional guarantees concerning the protection of person and property and democratic freedoms.

Applicants therefor may be accepted for service in the Regular Army or local police formations if they satisfy the conditions required for current recruitment of the Army and Police Corps.

The same procedure shall apply to those persons who have returned to civilian life and who may apply for civilian employment on the same terms as other nationals.

B.—BAN ON THE INTRODUCTION OF FRESH TROOPS, MILITARY PERSONNEL, ARMAMENTS AND MUNITIONS. MILITARY BASES

Article 7

In accordance with the Declaration made by the Delegation of Cambodia at 2400 hours on July 20, 1954 at the Geneva Conference of Foreign Ministers:

"The Royal Government of Cambodia will not join in any agreement with other States if this agreement carries for Cambodia the obligation to enter into a military alliance not in conformity with the principles of the Charter of the United Nations, or, as long as its security is not threatened, the obligation to establish bases on Cambodian territory for the military forces of foreign Powers.

"During the period which will elapse between the date of the cessation of hostilities in Viet Nam and that of the final settlement of political problems in this country, the Royal Government of Cambodia will not solicit foreign aid in war material, personnel or instructors except for the purpose of the effective defence of the territory."

C.—CIVILIAN INTERNEES AND PRISONERS OF WAR.—BURIAL

Article 8

The liberation and repatriation of all civilian internees and prisoners of war detained by each of the two parties at the coming into force of the present Agreement shall be carried out under the following conditions:—

(*a*) All prisoners of war and civilian internees of whatever nationality, captured since the beginning of hostilities in Cambodia during military operations or in any other circumstances of war and in any part of the territory of Cambodia shall be liberated after the entry into force of the present Armistice Agreement.

(*b*) The term "civilian internees" is understood to mean all persons who, having in any way contributed to the political and armed struggle between the two parties have been arrested for that reason or kept in detention by either party during the period of hostilities.

(*c*) All foreign prisoners of war captured by either party shall be surrendered to the appropriate authorities of the other party, who shall give them all possible assistance in proceeding to the destination of their choice.

Article 9

After the entry into force of the present Agreement, if the place of burial is known and the existence of graves has been established, the Cambodian commander shall, within a specified period, authorise the exhumation and removal of the bodies of deceased military personnel of the other party, including the bodies of prisoners of war or personnel deceased and buried on Cambodian territory.

The Joint Commission shall fix the procedures by which this task is to be carried out and the time limit within which it must be completed.

Chapter IV

Joint Commission and International Commission for Supervision and Control in Cambodia

Article 10

Responsibility for the execution of the Agreement on the cessation of hostilities shall rest with the parties.

Article 11

An International Commission shall be responsible for control and supervision of the application of the provisions of the Agreement on the cessation of hostilities in Cambodia. It shall be composed of representatives of the following States: Canada, India and Poland. It shall be presided over by the representative of India. Its headquarters shall be at Phnom-Penh.

Article 12

The International Commission shall set up fixed and mobile inspection teams, composed of an equal number of officers appointed by each of the above-mentioned States.

The fixed teams shall be located at the following points: Phnom-Penh, Kompong-Cham, Kratié, Svay-Rieng, Kampot. These points of location may be altered at a later date by agreement between the Government of Cambodia and the International Commission.

The zones of action of the mobile teams shall be the regions bordering on the land and sea frontiers of Cambodia. The mobile teams shall have the right to move freely within the limits of their zones of action, and they shall receive from the local civil and military authorities all facilities they may require for the fulfilment of their tasks (provision of personnel, access to documents needed for supervision, summoning of witnesses needed for enquiries, security and freedom of movement of the inspection teams, &c.). They shall have at their disposal such modern means of transport, observation and communication as they may require.

Outside the zones of action defined above, the mobile teams may, with the agreement of the Cambodian Command, move about as required by the tasks assigned to them under the present Agreement.

Article 13

The International Commission shall be responsible for supervising the execution by the parties of the provisions of the present Agreement. For this purpose it shall fulfil the functions of control, observation, inspection and investigation connected with the implementation of the provisions of the Agreement on the cessation of hostilities, and shall in particular:

(a) control the withdrawal of foreign forces in accordance with the provisions of the Agreement on the cessation of hostilities and see that frontiers are respected;
(b) control the release of prisoners of war and civilian internees;
(c) supervise, at ports and airfields and along all the frontiers of Cambodia, the application of the Cambodian declaration concerning the introduction into Cambodia of military personnel and war materials on grounds of foreign assistance.

Article 14

A Joint Commission shall be set up to facilitate the implementation of the clauses relating to the withdrawal of foreign forces.

The Joint Commission may form joint groups the number of which shall be decided by mutual agreement between the parties.

The Joint Commission shall facilitate the implementation of the clauses of the Agreement on the cessation of hostilities relating to the simultaneous and general cease-fire in Cambodia for all regular and irregular armed forces of the two parties.

It shall assist the parties in the implementation of the said clauses; it shall ensure liaison between them for the purpose of preparing and carrying out plans for the implementation of the said clauses; it shall endeavour to settle any disputes between the parties arising out of the implementation of these clauses. The Joint Commission may send joint groups to follow the forces in their movements; such groups shall be disbanded once the withdrawal plans have been carried out.

Article 15

The Joint Commission shall be composed of an equal number of representatives of the Commands of the parties concerned.

Article 16

The International Commission shall, through the medium of the inspection teams mentioned above and as soon as possible, either on its own initiative or at the request of the Joint Commission or of one of the parties, undertake the necessary investigations both documentary and on the ground.

Article 17

The inspection teams shall transmit to the International Commission the results of their supervision, investigations and observations; furthermore, they shall draw up such special reports as they may consider necessary or as may be requested from them by the Commission. In the case of a disagreement within the teams, the findings of each member shall be transmitted to the Commission.

Article 18

If an inspection team is unable to settle an incident or considers that there is a violation or threat of a serious violation, the International Commission shall be informed; the Commission shall examine the reports and findings of the inspection teams and shall inform the parties of the measures to be taken for the settlement of the incident, ending of the violation or removal of the threat of violation.

Article 19

When the Joint Commission is unable to reach agreement on the interpretation of a provision or on the appraisal of a fact, the International Commission shall be informed of the disputed question. Its recommendations shall be sent directly to the parties and shall be notified to the Joint Commission.

Article 20

The recommendations of the International Commission shall be adopted by a majority vote, subject to the provisions of Article 21. If the votes are equally divided, the Chairman's vote shall be decisive.

The International Commission may make recommendations concerning amendments and additions which should be made to the provisions of the Agreement on the cessation of hostilities in Cambodia, in order to ensure more effective execution of the said Agreement. These recommendations shall be adopted unanimously.

Article 21

On questions concerning violations, or threats of violations, which might lead to a resumption of hostilities, and in particular,

(a) refusal by foreign armed forces to effect the movements provided for in the withdrawal plan,

(b) violation or threat of violation of the country's integrity by foreign armed forces,

the decisions of the International Commission must be unanimous.

Article 22

If one of the parties refuses to put a recommendation of the International Commission into effect, the parties concerned or the Commission itself shall inform the members of the Geneva Conference.

If the International Commission does not reach unanimity in the cases provided for in Article 21, it shall transmit a majority report and one or more minority reports to members of the Conference.

The International Commission shall inform the members of the Conference of all cases in which its work is being hindered.

Article 23

The International Commission shall be set up at the time of the cessation of hostilities in Indo-China in order that it may be able to perform the tasks prescribed in Article 13.

Article 24

The International Commission for Supervision and Control in Cambodia shall act in close co-operation with the International Commissions in Viet Nam and Laos.

The Secretaries-General of these three Commissions shall be responsible for co-ordinating their work and for relations between them.

Article 25

The International Commission for Supervision and Control in Cambodia may, after consultation with the International Commissions in Viet Nam and in Laos, and having regard to the development of the situation in Viet Nam and in Laos, progressively reduce its activities. Such a decision must be adopted unanimously.

CHAPTER V

Implementation

Article 26

The Commanders of the forces of the two parties shall ensure that persons under their respective commands who violate any of the provisions of the present Agreement are suitably punished.

Article 27

The present Agreement on the cessation of hostilities shall apply to all the armed forces of either party.

Article 28

The Commanders of the forces of the two parties shall afford full protection and all possible assistance and co-operation to the Joint Commission and to the International Commission and its inspection teams in the performance of their functions.

Article 29

The Joint Commission, composed of an equal number of representatives of the Commands of the two parties, shall assist the parties in the implementation of all the clauses of the Agreement on the cessation of hostilities, ensure liaison between the two parties, draw up plans for the implementation of the Agreement, and endeavour to settle any dispute arising out of the implementation of the said clauses and plans.

Article 30

The costs involved in the operation of the Joint Commission shall be shared equally between the two parties.

Article 31

The signatories of the present Agreement on the cessation of hostilities and their successors in their functions shall be responsible for the observance and enforcement of the terms and provisions thereof. The Commanders of the forces of the two parties shall, within their respective commands, take all steps and make all arrangements necessary to ensure full compliance with all the provisions of the present Agreement by all personnel under their command.

Article 32

The procedures laid down in the present Agreement shall, whenever necessary, be examined by the Commands of the two parties and, if necessary, defined more specifically by the Joint Commission.

Article 33

All the provisions of the present Agreement shall enter into force at 00 hours (Geneva time) on July 23, 1954.

Done at Geneva on July 20, 1954.

For the Commander-in-Chief of the Khmer National Armed Forces:

NHIEK TIOULONG,
General.

For the Commander-in-Chief of the Units of the Khmer Resistance Forces and for the Commander-in-Chief of the Vietnamese Military Units:

TA-QUANG-BUU,
Vice-Minister of National Defence
of the Democratic Republic of Viet Nam.

DOCUMENT 3

Agreement on the Cessation of Hostilities in Laos

July 20, 1954

CHAPTER I

Cease-Fire and Evacuation of Foreign Armed Forces and Foreign Military Personnel

Article 1

The Commanders of the armed forces of the parties in Laos shall order and enforce the complete cessation of all hostilities in Laos by all armed forces under their control, including all units and personnel of the ground, naval and air forces.

Article 2

In accordance with the principle of a simultaneous cease-fire throughout Indo-China the cessation of hostilities shall be simultaneous throughout the territory of Laos in all combat areas and for all forces of the two parties.

In order to prevent any mistake or misunderstanding and to ensure that both the cessation of hostilities and the disengagement and movements of the opposing forces are in fact simultaneous,

(*a*) Taking into account the time effectively required to transmit the cease-fire order down to the lowest échelons of the combatant forces on both sides, the two parties are agreed that the complete and simultaneous cease-fire throughout the territory of Laos shall become effective at 8 hours (local time) on August 6, 1954. It is agreed that Peking mean time shall be taken as local time.

(*b*) The Joint Commission for Laos shall draw up a schedule for the other operations resulting from the cessation of hostilities.

Article 3

All operations and movements entailed by the cessation of hostilities and re-groupings must proceed in a safe and orderly fashion.

(*a*) Within a number of days to be determined on the spot by the Joint Commission in Laos each party shall be responsible for removing and neutralising mines, booby traps, explosives and any other dangerous substance placed by it. In the event of its being impossible to complete the work of removal and neutralisation in time, the party concerned shall mark the spot by placing visible signs there.

(*b*) As regards the security of troops on the move following the lines of communication in accordance with the schedule previously drawn up by the Joint Armistice Commission in Laos, and the safety of the assembly areas, detailed measures shall be adopted in each case by the Joint Armistice Commission in Laos. In particular, while the forces of one party are withdrawing by a line of communication passing through the territory of the other party (roads or waterways) the forces of the latter party shall provisionally withdraw two kilometres on either side of such line of communication, but in such a manner as to avoid interfering with the movements of the civil population.

Article 4

The withdrawals and transfers of military forces, supplies and equipment shall be effected in accordance with the following principles:

(*a*) The withdrawals and transfers of the military forces, supplies and equipment of the two parties shall be completed within a period of 120 days from the day on which the present Agreement enters into force.

The two parties undertake to communicate their transfer plans to each other, for information, within 25 days of the entry into force of the present Agreement.

(*b*) The withdrawals of the Vietnamese People's Volunteers from Laos to Viet Nam shall be effected by provinces. The position of those volunteers who were settled in Laos before the hostilities shall form the subject of a special convention.

(*c*) The routes for the withdrawal of the forces of the French Union and Vietnamese People's Volunteers in Laos from Laotian territory shall be fixed on the spot by the Joint Commission.

(*d*) The two parties shall guarantee that the withdrawals and transfers of all forces will be effected in accordance with the purposes of this Agreement, and that they will not permit any hostile action or take action of any kind whatever which might hinder such withdrawals or transfers. The parties shall assist each other as far as possible.

(*e*) While the withdrawals and transfers of the forces are proceeding, the two parties shall not permit any destruction or sabotage of any public property or any attack on the life or property of the local civilian population.

(*f*) The Joint Commission and the International Commission shall supervise the implementation of measures to ensure the safety of the forces during withdrawal and transfer.

(*g*) The Joint Commission in Laos shall determine the detailed procedures for the withdrawals and transfers of the forces in accordance with the above-mentioned principles.

Article 5

During the days immediately preceding the cease-fire each party undertakes not to engage in any large-scale operation between the time when the Agreement on the cessation of hostilities is signed at Geneva and the time when the cease-fire comes into effect.

CHAPTER II

Prohibition of the Introduction of Fresh Troops, Military Personnel, Armaments and Munitions

Article 6

With effect from the proclamation of the cease-fire the introduction into Laos of any reinforcements of troops or military personnel from outside Laotian territory is prohibited.

Nevertheless, the French High Command may leave a specified number of French military personnel required for the training of the Laotian National Army in the territory of Laos; the strength of such personnel shall not exceed one thousand five hundred (1,500) officers and non-commissioned officers.

Article 7

Upon the entry into force of the present Agreement, the establishment of new military bases is prohibited throughout the territory of Laos.

Article 8

The High Command of the French forces shall maintain in the territory of Laos the personnel required for the maintenance of two French military establishments, the first at Seno and the second in the Mekong valley, either in the province of Vientiane or downstream from Vientiane.

The effectives maintained in these military establishments shall not exceed a total of three thousand five hundred (3,500) men.

Article 9

Upon the entry into force of the present Agreement and in accordance with the declaration made at the Geneva Conference by the Royal Government of Laos on July 20, 1954, the introduction into Laos of armaments, munitions and military equipment of all kinds is prohibited with the exception of a specified quantity of armaments in categories specified as necessary for the defence of Laos.

Article 10

The new armaments and military personnel permitted to enter Laos in accordance with the terms of Article 9 above shall enter Laos at the following points only: Luang-Prabang, Xieng-Khouang, Vientiane, Seno, Paksé, Savannakhet and Tchépone.

CHAPTER III

Disengagement of the Forces—Assembly Areas—
Concentration Areas

Article 11

The disengagement of the armed forces of both sides, including concentration of armed forces, movements to rejoin the provisional assembly areas allotted to one party and provisional withdrawal movements by the other party, shall be completed within a period not exceeding fifteen (15) days after the cease-fire.

Article 12

The Joint Commission in Laos shall fix the site and boundaries:—

of the five (5) provisional assembly areas for the reception of the Vietnamese People's Volunteer Forces,
of the five (5) provisional assembly areas for the reception of the French forces in Laos,
of the twelve (12) provisional assembly areas, one to each province, for the reception of the fighting units of "Pathet Lao."

The forces of the Laotian National Army shall remain *in situ* during the entire duration of the operations of disengagement and transfer of foreign forces and fighting units of "Pathet Lao."

Article 13

The foreign forces shall be transferred outside Laotian territory as follows:—

(1) FRENCH FORCES
The French forces shall be moved out of Laos by road (along routes laid down by the Joint Commission in Laos) and also by air and inland waterway;

(2) VIETNAMESE PEOPLE'S VOLUNTEER FORCES
These forces shall be moved out of Laos by land, along routes and in accordance with a schedule to be determined by the Joint Commission in Laos in accordance with the principle of simultaneous withdrawal of foreign forces.

Article 14

Pending a political settlement, the fighting units of "Pathet Lao," concentrated in the provisional assembly areas, shall move into the Provinces of Phongsaly and Sam-Neua, except for any military personnel who wish to be demobilised where they are. They shall be free to move between these two Provinces in a corridor along the frontier between Laos and Viet Nam bounded on the south by the Line Sop King, Na Mi, Sop Sang, Muong Son.
Concentration shall be completed within one hundred and twenty (120) days from the date of entry into force of the present Agreement.

Article 15

Each party undertakes to refrain from any reprisals or discrimination against persons or organisations for their activities during the hostilities and also undertakes to guarantee their democratic freedoms.

Chapter IV

Prisoners of War and Civilian Internees

Article 16

The liberation and repatriation of all prisoners of war and civilian internees detained by each of the two parties at the coming into force of the present Agreement shall be carried out under the following conditions:—

(a) All prisoners of war and civilian internees of Laotian and other nationalities captured since the beginning of hostilities in Laos, during military operations or in any other circumstances of war and in any part of the territory of Laos, shall be liberated within a period of thirty (30) days after the date when the cease-fire comes into effect.

(b) The term "civilian internees" is understood to mean all persons who, having in any way contributed to the political and armed strife between the two parties, have been arrested for that reason or kept in detention by either party during the period of hostilities.

(c) All foreign prisoners of war captured by either party shall be surrendered to the appropriate authorities of the other party, who shall give them all possible assistance in proceeding to the destination of their choice.

Chapter V

Miscellaneous

Article 17

The Commanders of the forces of the two parties shall ensure that persons under their respective commands who violate any of the provisions of the present Agreement are suitably punished.

Article 18

In cases in which the place of burial is known and the existence of graves has been established, the Commander of the forces of each party shall, within a specified period after the entry into force of the present Agreement, permit the graves service of the other party to enter that part of Laotian territory under his military control for the purpose of finding and removing the bodies of deceased military personnel of that party, including the bodies of deceased prisoners of war.

The Joint Commission shall fix the procedures by which this task is carried out and the time limits within which it must be completed. The Commander of the forces of each party shall communicate to the other all information in his possession as to the place of burial of military personnel of the other party.

Article 19

The present Agreement shall apply to all the armed forces of either party. The armed forces of each party shall respect the territory under the military control of the other party, and engage in no hostile act against the other party.

For the purpose of the present article the word "territory" includes territorial waters and air space.

Article 20

The Commanders of the forces of the two parties shall afford full protection and all possible assistance and co-operation to the Joint Commission and its joint groups and to the International Commission and its inspection teams in the performance of the functions and tasks assigned to them by the present Agreement.

Article 21

The costs involved in the operation of the Joint Commission and its joint groups and of the International Commission and its inspection teams shall be shared equally between the two parties.

Article 22

The signatories of the present Agreement and their successors in their functions shall be responsible for the observance and enforcement of the terms and provisions thereof. The Commanders of the forces of the two parties shall, within their respective commands, take all steps and make all arrangements necessary to ensure full compliance with all the provisions of the present Agreement by all military personnel under their command.

Article 23

The procedures laid down in the present Agreement shall, whenever necessary, be examined by the Commanders of the two parties and, if necessary, defined more specifically by the Joint Commission.

CHAPTER VI

Joint Commission and International Commission for Supervision and Control in Laos

Article 24

Responsibility for the execution of the Agreement on the cessation of hostilities shall rest with the parties.

Article 25

An International Commission shall be responsible for control and supervision of the application of the provisions of the Agreement on the cessation of hostilities in Laos. It shall be composed of representatives of the following States: Canada, India and Poland. It shall be presided over by the representative of India. Its headquarters shall be at Vientiane.

Article 26

The International Commission shall set up fixed and mobile inspection teams, composed of an equal number of officers appointed by each of the above-mentioned States.

The fixed teams shall be located at the following points: Paksé, Seno, Tchépone, Vientiane, Xieng-Khouang, Phongsaly, Sophao (province of Sam Neua). These points of location may, at a later date, be altered by agreement between the Government of Laos and the International Commission.

The zones of action of the mobile teams shall be the regions bordering the land frontiers of Laos. Within the limits of their zones of action, they shall have the right to move freely and shall receive from the local civil and military authorities all facilities they may require for the fulfilment of their tasks (provision of personnel, access to documents needed for supervision, summoning of witnesses needed for enquiries, security and freedom of movement of the inspection teams, &c. . . .). They shall have at their disposal such modern means of transport, observation and communication as they may require.

Outside the zones of action defined above, the mobile teams may, with the agreement of the Command of the party concerned, move about as required by the tasks assigned to them by the present Agreement.

Article 27

The International Commission shall be responsible for supervising the execution by the parties of the provisions of the present Agreement. For this purpose it shall fulfil the functions of control, observation, inspection and investigation connected with the implementation of the provisions of the Agreement on the cessation of hostilities, and shall in particular:—

(a) Control the withdrawal of foreign forces in accordance with the provisions of the Agreement on the cessation of hostilities and see that frontiers are respected;

(b) control the release of prisoners of war and civilian internees;

(c) supervise, at ports and airfields and along all the frontiers of Laos, the implementation of the provisions regulating the introduction into Laos of military personnel and war materials;

(d) supervise the implementation of the clauses of the Agreement on the cessation of hostilities relating to rotation of personnel and to supplies for French Union security forces maintained in Laos.

Article 28

A Joint Commission shall be set up to facilitate the implementation of the clauses relating to the withdrawal of foreign forces.

The Joint Commission shall form joint groups, the number of which shall be decided by mutual agreement between the parties.

The Joint Commission shall facilitate the implementation of the clauses of the Agreement on the cessation of hostilities relating to the simultaneous and general cease-fire in Laos for all regular and irregular armed forces of the two parties.

It shall assist the parties in the implementation of the said clauses; it shall ensure liaison between them for the purpose of preparing and carrying out plans for the implementation of the said clauses; it shall endeavour to settle any disputes between the parties arising out of the implementation of these clauses. The joint groups shall follow the forces in their movements and shall be disbanded once the withdrawal plans have been carried out.

Article 29

The Joint Commission and the joint groups shall be composed of an equal number of representatives of the Commands of the parties concerned.

Article 30

The International Commission shall, through the medium of the inspection teams mentioned above, and as soon as possible, either on its own initiative, or at the request of the Joint Commission, or of one of the parties, undertake the necessary investigations both documentary and on the ground.

Article 31

The inspection teams shall transmit to the International Commission the results of their supervision, investigations and observations; furthermore, they shall draw up such special reports as they may consider necessary or as may be requested from them by the Commission. In the case of a disagreement within the teams the findings of each member shall be transmitted to the Commission.

Article 32

If an inspection team is unable to settle an incident or considers that there is a violation or threat of a serious violation, the International Commission shall be informed; the latter shall examine the reports and findings of the inspection teams and shall inform the parties of the measures which should be taken for the settlement of the incident, ending of the violation or removal of the threat of violation.

Article 33

When the Joint Commission is unable to reach agreement on the interpretation of a provision or on the appraisal of a fact, the International Commission shall be informed of the disputed question. Its recommendations shall be sent directly to the parties and shall be notified to the Joint Commission.

Article 34

The recommendations of the International Commission shall be adopted by majority vote, subject to the provisions of Article 35. If the votes are equally divided, the chairman's vote shall be decisive.

The International Commission may make recommendations concerning amendments and additions which should be made to the provisions of the Agreement on the cessation of hostilities in Laos, in order to ensure more effective execution of the said Agreement. These recommendations shall be adopted unanimously.

Article 35

On questions concerning violations, or threats of violations, which might lead to a resumption of hostilities and, in particular,

(*a*) refusal by foreign armed forces to effect the movements provided for in the withdrawal plan,

(b) violation or threat of violation of the country's integrity, by foreign armed forces,

the decisions of the International Commission must be unanimous.

Article 36

If one of the parties refuses to put a recommendation of the International Commission into effect, the parties concerned or the Commission itself shall inform the members of the Geneva Conference.

If the International Commission does not reach unanimity in the cases provided for in Article 35, it shall transmit a majority report and one or more minority reports to the members of the Conference.

The International Commission shall inform the members of the Conference of all cases in which its work is being hindered.

Article 37

The International Commission shall be set up at the time of the cessation of hostilities in Indo-China in order that it may be able to fulfil the tasks prescribed in Article 27.

Article 38

The International Commission for Supervision and Control in Laos shall act in close co-operation with the International Commissions in Viet Nam and Cambodia.

The Secretaries-General of these three Commissions shall be responsible for co-ordinating their work and for relations between them.

Article 39

The International Commission for Supervision and Control in Laos may, after consultation with the International Commissions in Cambodia and Viet Nam, and having regard to the development of the situation in Cambodia and Viet Nam, progressively reduce its activities. Such a decision must be adopted unanimously.

CHAPTER VII

Article 40

All the provisions of the present Agreement, save paragraph (a) of Article 2, shall enter into force at 24 hours (Geneva time) on July 22, 1954.

Article 41

Done at Geneva (Switzerland) on July 20, 1954, at 24 hours, in the French language.

For the Commander-in-Chief of the forces of the French Union in Indo-China:

DELTEIL,

Général de Brigade

For the Commander-in-Chief of the fighting units of "Pathet-Lao" and for the Commander-in-Chief of the People's Army of Viet Nam:

TA-QUANG-BUU,

Vice-Minister of National Defence

of the Democratic Republic of Viet Nam.

DOCUMENT 4

Agreement on the Cessation of Hostilities in Viet Nam

July 20, 1954

CHAPTER I

Provisional Military Demarcation Line and Demilitarised Zone

Article 1

A provisional military demarcation line shall be fixed, on either side of which the forces of the two parties shall be regrouped after their withdrawal, the forces of the People's Army of Viet Nam to the north of the line and the forces of the French Union to the south.

The provisional military demarcation line is fixed as shown on the map attached.

It is also agreed that a demilitarised zone shall be established on either side of the demarcation line, to a width of not more than 5 kms. from it, to act as a buffer zone and avoid any incidents which might result in the resumption of hostilities.

Article 2

The period within which the movement of all forces of either party into its regrouping zone on either side of the provisional military demarcation line shall be completed shall not exceed three hundred (300) days from the date of the present Agreement's entry into force.

Article 3

When the provisional military demarcation line coincides with a waterway, the waters of such waterway shall be open to civil navigation by both parties wherever one bank is controlled by one party and the other bank by the other party. The Joint Commission shall establish rules of navigation for the stretch of waterway in question. The merchant shipping and other civilian craft of each party shall have unrestricted access to the land under its military control.

Article 4

The provisional military demarcation line between the two final regrouping zones is extended into the territorial waters by a line perpendicular to the general line of the coast.

All coastal islands north of this boundary shall be evacuated by the armed forces of the French Union, and all islands south of it shall be evacuated by the forces of the People's Army of Viet Nam.

Article 5

To avoid any incidents which might result in the resumption of hostilities, all military forces, supplies and equipment shall be withdrawn from the demilitarised zone within twenty-five (25) days of the present Agreement's entry into force.

Article 6

No person, military or civilian, shall be permitted to cross the provisional military demarcation line unless specifically authorised to do so by the Joint Commission.

Article 7

No person, military or civilian, shall be permitted to enter the demilitarised zone except persons concerned with the conduct of civil administration and relief and persons specifically authorised to enter by the Joint Commission.

Article 8

Civil administration and relief in the demilitarised zone on either side of the provisional military demarcation line shall be the responsibility of the Commanders-in-Chief of the two parties in their respective zones. The number of persons, military or civilian, from each side who are permitted to enter the demilitarised zone for the conduct of civil administration and relief shall be determined by the respective Commanders, but in no case shall the total number authorised by either side exceed at any one time a figure to be determined by the Trung Gia Military Commission or by the Joint Commission. The number of civil police and the arms to be carried by them shall be determined by the Joint Commission. No one else shall carry arms unless specifically authorised to do so by the Joint Commission.

Article 9

Nothing contained in this chapter shall be construed as limiting the complete freedom of movement, into, out of or within the demilitarised zone, of the Joint Commission, its joint groups, the International Commission to be set up as indicated below, its inspection teams and any other persons, supplies or equipment specifically authorised to enter the demilitarised zone by the Joint Commission. Freedom of movement shall be permitted across the territory under the military control of either side over any road or waterway which has to be taken between points within the demilitarised zone when such points are not connected by roads or waterways lying completely within the demilitarised zone.

CHAPTER II

Principles and procedure governing implementation of the present agreement

Article 10

The Commanders of the Forces on each side, on the one side the Commander-in-Chief of the French Union forces in Indo-China and on the other side the Commander-in-Chief of the People's Army of Viet Nam, shall order and enforce the complete cessation of all hostilities in Viet Nam by all armed forces under their control, including all units and personnel of the ground, naval and air forces.

Article 11

In accordance with the principle of a simultaneous cease-fire throughout Indo-China, the cessation of hostilities shall be simultaneous throughout all parts of Viet Nam, in all areas of hostilities and for all the forces of the two parties.

Taking into account the time effectively required to transmit the cease-fire order down to the lowest échelons of the combatant forces on both sides, the two parties are agreed that the cease-fire shall take effect completely and simultaneously for the different sectors of the country as follows:—

Northern Viet Nam at 8:00 a.m. (local time) on July 27, 1954.
Central Viet Nam at 8:00 a.m. (local time) on August 1, 1954.
Southern Viet Nam at 8:00 a.m. (local time) on August 11, 1954.

It is agreed that Peking mean time shall be taken as local time.

From such time as the cease-fire becomes effective in Northern Viet Nam, both parties undertake not to engage in any large-scale offensive action in any part of the Indo-Chinese theatre of operations and not to commit the air forces based on Northern Viet Nam outside that sector. The two parties also undertake to inform each other of their plans for movement from one regrouping zone to another within twenty-five (25) days of the present Agreement's entry into force.

Article 12

All the operations and movements entailed in the cessation hostilities and regrouping must proceed in a safe and orderly fashion:—

(*a*) Within a certain number of days after the cease-fire Agreement shall have become effective, the number to be determined on the spot by the Trung Gia Military Commission, each party shall be responsible for removing and neutralising mines (including river- and sea-mines), booby traps, explosives and any other dangerous substances placed by it. In the event of its being impossible to complete the work of removal and neutralisation in time, the party concerned shall mark the spot by placing visible signs there. All demolitions, mine fields, wire entanglements and other hazards to the free movement of the personnel of the Joint Commission and its joint groups, known to be present after the withdrawal of the military forces, shall be reported to the Joint Commission by the Commanders of the opposing forces;

(*b*) From the time of the cease-fire until regrouping is completed on either side of the demarcation line:—

(1) The forces of either party shall be provisionally withdrawn from the provisional assembly areas assigned to the other party.

(2) When one party's forces withdraw by a route (road, rail, waterway, sea route) which passes through the territory of the other party (see Article 24), the latter party's forces must provisionally withdraw three kilometres on each side of such route, but in such a manner as to avoid interfering with the movements of the civil population.

Article 13

From the time of the cease-fire until the completion of the movements from one regrouping zone into the other, civil and military transport aircraft shall follow air-corridors between the provisional assembly areas assigned to the French Union forces north of the demarcation line on the one hand and the Laotian frontier and the regrouping zone assigned to the French Union forces on the other hand.

The position of the air-corridors, their width, the safety route for single-engined military aircraft transferred to the south and the search and rescue procedure for aircraft in distress shall be determined on the spot by the Trung Gia Military Commission.

Article 14

Political and administrative measures in the two regrouping zones, on either side of the provisional military demarcation line:—

(*a*) Pending the general elections which will bring about the unification of Viet Nam, the conduct of civil administration in each regrouping zone shall be in the hands of the party whose forces are to be regrouped there in virtue of the present Agreement.

(*b*) Any territory controlled by one party which is transferred to the other party by the regrouping plan shall continue to be administered by the former party until such date as all the troops who are to be transferred have completely left that territory so as to free the zone assigned to the party in question. From then on, such territory shall be regarded as transferred to the other party, who shall assume responsibility for it.

Steps shall be taken to ensure that there is no break in the transfer of responsibilities. For this purpose, adequate notice shall be given by the withdrawing party to the other party, which shall make the necessary arrangements, in particular by sending administrative and police detachments to prepare for the assumption of administrative responsibility. The length of such notice shall be determined by the Trung Gia Military Commission. The transfer shall be effected in successive stages for the various territorial sectors.

The transfer of the civil administration of Hanoi and Haiphong to the authorities of the Democratic Republic of Viet Nam shall be completed within the respective time-limits laid down in Article 15 for military movements.

(*c*) Each party undertakes to refrain from any reprisals or discrimination against persons or organisations on account of their activities during the hostilities and to guarantee their democratic liberties.

(*d*) From the date of entry into force of the present Agreement until the movement of troops is completed, any civilians residing in a district controlled by one party who wish to go and live in the zone assigned to the other party shall be permitted and helped to do so by the authorities in that district.

Article 15

The disengagement of the combatants, and the withdrawals and transfers of military forces, equipment and supplies shall take place in accordance with the following principles:—

(*a*) The withdrawals and transfers of the military forces, equipment and supplies of the two parties shall be completed within three hundred (300) days, as laid down in Article 2 of the present Agreement;

(*b*) Within either territory successive withdrawals shall be made by sectors, portions of sectors or provinces. Transfers from one regrouping zone to another shall be made in successive monthly instalments proportionate to the number of troops to be transferred;

(*c*) The two parties shall undertake to carry out all troop withdrawals and transfers in accordance with the aims of the present Agreement, shall permit no hostile act and shall take no step whatsoever which might hamper such withdrawals and transfers. They shall assist one another as far as this is possible;

(*d*) The two parties shall permit no destruction or sabotage of any public property and no injury to the life and property of the civil population. They shall permit no interference in local civil administration;

(*e*) The Joint Commission and the International Commission shall ensure that steps are taken to safeguard the forces in the course of withdrawal and transfer;

(*f*) The Trung Gia Military Commission, and later the Joint Commission, shall determine by common agreement the exact procedure for the disengagement of the combatants and for troop withdrawals and transfers, on the basis of the principles mentioned above and within the framework laid down below:—

1. The disengagement of the combatants, including the concentration of the armed forces of all kinds and also each party's movements into the provisional assembly areas assigned to it and the other party's provisional withdrawal from it, shall be completed within a period not exceeding fifteen (15) days after the date when the cease-fire becomes effective.

The general delineation of the provisional assembly areas is set out in the maps annexed to the present Agreement.

In order to avoid any incidents, no troops shall be stationed less than 1,500 metres from the lines delimiting the provisional assembly areas.

During the period until the transfers are concluded, all the coastal islands west of the following lines shall be included in the Haiphong perimeter:

meridian of the southern point of Kebao Island,
northern coast of Ile Rousse (excluding the island), extended as
    far as the meridian of Campha-Mines,
meridian of Campha-Mines.

2. The withdrawals and transfers shall be effected in the following order and within the following periods (from the date of the entry into force of the present Agreement):—

Forces of the French Union

Hanoi perimeter	80 days
Haiduong perimeter	100 days
Haiphong perimeter	300 days

Forces of the People's Army of Viet Nam

Ham Tan and Xuyenmoc provisional assembly area	80 days
Central Viet Nam provisional assembly area—first instalment	80 days
Plaine des Joncs provisional assembly area	100 days
Central Viet Nam provisional assembly area—second instalment	100 days
Pointe Camau provisional assembly area	200 days
Central Viet Nam provisional assembly area—last instalment	300 days

Chapter III

Ban on the introduction of fresh troops, military personnel, arms and munitions. Military bases

Article 16

With effect from the date of entry into force of the present Agreement, the introduction into Viet Nam of any troop reinforcements and additional military personnel is prohibited.

It is understood, however, that the rotation of units and groups of personnel, the arrival in Viet Nam of individual personnel on a temporary duty basis and the return to Viet Nam of the individual personnel after short periods of leave or temporary duty outside Viet Nam shall be permitted under the conditions laid down below:—

(*a*) Rotation of units (defined in paragraph (*c*) of this Article) and groups of personnel shall not be permitted for French Union troops stationed north of the provisional military demarcation line laid down in Article 1 of the present Agreement during the withdrawal period provided for in Article 2.

However, under the heading of individual personnel not more than fifty (50) men, including officers, shall during any one month be permitted to enter that part of the country north of the provisional military demarcation line on a temporary duty basis or to return there after short periods of leave or temporary duty outside Viet Nam.

(*b*) "Rotation" is defined as the replacement of units or groups of personnel by other units of the same échelon or by personnel who are arriving in Viet Nam territory to do their overseas service there;

(*c*) The units rotated shall never be larger than a battalion—or the corresponding échelon for air and naval forces;

(*d*) Rotation shall be conducted on a man-for-man basis, provided, however, that in any one quarter neither party shall introduce more than fifteen thousand five hundred (15,500) members of its armed forces into Viet Nam under the rotation policy.

(*e*) Rotation units (defined in paragraph (*c*) of this Article) and groups of personnel, and the individual personnel mentioned in this Article, shall enter and leave Viet Nam only through the entry points enumerated in Article 20 below;

(*f*) Each party shall notify the Joint Commission and the International Commission at least two days in advance of any arrivals or departures of units, groups of personnel and individual personnel in or from Viet Nam. Reports on the arrivals or departures of units, groups of personnel and individual personnel in or from Viet Nam shall be submitted daily to the Joint Commission and the International Commission.

All the above-mentioned notifications and reports shall indicate the places and dates of arrival or departure and the number of persons arriving or departing;

(*g*) The International Commission, through its Inspection Teams, shall supervise and inspect the rotation of units and groups of personnel and the arrival and departure of individual personnel as authorised above, at the points of entry enumerated in Article 20 below.

Article 17

(*a*) With effect from the date of entry into force of the present Agreement, the introduction into Viet Nam of any reinforcements in the form of all types of arms, munitions and other war material, such as combat aircraft, naval craft, pieces of ordnance, jet engines and jet weapons and armoured vehicles, is prohibited.

(*b*) It is understood, however, that war material, arms and munitions which have been destroyed, damaged, worn out or used up after the cessation of hostilities may be replaced on the basis of piece-for-piece of the same type and with similar characteristics. Such replacements of war material, arms and ammunitions shall not be permitted for French Union troops stationed north of the provisional military demarcation line laid down in Article 1 of the present Agreement, during the withdrawal period provided for in Article 2.

Naval craft may perform transport operations between the regrouping zones.

(*c*) The war material, arms and munitions for replacement purposes provided for in paragraph (*b*) of this Article, shall be introduced into Viet Nam only through the points of entry enumerated in Article 20 below. War material, arms and munitions to be replaced shall be shipped from Viet Nam only through the points of entry enumerated in Article 20 below.

(*d*) Apart from the replacements permitted within the limits laid down in paragraph (*b*) of this Article, the introduction of war material, arms and munitions of all types in the form of unassembled parts for subsequent assembly is prohibited.

(*e*) Each party shall notify the Joint Commission and the International Commission at least two days in advance of any arrivals or departures which may take place of war material, arms and munitions of all types.

In order to justify the requests for the introduction into Viet Nam of arms, munitions and other war material (as defined in paragraph (*a*) of this Article) for replacement purposes, a report concerning each incoming shipment shall be submitted to the Joint Commission and the International Commission. Such reports shall indicate the use made of the items so replaced.

(*f*) The International Commission, through its Inspection Teams, shall supervise and inspect the replacements permitted in the circumstances laid down in this Article, at the points of entry enumerated in Article 20 below.

Article 18

With effect from the date of entry into force of the present Agreement, the establishment of new military bases is prohibited throughout Viet Nam territory.

Article 19

With effect from the date of entry into force of the present Agreement, no military base under the control of a foreign State may be established in the re-grouping zone of either party; the two parties shall ensure that the zones assigned to them do not adhere to any military alliance and are not used for the resumption of hostilities or to further an aggressive policy.

Article 20

The points of entry into Viet Nam for rotation personnel and replacements of material are fixed as follows:—

— Zones to the north of the provisional military demarcation line: Laokay, Langson, Tien-Yen, Haiphong, Vinh, Dong-Hoi, Muong-Sen;
— Zone to the south of the provisional military demarcation line: Tourane, Quinhon, Nhatrang, Bangoi, Saigon, Cap St. Jacques, Tanchau.

CHAPTER IV

Prisoners of War and Civilian Internees

Article 21

The liberation and repatriation of all prisoners of war and civilian internees detained by each of the two parties at the coming into force of the present Agreement shall be carried out under the following conditions:—

(a) All prisoners of war and civilian internees of Viet Nam, French and other nationalities captured since the beginning of hostilities in Viet Nam during military operations or in any other circumstances of war and in any part of the territory of Viet Nam shall be liberated within a period of thirty (30) days after the date when the cease-fire becomes effective in each theatre.

(b) The term "civilian internees" is understood to mean all persons who, having in any way contributed to the political and armed struggle between the two parties, have been arrested for that reason and have been kept in detention by either party during the period of hostilities.

(c) All prisoners of war and civilian internees held by either party shall be surrendered to the appropriate authorities of the other party, who shall give them all possible assistance in proceeding to their country of origin, place of habitual residence or the zone of their choice.

CHAPTER V

Miscellaneous

Article 22

The Commanders of the Forces of the two parties shall ensure that persons under their respective commands who violate any of the provisions of the present Agreement are suitably punished.

Article 23

In cases in which the place of burial is known and the existence of graves has been established, the Commander of the Forces of either party shall, within a specific period after the entry into force of the Armistice Agreement, permit the graves service personnel of the other party to enter the part of Viet Nam territory under their military control for the purpose of finding and removing the bodies of deceased military personnel of that party, including the bodies of deceased prisoners of war. The Joint Commission shall determine the procedures and the time limit for the performance of this task. The Commanders of the Forces of the two parties shall communicate to each other all information in their possession as to the place of burial of military personnel of the other party.

Article 24

The present Agreement shall apply to all the armed forces of either party. The armed forces of each party shall respect the demilitarised zone and the territory under the military control of the other party, and shall commit no act and undertake no operation against the other party and shall not engage in blockade of any kind in Viet Nam.

For the purposes of the present Article, the word "territory" includes territorial waters and air space.

Article 25

The Commanders of the Forces of the two parties shall afford full protection and all possible assistance and co-operation to the Joint Commission and its joint groups and to the International Commission and its inspection teams in the performance of the functions and tasks assigned to them by the present Agreement.

Article 26

The costs involved in the operations of the Joint Commission and joint groups and of the International Commission and its Inspection Teams shall be shared equally between the two parties.

Article 27

The signatories of the present Agreement and their successors in their functions shall be responsible for ensuring the observance and enforcement of the terms and provisions thereof. The Commanders of the Forces of the two parties shall, within their respective commands, take all steps and make all arrangements necessary to ensure full compliance with all the provisions of the present Agreement by all elements and military personnel under their command.

The procedures laid down in the present Agreement shall, whenever necessary, be studied by the Commanders of the two parties and, if necessary, defined more specifically by the Joint Commission.

CHAPTER VI

Joint Commission and International Commission for Supervision and Control in Viet Nam

Article 28

Responsibility for the execution of the agreement on the cessation of hostilities shall rest with the parties.

Article 29

An International Commission shall ensure the control and supervision of this execution.

Article 30

In order to facilitate, under the conditions shown below, the execution of provisions concerning joint actions by the two parties, a Joint Commission shall be set up in Viet Nam.

Article 31

The Joint Commission shall be composed of an equal number of representatives of the Commanders of the two parties.

Article 32

The Presidents of the delegations to the Joint Commission shall hold the rank of General.

The Joint Commission shall set up joint groups, the number of which shall be determined by mutual agreement between the parties. The joint groups shall be composed of an equal number of officers from both parties. Their location on the demarcation line between the re-grouping zones shall be determined by the parties whilst taking into account the powers of the Joint Commission.

Article 33

The Joint Commission shall ensure the execution of the following provisions of the Agreement on the cessation of hostilities:—

(*a*) A simultaneous and general cease-fire in Viet Nam for all regular and irregular armed forces of the two parties.

(*b*) A re-groupment of the armed forces of the two parties.

(*c*) Observance of the demarcation lines between the re-grouping zones and of the demilitarised sectors.

Within the limits of its competence it shall help the parties to execute the said provisions, shall ensure liaision between them for the purpose of preparing and carrying out plans for the application of these provisions, and shall endeavour to solve such disputed questions as may arise between the parties in the course of executing these provisions.

Article 34

An International Commission shall be set up for the control and supervision over the application of the provisions of the agreement on the cessation of hostilities in Viet Nam. It shall be composed of representatives of the following States: Canada, India and Poland.

It shall be presided over by the Representative of India.

Article 35

The International Commission shall set up fixed and mobile inspection teams, composed of an equal number of officers appointed by each of the above-mentioned States. The mixed teams shall be located at the following points: Laokay, Langson, Tien-Yen, Haiphong, Vinh, Dong-Hoi, Muong-Sen, Tourane, Quinhon, Nhatrang, Bangoi, Saigon, Cap St. Jacques, Tranchau. These points of location may, at a later date, be altered at the request of the Joint Commission, or of one of the parties, or of the International Commission itself, by agreement between the International Commission and the command of the party concerned. The zones of action of the mobile teams shall be the regions bordering the land and sea frontiers of Viet Nam, the demarcation lines between the re-grouping zones and the demilitarised zones. Within the limits of these zones they shall have the right to move freely and shall receive from the local civil and military authorities all facilities they may require for the fulfilment of their tasks (provision of personnel, placing at their disposal documents needed for supervision, summoning witnesses necessary for holding enquiries, ensuring the security and freedom of movement of the inspection teams, &c. . . . .). They shall have at their disposal such modern means of transport, observation and communication as they may require. Beyond the zones of action as defined above, the mobile teams may, by agreement with the command of the party concerned, carry out other movements within the limits of the tasks given them by the present agreement.

Article 36

The International Commission shall be responsible for supervising the proper execution by the parties of the provisions of the agreement. For this purpose it shall fulfil the tasks of control, observation, inspection and investigation connected with the application of the provisions of the agreement on the cessation of hostilities, and it shall in particular:—

(*a*) Control the movement of the armed forces of the two parties, effected within the framework of the regroupment plan.

(*b*) Supervise the demarcation lines between the regrouping areas, and also the demilitarised zones.

(*c*) Control the operations of releasing prisoners of war and civilian internees.

(*d*) Supervise at ports and airfields as well as along all frontiers of Viet Nam the execution of the provisions of the agreement on the cessation of hostilities, regulating the introduction into the country of armed forces, military personnel and of all kinds of arms, munitions, and war material.

Article 37

The International Commission shall, through the medium of the inspection teams mentioned above, and as soon as possible either on its own initiative, or at the request of the Joint Commission, or of one of the parties, undertake the necessary investigations both documentary and on the ground.

Article 38

The inspection teams shall submit to the International Commission the results of their supervision, their investigation and their observations, furthermore they shall draw up such special reports as they may consider necessary or as may be requested from them by the Commission. In the case of a disagreement within the teams, the conclusions of each member shall be submitted to the Commission.

Article 39

If any one inspection team is unable to settle an incident or considers that there is a violation or a threat of a serious violation, the International Commission shall be informed; the latter shall study the reports and the conclusions of the inspection teams and shall inform the parties of the measures which should be taken for the settlement of the incident, ending of the violation or removal of the threat of violation.

Article 40

When the Joint Commission is unable to reach an agreement on the interpretation to be given to some provision or on the appraisal of a fact, the International Commission shall be informed of the disputed question. Its recommendations shall be sent directly to the parties and shall be notified to the Joint Commission.

Article 41

The recommendations of the International Commission shall be adopted by majority vote, subject to the provisions contained in Article 42. If the votes are divided, the chairman's vote shall be decisive.

The International Commission may formulate recommendations concerning amendments and additions which should be made to the provisions of the agreement on the cessation of hostilities in Viet Nam, in order to ensure a more effective execution of that agreement. These recommendations shall be adopted unanimously.

Article 42

When dealing with questions concerning violations, or threats of violations, which might lead to a resumption of hostilities, namely:—

(*a*) Refusal by the armed forces of one party to effect the movements provided for in the regroupment plan;

(*b*) Violation by the armed forces of one of the parties of the regrouping zones, territorial waters, or air space of the other party;

the decisions of the International Commission must be unanimous.

Article 43

If one of the parties refuses to put into effect a recommendation of the International Commission, the parties concerned or the Commission itself shall inform the members of the Geneva Conference.

If the International Commission does not reach unanimity in the cases provided for in Article 42, it shall submit a majority report and one or more minority reports to the members of the Conference.

The International Commission shall inform the members of the Conference in all cases where its activity is being hindered.

Article 44

The International Commission shall be set up at the time of the cessation of hostilities in Indo-China in order that it should be able to fulfil the tasks provided for in Article 36.

Article 45

The International Commission for Supervision and Control in Viet Nam shall act in close co-operation with the International Commissions for Supervision and Control in Cambodia and Laos.

The Secretaries-General of these three Commissions shall be responsible for co-ordinating their work and for relations between them.

Article 46

The International Commission for Supervision and Control in Viet Nam may, after consultation with the International Commissions for Supervision and Control in Cambodia and Laos, and having regard to the development of the situation in Cambodia and Laos, progressively reduce its activities. Such a decision must be adopted unanimously.

Article 47

All the provisions of the present Agreement, save the second sub-paragraph of Article 11, shall enter into force at 2400 hours (Geneva time) on July 22, 1954.

Done in Geneva at 2400 hours on the 20th of July, 1954, in French and in Vietnamese, both texts being equally authentic.

For the Commander-in-Chief of the French Union Forces in Indo-China:

DELTIEL,
Brigadier-General.

For the Commander-in-Chief of the People's Army of Viet Nam:

TA-QUANG-BUU,
Vice-Minister of National Defence
of the Democratic Republic of Viet Nam.

DOCUMENT 5

Declaration by the Royal Government of Cambodia[11]

July 21, 1954

The Royal Government of Cambodia,

In the desire to ensure harmony and agreement among the peoples of the Kingdom,

Declares itself resolved to take the necessary measures to integrate all citizens, without discrimination, into the national community and to guarantee them the enjoyment of the rights and freedoms for which the Constitution of the Kingdom provides;

Affirms that all Cambodian citizens may freely participate as electors or candidates in general elections by secret ballot.

DOCUMENT 6

Declaration by the Royal Government of Laos

July 21, 1954

The Royal Government of Laos,

In the desire to ensure harmony and agreement among the peoples of the Kingdom,

Declares itself resolved to take the necessary measures to integrate all citizens, without discrimination, into the national community and to guarantee them the enjoyment of the rights and freedoms for which the Constitution of the Kingdom provides;

Affirms that all Laotian citizens may freely participate as electors or candidates in general elections by secret ballot;

Announces, furthermore, that it will promulgate measures to provide for special representation in the Royal Administration of the provinces of Phang Saly and Sam Neua during the interval between the cessation of hostilities and the general elections of the interests of Laotian nationals who did not support the Royal forces during hostilities.

DOCUMENT 7

Declaration by the Royal Government of Cambodia[12]

July 21, 1954

The Royal Government of Cambodia is resolved never to take part

[11] This and the following Declaration (Document 6) refer to paragraph 3 of the final declaration (referred to herein as FD and reproduced as Document 1 above).

[12] This and the following Declaration (Document 8) refer to FD 4 and 5.

in an aggressive policy and never to permit the territory of Cambodia to be utilised in the service of such a policy.

The Royal Government of Cambodia will not join in any agreement with other States, if this agreement carries for Cambodia the obligation to enter into a military alliance not in conformity with the principles of the Charter of the United Nations, or, as long as its security is not threatened, the obligation to establish bases on Cambodian territory for the military forces of foreign Powers.

The Royal Government of Cambodia is resolved to settle its international disputes by peaceful means, in such a manner as not to endanger peace, international security and justice.

During the period which will elapse between the date of the cessation of hostilities in Viet Nam and that of the final settlement of political problems in this country, the Royal Government of Cambodia will not solicit foreign aid in war material, personnel or instructors except for the purpose of the effective defence of the territory.

DOCUMENT 8

Declaration by the Royal Government of Laos

July 21, 1954

The Royal Government of Laos is resolved never to pursue a policy of aggression and will never permit the territory of Laos to be used in furtherance of such a policy.

The Royal Government of Laos will never join in any agreement with other States if this agreement includes the obligation for the Royal Government of Laos to participate in a military alliance not in conformity with the principles of the Charter of the United Nations or with the principles of the agreement on the cessation of hostilities or, unless its security is threatened, the obligation to establish bases on Laotian territory for military forces of foreign Powers.

The Royal Government of Laos is resolved to settle its international disputes by peaceful means so that international peace and security and justice are not endangered.

During the period between the cessation of hostilities in Viet Nam and the final settlement of that country's political problems, the Royal Government of Laos will not request foreign aid, whether in war material, in personnel or in instructors, except for the purpose of its effective territorial defence and to the extent defined by the agreement on the cessation of hostilities.

DOCUMENT 9

Declaration by the Government of the French Republic

July 21, 1954

(*Reference: Article 10 of the Final Declaration*)

The Government of the French Republic declares that it is ready to withdraw its troops from the territory of Cambodia, Laos and Viet Nam, at the request of the Governments concerned and within a period which shall be fixed by agreement between the parties, except in the cases where, by agreement between the two parties, a certain number of French troops shall remain at specified points and for a specified time.

DOCUMENT 10

Declaration by the Government of the French Republic

July 21, 1954

(*Reference: Article 11 of the Final Declaration*)

For the settlement of all the problems connected with the re-establishment and consolidation of peace in Cambodia, Laos and Viet Nam, the French Government will proceed from the principle of respect for the independence and sovereignty, the unity and territorial integrity of Cambodia, Laos and Viet Nam.

Bibliography

Documents and Government Publications

Cole, A. B., ed. *Conflict in Indo-China and International Repercussions.* Ithaca, 1956.

Curl, Peter V., ed. *Documents on American Foreign Relations, 1953; 1954.* New York, 1954; 1955.

Dennett, R., and Turner, R. K., eds. *Documents on American Foreign Relations, January 1–December 31, 1950.* Princeton, 1951.

DRVN. *Facts and Dates on the Problem of the Reunification of Viet-Nam.* Hanoi, 1956.

————. *On the Re-establishment of Normal Relations between the Northern and Southern Zones of Vietnam.* Hanoi, 1955.

————. *The Problem of Reunification of Viet-Nam.* Hanoi, 1959.

The Dulles Oral History Collection, Princeton University Library, Princeton, New Jersey. Transcripts of Sherman Adams, George V. Allen, Joseph Alsop, Stewart Alsop, John R. Beal, Sir Howard Beale, Loftus E. Becker, Richard M. Bissell, Charles E. Bohlen, Robert R. Bowie, David K. E. Bruce, Arleigh Burke, Charles P. Cabell, Chang Myun, Marquis Childs, Chung Il Kwon, J. Lawton Collins, C. Douglas Dillon, Robert J. Donovan, Dwight D. Eisenhower, Thomas K. Finletter, Carlos P. Garcia, Thomas S. Gates, James C. Hagerty, John W. Hanes, Jr., Emmet J. Hughes, George M. Humphrey, U. Alexis Johnson, Thanat Khoman, Arthur Larson, Curtis Le May, Henry Cabot Lodge, Sir Thomas MacDonald, Michael J. Mansfield, Carl W. McCardle, G. L. Mehta, Pierre Mendès-France, Thruston B. Morton, Sir Leslie Knox Munro, Richard M. Nixon, Frederick E. Nolting, Jr., Paik Too-Chin, Herman Phleger, Christian Pineau, Pote Sarasin, Pyun Yung Tai, Matthew B. Ridgway, Chalmers M. Roberts, Carlos P. Romulo, James R. Shepley, Lord Sherfield (Sir Roger Makins), Sohn Won Yil, Paul Henri Spaak, Felix B. Stump, Maxwell D. Taylor, Nathan F. Twining, Prince Wan Waithayakon, Charles W. Yost.

John Foster Dulles Papers, Princeton University Library, Princeton, New Jersey.

France, Assemblée Nationale. *Journal Officiel de la République Française.* Débats Parlementaires, Jan.-Sept., 1954. Paris, 1954.

Great Britain, Foreign Office. *Documents relating to the Discussion of Korea and Indochina at the Geneva Conference.* Misc. No. 16 (1954), Cmd. 9186. London, 1954.

———— ————. *Further Documents relating to the Discussion of Indochina at the Geneva Conference.* Misc. No. 20 (1954), Cmd. 9239. London, 1954.

Great Britain, Foreign Office. *Interim Reports of the International Commission for Supervision and Control in Laos.* Command Papers, London, 1955-58.

—— ——. *Interim Reports of the International Commission for Supervision and Control in Vietnam.* Command Papers, London, 1955-61.

—— ——. *International Conference on the Settlement of the Laotian Question.* Laos No. 1 (1962), Cmnd. 1828. London, 1962.

—— ——. *Memorandum regarding United Kingdom Association with the European Defense Community.* Misc. No. 10 (1954), Cmd. 9126. London, 1954.

—— ——. *Progress Reports of the International Commission for Supervision and Control in Cambodia.* Command Papers, London, 1955-59.

—— ——. *Recent Exchanges Concerning Attempts to Promote a Negotiated Settlement of the Conflict in Viet-Nam.* Viet-Nam No. 3 (1965), Cmnd. 2756. London, 1965.

—— ——. *Special Report to the Co-Chairmen of the Geneva Conference on Indo-China.* Vietnam No. 1 (1962), Cmnd. 1755. London, 1962.

—— ——. *Special Report to the Co-Chairmen of the Geneva Conference on Indo-China.* Vietnam No. 1 (1965), Cmnd. 2609. London, 1965.

—— ——. *Special Report to the Co-Chairmen of the Geneva Conference on Indo-China.* Vietnam No. 2 (1965), Cmnd. 2634. London, 1965.

—— ——. *Text of a Note from the Soviet Government Regarding Collective Security.* Misc. No. 9 (1954), Cmd. 9122. London, 1954.

—— ——. *Text of a Note from the Government of the United Kingdom.* Misc. No. 13 (1954), Cmd. 9146. London, 1954.

—— ——. *Further Correspondence.* Misc. No. 26 (1954), Cmd. 9281. London, 1954.

—— ——. *Further Correspondence.* Misc. No. 34 (1954), Cmd. 9327. London, 1954.

—— ——. *Vietnam and the Geneva Agreements.* Vietnam No. 2 (1956), Cmd. 9763. London, 1956.

——. House of Commons. *Parliamentary Debates.* 5th ser., vols. 522-34 (1954). London, 1954.

Royal Institute of International Affairs. *Documents on International Affairs.* 8 vols., London, 1959-61.

RVN. *Violations of the Geneva Agreements by the Viet-Minh Communists.* Saigon, 1959-1960.

U.S. Congress. *Congressional Record.* 83d Cong., 2d sess., vol. 100 (1954). Washington, D.C., 1954.

U.S., Congress, House of Representatives, Committee on Foreign Affairs. *Report on H.R. 5710, A Bill to Amend Further the Mutual Security Act of 1951, as Amended, and for other Purposes.* H.R. Report No. 569, 83d Congress, 1st sess., June 16, 1953. Washington, D.C., 1953.

U.S., Congress, Senate, Committee on Foreign Relations. *Background Information Relating to Southeast Asia and Vietnam.* Washington, D.C., 1966.

U.S., Department of State. *American Foreign Policy: 1950-1955.* Washington, D.C., 1957.

―――. *Aggression from the North.* Washington, D.C., 1965.

―――. *A Threat to the Peace.* Washington, D.C., 1961.

―――. *Department of State Bulletin.* Vols. 30, 31. Washington, D.C., 1954.

―――. *Foreign Ministers Meeting, Berlin Discussions, January 25-February 18, 1954.* Department of State Publication 5399. Washington, D.C., 1954.

―――. *Treaties and Other International Acts Series.* Washington, D.C., 1946, 1949, 1953-55, 1962.

Memoirs and Collected Works

Adams, Sherman. *First Hand Report.* New York, 1961.

Bidault, Georges. *Resistance.* New York, 1967.

Eden, Anthony. *Full Circle.* Boston, 1960.

Eisenhower, Dwight D. *Mandate for Change, 1953-1956.* Garden City, New York, 1963.

―――. *Public Papers of the Presidents of the United States: 1953; 1954.* Washington, D.C., 1960.

Ely, Paul. *Mémoires—L'Indochine dans la Tourmente.* Paris, 1964.

Frédéric-Dupont, *Mission de la France en Asie.* Paris, 1956.

Ho Chi Minh. *On Revolution.* Edited by Bernard B. Fall. New York, 1967.

―――. *Selected Works.* Hanoi, 1961.

Laniel, Joseph. *Le Drame indochinois. De Dien Bien Phu au pari de Genève.* Paris, 1957.

Navarre, Henri. *Agonie de L'Indochine (1953-1954).* Paris, 1956.

Nehru, Jawaharlal. *Jawaharlal Nehru's Speeches.* New Delhi, 1958.

Ridgway, Matthew B. *Soldier.* New York, 1956.

Tournoux, Jean-Raymond. *Secrets d'État.* Paris, 1960.

Legal Materials

CASES

The Aaland Islands Question. Report of the Committee of Jurists,

League of Nations Official Journal, Special Supp. No. 3 (October, 1920).

Factory at Chorzów. P.C.I.J. (1928), Series A, No. 17, 1 Hudson, *World Court Reports* 646 (1934).

Free Zones of Upper Savoy and the District of Gex. P.C.I.J. (1932), Series A/B No. 46, 2 Hudson, *World Court Reports* 508 (1935).

German Interests in Polish Upper Silesia. P.C.I.J. (1926), Series A, No. 6, 1 Hudson, *World Court Reports* 482 (1934).

The International Status of South West Africa (Advisory Opinion). I.C.J. Reports 128 (1950).

Status of Eastern Greenland. P.C.I.J. (1933), Series A/B, No. 53, 3 Hudson, *World Court Reports* 148 (1938).

TREATISES, TEXTS AND ESSAYS

Brownlie, Ian. *Principles of Public International Law.* London, 1966.

Committee on American Policy Towards Vietnam. *Vietnam and International Law.* Flanders, New Jersey, 1967.

de Muralt, R.W.G. *The Problem of State Succession with Regard to Treaties.* The Hague, 1954.

Falk, Richard A. *Legal Order in a Violent World.* Princeton, 1968.

———, ed. *The Vietnam War and International Law.* Princeton, 1968.

Fauchille, Paul. *Traité de Droit International Public.* 8e edn., Paris, 1926.

Fenwick, Charles G. *International Law.* 2nd edn., New York, 1934.

Hannon, John. "A Political Settlement for Vietnam: The 1954 Geneva Conference and Its Current Implications," *Virginia Journal of International Law*, Vol. 8 (1968).

Harvard Research in International Law, Treaties. *American Journal of International Law*, Vol. 29 Supplement (1935).

Hyde, Charles Cheney. *International Law, Chiefly as Interpreted and Applied by the United States.* 2nd rev. edn. Boston, 1945.

Lauterpacht, H. *Oppenheim's International Law.* 8th edn. London, 1958.

O'Connell, Donald P. *The Law of State Succession.* Cambridge, 1956.

Roxburgh, Ronald F. *International Conventions and Third States.* London, 1917.

Scelle, Georges. *Cours de Droit International Public.* Paris, 1948.

Stone, Julius. *Aggression and World Order.* Berkeley, 1958.

U.S., Department of State, Legal Advisor. "The Legality of United States Participation in the Defense of Viet Nam," *American Journal of International Law*, Vol. 60 (1966).

Verdross, Alfred. *Völkerrecht.* 4th edn. Vienna, 1959.

Wengler, Wilhelm. *Völkerrecht.* Berlin, 1964.

Whiteman, Marjorie M. *Digest of International Law.* Washington, D.C., 1963.

JOURNALS

American Journal of International Law, 1935, 1966.
British Yearbook of International Law, 1947.

Newspapers and Magazines

Christian Science Monitor, 1954-55.
Current Digest of the Soviet Press, Vols. 5-6 (1953-1954).
The Economist (London), 1954.
Le Monde, 1954-55.
Manchester Guardian, 1954.
The New York Herald Tribune, 1953-55.
The New York Times, 1953-55.
Overseas Hindustan Times, 1954.
People's China (Peking), 1954.
Relazioni internazionali, Series 2, Vol. 18 (Milan, 1954).
Saturday Evening Post, 1954.
Survey of China Mainland Press (American Consulate General, Hong Kong), 1954.
The Times of London, 1954.
U.S. News and World Report, 1954.

Books and Other Writings

INDOCHINA AND SOUTHEAST ASIA

Bator, Victor. "Geneva, 1954: The Broken Mold," *The Reporter,* Vol. 34 (June 30, 1966).
———. *Vietnam: A Diplomatic Tragedy.* Dobbs Ferry, New York, 1965.
Blanchet, Marie Thérèse. *La Naissance de l'État associé du Viêt-Nam.* Paris, 1954.
Buttinger, Joseph. *Vietnam: A Dragon Embattled.* New York, 1967.
Champassak, S. N. *Storm over Laos.* New York, 1961.
Chatham House Study Group. *Collective Defense in South East Asia.* London, 1956.
Child, Marquis. *The Ragged Edge, The Diary of a Crisis.* New York, 1955.
Dommen, Arthur J. *Conflict in Laos.* New York, 1964.
Duncanson, Dennis J. *Government and Revolution in Vietnam.* New York, 1968.

Dutt, Vidya Prakash, and Singh, Vishal. *Indian Policy and Attitudes towards Indo-China and SEATO.* New York, 1954.

Fall, Bernard B. "The Cease-Fire in Indo-China—An Appraisal," *Far Eastern Survey* (October, 1954).

———. *The International Position of South Viet Nam, 1954-58.* New York, 1958.

———. *Street Without Joy.* Harrisburg, Pennsylvania, 1963.

———. *The Two Viet-Nams.* New York, 1963.

———. *The Viet-Minh Regime: Government and Administration in the Democratic Republic of Viet-Nam.* Ithaca, 1954.

———. *Viet-Nam Witness: 1953-1966.* New York, 1966.

Guillain, Robert. *La Fin des illusions: Notes d'Indochine (février-juillet, 1954).* Paris, 1954.

Gurtov, Melvin. *The First Vietnam Crisis.* New York, 1967.

Halpern, A. M., and Fredman, H. B. *Communist Strategy in Laos.* Santa Monica, 1960.

Hammer, Ellen J. *The Struggle for Indochina, 1940-1955.* Stanford, California, 1954.

Hinton, Harold C. *China's Relations with Burma and Vietnam.* New York, 1958.

Honey, Patrick J. *Communism in Viet-Nam.* Cambridge, Mass., 1963.

Hougron, Jean. *La Nuit indochinoise.* 6 vols. Paris, 1950-58.

Isaacs, Harold R. *New Cycle in Asia.* New York, 1947.

Isoart, Paul. *Le Phénomène national viêtnamien: de l'indépendence unitaire à l'indépendence fractionée.* Paris, 1961.

Lacouture, Jean. *Vietnam Between Two Truces.* New York, 1966.

——— and Devillers, Philippe. *La Fin d'une Guerre, Indochine 1954.* Paris, 1960.

Lancaster, Donald. *The Emancipation of French Indochina.* London, 1961.

Lindholm, Richard W. *Viet-Nam: The First Five Years.* Lansing, Mich., 1959.

Modelski, George. *The International Conference on the Settlement of the Laotian Question, 1961-2.* Canberra, 1962.

———, ed. *SEATO: Six Studies.* Melbourne, 1962.

Murti, B.S.N. *Vietnam Divided.* Bombay, 1964.

Mus, Paul. *Le Destin de l'Union Française: de l'Indochine à l'Afrique.* Paris, 1954.

Ngo Ton Dat. *The Geneva Partition of Vietnam and the Question of Reunification during the First Two Years.* Unpublished Ph.D. dissertation, Cornell University, Ithaca, New York, 1963.

Kien, Nguyen. *Le Sud-Vietnamese depuis Dien Bien Phu.* Paris, 1963.

Pike, Douglas. *Viet Cong.* Cambridge, Mass., 1966.

Renald, Jean. *L'Enfer de Dien Bien Phu.* Paris, 1955.

Roberts, Chalmers H. "The Day We Didn't Go to War," *The Reporter,* XI (September 14, 1954), 31-35.

Roy, Jules. *The Battle of Dienbienphu.* New York, 1965.

Sar Desai, D. R. *Indian Foreign Policy in Cambodia, Laos and Vietnam, 1947-1964.* Berkeley, 1968.

Vo Nguyen Giap. *Big Victory, Great Task.* New York, 1968.

————. *Peoples' War, Peoples' Army: The Viet-Cong Insurrection Manual for Underdeveloped Countries.* New York, 1962.

DIPLOMATIC AND POLITICAL STUDIES

Barnett, A. Doak. *Communist Strategies in Asia.* New York, 1963.

Beal, J. R. *John Foster Dulles: A Biography.* New York, 1957.

Berding, Andrew. *Dulles on Diplomacy.* Princeton, 1965.

Black, Cyril E., *et al. Neutralization and World Politics.* Princeton, 1968.

Bromke, A., ed. *The Communist States at the Crossroads: Between Moscow and Peking.* New York, 1965.

Cobban, Alfred. *National Self-Determination.* Chicago, 1944.

Cranshaw, Edward. *Khrushchev's Russia.* London, 1962.

Dallin, David J. *Soviet Foreign Policy after Stalin.* Philadelphia, 1961.

Dinerstein, Herbert S. *War and the Soviet Union.* New York, 1959.

Drummond, Roscoe, and Coblentz, Caston. *Duel at the Brink.* Garden City, New York, 1960.

Dulles, Eleanor Lansing. *John Foster Dulles: The Last Year.* New York, 1963.

Dulles, John Foster. "Policy for Security and Peace," *Foreign Affairs,* Vol. 32, No. 3 (April, 1954), 353-364.

————. *War or Peace.* New York, 1950.

Eckstein, Harry, ed. *Internal War.* New York, 1964.

Emerson, Rupert. *From Empire to Nation.* Boston, 1960.

————. *Self-Determination Revisited in the Era of Decolonization.* Cambridge, Mass., 1964.

Fauvet, Jacques. *La IVe Republique.* Paris, 1959.

Fox, Annette Baker. *The Power of Small States.* Chicago, 1959.

Goold-Adams, Richard. *The Time of Power: A Reappraisal of John Foster Dulles.* London, 1962.

Guiton, Raymond J. *Paris-Moskau: die Sowjetunion in der auswärtigen Politik Frankreichs seit dem zweiten Weltkrieg.* Stuttgart, 1956.

Halperin, Morton H. *China and the Bomb.* New York, 1965.

Horelick, A. L., and Rush, M. *Strategic Power and Soviet Foreign Policy.* Chicago, 1966.

Hsieh, Alice Langley. *Communist China's Strategy in the Nuclear Era*. Englewood Cliffs, New Jersey, 1962.

Hughes, Emmet J. *The Ordeal of Power*. New York, 1963.

Huntington, C. P. *The Common Defense*. New York, 1961.

Lall, Arthur. *How Communist China Negotiates*. New York, 1968.

Leonhard, Wolfgang. *The Kremlin Since Stalin*. New York, 1962.

Lerner, Daniel, and Aron, Raymond, eds. *France Defeats EDC*. New York, 1957.

Liska, George. *Alliances and the Third World*. Baltimore, 1968.

———. *Nations in Alliance*. Baltimore, 1962.

Paloczi-Horvath, G. *Khrushchev: The Road to Power*. London, 1960.

Rosenau, John N., ed. *International Aspects of Civil Strife*. Princeton, 1964.

Rothstein, Robert L. *Alliances and Small Powers*. New York, 1968.

Rouanet, Pierre. *Mendès-France au Pouvoir, 1954-1955*. Paris, 1965.

Rush, Myron. *The Rise of Khrushchev*. Washington, D.C., 1958.

Schilling, W. R., *et al*. *Strategy, Politics and Defense Budgets*. New York, 1962.

Shepley, J. "How Dulles Averted War," *Life*, January 16, 1956.

Tang Tsou. *The Embroilment over Quemoy: Mao, Chiang and Dulles*. Salt Lake City, 1959.

Taylor, Maxwell D. *The Uncertain Trumpet*. New York, 1959.

Vital, David. *The Inequality of States*. London, 1967.

Williams, Philip. *Politics in Post-War France*. 2nd edn. London, 1958.

Young, Kenneth T. *Negotiating with the Chinese Communists*. New York, 1968.

Young, Oran R. *The Intermediaries*. Princeton, 1967.

Zagoria, Donald S. *The Vietnam Triangle*. New York, 1967.

HISTORICAL SURVEYS

Barraclough, Geoffrey. *Survey of International Affairs, 1956-1958*. London, 1962.

———, and Wall, R. F. *Survey of International Affairs, 1955-1956*. London, 1960.

Bell, Coral. *Survey of International Affairs, 1954*. London, 1957.

Stebbins, R. P. *The United States in World Affairs, 1954*. New York, 1956.

Index

Unless otherwise indicated, the office, rank or positions of the persons identified in this index are for 1954.